Territoire de Cuyaba

GOUVERNEMENT DE GOYAZ

los Guyazas

VILLA BOA

M.T DE MATTO GROSSO

Cayapos

Ar ae

S.t An

R. Grande

R. de las Velhas

de Parana

GOUV. DE

R. Parao ou Colorado

R. Tiete

R. des Mortes

R. Sapacu

R. Yuaguari

sierra de Ibatucatu

R. Parana Pane

S. PAUL

R. Ybay

R. Pecueri

GOUVERNEMENT DE

R. Minas de Parana

M. Paranonbiacapa

S. Vincent

Iguitpe

Tarana R.

Ygassu R.

R. Parnagua

R. Sagasuy

uption

Gumanas

Inpeba R.

Ipinuba

S. François

Biturmas

R. Uruguay

GOUVERNEMENT

Tapes

M. de Mariachu

Caribes

I. S.t Cather

Candelaria

Arboreda

R. Igay

R. Trevigueri

Villa d. Lagu

LAND WITHOUT EVIL

v

Frontispiece: CHIQUITOS ARCHERS. Drawn by Alcides d'Orbigny, 1831.

LAND WITHOUT EVIL

UTOPIAN JOURNEYS ACROSS THE
SOUTH AMERICAN
WATERSHED

———

RICHARD GOTT

VERSO

London · New York

First published by Verso 1993
© Richard Gott 1993
All rights reserved

Verso
UK: 6 Meard Street, London W1V 3HR
USA: 29 West 35th Street, New York, NY 10001-2291

Verso is the imprint of New Left Books

ISBN 0-86091-398-8

British Library Cataloguing in Publication Data
A catalogue record for this book is available from the British Library

Library of Congress Cataloging-in-Publication Data
A catalogue record for this book is available from the Library of Congress

Typeset by York House Typographic Ltd, London W13
Printed in Great Britain by The Bath Press, Avon

CONTENTS

PART II The Upper Paraguay

PART III The Missions of Chiquitos

Ever since the European conquest of their lands in the sixteenth century, the Guaraní Indians to the east of the Paraguay river have been stirred up from time to time by messianic revivals. Sometimes a prophet announces the end of Spanish rule and the beginning of a new golden age. Sometimes the nation abandons its territory and goes on a great pilgrimage to the west, in search of the Land Without Evil.

The Guaraní seem always, with good reason, to have had a pessimistic view of the future of their present world, convinced that the end is near. They know for certain that one day the Great Father will set the earth on fire, unleashing the Eternal Bat and the Celestial Jaguar on a mission to destroy the stars and all mankind.

Yet at the beginning of their world, when the Eternal Bats fought in the night, and the Great Father, Ñanderuvucú, created the earth, he also created a woman, Ñandecy, Our Mother. The Guaraní believe that she lives in the west, in the Land Without Evil, a place to which everyone yearns to go.

Taken from Alfred Métraux, *The Guaraní*,
in *Handbook of South American Indians,
Volume 3: The Tropical Forest Tribes*,
ed. Julian Steward, Washington 1948

PREFACE AND ACKNOWLEDGEMENTS

The strange flat area between the Amazon and the River Plate began first to intrigue me some twenty-five years ago when I travelled to eastern Bolivia in 1967 to report on Che Guevara's guerrilla campaign. Flying over the route that skirts the western edge of the great Bolivian cordillera, from Santa Cruz de la Sierra to the southern oil town of Camiri, I was unaware then that this was one of the great frontier zones of the Spanish empire. I knew nothing of the string of Franciscan missions built here to provide a cheap buffer against the Chiriguano nation living in the Chaco, a people that never accepted Spanish rule.

Yet these miserable former mission villages were among those visited by Guevara during his desperate six-month campaign. Here was Florida, site of a great battle during the guerrilla wars for independence against the Spanish in the early nineteenth century. Now a forgotten village, its name is commemorated only by a famous shopping street in Buenos Aires. Here too was Samaipata, captured briefly by Guevara, but once the great redoubt of the Incas as they protected themselves against the Chiriguanos; and Vallegrande, the hill town that housed the head-quarters of the Bolivian army's counter-guerrilla command, once an important staging post on the old Spanish road from Charcas (Sucre) to Santa Cruz, a road that went on to Chiquitos and the upper Paraguay.

Of all this, I knew nothing at the time. But I did learn that there was more to Bolivia than the travel posters of the altiplano, the dramatic Andean wasteland at 12,000 feet with its Quechua and Aymara Indians; its tin mines and silver mountain. That for me then, as for most outsiders, was the only Bolivia that mattered. But at least I now knew that there was something else.

A year later, in 1968, I crossed the waist of Latin America by jeep, travelling from Curitiba in Brazil on the Atlantic to Tacna on the Pacific in Peru, passing through Paraguay and Bolivia on the way. There is a dirt road across the Chaco, built by the Paraguayan military, that runs past the Mennonite mission at Filadelfia, through the old battlefields of the Chaco War in the 1930s, with wrecked tanks and lorries fast disappearing in the scrub, past the metal pylons installed at the request of the League of Nations to mark the newly agreed frontier, and on through to Boyuibe and Camiri.

That journey gave me a taste for this strange, hot, semi-desert area, but I still had no inkling of how it fitted into the rest of South America. It seemed a place apart. The English Protestant missionary, Barbrooke Grubb, writing about the Lengua Indians in his Chaco mission near the Paraguay river at the end of the last century, called them "an unknown people in an unknown land". This, I have since come to feel, is an unfair characterization of these people and that territory. But twenty years ago I would probably have shared his opinion.

I returned to these parts nearly ten years later, in 1977, travelling down the Madre de Dios river from Puerto Maldonado in eastern Peru to Riberalta, in the Mojos area of northern Bolivia, now called the Beni. The first part was easy: a motor launch to the Peru–Bolivia frontier and then across the Rio Heath in a canoe to the Bolivian settlement of Puerto Heath, named after a nineteenth-century explorer. Here the Bolivian navy maintained a small border station. Rations were low, but the naval commander's cook provided monkey to eat, and the conscript sailors shot a tapir (not a recommended dish). It was an early introduction to the fact that, even in the jungle and surrounded by hostile Indians, the worst enemy of the early European conquistadores was hunger and famine.

The second part of the journey, escaping from Puerto Heath, was not so simple. The river was low, and few boats were travelling downstream. Riberalta, the closest outpost of civilization, was at least three days' journey away. Eventually, the Bolivian naval commander was prevailed upon to make the trip, steering down the Madre de Dios to Riberalta, a journey once made in the fifteenth century by the Indians of the Inca Yupanqui. Riberalta was established as a rubber town at the end of the last century, and that is what it still is, though a shadow of its former self. This was my first introduction to the Jesuit territory of Mojos, though I didn't know it as such at the time. My impressions were filed away.

Earlier in the 1970s, like everyone who has ever been there, I had begun to be fascinated by the history of Bolivia's eastern neighbour, Paraguay. My interest had been awoken by the expedition across the Chaco, but later I became intrigued by the extraordinary figure of José Gaspar Rodríguez de Francia. As left-wing nationalists began to gain control of the Peronist movement in Argentina in the early 1970s, radical activists in the River Plate countries started to revive the history of Francia. In search of a socialist model, they uncovered the improbable figure of this nineteenth-century Paraguayan dictator who closed the frontiers of his country, locked up the local upper class, kept out the English imperialists with their ideology of free trade, and – over twenty-five years – turned his state into one of the richest and most advanced in South America. Eventually, in the 1860s, his legacy was destroyed in a terrible war, from which Paraguay never recovered.

Gradually, at secondhand bookshops around the country and occasionally at Sothebys, I accumulated a small library about nineteenth-century Paraguay. Increasingly I wanted to understand why Francia had embarked on his unique autarkic course. What was it in Paraguayan history that had thrown up this unique and extraordinary figure?

Trying to answer this question, and moving back another century, I had soon transferred my enthusiasm to the Jesuits. For their mission experiment in Paraguay in the seventeenth and eighteenth centuries – virtually a state within a state – provides at least part of the answer, and an explanation of the subsequent history of Paraguay.

When I first came travelling through Paraguay in 1968, I knew nothing of the Jesuit missions except for the intriguing entry about them in the *South American Handbook*, that perennial source of so much wonderful information about the continent. But the missions themselves lay well off the east–west track from Iguaçú to Asunción. Not until 1983, after the Falklands/Malvinas war, did I have the chance to travel through southern Paraguay, pausing at each and every mission ruin, and photographing the magnificent carved and painted wooden sculptures from the eighteenth century that have been recovered, restored, and preserved.

Pushing on over the Paraná river, I stopped at the many ruined missions that lie in the narrow strip of land between the Paraná and the Uruguay rivers (in the Argentine province of Misiones). The ruins of San Ignacio Mini, in rose-hued brick, still stand as an impressive monument to what once was, but most of the others are now covered in woodland and scrub, and take some finding.

Later on that same trip, I came once again to Santa Cruz de la Sierra in eastern Bolivia, and visited for the first time one of the Jesuit missions of Chiquitos that form an important part of this book. Hiring a small plane, I visited Concepción, then in its last year of restoration work. In a dusty attic I chanced, like some nineteenth-century explorer, on a manuscript copy of music by Doménico Zípoli, the pupil of Scarlatti who died in Córdoba but enriched the music of the Paraguay missions.

From the experience of these different expeditions, I conceived the idea of making another journey across the middle of South America. This time I would travel further to the north, taking in the Brazilian territory of Mato Grosso do Sul, the Pantanal swamp, the Chiquitos province of eastern Bolivia, and the missions of Mojos in the Bolivian Beni. This was the old historic route across the heart of South America, made by the Guaraní before the conquistadores arrived in search of silver. I made the journey with my wife Vivien, and we travelled in July and August 1990. What we saw and discovered on that occasion forms the basic framework of this book.

As important as the journeys on the ground have been the expeditions into libraries. A visit to the British Museum library is often more revealing than a trip to a jungle mission. On one occasion I found a set of nine Bolivian volumes in Bloomsbury whose pages for the best part of seventy years had remained uncut. I soon discovered that what I had originally thought to be an obscure part of the world, largely bypassed by history and hardly mentioned in traditional textbooks, has in fact been a dramatic cockpit of endless struggle, visited by an unceasing stream of outsiders, and discussed, dissected, and written about over hundreds of years.

When I began, I was unaware that such a huge cast of eager travellers had beaten a path across the Pantanal and through Chiquitos and Mojos. They were virtually unknown to me. I had thought that I was revealing something, if not new, then at least fresh and under-noticed. But it is not so. Across this obscure tract of South America, obscure to the late twentieth century, hundreds of foreign visitors, report-makers, note-takers, and letter-writers, have passed – over a period of nearly five hundred years.

Whatever distant part of the globe you choose to travel in, you will nearly always find that others have been there before you. This is not just a question of humility before the original inhabitants, for even they may have frequently shifted their position over recorded time, but rather a recognition that travel and exploration are both part of a seamless web with conquest and exploitation.

So this is a travel book that tries to illuminate the past as much as the present. While telling the story of a single ordinary journey in the late twentieth century, I have also tried to give an account of a particular area as it developed (or in this case under-developed) over several centuries, and of the people in whose footsteps we trod. As the globe shrinks, and travel becomes more commonplace and banal, we can measure in the excitements and discoveries contained in the accounts of dead explorers the dimensions of our loss.

The book takes the form of a journey across the central belt of South America. We went from the town of Campo Grande in western Brazil to the mission settlement of Exaltación de la Cruz in Mojos, the northern territory of Bolivia now known as the Beni. We passed on the way the swamps of the upper Paraguay river in Mato Grosso do Sul, and the flat plains of Chiquitos in eastern Bolivia.

Woven into the story, in a way destined to be understandable and illuminating, are the tales of earlier visitors to this zone, and a description of some of the episodes of conquest, war and diplomacy to which it has been a witness over several centuries.

The story of a journey across a finite geographical area cannot at the same time be a chronological history. It is, inevitably, a switchback journey. Sometimes events in the nineteenth century seem to precede those in the sixteenth, sometimes the same figure appears again further along the line. Eventually, I hope, everything will become clear. It may make the reading easier to think of this book as a blank canvas on which the shape of the sketched-out design takes the form of a map. Gradually, as the pages turn, the colours – taken from the well-endowed palette of the past – are blocked in to create a completed picture.

Thanks are due to many people with whom I have travelled in Latin America in the past, or who have helped form my view of the continent: to Alma Guillermoprieto, Sven Lindqvist, Brian Moser, Jenny Rathbone, John Rettie, and Ann Zammit, as well as, of course, to my children, Inti and Araucana, now themselves capable of exploring their continent on their own, with their own children.

I also owe a great debt to successive foreign editors at the *Guardian*, Geoffrey

Taylor, Ian Wright, Campbell Page, Martin Woollacott, and Paul Webster, who have allowed me great latitude over the years in reporting from places not normally considered to be newsworthy; to Peter Preston, the *Guardian*'s editor, who gave me a year off to complete this book; and to Leslie Bethell, who provided me with a perch at the Institute of Latin American Studies at the University of London.

Much of this book was written and researched in the Reading Room of the British Museum, "a place," Ben Pimlott has written, "where there's this sort of practical socialism, with nice charming people who hand you books, and provide wonderfully efficient service." Thanks to all of them, and to the staff of the British Library's photographic and reproduction department, who made copies of the nineteenth-century prints with which this book is illustrated. The contemporary photographs were taken by Vivien Ashley and by me; the maps were drawn by Mandy Watson.

In recent years, I have travelled everywhere – in Eastern Europe, in Mexico and Central America, and on this particular journey across Latin America – with Vivien Ashley, my friend, companion and wife. An incomparably cheerful adventurer, she has invariably urged me to continue when I was keen to stop, and made me stop whenever I foolishly wished to press on. I could not now contemplate travelling without her.

Richard Gott
London 1992

INTRODUCTION

This is a book about places you have never been to, about a history you have never read, and about people you have never heard of. It is a story of many fruitless journeys across a great swamp, of innumerable forgotten travels through impenetrable marsh and desert, of utopian expeditions into a region of trackless scrub, a land that lies at the very heart of South America.

Little known by outsiders today, these territories have been travelled across by Europeans – and written about – for more than four centuries. Their original inhabitants – infinitely more numerous in the sixteenth century than they are in the twentieth – had moved around in these latitudes for thousands of years before they discovered the Spaniards and the Portuguese disembarking on their river shores. The Guaraní and the Guana, the Guaycurus and the Payaguas, the Chiriguanos and the Chiquitos, the Mojos and the Canichanas and the Cayubabas have now all but disappeared. Yet all these great nations had a history and an identity with which, two hundred years ago, many people were familiar. A memory of them deserves to be resurrected.

Over the centuries, the obscure and inhospitable frontier land at the centre of South America where these peoples lived, has attracted a polyglot collection of foreign visitors. They travelled across it, mostly from east to west, in search of silver and Indians, insects and animals – and adventure. Spanish conquistadores, Portuguese slavers, French explorers, Swedish ethnologists, German engineers and anthropologists, English surveyors, North American navigators, Italian traders, Norwegian farmers, Russian students, as well as Catholic missionaries from all over Europe, and a legion of scientists, botanists, and naturalists: all have found themselves irresistibly drawn to this remote area of the globe.

Many have left a written record of their passage. Some of the principal conquistadores wrote reports of their explorations; so too did the Jesuit missionaries, encouraged by Ignatius Loyola to write regular letters home. Later, in the nineteenth century, European scientists and adventurers left bulky volumes detailing their discoveries, mapping their journeys, and boasting of their exploits.

The great swamp at the heart of South America – the Pantanal – is also a watershed, the divide between the subcontinent's two great rivers. Out of it come some of the upper tributaries of the Amazon flowing to the north, and through it runs the mighty River Paraguay flowing south to the River Plate. In the rainy season, when the swamp expands during half the year into one enormous stretch of water, it is possible to travel by canoe from one river system into the other.

On all the early European maps of South America, the swamp of the Pantanal is clearly marked with a name: the Laguna de Xarayes. On these maps, the River Paraná and then its tributary the River Paraguay, well charted, ascend due North to the lake from the estuary of the River Plate.

Tracing that estuary from the south Atlantic ocean, the early mapmakers clearly knew where they were and what they were about. But as their maps move up the page to the north, from the Paraná into the Paraguay, the information becomes scantier, the outline more hazy, the detail more imaginative. The Laguna de Xarayes itself is often depicted simply as a large ink blot. Not until the end of the eighteenth century do the mapmakers begin to give the contours of the swamp a shape that is familiar today, an immense geographic area that reduces and inflates according to the season.

A watershed is both a unity and a division, and as in geography so in politics. History here, in part, is about borders and boundaries. The lands and swamps of the upper Paraguay have been fought for, and fought over, for hundreds of years.

Even before the Europeans arrived, these regions were the subject of armed dispute between the principal Indian nations of the Amazon and the River Plate – the Arawak and the Tupi-Guaraní – and the innumerable other nations that defended their local territory.

Then, in early colonial times, fresh participants continued the struggle in different forms: Spaniards and Indians, Spaniards and Portuguese, Jesuits and Mameluke slave-traders. All fought to maintain their predominance, or at the very least their presence, in this strategic region. For through the Pantanal and Chiquitos ran the road from the trade routes of the Atlantic to the silver mines of Peru.

Throughout the colonial period, until the beginning of the nineteenth century, this area of scrub and swamp was the fluid and flexible frontier between Portugal and Spain. As the fortunes of the royal families in Madrid and Lisbon waxed and waned and interlinked, so too did the fate of their South American possessions. In the fifteenth century, the Treaty of Tordesillas had drawn a straight line through the hemisphere, but it was rarely observed. No agreement to replace it was reached until the middle of the eighteenth century: the Treaty of Madrid of 1750. Even then, the properties of Spain and Portugal were never delineated adequately on the ground.

In the seventeenth and eighteenth centuries, the territory west of the upper Paraguay was one of the great Jesuit possessions in South America, "Greater Paraguay" as it might be called, though what is left of it now lies in eastern Bolivia and is known as Chiquitos. This was an area perceived by the Jesuits at the time as a crucial strategic link. They had always sought to establish an easy line of contact between their southern missions along the Paraná (in Paraguay proper) and the ones to the north. That line, never quite completed, would have run from Paraguay to Chiquitos, and then on to Mojos in Bolivia, to Maynas in Ecuador, and to Casanare in Colombia: a band of Jesuit-held territory skirting the western edge of the Amazon basin.

Later, in the nineteenth century, the newly independent countries of Paraguay and Bolivia inherited territory with no fixed frontiers. They had to fight to define them and to secure them. Embryonic Bolivians fought against Spaniards in the wars of independence and against Portuguese to protect their frontiers. Brazilians fought Paraguayans to the death in the War of the Triple Alliance (the Paraguayan War) from 1864 to 1870.

Having lost its Pacific sea coast to the Chileans in the War of the Pacific, 1879–83, Bolivia tried desperately – but to no avail – to obtain adequate access from Chiquitos to the River Paraguay, and thence to the Atlantic. Portugal had forestalled Bolivia by seizing both banks of the upper river at the end of the eighteenth century, and Paraguay did the same for the lower river in the nineteenth. Bolivia was successfully bottled up, as it remains to this day.

Even part of its northern region, the territory of Acre, adjacent to the old Jesuit province of Mojos, was detached in 1903 during the rubber boom, seized by Brazil. In the twentieth century, to complete the triangle, Paraguayans fought against Bolivians, in the Chaco War of the 1930s, for land that was barely fertile and for oil that was not there.

Today this frontier land, on either side of the upper Paraguay, is divided politically between three independent states. The western part stretches into the Bolivian provinces of Chiquitos and the Beni, formerly Mojos; the eastern section lies in the modern Brazilian state of Mato Grosso do Sul; to the south lie the still almost uncharted regions of the Paraguayan Chaco.

The Indian nations have not been bystanders in this endless struggle for frontiers. The Chiriguanos defeated an army led by the Spanish viceroy from Lima in the middle of the sixteenth century. This proud and independent nation, from its bases in the Chaco, was still fiercely defending its territory until a hundred years ago. The Guaycurus, on the eastern side of the Chaco, maintained a comparable struggle against the Spaniards and the Portuguese until the end of the eighteenth century. More than in any other part of South America, the Indian nations here fought – over several centuries – for their right to survive.

For many years, the eventual outcome remained in doubt. It was rare for an early conquistador to die in his bed, and the Jesuit missionaries who set up strategic hamlets to protect the Spanish frontier were also frequently killed. It was a long and bloody struggle, if ultimately an unequal one.

This is also a story of decline, of the steady deterioration of the condition of the people over the years since the Spanish conquest nearly five hundred years ago. As century has succeeded century in this part of the world, the lot of the local population has grown progressively worse. Bolivia, in particular, is now one of the poorest countries in South America, often linked in the statistical tables with Haiti.

Yet, clearly, the people of the watershed were better off in the nineteenth century than they are in the twentieth. They were far better off in the eighteenth century than in the nineteenth. And in the sixteenth and seventeenth centuries, in spite of the disruptions of conquest and slavery, the people were infinitely better off than in the eighteenth. One does not need to be a retrospective utopian to perceive that the early accounts of the state of the local population, written by the Spanish conquistadores in the sixteenth century, are infinitely more optimistic than anything written by a visiting journalist today.

In those early accounts, in the regular reports of the Jesuit missionaries, and in the later tales of travellers and adventurers from all over the world, it is possible to chart the course of a dismal collapse.

So this is the story of a particular piece of territory where more than four hundred years of externally induced "development" have had a disastrous impact, both on the original inhabitants and on the settler communities that arrived to replace the slaughtered natives.

The Indian nations were decimated and in many cases annihilated – by conquest, battle, slavery, and disease. But the economic decline is clear in the case of nearly all groups in society. European colonialism in this part of South America was a disaster not just for the colonized – the Indians – but for many others as well, black slaves and poor white settlers among them.

In recent years, historians and anthropologists have been estimating upwards the number of Indians to be found in the Americas at the time of Columbus's voyage. Where once it was fashionable or convenient to believe that the pre-Conquest Americas, north and south, had fewer than ten million people, there is now an entirely believable thesis, put forward particularly by French anthropologists and demographers, that one hundred million might be nearer the mark. The highest previous estimate (over forty million by Paul Rivet in 1924) has been more than doubled.

Recent research, Pierre Chaunu argued in 1964, leads to "a complete revision of our perception of American history".

It is no longer Dr Rivet's 40 million men, a figure held to be excessive, that must be assumed for pre-Columbian America, but 80 and perhaps 100 million souls. The catastrophe of the Conquista . . . was as great as Las Casas proclaimed it to be. . . . It appears that one-fourth of mankind was annihilated by the microbic shocks of the sixteenth century.[1]

One quarter of the population of the globe killed off by the arrival of the European. If the evidence can sustain the statistic, it is a frightening indictment. Unquestionably the area of the Pantanal, Chiquitos and Mojos – today a sparsely inhabited and inhospitable region with more cows than human beings – once sustained a huge population numbered in hundreds of thousands, if not millions.

The story of the European conquest and its aftermath, in the central part of South America, is not just a tale of slavery and rapine. Throughout the entire period there is a slender thread of opposition from within the colonial ranks. Almost from the beginning of the European period, in the 1540s, there were well-meaning people with progressive blueprints for development who sought to mitigate the worst effects of the colonial impact. The extraordinary activities of the Jesuits in this area, in the seventeenth and eighteenth centuries, form an important part of the story. Their unique mission experiment – introducing Indian farmers to a more urban experience – was a source of wonder at the time, and has remained so in the twentieth century.

The story of the Jesuit missions in southern Paraguay – the thirty mission towns close to the Paraná and Uruguay rivers that formed a significant enclave on territory that now lies on the frontiers of Paraguay, Argentina and Brazil – has been familiar in Europe ever since the eighteenth century. After 1767, when the Jesuits were finally expelled, their justificatory accounts of what had gone on in their mission towns were published in many editions and many languages, providing much-needed detail for a European public thirsty for information about Spain's collapsing empire. A recent film, *The Mission*, has put a twentieth-century gloss on their political difficulties.

To Chiquitos and Mojos, the Jesuits came late, at the end of the seventeenth century. But they brought with them more than a hundred years of missionary experience further south. They were no longer on a learning curve. They knew exactly what to do and how to run a successful mission in difficult territory.

Their success was remarkable. This unpropitious land, so arid and neglected and underpopulated today, was, in the eighteenth century, one of the greatest zones of Jesuit missionary endeavour anywhere at any time. Large mission towns were established, magnificent churches built, Indians rescued from slavery, farms and ranches developed, new societies created.

The ten missions of Chiquitos (the flatlands between the Paraguay and the Rio Grande), and the fifteen further to the north-west in Mojos (in northern Bolivia in the upper waters of the Amazon), were models of the kind of separate development that the Jesuits had patented in Paraguay proper: a garden economy, music and sculpture, monumental public buildings, a paternalist politics, a reverence for local language and custom. It was not paradise on earth, but it was a pretty impressive achievement in the circumstances of a South American swamp.

Yet this entire extraordinary endeavour collapsed utterly. This region today is bleak and backward, largely forgotten and ignored. The gardens have gone. The farms have disappeared. The towns are a shadow of what they once were. The people – the few that remain – live with little hope that their lives will improve. The ''holy experiment'' of the Jesuits, the ''socialist utopia'' of the missions, has disappeared for all time, leaving nothing but a few buildings and some scattered artefacts, and a faded memory in people's minds.

Even today, these ruins retain an aura of some ancient civilization that seems in some ways to have been more impressive than our own. Of this, nothing now survives. The people who live there today eke out their lives at a material level far below that which obtained two hundred years ago.

The story of this collapse is a significant part of the more general tragedy of South America's rape and pillage over the years. It is also a history worth reflecting on at the end of the twentieth century as another part of the world emerges from a utopian socialist experiment that took place on an infinitely greater scale.

So this is also the story of what now seems to have been wasted endeavour, of utopian efforts to promote development that ended in tragedy, and of well-meaning attempts to blunt the rapacity of colonial settlement that collapsed in failure. These were schemes that ran into the sand, leaving little behind but an occasional ruin.

In the 1980s, some of the great mission churches of Chiquitos were restored. Guilty Europeans – the West Germans in this case – sought to assuage their guilt about present poverty by funding the restoration of what they perceived to have been a great European development effort of the past. Yet the recovered churches, awash with fresh paint and gold leaf, flaunt an almost obscene opulence amid the surrounding gloom. The inhabitants of the old mission towns, sole inheritors of the utopian dreams of yesteryear, survive for the most part in a world of backwardness and apathy.

Disaster struck in the late eighteenth century because the Jesuits, like the enthusiasts for Third World development today, could only operate within a framework of thought and action devised in the colonial metropolis. When the Spanish king commanded, in 1767, that all Jesuits should be expelled from his dominions, they meekly withdrew. They abandoned their churches, their towns, their Indians. They had no choice but to be escorted to the frontier ports and embarked on ships that took them to Europe. They had been part of the state machine, and when the state decreed that they should cease their operations, they had no alternative strategy.

The great mission towns in South America that they left behind – with their music and art, their architecture and agriculture – returned to scrub and swamp. The Indians were soon worse off than they had ever been before. They survived into the nineteenth century only to be exterminated by the successor regimes to the Spanish crown. When a butterfly's wing flapped in Europe, a hurricane of destruction was visited on South America.

Note

1. Pierre Chaunu, *L'Amérique et les Amériques*, Paris 1964, p. 117. See also Pierre Clastres, *Society Against the State*, New York 1989 (Paris 1974); and John Hemming, ''The population of Brazil in 1500'', in his *Red Gold: the conquest of the Brazilian Indians*, London 1978.

PART I
Across the Pantanal

The Tacuary river comes down with numerous windings through pleasant grassy plains into the lowlands, towards the Paraguay, and empties itself by many mouths into the main stream . . .

All travellers agree in the praise of these lands, where they say that the stranger is constantly surprised by an abundance of new and remarkable objects. According to their accounts, these islands and the banks of the river are inhabited by innumerable flocks of birds; the shoals of fish in this river, which come from the Paraguay, are incredible. Palms of singular forms stand upon the banks, alternating with a beautiful vegetation of aromatic grasses and shrubs.

The scenery is said to be still more remarkable and pleasing when the travellers have arrived in the canals, between the Pantanals themselves; thousands of ducks and waterhens rise in the air on the approach of the boats; storks of immense size wade the boundless swamps, and divide the sovereignty over the waters with the terrible crocodiles; sometimes they sail for leagues together between thick plantations of rice, which here grows spontaneously; and thus this solitary tract, which is but seldom animated by a canoe of the Guaycurus engaged in fishing, recalls to mind the plantations and agriculture of Europe.

The diversity and grandeur of the scenery announce the vicinity of a great river, and after four or five days' journey the navigators reach the Paraguay, which, at this place, is almost a league in breadth, even in the dry season, but during the rains overflows the Pantanals, and spreads into a vast lake above a hundred square leagues in extent.

Johann Spix and Carl Friedrich von
Martius, *Travels in Brazil in the Years
1817–1820*, London 1824

1

CAMPO GRANDE

The city on the plateau

Campo Grande is a small city in the middle of nowhere. From the air it seems but a dot at the centre of a vast expanse of cattle land, huge fields stretching to a distant horizon. From the train – a long weary journey from São Paulo – it springs up from the hot plateau like a mirage, a jumble of skyscraper megaliths and shantytowns, home to 300,000 people.

The train created the city, for like so much of modern Brazil, Campo Grande is a twentieth-century settlement. It owes its existence to its position on a junction of the great Trans-Brasil railway, completed to the shores of the Paraguay river in 1915.

This southern part of the Mato Grosso was invaded and occupied by Paraguay in 1865, in an almost forgotten campaign. When the Paraguayan War was over, and the invaders ousted, the Brazilians took steps to keep a firmer grip on this distant piece of territory, contested between Spain and Portugal since the sixteenth century. They planned the construction of a strategic railway to reach out to their threatened frontiers. Surveyed by British engineers in the 1870s, the line took forty years to complete. In 1920 Colonel Fawcett, inveterate traveller in these parts, described it as "the worst constructed and least efficiently maintained in the whole republic. It is quite usual for the train to be derailed once or twice west of the Paraná river, and the continual rocking never lets the passenger forget the imminent perils."[1]

Here at Campo Grande, the railway turns south to the Paraguayan border at Ponta Pora (San Juan Caballero), and continues west to the frontier with Bolivia at Corumbá.

A large military barracks still stands on the edge of the city, with helicopters and army lorries stacked up by the line. Like most such installations in South America, it now exists to intimidate a potential internal enemy as much as a foreign invader.

The railway serves little economic purpose. It is cheaper and quicker to send things by road. Frequent rumours suggest that the line will be closed. But the military still like it, and so do the tourists. They come now in ever-increasing numbers to the great swamp known as the Pantanal, the historic wetlands that lie to the north-west of Campo Grande in the flood plain of the upper Paraguay.

Pantanal was the name of a popular Brazilian television soap opera in the late

1980s. Its popularity was partly due to the torrid scenes in which naked women dived into the apparently limpid waters of the swamp while square-jawed cattle-men fought it out in canoes above, against a backdrop of sunsets in purple bronze.[2]

The tele-series has given this hitherto remote area a degree of external fame only achieved previously when gold was found to the north, near Cuiabá, in the early eighteenth century. The gold-diggers of 250 years ago have been replaced by families with cameras. Brazil's now ecologically conscious middle class is as keen to preserve the Pantanal, the world's largest wetland swamp, as it is to save what is left of the Amazon rainforest.

Many of these new ecological tourists are staying at the Hotel Gaspar, a splendid 1930s concrete building on the corner by the railway station. It has seen more prosperous times but still has a period charm. I am travelling with my wife, Vivien, and we sign in and take a first-floor room overlooking the tracks. It comes complete with television set and the famous kind of electric shower in which Brazilian hotels specialize. Bare wires protrude close to the switch. The hotel is both comfortable and cheap.

Anxious to explore, we walk out into the town in search of God and Indians, the key combination that characterizes so much of the history of this part of Latin America. Soon we have found traces of both.

Jesuit missionaries came to Guaíra and Itatín, the land south and west of here between the Paraná and the Paraguay, at the end of the sixteenth century, but nothing remains of their work. In the Brazilian outback, as in so much of today's South America, the Protestants now call the tune. Protestant missionaries, keen to convert the Indians (and feeling that the Catholics were doing the Devil's work), first arrived in Mato Grosso – from Scotland and the United States – early in the twentieth century. West of here, they established mission stations along the railway line.

Their successors, evangelicals with the enthusiasm of would-be pop stars, have a thriving practice in Campo Grande. It is a familiar scene in all the new settlements of South America, where the Catholic Church now has a wholly inadequate reach. Here on a busy street, behind a modern façade, is the Comunidade Evangélica Vida Nova, the New Life mission.

The doors, several of them, are symbolically thrown wide open, giving the impression that the entire width of the temple is open to the road. Inside, some three hundred people, mostly young, sitting in rows with five aisles between them, are clearly having a cheerful time.

Carelessly but cleanly dressed, in jeans and gay cotton tee-shirts, they sit in colourful contrast to the bare whitewashed walls of their makeshift temple. Here there is not a single statue or image, not even a crucifix. The pastor strides up and down across a low stage, microphone in hand. The audience stands or kneels at his command.

Outside it is hot, inside it is enticingly cool. The doorkeeper gestures to us with an inviting hand to come in to partake of this friendly gathering. We do not resist, but sit at the back admiring the economy of the scene. Unlike the Catholic Church, this Protestant enterprise is neither labour- nor capital-intensive. The temple is little more than a garage. The pastor has the minimum of training. But the congregation is clearly enjoying an experience closer to a football match or a pop concert than to the neurotic mysteries of an ancient religion.

Scenes like this represent a challenge to the hegemony of the Catholic Church in Latin America to which it has been extraordinarily slow to respond. The current answer of Pope Woytila – as Brazil's largest city, São Paulo, moves to the left – has been to reorganize the diocese and fill it with appointees from Rome. No more liberation theology. And Brazil's black bishops have appealed to Rome to be allowed to put some Afro-Brazilian "cultural elements" into their services: a nod, their critics think, in the direction of voodoo. But none of this is likely to stop the inroads made by the evangelical churches into the traditional flocks of the Catholic Church, a development that is changing the face of Latin America.

As for Indians, these are mostly in a museum. A few hundred Indians live in the shantytowns of Campo Grande – Terenos, Caduveos, Guatos, Xavantes, Guaraní, and Kaiowas – but they are unlikely to last for more than another generation. All that is left of their aboriginal culture is assembled in the Museu Don Bosco, an eclectic collection of birds and animals, and snakes and alligators – and Indians. The artefacts come from the Bororo Indians, and the museum's material was assembled over the years by the Salesian Fathers who worked among them.

There are many rooms and many visitors, and all the exhibits are crammed together in great confusion. But it seems a cheerful, secular place, with everyone laughing and joking and enjoying themselves, not at all intimidated by the atmosphere of a museum.

Just as the Brazilians are beginning to take a new interest in their swamps and forests, so they are also starting to investigate their Indian heritage. Catholic Fathers and European and North American anthropologists have been accumulating material for decades – Claude Lévi-Strauss worked near here in the 1930s – but only in the 1980s have these investigations acquired a wider audience.

Once it was argued that the forest Indians of the Amazon basin had an inferior civilization to that of the Andean, Maya, or Mexican Indians of the highlands. Such an argument, which reflected the cultural preconceptions of the time, is no longer tolerated, and Brazilians are at last beginning to take pride in their pre-Conquest cultures – what is left of them. Even in the little museum in Campo Grande it is possible to get a flavour of the advanced civilization of the local Indians from the forest and plain, settled farming people with their own art and artefacts, their own customs, traditions and philosophies. These were the people that the Spaniards and the Portuguese ran into – hundreds of thousands of them – when they advanced inland in the sixteenth century.

From the Museu Don Bosco we walked slowly back to the Hotel Gaspar, pausing for a fruit juice whipped up in an electric machine with milk and ice. Too hungry and tired to search further, we collapsed into a North American style fast-food restaurant which sold cheesy nibbles in batter. We lost our way on the return journey to the hotel, walking for several blocks in the wrong direction.

The expedition of Aleixo García, the first European traveller across South America, in 1524

These journeys across South America have been made before. This is no tabula rasa. Across the plateau of Campo Grande, down through the Pantanal and across the Paraguay river to the west, an endless procession of European traders and slavers, farmers and miners, priests and explorers, has made its way over the centuries. Written records of the visitors' presence were often made, and many have survived.

For the most part unsung and unrecorded, but increasingly available to the archaeologist's art and the anthropologist's interview, are the journeys of Indians in the pre-Columbian era. Many Indians, individually and collectively, migrated westward across the swamps and deserts of Chiquitos and the Chaco in the fifteenth century, from the banks of the Paraguay to the foothills of the Andes. Other Indian nations made the return journey. The outlines of the framework of pre-Columbian history in this area, for so long ignored, are at last beginning to be drawn.

Certainty only begins, however, with the first European to come this way. He was Aleixo García, a Portuguese adventurer who had come to Brazil some thirty years after Columbus first sailed into the Caribbean. Most accounts suggest that García came through this part of what is today the Brazilian state of Mato Grosso do Sul some time around the year 1524.

Of all the European conquistadores to arrive in the early rush to the shores of Brazil, Aleixo García is remembered not just because he was the first to move inland, but because he was the first to cross the continent from east to west. He reached the Inca empire a full decade before Pizarro, touching its eastern borders in the area that is now Bolivia. Since he was almost incontrovertibly Portuguese, his historic presence in the foothills of the Andes was used by the Brazilians over the centuries to justify their persistent westward move into territory traditionally considered Spanish.[3]

In spite of continual references to García in the near-contemporary reports and chronicles of the sixteenth century, he is a man of whom we know little. Shipwrecked off Santa Catarina in southern Brazil, he was tipped on shore in 1516 with a handful of Spaniards, perhaps from the ships of the expedition of Juan Diaz de Solís. We know nothing for certain of his ship or of its origins, though Argentine and Brazilian historians have long fought for the right to claim its nationality, Spanish or Portuguese.[4]

Unlike other early shipwrecked mariners in these latitudes, who usually stayed put and waited to be rescued, García and his companions were uncommonly adventurous. They advanced into the interior, learnt the language of the Guaraní Indians, and were lured westward across the swamps of the Chaco and Chiquitos by tales of gold and silver. They were the first of many.

García travelled to the west with four Portuguese and several friendly Indians. Moving up the coast to São Vicente (Santos), they would have climbed up onto the São Paulo plateau and travelled down the eastern rivers that lead to the Paraná. Sailing up that great stream and into its western tributaries, they would have arrived at the plains of Campo Grande.

From here, taking the gentle curves of the Aquidauana and then the Miranda river (called by the Indians and the first Spanish settlers the Mbotetei), they moved down into the swamps of the Pantanal to the Paraguay river. They crossed the Paraguay at a place called San Fernando.[5] The placename no longer exists, but the evidence suggests that it corresponds to the village of Albuquerque, across the river from Pôrto Esperança.

This spot marks the age-old entry to the Chiquitos route across the northern Chaco to the Andes. This was the route of the pre-Columbian Indians, of the Spanish conquistadores, of the Jesuit Fathers, of the Portuguese bandeirantes, and of the nineteenth-century commercial travellers. Today it is the route of the transcontinental railway line.

Somewhere near this traditional assembly point, García gathered together a large army of two thousand Guaraní Indians, the one settled group of Indians in the upper stretches of the Paraná and the Paraguay with whom the Europeans established an initial rapport. Marching with this great troop across Chiquitos, through what are now the flatlands of eastern Bolivia, he arrived at the frontiers of the Inca empire.[6]

This was a journey that the Guaraní Indians from the Paraguay basin had made often before – in search of the Land-Without-Evil or, more prosaically, in search of treasure. Many accounts exist of their great migrations westward across the Chaco in the fifteenth century, and it seems that García either joined or inspired a new one. The desert and swamp that characterize this land made it difficult for the Europeans to cross, and parts of it are still unmapped. But, for the Indians in the fifteenth and sixteenth centuries – familiar with the routes and the seasons – the road would have been much easier.[7]

García reached the rugged territory that lies between the towns of Mizque and Tomina (in what is now Bolivia). By all reports he got as far as the town of Tarabuco, on the eastern slopes of the Andes not far from the city of Sucre (known in colonial times as Charcas or Chuquisaca). Then it was ruled by the Incas. Today it is a famous market town, much admired by foreign visitors. There, like any contemporary tourist, García loaded up with treasure: cloth, clothing, jewellery, and artefacts of copper and silver.

The first European to find the treasure of the Inca empire, García now had to return to the east to tell the outside world of his discovery. With his makeshift Guaraní army and his supply of silver, he left Tarabuco and made his way back across Chiquitos. He arrived safely on the shores of the Paraguay, but was to get no further.

"Being loaded with this booty," the Jesuit chronicler Nicolás del Techo records, "he sent away two of his Portuguese companions to Brazil for succour." But help was not forthcoming in time. García himself "was cruelly murdered by the barbarians", although his son was spared "because of his tender years".

Father del Techo paid tribute to García's achievement and was the first to emphasize his historic importance as a transcontinental traveller. "His memory will last forever, because he durst with so small a company traverse almost all the land between the two seas that encompass South America, travelling unknown ways, where no European had been before."

The pattern of the future was etched out in these early years. The conquest and occupation of this land was not going to be easy. The Europeans were often isolated and beleaguered. For the next three centuries, until well after the wars of independence in the early nineteenth century, the Indians maintained the upper hand.

Aleixo García never returned to the Atlantic, but the remnants of his booty were found by the next group of European explorers who came thirsting up the Paraguay in search of silver. Journeying up the Paraguay north of Asunción in 1527, Sebastian Cabot came upon some Indians who had participated in García's expedition. They were the all too obvious beneficiaries of it.

Father del Techo records the encounter, though he suggests that Cabot was not fully aware of its significance:

> Cabot came to that place where 'tis said Alexius García the Portuguese was robbed and killed by the people of Paraguay. There, as he pryed into all things, finding many utensils of plate in the huts of the Indians, and not knowing anything of García's travel and death, thinking them to be the natural riches of the country, he hastily bought up all the Indians' silver plate, and . . . hasted back to Spain.

The remains of García's silver, enticingly glimpsed by Cabot, was to bring yet more foreign explorers hotfoot to the region. The rush for riches caused the River Plate to be called "the silver river", an overly optimistic prospectus as things were to turn out. The middle years of the sixteenth century were taken up with innumerable Spanish expeditions up the Paraguay – and across Chiquitos to the Andes.

Notes

1. Percy Harrison Fawcett, *Exploration Fawcett*, Hutchinson, London 1953, p. 212.

2. Described as the first ecological soap, *Pantanal* ran for 250 episodes. Its author, Benedito Ruy Barbosa, who wrote the original novel, spent years trying to find someone to turn it into a film.

3. Reporting a discussion in 1680 between Portuguese sailors and the governor of Buenos Aires, the Jesuit historian Father Charlevoix records that "some of the Portuguese had the assurance to advance [the argument] that the dominions of his Portuguese Majesty extended as far as the mines of Potosí, founding their pretensions, it is probable, on the expedition of Alexis García". The silver of Potosí (now a town in the Bolivian Andes) was by that time one of the main sources of Spanish wealth. (Pierre François Charlevoix, *The History of Paraguay*, 1769, vol. 2, p. 80. Father Charlevoix, who had not been to Paraguay, wrote originally in French. He also wrote a history of the Jesuits in Canada.)

4. The first detailed story of García's journey was written by Ruy Díaz de Guzmán, the chief, though not always reliable, chronicler of the first century of the Spanish conquest of Paraguay. His account was first published in 1612. He had a certain amount of nearly first-hand information in that his mother was one of the daughters of Domingo de Irala, one of the first European caciques of Paraguay. His grandmother was an Indian. (Irala was himself to make the journey across the Chaco in the 1540s, and, like other early conquistadores, he met Indians who had travelled with García or who were familiar with his story – see note 11, page 124.) Ruy Díaz de Guzmán, *Anales del descubrimiento, población y conquista de las provincias del Río de la Plata*, Ediciones Comuneros, Asunción 1980.

5. This is Guzmán's version. San Fernando is one of the names of the range of hills that stretch above the Paraguay between Coimbra and Corumbá. Some chroniclers suggest that García's expedition crossed Brazil further to the south, passing the great waterfall at Foz do Iguaçú.

6. "In martial manner," wrote Nicolás del Techo, the Jesuit historian who put together a synthesis of the tales of the early chroniclers towards the end of the seventeenth century, "he made his way to the borders of Peru, whilst the Inca was first living." There, through plunder, he collected "a vast quantity of wrought and unwrought silver". (Nicolás del Techo, *The History of the Provinces of Paraguay, Tucumán, Río de la Plata, Paraná, Guaíra, and Urvaica*. Father del Techo's history was written and first published in the seventeenth century in Latin. An edited and severely truncated version was published in English in A. and J. Churchill's *Collection of Voyages and Travels*, vol. 4, 1746.

7. Baron Erland Nordenskjöld, "The Guarani invasion of the Inca empire in the 16th century: an historical Indian migration", *Geographical Review*, New York, vol. 4, July–December 1917.

2

TERENOS

On the train from Campo Grande

The hotel in Campo Grande is buzzing with the sound of early travellers. The two trains of the day – going south to Paraguay and west to Bolivia – leave betimes. We have a powerful German breakfast in the Hotel Gaspar's commodious dining room, coffee and rolls, cheese and ham. The room is full of Brazilian couples and families, all on holiday and looking cheerful.

The train comes in at eight, having brought a tired group of passengers through the night from Baures. We scrabble for seats in the foetid first-class carriage, bundling our luggage through the open window. The train sets off punctually at quarter to nine.

First we go slowly through the town, the klaxon blowing at the level-crossings, with cars and lorries patiently waiting for us to pass. Then we go past oil depots and gas deposits and endless warehouses, till finally, beyond the barracks and the airport, we come to the wide grasslands that stretch to the furthest distance. This is the cattle country that makes Mato Grosso do Sul such a prosperous state.

At the first small halt, Indubrasil, the lines diverge. The left-hand fork goes to Ponta Pora and the Paraguayan frontier. We take the right-hand fork towards Corumbá and Bolivia. A man comes down the corridor selling coffee from a thermos. Then we stop at Terenos, a leafy village with a name to remind us that this is the beginning of what was once Indian territory. The original Terenos – the Guana or Chané – came from the eastern slopes of the Andes, but there are few survivors left in the village today.

After a couple of hours through fields of white cattle, skeletal like old men, the train begins to climb a low pass through the Serra do Maracajú. For miles ahead a great gap is visible in the hills, a path through to the Pantanal and the west that has been used for thousands of years. For a while we follow the course of the Aquidauana, a river that eventually runs into the Paraguay. We pause briefly at the station of Palmeiras and again at Piraputanga.

Once past the line of hills, the land is mostly flat again – swamp, palm trees and scrub. Burnt and blackened trees stick up out of the water, birds cling to tree stumps, herds of great white cattle seize the high ground. We see the occasional alligator, a few ostriches and innumerable herons and parrots. This is the beginning of the Pantanal, the great wetland that stretches from the hills of Maracajú to the Paraguay river.

The first written description of this immense area of swamp, and of the people who originally lived here, comes from the pen of Pero Hernández, the secretary and lawyer of Alvar Núñez Cabeza de Vaca who led one of the first Spanish expeditions to the upper Paraguay in the 1540s.

Hernández wrote an account of the upriver journey, at Cabeza de Vaca's direction, and he gives a picture of an enchanting and prosperous province, where the local Indian population had adapted itself to the demands of the changing seasons:

> When the waters are low, the people from the interior come and live on the banks of the river with their wives and children, and pass their time in fishing, for the fish are abundant and very fat at this season. They lead pleasant lives, dancing and singing night and day, like persons who are relieved of all anxiety about food; but when the water begins to rise, which is in January, they retire inland, because at that season the floods begin, and the waters rise six fathoms above the banks of the river. At such time the country is under water for over one hundred leagues inland, spreading over everything like a sea, so that even tall palms and other trees are covered, and vessels may pass over their summits. This usually happens every year.[1]

At such times, Hernández wrote, the Indians became floating nomads, taking home and family with them on the rising waters.

> The natives keep very large canoes in readiness for this emergency; and in the middle of these canoes they throw two or three loads of mud, and make a hearth. The Indian then enters with his wife, children, and household goods, and floats on the rising tide wherever they like. He lights a fire on the hearth to cook his food and for warmth, and thus he voyages for four months of the year, or as long as the floods last. As these retire into their channels, he returns the same way, hunting and fishing, and not leaving his canoe till the banks whereon he is wont to dwell are uncovered.

These were the Terenos, the great nation that came originally from the Amazon side of the Chaco and now survives as the name of a railway station. In Hernández's day in the sixteenth century, known as the Chané or the Guana, this nation lived along the banks of the upper Paraguay. Today its survivors are gathered in dispiriting reservations not far from here.

In the early years of Spanish conquest and settlement, this area was called Itatín. Tens of thousands of Indians were living here when the Europeans first arrived. Travelling up from Asunción, where they were already familiar with the Guaraní Indians of the lower Paraguay, the Spaniards called them the Itatines. Father Charlevoix, a Jesuit historian living in the middle of the eighteenth century, says that they "spoke the same language with the Guaraní, and seemed to be of the same origin". At that time, however, "they kept up very little communication with them".[2]

The Spaniards were impressed by the Itatines. They found them to be "extremely vigorous and nimble". They were particularly intrigued by their enthusiasm for handicap racing. "Running was so well studied and so favourite a diversion among them, that they obliged the runners to carry stones of a fixed weight, and even distributed prizes among them." The Itatines of Mato Grosso do Sul have now all but disappeared.[3]

Over the centuries, the old region of Itatín has been laid waste by conflict and war. This conflict was not just the generalized onslaught associated with the European conquest – disease and famine – but two very specific instances of battle: once in the 1630s when the slave-traders from São Paulo came sweeping through, and again in the 1860s when the forces of Brazil and Paraguay fought for supremacy over the upper Paraguay.

The arrival of the Jesuits in Brazil in the sixteenth century

The country south of here is immensely wealthy cattle land. It must always have been fertile. Spanish colonists came to this area late in the sixteenth century. Jesuit priests soon followed them, first to minister to the whites, then, increasingly, to corral the Indians into mission settlements. This attractive region, the broad acres that stretch from the Serra do Maracajú to the Paraguay river, was once – in the 1630s – the short-lived Jesuit missionary province of Itatín.

In some parts of South America, many of the old Jesuit mission towns still survive. In Paraguay and Argentina, in southern Brazil and eastern Bolivia, great ruins can still be found, many of them almost lost in the jungle. But in the area that was once Itatín, nothing remains. There is no physical memorial to the particular Jesuit endeavour of the 1630s, when a group of charismatic Belgian priests sought to hold this land and resist the westward push of the Portuguese.

Itatín was the most northerly part of the early Jesuit province of Paraquariae, an area that embraced virtually the entire southern region of South America. The story of Paraquariae, and of the utopian missions that were established there among the Indians, has been told and retold ever since the eighteenth century, when tales of the Jesuits' activities first began to surface in the compilations of exploration and travel that so excited the jaundiced palate of pre-revolutionary Europe. After the Jesuits were expelled from South America in 1767 (and their Society of Jesus closed down by Pope Clement XIV in 1773), a further cornucopia of mission writings and memoirs appeared, from the pens of the exiled priests.

Because of the volume, and indeed quality of this material, the Paraguayan Jesuits sometimes seem to have a monopoly on the information that has been passed on to later generations about the early years of South American colonial endeavour. Their observations and insights are the ones that inform much of the historical writing about this part of the world.

But the Jesuits were not the first priests or missionaries in South America – that distinction belongs to the Franciscans and the Dominicans – and their first major efforts were not in Spanish Paraguay but in Portuguese Brazil. Indeed, the model for the famous Paraguay missions of the eighteenth century was first tested, over a considerable period, in the second half of the sixteenth century, in Brazil.

Portuguese mission practice was later to differ considerably from that of the Spanish missions. The latter were to enjoy somewhat greater freedom from the Spanish state, in both its local and peninsular form, than the Brazilian ones did from the Portuguese state. But the first religious experiments – seeking to control the Indian population of this part of the New World – were made in Brazil.

The history of the watershed between the Paraguay and the Amazon is inextricably linked with the colonization schemes of the Spanish Jesuits, and with the journeys they made between the different areas under their control. But to understand the history of the great string of missions that these Jesuits were to establish – stretching in a wide semicircle in the shadow of the Andes from Paraguay in the south, through Bolivia, Peru and Ecuador, to Colombia in the north – it is necessary to see how that endeavour was first experienced in Brazil.

The Society of Jesus, the advance guard of the Counter-Reformation, was founded in 1539, at a time when Portuguese settlers were already farming on the island of São Vicente, off Santos (1532), and when Spanish conquistadores had already begun to penetrate into the waters of the upper Paraguay (1537). The Basque founder of the society, Ignatius Loyola, had not originally conceived it as a missionary order operating in distant parts. Founded as a Catholic response to the Reformation, its first task was to attack Protestants, not to convert Indians. But since its message fell on particularly fertile ground in Portugal, the society soon hitched its waggon to the overseas activities of the Portuguese empire, first in Asia and later (in 1549) in Brazil.

In 1553, Brazil became the Jesuits' first foreign province. Manoel da Nóbrega, the first Brazilian Provincial of the Society, came out to Bahía with five other priests. Fifty years later, in 1600, there were 128 Jesuits in Brazil, and a similar number in Peru. By that time, Jesuits had also begun to filter through to the Paraguay river, and even to the area of Chiquitos.

These men were soldiers of Christ. They saw themselves as soldiers in priestly garb. Some of them, like Ignatius himself, had actually been in the armed forces. They belonged to the same adventurous elite as the second- or third-generation conquistadores with whom they shared administrative responsibilities in the new colonial territories. A century later, these priests were to be more overtly spiritual, more interested in the life of the Church than that of the State. But a Jesuit priest at the end of the sixteenth century was more like a member of the Special Boat Squadron than a pastor bearing witness to the pacifistic message of the pale

Galilean. Tough, athletic and entrepreneurial, the Jesuits were the intellectual shock troops of European expansion.

Although the initial emphasis of the Society of Jesus was on the Portuguese territory of Brazil, Ignatius Loyola survived long enough to take a personal interest in Paraguay. Shortly before he died, on 31 July 1556, he wrote enthusiastically of the contacts made by Jesuits in São Vicente "with a town of Spaniards called Paragay [sic] on the River Plate". He told his correspondent that Father Nóbrega was planning to go there, and hoping to secure a base from which to send out priests "to preach and baptize, and to help those people to salvation".[4]

With a keen eye for worldly realities, Loyola added that Nóbrega's priests would be able "to help the Christians of the town as well, for whom I think it will be most necessary". He had perceived that the European settlers would be in at least as much need of spiritual guidance as the Indians.

Loyola did not live to hear that this early plan was to be frustrated. A letter from his man in São Paulo, arriving in Rome after his death, revealed that Nóbrega's initial scheme to send priests to Paraguay had been sabotaged by the Spanish governor. The road from Portuguese Brazil to Spanish Paraguay was to be closed.[5]

The Jesuits in Brazil, like almost all Europeans in the sixteenth century arriving in South America for the first time, had been notably impressed by the Indians that they encountered. Adjectives like "barbarian" and "savage" came much later, when the Indians openly rebelled and refused to accept their secondary status. Father Nóbrega was amazed by the quality and character of the Indians he found in the country inland from Bahía. In many things, he wrote, they are "superior to Christians, for they live better morally and observe natural law better".[6] Ignatius Loyola would not have been surprised. It was not difficult to live a more moral life than the average European settler of the sixteenth century.

A couple of years after landing in Brazil, Nóbrega wrote to the Portuguese king with a glowing description of the putty that he had found in his hands. "They believe in nothing – they are a blank page on which one can write at will, provided one sustains them by example and continual converse."

This initial sense of delight proved to be short-lived. The early Portuguese Jesuits soon found that it was difficult to get their message to stick to "the blank page". It was, writes John Hemming, the historian of the Brazilian Indians, more like "writing on the sand of a beach, washed clean by the first wave".[7]

Nevertheless the Portuguese on their coastal strip, and the Spaniards on the upper Paraguay, do seem – on their first arrival – to have come into contact with a number of Indian nations that were prepared to be friendly. Some seem to have displayed considerable interest in the activities of the Jesuits. Even allowing for the excitement that doubtless grew in the telling, many Indians fell over themselves to get converted and baptized. The potential harvest, as the priests kept writing home, was enormous. Indeed it was so large and so widespread that the Brazilian Jesuits devised the idea of creating mission settlements: a kind of human granary in which the converts could be stored. Nóbrega wrote:

> The first step, which is already a great success, is to concentrate the Indians from scattered villages into one large village. Whereas before many of us were needed to teach and indoctrinate them because they were so scattered about, now that they are concentrated together, fewer of us are needed.

The early Portuguese settlers were keen supporters of these Jesuit villages. The assembled Indian population gave the priests a ready audience for their ideological indoctrination sessions, and provided the settlers with a convenient and ever available pool of labour. Inevitably and unsurprisingly, as time went by, the enthusiasm of the Indians for this new way of life began to wane. Christianity was one thing, forced labour quite another. The Indians grew reluctant to accept the bait.

Increasingly, forced settlement became the Portuguese response. Soon settler and priest were helping each other – changing the metaphor – to drive the fish into the net, by force when necessary. Father Nóbrega grew increasingly disillusioned with the Indians who had once so impressed him. His early favourable opinions changed. His language grew more harsh. "Nothing can be done with them if they are left at liberty," he wrote, "for they are brutish people."

Nóbrega's successor, Father José de Anchieta, was equally tough and uncompromising. "For these people there is no better preaching than by the sword and iron rod. Here more than anywhere it is necessary to adopt the policy of compelling them to come in."

Not having much luck with the adults, the Brazilian Jesuits began to concentrate their efforts on Indian boys. Initially, and with the very young, this strategy was quite successful. But it did not last. "All I can say of them," wrote a disappointed José de Anchieta, "is that on reaching puberty they began to take charge of themselves. They then reached such a state of corruption that they now exceed their parents in evil by as much as they formerly did in good." The next generation was to prove as intransigently hostile as the previous one.

In spite of these setbacks, the Portuguese policy of driving Indians into mission villages continued throughout the sixteenth century. The only successful form of Indian protest was to die. And this, in ever-increasing numbers, is what the Indians did. A Jesuit in Brazil reported in the 1580s: "the number of people who have died here in Bahía in the past 20 years seems unbelievable. No one ever imagined that so many people could ever be expended, far less in so short a time."[8]

Another Brazilian Jesuit, Father Antônio Blasques, was equally shocked.

> Anyone who saw them in this distress, remembering the time past and how many there were then and how few now, and how previously they had enough to eat but now they die of hunger, and how previously they used to live in freedom but now find

themselves beyond misery, assaulted at every step and enslaved by force by the Christians – anyone who considered and pondered this sudden change cannot fail to grieve and weep many tears of compassion.

This was the situation in the Portuguese towns in Brazil at the end of the sixteenth century. After sixty years of conquest and occupation, the Indian population had already been decimated.

Those surviving outside the European sphere did not necessarily fare much better. They were the prey of the Portuguese slave-traders, the middlemen who went out into the plains and jungles to collect Indians, to make the fragile economy of Portugal's new colonies viable. Father José de Anchieta calculated that as many as two to three thousand Indians might be brought in to Bahía as slaves each year.

A pattern had been established in the coastal regions of Brazil. It was soon to spread westwards into Paraguay, bringing Portuguese slave-traders into dramatic conflict with Spanish missionaries, and causing the eventual destruction of all the early Jesuit missions in Paraguay. As so often in South America, disputes between Europeans were far more lethal and damaging to the local inhabitants than any arguments that they might have had among themselves.

Notes

1. "The Commentaries of Alvar Núñez Cabeza de Vaca", in Luis Domínguez (ed.), *The Conquest of the River Plate*, Hakluyt Society, London 1891, p. 193.
2. Pierre François Charlevoix, *The History of Paraguay*, London 1769, vol. 1, p. 354.
3. Some say that they survive as the Guarayu of eastern Bolivia, for many of them migrated to the west in the 1550s with Nuflo de Chávez, the founder of Santa Cruz de la Sierra.
4. Letter from Ignatius Loyola to Pedro da Ribadeneira, 3 March 1556, printed in Serafim Leite, *Cartas dos primeiros Jesuitas do Brasil*, vol. 2, *1553–1558*, São Paulo, 1957, pp. 263–5. Nóbrega had received first-hand information about Paraguay from Antônio Rodrigues, a Portuguese adventurer who had travelled to the River Plate with Pedro de Mendoza in 1535 and subsequently crossed "near to the Marãnon and the Amazon" with Domingo de Irala. Rodrigues had then, in 1552, travelled to Brazil and persuaded Nóbrega to enrol him in the Company of Jesus. Rodrigues was the first conquistador to become a Jesuit priest. In return, Nóbrega asked him to write a long report for the Jesuit college in Coimbra. One of the earliest accounts of the Spanish campaign on the upper Paraguay, it is published in Serafim Leite, *Cartas*, vol. 1, pp. 468–81.
5. Letter to Ignatius Loyola from Luis da Grao, dated Piratininga, 7 April 1557. Serafim Leite, *Cartas*, vol. 2, pp. 359–63. This is the first recorded instance of the closure of the east–west road across South America, but by no means the last. Sometimes it was closed by the Indians, sometimes by the climate, and quite frequently by administrative fiat.
6. Quoted in John Hemming, *Red Gold: the conquest of the Brazilian Indians*, Macmillan, London, 1978, p. 99.
7. Hemming, p. 102.
8. Quoted in Hemming, p. 144.

3

AQUIDAUANA

By train and road to Aquidauana

Our train from Campo Grande moves steadily on, arriving at midday at the large and prosperous town of Aquidauana, the largest settlement on the eastern edge of the Pantanal. Across the track, there is a circular concrete stadium: football rather than running is the passion of the local inhabitants of the twentieth century. The station here has long platforms and buildings of brick to match the historical pretensions of the town. Food sellers parade up and down the platform doing a useful trade. The train stops here for half an hour while passengers and their baggage are disentangled.

Almost the same journey, from Campo Grande to Aquidauana, can be made by car. The road and the railway run parallel for much of the way. By car the journey takes about three hours, along a good metalled road. As far as Terenos, the land is flat, and then the hills begin. Travelling along the route one hot afternoon, I found the road gap into the Pantanal through the Serra do Maracaju to be rather more impressive than the route taken by the Aquidauana river and the railway. The road carves its way through beside a great rock cliff that rears high up into the sky. Red and bare at the top, it is covered with thick green vegetation at the bottom.

The climate usually matches the majesty of the geological formation, sometimes roasting hot, sometimes cooled by the arrival of a tropical storm, the sky constantly illuminated by lightning flash. Flagged down by a broken-down lorry, I gave a man a lift to the next garage. There are a lot of lorries on the road. Outside Campo Grande I counted 24 great ten-wheelers parked by the roadside. Sometimes you pass a stall loaded high with yellow squashes, or lemons. But this is mostly fazenda country, poorly farmed. You don't see many people.

The main road goes on to Corumbá and the Bolivian frontier, but I turned off at the sign to Aquidauana, and found the town rather more one-horse than I had expected: a strip of road with a line of garages for repairing trucks, and men playing chess in the shade. But these were only the outskirts, south of the river.

Crossing the broad and majestic Aquidauana on a narrow concrete bridge, you come to the town proper, a criss-cross of paved streets lying between the river and the railway line. Aquidauana seems to have no street lights, but the pavements are lit from the glow of houses, shops and bars.

Down the road is the town square: all gardens and a children's playground. On each corner are the busts of distinguished citizens of the region, with a simple placard announcing that they had instilled into the town a love of work.

Missionary work above the Sete Quedas at the end of the sixteenth century

Far to the south of Aquidauana, across the basin of the Paraná river and close to the twentieth-century frontier where Paraguay and Brazil meet Argentina, are some of the most splendid waterfalls in the world. For long a famous tourist attraction, these falls on the Iguaçú river acquired a wider fame in the 1980s as the backdrop to a film, *The Mission*, about the downfall of the Jesuits in South America in the 1760s. The Iguaçú falls were known to the first Spanish explorers who came this way from the coast in the 1540s, though at that time they went largely unremarked. Travellers in the sixteenth century had little time for the aesthetic achievements of nature.

Below the falls, the Iguaçú runs into the Paraná, and on that river, just upstream from the junction, a mighty dam now stands, one of the largest in the world. Finished in the 1980s, the Itaipú dam rivals the Iguaçú falls in its immensity, a man-made competitor with nature.

Like many such great engineering projects in the Third World, the hydro-electric scheme at Itaipú is dumbfounding in its presumption. To the north, upstream, a vast all-embracing lake has been created in the jungle by the rising waters of the dam. It stretches for miles, drowning the river and absorbing immense tracts of land on either side. Underneath its placid surface, another great and turbulent waterfall has been submerged – for all time.

The Sete Quedas, the Seven Falls – known in Spanish Latin America as the Guaíra Falls – were a dramatic series of waterchutes and cataracts, divided by rocky islands, blocking the downward path of the Paraná river. "Amongst all the things capable of exciting admiration in these provinces," a Jesuit father wrote in 1626, "this cataract easily obtains the first place." I know not, he added, "whether the whole terra-queous globe contains anything more wonderful".

The river precipitates itself, with the utmost violence, down an immensely high rock, twelve leagues in descent, and dashes in its downward course against huge rocks of horrible form, from which the waters, being reverberated, leap up to a great height, and as the channel is in many places intersected, on account of the exceeding roughness of the rocks, the waters are separated into various paths, and then meet together again, causing stupendous whirlpools.

In other places also, the waters, leaping down, rush into the rocks themselves, and are concealed from the view: then, after having remained hidden for some time, again break forth, as if they had sprung from various fountains, and swallow up vast masses of rock.

Lastly, so great is the violence of the waters in the descent of the stream, that, during the whole course of twelve leagues, they are covered by a perpetual foam, which, reflecting the rays of the sun, dazzles the eyes of beholders with its brightness.[1]

These waterfalls, now gone forever as a result of twentieth-century technology, are famous in history for an extraordinary event in the early seventeenth century. In 1631, they bore witness to a quasi-religious exodus as a messianic Jesuit priest, Antonio Ruíz de Montoya, sought to lead his Indian people out of danger into a new, unpromised, land. It is one of the great stories of missionary history, told and retold over the years. Yet in its ill-planned execution, as Father Montoya led his flock around the cataracts, the exodus proved to be yet another of the many disasters visited on the Indians by the Europeans.[2]

The first Jesuits had arrived in the lush territory above the Sete Quedas at the end of the sixteenth century. The province was called Guaíra, a fertile land on the eastern banks of the upper Paraná. Inhabited by Guaraní-speaking Indians, it had been occupied by Spanish colons from Asunción since the 1560s. Though now today in Brazil, at that time it formed part of the Spanish territory of Paraguay.

Evangelical work among the Indians of Paraguay, frustrated in the 1550s by the closing of the road from Brazil, had begun two decades later. The first European missionary here was a Franciscan from Spain, Father Luis de Bolaños, who arrived in Asunción in 1575. According to later reports, he began encouraging the Indians to move into mission villages, along the lines of the pattern already established by the Jesuits in Brazil. Pushing eastwards into Guaíra province, by the end of the 1580s he had established some eighteen Christian villages there among the Indians. Father Bolaños was a notable pioneer, learning the Guaraní language, writing a Guaraní grammar, and translating the prayer book.

Two Jesuits then arrived from Brazil – Manoel Ortega and Tomás Fíldio. Ortega was Portuguese, and Fíldio was an Irishman from Limerick, Tom Fields, who had been one of the companions of José de Anchieta.[3] Like the early Jesuits in Brazil, the two priests were favourably impressed by the Indians they encountered, and amazed by their obvious capacity to dominate and control their environment. Father Alonso de Barzana, writing from Asunción in 1594, reported that they were excellent farmers. "They have great quantities of food, especially maize, various kinds of manioc and other fine roots, and a great amount of fish."

Yet already, some fifty years after the original Spanish settlement in Paraguay had been established, disease and epidemic had begun to wreak havoc in the new Indian towns and villages, just as they had done in Brazil. Father del Techo, writing half a century later, tried to calculate the scale of the disaster. There were three hundred thousand Indians in Guaíra when the Spaniards first arrived, he wrote, and "scarce the fifth part of that number remains''. Sixty thousand now lived where once there had been three hundred thousand.

His mention of ''the ruins of an abundance of villages, which appear thick and contiguous'' makes this number seem credible. The whole nation, he went on, now ''lives miserably, having no bread but what is made of the root mandioca, or any flesh to eat but that of wild beasts''. The deserted villages were caused ''by sickness and the driving away of the Indians''.[4] The Spaniards brought the sickness, the Portuguese were responsible for driving the Indians away.

For the handful of early Jesuits in Guaíra at the end of the sixteenth century, the circumstances were hardly propitious. In 1590 ''the worst plague of smallpox in South American history'' interrupted their teaching. The priests withdrew to the west, down the Ipané river to the Paraguay and thence back to Asunción. Despair set in. Converting the Indians of Guaíra seemed to be a hopeless cause.

All the Jesuits from Paraguay were summoned to a crisis meeting in Salta, in the north of Argentina, in 1602. There was no future for their work in Paraguay, according to the Jesuit Provincial, Father Paez. It should be abandoned. It was not an easy decision, since ''they had left behind them two hundred thousand Indians, quite ripe for the kingdom of Christ''.[5]

The strategic hamlets established by the Spanish Jesuits in Guaíra, 1590–1630

The outlook seemed bleak, and not just for the Jesuits. At the beginning of the seventeenth century, the entire Spanish project in this part of South America was at risk. The Spanish authorities were faced with a difficult problem. Their colons in Paraguay, poised along an uncertain frontier with Brazil, were in desperate need of indigenous labour to make a success of their settlements. As in Brazil, the settlers needed Indians to work on their farms and plantations. But the pool of Indians was so huge – there were hundreds of thousands of them – that if the settlers were not careful in their demands, they were in danger of being destroyed by revolt. An additional danger was the prospect of such a slave revolt being organized or manipulated by the Portuguese.

These threats were genuine. Within fifty years of the start of the century, the frontier territory in question – Guaíra and Itatín, first settled by Spaniards – was in the hands of the Portuguese. In some circumstances, and nearer home, the Spanish crown might have offered to protect its colonists with military force. But this was the Spanish way. South America was far away, and there was little spare money available for imperial defence.

So a cheap and, in the circumstances, sophisticated policy was devised: the useful but potentially threatening Guaraní Indians were to be placed under the ideological control of the priests; the small numbers of Spanish military were to adopt a low profile and keep their powder dry; and the settlers were to be allowed cheap, but not free, labour. In this way an inexpensive buffer would be placed between the Spaniards and the Portuguese.

In 1609, acting under instructions from the government of Philip III in Madrid, the Spanish governor of Asunción, Hernando de Saavedra, made a deal along these lines with the Jesuit Provincial of Paraguay, Father Diego de Torres. The Jesuits would set up strategic hamlets in the frontier province of Guaíra, along the upper Paraná river. These would be populated by Indians and be separate from the existing established Spanish towns. They would help to stabilize the frontier area. As a further inducement, the new Jesuit missions were to enjoy a tax holiday for ten years: a concession that in practice was almost indefinitely extended. There was only one charge on the Spanish crown: the salary of the Jesuit priests, two in each town, was paid by Madrid.[6]

The groundwork had been laid for a mission strategy that was to last for 150 years, until the Jesuits were expelled in 1767. It was modified over time, and its implementation varied from place to place. But the fundamental purpose of the Jesuit missions, to guard the Spanish frontier cheaply against the Portuguese and, later, against a number of incorrigibly hostile Indian nations, was etched out in the first decade of the seventeenth century.

The Jesuits called their mission towns "reducciones", reductions, places where the Indians were "reduced" into European "civilization". They were hamlets, Father Ruíz de Montoya wrote, "where the Indians who had been living according to their ancient customs – in the bush and the hills, in the valleys and the hidden watercourses – separated from each other in scattered huts of three or four or six, were united by the efforts of the Jesuit fathers into large villages, and then 'reduced' to political and human existence".[7]

The pilot project in Guaíra, started in 1610, began rather hopefully. Two Italian Jesuits, Simón Maceta and José Cataldino, set off on the familiar route from Asunción, up the Paraguay and the Ipané, to Ciudad Real, another new Spanish town in Guaíra. From this base, they travelled up the Paraná to the Paranapanema where they established their first mission town: Loreto. The following year, 1611, they founded another: San Ignacio.

The two new missions began to prosper, but as Father Charlevoix rather caustically observed, "they were not as yet overstocked with Christians". The Jesuits themselves were often depressed by the huge gap that existed between their own mystical belief that they were there to save souls from hellfire, and the overtly secular motives that led Indians to join their settlements. Father Charlevoix noted that "most of their proselytes repaired to them merely to avoid being molested by the Spaniards or the Portuguese of Brazil, and in order to be the better able to defend themselves against their own enemies". (Later, in the eighteenth century, it became standard practice for the mission Indians of Paraguay and Chiquitos to march out to attack their traditional enemies, and then to retreat to the relative safety of the mission compound.)

In Guaíra, the missionaries grew increasingly unhappy about the motives of their flock. They "began to admit them with some reserve", wrote Charlevoix, particularly when they realized that "many of those who had been too readily received soon grew tired of the regular life they were made to lead". To the intense irritation of the Jesuits, these Indians returned "to the woods and mountains when the missionaries least expected it".[8]

Sometimes, even the missionaries must have admitted to themselves that their mission towns were less than satisfactory, and that the Indians had good cause for mistrust. Almost inevitably, the Guaíra settlements became major health hazards. When the mission towns were once again struck by smallpox in 1618, many Indians abandoned them, retiring to the forest. They believed, not without reason, that life there would be healthier.

Disease apart, the Indians of Guaíra still remained vulnerable, both to the Spanish colons seeking labour, and to the slave-raiding expeditions of the Portuguese. In the original deal made in 1609 between the governor and the Jesuits, it was agreed that Spanish soldiers should be kept out of the mission towns. Overt signs that Indian territory was being violated had to be kept to a minimum. A later governor, Fernando Arias, failed to obey this clause. When making a tour of the new settlements, he arrived with an armed retinue. At one of them, "the appearance of about fifty soldiers caused such an alarm among the neighbouring Indians that . . . a large body assembled to cut him off on his return."

Governor Arias compounded his initial error. He made the mistake of "disposing of all the civil and military employments of the new establishment with the same authority he could have done in any Spanish town of his government". Only the intervention of the local Jesuit priest, who by happenstance was his brother-in-law, saved him from the wrath of the Indians.

The Indian cacique had the last word. Governor Arias thought that it would be a good idea, in smoothing over this outrage, to present the cacique with a staff of command, given in the name of the king. "The barbarian prince nobly answered that he had, for a long time past, commanded in the country without any such staff, and therefore desired him to keep the bauble for somebody else, who might think it worth his acceptance."[9]

In 1620, a new missionary arrived in Guaíra, a controversial priest from Peru blessed with unquenchable enthusiasm and energy. This was Antonio Ruíz de Montoya, famous in the annals of the Jesuit order. In the six years between 1622 and 1628, he is credited with the foundation of no less than eleven new Indian missions, with a combined population of more than forty thousand.

Montoya was the only son of a wealthy landowner in Peru. As a young man, he had volunteered to join the army, offering to fight the Araucanian Indians of Chile at his own expense. He was dissuaded from doing so on the ground that, were he to be killed, his estates would be left without a legitimate owner. On joining the Society of Jesus, he was despatched to Paraguay and to Guaíra.

His labours in that vineyard, though dramatic, were of no permanent value. The missions near the Spanish town of Villa Rica proved to be endlessly vulnerable to the depredations of the Spanish colons. Charleroix records that they "let slip no opportunity of carrying off all the new Christians they could surprise". They were then treated "in a manner that exposed them to the danger of losing their faith along with their liberty".

Father Montoya thought that he could remedy this problem by moving further away from the Spanish towns, to the east, establishing mission towns on the other side of the Paranapanema river. But there, of course, they were vulnerable to the Portuguese, in the shape of the famous Mameluke slave-traders, advancing westward from São Paulo.

The destruction of the Guaíra missions by the Mamelukes

In the writing of the history of the Spanish- Brazilian border, no subject has aroused so much controversy among the nationalist historians of South America (and there are no others) as the description of the inhabitants of São Paulo in the early seventeenth century.

Were they barbaric murderers, little better than the Indian savages they enslaved, who forced their way into territory that was not theirs? This is the Jesuit, Spanish, and Argentine version, and they are known to their history as Mamelukes.[10]

Or were they fearless patriots, exploring unknown lands and acquiring them for the Portuguese empire, earning an honest crust by advancing into hostile territory and securing the labour needed to keep the colonial settlements economically alive? This is the Portuguese and Brazilian version, and in Brazilian history they are known as "bandeirantes" – a noble word with a positive meaning, suggesting pioneers with flags (bandeiras) who open up new country.

For several centuries it was sufficient for the hostile Spanish chronicler to explain to the reader that the Paulistas were half-castes: perceived as a most undesirable mixture of Portuguese colon, black slave and native Indian. Most early writers were anxious to explain that the Mamelukes were also the fruit of the riff-raff of half Europe, scoundrels of one sort or another who had crossed the Atlantic, been thrown out of Bahía, and moved down to São Paulo in the company of thieves and prostitutes and other assorted rogues.

Nicolás del Techo was the first among many to denounce their cross-breed origins:

> The European planters for a long time preserved their native honour, till, the European women failing, they began to mix with that barbarous race, and corrupted the noble Portuguese blood. This mixture, in process of time, running through them all, and bad sons succeeding good fathers, and worse grandsons, the sons that the generous

Portuguese bred being so often mixed, degenerated, so that there nothing remained among the posterity of those first renowned conquerors of Brazil but their names. The Portuguese disdaining to call this generation by their name . . . gave them the barbarous name of Mamelukes, that since they are like them in nothing else, they may not be alike in name.

No one wrote about the Mamelukes in such offensive terms as Jesuits like Father del Techo, for these Portuguese slavers destroyed all their initial missionary work in Guaíra and Itatín. Father Martín Dobrizhoffer gives a heart-rending account of the Mamelukes' activities as they advanced on the missions of Guaíra in search of slaves, a description that bears comparison with the accounts of the Germans marching into eastern Europe in the 1940s:

The sucking babes were torn from the bosoms of their mothers, and cruelly dashed upon the ground by the way. All whom disease or age had rendered imbecile were either cut down or shot, as being unequal to the daily march. Others, in sound health, were often thrown by night into trenches that were prepared for them, lest they should take advantage of the darkness and flee. Many perished by the way, either from hunger or the hardships of a journey protracted for many leagues.

Historians of Brazil, however, depict the Mamelukes as pioneers of Brazilian nationhood. They suggest that they started as self-defence units. These were made up of whites and Indians, banded together for self-protection against a hostile environment (and later against the threat from the Dutch). Their "bandeiras" expanded from São Paulo at the beginning of the seventeenth century, first to the south and then west across the Paraná river to the Paraguay.[11]

By the 1630s, however, these groups' reason for existence had gone beyond mere self-defence; they had become a way of life. The Portuguese/Brazilian historian Jaime Cortesão makes the point that a bandeira was essentially a collaborative enterprise between a few whites and a very large number of Indians. To survive, it relied significantly on the nomadic experience of the Indians.

This is an intriguing and attractive argument, since it goes halfway towards suggesting that the Mamelukes were really one more form of Indian resistance to European conquest. If the Mamelukes/bandeirantes were half-castes, then it is perfectly legitimate to argue that the Indians were the dominant element. Noting their skill in shooting and robbing, Dobrizhoffer had perceived them as true Europeans, "a set of people born of Portuguese, Dutch, French, Italians and Germans, and Brazilian women". But contemporary Jesuits were often impressed by their resilience and endurance, reflecting that they were as hardy as the Jesuits themselves, even though they lacked the spiritual backbone of faith with which the Jesuits were provided.[12]

However they are defined, whether Indian or European, the Mamelukes of the

1620s were delighted with the Jesuit missions of Guaíra. Instead of having to capture Indians dispersed in the jungle, the Mamelukes found them already conveniently bundled together in the mission towns.

"In this hunting of the Indians," Father Dobrizhoffer wrote, "they sometimes employed open violence, sometimes craft, equally inhuman in both." The Mamelukes would usually enter the town in Indian file "when the people were assembled in the church at divine service". Then, "blocking up every street and corner", they would leave "the wretched inhabitants no way of escape". In addition, a favourite trick, they would frequently disguise themselves as Jesuits, "wearing rosaries, crosses and a black gown".[13]

Dobrizhoffer complained bitterly that the Mamelukes took the Indians from the mission towns that the Jesuits had laboured so long to establish. With the exception of a few who escaped by flight, these Indians "were led away to Brazil, chained and corded, in herds, like cattle, and there condemned to perpetual labour in the working of sugar, mandioc, cotton, mines, and tobacco".

Faced with the continuing threat from the Mamelukes, Father Montoya decided in 1631 that there was no alternative except to withdraw from the thirteen Guaíra mission towns that had by then been established, and to take their Indian populations on a great march to the south. There, behind the barrier of the Paraná and the Uruguay rivers, they might be able to establish new missions free from the Portuguese menace.

Abandoning the two original settlements in Guaíra – Loreto and San Ignacio – must have been a fearful blow. These two colonies, Father del Techo wrote, were so improved "by the industry of the fathers" that they could bear comparison with the best Spanish towns in those parts:

> The churches in them were more stately and better adorned than any in Tucumán or Paraguay. Father Vaz had brought up such choirs of music in those places that they differed but little from those in Europe, and the behaviour of the converts was scarce inferior to that of the most polite nations. There began to be a good increase of kine and other cattle, brought thither with much trouble by the Society. There grew enough of cotton and corn, not only to supply the natives, but to furnish the Spaniards.[14]

All in vain. Nine hundred families from Loreto, eight hundred from San Ignacio, and hundreds more from elsewhere were assembled for evacuation. To travel to the south, they had first to negotiate the waterfalls of the Sete Quedas on the Paraná. Upstream from the precipice, a total of some 12,000 Indians were loaded onto a huge fleet of rafts and canoes. When they came to the great cataracts, it was necessary to do a portage. Normally, the Indians would have carried the canoes through the jungle around the falls to the waters further down. It was not an easy task, but feasible.

Father Montoya, however, had the mistaken idea of sending three hundred canoes over the rapids, hoping to use them again further down. Inevitably, they were smashed to pieces. "In a moment, they were shattered into chips, beaten against the rocks and swallowed by whirlpools."

The priests and the Indians in their thousands managed to climb round the falls and reconstruct some of the boats on the river far below. But the cost of this great exodus was high.

Further down the Paraná, the remnants of the expedition eventually established new settlements between the Paraná and the Uruguay. But of the people from "the remains of the thirteen towns of Guaíra, scarce four thousand survived the first year after the transmigration; all the rest either dying on the way, dispersing themselves about, or perishing by hunger or famine".

Today, the physical remains of the Spanish towns and the Jesuit missions of Guaíra have disappeared completely. Yet a hundred years ago Franz Keller, a German engineer who came travelling through these parts, recalled finding their ruins. At that time, in the 1870s, in the aftermath of the Brazilian war against Paraguay, Keller found several villages where the Brazilian government had been establishing settlements for the Coroado Indians, two hundred and fifty years after the Jesuits had done exactly the same thing. These villages included San Ignacio and Nossa Senhora do Pirapo, two settlements which, wrote Keller, had been built on the site of the missions destroyed by the Paulistas in 1630. "We could easily construct the plan on which these missions were laid out. . . . In the centre a large square, with the church and the colegio on one side; and the low rectangular streets all around it."[15]

Keller claimed to have seen the remains of walls and trenches, "fortifications evidently necessitated by the repeated attacks of the Paulistas". Two hundred and fifty years later, that was all that remained of the Jesuit experiment in the province of Guaíra.

Notes

1. Quoted in Martín Dobrizhoffer, *An Account of the Abipones: an equestrian people of Paraguay*, translated from the Latin by Sarah Coleridge, London 1822, vol. 1, pp. 186–7. The original was published in 1784. Dobrizhoffer credits Father Ransonnier with this description, but Ransonnier did not arrive in Paraguay until 1628.

2. See Francisco Jarque, *Ruíz Montoya en Indias (1608–1652)*, published in the *Colección de libros raros y curiosos que tratan de America*, volumes xvi–xix, edited by Victoriano Suárez, Madrid, 1906. Father Jarque's *Vida prodigiosa de Montoya* was originally published in Zaragoza in 1662. Jarque himself was a Jesuit priest in Paraguay (and later in Potosí) who was invalided out of the Society of Jesus and returned to Spain.

3. The two priests did not travel directly by land from São Paulo for the route was still closed. They sailed down the Atlantic coast of Brazil to the River Plate and travelled up the Paraguay to Asunción. From there they were sent eastwards, up the Jejui river, to Villa Rica, one of the Spanish towns newly established in Guaíra. This cross-country route avoided the waterfalls of the Sete Quedas on the Paraná, which were difficult to negotiate. Dense jungle surrounded the cataracts. From Villa Rica,

they moved out into the countryside to preach the gospel to the Indians. It was, says Philip Caraman, the modern historian of the Paraguayan missions, "pioneer, ill-coordinated work that held out little promise of development" (Philip Caraman, *The Lost Paradise: an account of the Jesuits in Paraguay, 1607–1768*, Sidgwick and Jackson, London 1975, p. 28).

4. Nicolás del Techo, *The History of the Provinces of Paraguay*, pp. 29–30. Father del Techo took his figure of 300,000 from the account of Ruy Díaz de Guzmán.
5. Pierre François Charlevoix, *The History of Paraguay*, London 1769, vol. 1, p. 208–9.
6. See Magnus Moerner, *Actividades políticas y económicas de los Jesuitas en el Río de la Plata*, Hyspamerica Ediciones, Buenos Aires 1985.
7. Quoted in Jaime Cortesão, *Jesuitas e bandeirantes no Guaíra, 1549–1640*, Rio de Janeiro 1951, volume 1 of the *Manuscritos da Coleção de Angelis*, p. 493.
8. Charlevoix, vol. 1, p. 309.
9. Charlevoix, vol. 1, p. 311. The alarm of the Indians at the Spanish encroachment into their territory can be measured by the figure quoted by Marion Mulhall. At the new Spanish town of Ciudad Real de Guaíra, twenty-six thousand Indians were granted as slaves to the hundred white settlers who established the town (Marion Mulhall, *Explorers in the New World*, London 1909, p. 279).
10. The original Mamelukes (the name derives from the Arabic word, *mamluk*, for slave) were Turkish slaves who seized power in Egypt in the middle of the thirteenth century and established themselves as sultans. For the Spanish in South America, the Mamelukes of Brazil were slavers, not slaves, who had successfully usurped power in São Paulo and were effectively out of the control of Lisbon. But much was made of their black and Indian (that is, slave) origins.
11. Jaime Cortesão, *Rapôso Tavares e a formação territorial do Brasil*, Lisbon, 1966.
12. These race-conscious arguments of the past do not, however, explain why the Paulistas have come down to us in the historical record in such a different form from the half-Indian, half-Spanish gangs that roamed the lands of Paraguay and also recruited large numbers of Indians to fight their wars.
13. Martín Dobrizhoffer, *An Account of the Abipones*, London 1822, p. 160.
14. Nicolás del Techo, p. 82.
15. Franz Keller, *The Amazon and Madeira Rivers*, London 1874, p. 168. A third ruined village Keller came across was São Pedro de Alcántara on the Tibagy river, "in the heart of the endless region of primaeval forest lying between the Tiete and the Iguaçú".

4

MIRANDA

The Spanish town of Santiago de Xerés in the sixteenth century

From the Aquidauana river to the Miranda river is but a short stretch through undulating cattle land. Not long after leaving the forgotten halt at Taunay, the trans-Pantanal train pulls into the station of Miranda, the last large town before Corumbá. Arriving in one of those heavy storms in which the Pantanal excels, we found it to be a damp and lugubrious town.

The railway cuts through the centre of Miranda in a narrow ravine, and most of the town's inhabitants have to cross the tracks three or four times a day. North are the houses with gardens, and the cafés and garages that service the main road west to Corumbá. South lies the town proper, with one-storey houses and straight streets, small shops and a modern church, and government buildings and municipal squares.

Beyond flows the Miranda river, one of the historic tributaries of the Paraguay. Though not as wide as the Aquidauana, it seems to be more used, more travelled along. Boats are moored by the mud cliff banks, and a few houses stand up on stilts above the flood plain. The river is crossed by a concrete bridge with a disused guard house in the middle – reminiscent of more troubled times.

To the Indians and the Spanish at the end of the sixteenth century, this was the River Mbotetei. At another stage in its history, it was called the Mondego. For the last two centuries, it has been known simply as the Miranda.

For a brief moment in the early twentieth century, when the railway line was being built, Miranda witnessed a minor gold and diamond rush. Sir Christopher Gibson, an Anglo-Argentine landowner who managed a cattle ranch near here – the Miranda Estancia – in the 1930s, recalls in his memoirs the atmosphere that prevailed:

> A workman picked up ''a pretty stone'' about the size of a pigeon's egg, and sold it for a few milreis to a Miranda shopkeeper. It proved to be a diamond of enormous value, which set off a handful of Negroes panning for gold and diamonds – with almost indecent results – in the Rio Aquidauana close to the eastern boundary of the Miranda Estancia.[1]

These sightings of diamonds and gold must also have occurred in the early colonial period. Father Charlevoix, the Jesuit historian writing in the eighteenth century, noted that "people for a long time thought they could discern some indications of gold mines in the neighbourhood of a town which the Spaniards built under the name of Xerés". They were an illusion, he wrote, adding that "the inhabitants of Xerés were always wretchedly poor".[2]

Santiago de Xerés was the name the Spanish settlers gave to Miranda when they came here in the 1590s. Always a meagre settlement, far away on the frontier, Xerés survived under constant threat from the local Indians, the Itatines. Numerically far superior to the Spaniards, the Itatines occupied land that was attractive and fertile, and worth fighting for. Even today, parts of the great rolling acres round here, formed into huge modern Brazilian cattle fazendas, look as though they have been modelled on English parkland.

The Spanish colons, led by one of the second-generation conquistadores, Ruy Díaz de Melgarejo, came to Xerés from Guaíra, to the south-east, on the upper waters of the Paraná. Earlier, in the 1550s, they had travelled from Asunción to create the new Guaíra settlements – Ciudad Real and Villa Rica – on what had once been Indian land.

At that time, nervously isolated at the heart of the continent, the Asunción settlers had been trying to safeguard the land route from the Paraguay to the Atlantic. The Asunción governor was much irritated by the decision of some of the Ciudad Real settlers to decamp to Santiago de Xerés, leaving the Guaíra frontier dangerously undermanned. Nor was the new Xerés settlement secure. Twice in the early years, in 1602 and 1604, rescue parties had to go out to it from Asunción, with arms, food and soldiers.[3]

After only one generation of European settlement, Xerés was threatened by the Portuguese. Marauding bands were first reported in the neighbourhood in 1617. By the 1630s they were to be found regularly on the Aquidauana, pushing their way ever more energetically from their bases on the Atlantic coast towards the Pacific shore. By 1648, they had joined forces with the Guaycurus from the Chaco to make life impossible for the Spanish colons. Some of the settlers joined up with Portuguese marauders, others made their way down to Asunción. The town returned to the jungle. On some French maps of the seventeenth century, it is marked as "ville ruinée". The three or four Jesuit missions that had been established near here, in the province of Itatín, succumbed to the Portuguese onslaught at much the same time.

The missions of the Jesuits in Itatín, 1630–45, and their wooing of the cacique Nianduabusuvius

Into the great fertile area between the Aquidauana river and the Paraguay, the Jesuits first began to penetrate in 1631, the year that Father Montoya so recklessly took his canoes over the Sete Quedas. Driven out of Guaíra by the Portuguese Mamelukes, the Jesuit fathers now had a chance to make a fresh start elsewhere, in areas that might prove to be less accessible to the Paulista slave-traders than Guaíra had been. Whilst Montoya himself went south to the River Uruguay with the bulk of the Indian population of Guaíra, he sent a handful of priests to the north, to the Aquidauana province that the Spaniards had labelled Itatín.

Itatín was not regarded by the Jesuits as important in itself. It was perceived, rather, as a stepping stone to more significant areas to the north-west, at the heart of the continent. Father del Techo was well aware of the region's geo-strategic importance. It was on the old road across the continent to the west. There were hopes, he wrote, "that when the province of Itatín was once subdued, the light of the gospel might be carried beyond Paraguay, as far as Peru one way, and the other way to the lands about the river Marañón, all famous for multitudes of Indians".[4] The strategic ambitions of the Jesuits in the heart of South America were already being sketched out.

The first Jesuit missionary to arrive in Itatín was a Belgian, Father Jacobo Ransonnier. Born in 1600, he had arrived in Buenos Aires from Europe in 1628. He had gone straight on to Guaíra, working for three years in the mission villages on the banks of the tributaries of the upper Paraná. Now he was to investigate new opportunities for mission development to the north.[5]

Father Ransonnier went first to Santiago de Xerés, on the Miranda river. After a brief spell there, looking after the neglected souls of the Spanish colons, Father Ransonnier set out into the country to contact the Indians, in much the same place that the French explorer Francis de Castelnau was to find them two centuries later, in the 1840s.

Initially Father Ransonnier had little luck in finding likely converts. He was alarmed to find that the Mamelukes had already begun to make inroads. The Itatínes, as a result, had become mistrustful of all Europeans. Father Ransonnier was told the story of a Portuguese priest, a certain Father Acosta, who had cleverly assembled a number of Indians into a mission town – and then tried to pack them off to Brazil as slaves. This had been a familiar tactic of the Portuguese slave-traders in Guaíra. It produced inevitable suspicion when real priests came along.

In the case of the bogus Father Acosta, the Itatines had rebelled in time, rather belatedly made aware that they were about to be taken off as slaves. They captured and killed him, though this did not make the missionary task of a Spanish Jesuit any easier. The Itatines assumed and feared that Father Ransonnier was cut from the same cloth.

First, the Jesuit had to establish his own credentials as a potential adviser to the Indian nation. Yet the Indians already had their own advisers, and were suspicious. One local priest of the Itatines (described by del Techo as a sorcerer) warned against all contact with Europeans, prophesying, correctly, that the arrival of the Jesuits would be but "the forerunner of slavery and other calamities".

Through perseverance, Father Ransonnier survived and prospered. He managed to persuade the Indians, at least for a while, that Jesuit magic was preferable to their own, and superior to that of the Portuguese. "By his discreet and religious behaviour," del Techo noted obsequiously, "he so gained the hearts of those people that they were absolutely at his disposal."

Ransonnier was soon joined by three other Belgian Jesuits, priests evacuated from Guaíra and sent north by Father Montoya. Soon they had established a string of mission towns along the Miranda river: San José run by Father Enartius, Los Angeles by Father Martínez, Encarnación by Father van Suerck, and San Pedro y Pablo by Father Ransonnier. As in Guaíra, none of these missions now survives, not even as names of villages.

The key to successfully starting a mission in South America in the seventeenth and eighteenth centuries was to secure the support of the local cacique, or chief. If he could see benefit to his people in establishing some kind of new relationship with the Europeans, a deal could be struck. Without his support, missionary activity was nearly always doomed. In Itatín, the task of the Jesuits was made easier by the fact that they were able to convert an important cacique called Nianduabusuvius, who controlled a sizeable patch of territory.

Looking at the course of colonial history in South America, it is not easy to highlight the leaders of the Indian nations ranged against the Spanish invaders. There are innumerable written portraits to be found of the Spanish and the Portuguese – soldiers, settlers, administrators and priests – almost none of the caciques that opposed them. The Indian nations did not write the chronicles or the histories. Even their oral traditions have for the most part disappeared.

Yet sometimes a picture of their leaders emerges in the interstices of stories about other men. One such is Nianduabusuvius, cacique of the Itatines in the 1630s. The Spaniards credited him with wider ambitions. "He did not only boast himself to be lord of the Itatines," Father del Techo wrote, "but extending his imaginary power beyond the bounds of his country, he pretended that all the Indians as far as the city of Asunción ought to be subject to him."[6] Yet despite this ambition, so disapproved of by the Spanish Jesuits (and perhaps because of it), Nianduabusuvius "was almost adored by the Itatines".

Perceiving him to be an influential figure, the Spanish colons in Santiago de Xerés had, before the arrival of the Jesuits, tried to make contact with him, but without success. The cacique had a clever way of maintaining his distance. He never allowed himself to be seen by Europeans. Whenever Spaniards came to negotiate, he remained behind the scenes, appointing another Indian to impersonate him.

Initially, Father Ransonnier received the same treatment. Seeking an interview with the cacique, he was met by a man who claimed to be him. Nianduabusuvius had "strictly enjoined his people not to discover him to the stranger priest till he had observed his life and conversation".

Over a period of four months, Nianduabusuvius observed the actions of the missionary without revealing himself. Finally, del Techo wrote, perceiving "that the father truly favoured the Indians . . . and would protect them against their ene-mies", the cacique agreed to an alliance. It was a breakthrough for the Jesuits. They were to be allowed to establish mission towns among the Itatines.

Trouble was not slow in coming to these missions, as it had come to those in Guaíra. "The fathers had not been long settled in their new towns", del Techo wrote, "before they received the dismal news that the Mamelukes were broke into the province." They had simply followed the Jesuit withdrawal from Guaíra to Santiago de Xerés.

Once again the work of the Jesuits was threatened. And once again the Portu-guese slave-traders pretended that they were themselves Jesuits, or were working with them. This was the scheme they put into practice at the mission of San José, ruled over by Father Enartius. "They sent messengers to San José in the absence of Father Enartius, fraudulently to insinuate to the people there that they were not come to plunder, or do any mischief, but to revenge the wrongs done to Father Ransonnier by the Indians further up the country – and if they joined their forces with them, it would oblige the Society."

The cacique at San José, "innocently giving credit to the robbers, ordered his men to go out armed to take revenge, and led them directly to the Mamelukes' camp". There, "they were all disarmed and bound; the women and children, thus deprived of all defence, being after this easily conveyed from off the town to the camp".

When Father Enartius eventually returned to his mission town, he found it empty. Following his Indians to the Mamelukes' camp, he got a frosty reception. Threatening to kill him, "they forced him from among them, giving him abusive language, tearing his clothes, and treating him in an outrageous manner".

At San Pedro y San Pablo, in the territory of Nianduabusuvius, the Mamelukes used their favourite ploy yet again:

> Having drawn the chief of the nation to a conference, they gave out that they were not come as enemies, but to gather the Indians who lived scattered abroad into a great town, for instructing them in religion, and if they would lend their helping hand they would all live friendly together.

This was the familiar Jesuit patter, and again the Indians fell for it.

> The poor people deluded by this pretence came in crowds to them, who the Mamelukes cruelly bound, secured Nianduabusuvius, and appeared as open enemies; but then prosecuting their deceitful villainy, they told the principal men they had no way to escape being made slaves but by delivering up their people; who being produced, were perfidiously secured without releasing the caciques.

Father Enartius managed to persuade the Mamelukes to release both Nianduabusuvius and the cacique from his own mission. The rest were carted off to Brazil in chains. Del Techo forlornly records that "all the caciques of Itatín were drowned in passing a river, they being all in a chain and a sudden storm arising".

Faced with this challenge to the work of the order, Father Ransonnier, as the man in charge of all the mission towns of Itatín, toured the province to inspect the damage. He travelled "very often in danger of his life", for the Itatines had grown suspicious. "They kept in mind the words of some of the Mamelukes who had the impudence to say they had been called in to plunder the province by the fathers." One group of Indians tried to murder him "saying he was the forerunner of them, and they had come the same way he did".

Del Techo records the dismal scene:

> The Indian villages everywhere smoked, the Indians being hid or running about like madmen. Because the Mamelukes had given out that another troop of them was gone to destroy the villages of Paraguay, neither the fathers nor the Indians knew which way to turn themselves.

To make matters worse, Father Martínez had been despatched to Asunción to get help from the Spanish governor. "Two troops" of Spanish soldiers were sent up to Itatín, but they arrived too late "and the soldiers being eager to make slaves of the Indians did more harm than good".

Over the next few years, things continued to go badly for the Jesuits in Itatín, and for their relationship with Nianduabusuvius. There were several problems. The Mameluke attacks became more regular and more successful. Even when the Jesuits were allowed to arm the Indians, the Portuguese often had the upper hand. Help came occasionally from Asunción, but it could never be relied on and was frequently counter-productive. Assistance from Santiago de Xerés was almost non-existent. The beleagured Spanish colons liked recruiting cheap Indian labour, and they often did so by joining together with the Mamelukes.

Under these pressures, the Jesuit missions were forced to move further south, to be closer to Asunción. The province of Itatín was effectively abandoned, and the Jesuits retreated to an area that lies today along the Paraguayan border with Brazil.

This retreat did not please the Indians. Their original understanding with the Jesuits was that they would be protected in their own homes and lands. Adequate protection had not been forthcoming. Finally, in 1644, "at the instigation" of Nianduabusuvius, the Indians rebelled.

Three of the Jesuit priests, "offering to reprimand them for their insolence, were not only abused in words, but struck". Father Mannoa was hit in the face by Borobebus, the nephew of Nianduabusuvius. Father Arenos was hit on the head. Father Badia, attempting to remonstrate with Nianduabusuvius and "reproving their base proceedings", got nothing but "very ill language" in reply.

Rejecting the Jesuit way of life, Nianduabusuvius told Father Badia that in future "he would transmit those customs he had received from his ancestors to posterity". The cacique of the Itatines had declared conclusively that he would have no further truck with the god of the Jesuits.

For the Jesuits, worse was to come. Nantabagua, another member of Nianduabu-suvius's family, was "enraged because one of the fathers had taken away the rod of his office as a punishment for his offence". He went on the warpath, interrupting a sermon in church, and stirring up the people to revolt. He attacked "the doctrine of the fathers" for being opposed "to the manners and customs" of his forefathers.

The Jesuits had lost their ideological control over the mission Indians and Nantabagua had no difficulty in persuading the congregation "to foresake the preacher". Things looked serious for the priests. Their authority had gone. "They themselves were scorned by all degrees, no honour was given to religious things, and no body was left to attend the fathers, not even in church."

At this stage, the Jesuits resorted to force. Faced with Portuguese Mamelukes or with Spanish colons, the Jesuit fathers invariably behaved with meekness and submission. Challenged with rebellion by their Indian converts, they had no strategy except to crush it with whatever means they had at their command. Rebellion struck at the very heart of their colonial purpose and could not be allowed to succeed. "Having in vain tried fair words and threats, and finding it necessary to take a harsher course, the fathers artfully drew Nianduabusuvius' son and two nephews out of the town."

The rebels were taken to a place of exile far to the south of the Uruguay river, some two hundred leagues away. Peace at once broke out. "The heads being removed, the face of things immediately changed. The people flocked to the church and performed all Christian duties, all lewdness and barbarous customs were banished, and virtue and submission succeeded in their place."

But the victory was temporary. Itatín had been lost to the Spaniards, and the Jesuits soon found it difficult to hold their position in northern Paraguay. For a hundred years, between 1650 and 1750, this entire area reverted to Indian control. Portuguese slave-raiders still crossed it with impunity, but no permanent European settlements were established. The heirs of Nianduabusuvius, and the Guaycurus from across the Paraguay, were to reign supreme.

The Jesuits move west across the Paraguay river, 1645

To the west of Miranda lies the road through to the Paraguay and, crossing the river, the road to Peru. In the 1630s, when Jesuit pioneers established mission towns in the territory of the cacique Nianduabusuvius, they also founded two missions near the Paraguay river itself. One was San Ignacio de Caaguaçú, another Nuestra Señora de Fé de Taré.

Like the other missions of Itatín, these too have long disappeared. They were in any case forced to move to the south in the decade after they were first established. But near Pôrto Esperança, where the railway now crosses the Paraguay, is an old river crossing known as the Paso de los Jesuítas – the Jesuits' Ford. The crossing, like the missions, can no longer be placed precisely on the map, but there is a place on the great bight described by the Paraguay river between Bahía Negra and Corumbá where – according to the *South American Pilot* – the water level drops. There are shallows of "about 7 feet at extraordinarily low levels. The period of low level is very regular and lasts for about 90 days, covering almost invariably the months of November, December, and January."[7]

This ford or crossing, going approximately from Pôrto Esperança to Albuquerque, was the traditional route for travellers coming down the Miranda river and then moving on across Chiquitos towards the Andes. It predates the Spanish conquest and was much used by the early Spanish conquistadores and missionaries.

The mission of Nuestra Señora de Fé was positioned close to the Jesuits' Ford. It got its name from a famous Belgian statue of the Madonna. The Belgian Jesuits had brought a model of it with them from Belgium.

To begin with, the missionaries had kept strictly to the east bank of the river. Nicholas del Techo gives three reasons for their reluctance to cross into Chiquitos: "their small numbers, the invasions of the Mamelukes, and trouble among the converts".[8] These were powerful reasons, but if the Portuguese bandeirantes were to be stopped from reaching Peru, there was also a clear strategic imperative to expand into the territory west of the Paraguay. The Spanish authorities had an obvious interest in encouraging the Jesuits to move into this area. Jesuit missions were needed, as they had been in Guaíra and indeed in Itatín itself, as a first – and cheap – line of defence against the Portuguese.[9]

Although at first reluctant, the Jesuits too had their own good Christian reasons for making the move. The country west of the Paraguay was replete with Indians ripe for conversion. The Jesuits already knew "by information given by many" that the vast tract of land stretching for 150 leagues from Itatín to Peru was "very full of Indian villages where the Christian faith was not yet professed, and where many towns might be built if the Society were once admitted".

And of course the Jesuits still had the old geo-strategic reasons of their own. Their ambition to link up with the Jesuit missions around the Amazon basin – in Peru, Ecuador and Colombia – was still very much alive.

So in 1645, after the disasters in Itatín with Nianduabusuvius, Father Francisco Lupercio de Zurbano, the Jesuit Provincial in Asunción, gave orders for a new mission to be established. It was to be set up west of Itatín on the further bank of the Paraguay river. Two veteran missionaries, men with experience of the pioneering efforts in both Guaíra and Itatín, were given the job. They set off across the river at the Paso de los Jesuítas from the mission town of Nuestra Señora de Fé de Taré. The two men, Father Pedro Romero and Father van Suerck, were accompanied by a large group of Indians from the Itatín missions.

Initially, the going was tough. As all travellers before and since have found, the entrance to Chiquitos from the Paraguay river – to those unfamiliar with the path – is hilly, swampy, and covered with almost impenetrable thorn and scrub. The missionary party took three weeks to reach their first Indian settlement.

Here they were well received by the Indian cacique, Curapaio, and Father Romero had soon mapped out a new mission town. It was to be called Santa Bárbara. Father van Suerck, meanwhile, was sent back through the scrub and swamp to the river, to sail down to Asunción to collect tools and building equipment for the new town.

While waiting for him to return, most of the accompanying Indians went back to their missions in Itatín. Father Romero was left at the embryonic site of Santa Bárbara with only six Indian supporters. Since this was the territory of the Guaycurus and the Payaguas, and since this was also the zone where Aleixo García and Juan de Ayolas had come to grief a century earlier, he was clearly in danger.

Nicolás del Techo takes up the story, in the New Testament style beloved of historians about to recount a succulent tale of martyrdom:

> It happened at that time that one Guiraguera, a heathen from remote parts, was come to the same place on account of trade, who Father Romero laboured to win. And Guiraguera craftily promised to use his endeavours to reduce his country people to the new town. But being a cruel and deceitful man, he made it his business, when he came thither, to incense them against the Christian preachers.
>
> Many, who had fled out of Peru and other parts to live more at liberty, seconded him; and above all, one Mborosenius, an imposter, who being skilled in sorcery, assumed the title of a deity.

It is an intriguing story, for it suggests that del Techo was keen to emphasize that the people responsible for opposing Father Romero were not the local people from Santa Bárbara, but Indians who had already come into contact with – and fled from – the Spaniards from Peru at the western end of Chiquitos (probably the Chiriguanos). Guiraguera and his people were understandably angry at running into more white conquerors in an area that had hitherto been safe.

Together with the sorcerer Mborosenius, it was apparently easy to persuade an Indian by the name of Tucumbaius "to manage the design of murdering the father. Taking Guiraquera and forty more assassins with him, he set out as if they were to desire to be baptised."

Father Romero was warned of the danger and advised to make a rapid escape:

> But despising that which looked like fear, he went out to meet them, and having exhorted them to embrace the opportunity, he offered them of being admitted into the number of the sons of God, gave them some presents, and went away to say mass.
>
> Thinking no time was to be lost, Tucumbaius gave the signal to the murderers; one of them gave him three blows on the head with his club which laid him flat on the ground.

The rest of them murdered the father's companion, Fernández, as yet only a novice, and a convert, Gonzalo. Which done, and perceiving that the father was still alive, they ripped open his belly, pulled out his tongue, cut his throat, chopped off his fingers, and thrust them into his belly, superstitiously believing that would prevent any revenge being taken for murder committed.

Then they plundered all they found, and whilst they were so employed, the other four converts fled, and all of them returned safe home and gave an account of what had happened.

When the murderers were gone, the natives of the place, returning from their country affairs, were extremely grieved at this action. Having laid the bodies decently together, men and women (as is the custom of the country) made dismal howlings in their turns, like singing in a choir, and then were silent by fits, which are the funeral ceremonies. And thus they committed them to the ground, till seven months after when those same heathens put the bones of the father and his companions into several coffins, and sent them honourably to the fathers in the province of Itatín.[10]

This attempt by the Jesuits to move west across the Paraguay, though in practice unsuccessful, is all the more remarkable if it is recalled that the 1640s was a decade in which the entire Paraguayan area was wrapped in a prolonged crisis of colonial government. This was to leave a legacy of bitterness that lasted throughout the Spanish period and on into the twentieth century. An obvious external influence was the Portuguese rebellion in 1640 that brought about the division between Spain and Portugal, whose two monarchies had been united since 1580. From this time on, the Portuguese were not only able, but were officially encouraged to explore further west into Spanish territory: to resume the search not just for Indian slaves but for the silver of the Andes.

At the same time, the Spanish royal decision to give greater protection to the Indians and more autonomy to the Jesuits, and to allow the mission towns to hand out arms to the Indians when necessary, caused a rebellion among the Spanish colons in Asunción. Led by their bishop, the charismatic Franciscan from Sucre, Bernadino de Cárdenas, the colons struggled to maintain their privileges – of which the most essential was the right to enslave Indians.

For a decade there was sporadic fighting, verging on civil war, though the moments of actual conflict were brief and localized. Sometimes the Jesuits used Indian troops to defend their position, sometimes the colons had the upper hand, expelling the Jesuits from Asunción and closing down their missions. As the crisis continued, the Portuguese were able to reinforce their position in Itatín and to plan journeys across the continent.

As for the Indians, they had a brief moment of triumph. The Guaycurus and the Payaguas, in particular, foresaw an end to Spanish control, and took advantage of the state of civil war to re-establish their pre-eminence.

The first wave of new Portuguese attacks came in 1647 when a bandeira, moving west, attacked and destroyed Nuestra Señora de Fé de Taré. The Jesuits withdrew, taking some of their Indians to establish a new mission further south on the River Apa.

The following year, the bandeira of Antônio Raposo Tavares came steamrollering through the province.[11] In the same year, Tavares was given the task of opening a route through to Peru. Ever since the separation of Spain and Portugal in 1640, the Brazilians had been seeking ways to establish a position in the centre of South America. Setting out from São Paulo, Raposo Tavares crossed the Paraguay and travelled across Chiquitos to the headwaters of the Amazon. In fact he circumnavigated what was then Brazil, arriving home some three years later. It was a tough, pioneering journey, and it is said that his family hardly recognized him on his return.

Passing through Itatín on its way west, the bandeira mopped up what was left of the Jesuit missions. In November 1648, one of Raposo Tavares's lieutenants, Antônio Pereira de Azevedo, destroyed the new mission that had been settled on the River Apa. The father in charge, Cristóbal de Arenas, was captured by Raposo Tavares's men, and he learnt at first hand that the bandeira was on a trip to Peru to get silver.[12]

Hearing of his capture, the Jesuit father at the neighbouring mission of Caaguaçú, Father Justo Mancilla, sent out a troop of armed Indians, led by Father Alonso Arias, to rescue Father Cristóbal de Arenas. Although this expedition was successful, in that Father Arenas was rescued, Father Arias was killed.[13]

Notes

1. Sir Christopher Gibson, *Enchanted Trails*, Museum Press, London 1948, p. 167.
2. Pierre François Charlevoix, *The History of Paraguay*, London 1769, vol. 1. p. 10.
3. Regina Maria A.F. Gadelha, *As Missões Jesuiticas do Itatim, um estudo da estruturas socio-economicas coloniais do Paraguai (seculos xvi e xvii)*, Paz e Terra, Rio de Janeiro 1980, p. 170.
4. Nicolás del Techo, *A History of the Provinces of Paraguay*, London 1746, p. 86.
5. Father Ransonnier is elsewhere called Rancioneri, and is sometimes known as Diego Ferrer. He died at San Ignacio in 1636. See Ernesto J.A. Maeder, *Cartas Anuas de la Provincia del Paraguay, 1637–1639*, Fundacion para la educacion, la ciencia, y la cultura, Buenos Aires 1984. (This volume for 1637–39 continues the series of Annual Letters from Paraguay formerly edited by Emilio Ravignani and Carlos Leonhardt, and published as volumes 19 and 20 of the *Colección de documentos para la historia argentina*, and unfortunately abandoned in 1929.) Other accounts of the history of Guaíra and Itatín are collected in: Jaime Cortesão, *Jesuitas e bandeirantes no Guaíra (1549–1640)*, Rio de Janeiro, Biblioteca Nacional, 1951 (volume 1 of the Pedro de Angelis manuscript collection); and Jaime Cortesão, *Jesuitas e bandeirantes no Itatim*, Rio de Janeiro, Biblioteca Nacional, 1952 (volume 2 of the Pedro de Angelis manuscript collection).
6. Nicolás del Techo, p. 87.
7. *South American Pilot*, vol. 1, tenth edition, 1959, p. 504.
8. Nicolás del Techo, p. 115.
9. In May 1637, the governor of Paraguay, Pedro de Lugo e Navarra, had written to Madrid requesting at least twenty more Jesuit priests. Six were needed for Itatín, he said, since three of the priests who lived there had died, two from overwork. Another four were needed for exploring the upper Paraguay "and on the other bank towards Santa Cruz de la Sierra and the cordilleras of Peru where

there are many people ready to receive the gospel and where they could shortly establish new reductions'' (Helio Vianna (ed.), *Manuscritos da colecao de Pedro de Angelis*, Rio de Janeiro, vol. 4, p. 153).

10. Nicholas del Techo, p. 115.

11. The most famous of all the Portuguese bandeirantes, Raposo Tavares was born about 1598 (and died in 1658) in the Alentejo in southern Portugal. His father came to Brazil and became the governor of São Vicente. As a young man, Raposo Tavares participated in the bandeira that caused so much trouble to the Spaniards and to Ruiz Montoya in Guaíra in 1629. Later, in the 1630s, he fell foul of the São Paulo Jesuits as a result of his slaving activities.

12. Jaime Cortesão, *Raposo Tavares e a formação territorial do Brasil*, Rio de Janeiro 1958, p. 285.

13. From the second half of the eighteenth century, Cortesão writes, it was known that, between the tributaries of the Jauru and Guaporé (or more precisely between the Aguapei and the Alegre), there was a small space where the two rivers run in parallel but opposite directions. They join at a place called Istmo de Varadouro, where canoes can cross from one river to another. Cortesão believes that Raposo Tavares may have found this place when wandering around Chiquitos (Cortesão, *Raposo Tavares*, p. 362).

5

GUAYCURUS

In the steps of Claude Lévi-Strauss

The train moves slowly across the plain in the afternoon light, and we come to the next station, just another halt really, sheltered by a few trees. Beyond is a blue line of low hills, the Serra do Bodequeña, the last bump in the Pantanal before the Paraguay river. A dozen people climb down from the carriages, laden with bags and parcels. They disappear down a dirt track beside a cornfield. A man bends down to tie the shoelaces of one of his small children before joining the others on their trek across the fields.

On a plank supported by two posts is the station's painted signboard, GUAICURUS, perpetuating, Claude Lévi-Strauss wrote in his memoirs, "the name of the great warlike tribes who formerly controlled the area".[1]

All that now remains of the Guaycurus is a small group of Indians now referred to as the Caduveo.[2] This once formidable nation from the Chaco, sometimes known as the Mbaya, had kept the Europeans – settlers and priests alike – at bay for more than four centuries. Today they bleakly survive in this area of Mato Grosso do Sul, corralled into small reservations, and visited from time to time by anthropologists.

The famous French one came travelling along this railway line in 1935. Making his base near Guaicurus station, at a fazenda run by two Frenchmen, he set out on horseback with a team of oxen along the Serra to an area that is still today a Caduveo reserve. His account of the ninety-mile journey to Nalique, the Caduveo capital, reads like that of a conquistador or a Jesuit missionary travelling through the same country centuries before:

> We soon found ourselves in narrow valleys, overgrown with tall grasses through which the horses had difficulty in forcing their way. Progress was made more difficult by the swamp mud underfoot. The horses would slip and scramble back onto solid ground as best they could, and where they could, and we might find ourselves completely surrounded by vegetation.

At Nalique, Lévi-Strauss found only a handful of huts, and was oppressed by the sense of decline. "One felt very removed from the past in this wretched hamlet,

GUAYCURU. Man drawn by the Count of Castelnau, 1845. The Guaycurus, known later as the Caduveo or the Mbaya, were treated with admiration and respect by the Spaniards in the sixteenth century. Cabeza de Vaca noted that "they are nimble and vigorous, swift of foot, and so long-winded that they tire out the deer, and catch them with their hands." Although endlessly harried and betrayed, the Guaycurus were not defeated until the nineteenth century.

TERENO. Man drawn by Castelnau, 1845. The Tereno (known to the conquistadores as the Chane or the Guana) were of Arawak origin. At some stage in the fifteenth century they came from the Amazon basin on the western edge of the Chaco and settled in the area of the Pantanal, attaching themselves to the Guaycurus in a subservient semi-slave relationship. It was their job, wrote the German adventurer Ulrich Schmidl, to "generally do whatever they are ordered, just as at home the peasants are subject to the noble lords." Today a few survive in miserable reservations in Mato Grosso do Sul.

PAYAGUA. A chief of the Payaguas drawn by Colonel Alfred Graty and published in his book on Paraguay, 1862. The Payaguas, known in the sixteenth century as the Agazes, were traditionally a riverine nation, often working in cooperation with the Guaycurus against the Spaniards and the Portuguese. They were "the most formidable opponents of European rule until the end of the eighteenth century."

GUACHI. A chief of the Guachis, detained in Miranda, drawn by Castelnau, 1845. According to Castelnau, the Guachis had once been the most powerful group on the Miranda river (the Mbotetei).

GUATO. Man drawn by Castelnau, 1845. The Guatos were described by Castelnau as "different from the rest; intelligent and attractive."

GUAYCURU. A chief's wife drawn by Castelnau, 1845. Castelnau noted that she appeared to have white blood.

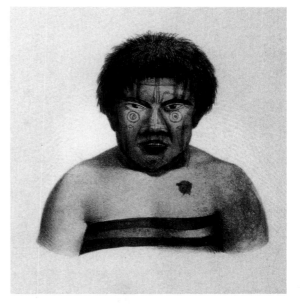

GUAYCURU. A woman drawn by Castelnau, 1845. Castelnau noted that she had a brandmark of her husband's above her left breast, and he claimed that this was the same brand that he used for his dogs and his horses.

ALBUQUERQUE. Encampment of Guaycurus close to the settler village of Albuquerque, drawn by H.A. Weddell, one of the members of Castelnau's expedition, 1845.

ALBUQUERQUE. Brazilian settler village drawn by H.A. Weddell, 1845. One of the earliest Spanish settlements on the west bank of the Upper Paraguay, and one of the traditional entrance points into Chiquitos from the east. It was known in the sixteenth century as San Fernando or Puerto Itatín. From near here, circa 1524, Aleixo Garcia assembled two thousand Guaraní and marched across the Chaco to the Andes. Occupied by the Portuguese at the end of the eighteenth century, it was, by the 1850s, Brazil's "central and principal post on the Paraguay frontier." Castelnau described it in 1845 as a "ravishing spot, in the middle of a great plain, surrounded by Indian hamlets."

TERENO. Message on the church wall at Bananal, the Tereno reservation near Taunay, Mato Grosso do Sul. It reads: Welcome to this house. A mission originally dominated by Protestant missionaries, this church is now run by a Catholic nun from Colombia.

GRAN CHACO. Drawn by H.A. Weddell, 1845. The view over the Paraguayan Chaco, looking west from the Paraguay river. This was the route, familiar to many Indian nations, that had to be taken by the early Spanish conquistadores in the 1540s. "Vast airy plains drop away to the horizon," wrote Julian Duguid in 1928.

COIMBRA. The Portuguese fort established on the west bank of the Paraguay river at the end of the eighteenth century. Drawn by H.A. Weddell, 1845.

COIMBRA. The ruins of the by-then-Brazilian fort at Coimbra, photographed by a member of ex-President Theodore Roosevelt's expedition up the Paraguay in 1913.

CORUMBÁ. View northward from this Brazilian town on the western shore of the Paraguay river which "flows towards the town from far on the northern horizon, sweeping down in majestic curves until it almost washes the lower streets." The entrance to the Tamengo channel, and the way through to Lake Cáceres and Bolivia, is on the left.

CORUMBÁ. Paradise Hotel, "a low one-storey building with a room on the street. It looks and feels as though this is a room that is normally rented by the hour."

PUERTO QUIJARRO. Stall on the station platform. The eastern entrance to Bolivia, Puerto Quijarro is "a dismal place surrounded by filthy shacks, hovels and doss-houses."

LAKE GAIBA. Drawn by H.A. Weddell, 1845. Lake Gaiba was "hardly known before our journey", wrote the Count of Castelnau in 1845. The Spanish conquistador, Alvar Núñez Cabeza de Vaca, established a base on its shores in 1543 for the purpose of moving west into Chiquitos, and called it Puerto de los Reyes. "We found a great assemblage of natives with their wives and children waiting for us." In 1927 the remnants of the Prestes column arrived here to find a British pioneer camp.

LAKE GAIBA. Ancient carvings on the rocks at the entrance to the lake, copied by the German anthropologist Max Schmidt during his exploration on the Upper Paraguay in 1900. A British explorer, Whitfield Ray, who visited Lake Gaiba the same year, noticed "with mingled feelings of curiosity and wonder, that the face of these rocks was rudely carved by unmistakeable Indian art. There were portrayed a rising sun, tigers' feet, birds' feet, etc."

where there is hardly even a memory of the prosperity that Guido Boggiani had found there forty years before."

Boggiani, an Italian ethnographer based in Paraguay, had spent time in Nalique in 1892 and 1897, and had written enthusiastically about what he had found. He was killed exploring on the other side of the Paraguay, in the Chaco, in 1901.[3]

In spite of Nalique's material poverty, Lévi-Strauss, like Boggiani, was excited by the body paintings and tattooed designs that gave the Guaycurus/Caduveo a certain grandeur. He compared them with the creations in *Alice in Wonderland*:

> Their civilisation is undeniably reminiscent of one that European society playfully invented in a traditional pastime, and the model of which was imaginatively defined with such success by Lewis Carroll: these knightly Indians looked like the court figures in a pack of cards. The resemblance was noticeable first of all in their attire: leather tunics and cloaks that broadened the shoulders fell in stiff folds and were decorated in black and red patterns which the old writers compared to Turkish carpets and which had recurrent motifs in the shape of spades, hearts, diamonds and clubs.

So there was still something in the lifestyle of the Guaycurus/Caduveo to remind an anthropologist of their past. In his memoirs, Lévi-Strauss recalls the rich haul he collected from them on that occasion. "We brought back huge painted and engraved pottery jars, deerskins illuminated with arabesques, and wood carvings representing the pantheon of a forgotten religion."

A few artefacts remained of what had once been an extraordinary civilization. When he got back to the fazenda of the two French farm managers near Guaicurus station, Lévi-Strauss found that they had a less elevated view of the Guaycurus/Caduveo. In the prosaic perception of the twentieth-century colon, they were "lazy, degenerate thieves and drunks". For a French farm manager in the 1930s, the Guaycurus/Caduveo were simply people to be expelled from the grazing lands "whenever they ventured there".[4] This indeed was the alternative view that had flourished among the Spanish colons ever since the first century of European conquest.

Four hundred years earlier, when the Europeans first came up the Paraguay river in the 1530s, they had identified three important nations out of the large number with which they were faced. These were the Guaycurus, the Guaraní and the Payaguas.

The Guaycurus/Caduveo to the north of Asunción were the subject of admiration, almost of awe. The memoirs of the governor of Paraguay, Alvar Núñez Cabeza de Vaca, describing events in the 1540s, devote considerable space to what was clearly perceived to be an impressive nation.

> These Indians are great warriors and valiant men, who live on venison, butter, honey, fish, and wild boar, eating nothing besides, neither they nor their wives and children.

They go daily to the chase for it is their only occupation. They are nimble and vigorous, swift of foot, and so long-winded that they tire out the deer, and catch them with their hands, besides slaying many more with their arrows, as well as tigers and other animals.

They are kind to their wives, and not only to those of their own tribe, who are greatly esteemed by them, but also to women generally; thus, if any fall into their hands when they are making war, they set them at liberty and do them no wrong.

They are much feared by all the other tribes. They never remain more than two days in one place, but quickly remove their houses, made of matting, to distances of one or two leagues when they are in pursuit of game.[5]

The tone of admiration is unmistakable, and the early Spaniards were not alone in having a marked respect for the Guaycurus. Martín Dobrizhoffer relates that Alaykin, a cacique of the Abipones, told him how "persons blown upon by their breath fell to the ground, as if struck by thunder".[6] The Guaycurus inspired fear and respect among other Indian nations.

The Spanish battle against the Guaycurus in the Chaco in 1542

The first contacts made between the Europeans and the Indian nations of the Paraguay almost invariably involved a battle. The meeting between the Spaniards and the Guaycurus followed the same pattern, but was nevertheless unusual. In this particular case, the Spaniards launched an attack against an important Indian nation without ever having encountered it before. They had been egged on to do so by their Guaraní allies, some five years after the Guaraní had made their own initial uneasy truce with the white invaders.

In 1542, the Guaraní caciques, who controlled huge territories on the east bank of the Paraguay river, came to see the Spanish governor in Asunción, Alvar Núñez Cabeza de Vaca, to complain about the Guaycurus. The latter, the Guaraní alleged, had crossed to the east of the Paraguay and had dispossessed the Guaraní of their land, killing "their fathers, brothers, and relatives".[7]

The caciques pointed out that since the Guaraní were now vassals of the Spanish king, they were justified in claiming "protection and restitution of their property".

The governor, who had only just arrived from Europe after a difficult cross-country journey, was in a difficult position. He was being called upon to attack an Indian nation with which he had as yet no quarrel. Cabeza de Vaca was the most experienced conquistador ever to reach the Paraguay, for he had served his apprenticeship in Florida, and had himself been captured by Indians. Anxious to spread responsibility for any decision he might take, he first sought permission from his ideological cadres, four Spanish priests. He asked them whether it would be morally justifiable to attack the Guaycurus. Conveniently, the priests replied that it would be.

So a great army was assembled, of Spaniards and Guaraní Indians, and it crossed the Paraguay into the Chaco desert on the other side. There it planned to seek out and fight the Guaycurus, a nation that hitherto had believed themselves to be the lords of all mankind. It was the first major battle that the Spaniards undertook in this part of South America. They paid heavily for their presumption, for the Guaycurus were to be an enemy that would threaten them for the next three hundred years.

The memoirs of Alvar Núñez Cabeza de Vaca devote several pages to the battle, which at the time was recognized as an important event. Although it was claimed as a victory by the Spaniards, a close reading of his story suggests that, although the Guaycurus were humiliated by the presence of the Spaniards' horses, the end result was more like a truce. The Guaraní, in particular, seem to have behaved in a somewhat pusillanimous fashion.

When the army of Guaraní and Spaniards first marched out of Asunción, crossing the river and moving on into the Chaco, they were an impressive sight. In front was a troop of Guaraní, extending over a league in length, and "numbering some ten thousand men, all painted and bedizened with necklaces of beads and plumes, and plates of copper which glistened marvellously well in the sun". They were followed by the Spaniards – Cabeza de Vaca himself and twelve men on horseback, with two hundred arquebusiers and crossbowmen. "After these came the women, bearing the munitions and the provisions of the Spaniards. The Indians carried their own supplies."

Although the Spaniards and the Guaraní were ostensibly friends, neither trusted the other. At one stage, at twilight, the Guaraní simply abandoned the Spaniards to their fate. Without Guaraní supplies of food and water, the Spaniards would simply have died in the Chaco desert, as both Paraguayans and Bolivians were to do in the Chaco Wars of the 1930s. Cabeza de Vaca managed to haul the Guaraní deserters back, and read them the riot act. "You know that the war we are about to engage in is in your interest and on your behalf only, for the Guaycurus have never seen the Spaniards or had any trouble or grievance with them. We are proceeding against them to protect and defend you." The Guaraní meekly returned and eventually the Spaniards found the Guaycurus' settlement. Battle was joined, though in the event the Guaraní soldiers continued to be of little use. "Whilst waiting in expectation, the Guaraní were almost paralysed with fear; nothing would induce them to begin the attack."

The Guaycurus attacked first, with "impetuosity and courage", but they had not reckoned on the horses the Spaniards had brought from Spain. "When the enemy saw the horses for the first time, a great fear fell upon them, and they fled to the mountains as fast as they could."

Essentially the Guaycurus evaporated, leaving the Spaniards masters of the day but with little to show for it. The Guaycurus harassed the Guaraní all the way back to

Asunción, killing a thousand of them. Only four hundred Guaycurus, men, women and children, were taken prisoner. It was not an impressive number by the standards of the time.

For a few years there was peace on the eastern shores of the Paraguay. There the Spaniards and the Guaraní maintained their control. The Guaycurus remained in the Chaco, to the west of the Paraguay. But as the Spaniards pressed into Chiquitos and the Chaco through the rest of the sixteenth century, war between the Europeans and the Guaycurus was inevitable. It could only be a fight to the death. Both sides believed that they were born to rule, and neither could accept that there was any limit to their territory.

José de Avalos and the massacre of the Guaycuru caciques in 1678

Early in the seventeenth century, the king of Spain authorized a twin policy to deal with the security problem faced by his colons: he formally declared war on the Guaycurus and, at the same time, he sent Jesuit missionaries into the Chaco to be nice to them. The Jesuits did not last long in that area, and nor indeed did the punitive expeditions of the Spanish against the Guaycurus. There was one in 1623, two in 1626, and another in 1631. Later, between 1650 and 1700, there were no less than fifty military expeditions against the Guaycurus, one every year.[8]

Times of peace alternated with times of war. One particular and traumatic event, in 1678, brought permanent war again. This lasted until the middle of the eighteenth century, with the Guaycurus occupying much territory to the east of the Paraguay.

There are many versions of this event, but the man who probably knew most about it was Father José Sánchez Labrador, a Jesuit priest sent to establish missions among the Guaycurus a hundred years later, in the 1760s. There he met a very old man who remembered the events of the 1670s.[9] This is his tale.

At the end of 1677 the Spaniards suspected that the Guaycurus were planning to attack Asunción. They seemed to be preparing for something, and were often to be seen in the city bearing arms, itself somewhat unusual. Something was in the wind.

Then a Guaycuru slave girl, working for a Spanish woman and anxious less any harm should befall her, told her mistress what was afoot. An Indian attack against the Spaniards was imminent. Hearing the story, the governor consulted the bishop in the time-honoured fashion. As usual, the bishop said that war against the Guaycurus would be completely justifiable.

It seemed difficult, however, to go to war without an excuse. In the sixteenth century, this had caused no problem. In the seventeenth century, times were different. The Spanish commander-in-chief, José de Avalos, was asked to think up a reason for going to war.

General Avalos had the bright idea of telling the Guaycuru caciques that he would like to marry one of their daughters. He dressed himself up in Guaycuru clothes to please and impress them – not many clothes and plenty of feathers – and the wedding date was fixed for 20 January 1678, a day of infamy in the history of Paraguay. The Spanish plan was to kill the wedding guests.

All the most distinguished Guaycuru caciques and their families were invited to the festivities. They were lodged in three of the most important houses in Asunción. At the same time, many Spanish soldiers were hidden in the houses. Their task – at the sound of a signal bell – was to fall on the drunken guests and kill them.

Spanish infantry and cavalry, meanwhile, were sent secretly across the river to destroy the nearby Guaycuru settlement in the Chaco.

This, the second part of the plan, was a failure. A Guaycuru sentinel noticed the soldiers crossing the river and thought it a trifle odd that there should be so much movement on a day devoted to a great fiesta. Thus warned, the Guaycurus in the settlement prepared themselves for a fight.

But in the city, where General Avalos himself had been priming the wedding guests with drink, the Spanish soldiers turned on the Guaycurus. In the ensuing massacre, three hundred were killed.

This terrible event, kept alive so vividly in the Guaycuru folk memory for a hundred years that Father Sánchez Labrador was able to write it all down, coloured the history of Paraguay until the nineteenth century. The Guaycurus remained implacable foes of the Spaniards.

Throughout the eighteenth century, they still controlled vast areas of territory on both sides of the Paraguay. The Spaniards tried to maintain a system of military forts in the Guaycurus' land, but these were often overrun. Martín Dobrizhoffer recalls that in 1745, the Guaycurus "laid waste the lands of Paraguay with exceeding pertinacity".

> The greater part of the province was more employed in regretting the slaughters and the rapine, than in preventing them, nor could they devise any remedy for the evil. The soldiers were now baffled by their swiftness, now unexpectedly surprised by their designs, and now discomfited by their powerful assaults.
>
> The savages, elated by the daily victories they had gained for many years, could neither be restrained by the arms of the Spaniards nor appeased by fair words.[10]

Two hundred years after the Conquest, the Guaycurus were still recognizably the nation that Cabeza de Vaca had encountered. Dobrizhoffer describes them as "large and generally tall, hostile in the highest degree to the Spaniards, full of the absurdest superstition and arrogance, and, as appears from the clothing and manners, ignorant of the very name of modesty".

The horses that had instilled so much terror among them in 1542 had now become an essential part of their equipment. "Their only care is that of their horses and arms, in the management of which their skill is admirable. War, or more correctly pillage, is the occupation they reckon most honourable."

In the 1760s, there was a curious interlude. For something like a decade, peace broke out, and the Jesuits were once again given the task of establishing missions among the Guaycurus. The reason was military and strategic. In the middle of the eighteenth century, the Spaniards deemed it necessary to establish a real line of defence across the subcontinent, to guard their territory against both the Indians and the Portuguese. There was a serious gap in those defences on the upper Paraguay. If it was not filled, the Portuguese would move in and, what was worse, the Portuguese might move to the west in alliance with the Guaycurus.

The Guaycurus had made life difficult for Portuguese travellers across the Pantanal ever since the seventeenth century. But the threat of a Portuguese–Guaycurus alliance against the Spaniards was always there. (Karl von Steinem, the first German ethnographer up the Paraguay in the 1880s noted that though the Guaycurus were "continually at war with their neighbours", they were "at peace with Brazil".[11]) So the Spaniards and the Guaycurus agreed to make peace. Two caciques, Epaquini and Napidrigi, sent Epaquini's son, Epilig Iyegi, to negotiate peace terms with the governor in Asunción, Jaime de San Justo. The Guaycurus agreed to return some of the Christian captives that they held, the Spaniards agreed to send the Guaycurus development aid, in the shape of some Jesuit missionaries.

It seems to have been a controversial agreement, particularly with the Spanish colons, though the Jesuits were overjoyed. Father Sánchez Labrador was given the task of setting up the first mission. He called it Nuestra Señora de Belén and established it on the north bank of the river Ipaneguazú, a tributary of the Paraguay, in the middle of Guaycuru territory. It is near to the modern town of Concepción.

A wry report on the Spanish reaction to this new Jesuit initiative came from Martín Dobrizhoffer. At a time when they feared the Guaycurus as enemies, he wrote, "and remembered the slaughter they had sustained", the Spaniards had promised "mountains of gold for the maintenance of the colony". But when their fears subsided, "they began to supply them sparingly, or at least tardily, with those things necessary for living in a town". Many of the Guaycurus brought into Sánchez Labrador's mission town "would have died of hunger had not the fruit of the palm tree and wild animals supplied the want of beef".[12]

Sánchez Labrador was the last of the great explorer–naturalists (and indeed theologians) produced by the Jesuits in the eighteenth century. His work among the Guaycurus lasted for seven years, and during that time, as well as pioneering a route through to the missions of Chiquitos, he wrote a Guaycuru dictionary, and translated the catechism into Guaycurus. Then in 1767, along with all members of the Society of Jesus, he was expelled from Belén, from Paraguay, and from South America. In exile in Ravenna, he produced several magnificent volumes, not only on his explorations, but also on the flowers and birds, fishes and animals of Paraguay.[13]

For a brief moment, it had looked as though the Jesuits would be able to provide the Guaycurus with some elementary protection against the Spaniards. But with the departure of the Jesuits, that protection was withdrawn. When James Henderson, a

British visitor to Brazil, wrote about the Guaycurus fifty years later, in the 1820s, they had already begun to lose the independent spirit that had characterized them in the first three centuries of Spanish rule:

> The Guaycurus are of medium stature, well-made, healthy, robust, and appear formed to the most painful and laborious undertakings. They eat many times in the day, very slowly, and their provisions are generally over-dressed, and cooked without any attention to cleanliness. They never suffer from indigestion. They are most particular in their diet which they use on occasions of their unfrequent indispositions. The scurvy never makes its appearance, and sudden deaths are never known. Bodily defects are exceedingly rare; blind persons are sometimes seen, but none are ever bald.[14]

Fifty years later, in 1875, Marion Mulhall caught a glimpse of them when she travelled up the Paraguay with her husband in the aftermath of the Paraguayan War. Near the Portuguese fort of Coimbra, they encountered some Indians who came out to their boat in canoes. Fodder for tourists, they had become a tragic caricature of their former selves:

> At least 20 canoes surround us, although the steamer does not stop . . . Some have soldiers' jackets, others pantaloons, and the cacique wears an officer's cap with linen cover, but most of them are nearly naked.
>
> Muscular, broad-chested, copper-coloured, with a bold and daring expression, decidedly handsome, or at least manly in their physiognomy, they seem undisputed lords of these vast wilds.
>
> As our captain throws them ships' biscuits, they dart after the prizes in their swift canoes, some throwing themselves into the water, others grinning and displaying fine sets of teeth, others calling for more or holding up tiger skins to signify their readiness to trade if our steamer will only let them come aboard. Over 100 Indians are looking at us from the shore, and we keep on at full speed.[15]

In the twentieth century, the outlook for the Guaycurus/Mbaya/Caduveo was yet more bleak. Kalervo Oberg, an anthropologist who did fieldwork here in 1947, in the area between the Miranda and the Paraguay, found the Caduveo – "the survivors of the once mighty Mbaya" – even more decayed than Lévi-Strauss had done a decade earlier. By the middle of the twentieth century, they had become "an impoverished and demoralised people".

> From conquerors, raiders, and tribute gatherers, they have been reduced to itinerant labourers, hunters, and indifferent agriculturalists. Once the aristocrats of the Chaco, with a class and military organisation, they are now counted among the less fortunate Indians living as wards of the Brazilian government.[16]

Now remembered, one might add, almost solely by a railway station.

The Spanish encounter with the Payaguas on the Paraguay

The Guaycurus were not the first Indians that the Spaniards met when they fought their way up the Paraguay river in the 1530s. The conquistadores encountered thousands of Indians from many different nations and, to begin with, they could find no allies at all. Taking no chances, they killed any group they encountered that looked as if it might prove hostile.

The chronicle of Ulrich Schmidl, the German adventurer who travelled with the main Spanish expedition of 1536, is an eyewitness account of endless atrocities. Different Indian nations controlled the Paraná and the Paraguay, and came out to block the Spaniards' upriver passage. To get through at all, the Spaniards found themselves obliged to kill anyone who got in their way. They also had to kill to get food, since the Indians controlled the river banks as well as the rivers. The conquistadores also knew that they would have to return the way they had come.

Several Indian nations, including the Abipones and the Payaguas, tried to stop the Spaniards. While the conquistadores were still on the Paraná, an army of some ten thousand Abipones tried to stop their upriver journey. "This people", Schmidl wrote, "received us on the river in a hostile and warlike manner, with 500 canoes, but with little profit to themselves from us, for we slew a goodly number of them with our guns, they having never in their lives before seen either a gun or a Christian."[17]

Near Asunción, the Guaraní (called Carios by Schmidl) were blocking the Spaniards' path. The Guaraní, a settled agricultural people with a food surplus, were an attractive target, for at this stage the Spaniards were more interested in finding food than in travelling further up the Paraguay. "The country and the people pleased us very well, as did also their food, for we had not seen or eaten better bread during the last four years, fish and meat having been our only sustenance."

The Guaraní were initially friendly, offering to provide "victuals and other necessaries", but their gestures of friendship were insufficient. The Spaniards, needing food and security on their own terms, attacked:

> When we came near them we fired at them, so that they heard it, and saw their people fall to the ground, although they saw not any bullet or arrow or aught else but a hole in their body; and they wondered and were frightened and soon all took to flight.

Two hundred Indians from the Guaraní resistance fell into pits the Spaniards had dug outside their town, but even so they were able to sustain a battle against the European soldiers that lasted for three days. Finally, they were obliged to give in. The Spaniards forced them to build a stockade behind which the members of the small European expedition could live protected.

In the area in and around what is now Asunción, the Spaniards were able to establish a *modus vivendi* with the Guaraní-speaking farming people they found there. Indeed, it was the relatively friendly and peaceful reception they received, subsequent to the battle, that persuaded them to settle there.

Further downriver, at the entrance to the River Plate and the Paraná, the Indian nations were so hostile to the newcomers that it was years before it was possible to establish a permanent European base. The town of Asunción, in the heart of the continent, was developed several decades before Buenos Aires, the city on the Atlantic periphery.

The Guaraní were to become the greatest ally of the Spaniards, providing them with mutual protection and accompanying them on their transcontinental expeditions. Over the centuries, it may be argued that the strategy of the Guaraní has paid off. Almost alone of the Indian nations of the area of swamp and forest, they have survived into contemporary Paraguay, though transmogrified, with their language intact. Hundreds of other nations have entirely disappeared.

Having tamed and pacified the Guaraní, the Spaniards turned their attention to the Payaguas. They had already had an encounter with them on the Paraguay river before reaching Asunción. Schmidl called them the Agaces:

> When we came to them, they put themselves on their defence, and wished to make war against us by not allowing us to pass through. Finding this to be the case, and that there was no help for it, we put our trust in God, and then made our preparation to attack them by land and water; we fought them and killed a great number – fifteen of our men also being slain. God be merciful to them.

Once the Spaniards had reached Asunción and settled there, they needed to protect their exit to the sea. Effectively, the Payaguas blocked the river to the south. So once again the Spaniards set out to attack them, accompanied this time by their new friends, the Guaraní.

> We fell upon them by surprise in their houses while they were asleep, between three and four o'clock in the morning . . . and we killed everybody, young and old. . . . We took also more than 500 canoes or skiffs, and we burnt down all the villages we found, and wrought very much damage besides.

Although there were brief moments when the Spaniards and the Payaguas worked together, the Payaguas were the great allies of the Guaycurus against the European conquest. The Payaguas controlled the river, the Guaycurus the land. At the end of the eighteenth century, Martín Dobrizhoffer provides a typical comment on the Payaguas, the Indian nation the Spaniards had least reason to love, describing them as "atrocious pirates":

> They use their own language, though from their constant intercourse with the

Spaniards the majority can stammer a little Spanish and Guaraní. They abound in nuptial, funeral, natal, and military rites, and in the absurdest superstitions. Their weapons are a bow and arrows, long spears, and a club; but their craft is more formidable than their arms. Each family has its canoe, a narrow one indeed, but very long. They are managed with a single oar, pointed at the end like a sword, and fly at the slightest impulse in any direction. Their velocity is owing to their structure. The keel touches the water for little more than three palms in the middle; the remainder, towards the prow and poop, is curved like a bow, and rises out of the water. Both ends of the canoe are sharp alike, and either serves for poop or prow, as seems good. . . .

They have two sorts of canoes: the lesser for fishing and daily voyages, the larger for the uses of war. These latter will hold forty warriors. If their designs be against the Spaniards, many of them join together in one fleet, and are the more dangerous from their drawing so little water, which enables them to lurk within the shelter of the lesser rivers, or islands, till a favourable opportunity presents itself of pillaging loaden vessels, or of disembarking and attacking the colonies.

The Payaguas, with their control of the Paraguay river, proved to be one of the most formidable opponents of European rule until the end of the eighteenth century. Dobrizhoffer, who left Paraguay in 1767, records that their attacks on Spanish settlements were "yet fresh in the memory of man on my coming to Paraguay". They were famously crafty:

These savages, though more like beasts than men in their outward appearance, do nevertheless in the contrivance of their designs discover amazing subtlety.

For many years they continued to pillage the Spanish colonies. . . . Heaps of dead bodies, crowds of boys and girls driven away, houses reduced to ashes, wares and all kinds of precious furniture carried off, and churches laid waste – these are the monuments of the barbarous ferocity of these pirates.[18]

Eventually, the Spaniards got the upper hand. The Payaguas survive in the accounts of nineteenth-century travellers as a small depressed colony along the shores of the Paraguay near Asunción. C.B. Mansfield, a public-school adventurer who visited Paraguay in 1852, described their sad existence:

The Payaguas are very queer creatures: they are tame Indians . . . so far tame, at least, that they will live near white men, without mixing with them, irritating them, or cutting their throats. I believe their fathers made in ancient days an alliance with the Spaniards, after having been thrashed by them; and that in consideration thereof they have been allowed to drag on their miserable life unmolested, on the soil taken from them by the white men. . . .

They are miserable-looking creatures – a very few of them fair-haired; the men look just like women. One or two of them are large and well-built however, but ugly. . . . The women are distinguishable from any of the Paraguayan women by their extreme hideousness. . . . These Indians wear precious little clothing, but what they do is of a dirty bluish or greyish woollen or cotton cloth, a sort of pinafore without sleeves, and a kind of sack frock; they wander about the town and pick up a living by selling birds and little things which they make, wherewith they buy in the market such food as they cannot catch for themselves.[19]

Today, one hundred and fifty years later, the once great nation of the Payaguas is effectively extinct.

Notes

1. Claude Lévi-Strauss, *Tristes Tropiques*, London, Peregrine Books 1984, p. 212.
2. One of the difficulties of tracing the history of the Indians in this part of the world is that although the relationship between Europeans and Indians is well documented (by the Europeans), the names given to the Indian nations by the various European chroniclers tend to change over the centuries. In addition, forced out of the places where they were to be found in the early sixteenth century, the Indian nations have often ended up in the twentieth century far from where they were four hundred years earlier.

   The Indians to the north of Asunción, on either side of the upper river, were Guaycuru-speakers. They were often referred to simply as the Guaycurus (or Guaicurus). Included in this large, and nearly always intransigent, group were the Mbayas, for the most part hunters in the Chaco.

   Allied to the Guaycurus/Mbayas were the Payaguas, who lived by fishing on the Paraguay river, passage up or down which they largely controlled. Both the Guaycurus/Mbayas and the Payaguas maintained a fierce hostility to the Spaniards from the sixteenth to the nineteenth century.

   Other members of the Guaycuru linguistic family who once occupied the drainage basin of the Paraguay and Paraná rivers, from Santa Fé (in Argentina) to Corumbá (on the Brazil–Bolivia border), were the Abipones, the Mocovi, the Pilaga and the Toba. Of these, only the last two have survived to the twentieth century.
3. Guido Boggiani, "Etnografia del Alto Paraguay", *Boletin del Instituto Geográfico Argentino*, vol. 18, 1897.
4. Lévi-Strauss, p. 216. Influenced by the visiting anthropologists, the two farmers began to take a more sympathetic interest in the Indians. But it did not do them much good. One of them, Don Felix, was killed a few years later, and the French sage reflects pensively that he was "not so much a victim of the Indians as a victim of the mental confusion into which he had been plunged ten years previously by the visit of a party of young anthropologists".
5. "The commentaries of Alvar Núñez Cabeza de Vaca", in Luís Domínguez (ed.), *The Conquest of the River Plate*, Hakluyt Society, London 1891.
6. Martín Dobrizhoffer, *An Account of the Abipones*, London 1822, volume 2, p. 422.
7. "Commentaries of Alvar Núñez Cabeza de Vaca".
8. See Raúl del Pozo Caño, *El Chaco Paraguayo y el Vaticano*, Asunción 1927, p. 52. Captain Martín Sánchez de Arzamendia led the expedition into the Chaco in 1623, and Governor Céspedes Xeria organized that of 1631.
9. José Sánchez Labrador, *El Paraguay Católico*, Buenos Aires, 1910.
10. Dobrizhoffer, vol. 1, p. 97.
11. Karl von Steinem, *Reiseschilserung und Ergebnisse der Zweiten Schingu*, Berlin 1894 (a report of an expedition in 1887–88).
12. Dobrizhoffer, vol. 1, p. 98.
13. José Sánchez Labrador, *El Paraguay Católico*; see also José Sánchez Labrador, *Peces y aves del Paraguay Natural*, edited by Mariano Castex, Buenos Aires 1968.
14. James Henderson, *A History of the Brazil*, London 1821, p. 208.
15. Marion Mulhall, *From Europe to Paraguay*, London 1877, p. 38.

16. Kalervo Oberg, *The Tereno and the Caduveo of Southern Mato Grosso, Brazil*, Smithsonian, Washington 1949.
17. "Voyage of Ulrich Schmidt to the rivers La Plata and Paraguai", in Domínguez. (The original German edition was published in 1567.) There have been various ways of spelling the name Schmidl over the years – Schmidt and Schmidel – but current opinion seems to think he was called Schmidl and not Schmidt.
18. Dobrizhoffer, vol. 1, p. 118.
19. C.B. Mansfield, *Paraguay, Brazil, and the Plate: letters written in 1852–53*, London 1856. Mansfield (1819–55) was educated at Winchester and Cambridge, trained as a chemist, and was killed as the result of a disastrous experiment.

6

TAUNAY

The Tereno (Guana) reservation at Bananal

Some miles further back along the railway line from Guaicurus, between Aquidauana and Miranda, lies the small settlement of Taunay. The station here is little
more than a small shed, and the line seems to run down the middle of the unpaved
main street. The train only stops for a minute or two.

I came here once by car, travelling on the red mud track from the main road.
Stopping at the Casa Taunay, a corner store selling a variety of useful things
including hats, I asked for a coffee. I had seen it advertised on the outside. The
owner, rather surprised, retired into the kitchen and brought out a cup of the
breakfast brew from a thermos flask.

Taunay is a small and forgotten place. Opposite the Casa Taunay, on the far side of
the railway line, stands a Pentecostal church. A bar and a couple of shops in the mud
street behind make up the bulk of the settlement's public buildings. Up the hill on
the south side is a Catholic church, next to a playing field and a school.

The halt at Taunay, and indeed the shop that provided me with coffee, is named
after a writer and soldier famous in the nineteenth-century history of Brazil. In the
1860s, in the middle of the great War of the Triple Alliance (in which Paraguay
fought single-handed against Brazil and Argentina and Uruguay), Alfredo Taunay
reconnoitred a strategic route across the Pantanal. Paraguay had invaded this
section of the Mato Grosso, the old Jesuit province of Itatín, and the Brazilians were
trying to recover the territory they had lost.[1]

A mile or two to the north, there is an Indian settlement, Bananal, where a handful
of Terenos maintain a meagre, semi-segregated existence. A couple of streets from
the railway line, where the mud track heads to the north, there is a small wooden
bridge over a stream. Above the bridge, on both sides of the track, is a stern official
notice: "THIS IS NATIVE LAND. NO STRANGERS MAY ENTER."

I felt a momentary frisson, and the stirring of a distant memory. I had travelled a
long way in order to cross this bridge and enter this forbidden territory, but I was
undoubtedly a stranger and I had no permission to be here. I recalled that, centuries
earlier, the Jesuit mission towns of Paraguay had refused to allow strangers to enter.

In the Indian missions, the local languages prevailed and no trade or commerce was permitted. I crossed the bridge and walked on.

This is the Indian reservation of Bananal, established here in the early years of the twentieth century with Tereno Indians. The Terenos are the descendants of the nation that was known in the early years of the Spanish conquest as the Guanas. They are by origin an Arawak nation from the western side of the Chaco and the headwaters of the Amazon, but at some stage before the arrival of the Spanish they had moved east and established themselves along the upper Paraguay river, where they formed a close, though subservient, relationship with the Guaycurus/Caduveo.

Domingo de Irala, the Spanish conquistador who took over in Paraguay from Núñez de Cabeza, had encountered the Guana when he advanced into Chiquitos in 1546 and slaughtered the Guaycurus. His chronicler, Ulrich Schmidl, had been particularly interested that the Guaycurus appeared to have slaves. Schmidl liked collecting slaves himself. Describing the Guaycurus as ''a very numerous people'', he went on to identify the Indians who appeared to be their ''subjects''. It was the job of these subject peoples, Chanas, Chane, or Guanas, to ''plough the land and fish'' for the Guaycurus ''and generally do whatever they are ordered, just as at home the peasants are subject to the noble lords''.[2]

The survivors of this nation today, the Terenos, speak Arawak, the language not of the Paraguay but of the Amazon. Their speech is quite different from that of the Indians of the River Plate.

The Guana/Tereno seem to have been a relatively peaceful and primarily agricultural people. Kalervo Oberg, who studied them in the 1940s, had this to say:

> In time, the interaction between the Guana [Tereno] and the Mbaya [Guaycuru/Caduveo] led to a symbiotic relationship based on intermarriage between Mbaya chiefs and Guana women of chiefly rank, exchange of goods, and the rendering of services by the Guana for military protection provided by the Mbaya.
>
> In this system of accommodation, the Mbaya maintained a position of ascendancy owing to their military superiority. This seems to have been the existing situation when the Spaniards made contact with the Guana and the Mbaya around the middle of the 16th century.[3]

The Guana/Tereno were to prove essential contacts for the Spanish conquistadores when they set off across Chiquitos to Peru, since they were familiar with the other side of the great swamp and desert.

At first sight, the Guana/Tereno settlement at Bananal looks just like an ordinary poor village, stretched out for several kilometres on either side of a broad track. The houses are made of wood, and the inhabitants wear ordinary Western clothes – trousers and tee-shirts. I saw a tractor hauling logs, a youth carrying a transistor radio, and a hut with a television aerial. Up the hill, by a flagpole, stands a brick-built whitewashed school. It was built in 1940 and named after Colonel Rondón.

But beneath the surface similarity, the people here look different from the mestizos in the neighbouring railway settlement of Taunay. The people here have shining black hair, often worn extremely long, and sweet, smiling faces. They seemed open and cheerful, and gave a wave as I walked by.

Eventually, and inevitably, I came to a church. An unpretentious building, built in 1932, it had some words in Tereno written on one wall: "YAHI KAPU NE'NOE". There was no one around, and I wandered to the outhouses at the back, calling out "Bom Dia" in a rather unconvincing way. I still had in my mind's eye the notice at the entrance to the settlement demanding that no strangers should enter.

Suddenly from nowhere a nun appeared, speaking, to my surprise, in Spanish. She was Colombian, she said, from Medellín, and we immediately began discussing the charms of that distant city. She belonged to a missionary order known as Las Misioneras de la Madre Laura, an extraordinary and unusual grouping set up in 1914 with the specific aim of helping Indians. It had no other purpose, and there were now, she said, some twelve hundred missionaries spread all over Latin America. Their work is mainly as teachers and nurses and, as we talked, an Indian woman and her daughter arrived to seek medical attention.

I was impressed by the secular approach of the Colombian nun. She seemed more interested in the physical well-being of her flock than their spirituality and, despairing of the expense of Western medicine, she was trying to revive the arts of Indian doctoring.

Bananal has a population of nearly three thousand, and is served by two other churches, one Pentecostal, the other a Church of God. Most of the inhabitants can speak Portuguese, but they stick firmly to their own language.

Protestant missionaries first came to this area – to mingle their message to the Indians with that of the Catholics – in the twentieth century. They came from Scotland and from the United States. The record suggests that they did not have an easy time of it, either from the Indians or from the local Catholics.

One of the first was Harry Whittington. He came here from Paraguay in 1912, soon after the reservation had been established. He talked to various Tereno caciques about the possibility of setting up a school, but he took a long time getting permission from the Brazilian authorities.

Whittington came originally from Glasgow. He had started work as a missionary in 1907 in a small village in Paraguay. There he had fallen foul of the local Catholic priest. No one was even prepared to rent a room to "the pedlar of the devil's heresies".[4]

Then he came to Mato Grosso. He travelled up the Paraguay from Asunción to Concepción, and then took the old Paraguayan War route across country, through Bella Vista and Nioaque to Miranda and Taunay. He eventually got permission to settle in Bananal in 1915, proudly proclaiming the establishment of "the first Indian church in Brazil". But as in Paraguay, he was caught in the sights of the local Catholic priest, who preached fiercely against the Protestant newcomers. The sermon was followed, a fortnight later, by a great tropical storm and Whittington and his wife were struck by lightning. It was an inauspicious start to their ministry.

The Whittingtons pulled out of Bananal ten years later, in 1925. They had been joined in 1919 by an American missionary, the Reverend John Hay. Hay had had plans to move north to convert the Bororo Indians when the situation "suddenly and completely changed, Satan had bestirred himself".[5]

But the Protestant missionaries at Bananal remained well dug in, as Kalervo Oberg observed:

> The activities of the missionaries go far beyond the inculcation of Protestant religious doctrine. Besides religious teaching, the missionaries supervise the moral behaviour of their followers. Smoking, drinking, dancing, and sex irregularities are prohibited, and the breaking of these rules results in a loss of status, and of economic, medical and educational assistance.

Oberg tells the story of the son of a cacique who had made a village girl pregnant. The missionaries told him to marry the girl, but he refused. The missionaries were powerful enough at that time to have him exiled from the village.

> This caused considerable disturbance among the Indians, as neither the Indians nor the Brazilians take the same view of the unmarried mother as do the American Protestant missionaries.

The trouble eventually led the state's Indian Service to close the Protestant school for several months.

In Bananal today, peace and apathy reign. I asked the Colombian missionary if she knew where the Terenos came from. She said she knew that they had come originally from the Chaco, but that their lives had been disrupted in the 1860s by the Paraguayan War. They had been provided with this chunk of land by Colonel Rondón some eighty years earlier. They were very poor, and getting poorer.

And the Tereno message on the church wall?

It means welcome, she said, welcome to this house.

The expedition of the Count of Castelnau in 1845

A nineteenth-century account of the Terenos comes from the reports of Francis Laporte, the Count of Castelnau. He and his party had paddled up the Miranda river from the Paraguay in 1845 in search of fresh oarsmen for their canoes. Early in April, he set off from the town of Miranda to a Tereno settlement a couple of leagues to the north-east. "We left at seven in the morning, escorted by a dozen soldiers and villagers, including the priest, all of them on horseback and well-armed."[6]

The Tereno settlement that Castelnau came to was large and impressive. When his party first arrived, hundreds of men, women and children were bathing in a great lake beside the settlement. There were more than a hundred houses, long huts in a circle around a great central space. In the settlement were some 1500 to 2000 people, all preparing for a fiesta. The Europeans were greeted politely, but the Tereno caciques indicated that they would not provide them with oarsmen, and nor would they permit them to attend their fiesta. Castelnau was obliged to make as dignified a retreat as he could.

Castelnau had innumberable misfortunes. One of the most energetic and experienced French explorers of South America, and one who left an immense amount of published material – diaries, maps and drawings – he has always received rather less attention than his near-contemporary Alcides d'Orbigny, who travelled extensively in neighbouring Bolivia in the 1830s.

Castelnau's principal disaster was to lose most of the records of the expedition at a later stage, in Peru, when one of its members was murdered. Castelnau had to reconstruct almost everything from scratch. Then, when he returned to Paris in 1848, exhausted and half blind, he found that revolution had broken out. Although his work eventually found a publisher, the return of his expedition was hardly headline news in such an eventful year. By the time the book was published, he had had to travel to Bahía, securing work as the French consul, presumably to earn some money.

Before coming to South America, he had journeyed all over North America, from Texas to Canada, and had even been offered the job of American consul in Lima. His travels to South America were specifically aimed at the central area, "the watershed where the rivers flow, one to the north to join the Amazon, the other to the south to form the River Plate".[7] He even had a rather modern ambition to see if it was possible to travel from the north to the south of the continent by water.

As with all French explorers in the nineteenth century, the French state took an eager interest in his expedition. He was assisted by nearly all the great departments of government. The war department provided pistols and hunting rifles, the navy shipped the entire party across the Atlantic, the education ministry footed part of the bill. Intriguingly, only the department of trade refused to take an interest. The minister said that France had no interest in importing new products. One of Castelnau's team subsequently wrote a pamphlet extolling the merits of alpaca farming and advocating its introduction into France.[8] Castelnau was in effect operating as a French spy. He collected an enormous amount of useful military information about the area, and published it all when he got home.

Castelnau and his party came paddling up the Miranda from the Brazilian post at Albuquerque on the Paraguay. He had travelled down from Cuiabá, and although he was interested in exploring the inhabited parts of the Brazil–Paraguay border, his real purpose in coming up the Miranda was to find Indian oarsmen to take his boats back to Cuiabá. The Indians at Albuquerque had not been forthcoming, but they told him that he might have better luck at Miranda, as several thousand Terenos lived in the villages nearby.

The upriver journey to Miranda took twelve days. There he found some two hundred Brazilians, living in thatched huts surrounded by orange trees. The small military fort, defended by a ditch and a staked palissade some two or three metres high, was not in a good state. "Today it would be unable to sustain the attacks of an enemy. Most of the wooden stakes have fallen down, the ditch has been filled in, and the fortifications have all collapsed."[9]

In the settlement he found a small church "in the charge of a priest who, like most of his Brazilian colleagues, is rather too fond of the pleasures of this world". The priest did, however, prove to be an excellent hunter who produced useful material for the expedition's natural history collection.

The garrison behind the useless fort consisted of forty soldiers commanded by a lieutenant. Every month it was his job to send a small troop of seven men down to the Paraguayan frontier, a journey, on horseback, taking some fifteen to twenty days. The purpose was not so much to keep an eye on the Paraguayans as "to guard against attacks from the Indians".

A hundred years later, in the mid twentieth century, these great Indian settlements near Miranda had all but disappeared. Castelnau saw them when they were still flourishing, but even in his day, their decline was on the agenda. The Indians, he wrote, "seem to be the blind instruments of a mysterious decree of fate that orders the destruction, in a thousand different ways, of all those who no longer serve its purposes".

The workings of fate were by no means as mysterious as Castelnau had liked to believe. For most of its existence at the heart of a zone suitable for European settlement, Miranda/Xerés had been a centre for farming. Sir Christopher Gibson's description of his estancia near Miranda in the 1930s explains the economic attraction of the area to the Europeans over the centuries. With cheap labour, provided by the Indians and by black slaves, almost anything could be achieved.

It was a paradise for cattle farmers. Half Gibson's property was covered by dense jungle, but this "was so distributed that it was an easy though costly matter to separate it from the open grazing lands with many thousand miles of fencing". Wherever these lands bordered the Aquidauana and Miranda rivers, "they were known as pantanales, and carried the bulk of the Company's Zebu cattle – Brazil's preferred breed – which flourished exceedingly on the lush swamp grasses".[10]

Even when the rivers flooded, "the cattle had access to higher ground where they could take refuge". And Gibson found that "the insect pests, with the exception of ticks, were far less offensive than those to which we had been accustomed" in the Paraguayan Chaco.

Gibson had been ranching previously in western Paraguay, on the Chaco side of the Paraguay river, and he could hardly believe his luck when he arrived at Miranda. "In whatever way we looked at it, the thing was money for jam after the appalling difficulties of the Chaco." The Spanish settlers of the 1580s must have felt much the same way.

By the 1930s, the Miranda estancia had acquired all the trappings of modernity.

Where the terrain permitted, good motor roads had been constructed; windmills supplemented the already excellent water supply; a private telephone system linked up every retiro or outpost with the fazenda and Miranda Town; there was a sawmill to work the beautiful cedar which went off to São Paulo by rail; the buildings and peons' quarters were very well appointed.

This Elysian picture had little room in it for the Guaycurus or the Terenos, the inheritors of the Itatines. The huge and prosperous Tereno villages that Castelnau visited in 1845 had become, a century later, the depressed and hopeless reservations that provided grist to the mill of visiting anthropologists but little comfort to their inhabitants.

The Indians turn white: the Kaiowa reservation at Dourados

Once a year in the province of Mato Grosso do Sul, on 19 April, they celebrate the Day of the Indian. It is a ritual obeisance by the well-meaning authorities of the late twentieth century, a gesture of contrition for the iniquities of the past – with one eye open to the potential of the tourist trade. In the marketplace at Campo Grande, there is dancing in the streets. Some 4000 Indians now live in the great expanse of shanty settlements that surround the town, and the descendants of many nations are there to perform: Terenos, Caduveos, Guatos, Afoie-Xavantes, Guaranís, and Kaiowas.

Some 250 kilometres to the south, at a reserve of Kaiowas near Dourados, official Brazil came out in force in April 1991 to do its bit. Not surprisingly. There had been 59 suicides at the Dourados reservation since 1987. In the first three months of 1991, there had been 7, mostly teenagers.

So the prefect turned up at the local celebrations of the Day of the Indian, and a couple of federal deputies. There were representatives, too, of Funai, the government's Indian agency, and students and lecturers from local colleges. According to Benedito Benjamín Bernárdes, the pastor of the local Missão Evangelica Kaiowa, this was the first time in seven years that there had been such a distinguished attendance.

The reserve here is home to rather more than 7000 Indians. They come from three separate nations: Kaiowa, Guaraní and Tereno. Together they own about 3500 hectares of land, one million less than the area that Funai thinks desirable.

The Kaiowa are the remnants of Guaraní groups once Christianized by the Jesuits in the seventeenth century, and contacted afresh after the Paraguayan War of the 1860s. They have occupied the Dourados reserve since the early twentieth century.[11]

An article in the local paper of Campo Grande, the *Diario da Serra*, gives a flavour of the occasion. The writer is Nicanor Coelho:

. . . "Ko Ape Xe Auya". This was the cry of the group of students and politicians as they headed for the reservation. "I'm Happy Here" was their message as they came through Jaguapiru, the entrance to the Indian poverty of Dourados. The Kaiowa headman, Bigua, was waiting to hear the good news from the prefect, Braz Melo. The community is to get a health centre and a school.

In a few minutes the caravan of six buses and dozens of cars has covered the mile or so that separates the town from the reservation. A group of catechists from an evangelical mission lead off with a service of thanksgiving. God is the watchword of the Indian children, and they carry thick bibles under their arms. "May God forgive the sins of the Indians," says the reverend. Maybe he will.

Then they sang a couple of songs in Guaraní, and the meeting began with the formal approval of the tender to build the health centre and the school. The most sensible of the speeches was made by the headman, Ailton de Oliveira, or Bigua. He advocated the continuing unity of the Guaraní and Kaiowa people so as to secure improvements to their reservation.

The regional manager of Funai held forth for a long time, about nothing. He was hopelessly stuck in the same old rhetoric. A lot of politicians spoke from the raised platform, and in the evening the students met in the lecture hall to discuss the topic: "Indians: we have rights too".

What should have been a festival to celebrate the Day of the Indian was not really a festival at all. Of the 7000 or so Indians on the reservation, only 400 took part in the celebrations. In any given month, dozens of them are laid up with tuberculosis in the hospital of the Kaiowa Evangelical Mission.

The Indian is not happy. "Ko Ape Xe Auya" means "Here I am Happy". And he is not happy because his daughters are raped, and everyone's stomach is empty. And Funai has effectively abandoned them. So far there has been no solution to the problem of the suicides, nor to the hundreds of other problems that afflict the settlement and its children. When the television cameras first sensationalised these problems, all of Brazil was horrified. But yesterday the same cameras showed the toothless mouths of boys and girls. Even their teeth are falling out.

The rain fell yesterday morning and the red mud of the settlement was trampled and then stolen by white men's feet. The mud was carried off to the town. And an Indian cried out: "They're even taking our earth away."

That cry will be heard for a long time to come. For not only is the earth carried away by the feet of the white man after a downpour; it is also removed surreptiously by the tenant farmers who suck it up year after year. One Indian whispers that the reservation has already lost some 15 per cent of its land to the neighbouring landholder. And Funai says nothing.

And the suicides? a journalist asks the Funai administrator.

Solutions are being looked into, comes the reply. "Overpopulation, shortage of land, hunger, poverty – this is the background. But there's another, deeper reason." In reality, the Dourados Indian has stopped being Indian. Today he is now white. When an Indian turns white, something has been done to him to make it happen.

The whole white world wants to have a finger in the Indian reservation. The university is helping it and teaching the Indians to sow seed. The Funai psychologist has been spending days and days at the settlement, and solved nothing. Seven Pentecostalists have arrived, to blind the god of the Indians. They create some kind of new consciousness, and take away a few cruzeiros.

There are many churches here. There are university professors, working for more than seven years on their theses, and still not coming to a conclusion. There is alcohol on sale with no restrictions. There is culture shock and the invasion of the white man's town, just down the road from the reservation.

The Indian is no longer a romantic figure. The real world in all its stark cruelty now forms part of his life. He no longer knows what to do. Is he white, or is he Indian? He doesn't know, and he chooses to be a little of each. He ends up being forced to be white. The president of the Dourados council of evangelical churches says that it's time for the Indian to be taken seriously – not as a savage, but as someone who participates in the life of the white man.

Braz Melo, the prefect, says that the settlement is a world within our own world. The First World and the Third World coexist on the Indian reservation. The Indians close to the Kaiowa mission form part of the First World, those from the Bororo and Guaraní settlement are part of the Third World. With a school and a health centre, perhaps there will be a Second World.

The celebrations finish with a race for the Indians. There is a barbecue and a football match. All these are amusements of the white man. The Indian doesn't run for medals. He runs to hide and to hunt. He doesn't go in for barbecues, nor does he play football. If he does all that, he is no longer Indian. He is white.

So as the Indian is no longer an Indian, there is a tee-shirt for each of them, with the inscription "Dourados – Ko Ape Xe Auya".

Translated it means "Dourados – Here I'm Happy". In other words, he's happy in the white man's town.[12]

Five hundred years ago, untold numbers of Indians roamed across the rich and fertile land in the area between the Paraná and the Paraguay. Today in Brazil, some groups in society have woken up to the tragedy of the prolonged war of physical and cultural extermination that has characterized the history of those centuries. They have woken up too late.

Notes

1. Still remembered in Brazil though almost entirely unknown or forgotten outside, Alfredo d'Escrag-nolle Taunay was a young lieutenant in the Brazilian expeditionary force sent to liberate Mato Grosso

from the Paraguayans. He wrote two famous books about the Mato Grosso campaign, one describing his journey across the Pantanal, and the other an eyewitness report of the Brazilian invasion of northern Paraguay and its defeat at a Paraguayan estate just over the frontier called La Laguna. No memorial exists to Taunay in the village of Taunay apart from the name, though there is a rain-soaked bust of him in the main square at Aquidauana. Alfredo d'Escragnolle Taunay, *Scenas de viagem: exploração entre os rios Taquary e Aquidauana no districto de Miranda*, Rio de Janeiro 1868; and Alfredo d'Escragnolle Taunay, *A Retirada de Laguna, épisode de la guerre du Paraguay*, Tours 1913. As so often in this part of South America, battles are lost not so much by bullets as by hunger and disease. The Brazilian force made a slow and terrible return journey from La Laguna. Taunay's book (The Retreat From Laguna), was translated into many languages and for several decades enjoyed fame as a minor military classic.

2. ''The voyage of Ulrich Schmidt to the rivers La Plata and Paraguai'', in Luis Domínguez (ed.), *The Conquest of the River Plate*, Hakluyt Society, London 1891.
3. Kalervo Oberg, *The Tereno and the Caduveo of southern Mato Grosso, Brazil*, Smithsonian, Washington 1949, p. 36.
4. Harry Whittington, *On the Indian Trail in Paraguay and Brazil: the struggles and triumphs encountered by a missionary seeking jewels*, Edinburgh 1968.
5. Alex Rattray Hay, *Saints and Savages: Brazil's Indian problem*, London 1921.
6. Francis Laporte, Count of Castlenau, *Expedition dans les parties centrales de l'Amérique du Sud, Histoire du voyage*, Paris 1850, vol. 2, p. 458.
7. Castelnau, vol. 1, p. 11.
8. Emile Deville, *Considérations sur les avantages de la naturalisation en France de la l'alpaca*, Paris 1851.
9. Castelnau, vol. 1, p. 7.
10. Sir Christopher Gibson, *Enchanted Trails*, Museum Press, London 1948 p. 168.
11. For the strange history of the Kaiowa, see John Hemming's account in *Amazon Frontier*, London 1987, pp. 444–8.
12. Nicanor Coelho, ''When the Indian turned white'', *Diario da Serra*, Campo Grande, 20 April 1991.

PART II

The Upper Paraguay

The river was like glass. In the white moonlight, the palms on the edge of the banks stood mirrored in the still water. We sat forward, and as we rounded the curves, the long silver reaches of the great stream stretched ahead of us, and the ghostly outlines of hills rose in the distance. Here and there prairie fires burned, and the red glow warred with the moon's radiance . . .

The Paraguay was known to men of European birth, bore soldiers and priests and merchants as they sailed and rowed up and down the current of its stream, and beheld little towns and forts rise on its banks, long before the Mississippi had become the white man's highway. Now, along its upper course, the settlements are much like those on the Mississippi at the end of the first quarter of the last century; and in the not too distant future it will witness a burst of growth and prosperity much like that which the Mississippi saw when the old men of today were very young . . .

We passed forests of palms that extended for leagues, and vast marshy meadows, where storks, herons, and ibis were gathered, with flocks of cormorants and darters on the sandbars, and stilts, skimmers, and clouds of beautiful swaying terns in the foreground.

About noon we passed the highest point which the old Spanish conquistadores and explorers, Irala and Ayolas, had reached in the course of their marvellous journeys in the first half of the sixteenth century – at a time when there was not a settlement in what is now the United States, and when hardly a single English captain had ventured so much as to cross the Atlantic. By the following day, the country on the east bank had become a vast marshy plain, dotted here and there by tree-clad patches of higher ground.

Theodore Roosevelt, *Through the Brazilian Wilderness*, London 1914

7

PÔRTO ESPERANÇA

Port on the Paraguay (1)

As darkness falls over the Pantanal, our train moves slowly out over the Paraguay river on a great box-girder bridge. Pôrto Esperança, a tiny settlement on the bank below, has been left forever bypassed. Before the bridge was finished in the 1950s, the train journey across the Pantanal used to end at this ramshackle port, perched precariously above the eastern bank of the river. Passengers for the Brazilian town of Corumbá – on the western side – were obliged to disembark, and to take canoes out to a river steamer. It might be a further twenty-four hours before they arrived at Corumbá. Then, in the 1940s, Brazil made good its promise to create a rail connection with Bolivia. This great bridge was built, spanning not just the wide river but a huge expanse of seasonal swamp on either side.

With or without a bridge, this is one of the most significant river crossings in the history of South America. The modern railway bridge lies just below the place where the Miranda river flows into the Paraguay, and the Miranda was one of the tributaries that brought the first European travellers from the Atlantic to the west. Aleixo García and his Guaraní army came this way in the 1520s.

Here, between the 18th and 19th degree of latitude, the Paraguay river describes a great bight, a large bulge to the east. It runs from Corumbá in the north to Bahía Negra in the south, passing the eighteenth-century Portuguese forts of Albuquerque and Coimbra as well as the seventeenth-century ford used by the Jesuits – the Paso de los Jesuitas.

Within the bight, to the north, are the great iron mountains associated with Urucum and Mutún (the largest iron deposit in the world). Here is Lake Yacadigo, crossed by the Jesuits in the eighteenth century on their way through to their missions in Chiquitos. To the south, forever stagnant, are the impenetrable swamps of the Otuquis river, stretching deceptively north-west into Bolivia towards Chiquitos, the scene of many attempts to find a navigable river route to the west. To the east, on the outward side of the bight, run the many tributaries that flow down through the Pantanal from Brazil: the Taquari, the Negro, and the Miranda.

This great curve in the river marks the traditional crossing for journeys across the continent, from east to west. It was the point of departure for most of the early European attempts to reach the silver mines of Upper Peru (in what is now Bolivia).

According to geography and historical logic, the Paraguay river ought to be the frontier between Brazil and Bolivia, but late in the eighteenth century, the Portuguese seized the west bank. Neither the Spaniards nor, later, the Bolivians were able to recover this strategic territory – though Paraguay wrested it back briefly in the Paraguayan War of the 1860s.

Almost everywhere around here, at one time or another, has been a battleground or a disputed fort. Spanish conquistadores and Indians fought here in the sixteenth century, Jesuits and bandeirantes clashed here in the seventeenth century. Albuquerque and Coimbra were military settlements. Ladário, near Corumbá, was once the Portuguese arsenal for the entire Mato Grosso area. And in the nineteenth century, the Paraguayan forces of President Francisco Solano López swept up here in 1864 to recover the territory that the Spaniards had lost.

Pôrto Esperança, half a mile downstream from the railway bridge, is a twentieth-century creation, but the site dates back to the first years of the Spanish conquest. Juan de Ayolas, the first Spaniard conquistador in the upper Paraguay, set off to Peru from here in 1537, in the footsteps of Aleixo García. For Pôrto Esperança, latitude 19.75 degrees, is the place once called Puerto de la Candelaria, the jumping-off point for most of the Spanish expeditions across Chiquitos and the northern Chaco in the sixteenth century. Ayolas called it La Candelaria because he arrived on Candlemas Day, 2 February 1537.

No trace of the old Spanish port now remains, and some authorities place it a little further downstream, near the Sugar Loaf mountain north of Pôrto Murtinho. But the weight of early evidence seems to suggest that Pôrto Esperança was the likely spot.

Early in the twentieth century, the completion of the railway line brought a steady stream of explorers, traders and adventurers to Pôrto Esperança. One of the first travellers to come on the railway from the east – and to write about his journey – was George Cherrie, a freebooting North American naturalist who had accompanied Theodore Roosevelt's expedition up the Paraguay river in 1914.

Cherrie had come up the river on that occasion, by steamer from Buenos Aires. The following year, he took the train from São Paulo, travelling through Bauru, Campo Grande, Aquidauana and Miranda. It was a long journey, for the line had only just been completed. With the track still in poor and unsettled condition, the travellers were obliged to stop every night at little rest houses erected along the route. It was not considered safe to run the train in the dark.[1]

At Pôrto Esperança, Cherrie boarded the ferry that took the train passengers on to Corumbá. He recorded a scene of "noisy confusion, hurry and bustle; Indians, natives, and halfbreeds were all in a mad struggle to get their belongings transferred from the train to the little river steamer". Only after much haggling was "the almost inextricable mass of boxes, bundles and bags" got aboard.

Four years later, in 1919, two of the North American Protestant missionaries from the Indian reservation at Bananal came this way: John and Alex Hay, father and son.

> The station platform was filled as usual with changadores, all clamouring for the privilege of carrying the passengers' baggage, and all on the look-out for a foreigner to fleece. They were a ruffianly-looking crowd of all shades from black to white.[2]

In 1928, Julian Duguid, an English writer who had come up the Paraguay by boat to take part in a trans-Chiquitos expedition, recorded his halt here in his best-selling travel book of the 1930s, *Green Hell*. Gazing across the Pantanal, he unleashed his capacity for purple prose.

> Vast airy plains drop away to the horizon, brittle spear-grass that lacerates like a sabre covers the drab landscape, and drowsy bullocks meander from clump to clump at great risk to their tongues. From time to time a tiny breed of deer, yellow as a hare, with a white scut, dodges and leaps across the open, and a flaming sun scorches the ground for ten hours a day.
>
> In the rains this flat prairie is a huge sea, and river steamers drop their anchors off the booking office two stations down the line. We hitched up to the bank, near a pile of sleepers, and started to unload salt for the meat factories.[3]

Growing tired of "an endless chain of sweating negroes, and the monotonous rumble of cranes", Duguid and his companions escaped for a brief dinghy expedition into the Pantanal before moving on to Corumbá.

He was followed a few years later by an intrepid North American woman, Grace Thompson Seton, who recorded the journey of a scientific expedition up the Paraguay in 1931. Much of her account is taken up with the story of an affair between a male ornithologist and a woman who had financed the expedition. Like George Cherrie before her, she had travelled on the railway from São Paulo and made a trans-shipment stop at Pôrto Esperança. "The little frontier port presented a picturesque scene as the coughing, screaming engine hauled our two cars out onto the water, the tracks lying only a few feet above the flooded area. All around was water gleaming palely in the moonlight."[4]

She watched while the luggage was transferred "by means of dugout canoes and one wide-bodied dory to the little craft that was to take us up the Paraguay river".

Next to write about this river bank was the youthful Claude Lévi-Strauss, who first came in search of the Caduveos in 1935. "Dismal Pôrto Esperança," he wrote later, "so wrongly named, remains in my memory as the weirdest spot one could hope to find on the face of the earth, with the possible exception of Fire Island in New York State."[5] Lévi-Strauss described the local community as "hopelessly damned", correctly as it turned out since the railway bridge was soon to be built.

There is no reason for its existence, except that this happens to be where the railway line comes to an end at the river. . . . The only inhabitants were the railway employees, and there were no houses apart from theirs – wooden shanties built right in the middle of the swamp, and reached by shaky planks.

Unlike most visitors to Pôrto Esperança, Lévi-Strauss was not simply passing through. He actually stayed here, "in a chalet put at our disposal by the company". He remembers it as "a cube-shaped box, one small room perched high on piles and reached by a ladder. The door opened on to the void above a siding; at dawn we were wakened by the whistle of a locomotive." From here, he set out to begin his investigations into the habits of the local Indians.

Sir Christopher Gibson, the cattleman from Miranda estancia, also stayed in Pôrto Esperança that year. Coming upriver by steamer from Asunción, he disembarked here with a companion for the night, planning to take the train east the following day. The river was unusually high, flowing over its banks, and they were obliged to transfer from their boat to the land in a canoe. They were paddled across to the customs house, "where the baggage was submitted to a lengthy inspection".[6]

The two men were taken off to a two-storey "hotel", the river running through the ground floor. "The upper floor was gained by a flight of rickety wooden steps fixed outside the wall, and skirted by a narrow veranda whereon lounged some 20 half-caste negro stevedores – all of them drunk, for it was Sunday and they had been paid off."

Inside this insalubrious construction, things were not much better:

Our arrival at the pub was greeted with a salvo of revolver shots. Forcing our way past this outcast rabble of Brazil's most primitive state, we found ourselves in a large room, open on two sides to the winds of heaven. . . . A delicious aroma of bar soap, stale cheese and tar assailed our nostrils. For the sake of appearance, the bar-cum-post-office next door had been partitioned off with quarter-inch deal boarding, so arranged as to magnify the sounds of uproarious revelry proceeding from that quarter. And on the other side of the room was the brothel. . . . The joint was tough, all right; just as tough as they come.

Latin America's Anglo community has always lived in a time-warp, and Gibson tells his story of 1935, written in 1945, as though it were an Edwardian adventure story taking place in Africa in 1895. He records how his companion, faced with a dramatic situation in which two white men are about to be set upon by savages, suggests – in true imperial style – that they should calm the atmosphere down by doing some fishing.

I grasped at the straw. On looking over the veranda rail, we saw that shoals of salmon were cruising round the building in the crystalline water, exploring the lower rooms and greedily snatching at scraps of food. Pert and hungry, they seemed easy game. Tackle was hastily produced, and the contest began.

The half-castes eyed our rods with puzzled curiosity. When they grasped what we were about, they shrugged their shoulders and made indirect – and extremely rude – remarks about mad foreigners.

Soon fish were caught, the atmosphere calmed down, and the mad white men were left to stand drinks all round.

The cultural clash between the local population and the outsider has been a phenomenon of life on the upper Paraguay for more than four centuries. The first Spaniards came to Pôrto Esperança in 1537. Juan de Ayolas, their leader, doubtless had comparable difficulties in dealing with the indigenous inhabitants, but he was less successful in keeping them amused. Returning to Paraguay from Peru, loaded with treasure, he and his companions were set upon along this reach of the river, and here they were killed.

The expedition of Juan de Ayolas from Puerto de la Candelaria in 1537

In February 1537, four hundred years before Sir Christopher Gibson's bar-room exploits, Juan de Ayolas spent a week in the settlement that he named Puerto de la Candelaria. Here he prepared to launch what was to be the first Spanish expedition to the west across Chiquitos, in search of silver.

The immediate cause of Ayolas's presence on the upper Paraguay was the return to Spain at the beginning of 1534, three years earlier, of Francisco Pizarro. The Spanish conqueror of Peru had returned to Seville with the immense treasure of Atahualpa. He brought gold and silver on such an unprecedented scale that innumerable adventurers began descending on the Spanish town in the hope of taking passage to the New World. Their ambitions focused on a fleet that had already planned to leave for the south Atlantic.

In the previous decade, details of a possible route across the heart of the continent to Peru had been obtained by Sebastian Cabot when he had sailed into the River Plate and up the Paraguay. Cabot had met Indians with silver, and he called the great river he had sailed up the "silver" (Plata) river. His information, though inconclusive, was intriguing: if there really was an easy way through to the treasure of Peru from the upper Paraguay, it would make the long northern journey from Peru to Spain, via the Panamanian isthmus, unnecessary.

The man charged with opening up the potential Paraguay route to Peru was Pedro de Mendoza, a Spanish nobleman who had made his name as a commander during the recent Spanish campaigns in Italy. As a reward, and in exchange for organizing and funding the expedition to South America, he was to be made Adelantado –

supreme governor and effective owner – of the entire southern region of South America.

Mendoza set out for the River Plate in 1535 with an armada of fourteen ships. On board were 1500 Spaniards, 150 Germans and a handful of Portuguese. The expedition was put together in a great hurry, lest others might get there first. Portugal, in particular, was a threat. It had already laid claim to both the Plate and the Paraguay, and was thought to be organizing a comparable fleet.

Perhaps because of the speed with which it had been put together, Mendoza's expedition was dogged with misfortune from the start. Later, when it arrived at the River Plate, the Adelantado was forced through ill-health to return to Spain. He was never able to sail up the Paraguay, and died on the return journey.

Several of his officers, however, made the journey up the river. Two of them, Juan de Ayolas and Domingo de Irala, embarked on historic expeditions to the west – to Peru. They were successful in finding a new cross-country route to the gold and silver of the Incas.

Juan de Ayolas came from Burgos. He had been the chief administrator of Mendoza's expedition and was the Adelantado's natural successor. With three small ships and 175 European adventurers, he sailed into the upper waters of the Paraguay. The stated ambition and purpose of his expedition was to reach the silver mountains of Peru.

When he arrived at La Candelaria in February 1537, he found himself in the territory of the Payaguas, the nation of champion canoeists that dominated the waters of upper Paraguay until the end of the eighteenth century.

Initially, the Payaguas reacted passively to the presence of the Europeans. Ulrich Schmidl, one of the Germans on the upriver journey (and the only one to leave a written account), notes that the Payaguas met them "peaceably . . . and took us into their houses and gave us fish and also fenugreek".[7]

Ayolas interrogated the cacique of the Payaguas and asked if he knew anything about a nation called "Karchkareisso". This was Schmidl's transliteration of the "Charcas" people who lived in the Andes around Potosí, and spoke Quechua. These were the people the Spaniards had already heard about from Cabot – and needed to find.

The cacique replied that the Payaguas "knew nothing indeed of such people but what they had heard of them by report, and that they dwelt far away in the country, and that they had much gold and silver".

The Payaguas, the cacique added, "had never seen any of them", but he knew that they were "wise men, like as we Christians are, and that they had plenty of victuals . . . as well as deer and rabbits, geese and hens".

The Spaniards clearly felt that they were hot on the silver trail, especially when, like almost everyone else who came this way in the first decades of conquest, they met someone who had travelled to the west with Aleixo García in the 1520s. At Puerto de la Candelaria they were introduced to a man, a Chane (or Guana) Indian, who claimed to have been García's slave. Ayolas immediately secured him as his guide, to plot a path through the forests and swamps of Chiquitos and the northern Chaco on the way to Peru.

The Payaguas and their cacique appear to have approved of Ayolas's trip. They too liked going west in search of silver. The cacique presented Ayolas with his daughter so that she might travel with him, an unambiguous expression of good will.[8]

When Ayolas crossed the Paraguay, he took with him 135 of the assortment of European adventurers with whom he had sailed up the river. A further 33 Europeans, under the command of Domingo de Irala, were left behind on the banks of the river. Their task was to maintain a rearguard base, and to wait where they were until Ayolas returned.

Ayolas and his Europeans were accompanied by a troop of three hundred Payaguas Indians. These were locals, their homes nearby on the river. As with the expeditions made later by the Jesuits, the Indians were used by the Europeans to carry their gear, to forage and to prepare the food. These early expeditions were extremely large. Their chief problem was to secure sufficient food to keep them going. Since they could not take much with them, they were obliged to live off the land, and this meant obtaining the cooperation of the local inhabitants. Today it would be difficult for four hundred men to cross Chiquitos without taking adequate provisions, but four hundred years ago it was perfectly possible. Large local populations produced more than enough for their own needs. With little capacity for storage, they were often willing and able to share their production – when available at harvest time – with those who came past, provided such people were prepared to be friendly.

At times, the Spaniards were able to secure food through friendship. The Payaguas on the upper Paraguay had provided them with fish. At other times, however, food could only be obtained by force, and this was not always easy. In the early years, skilled Indian archers, enjoying numerical superiority, were usually a match for the Spaniards. For although the Spaniards had rudimentary firearms, these were more useful as frighteners than as machines for killing. When the Spaniards ran out of food and ammunition, they became exceptionally vulnerable, liable to suffer attack even from the "friendly" Indians with whom they had been travelling.

Ulrich Schmidl, the German soldier of fortune, remained behind with Irala on the Paraguay, so no direct record of the Ayolas expedition across Chiquitos survives. It is known, however, that Ayolas and his men, like Aleixo García before them, successfully made the journey through the swamps of the northern Chaco. They crossed the Rio Grande, the river near Santa Cruz de la Sierra that the Indians called the Guapay, a river that drains the water from the eastern Andes into the Amazon.

Like García, Ayolas found himself at the foothills of the Andes and at the frontiers of the Inca empire. At exactly what spot is not known. According to a story told to

Irala three years later by a group of Indians who survived the trip, Ayolas built a large fort and filled it with gold and silver.

But his presence did not go unchallenged. Soon he was attacked by the local Indian nation, the Caracaraes, the Quechua-speaking Indians then to be found in the neighbourhood of Potosí, the "Charcas" that he had asked about on the Paraguay river. Irala, who came this way later, described them as "the richest and most powerful people in these parts; they have stockaded towns that are well-policed".[9]

Ayolas survived the battle against the Caracaraes, but was by now isolated and in need of additional support. He began the return journey to the Paraguay to seek Spanish reinforcements. Members of another Indian nation, the Tereno (the Chane or Guana), had been dragooned into his service, and a considerable number returned across Chiquitos with him, to carry the metal collected and the provisions for the journey. Fifteen Spaniards were left behind "as hostages".

Ayolas got back safely to the Paraguay with about eighty of his men. He must have lost a similar number on the way, or perhaps in battle with the Caracaraes. When he arrived at Pôrto Esperança, he found plenty of Payaguas waiting, but no sign of Domingo de Irala, the Spanish commander, who had been ordered to await his return. Replete with treasure, but low in food and ammunition, his position was precarious.

The expedition of Domingo de Irala from Puerto de la Candelaria in January 1540, and the torture of the Payaguas

When Juan de Ayolas set off across Chiquitos from Pôrto Esperança in February 1537, Domingo de Irala had been left behind with two ships and thirty-three men. His orders were to stay there. He did in fact wait until June that year, feeding his men with the help of the local Payagua fishermen. Then another Spanish flotilla arrived from Asunción, two ships with soldiers commanded by Juan de Salazar de Espinosa, and accompanying canoes filled with Guaraní Indians from lower down the river.

It was a welcome meeting of old friends, for Juan de Salazar and Domingo de Irala had both sailed over to South America with the expedition of Pedro de Mendoza. But the encounter had an unfortunate side effect. The act of firing their guns in greeting so terrified the hitherto friendly Payaguas that they disappeared into the forest. They did not return.

Hungry and tired of waiting for Ayolas, Irala retreated downriver to Asunción with Juan de Salazar to repair his boats. He came back a few months later, as he had been commanded to do, to continue his watch. The Payaguas, meanwhile, had returned to their traditional haunts on the river banks. Initially, they seemed once again to be friendly.

After a couple of weeks, however, they again disappeared into the forest. Life now became extremely difficult for Irala. He had relied on the Payaguas to provide his squadron with fish. Without food supplies, he was once again forced to take his boats down to Asunción. He was apparently unconcerned by Ayolas's prolonged absence. He had heard a rumour from the Indians that his commander was still a long way away from the river and unlikely to return for some time.

Irala came back to Pôrto Esperança the following year, in August 1538. This time, the Payaguas were no longer prepared to be friendly. They greeted him in battle array. In a skirmish on the river, for which the Spaniards were ill prepared, Irala himself was wounded. Four of his men were killed. In hostile country and without the possibility of foraging for food – the now hostile Payaguas controlled the river banks – Irala was forced once again to retreat to the Spanish base camp at Asunción. He had abandoned his post three times.

Before he left, he pinned a note to a tree. His message warned Ayolas that the once friendly Payaguas had a potential for treachery. "This advice", Father Charlevoix wrote rather unctuously in his history of these events, "was the more necessary, as there is not perhaps a more dangerous nation on the face of the earth. They cover the most savage dispositions with the most engaging manners, and never make greater protestations of friendship than when they are treacherously meditating some mischief."[10] The Payaguas, had they been blessed with a chronicler, might well have used the same phrases about the Spanish.

While not the master of the upper river – the Payaguas were still in effective control – Irala grew to know it better than any other Spanish captain. He had sailed up it twice in 1537, and again in 1538. Finally, in November 1539, he made one last effort to find Ayolas, sailing up from Asunción.

This time, taking no chances, he came with a larger and more powerful force, nine ships and 280 men. On the way up he met some Indians (Carios) who informed him that some Spaniards from Ayolas's expedition had returned to the Paraguay.[11] Irala paused at San Sebastián which lay eight leagues below La Candelaria (now the fort of Coimbra), leaving three ships and 80 men behind as a rearguard.

When he arrived at Pôrto Esperança, there was no sign of the Payaguas settlement. But he did find a canoe with six Payaguas Indians in it, one of whom claimed to have been with Ayolas. This Indian said that a dozen Spaniards had returned with Ayolas from the other side of the Chaco. They had brought much metal with them, but all of them had been killed.

Hearing this news, Irala decided to go in search of survivors. In January 1540, having left 60 men behind at Pôrto Esperança, he crossed the river and plunged into the hills and swamps of the further side. He went with 140 soldiers, taking the six Payaguas as guides.

It was the worst time of year for such a venture. For three weeks they struggled through waist-high swamps. By the middle of February, they had had enough. They felt obliged to return to the river. The floods were rising and they had nothing to eat.

It took them a month to get back to Pôrto Esperança. There was nothing more that they could do.

Just as they were preparing to leave the port to sail downstream, a teenage Tereno boy appeared. He said that he had been a member of the escort that had accompanied Ayolas on his return journey across Chiquitos. Ayolas and his men, he said, had returned to the Paraguay, ill and lacking munitions and powder. Their troop of accompanying Tereno Indians had come laden with twenty cargoes of metal.

The Tereno boy told Irala what had happened:

> "We crossed vast deserts to avoid meeting with some nations of which he was suspicious. At last, we arrived at the place where he had left his boats; but they were no longer to be found.
>
> "We thought it proper to remain with him some days longer, in the hope that he might get some intelligence of them. In the meantime, some Indians who were allies of the Payaguas, after having feasted us with their game, invited us to take some repose among their friends.
>
> "But this was but a snare laid by the traitors to deceive the Spaniards, who never suspected it. For they had brought us into some marshes, where our march was attended with great difficulty, and the Payaguas, whom they had informed of their designs, fell suddenly upon us, and massacred the Spaniards.
>
> "Many of my countrymen likewise, lost their lives; and I, and all the rest, were made slaves."[12]

Ayolas meanwhile, according to this eyewitness account, had made his escape and hid himself in the bushes. "But they soon discovered him, and conducted him to an island, whence they put him to a much more cruel death than they had done the rest of the Spaniards."

Ayolas and his eighty Spaniards, with the Tereno Indians they had brought from the other side of Chiquitos, were no match for the Payaguas and the Guaycurus ("the Indians who were allies of the Payaguas"). This powerful alliance effectively controlled the upper Paraguay, and was to do so for the next two centuries. Other expeditions came through, but only with their consent.

The Tereno lad who had managed to escape to talk to Irala was clearly telling the truth since he knew a dozen of Ayolas's men by name. He also said that the famous slave who had once belonged to Aleixo García, and who had travelled west as Ayolas's guide, had been killed by the Payaguas.[13]

The six Payaguas who had travelled into the swamps to the west of the Paraguay with Irala, on the futile search for his commander, were much alarmed when they saw the youth. They admitted that they had known the story all along. Irala detained two of them, accusing them of the murder of Ayolas, and tortured them until they confessed.

Ulrich Schmidl describes what happened.

Our commander then obtained permission from the judge and the provost-marshal that the two prisoners should be put to the torture in order that they might tell the truth. And by his order they were tormented in such a manner that they were compelled to confess that they had killed the Christians and their chief.[14]

Retribution was swift. They were "tied to a tree around which a great fire was made in order to burn them". The Payaguas of the upper Paraguay could be brutal, but no more brutal than their European conquerors.

It was a short-sighted action, for the Payaguas were now to be the mortal enemies of the Spaniards. The conquistadores were never again able to use the settlement of Puerto de la Candelaria. Pôrto Esperança was effectively closed to the Europeans until the twentieth century. Future Spanish expeditions up the Paraguay had to pass through this stretch of the river tensely, prepared for hostile action. Irala had scored a pyrrhic victory.

Although an example had been made of the two Payaguas, a reprisal that was both real and symbolic – since it was designed to emphasize the long arm of Spanish power – the Indians along the banks of the upper Paraguay must in 1540 have had reason to believe that this European incursion into their territory would be short-lived. Not only was Ayolas killed and Mendoza dead, but Irala's men were soon scuttling back to Asunción from Pôrto Esperança faint with hunger. Of the two hundred soldiers who had marched ashore with Irala and waded through the swamp, more than fifty died during their return to Asunción later that year. They were ill and lacked food. More significant, they lacked slaves to look after them.

Food, women and land along the Paraguay in the sixteenth century

Such was the political economy of the early settlements of the conquistadores along the middle reaches of the Paraguay river that only those adventurers who secured the rights to a female Guaraní slave, or several, were likely to survive. They needed the women slaves to grow and prepare their food.

Spaniards who were already rich and influential had no difficulty in being allotted Guaraní slaves, indeed they often acquired a superfluity. But the poorer Spanish soldiers often lived on the breadline. Without enough slaves, they lived without enough food.

Guaraní women in the area of Asunción were accustomed in their own society to perform a variety of tasks. They cultivated the land, harvested the crops and prepared the food. And they looked after the children. This was the local practice. The men, meanwhile, were hunting and fishing – and, doubtless, lazing about.

The primary need of the Spanish conquistadores was for food. They had arrived famished, after a long and exhausting sea voyage. Early settlements on the River Plate collapsed for want of regular supplies. In Asunción, in the 1540s, if you wanted to survive you needed women slaves to provide you with food to eat. If you wanted to eat well, and provide for your own dependants, you would need a lot of women.

A woman's work, of course, was by no means confined to the field and the kitchen. It also went on in the bedroom. There is some evidence to suggest that it was customary in these parts, before the Spaniards arrived, for women to be handed over to others by the men. In the power relationships between various Indian nations, the caciques often seem to have been very free with the women of their own nation, giving them away as prizes, or bribes, or simply as a gesture of friendship.

The female Guaraní Indians, in and around Asunción, were not, of course, party to these arrangements. No one asked them if they wished to be the slaves of the newcomers. Less warlike than the Payaguas and the Guaycurus, the Guaraní men succumbed to Spanish power in the early years almost without a fight – though later they were to rebel, again and again. Surrendering their women was the least of their problems.

The Spanish settlers had come to the regions of the upper Paraguay not as colonists, but as conquerors. They planned to put their feet up and enjoy life. They had not, like later generations of emigrants to South America, crossed the ocean – braving the hazards of the unfamiliar and the unknown – in search of work. Far from it. They wanted a life of ease. Some sought to secure the aristocratic privileges that they were accustomed to in Europe. Others sought these privileges because they had been denied them at home. Just as mediaeval Europe was full of serfs, propping up the unproductive military and priestly castes, so in South America a subclass of local people had to be found to sustain the comfortable lives of the conquerors. It is a pattern that has continued to this day.

Ideally, the Spaniards in Paraguay would have lived off gold and silver, as their more fortunate compatriots were able to do in Peru and Mexico. Failing that, since there were no precious metals to be found, they had to make do with land. But people were needed to work the land. The Spaniards had not brought their serfs with them. Labour had to be found locally. Thus much of the early colonial history of South America consists of too many conquerors chasing too few Indians. The Spaniards were often forced to move from their established settlements in search of fresh sources of labour.

To begin with, there were plenty of Indians on the upper Paraguay. Indeed, the conquerors were hugely outnumbered. But very soon after the initial conquest, the Indians began to evaporate. They vanished for four main reasons: they disappeared into the forest, they were captured and enslaved by the Portuguese, they died of disease, or they were killed. One estimate suggests that there were one and a half million Indians in the area between the Paraguay and the Atlantic when the Spaniards first arrived, in the 1530s. Two centuries later, in 1730, there were barely 150,000 – a tenfold decline.[15]

There was an existential problem too. Like the Spanish conquerors, Indian men also enjoyed putting their feet up. The late Pierre Clastres, a French anthropologist who worked in this region, points out that Indian men devoted relatively little time "to what is called work".

Women worked rather harder than men, but neither man nor woman had to strain themselves unduly to survive. Many early observers were intrigued by the Indians' longevity. Their relative idleness by European standards (in the nascent era of the Protestant ethic) does not seem to have affected their diet. It is clear that when the Spaniards first arrived on the Paraguay, the local Indians ate extremely well. "The chronicles of the period," Clastres writes, "are unanimous in describing the fine appearance of the adults, the good health of the many children, and the abundance and variety of things to eat."

The subsistence economy of the Guaraní, Clastres suggests, "did not by any means imply an anxious, full-time search for food". Quite the reverse. Clastres produces some astonishing arithmetic to prove that half the Tupi–Guaraní population of Paraguay only needed to work for the equivalent of two or three weeks a year:

> The economic life of those Indians was primarily based on agriculture, secondarily on hunting, fishing and gathering. The same garden plot was used for from four to six consecutive years, after which it was abandoned, owing either to the depletion of the soil, or, more likely, to an invasion of the cultivated space by a parasitic vegetation that was difficult to eliminate.
>
> The biggest part of the work, performed by the men, consisted of clearing the necessary area by the slash and burn technique, using stone axes. This job, accomplished at the end of the rainy season, would keep the men busy for a month or two. Nearly all the rest of the agricultural process – planting, weeding, harvesting – was the responsibility of the women, in keeping with the sexual division of labour.
>
> This happy conclusion follows: the men (i.e. one half of the population) worked about two months every four years! As for the rest of the time, they reserved it for occupations experienced not as pain but as pleasure: hunting and fishing; entertainments and drinking sessions; and finally for satisfying their passionate liking for warfare.[16]

Given this background, it is hardly surprising that the Spaniards found it extremely difficult to find and keep indigenous labour. The Indians had never needed to do much work to keep themselves going. It is symbolic that one of the great inventions that the South American Indians have given the world is the hammock, arguably a more agreeable invention than the wheel. Lying in a hammock was an infinitely more pleasurable experience than working for some European slob who wanted food and sex all the time. Unless physically cowed or coerced, the Indians began to withdraw their labour. Without it, the settlers died.

The original settlement at Buenos Aires, at the entrance to the River Plate, collapsed for this reason; it was a contributory factor in the decay of the Spanish towns in Guaíra on the upper Paraná; and it seriously affected the viability of Asunción.

This simple fact goes some way to explain why the Spaniards were always so rapaciously searching for slaves. They were absolutely necessary for their survival. It also explains why people were prepared to go on a succession of (ultimately unsuccessful) expeditions in search of gold and silver when they might have been more profitably occupied in growing their own vegetables in Asunción. On such expeditions, it was the responsibility of the leader to ensure that food was found for his troops. Invariably, when supplies ran low, there was a mutiny.

Even when no metals were found – which happened on nearly every occasion – the ordinary soldier might well hope to return with a few Indian slaves. This was to be the pattern of life on the Paraguay for the first thirty years of the Conquest.

Presenting every Spanish conquistador with a Guaraní woman slave to grow his food did, of course, have other inevitable consequences. When the Spaniards first came to settle on the shores of the Paraguay river in the late 1530s, there was a population of Spaniards (mostly men) and Indians. Very few Spanish women came in the armada of Pedro de Mendoza in 1536. Quite soon afterwards, however, there was a large mestizo population as well.

The arithmetic (for the town of Asunción) goes something like this. In 1538 there were approximately 250 Spanish men in the town. Four years later, in 1542, Núñez Cabeza de Vaca arrived from Spain with another 350 men. By 1545, there were reported to be 1500 small mestizo children in Asunción. A considerable amount of inter-ethnic procreation had already taken place.

The original 250 Spaniards, according to a report made by Domingo de Irala in 1541, had more than 700 Guaraní women at their disposal: about three women to each man. By all accounts this was a low ratio. A Spaniard who owned only two or three women was considered to be rather impoverished. Francisco González Paniagua, a Spanish chaplain in Asunción, wrote to the king in 1545 to outline the problem. "Here some have up to seventy women; if you're poor, you may have five or six; most have fifteen or twenty; or even thirty or forty."[17]

This situation, easily sketched, soon got out of hand. Asunción was referred to in early reports as "the paradise of Mahomet", and there were subsequent references to the fact that even "the Koran of Mahomet" would not give permission for what was going on. The Spaniards, of course, had only thrown out the Moslems from metropolitan Spain in the course of the previous century. Images of a many-wived Moslem male lifestyle were still part of a very recent folk memory.

This picture of Paraguay as an earthly paradise is a significant aspect of all travellers' tales for the next four centuries, though in the case of *A Vanished Arcadia* by Robert Cunninghame Graham, who was familiar with the country in the aftermath of the Paraguayan War, the "arcadia" is perceived to have existed in the past rather than the present.[18] Was this portrayal of Paraguay's charms not simply based on the originally favourable (to men) ratio of men to women? And when, both in the 1870s and the 1930s after disastrous wars, visitors commented on the notable lack of men – indeed one novel about Paraguay in the 1930s is called *Land Of Women*[19] – were they not merely echoing tales of an historic imbalance that had existed since the mid sixteenth century?

Intriguingly, one British observer commented on the shortage of Paraguayan men before the outbreak of the Paraguayan War, blaming it on the incidence of child labour. "It is said that the women are much more numerous than the men," Edward Thornton wrote from Asunción to Lord Russell in London in September 1864, "and that this disproportion arises from the number of males who are destroyed by being forced to the severest labour with scanty food, long before they have arrived at their full strength."[20]

There is no answer to these questions, nor is it possible to discover what the Guaraní Indian women (or indeed the men) thought about the situation in which they found themselves when the Spaniards first arrived. Among some nations – notably the Tereno (Guana) and the Guaycurus (Mbaya/Caduveo) – there was undoubtedly a tradition whereby weaker national groups teamed up with stronger ones. The arrival of the Spaniards may initially have seen no departure from this norm, with the submissive Guaraní playing the role of the "Guanas" to the dominant Spaniards' "Guaycurus". If so, the relationship did not last for long. Guaraní rebellions against this alien influx began very soon after the Spanish arrival. The famous rebellion at Asunción in 1560 lasted for nearly six months. Thousands took part, and thousands were killed.

Anecdotal evidence about individuals can be used either way. Some Indian women murdered their Spanish "husbands". Others went to great lengths to protect them, betraying their nation rather than their lovers.

The voice of Spanish women is not altogether absent from the record. Cunninghame Graham published a remarkable letter from Isabel de Guevara, who had travelled to the River Plate with her husband, Pedro de Esquivel, with the Mendoza expedition of 1536. Writing twenty years later from Asunción, she requested assistance from Madrid, arguing that Spanish women had played a crucial role in establishing the colony in Paraguay. When Mendoza's fleet first sailed into the River Plate, exhausted and starving, many had died in the famine:

> The men became so weak that the poor women had to do all their work; they had to wash their clothes, and care for them when sick, to cook the little food they had; stand sentinel, care for the watch-fires and prepare the crossbows when the Indians attacked, and even fire the petronels; to give the alarm, crying out with all our strength, to drill and put the soldiers in good order, for at that time we women, as we did not require so much food, had not fallen into the same state of weakness as the men.

The story was much the same when the expedition sailed up the Paraná and the Paraguay:

They arrived at this city of Asunción, which, though it is now fertile and full of food, was then in wretchedness, so that it became necessary that the women should return to their labours, making plantations with their own hands, digging, weeding, and sowing and gathering in the crops without the help of anyone, until the soldiers recovered from the weakness and commenced to rule the country and to acquire Indians [male and female] as their servants, and so get the land into the state in which it is.[21]

After this heartfelt outpouring, Isabel de Guevara requested a job for her husband and some recognition of the ingratitude to which she had been subjected: "they have left me without assigning me a single Indian girl to be my servant".

Isabel de Guevara was one of the very few European women in the first wave of conquest and settlement. In the 1550s, Madrid felt that something should be done to redress the balance, and a boatload of forty unmarried Spanish women was dispatched from Spain to Paraguay. They were all of some class in society, the stowaway prostitutes being discovered and thrown off. As a result of various adventures on the way, it took five years for this boatload to get to Asunción. After a long transatlantic journey, one of the women was not available for the Spanish settlers. When they landed in Brazil, she married the priest with whom she had had such a good time on the boat.

For the beleagured settlers in Asunción, meanwhile, a fresh problem was looming. The lack of new recruits from Spain, men or women, meant that there were only about 250 pure Spaniards left in Asunción in the 1570s – "a hundred useless, and the rest old". They were surrounded by their offspring. By 1575, the 1500 small children of 1545 and their successors had become 10,000 teenage mestizos. By all accounts, they were unusually unruly and unmanageable.

Notes

1. George Cherrie, *Dark Trails*, Putnams, New York 1930.
2. Alex Rattray Hay, *Saints and Savages: Brazil's Indian problem*, London 1921, p. 6.
3. Julian Duguid, *Green Hell: a chronicle of travel in the forests of eastern Bolivia*, London 1931.
4. Grace Thompson Seton, *Log of the Look-See: a half year in the wilds of Mato Grosso and the Paraguayan forest, over the Andes to Peru*, London 1932.
5. Claude Lévi-Strauss, *Tristes Tropiques*, Jonathan Cape, London 1973.
6. Sir Christopher Gibson, *Enchanted Trails*, Museum Press, London 1948.
7. "Voyage of Ulrich Schmidt to the rivers La Plata and Paraguai (a true and agreeable description of some principal lands and islands which have not been recorded in former chronicles, but have now been first explored amid great danger during the voyage of Ulrich Schmidt of Straubing and most carefully described by him)", in Luis Domínguez (ed.), *The Conquest of the River Plate*, Hakluyt Society, London 1891, p. 25.
8. Enrique de Gandia, *Historia crítica de los mítos de la conquista americana*, Madrid 1929, p. 186.
9. "Relación de Irala", quoted in Enrique de Gandia, *Historia crítica*, p. 154. The fullest biography of Irala, with the most extensive documentary material, is Lafuente Machain, *El gobernador Domingo Martinez de Irala*, Buenos Aires 1939.
10. Pierre François Charlevoix, *The History of Paraguay*, London 1769, vol. 1, p. 51.

11. Manuel Serrano Sanz (ed.), *La relación de los naufragios y comentarios de Alvar Núñez Cabeza de Vaca*, Madrid 1906, vol. 2, p. 381.
12. Charlevoix, vol. 1, p. 56. Ayolas was probably killed in 1538, but the news did not reach Asunción until 1540.
13. Julio César Chávez, *Descubrimiento y conquista de Rio de la Plata y el Paraguay* (volume 1 of the *Historia General de Paraguay*), Ediciones Nizza, Asunción 1968.
14. "Voyage of Ulrich Schmidt", p. 28.
15. Pierre Clastres, *Society against the State: essays in political anthropology*, Zone Books, New York 1989, p. 93.
16. Pierre Clastres, p. 194.
17. Quoted in Enrique de Gandia, *Indios y conquistadores en el Paraguay*, Buenos Aires 1932.
18. Robert Cunninghame Graham, *A Vanished Arcadia: being some account of the Jesuits in Paraguay, 1607–1767*, Century, London 1988 (first published in 1901).
19. Katharina von Dombrowski, *Land of Women: the tale of a lost nation*, Putnam, London 1935. "Far away, in the heart of a continent, lies a land that for many years has been called The Land of Women, because the men were almost entirely wiped out in the great war of South America."
20. Cited in Pelham Horton Box, *The Origins of the Paraguayan War*, Urbana 1930, p. 298.
21. Robert Cunninghame Graham, *The Conquest of the River Plate*, Heinemann, London 1924, pp. 280–87.

8

ALBUQUERQUE

Port on the Paraguay (2)

Upstream from Pôrto Esperança on the west bank of the Paraguay, opposite the place where the Miranda flows into the main river, stands Puerto Albuquerque. The early Spanish conquistadores called it San Fernando. When the hostile activity of the antagonized Payaguas prevented the Spaniards from using Puerto de la Candelaria to the south, they established themselves here.

Albuquerque, as it is today, marks the entrance to an ancient trail across Chiquitos, one taken by many of the first European travellers who made the east–west crossing. Since the village lies on the river bank, however, and is liable to be flooded in the rainy season, the main settlement is a few miles inland.

The Count of Castelnau, who came here on his great South American expedition early in 1845, was enchanted by what he found:

> Albuquerque is situated in a ravishing spot, in the middle of a great plain, surrounded by Indian hamlets. Above the roofs hang huge leaves of banana and the fronds of beautiful clumps of palm. Beyond lie high hills thickly covered with vegetation.[1]

On landing, the French traveller found himself surrounded "by Indian women who sang strange songs in our honour".

In Castelnau's day, this was a Brazilian camp, manned by about forty soldiers. The village had some sixty Brazilian inhabitants, and perhaps two thousand Indians: Guana and Guaycurus. Castelnau noted that some of the Guaycurus, recently arrived from the Chaco, had hardly ever seen white people before. These new arrivals, according to his account, had massacred a Spanish settlement further to the south – and then taken refuge with the Brazilian garrison. Over the centuries, the Indians of this frontier area had learnt how to exploit the differences between the Europeans.

By the middle of the nineteenth century, Albuquerque was Brazil's "central and principal post on the Paraguay frontier" – the description of Captain Thomas Page of the United States Navy who came here ten years after Castelnau. Captain Page steamed up the Paraguay in his ship the *Water Witch* in 1853, stopping at Albuquerque on his way downstream from Corumbá. He too was delighted with the town. "The whole aspect of the place was cheerful and pleasant; it consisted of sixty or seventy adobe houses, built round a plaza, at one end of which, as usual, stood the chapel, with its white-washed gable and cross."[2] Captain Page spent a day visiting various Indian settlements in the neighbourhood, in the company of Captain Peixoto de Azevido, the commander of the Brazilian garrison at Coimbra, lower down the river. "We called at two establishments of Guaycurus. They live in neat huts, and occupy themselves so successfully in cultivating the ground as to supply nearly all the vegetables used at Albuquerque, and many of those sent to Coimbra and Corumbá." The following day they went to a Tereno mission town run by the Franciscans, the Missão da Nossa Senhora de Bom Conselho, about eight miles from Albuquerque. This, Captain Page noted, "is still more interesting, as exhibiting the aptness of the Indian for civilisation. The subjects of this mission are Guanos, under the immediate charge of a Franciscan friar. . . . We were scarcely prepared for the neatness, order, and cultivation immediately around the mission."

This mission had in fact been planned as a Jesuit settlement nearly a century before. The area was visited by Father Sánchez Labrador who went on a great expedition from the Paraguay to Chiquitos in 1766. But the expulsion of the Jesuits from South America in 1767 put an end to his initiative.[3] An Italian Capuchin, José María de Macerata, re-established a mission here in the 1820s.[4] When the Portuguese military surveyor, Luiz d'Alincourt came here at the same time, he was extremely impressed. He recommended that its strategic position, dominating the entrance to the Miranda, should be taken advantage of. Here the Portuguese should establish a fort.[5]

The Portuguese did garrison the settlement, but it was overrun in the Paraguayan surge up the river in 1864. The Brazilians recovered it in 1868.

Domingo de Irala's two-year expedition to Peru from Albuquerque, 1547–49

The conquistador Domingo de Irala launched a great expedition from the settlement the Spaniards called San Fernando in 1547. After three years of preparation, and a number of tentative explorations across the Paraguay into the Chaco from the main Spanish base at Asunción, Irala was ready to make another cross-country attempt to reach the silver mines of Peru: the Sierra de las Minas.

First he assembled a huge armada at Asunción, with 7 ships and 200 canoes. With him he took 250 Spaniards, 27 horses, and 200 Indians. The expedition was so large that only 240 Spaniards remained behind in Asunción. The possibilities of San Fernando had been reconnoitred a couple of years earlier, in 1545, by one of Irala's lieutenants, Nuflo de Chávez, with fifty Spaniards and "hundreds" of Indians. They had given a positive report.

Irala's armada sailed up the Paraguay from Asunción, and on arrival at San

Fernando, the Spanish commander made considerable efforts to learn from the mistakes of past expeditions. A stockade was constructed, with food and provisions for forty Spaniards who were to stay behind and form a base camp near the river. There would be no repeat of the disaster that had destroyed the returning expedition of Juan de Ayolas nearly ten years earlier (see pages 77–80).

Irala's troop set off westward into the swamps of Chiquitos without too much initial difficulty. The rainy season had not yet begun. Soon they were advancing across the territory of the Guaycurus, whom the Spaniards sometimes called the Mbayas. To begin with, the Indians appeared to receive them with friendship, even offering the sixty-year-old Irala three young girls for his delectation.

But this was nothing more than a ritual. The girls disappeared in the night, and early the next morning the Spanish camp was under attack from the Guaycurus. The Spaniards were ready for them and counterattacked, pursuing the Indians for three whole days.

On the third day, Ulrich Schmidl records, they came upon a group of Indians, with their women and children gathered together in a forest. The fact that these were not the Guaycurus who had attacked their camp, and were perfectly friendly, was of only momentary interest to the Spaniards:

> These were not the people we sought, but their friends. They did not fear at all our coming to them. Nevertheless the innocent had to pay for the guilty, for when we lighted upon them we killed many, and took over 3000 prisoners, men, women, and children; and if it had been daytime instead of night, none of them would have escaped, for there was a goodly number of people gathered together on the hill, at the summit of which was a great wood.[6]

Having made its point, the Spanish expedition continued across the northern Chaco. Once past the swamps and into the pitiless desert, they began to lose men from thirst. The friendly Indians they had with them taught them how to survive by sucking the Chaco thistle.

Eventually they clashed with another Indian nation, the Payzunoes, and captured many of them for use as slaves. These people gave them news of the expedition of Ayolas ten years earlier, saying that several of its members had been kept as prisoners by the Payzunoes. They had survived until recently, having been executed just before the arrival of Irala's troop. Enraged at this news, Irala ordered that the Payzunoes prisoners who had brought it should be killed as a reprisal.

Pushing on to the west, Irala's men crossed the Rio Grande and reached the eastern folds of the Andes. Here they received the greatest shock of their expedition. They encountered a group of Indians who spoke Spanish.

The soldiers from the Paraguay were dumbfounded. They had marched across the centre of the continent, waging war on all who blocked their path. Without suffering either mutiny or famine, they had emerged victorious on the other side.

They were ready to claim the treasure they believed to be theirs. Yet the Spanish words of the Indians revealed that others had got there before them. The local Spanish cacique, already well established in Cochabamba, was Pedro Anzures, sent there with a commission from the viceroy in Lima. This land that Irala's men had come to was no longer virgin Indian territory. It had already been conquered for Spain – by someone else.

Irala retraced his steps to the land of the Corocotoquis Indians, close to the Rio Grande. There he wrote a letter to the viceroy, pleading his case. He entrusted it to Nuflo de Chávez.

Travelling with five Spaniards and one hundred Indians, Chávez crossed the Andes to Lima, arriving in November 1548. The viceroy's message was clear. Irala and his men were to return to the Paraguay. The last thing the authorities in Lima wanted was a large and potentially hostile army on their frontier carving out chunks of their land.

Irala wanted to wait for Chávez's return and then to go north, into the territory called Mojos, the land about which the Spaniards on the Paraguay had already heard rumours. But the encounter with the men of Pedro Anzures had brought disappointment and anger to his troops. He had a rebellion on his hands, which was quelled only by his temporary retirement from the leadership of the expedition. With considerable misgivings, the expedition made its way back across Chiquitos to the Paraguay.

It arrived at Albuquerque in March 1549, after great battles with the Corocotoquis Indians. The Spaniards secured a vast quantity of slaves, two thousand according to one report. It was all they could show for their expedition. Nuflo de Chávez returned to Asunción at the beginning of 1550, bringing with him one hundred Spaniards from Peru. Ten years later, he was to make another attempt to occupy the land between the Paraguay and the Rio Grande.

Notes

1. Francis Laporte, Count of Castelnau, *Expedition dans les parties centrales de l'Amérique du Sud*, Paris 1850.
2. Thomas Page, *La Plata, the Argentine Confederation, and Paraguay: being a narrative of the exploration of the tributaries of the River La Plata and adjacent countries during the years 1853, 54, 55, and 56, under the orders of the United States Government*, London 1859.
3. José Sánchez Labrador, *El Paraguay Católico*, Buenos Aires 1910.
4. Lecio Gomes da Souza, *Historia de Corumbá*, Corumbá n.d.
5. Luiz d'Alincourt, *Memoria sobre a viagem do porto de Santos a cidade de Cuiaba*, São Paulo 1953.
6. "Voyage of Ulrich Schmidt", in Luis Domínguez (ed.), *The Conquest of the River Plate*, Hakluyt Society, London 1891, p. 65.

9

CORUMBÁ

The town on the hill

The train pulls in to the ill-lit station of Corumbá at eight in the evening. By now it is quite dark, and we are unsure how to proceed. The railway station seems to be on the outskirts of town, and there are no hotels in sight. Do we walk out into the darkness and make for the town? Or do we stand around, hoping for a taxi to turn up? Exhausted, we do the latter, and eventually one appears. The driver is pessimistic. There will, he suggests, be nowhere to stay.

He takes us on a tour of the town, from one hotel to another. We must have stopped at more than ten, moving further and further down the scale. Then, on the verge of despair, we stop at the Hotel Paraíso, a low one-storey building with a room on the street. It looks and feels as though this is a room that is normally rented by the hour, but we are only too happy to be allowed to take it for the night. In the morning we will explore.

Corumbá is dominated by the Paraguay river, wide and brimming. It flows towards the town from far on the northern horizon, sweeping down in majestic curves until it almost washes the lower streets, passing from left to right. Then it moves on to the east, round the corner on which the old fort of Ladário stands.

Sometimes a great barge comes past, towing smaller ones upstream. Boats large and small are moored at the bank, including a number of double-deck river steamers, nostalgic and photogenic, that take Brazilian tourists on expeditions deep into the swamp. "PRESERVE THE PANTANAL", says a heartfelt sign on the bank, not unaware that this will help preserve jobs in Corumbá too.

An enlightened municipal authority of the past has created a small park of trees by the river bank, edged with a white-painted balustrade. On the land side of a cobbled street are small bars and restaurants, workshops and places for repairing engines. Here stands a boatyard, there a once-imposing state building, the customs house perhaps, or the former emporium of some wealthy river trader.

The harbour road winds slowly up the hill, cutting a transverse line across the slope. Here are more white balustrades, a line of ornamental palms, and some splendid and ornate buildings, once hotels but now mere rooming houses.

The town is a creation of the late eighteenth century, though most of its faded

94

splendour dates only from a hundred years ago. It started life as a military outpost of the Portuguese. But there must always have been an Indian settlement here, on this great rock above the river, observing the endless procession of foreign travellers and adventurers moving up and down the river and manoeuvring round the turn.

Many of these travellers have left accounts of their journeys, for the waters of the upper Paraguay long had strategic significance. And for later travellers these latitudes have always been overly endowed with charm. In earlier centuries, long before the Spaniards or the Portuguese arrived, dozens of Indian nations made full use of this great waterway.

Claude Lévi-Strauss came here in 1935 and his first impressions were not too far removed from the ones we have just had. "There is only one hotel," he noted, "and it is always full." But he clearly liked the way this luminous place was "perched at the top of a limestone cliff overlooking the river". Nothing much has changed in half a century. "Surrounded by a mass of canoes, one or two small paddle boats, with low hulls and two layers of cabins surmounted by a slender funnel, are moored at the quayside, from where the road climbs up."[1]

Grace Thompson Seton, the loquacious North American who arrived here four years earlier, also had trouble finding rooms. "So here we are, bag and can, at the hotel clamouring for rooms and a bath! No rooms, 'nadamas'."[2]

But on the whole she liked its brick-built one-storey houses surrounding mysterious patios. "The streets present a blank face to the passer-by and all the life of the house goes on within its walls." She had soon located the Bar Venizelos, which "with its tropical garden and cafe tables, proved to be the most agreeable gathering place for the afternoon coffee or light beer of Corumbá". There was nowhere quite like Corumbá, "with its dock, its few streets, its public square where the band plays for paseo on Sunday nights, its hotel, its wineshops and stores for tinned food and merchandise".

On her way upriver to the north, she felt the town to be "the last outpost of civilisation". It had mail, telegraph and cable service – "somewhat fitful, but service". It must indeed, she thought, seem "a teeming metropolis to the farflung ranch owners who are days, sometimes weeks, of travel away".

Some sixty years before the arrival of the French anthropologist, an adventurous Irishwoman, Marion Mulhall, stopped here with her husband on her way up the Paraguay river to Cuiabá. This was in 1875, only five years after the death of President Solano López and the end of the Paraguayan War. Her husband was the editor of the *Review of the River Plate* in Buenos Aires, and she was on the journey to accompany the wife of the new Brazilian governor of Mato Grosso.

She was enchanted by Corumbá and published a vivid account of her travels. She found a fort "newly built on the barranca" or cliff, with its guns "pointed east, north and south". After the Paraguayan War and the shock of invasion, the Brazilians were taking no chances. She walked the zigzag road up the hill, still there today, with the rocks "overhanging on either side". And she was impressed by the shopping. "Several of the shops are as well-stocked as in Buenos Aires, and the merchandise is cheaper."[3]

British goods had already forced their way up the river, closed for so many centuries but now open after the victory of the British-backed triple alliance of Brazil, Argentina, and Uruguay. "I am told the hammocks are made in Manchester," she wrote, "and are excellent imitations of those made here." Local hammocks, of course, were "much dearer".

She also commented on the huge success of the local landowners. "The farmers round here are very wealthy and often spend $1000 when they come into town." Indeed Mrs Mulhall was a fan of all things Brazilian.

> It is very pleasant to see the air of security and good order that pervades every Brazilian town however remote, the unmistakeable sign of good government. . . . There are no iron bars on the windows, which are thrown wide open to admit the morning breeze and sunshine. The inhabitants have not the anxious look of people who sleep with revolvers under their pillows or get up every morning with rumours of revolution. Corumbá must be a dull place to live in, but it possesses that security for life and property which is the first right of every peace-abiding citizen.

A visiting Brazilian doctor, João Severiano da Fonseca, testified that in a town of five thousand inhabitants "you didn't see a single beggar".[4]

Yet in 1877, barely two years after Mrs Mulhall's visit, that feeling of security had gone. Corumbá was like a town struck by the plague. Doctor Fonseca described it as a place where:

> the streets were filled with beggars, little more than walking corpses; where poverty ravaged the poorest people; where vast numbers of men, women and children, badly dressed, badly housed, and worse fed, lived, most of them, in miserable huts in the woods surrounding the town".

What had gone wrong? The cause of the problem was simple. The Brazilian army, which had been occupying Paraguay ever since the war had ended in 1870, was now being withdrawn. Hundreds of Paraguayans employed by that army, chiefly in keeping the soldiers fed – that traditional task of the Indians since colonial times – had withdrawn with them up the Paraguay river. They were followed by thousands of others, "forced by the fear of famine to abandon their unfortunate country".

In a single span of four months, from May to July 1876, some three thousand impoverished refugees had arrived at Corumbá and the neighbouring settlement of Ladário. In an effort to try to prevent this huge influx turning into an even greater tragedy, Doctor Fonseca set up a hospital in Ladário. But it did not long survive his own departure.[5]

By the early twentieth century, however, Corumbá had recovered. Trade and commerce revived. The English manager of a Bolivian rubber plantation, passing through here in 1911 and staying at the Hotel Galileo, noted that "the accommodation was comfortable but the food was execrable – the worst I have had in any part of the world". The man's name was Henry Grey, and he was more familiar with Africa than South America. He was depressed to find that:

> Vegetables were a luxury, and what there was were nearly all imported in tins; and even tomatoes, which could have been easily grown there, were almost unheard of. The only place where a decent meal could be got was at a restaurant kept by an American negro called Bill Carter, who grew his own tomatoes and reared his own chickens – and was very proud of both.[6]

Theodore Roosevelt, the former United States president, who came up the Paraguay late in 1913, almost certainly stayed at the Hotel Galileo too, echoing Henry Grey's words that "the accommodation was comfortable but the food was execrable".[7]

Howard Clewes, passing through forty years later in 1953, had a similar view. "The town's one hotel was not too uncomfortable, though the provender was atrocious."[8]

Equally caustic in his opinions was Alex Rattray Hay, the North American evangelical missionary who passed through Corumbá in 1919, on his way to convert the Bororo Indians in the region of Cuiabá. Corumbá, he wrote, "is quite a prosperous-looking place, though it has suffered considerably during the Great War. Most of the business is in the hands of Syrians, who, because of their success and sharp practices, are well-hated by the Brazilians".[9]

Colonel Fawcett, however, who knew this region well and called in a year later, in 1920, noted that the town "had altered much for the better since 1909, for its traders and cattlemen had cleaned up tidy fortunes during the war".[10]

The Reverend Hay had also been to Corumbá before, and had other interests. He was relieved to find that the Catholic priests had few apologists "being generally considered as canting hypocrites. The great majority of the people had become nauseated by the Roman sham, and were antagonistic to religion in any form."

Out of the most uncompromising material, missionary Hay hoped to make converts. On the boat going north from Corumbá to Cuiabá, he caught sight of a couple of Paraguayans, rough clay that he longed to mould:

> Without exception their faces were sensual, brutish, bearing the marks of debauchery. They were of wretched physique. There was no manliness or self-respect in their bearing, or purpose in their expressions. The lewd jest and coarse laugh, and a pack of cards, were their only diversions. They were astonishingly godless, having little respect even for the Roman Catholic church, though they retain many of its corrupting superstitions, and carry its blighting influence stamped deep upon their characters.

> They are rough material, but, thank God, there is cleansing for even these, and power abundant to make new creatures.

Julian Duguid, the English writer who came here in 1928, was more fastidious. He didn't mind the people, but he disliked the town. "It is without dispute the most unpleasant place I ever saw." He was put off chiefly by the heat:

> A low range of limestone hills rears up out of the cattle plains, and the sun devours the yellow streets. The whiteness of the houses is blinding, the heat comes up in a haze, and a vast, heavy stillness broods over the terraced town. By day the porous stone sucks in the hot savagery of the tropics, and breathes it out like an evil odour by night.[11]

Nearly all the twentieth-century travellers spin a tale of frying eggs on the pavement in the afternoon heat. Henry Grey's account is the first of many. "The stone parapet of the wall banking the road leading down to the 'beach' would get so hot during the afternoon that one could almost have fried an egg on it; to touch it with the hand was unbearable."

Duguid tells of the proprietor of the Hotel Galileo who, in the hottest months, "wins many bets off strangers by pouring an egg on to the pavement and scraping it off baked".[12] Grace Thompson Seton also knew that "here one can cook eggs on the pavement". Did it really happen, or did they all read each other's books?

We enjoyed our rent-by-the-hour hotel, but decided the next morning that it would be nice to move. Across the road we found the Hotel Schabib, a charming Syrian hostel run for the benefit of backpackers, many of whom were setting off for a three-day hike into the Pantanal when we arrived. A round trip costs 66 dollars, and we were constantly asked by wistful jeep drivers if we would like to join in. According to the local paper, *Diario da Manha*, 12,000 tourists a year now come to Corumbá.

Like Alex Rattray Hay, we found Corumbá to be a town of Syrians, "Turcos" they are usually called in South America, refugees from the break-up of the Turkish empire. One family ran our hotel, others owned small shops in the town. In a shop selling tee-shirts covered with jaguars from the Pantanal, we found a man from Palestine who had once been in the British police.

On our way downhill to the river, we stopped at a bar selling sucos (fruit juices). It had three posters on the wall, one of Rambo, one of Charlie Chaplin and one of a Mercedes Benz. The pert serving-girl had a tee-shirt which said "Casual Hello", we sat there for a while, looking out across the central square towards the bandstand.

On the waterfront, we found the El Pacu restaurant, run by an aged German and his Brazilian wife. With a high ceiling and a tiny entrance, it is a cool oasis in the heat. On the walls are posters advertising *Deutschland* and *Oberbayern*, together with alligator skins and the obligatory mural of the Pantanal. There are also two pictures of conquistadores, looking suspiciously like Teutonic knights. Perhaps they are meant to be Ulrich Schmidl, who came this way. I ate fried pacu, Vivien tried urucum, a fish with the flavour of crab, cooked with cheese. You could stay a long time in Corumbá.

The United States comes to the Paraguay: the expedition of Captain Thomas Page USN in 1853

One of the first North Americans to report from the upper Paraguay in the nineteenth century was Thomas Page of the US Navy. He steamed upriver in 1853, a decade before the outbreak of the Paraguayan War, in the *Water Witch*, a sailing-ship-cum-paddle-steamer, one of the first of its kind.

Captain Page steamed up as far as Corumbá, but there he was obliged to turn back. He had no permission from the Paraguayans to go that far, the Brazilians did not wish him to go on to Cuiabá, and in any case the *Water Witch* was too large to make the journey further upriver.

He wrote a delightful account of his expedition and was much impressed by the surroundings of the Brazilian town.

> The country presents the appearance of a beautiful and recently-mown meadow, bounded by wooded mountains, artificially terraced to the plain. The silence and solitude is that of a desert. Not a sign of human life, not a vestige or germ of civilisation, except our little craft.[13]

Corumbá itself he did not much care for:

> . . . merely a collection of thatched huts forming two sides of a plaza, at one end of which is a chapel, distinguishable only by its cross from the humble tenements. A commander, fifteen soldiers, and about thirty women and children, apparently mixed breeds of whites, Indians, and negroes, are the inhabitants of this place, which has the appearance of a forlorn settlement of squatters.

But Captain Page had no doubts about the importance of his mission. He perceived his ship as a symbol of the new era that was about to start in South America. "She puffs over the waters," he wrote, proud of its new steam technology. "At her peak the 'Stars and Stripes' are spread by a gentle southern breeze. We are opening, I sanguinely hope, a new path to commerce and civilisation."

Captain Page was a naval surveyor. He had spent the years from 1848 to 1851 on the East India station, cruising in Chinese waters. Convinced of the importance of surveying for trade and commerce, he had tried to interest the authorities in Washington of the value of his perception. Denied the opportunity of putting his ideas into practice in Chinese waters (the command went to a more senior captain), he was sent to South America with a novel brief in February 1853.

The European nations had all sent expeditions in the early nineteenth century to enlighten themselves about the former Spanish empire. Now it was the turn of the United States. Captain Page's new job was to lead an expedition to explore and survey the tributaries of the River Plate. He was to report on the "navigability and adaptation to commerce" of these rivers and to examine their agricultural resources. Like his European predecessors, he was also commanded to make natural history collections.

The idea of a United States scientific expedition had first been floated with the Paraguayan president (Carlos Antonio López) by Edward Hopkins in 1845. Now, seven years later it had borne fruit. Indeed it was Hopkins's lecture to the American Geographical and Statistical Society in New York in 1852, on the commercial possibilities opening up in Paraguay, that had provided the impetus for the expedition.

Edward Augustus Hopkins was one of those strange semi-freelance US operatives common in Latin America in the nineteenth century. Briefly a midshipman in the US Navy, and with influential connections in Washington (he was the son of a bishop), he had somehow secured for himself in 1845, at the age of twenty-three, a post as US Special Agent to Paraguay – perhaps someone thought it was suitably far away.

Three years later, in 1849, Hopkins had travelled to the headwaters of the Paraguay, "a thousand miles above Asunción in a canoe", he later recalled, "with Indians of the Chaco for crew".[14] Hopkins became an ardent advocate of the charms of Paraguay, and soon became rather more deeply involved with commerce than diplomacy. In his New York lecture, he had reported on the wonderful trading opportunities to be secured in the upper Paraguay – trade to be carried on in boats in which Hopkins had an interest.

> Beginning with the headwaters of the River Paraguay, we find the productions upon the Brazilian side to be gold and precious stones, sugar, molasses, hides of extraordinary size, hair, tallow, wax, deer and tiger skins, with rice, corn, and the different manufactures of the mandioca root; in Bolivia, gold and precious stones, silver, coffee – considered by good judges to be equal to Mocha – and Peruvian bark. Though undoubtedly we could draw from these two countries many other productions of tropical America, yet it is in Paraguay that we find the greatest wealth of all these valleys.[15]

The enthusiasm of Hopkins was directly responsible for the expedition of Captain Page. The *Water Witch* left Buenos Aires in July 1853 and reached Asunción in October. There, in his lodgings, Captain Page wrote with admiration of finding "a dozen richly carved high-backed chairs, which dated from the time of the Jesuits", a time when "those missionaries were the Medici of La Plata". The chairs, he said, were "the pride of the establishment".

In Asunción, Captain Page met Hopkins, and they seem to have cordially disliked each other, a rivalry between imperial servants familiar from the Spanish era. Page got on better with President Carlos Antonio López, the inheritor of the mantle of Doctor Francia. Advised and encouraged by Hopkins, López had begun to open up his country to the outside world.

While intrigued to meet the American captain, López said that, were he to permit the *Water Witch* to ascend the river beyond Paraguayan jurisdiction into Brazil, Brazil would make the same demand for Brazilian boats. In the present state of their political relations, López said, "he was resolved not to grant her that privilege".

The three-centuries-old dispute in this area between Spain and Portugal had remained unresolved at the time of Paraguayan independence. Brazil and Paraguay continued at loggerheads over the course of their common frontier. Granting, or withholding, rights of passage up the river was one of the few weapons in Paraguay's arsenal.

Captain Page seems to have agreed with the president that he would remain in Paraguayan waters, but once on his way he was clearly tempted to continue his journey upstream to Brazil. Eventually his actions were to cause serious trouble, clouding relations between the United States and Paraguay throughout the 1850s.

But on his way upriver, such thoughts were far from the mind of Captain Page. Instead he waxed lyrical about the future of the fertile valley of the Paraguay, perceiving it as a new American frontier: "I found myself speculating upon the future of these favoured regions . . . presenting, with the exception of that of our Mississippi, the fairest unbroken extent of cultivable land in the world".

This was the common wisdom of the age. Similar thoughts had been expressed that year by an influential United States writer, Matthew Fontaine Maury, who argued passionately for the development of both the Amazon basin and the upper Paraguay. A geographer and a lieutenant in the US Navy, Maury first published his *The Amazon and the Atlantic Slopes* in Washington in 1853. In it, he described the Paraguay not as the Mississippi but as "the Missouri" of the River Plate basin.[16]

All that the area needed, Maury argued, was some modern technology, which the United States would be well able to provide. "In the valley of the Amazon the plough is unknown: and the American rifle and axe, the great implements of settlement and civilisation, are curiosities."

Lieutenant Maury had nothing but contempt for the European experience in South America:

> For more than 300 years the white man has been established in that Amazonian basin, and for more than 300 years it has remained a howling wilderness. Owing to the mismanagement of its rulers, the European has made no impression – none – no, not the least – upon its forests. How long shall this continue to be so?

The country drained by the Amazon, Maury wrote, "if reclaimed from the savage, the wild beast, and the reptile, and reduced to cultivation now, would be capable of supporting with its produce the population of the whole world".

Captain Page was not so much interested in feeding the world as in providing places for Europe's restless millions to settle in:

> Is this wealth of creation to remain unavailable for the comfort and happiness of men, while the powers holding dominion over it invite immigration, and the overcrowded cities of Europe teem with millions whose cry is bread? When the dungeons of southern Italy re-echo the sighs of men who have dared to aspire to political independence? And while the industrial nations are seeking new sources of supply in raw materials and outlets for their manufactures? And while, even in Constitutional England, in underground dens, or within the shadow of palatial precincts, are hid, not sheltered, men, women, and children, crushed, not by vice, but a poverty that generates crime?

An English visitor to Paraguay, C.B. Mansfield, gazing out at the Chaco the year before, had had similar thoughts, expressed with the Victorian schoolboy's enthusiasm for colonialism.

> One thing is abundantly clear to me, viz, that the Gran Chaco is the yet empty cradle of a mighty nation; it must be the theatre of a new era in history. . . . Besides the cultivation of the Chaco-land, there is the cultivation of the Indians to be effected. These are the "untameable Guaycurus", etc., which tradition says can never be tamed. . . . A traditional enmity has ever existed between the Indians and those whose ancestors looked upon them only as material for slavery; but I firmly believe that Englishmen with some real Christianity in their souls would civilise them in some degree.[17]

Steaming along in the *Water Witch*, Captain Page let his imagination run. He foresaw how it would be possible for European emigrants to the valley of La Plata to reach their new homes in ocean steamers.

> The steamers of maritime nations, bearing the products of industrial power, will cover her interior water-courses, and, in return, pour into the lap of those nations the indigenous agricultural and mineral wealth of the Western Indies. No overthrow of existent governments, no political revulsions are necessary to place the inhabitants of these regions under the beneficent influences of a great republican civilisation.

The *Water Witch*, the bearer of these utopian dreams, was the object of much attention in the upper Paraguay.

> People from a long distance in the interior flocked to see the wonderful bark. Men, women, and children crowded on board, and would sit for hours under the awning of

the deck, seemingly astonished and delighted at all they saw, and eagerly questioning the old Guaraní pilot as to the meaning of many things to them so incomprehensible.

Wherever they went, they were stopped by admirers on shore. Above Concepción, Captain Page invited a Lengua cacique and a few Indians on board. Three hundred years after Juan de Ayolas, Domingo de Irala, Núñez de Cabeza, and Nuflo de Chávez had made contact with the Indians on the Paraguay's shores, Captain Page made comparable overtures. He was not seeking a way through to the east, but the nineteenth-century El Dorado of trade and commerce. He recorded the reaction of the Indians:

> Not only no steamer, but no vessel approaching the size of our craft had ever before passed over these waters; but not a sound or movement betrayed either astonishment, admiration, or fear on the part of the chief. Some of those who accompanied him had less command over themselves, and manifested a little uneasiness; no persuasion could induce them to go below, after having been shown everything on deck.

Captain Page gave them "a few trinkets, fish-hooks, and cigars", and they seemed pleased. Indeed soon another party of mounted Indians appeared, "approaching the river at full speed". They proved to be "a part of the same tribe we had already seen, and wanted presents". The message had spread quickly.

Further up the river, another group of Indians made signs that they wanted "a talk". The steamer stopped and some of the crew landed.

> They proved to be one of the most warlike tribes, the Angaite, and were noble-looking creatures, above the normal stature, and well formed: their teeth were white and regular; hair luxuriant, and cut square upon the forehead. We gazed with interest upon these savages, for the warlike Chaco tribes have alone, amid the degradation and extirpation of the nation of their race upon the American continent, defied, for more than three centuries, the power of the white man. They still maintain their wild independence, but in intricate and inaccessible passes of mountain ranges – not in great sterile plains, or among the death-exhaling morasses, where the ingenuity or industry of the white man could obtain no remunerative return, but over a vast domain of two hundred thousand square miles, spreading out into noble forests of precious woods, lovely plains, accessible by navigable rivers, and irrigated by hundreds of their tributary streams; a land not figuratively, but literally flowing with milk and honey.

Here, mapped out by Captain Page, was the promised land for the prospective colonist. Europeans were to flock to the River Plate basin throughout the rest of the nineteenth century, and North American settlers were coming to the Chaco as late as the 1920s. All that remained was to throw out the Indians to make room for them.

European colonization in the nineteenth century

When the Spanish empire in South America collapsed at the beginning of the nineteenth century, the Indian nations that occupied the land had not yet lost their struggle for supremacy. In all parts of the territory, except for the sea coasts, the mining districts and the river valleys, they remained in control. While some Indian nations had worked with the Spanish invaders from the beginning, the majority had avoided the colonial embrace and could look back on nearly three centuries of successful resistance.

Although the Spaniards should have had the upper hand militarily, in practice the two sides were reasonably matched. Martín Dobrizhoffer, the Jesuit priest who had lived and worked on both sides of the Paraguay in the eighteenth century, had not been at all impressed with the local soldiery in Paraguay. The soldiers, he found, were often no match for the Indians, even when armed with guns:

> Whenever some hundreds of soldiers fiercely approached the stations of the savages, either the steel was rusty and would not explode, or the gunpowder so moist as to prevent its blazing, so that very few were able to discharge their guns.[18]

Dobrizhoffer gave an example of an occasion when twenty youths from the Abipones had slaughtered a group of thirty soldiers. "They had passed the night in the open air, and as the guns were very badly taken care of, the copious dew so moistened the gunpowder that Vesuvius itself would not have been able to kindle it."

Dobrizhoffer went further, pointing out that even regular troops from Spain would be insufficient:

> The soldiers would indeed be superior to the Americans in the skilful management of fire-arms, but very far inferior in the arts of swimming and riding, and in tolerance of fatigue, heat, hunger, and thirst. Encumbered with tents, waggons, boats, or pontoons, which they could not dispense with, they would be unable to pursue the flying horsemen of the savages, still less to reach their hordes, which are sometimes two hundred leagues distant from the cities.[19]

This farsighted critique of the problems facing imperial armies operating far from home goes some way to explaining why the Spanish after so many centuries were still only able to manage a holding operation in South America. Unable to remove the Indian threat by force, the Spanish imperial regime was obliged to deal with it by operating a twin policy of stick and carrot. Indians that could be attracted into the imperial web were rewarded, those that remained hostile were severely chastized.

The independence governments did not have such a sophisticated policy. From the beginning they made it clear that independence was for whites only. There was no such thing as a "good Indian". Indeed in some countries the "patriots" rose up against imperial rule because the Spanish were considered to be soft on the Indians. Yet now, with nothing to offer the Indians, the whites were faced with a dramatic security problem and no great imperial army at their disposal.

Outnumbered by the Indians, and with insufficient forces at their command, they embarked throughout the nineteenth century on a campaign to eradicate the indigenous nations. By the end of the century they had abandoned any notion of coexistence and were purposefully killing Indians on a comparable scale to that of the conquistadores and the early Spanish settlers in the sixteenth and seventeenth centuries.

The policy of extermination was coupled with a programme to people the lands that their forefathers had stolen with new generations of white settlers from Europe. Nor did they merely need settlers. Deprived of the old European civil service, and slow to produce new cadres of their own, they were forced to buy them from outside. John Lynch has argued that "in a sense the Paraguayan government [in the 1850s and 1860s] imported an entire middle class – engineers, architects, doctors, teachers, merchants and artisans".[20]

The new settlers from Europe did not find life easy, since for a long time they coexisted in frontier areas with the as yet undefeated Indians. A young Englishman, L. Dillon, who travelled to Córdoba in the middle of 1867, found some of the new immigrants "several very jolly English fellows". They had settled on the camps outside to farm. They told him the following:

> There is one great drawback to these camps – they are too near to the Indian tribes. About four or five months ago these savages made a raid upon the Frayle Muerto lands. They killed three Englishmen, and actually advanced within two leagues of the town. . . . The Indians mustered five to six hundred strong, and, had they chosen, could easily have advanced and taken the town. . . . This raid of the savage tribes will be a serious let to immigration, and until the government erects more forts and fills them with efficient garrisons, they must not expect Europeans to come and risk their lives in such a desert and uncultivated spot as this is.[21]

The new immigrants were in fact learning the hard lesson that their Spanish predecessors had had to learn. They were on their own, and no government was going to do much for them. Mr Dillon went on to quote from a letter he had read in the Buenos Aires *Standard* from an English correspondent in Frayle Muerto:

> Those of us who are here are seriously thinking of getting up, if possible, an expedition against the Indians; for as the government does not seem inclined to do anything for us, we must do something for ourselves in self-preservation. If we could get two hundred, or a hundred and fifty Englishmen, and have a sort of military discipline, with a little drill, we should do very well.

These campaigns against the Indians were taking place at the exact moment when the Argentines were involved in a war against Paraguay, a war which at that moment, they were not winning.

The expedition of Theodore Roosevelt in 1913–14

By the beginning of the twentieth century, such freelance vigilante operations were no longer necessary. The independent governments of South America, often importing European military expertise, had begun to create armies capable of destroying the surviving Indian nations: in Argentina in the 1880s, in Bolivia in the 1890s. The Paraguayan Indians had already been decimated in the 1860s.

When Theodore Roosevelt came up the Paraguay river in December 1913, he reflected on the beneficent nature of these new South American armies. He had sailed upriver from Asunción and arrived at Concepción. There he had inspected the local troops, who had been trained by a German lieutenant.

In every South American country where a really efficient army is developed, the increase in military efficiency goes hand in hand with a decrease in lawlessness and disorder, and a growing reluctance to settle internal disagreements by violence.[22]

This North American admiration for the Latin American military was to last throughout the twentieth century.

Theodore Roosevelt was still only in his fifties when he came travelling up the Paraguay. He had never found anything very satisfactory to occupy his time since leaving the presidency of the United States. A journey into the heart of South America would relieve the tedium of post-presidential life. Several members of his expedition have left accounts of it, but Roosevelt's is written in the ripest prose:

Under the brilliant sky we steamed steadily up the mighty river; the sunset was glorious as we leaned on the port railing; and after nightfall the moon, nearly full and hanging high in the heavens, turned the water to shimmering radiance. On the mudflats and sandbars, and among the green rushes of the bays and inlets, were stately waterfowl; crimson flamingoes and rosy spoonbills, dark-coloured ibis, and white storks with black wings.[23]

When the expedition arrived at Corumbá, it was difficult for the local inhabitants to ignore the fact that Roosevelt was a celebrity. It was, after all, barely four years since he had been the United States president. "Several steamers came out to meet us," he wrote, "and accompanied us for a dozen miles, with bands playing and the passengers cheering, just as if we were nearing some town on the Hudson."[24]

He found the place to be rather more primitive than the towns he was familiar with on the Hudson river:

> Corumbá is on a steep hillside, with wide roughly-paved streets, some of them lined with beautiful trees that bear scarlet flowers, and with well-built houses, most of them one-storey, some of two or three stories. We were greeted with a reception by the municipal council, and were given a state dinner. The hotel, kept by an Italian, was as comfortable as possible – stone floors, high ceilings, big windows and doors, a cool, open courtyard, and a shower-bath. Of course, Corumbá is still a frontier town. The vehicles are ox-carts and mule carts; there are no carriages; and oxen as well as mules are used for riding.

Roosevelt's Brazilian expedition, like all such excursions at the time, had the trappings of a scientific exploration. The naturalist on the trip, Leo Miller, who later became a writer of children's stories, has also left a description of the town. He too was impressed by the trees:

> Corumbá is a very hot, dusty town built on a high rocky elevation on the west bank of the Paraguay. The settlement bears the unenviable reputation of being the rendez-vous for fugitives from justice from many climates, but we saw nothing of the lawlessness and disorder said to prevail. . . . The heat at midday was great, but frequently a breeze came up at night. Rows of low, spreading mimosa trees lined some of the streets and cast a welcome shade; their branches were covered with clumps of gorgeous scarlet flowers.[25]

Another member of the former president's expedition, George Cherrie, found this part of the world so fascinating that he came back the following year. He too was beguiled by Corumbá.

> Our first glimpse of Corumbá was enchanting. It lay bathed in the early morning sunshine, the red-tiled roofs and white walls in pleasing contrast to the rich green of banana trees and the fronds of waving palms. Much of the business and all of the residential part of the town was situated on a bluff some 200 feet above the river, affording an extensive view out over the low flat country which is so characteristic of the upper Paraguay River. . . . We found the place full of surprises. A city of 10,000 inhabitants without a market place, with no street cars, no automobiles and only a single carriage for hire.[26]

After stopping at Corumbá, Roosevelt's expedition sailed on up the Paraguay. He had been joined lower down the river by Colonel Candido da Silva Rondón, the doyen of Brazilian exploration. Rondón had travelled to Pôrto Esperança by train, and knew the entire area extremely well. He had spent the previous twenty years linking up all the major towns of Mato Grosso by telegraph wire.

The expedition travelled past the lakes of Mandiore, Gaiba and Uberaba, until they arrived at the great American-run ranch at Descalvados. This was the headquarters, Roosevelt noted, of one of

> the great outlying ranches of the Brazil Land and Cattle Company, the Farquhar syndicate, under the management of Murdo Mackenzie – than whom we have had in the United States no better citizen or more competent cattleman. On this ranch there are some 70,000 head of stock. We were warmly greeted by McLean, the head of the ranch, and his assistant Ramsay, an old Texan friend. Among the other assistants, all equally cordial, were several Belgians and Frenchmen.[27]

The Descalvados ranch had replaced the Jesuit missions of the eighteenth century as a local centre:

> At this ranch there was a tannery, a slaughterhouse, a cannery, a church, buildings of various kinds and all degrees of comfort for the 30 or 40 families who made the place their headquarters, and the handsome, white, two-storey big house, standing among lemon trees and flamboyants on the river bank.

But this was for Europeans and North Americans, for whites and cattle. Of the Indians there is little mention. "The hands were Paraguayans and Brazilians, and a few Indians – a hard-bit set, each of whom always goes armed and knows how to use his arms, for there are constant collisions with cattle thieves from across the Bolivian border."

Roosevelt's expedition continued and eventually, after many adventures, reached the Amazon. He returned to the United States from Manaus. The former president suffered severely on the journey, from illness, heart trouble and fatigue. He died five years later.

His travels have something of the flavour of earlier expeditions. Nearly all of them plunged into the unknown interior with very little understanding of what they would find, and little inkling of the trouble they would cause to those who went with them. Few had much interest in the people they met.

Notes

1. Claude Lévi-Strauss, *Tristes Tropiques*, Jonathan Cape, London 1973.
2. Grace Thompson Seton, *Log of the "Look See"*, London 1932, p. 60.
3. Marion Mulhall, *From Europe to Mato Grosso*, 1877, p. 45.
4. João Severiano da Fonseca, *Voyage autour du Brésil*, Rio de Janeiro 1899, p. 69. Published earlier, 1880–81, as *Viagem ao Redor do Brasil*.
5. Severiano da Fonseca was a well-connected figure in Brazilian politics. (His brother, Marshal Deodoro da Fonseca, was to become the President of Brazil in November 1889.) He was in fact the military doctor on a governmental expedition sent up the Paraguay river to settle the border between

Brazil and Bolivia. The eight-man survey team left Rio de Janeiro in May 1875, travelling by sea and then into the River Plate, and returned, after nearly three years, in January 1878.

6. Henry Grey, *The Land of Tomorrow*, London 1927, pp. 31–2.
7. Theodore Roosevelt, *Through the Brazilian Wilderness*, London 1914.
8. Howard Clewes, *The Way the Wind Blows*, London 1953, p. 95.
9. Alex Rattray Hay, *Saints and Savages*, London 1921, p. 8.
10. Percy Fawcett, *Exploration Fawcett*, London, Hutchinson 1948, p. 212.
11. Julian Duguid, *Green Hell*, London 1931, p. 56.
12. Julian Duguid, *Tiger Man: an odyssey of freedom*, London 1932, p. 255.
13. Thomas Page, *La Plata, the Argentine Confederation, and Paraguay: being a narrative of the exploration of the tributaries of the River La Plata and adjacent countries during the years 1853, 54, 55, and 56, under the orders of the United States Government*, London 1859.
14. Edward Hopkins, "My Life-Record", appendix 2 in Pablo Max Ynsfran, *La expedición Norteamericana contra el Paraguay, 1858–1859*, (2nd edition), Asunción 1988.
15. E.A. Hopkins, "Memoir on the geography, history, productions and trade of Paraguay", in *Bulletin of the American Geographical and Statistical Society*, vol.1, New York 1852.
16. Matthew Fontaine Maury, *The Amazon and the Atlantic Slopes*, Washington 1853.
17. C.B. Mansfield, *Paraguay, Brazil, and the Plate*, London 1856, p. 354.
18. Martín Dobrizhoffer, *An Account of the Abipones*, London 1822 vol. 2, p. 399.
19. Dobrizhoffer, vol. 2, p. 404.
20. John Lynch, "The River Plate countries", in Leslie Bethel (ed.), *Cambridge History of Latin America*, Cambridge 1985 vol. 3, p. 669.
21. L. Dillon, *A Twelve Month Tour, Brazil and the River Plate*, Manchester 1867.
22. Roosevelt, p. 45.
23. Roosevelt, p. 37.
24. Roosevelt, p. 58.
25. Leo Miller, *In the Wilds of South America: six years of exploration*, London 1919, p. 208.
26. George Cherrie, *Dark Trails*, New York 1930, p. 267.
27. Roosevelt, p. 117.

10

PUERTO SUÁREZ

From Corumbá to the shores of Lake Cáceres

Throughout our second night in Corumbá a great wind storm blew from the south, with such ferocity that it seemed as though the corrugated iron must be ripped from the roof. I wondered how those on safari in the Pantanal would be faring. This morning the temperature has dropped dramatically, with a strong breeze still blowing through the town, though the sun shines as bright as ever. We have coffee and omelettes for breakfast and prepare to leave Brazil.

Walking through a Friday street market, we come to the Rodoviario, the railway station where days ago we arrived in the dark. Here we are given our Brazilian exit stamps by an immigration officer reading *An Introduction to Greek Philosophy*. Then we return to say goodbye to the Hotel Schabib and its quota of cheerful Syrians who have served us so well. We take a taxi to the Bolivian frontier, a few miles out of town.

At the Brazilian border post we are waved through, but in the no-man's-land before crossing into Bolivia, we are expected to change taxis. A Bolivian driver materializes, most anxious to give us a lift. We are, after all, to be his best fare of the day. He assures us that, if we are quick, we should just manage to catch the train for Roboré. It is just ready to leave, he suggests, from the station at Puerto Quijarro down the road, and indeed is only just waiting for us.

A likely story, as we are under the impression that the train leaves in the evening. But since uncertainty is ever the keynote of travel in these parts, we are happy to fall for his tale – and pile into his ancient car. He tells us that he comes originally from Santa Cruz where he had had a chicken farm. But his chickens got the pest, his business failed, and he came to Puerto Quijarro to work as a taxi-driver.

At the Bolivian frontier, the officials go through the motions of stamping our passports and let us through without comment. We drive on, down dusty roads, to Quijarro station, a dismal place surrounded by filthy shacks, hovels and doss-houses. It is very poor and miserable compared with Corumbá.

The platform is almost deserted and the ticket office is closed. There will clearly be no train for a long time. Sometime in the evening, they say. So we go off with our friendly taxi-driver to drive round the village in search of the ticket office official. He is not in his house, but when we go back to the station he has reappeared. He says we can return after lunch to buy tickets to Roboré.

We get our taxi-driver, by now in effect our guide and chauffeur, to take us down to Puerto Suárez, the nearby port on Lake Cáceres that gives the Bolivians some access to the River Paraguay, though only for very small boats at certain times of the year.

Puerto Suárez, too, is a pitiful spot, with a deserted hotel looking over the lake. There is a mean main street with stalls selling tourist kitsch from the Bolivian altiplano to Brazilian day-trippers. We do find a reasonable place to have lunch, patronized by the local military.

This unlovely settlement has undergone innumerable changes over the years, of place, name and function. In spite of the historic nature of this route across the northern Chaco, there is no written record of settlement – either Spanish or Indian – before the nineteenth century, though the shores of Lake Cáceres must always have provided a home to Indians before the arrival of the Spaniards. Today it is in a state of terminal decline.

In 1900, an English explorer, Whitfield Ray, found a population of "perhaps a hundred inhabitants, chiefly civilised Chiquitanos Indians". He noted "a large customs house, and a regular trade in rubber brought in from the interior on mule back, a journey which often takes as much as four months".[1]

Throughout its existence, Puerto Suárez was the jumping-off ground for the long trek westward across Chiquitos to Santa Cruz de la Sierra. Leo Miller, the naturalist who travelled with Theodore Roosevelt in 1914, wrote of "the cart trail leading through the heart of the Chaco". To travel over it, he wrote, "is a difficult undertaking, the ox-drawn carts requiring a minimum of 30 days for the trip. During the rainy season a large part of the country is inundated, when the caravans must, of course, suspend their activity".[2] Nor was safety on the track guaranteed. One night, Miller noted, "but a short time before", a party of Indians had attacked and killed all the members of the caravan.

A little earlier, in 1911, an Englishman, Henry Grey, had come this way to take up his position as the business manager on a rubber estate north of Chiquitos on the Baures river. Having travelled up the Paraguay to Corumbá, he was promised that there would be "a cart and animals, with men who knew the route, to meet me at Puerto Suárez".[3] The men failed to turn up, and Grey was stuck for some time in Puerto Suárez. He paints a typically lugubrious picture:

> When I was there the rainy season had not yet begun, and the water had shrunk until the "port" was practically dry, and a dreary expanse of mud stretched before me in smelly unloveliness. . . . The previous year there had been a particularly long dry season. The water in front of the town entirely disappeared – not even a stream trickling through where before a great sheet of water had been – and thousands of dead fish and jacarees were left lying on the mud. The stench became so bad, and the fear of an

epidemic so strong, that, eventually, the soldiers of the garrison were ordered out to collect as much as possible of this fetid refuse and burn it.

For much of the nineteenth century, Bolivians hoped that Lake Cáceres would prove to be a good access point to the Paraguay – and from there to the Atlantic. Yet anyone who had ever been there knew that it was a vain hope. The peculiar difficulty of navigating through the lake was explained by a French explorer, Paul Walle, who wrote a book about the journey he had made through Bolivia in 1911.

The Cáceres bay, he wrote, is joined to the Paraguay river by a narrow and tortuous channel. "Sometimes the water flows from the bay to the river, and sometimes from the river to the bay, according to the season." The bay, he went on:

> . . . is full of floating masses formed of algae and weeds, known as camalotes. In the bay, which is covered with these islands for nearly a third of its surface, these camalotes, mingled with shrubs, lianas, and all sort of vegetable growths torn from the banks, form floating islands which are often three or four hundred yards in diameter and more than twelve feet thick.[4]

Bolivia's trade route to the Atlantic was hardly going to pass through Lake Cáceres.

Recalling these gloomy accounts, we abandoned Puerto Suárez and returned with our driver to the railway station at Puerto Quijarro. There, after much familiar delay, we secured two Pullman tickets for the night train to Roboré.

Lake Gaiba: the expedition of Domingo de Irala to Puerto de los Reyes in 1542–43

North of Lake Cáceres and the town of Puerto Suárez lie three other great lakes. They too are umbilically attached to the Paraguay river, but none of them is on the Paraguay proper. They lie a mile or two to the west, joined by narrow channels often choked by weed. The modern Brazil–Bolivia frontier runs through the middle of them.

Lake Gaiba is the middle lake, Lake Mandiore lies to the south, and Lake Uberaba to the north. In January, when the Pantanal floods, Lake Gaiba and Lake Uberaba form a continuous sheet of water. This is the central point of the great Pantanal swamp, marked on all the early European maps of South America as a gigantic spider, or an ink blot. The European conquistadores in the 1540s knew it as the swamp of Xarayes.

Today these lakes are little-frequented and almost inaccessible except by river. And river traffic is a shadow of what it once was. Valerie Fifer, the geographer of contemporary Bolivia, wrote in 1972:

With isolated exceptions, few sites on the outlets to the upper Paraguay river have been visited at all during the last forty years save by the Boundary Commissioners, toiling between 1957 and 1962 to erect the pyramidal concrete pillars in the swamps along the southern section of the border with Brazil.[5]

Yet however neglected today, these three lakes have borne witness over four centuries to a dramatic pageant of South American history. Lake Gaiba, in particular, lying just upstream from the place where the Sao Lourenço (or Cuiabá) river flows into the Paraguay, has had more than its fair share of visitors.

Once, in the early sixteenth century, this was the centre of a populated and prosperous region. On its western shores, when Europeans first arrived in the 1530s, there was a large Indian settlement with nearly a thousand houses, and a population ten times that number.

Yet by 1900, when members of a Bolivian expedition came here, they recorded their feeling that they were entering unexplored territory. Whitfield Ray, an English member of the team, described the lake in glowing terms:

> Lake Gaiba is a stretch of water ten miles long, with a narrow opening into the River Paraguay. The lake is surrounded by mountains, clad in luxuriant verdure on the Bolivian side, and standing out in bare, rugged lines on the Brazilian side. . . .
>
> On the shores of the lake the beach is covered with golden sand and studded with innumerable little stones, clear as crystal, which scintillate with all the colours of the rainbow. Among these pebbles I found several arrowheads of jasper. In other parts the primaeval forest creeps down to the very margin, and the tree-roots bathe in the warm waters.[6]

But there were still signs of a previous civilization. Describing the river entrance to Lake Gaiba, Whitfield Ray writes of the old Indian drawings that have always fascinated travellers here and elsewhere along the rivers of Amazonia.

> On our port bow rose frowning rocks of forbidding aspect. Drawing nearer, we noticed, with mingled feelings of curiosity and wonder, that the face of these rocks was rudely carved by unmistakeable Indian art. There were portrayed a rising sun, tigers' feet, birds' feet, etc.

The purpose of this expedition was to create a settlement that would give the Bolivians access to the Paraguay. Whitfield Ray and the others set to work to make a clearing in the jungle.

> Paths were cut in different directions and the wonders of nature laid bare. The ring of the axe and the sound of falling trees marked the commencement of civilisation in those far-off regions.

Once the land was cleared, the expedition paused for a little ceremony.

> Planting a huge palm in the ground, we then solemnly unfurled the Bolivian flag. This had been made expressly for the expedition by the hands of Señora Quijarro, wife of the Bolivian minister residing in Buenos Aires. As the sun for the first time shone upon the brilliant colours of the flag, nature's stillness was broken by a good old English hurrah.

Bizarrely, this ceremony had been paralleled rather more than 350 years earlier, when the Spanish conquistador Alvar Núñez Cabeza de Vaca, governor of Paraguay, sailed up to the lake in 1543 to claim it for the Spanish crown. His secretary Pero Hernández, has left an account of the event:

> We found a great assemblage of natives with their wives and children waiting for us. The governor and all his people landed, and the natives came towards them. He said he had been sent by His Majesty to warn them to be Christians. . . . He then convoked the clergy and told them he wished a church built where mass could be said. . . . He ordered a large wooden cross to be created on the bank of the river, under some tall palms. . . .
>   He took formal possession of the country in the name of His Majesty, and in the presence of the notary, as newly discovered land, and, having conciliated the natives by bestowing presents on them, he ordered the Spaniards and Guaranís to take up the quarters on the shore of the lagoon, cautioning them to do the natives no injury or violence, because they were friendly and vassals of the King.[7]

Cabeza de Vaca was not the first Spaniard at this spot. The previous year, in October 1542, Domingo de Irala had left Asunción on a reconnoitring expedition up the Paraguay. He took with him three ships and ninety-three Spaniards. His task was to try to find a new way through to the west that avoided the dangers of the earlier route that Juan de Ayolas had taken, starting from Pôrto Esperança (Puerto de la Candelaria).

Lake Gaiba seemed to be a safe harbour, and because he arrived on 6 January 1543, the day of Epiphany, Irala called the settlement Puerto de los Reyes, the "port of kings". He was delighted with what he found. "Such an excellent place and so well provided for, we have not seen before. It is well policed, and each person lives in his own house. Among them are many Indians of those who were slaves of [Aleixo] García." These were Terenos and came from the west side of the Chaco.

With a small troop of men, Irala made a probing march to the west of Puerto de los Reyes. After three days' travel through the swamp, the European expedition encountered a group of Guaraní who informed them of a well-populated region some two weeks' travel further west. But this first venture into Chiquitos had to be abandoned. The rising waters of the Pantanal in the early months of the year forced Irala to return to Lake Gaiba, and from there to Asunción.

For the next two centuries, Lake Gaiba was to be one of the important entry points for expeditions heading west to Peru, though the route was never uncontested. Although the Indians initially received the Spaniards in friendship, they were later to clash with both the Spaniards and the Portuguese. Sometimes the road west was closed because the Indians made it impassable. Sometimes the Spanish governor ordered it to be closed, for safety's sake. And for at least half of every year, it was closed anyway. The floods that create the swamp of the Pantanal left the entire zone under water, as they still do today.

Lake Gaiba: the expedition of Alvar Núñez Cabeza de Vaca from Puerto de los Reyes in 1543

Alvar Núñez Cabeza de Vaca, who came to Lake Gaiba towards the end of 1543, had been appointed as the new Adelantado or supreme governor of South America by the king of Spain. He had been sent out to replace the unfortunate Pedro de Mendoza, now long dead. Cabeza de Vaca was a conquistador with immense experience. He had been involved with expeditions in the Caribbean and had once made a famous journey from Florida to Mexico. Captured by North American Indians, he had retained from that experience a lasting respect for the civilizations of the New World. In consequence, he never found favour with the white settlers.[8]

Typical of his path-breaking approach to South American affairs was his journey to Asunción, not by river like his predecessors, but by land. He plunged across from the Brazilian coast to the Iguaçú falls, and then carried on through eastern Paraguay to the Paraguay river. But on his arrival at Asunción in 1542, he was received with considerable hostility by the Spanish settlers. By that time, they had been on the banks of the river for five years without any outside interference. For much of that period, Domingo de Irala had been their effective leader. They had got used to him, and had no wish to see him replaced.

Cabeza de Vaca, like his predecessors, had been enjoined by the authorities in Madrid to find a way through to the treasures of Peru. He was anxious to get started. But first there was much trouble in Asunción. The city itself, five years old and made of straw, flared up one night like a torch. All available manpower had to be employed in rebuilding it. Little could be done to rescue the seven thousand bushels of maize that were also destroyed, food stocks for expeditions.

Then there was an Indian rebellion upstream, on the route to Peru. The Payaguas on the river had started to attack the Guaraní on the land.[9] The aim of the Payaguas was to break the tactical alliance that existed between the Guaraní and the Spaniards. If the Guaraní could be persuaded to attack the Spaniards, the Indians could regain control and send the interlopers back to Spain.

The Indians had devised this strategy too late. Cabeza de Vaca had arrived in Paraguay with European reinforcements. At an earlier stage, the two sides had been evenly matched. Now the Spaniards – though still numerically inferior – had the military edge. An expedition was sent upriver to quell the incipient Indian sedition.

By September 1543, however, preparations for a new journey of discovery and conquest were ready. The prospect of an expedition to Peru would help clear the air in Asunción. Cabeza de Vaca's party set off in 10 sailing luggers, with 400 Spaniards and 10 horses. They were accompanied by 1200 Guaraní auxiliaries in 120 dugout canoes.

The expedition sailed up the Paraguay river and stopped initially at Puerto de la Candelaria, a settlement thought to be too dangerous after Irala's exemplary execution of the Payaguas he believed to have been responsible for the death of Juan de Ayolas (see pages 80–83). On this occasion, Irala was told to keep below deck out of sight, lest his presence might inflame the Indians. Cabeza de Vaca did the talking.[10]

They sailed on, past Corumbá, arriving eventually at Lake Gaiba, at the settlement of Puerto de los Reyes. Here they were met by the now familiar group of Terenos who said that they came originally from the west, from the feet of the Andes mountains.[11]

Cabeza de Vaca asked them if they knew the best place to take a road through to the west. They told him blithely that the easiest route was further north through the land of some Indians called the Xarayes. "Through that land the entire country is populated until you get to the settlements where there is gold and silver. Going from Puerto de los Reyes, you do not come so quickly to the populated area."[12]

How many days' march would it be to the land of the Xarayes? asked Cabeza de Vaca. "They answered that the journey could not be made by land, because the road was very bad, owing to the numerous swamps and lakes, but that if he chose to go thither by water in canoes, it would take eight or ten days."

So Cabeza de Vaca sent a small expedition up to the Xarayes to investigate. Today there is no place called Xarayes, nor does any twentieth-century Indian nation answer to that name. But north of Lake Gaiba lies Lake Uberaba, and when the Pantanal floods, a huge area to the north of Lake Uberaba goes underwater, creating an immense lake. Late in the year, this is what the Spaniards would have found.

The small expedition sent to the Xarayes consisted of two Spaniards who spoke Guaraní, two Guaraní from Asunción, and ten local Indians from Lake Gaiba. They appear to have ignored the advice to go by water, and had a difficult journey through the swamps:

> They had taken water to drink on their journey in gourds, and had marched all that day
> through swamps, sinking at each step to the knees in mud, and withdrawing their feet
> with great difficulty. The mud was so heated by the sun that it scorched their legs, and
> produced painful wounds on them. That day they certainly would have died of thirst,
> for the water in the gourds only lasted half a day. They slept on the open ground,
> between swamps, overcome with fatigue, thirst, and hunger.[13]

Eventually they encountered a group of twenty Xarayes Indians "laden with maize, bread, cooked geese, fish, and maize wine. They told the Spaniards that their chief had learned of their coming and had ordered them to bring food."

They made their way to an immense town:

> When they were a bow-shot off, upwards of five hundred Xarayes came forth to receive them with great joy. All were elegantly attired with parrots' feathers and aprons of white beads to cover their nakedness. They placed the Spaniards in their midst, and led them into the village, at the entrance to which large numbers of women and children were waiting for them. The women all had their privities covered, and many of them wore wide cotton dresses, this material being in use among them under the name of tipoyes.

An almost exact echo of this early description of an Indian town in the area of the upper Paraguay can be found in the descriptions written by nineteenth-century travellers arriving at the old mission towns of Chiquitos.

The two Spaniards sent by Cabeza de Vaca were clearly impressed by what they saw. The Xarayes settlement had a population of one thousand people, and there were four other similar settlements nearby.

> These Xarayes are tall men, and well made; they are agriculturalists, sowing and reaping twice a year – maize, potatoes, manioc and mandubies. They rear large numbers of geese and fowls like ours in Spain. They pierce the lip like the Artaneses. Everyone lives separately with wife and children; they hoe the ground and sow; the women gather the produce and carry it to their houses; they spin much cotton.

The two Spaniards were taken before the cacique, who was seated on a cotton hammock in the middle of a large open space "surrounded by three hundred Indians of very good appearance, mostly elderly men".

The Spaniards told him clearly what they wanted. They said that they had been sent by their governor, Cabeza de Vaca, "to learn from him the route he should follow to reach the settlements in the interior, and to know by what tribes and villages he would have to pass, and in how many days he might arrive at the Indians that had gold and silver".

The cacique of the Xarayes, whose name was Camire, was friendly but understandably distant. He professed ignorance of what they wanted to know. "Concerning the road leading to the settlements of the interior, I do not know of one, never having been there, because all the country is under water for two months, and when the waters subside, the country is impassable."

He did, however, offer to provide the Spaniards with a Guaraní guide who "has been in the interior and knows the road", and he gave them twenty of his local Indians to help them back over the swamps to Lake Gaiba.

On their return to the lake, Cabeza de Vaca interrogated the Guaraní Indian guide about the journey that he had once made into the interior.

> He said it was long ago that his countrymen advanced into that country, and that as they went they opened a road by cutting down trees and clearing the ground, which was quite wild. He thought that the roads then made would long ere this have been choked with weeds, for he had never been that way since. Nevertheless, he thought that if he once found the road he might continue in it. He added that the road began at a high, round mountain in sight of Puerto de los Reyes.

With this information, Cabeza de Vaca decided that he knew enough to set off for the west. By now it was late in November 1543. He took with him the Guaraní guide, three hundred Spaniards, provisions for twenty days, and one thousand Guaraní Indians. It was quite an expedition. As with previous expeditions, a small group – a hundred Spaniards and two hundred Guaraní – was left behind at Lake Gaiba to secure the return journey.

The poet Robert Southey, in his *History of Brazil* (which he derived essentially from the "Commentaries of Núñez de Vaca"), gives a good version of the story. This is the first detailed account of a Spanish expedition into the Chiquitos area of eastern Bolivia.

> The first day's journey lay through pleasant woods, where there was a track, though but little trodden; they slept beside some springs. On the morrow it was necessary to clear their way before them, and the farther they advanced the thicker they found the woods: they were also greatly impeded by a close grass, which grew to an exceeding height.
>
> Their second night's lodging was beside a lake, wherein the fish were so abundant that they caught them by hand. The guide was ordered to climb trees and ascend eminences as they went on, that he might survey the road well; and he maintained that they were in the right way. Honey was found in the trees, and there was plenty of game, but the noise of their march scared it, so that they profited little by this resource.
> . . .
> On the fifth day of their march, they came to a little river of hot water [Aguas Calientes], issuing from a mountain. The water was clear and good, and there were fish in it notwithstanding the heat.[14]

By this time, the expedition was already lost. The Guaraní guide they had been lent by the cacique Camire confessed that he had mistaken the road: the old marks were gone; it was many years since he had made the journey; he no longer knew which way to turn.

> The following morning, however, as they still advanced, cutting their path, two Guaranies ventured to approach them. These people were some of those who had

escaped from the great overthrow which the guide had related, and retired into the wildest part of the woods and mountains to hide themselves. Their hut was near, and the whole of this wreck soon made their appearance, consisting of only fourteen persons, the eldest of whom appeared to be about five and thirty. They were children, they said, at the time of the great destruction of their nation. . . .

Two days journey on, there was another family consisting of ten persons, the head of whom, this man told them, was his brother-in-law, and he knew the way to the country for which the Spaniards enquired, for he had often been there.

When the brother-in-law turned up, he told them they only had a journey of sixteen days still to do "through thickets and close high grass" and they would then reach "a lofty rock called Tapuaguazu". From the top of that rock "much cultivated country could be seen".

At this stage, as was usually the case in most of these early expeditions, the Spanish soldiers rebelled. The simmering resentment against Cabeza de Vaca that had been brewing in Asunción had continued all the way up the Paraguay river to Lake Gaiba. Now, after a few days' march into the swamps of Chiquitos, it had come to a head. The soldiers told Cabeza de Vaca that they were not prepared to go any further. They pointed out that their expeditionary force clearly did not have sufficient provisions to make a further sixteen-day journey. There was no alternative, they said, except to return to Puerto de los Reyes at Lake Gaiba without delay.

Much against his will, Cabeza de Vaca was obliged to comply, though he argued vigorously in favour of going on.

He said that it would be impossible to find sufficient provisions at Los Reyes for so many people; that the maize was not yet ripe for harvest, and that none could be obtained from the natives. He reminded them that the natives had told them that the floods would soon begin, and these would add seriously to their embarrassments.[15]

His arguments were to no avail, and he was obliged to return with the bulk of the Spanish force to Lake Gaiba. He got back after a trek of eight days, "much dissatisfied at having gone no further". Possibly, however, the speedy return was a blessing in disguise, for at this stage everyone became extremely ill. The chronicler records that of the four hundred Spaniards who had set out from Asunción, only four remained in good health. The diseases of this flat and unhealthy country, to which the Europeans were unaccustomed and had little resistance, had taken an early revenge.

Cabeza de Vaca made one further effort to recover something from what otherwise had proved to be a pretty disastrous expedition. He decided to send an exploring expedition to the north, further up the Paraguay, to the Xarayes lake of which much had been reported from the initial reconnaissance. The command was given to Hernando de Ribera, who was sent off with fifty-two Spaniards and six hundred Indians.

Unlike the earlier scouting expedition that had gone by land, Hernando de Ribera's men went upriver in a brigantine. They arrived at the Xarayes lake, and were once again "well received" by the cacique Camire.

Here they left their ship, and moved inland for three days to a settlement of Urtueses. There they heard many wonderful stories of Amazon women and rich countries further to the west, stories that were to feed the imagination of many generations of travellers in this area, from the first conquistadores in the 1540s to Colonel Fawcett in the 1920s:

> All these Indians told me that at ten days' march from there, towards the west-north-west, there were women inhabiting large villages, who possessed a large quantity of white and yellow metal, and all their domestic utensils and vessels were of this metal, and their chief was a woman.

Cabeza de Vaca would have liked to wait until the floods on the Pantanal subsided and then make another attempt on the westward route. But his rebellious soldiers insisted on returning to Asunción. But they did not depart before leaving their mark on the local people.

When they had first arrived at Lake Gaiba, Ulrich Schmidl had gone upstream a day's journey and found a nation called the Surukusis who lived on an island "30 miles wide and encompassed by the Paraguay". Schmidl records how they were "received in a friendly way", and he notes that he thought them to be "a great people".[16]

Rather to his surprise, on returning to Lake Gaiba from the north, with Hernando de Ribera's expedition, he was told to go out and slaughter the Surukusis. "We Christians fired at them and killed very many, and having made more than 2000 prisoners, men, women, boys and girls, we afterwards burnt down their town, and took all they possessed that could be carried away, as in such violent assaults is usual."

"God knows," he writes, "that we did them wrong."

The conquistadores got back to Asunción on 8 March 1544, and on 10 March the simmering rebellion came to a head. Cabeza de Vaca was overthrown. It was the first coup d'état in Paraguay.

Lake Gaiba: the encounter between British settlers and the revolutionary army of Luís Carlos Prestes in 1927

Some four hundred years after Cabeza de Vaca's expedition, in July 1922, a 30 million acre piece of land inland from Lake Gaiba was made available to a British company, the Bolivian Oil and Land Syndicate (Bolivian Concessions Ltd), for the settlement of British colonists. Founded by an Anglo-Norwegian engineer, Christian Lilloe-Fangan, the company had Sir Martin Conway and Henry Mond on the board of directors.

This was "some of the most inaccessible and difficult territory on the whole continent", Sir Christopher Gibson noted when he came here in 1940.[17] Now it was in the hands of the British. "Its original smaller holdings", Gibson wrote, "were strung out along the old mule-trail leading from Corumbá to Santa Cruz, where the new railroad was under construction and which were, therefore, fairly easy to control; but the bulk of its land, lying on the west of Lakes Mandiore, Gaiba and Uberaba, was a waterless waste of impenetrable jungle."

The company bought a Krupps boat, built in Essen in 1917, which had been used during the German occupation of Romania to tow barges full of German soldiers up the Danube. Renamed *El Presidente Saavedra*, it sailed from Dunkirk in 1926 with a load of prospective British settlers. They had spent some time beforehand at a farm near Cambridge, learning to fend for themselves. The ship steamed safely to Buenos Aires and then set off up the Paraná and the Paraguay, arriving at Lake Gaiba at the end of January 1927.

There were some misgivings, according to the chronicler of their activities, Charles Vivian, "before the pioneers started work, that the natives might prove hostile".[18] It was felt that they might "resent the development of their country". But fortunately for the settlers, these fears "proved to be unfounded". They found that "the natives in the vicinity of the lake, and on the property of Bolivian Concessions Ltd generally, were invariably friendly". What a relief!

An earlier group of one hundred colonists had arrived the previous year, and the new arrivals brought the total to four hundred. Their first task, Vivian wrote, was "to clear the land by the lakeside to make room for the various warehouses, staff buildings, and houses, forming the nucleus of the new town, and then to cut a way through the forest belt to link up the river port with the parklands, where cultivation would begin when the first regular settlers arrived".

The word "parklands" sounds rather optimistic in the context of Lake Gaiba, and indeed the pioneers soon ran into trouble. "The task of cutting through the belt of forest proved more difficult than was at first anticipated. The official maps of the district were found to be inaccurate in many essential particulars."

The belt of forest, shown on the maps to extend west from the lake for a mere 15 miles, proved to be at least double the estimated size, "and in all that distance there was no water, every drop having to be carted from the lake".

Had they been able to read the accounts of the early European visits to Lake Gaiba in the sixteenth century – the accounts of Domingo de Irala, Alvar Núñez Cabeza de Vaca, and Nuflo de Chávez – they would have known a bit more about what they were likely to face.

The work of the British settlers was made easier, however, by the surprise arrival of six hundred latter-day conquistadores, revolutionary soldiers from Brazil. These were the remnants of the famous Prestes column that had been roaming the backlands of Brazil for the previous two years.

Luís Carlos Prestes was an army officer who led a revolt against the Brazilian regime in 1925. Later he was to be the leader of the Brazilian Communist Party for many decades. He lived long enough to support the campaign of Lula, the Workers' Party candidate in the presidential elections of 1989, and he died early in 1990. In 1925, his "column" of rebels eluded capture for many months, marching through the country for some 25,000 kilometres. Eventually they were obliged to take refuge in Bolivia, just as Spanish royalist troops had found refuge in Brazil a century earlier.

One of the historians of the column, Neil Macaulay, describes how "the rebels lost almost all their horses in the Pantanal and at times marched in water up to their chests. Revolutionary soldiers spent some nights perched on top of huge anthills, the only dry ground available, where they were relentlessly tormented by thick clouds of mosquitoes".[19]

At the beginning of February 1927, what was left of the Prestes column, 620 soldiers, crossed into Bolivia at the frontier post of San Matías, some way to the north of Lake Gaiba. There they handed over their weapons to the Bolivian army – 90 Mausers, 4 machine-guns, and 8000 rounds of ammunition – and made their way through to Lake Gaiba to find work. They were employed in preparing the ground for a railway that was to run from Gaiba to the old Jesuit mission town at Santo Corazón, some sixty miles away. The former rebels built their own huts and secured their own food, and were paid two shillings and sixpence per head per day.

These ex-soldiers, according to Vivian, were a comic sight.

> They had undergone terrible hardships, and were in a very forlorn condition, their once smart uniforms tattered and torn, their hair unkempt, and most of them barefooted. For all that, however, they were still very much of the military caste; their own NCOs acted as foremen, and they never failed to salute their officers. . . . Many of their officers were cultured men and delightful companions, and their advent was very welcome.

Julian Duguid, arriving here the following year, wrote of the romance of a revolutionary army staggering into Gaiba "starving and ragged" after months of hardship in the forests of Brazil.[20] He felt that Prestes's men had done most of the work around the camp of the British pioneers, clearing a great semi-circle a mile in diameter. By the time Duguid got there, there were "houses and beds and a wireless station".

But the pioneering experiment, like so much missionary endeavour in these parts, was to end in tears. "The unfortunate families were decanted amid that howling abomination of desolation," Christopher Gibson wrote, "with absolutely nothing made ready for their reception. All felt sick, many died, the survivors dispersed." It was, as far as he knew, "the only blot on the shining escutcheon of British enterprise in the River Plate territories".

The British colonists complained bitterly that the company had misled them. The terrain was inhospitable, and their crops refused to grow. Rapidly, the situation deteriorated. One of the colonists, Mrs Constance Cline, sent a letter listing her complaints to the Prince of Wales. In the letter, dated July 1928, she gave "a harrowing tale of life at Gaiba, where no decent habitations and no marketable crops had been produced at all since her arrival there in March 1926".[21]

These mutinies by settlers had been going on since the sixteenth century. Usually they wanted to be bailed out and to return to civilization. Mrs Cline was no exception. Perhaps after the intervention of the Prince of Wales, or perhaps because it did not wish to see the British escutcheon dulled any further, the British Foreign Office agreed to provide financial assistance to help the colonists get home. This happened in October 1928, and the company went into liquidation in 1931.

Some years later, in 1940, Sir Christopher Gibson was employed to discover whether anything could be done about the Gaiba concession. He flew up from Corumbá and circled over the lake, but was too depressed by what he saw to make any positive proposals.

A trail shown on the map as leading westwards . . . had long since disappeared: not a vestige of it, nor of any habitation, remained. Beneath the shadow of a huge mountain rising sheer out of the eastern side of Gaiba, the river connecting the lake with the Paraguay, as in the case of Mandiore, was wholly choked up. And to the north, the dry bed of the Rio San Pedro linking Gaiba with Lake Uberaba had become an animal trail. No wisp of smoke, no sign of any living thing broke that incredible, grey solitude.[22]

Gibson's small plane then flew west from Lake Gaiba towards Santo Corazón, the route taken by Spanish conquistadores, Portuguese slave-traders and Jesuit missionaries for more than two centuries from the 1540s to the 1760s. Few people had seen it and described it from the air.

I cannot hope to give a convincing description of that frightful wilderness. There are not many places I never want to see again; but that is one of them. Hitherto we had at least had water and mountain to distract our attention, but now a parched, grey jungle stretched beneath us in every direction, absolutely unbroken by creek or stream or one single acre of open land. It undulated into low hillocks and ridges, covered with tightly-packed vegetation; the whole enveloped in that thin grey pall.

What had been Indian territory when the Europeans first arrived had returned to swampy desert. Conquistadores, missionaries and white settlers had all failed to make a permanent mark. Yet in the process of their attempted settlement, they had crushed the civilization of those who had once been able to make the swamp their home.

Notes

1. G. Whitfield Ray, *Through Five Republics on Horseback*, Cleveland 1925, p. 135. Ray noted that "when the women go down to the bay for water, with their pitchers poised on their heads, the sight is very picturesque". This sight is no longer to be seen, although when Julian Duguid came through Lake Gaiba in 1928, his cameraman, J.C. Bee-Mason, took some film of a similar magnificent procession, which I have seen in his film *Across Bolivia*.
2. Leo Miller, *In the Wilds of South America*, London 1919.
3. Henry M. Grey, *The Land of Tomorrow: a mule-back trek through the swamps and forests of eastern Bolivia*, London 1927, p. 11.
4. Paul Walle, *Bolivia, its People and Resources*, London 1914. Walle was a Frenchman commissioned by the ministry of commerce in Paris to wander round South America looking for trading opportunities.
5. Valerie Fifer, *Bolivia: land location and politics since 1825*, Cambridge 1972, pp. 234–5.
6. Whitfield Ray, pp. 118–34. The leader of the expedition was Captain Henry Bolland, an English naval officer born in Yorkshire in 1857. The German anthropologist Max Schmidt came to Lake Gaiba the same year, in November 1900. An illustration of the Indian drawings on the rocks at the entrance to the lake appears in his *Indianerstudien in Zentralbrasilien*, Berlin 1905.
7. The chief sources for these early expeditions up the Paraguay are contained in Manuel Serrano y Sanz (ed.), *La relación de los naufragios y comentarios de Alvar Núñez Cabeza de Vaca*, published in two volumes in Madrid in 1906. Volume 1 contains Cabeza de Vaca's Florida expedition and his Paraguay travails (as dictated to Pero Hernández); and volume 2 contains Cabeza de Vaca's own story, as well as Irala's letter of 1545 and Hernández's story of 1545, pp. 571–78. More about Irala's expedition can be found in "Relación de Domingo Martínez de Irala acerca de los descubrimientos que iba haciendo cuando fue navegando Paraguay arriba por orden del Gobernador Cabeza de Vaca desde el 18 de diciembre de 1542", in *Anales de la Biblioteca Nacional*, Buenos Aires 1912, vol. 8, pp. 346–7.
8. There is a large literature on Alvar Núñez Cabeza de Vaca, particularly on his North American exploits. An unsatisfactory Mexican film of his capture by Indians was made in 1990, directed by Nicolas Echevarria. North Americans are less familiar with his activities in Paraguay. Argentine and Paraguayan historians correspondingly ignore his Florida experience. In the political struggle that ensued between Cabeza de Vaca and Domingo de Irala, they tend to take the side of Irala, the victor, who is perceived to be an early embodiment of the spirit of South American nationalism against the centralism of Spain. Cabeza de Vaca left very full accounts of his expeditions. A useful biography is Morris Bishop, *The Odyssey of Cabeza de Vaca*, Century Co., New York 1933. The term *Adelantado*, "someone sent out in the vanguard", was originally used in Spain to refer to the governor, with plenipotentiary powers, of an area recaptured from the Moors. By extension, it came to mean the governor of a large colonial territory.
9. Or possibly it was the Guaycurus who attacked the Guaraní; the sources are divided. The Payaguas and the Guaycurus often operated in alliance.
10. Manuel Serrano y Sanz (ed.), *Cabeza de Vaca, relación de los naufragios y comentarios*, vol. 2, Madrid 1906, p. 46.
11. The Tereno (Chane) repeated what they had said to Ayolas in 1537: (see pages 77–80): they had met Aleixo García twenty years earlier and had travelled back with him across the northern Chaco. They had arrived at the Paraguay river further to the south, and it was there, they said, that García had been murdered by the local people.
12. Serrano y Sanz, vol. 2, p. 46.
13. Luis Domínguez (ed.), in *The Conquest of the River Plate*, "The commentaries of Cabeza de Vaca", Hakluyt Society, London 1891, p. 208.
14. Robert Southey, *History of Brazil*, London 1819, vol. 1, p. 149.

15. Domínguez, p. 221.
16. ''The voyage of Ulrich Schmidt to the rivers La Plata and Paraguai'', in Domínguez, p. 51.
17. Sir Christopher Gibson, *Enchanted Trails*, Museum Press, London 1948, p. 231.
18. Charles Vivian, ''Pioneering in wildest Bolivia'', *Wide World Magazine*, vol. 61, 1928.
19. Neil Macaulay, *The Prestes Column: revolution in Brazil*, New York 1974, pp. 234–5.
20. Julian Duguid, *Green Hell: a chronicle of travel in the forests of eastern Bolivia*, Jonathan Cape, London 1931, p. 105.
21. Fifer, p. 204.
22. Gibson, pp. 228–40.

PART III
The Missions of Chiquitos

The eastern department of Bolivia . . . is only partly explored. It consists of a great plain extending eastward from the base of the Andes to the frontiers of Brazil, broken by occasional isolated hills, and in the north-east by a detached group of low sierras known collectively under the name Chiquitos, which belong to the Brazilian highlands rather than to the Andes . . .

The Chiquitos contain a number of old missions, now occupied almost exclusively by Indians. The great plains, whose general elevation is about 900 feet above the sea, are so level that the drainage does not carry off the water in the rainy season, and immense areas are flooded for months at a time. Extensive areas are permanently swampy. There are forests in the north and west, but the larger part of the department consists of open grassy plains, suitable for grazing . . .

There are two river systems, one belonging to the Amazon and the other to the La Plata basins. The first includes the Guapay (or Rio Grande), Piray (or Sara), Yapacaní and Maraco, upper tributaries of the Mamoré, and the San Miguel, Blanco, Baures and Paraguá, tributaries of the Guaporé — both draining the western and northern parts of the department. In the extreme east a number of streams flow eastward into the Paraguay, the largest of which is the Otuquis; their channels are partly hidden in swamps and lagoons. The climate of the plains is hot and malarial, and the rainfall heavy . . .

There is a trade route across the plains from Santa Cruz de la Sierra to Puerto Suárez, on the Paraguay, and the Bolivian government contracted in 1908 for a railway between these two points (about 497 miles) but the traffic is inconsiderable.

Encyclopaedia Britannica,
eleventh edition, 1911

11

SANTO CORAZÓN

By train from Puerto Quijarro to Roboré

After we have been waiting for several hours on the platform of the shabby station of Puerto Quijarro, a small diesel train finally materializes in the evening heat. There is a great scrimmage to get on. What appears to be a crowd of two hundred people struggles to force its way into a single narrow opening to two carriages that might just hold fifty apiece. But miraculously, our tickets prove to be numbered. We have privileged, guaranteed seats. The hubbub subsides and the train sets off in good order at four minutes to six, exactly four minutes early.

A railway line across Chiquitos, from the Paraguay river to the eastern Bolivian town of Santa Cruz de la Sierra, has been a Bolivian national aspiration for more than a hundred years. One nineteenth-century president, Aniceto Arce, an enthusiastic railway promoter, authorized an English company to build a line in 1890. The company, Messrs Perry, Cutbill, de Lungo y Cia., were to build a port on the Paraguay and to develop colonization schemes along the frontier with Brazil. Nothing came of it. Then in 1901, a Belgian company, L'Africaine, was given a similar concession. Again, nothing happened. In 1905, the Bolivians themselves financed a study, and were ready in 1908 to sign contracts. But no money was forthcoming to embark on building the real thing.

When the Trans-Brasil line was finished in 1914, from São Paulo to Pôrto Esperança, there was an incentive to continue the line across Bolivia to the Pacific. But it was not until the late 1930s, after the end of the Chaco War between Bolivia and Paraguay, that work began. A joint Brazilian–Bolivian survey team flew along the proposed route in September 1938.

Nearly twenty years later, the line was ready, a single track crossing what had once been almost impenetrable swamps. A straight line from Corumbá to Santa Cruz is 598 kilometres. The railway makes a slight curve and the journey covers 680 kilometres.[1]

We soon find it too dark to see much of the scenery, though a great searchlight from the engine lights up much of the track ahead, carving a path through the forest. Few of the carriage windows fit properly and when the sun is gone, it is bitterly cold.

From a tiny cabin, a cook produces huge meals, chicken and potatoes piled so high on the plate that they threaten to fall off with each successive lurch of the train.

The first excitement comes when we stop at the town of Carmen. Here a bevy of enchanting Indian girls of great beauty and charm greets us on the platform, selling grapefruit and lemons and limes, and bread and cakes. "Toronja", they shout, thrusting forward great bunches of grapefruits as though they were Saint Agatha. After the grumpy mestizos on the train, they look ethereal.

We hurry through, recalling that near Carmen are the ruins of the old eighteenth-century mission town of Santo Corazón, the most easterly of the Chiquitos missions set up by the Jesuits in the eighteenth century. (Later the town was moved further to the north.) The ruins formed the basis for the settlement of Oliden, built by Manuel Oliden, a wealthy trader in the early nineteenth century who hoped to do business on the Paraguay river (see page 137 ff).

Subsequently we stop briefly at Candelaria and at Aguas Calientes, where Alvar Núñez Cabeza de Vaca and his disastrous expedition from Lake Gaiba had stopped more than four hundred years ago (see page 115). Nearby too is Florida, the site of another of the settlements established by Manuel Oliden. So much historical activity, so little to show for it today.

Late in the evening, the train pulls into the small military town of Roboré. Here we are to stop to explore. Forcing our way out of the by now sleeping carriage, we find ourselves on a dark and sandy track. We are almost alone, for most of the passengers from Puerto Quijarro are going on to San José and Santa Cruz.

The driver of a small lorry emerges from the dark night and rather surprisingly says "Taxi?" Gratefully we load our gear onto the back and clamber into his cab. He takes us on a long journey into town, leaving us at the Hotel Bolivia, a dark and apparently deserted two-storey building. Everyone inside is asleep. Heavy knocking eventually produces a sleepy woman with a torch. She guides us upstairs to a large room with three beds. It is pleasant enough, and warm.

The establishment of Jesuit missions in Chiquitos in the 1690s

We are now travelling into the historic Jesuit mission territory of Chiquitos. The remnants of ten mission towns are still be be found among the swamps and savannahs that stretch from the upper Paraguay to the Rio Grande, roughly between Corumbá in Brazil and the Bolivian town of Santa Cruz de la Sierra.

After their setbacks in Guaíra and Itatín in the early part of the seventeenth century, in the 1640s the Jesuits had made tentative efforts to move into the territory west of the Paraguay. But these too had ended in disaster, with the murder of Father Romero at the embryonic settlement of Santa Bárbara, and the temporary close-down of all Jesuit operations in Paraguay after a major political dispute in Asunción between priests and settlers.[2]

When expansion into Chiquitos did eventually come, at the end of the seventeenth century, it came not from the Paraguay side in the east, but from Santa Cruz in the west. It seems to have happened almost by accident.

A Spanish settlement called Santa Cruz had been established in the middle of the sixteenth century, with soldiers from both Paraguay and Peru. This was not the city of Santa Cruz that exists today, but a place that is now a ruin, close to San José de Chiquitos, almost exactly halfway between the Paraguay and the Rio Grande. Established in the 1560s, it moved to its present site in the 1590s.

The settlement had been born in conflict between two groups of conquistadores, from either side of the continent, and the white settlers of Santa Cruz (or Cruceños as they came to be called) were still, a century later, a small and embattled group. Surrounded by hostile Indians, they were also threatened by marauding bands of Portuguese.

Jesuits had been established in Santa Cruz since the end of the sixteenth century. They worked as priests and teachers. Occasionally they accompanied military expeditions into Indian territory. But they were not involved at that stage in missionary endeavours among the native population.

In the wake of the military "pacification" of numerous Indian settlements to the east of the town in the 1680s, the Santa Cruz governor, Agustín de Arce de la Concha, decided that the missionary solution, employed so successfully earlier in the century east of the Paraguay and the Paraná, could now be suitably proposed for the Chiquitos territory.

Chiquitos was under threat both from the Indians and from the Portuguese. If strategic hamlets filled with friendly Indians could be established along both the Portuguese border and the Chaco border (home to so many nations that had become eternally hostile to the Spanish occupation, notably the Guaycurus and the Chiriguanos), the security of Santa Cruz could be obtained rather more cheaply than through the expensive deployment of military force. The settlers had to finance soldiers themselves. The king in Madrid paid for Jesuits.

So Governor Arce de la Concha requested the local Jesuits to begin setting up new mission towns to combat the Indian and Portuguese threat. A large Jesuit college had already been set up to the south, at Tarija, in 1690, and there were ambitious plans to advance into the area occupied by the Chiriguanos in the western Chaco. A move into Chiquitos, where the Indians were known to be more tractable, would be most welcome.

Later reports, influenced by the settlers in Santa Cruz, give a poor account of the Chiquitos Indians. In the 1760s, at the end of the Jesuit period, the Lima chronicler Cosme Bueno wrote some unfavourable lines:

It took considerable work and much effort to reduce these people, not only to the faith, but to reason. They are extremely stupid and ferocious; indeed they are only men in their shape. Even today, they are only motivated by self-interest and material ambition.[3]

The man selected for the task of establishing mission towns, Father José de Arce, was a man of unusual energy and bravado, one of the toughest diplomats and explorers the Society of Jesus ever fielded in South America.

The Santa Cruz governor was an unusual figure too. In his history of Brazil, Robert Southey describes Arce de la Concha approvingly as a man who, "both from principle and policy, understood the importance of converting the natives". He had lived long enough in the country "to become acquainted with the character of the different tribes".[4]

The governor may also have been impressed by the famous capacity of the Jesuits to tackle the local Indian languages of eastern Bolivia, so much more difficult than those of Paraguay. According to a dissident Jesuit of the eighteenth century, Bernardo Ibáñez de Echavarri, "the language of the Guaraní is so widespread that a large part of America uses it; that of Chiquitos is so special and difficult that no one in the kingdom knows it except the Indians and their priests".[5]

Another chronicler wrote that "even after eight or ten years, some missionaries find it difficult to preach in the Chiquitos language". An additional problem was caused by the fact that the language is different for men and for women. An unwary priest referring to the Virgin in the language of the men would cause everyone in the church to titter.[6] Although the missionaries tried to simplify matters by making Chiquitano the lingua franca of Chiquitos, there were in fact more than fifty Indian nations in Chiquitos, each speaking a different language.[7]

Whatever the reason, Arce de la Concha's decision to seek Jesuit assistance in the further pacification of Chiquitos was somewhat out of the ordinary. Spanish Santa Cruz, like Portuguese São Paulo, was (though on a much smaller scale), a centre of the local slave trade. At the end of the sixteenth century, the settlers had secured the right, from the viceroy in Lima, to send out an armed band twice a year to collect Indian slaves. These were then employed on the settler lands around Santa Cruz.

As the years went by, this concession became a nice little earner. Extra money was made by sending the Indian slaves upcountry, to be sold to work in the mines and plantations of Peru. "From this traffic of the Indians," Martín Dobrizhoffer reports, "many thousands of crowns were yearly collected."[8]

The Jesuits in Santa Cruz had campaigned against this practice, though not always with much success. So they must have been surprised when the governor offered them the job of "reducing" the Indians of Chiquitos. For if the Jesuits were to control Chiquitos by establishing mission towns, this would put a stop to (or at least hinder) the slaving expeditions to which the white settler Cruceños had grown so accustomed.

In this light, it does not appear surprising to learn that the governor was soon dismissed. Hardly had the offer to the Jesuits been made, Southey writes, before he was replaced by "a man of different temper, who gave ear to a company of slave traders". Under the new regime, the Jesuits were to be discouraged.

Father José de Arce, however, was not a man to be trifled with. He had been given a job, and he intended to carry it out. "By his perseverance," Southey notes, "he overcame the opposition of the dealers in human flesh, and the cold unwillingness of the governor." Father Arce had made his plans for Chiquitos, and he stuck to them.

The first Chiquitos mission to be established, in 1692, was called San Javier. Today it is the most westerly and the closest to Santa Cruz of the mission towns. San Rafael was the next, in 1696. Further to the east, it was placed with a view to opening a route through to the Paraguay. Then came San José, built in 1698 on the ruins of the original Santa Cruz of the conquistadores established 150 years earlier. Then San Juan Bautista was set up, in 1699.

Four missions had been founded by the end of the century, and a further six were to be created in the eighteenth century: Santo Corazón, Santiago, Santa Ana, San Ignacio, San Miguel, Concepción.

For seventy years, until the Jesuits were expelled from South America in 1767, these ten mission towns became an extraordinary centre of missionary endeavour. Forests were cut down, houses built, and great churches constructed. Taught in their own languages, organized by their own caciques, the local Indians became the raw material of an astonishing social experiment that still, three hundred years later, has an enduring power to amaze anyone who comes in contact with its history.

This was no namby-pamby, turn-the-other-cheek Christianity. This was the church militant. Supported by friendly Indians, the Jesuit fathers marched out into the jungle with drums and portable altars – and arrows and guns – and seized the Indians just as the Santa Cruz slave-traders had done. They brought their captives back into their mission compounds and, in twentieth-century language, brainwashed them. With creature comforts, regular food and music, work and play, and strict ideological control, they forced the Indians to enjoy their new freedoms. The experiment was performed on a huge scale. The population of the Chiquitos missions in 1731 was 15,000. By the time the Jesuits were thrown out, just thirty-six years later, it had expanded to nearly 24,000.

The mission town of Santo Corazón, the resistance of the Guaycurus in the 1760s, and the Jesuits' search for a route to the Paraguay

During our night ride in the train from Puerto Quijarro to Roboré, we had passed close to the ruins of the old Jesuit mission of Santo Corazón. The ruins mark its earliest position, at the junction of the Tucabaca and San Rafael rivers.

The mission here was established very late, in 1760, and there was hardly time to consolidate it before the Jesuits were expelled. It was founded for a specific military purpose – to guard the Spanish frontier on the Paraguay river against the Guaycurus, and to ward off renewed threats from the Portuguese. The most easterly of the ten missions in Chiquitos, Santo Corazón was the one nearest to the Paraguay – only 20 leagues from Lake Gaiba. The Tucabaca and the San Rafael rivers, on whose banks it was set up, together become the Otuquis, the non-navigable river-cum-swamp that eventually runs into the Paraguay between Coimbra and Bahía Negra.

Arguably this is the most conflictive frontier in South America. Long after the threat caused by the Guaycurus and the Portuguese had disappeared into history, the area became a bone of contention between Bolivia and Paraguay. A Paraguayan attack on a Bolivian fort just south of here, in 1928, led to the Chaco War between the two countries in the 1930s.

In 1760, two Spanish Jesuits with long experience in the affairs of Chiquitos, Father Antonio Guaspe and Father José Chueca, were given the initial task of creating the mission town of Santo Corazón. Within its perimeter stockade, they brought together hundreds of Indians from four distinct nations. Initially their town had a population of 532 families, 2287 people in all.

Set up to guard the frontier, Santo Corazón was under continual threat from the Guaycurus, the proud nation that had refused to submit to Spanish rule. These Indians are notorious, it was noted in one of the Jesuit annual reports, "for their ferocity and great numbers. Everyone fears them and they fear none".[9]

Three years after the mission's foundation, the Jesuit Visitor to Chiquitos, Father Francisco Lizardi, gave permission for a military expedition to be mounted against the Guaycurus from Santo Corazón. The expedition, which set out in 1763, was formed from the combined troops of three missions: "a force of a thousand picked Christian men . . . strong and well-armed".

It had a twin purpose: "We hope to win over to God a very savage people," Lizardi wrote, "and at the same time to make safe the approach to Chiquitos from the Guaraní towns" of Paraguay. The old need to connect Asunción (in Paraguay) with Santa Cruz (in Bolivia) – which had been on the Spanish colonial agenda since the sixteenth century – was now being revived. To make the task easier, another Jesuit mission was set up at the same time east of the Paraguay, at Belén. This mission, established by Father José Sánchez Labrador, was in the heart of Guaycuru territory on the east bank of the Paraguay.

Accompanied by Fathers Guaspe and Chueca, the large expeditionary force of Chiquitos Indians that set out from Santo Corazón to hunt the Guaycurus was told "not to give battle, but to tame the barbarians and bring them to a better way of living". They arrived on the banks of Lake Yacadigo, not far from Corumbá, and confronted a group of some seventy Guaycurus, accompanied by a Christian Indian woman who spoke Portuguese. Perceiving that they were outnumbered, thirty Guaycurus agreed to return with the expedition to the Santo Corazón mission.

These Indians stayed in the mission for a month, subjected to the traditional wiles of the missionaries: a continuous supply of food and an unending series of church services and celebrations. They appeared to be so beguiled, and made such good progress in accepting the ways of mission life, that Father Guaspe was encouraged to believe that the conversion of other members of their nation would be relatively easy. He agreed to travel with them to their villages to find potential converts.[10]

He set out again in August 1763, unarmed, with some Guaycuru guides and half a dozen Chiquitos Indians. He was too trusting. His Father Superior wrote subsequently that he should never have dreamt of moving into this conflictive area without a troop of four hundred. Arriving at one of the mission's estancias, at La Cruz, close to Lake Yacadigo, he fell into a Guaycuru ambush organized by the cacique Oyomadigo. He was seized by two of Oyomadigo's Guana slaves. Then, according to Martín Dobrizhoffer's account, he "was taken by one Guana, knocked down by another with a blow on the forehead from a club, and slain by Oyomadigo".[11]

The following year, in December 1764, a Guaycuru army of some five hundred men assembled outside the mission, supported by Guanas, Payaguas and Tobas. They appear to have come with hostile intent, but the remaining Jesuit father, Antonio Chueca, went out to meet them with a smaller army of one hundred armed Chiquitos. Offering them the delights of the mission, he brought them into the settlement and spread them round the mission families for lunch. Then, in a sudden and dramatic move, he detained them all, including the cacique Oyomadigo. Subsequently, the prisoners were dispersed among the other Chiquitos missions.

Three years after these events, the Jesuits were expelled from Chiquitos. Their mission towns were handed over to secular administrators and to corrupt and untrained local priests. Under continuing threat from the Guaycurus, the mission at Santo Corazón was moved to the north in the 1780s, to its present site. The bulk of its Indian inhabitants – far from any central control – soon abandoned it. They went to live in the hills east of the town towards Lake Gaiba. During the last thirty years of Spanish rule, Santo Corazón was a remote military garrison. It no longer posed a threat to Guaycuru dominance of the upper Paraguay.

Half a century later, after the long period of civil war that characterized the wars of independence in eastern Bolivia, the administrator put in by the new republican regime was able to entice some of the Indians back. That was in 1829. Situated close to the Portuguese frontier, and far from the centres of Bolivian power, Santo Corazón was used for a while as a penal colony. But the Guaycurus continued to control much of the surrounding territory, both to the east and to the south.

In September 1831, the French explorer Alcides d'Orbigny arrived at Santo Corazón. He had travelled through all the mission towns of Chiquitos on an extraordinary journey that had taken many months. D'Orbigny was to spend several years in Bolivia and has left an immense and irreplaceable record of its state of development in the early years of independence.[12] He had left Santa Cruz in June, accompanied by the Bolivian governor of Chiquitos, Marcelino de la Peña.

Although ostensibly on a scientific expedition, d'Orbigny was charged by the Bolivian government to make recommendations about the future economic development of the area. He had nine people on his staff. One was Mauricio Bach, a recently arrived German. There was also a Belgian assistant and two young Bolivians provided by the government. He had two servants, one of whom was an interpreter who spoke Aymara and Quechua. Useful as this might have been in the Andes, it was of little use in Chiquitos where the languages are completely different. The other servant was a former inhabitant of the province of Mojos, an area with a different collection of languages again. In addition, there were two muleteers to look after the seven mules that carried the expedition's baggage.

No governor had ever visited Santo Corazón since the expulsion of the Jesuits, and the town turned out in force to welcome this strange party. D'Orbigny seems to have cut a more impressive figure than Marcelino de la Peña and, to the amusement of both of them, received the homage of the caciques.

He found the inhabitants to be "more corrupt" than those of the other mission towns he had visited. This turned out to mean that he had noted the rather forward behaviour of the Indian girls "who exchange their role for that of the boys and are everywhere to be seen making love publicly". He also noted that, in distinction to the other Chiquitos missions, the Indian women of Santo Corazón preferred Indians to whites.[13]

In a town where only eight hundred people now lived, d'Orbigny found that the homogenizing influences of the Jesuits had had little lasting effect. The population was still divided into the four distinct Indian nations with which it had been set up, though they were beginning to lose their different languages.[14] As with the other towns of Chiquitos, d'Orbigny concluded that the situation of the local inhabitants had deteriorated notably since the 1760s.

D'Orbigny's visit to Santo Corazón had a similar purpose to that of the Jesuits a century earlier, and of the Spanish conquistadores in the sixteenth century. It was to find a way through the swamps between Chiquitos and the Paraguay river. He had been specifically instructed by the Bolivian president, Andrés Santa Cruz, to examine the possibility of establishing a commercial route through to the Paraguay. When he first arrived at the mission town, he asked for a group of Indians from the area to be brought together to discuss the feasibility of finding such a route.

While they were being assembled, he went off on his own, on an expedition to the east, climbing the Taruoch range of hills. From the top, he was able to see the vast extent of boggy swamp that stretches all the way to Lake Gaiba and the Paraguay:

> The thought that I had arrived 600 leagues from the shores of the great [Pacific] Ocean to find myself in the centre of the continent at almost the same distance from the Atlantic gave me a sense of pleasure I was quite unable to express.

Returning to Santo Corazón, d'Orbigny found that the message from the assembled

Indians was not very hopeful. Perhaps, as their forefathers had done with the conquistadores and the Jesuits, they wished to preserve the only important secret they had: the route through the swamps.

There was no all-the-year-round route to the Paraguay, they told him. You could only get through the marshes with great difficulty, if the summer was extremely dry.

Undaunted, d'Orbigny sought further information. He persuaded Marcelino de la Peña to send a group of Indians to open up a route to the south, to the old site the Jesuits had chosen for the Santo Corazón mission on the Tucabaca river. Perhaps from there, a simpler way might be found through to the Paraguay.

Ten days later, his vision was seemingly rewarded. Returning from the south, the Indians brought news of a large stream with high banks: the Otuquis. According to their report, it looked as though this stream went through to the Paraguay and might well be navigable all the year round.

Excited by the news, d'Orbigny was eager to see the river for himself. But the governor had run out of time. They had been travelling for several months through eastern Bolivia, and it was now necessary for the expedition to retrace its tracks to the west. In October 1831, not without regret, d'Orbigny and his party left Santo Corazón and began their long march back to Santa Cruz and La Paz.

Before they left, d'Orbigny drew a detailed map of the area. Armed with this, he was able to make specific proposals to President Santa Cruz when he got back to La Paz. The route through to the Paraguay, he argued powerfully, should be developed.

Had he been able to stay longer, d'Orbigny might have been able to verify a fact with which the Jesuits were familiar in the eighteenth century, that the Otuquis was a most unreliable waterway. It was by no means as clean and tidy as he had hoped or had been led to believe. Seasonally dry and often clogged with weed when wet, the Otuquis was a false hope, but one that others continued to believe in . If d'Orbigny had been permitted another two weeks' exploration, the subsequent history of this part of the world might well have taken a different course.

The Bolivian government acted on his advice that a route through to the Paraguay should be considered a practical possibility. The Congress in La Paz made a grant of a huge expanse of eastern Chiquitos, bordering the Paraguay, to a wealthy merchant, Manuel Luis de Oliden. He was authorized to develop it on their behalf.

Manuel Oliden, the Otuquis Concession, and the attempt in the 1830s to find a way from Chiquitos to the Paraguay

Manuel Oliden was a rich trader from the Bolivian altiplano. Born in Buenos Aires towards the end of the eighteenth century, he had made his money in commerce during the last years of Spanish rule, in the towns of Potosí and La Paz. In Potosí, he had married Eustasia Amatller, whose nephew, Tomás Frias, was to be a future President of Bolivia. Oliden was well-connected.

Involved in 1809, as any rich trader would have been, with the first stirrings of Bolivian independence, Oliden had shown his hand too early. When the first anti-Spanish rebellions failed, he was forced to flee from Potosí to Buenos Aires. All his Bolivian property was confiscated by the Spaniards, who remained in control of what was to become Bolivia for another fifteen years. But in embryonic Argentina, now freed from Spain, Oliden prospered. He fought in the anti-Spanish campaigns of General Belgrano in Upper Peru, ending up with the rank of colonel. In 1815, he became the governor of Buenos Aires province.

Bolivia did not become independent from Spain until 1825, and Manuel Oliden did not return to Potosí until 1831. He had hoped to regain his confiscated property. Simón Bolívar, the liberator, had decreed that the goods and estates of premature independence supporters, taken from them by the Spanish, should be restored to their rightful owners. Manuel Oliden planned to take advantage of this offer.

But he had returned too late. The money for compensation (this is a typical Bolivian tale) had already run out. It was in these circumstances that the influential and well-connected Oliden persuaded the Bolivian Congress to give him land – subsequently known as the Otuquis Concession – along the Paraguay river. To show its enthusiasm for the project, in 1834 the Congress also offered a prize of 10,000 pesos to anyone who would successfully take a steamship from the Atlantic into the rivers of the republic "that run from north to south".[15]

Armed with his congressional gift, Manuel Oliden first travelled through Chiquitos in 1833. He came to the old Jesuit mission town of Santiago Apóstol. With him, as his aide-de-camp and publicist was Mauricio Bach, the German explorer who had travelled through Chiquitos with d'Orbigny two years earlier. Few descriptions exist of this elusive individual, who came originally from Frankfurt. The Count of Castelnau, who met him on the Paraguay in 1845, said that he spent much time sounding forth against the evil of absolute monarchs, denouncing Alexander, Julius Caesar, Louis XIV, and Napoleon with considerable gusto. "Apart from his infection of Voltairean liberalism," Castelnau observed, "he was an excellent fellow, well-educated and much travelled."

From Santiago, Oliden moved east to the ruins of an earlier Santiago, built near the hot springs called to this day Aguas Calientes. Alvar Núñez Cabeza de Vaca had visited these springs in the 1540s and the Jesuits knew them well in the eighteenth century (see page 118).[16]

At this tempting spot, Oliden founded the new village he called Florída after one of the battles in the independence war. In 1836 he built himself a house there.

Further to the south, on the spot d'Orbigny had favoured but never seen, on the ruins of the old Jesuit settlement of Santo Corazón, he began to plan a new town, to be called Oliden. A hundred years earlier "in the time of the Jesuits", Mauricio Bach wrote not altogether accurately, the place had been "a rich and blooming village with 3000 souls". In the 1830s, only ruins remained.[17]

The new settlement of Oliden, built on these ruins, was close to the banks of the Tucabaca river, the river that runs into the Otuquis. This, Oliden hoped, would make his fortune afresh by leading the way through to the Paraguay.

On 18 July 1836, he formally took possession of his new territory, in the presence in Oliden of d'Orbigny's old friend, the governor of Chiquitos, Marcelino de la Peña, and various other local dignitaries from Santiago Apóstol and Santo Corazón.

At that time, the new town of Oliden had a population of more than one thousand. Manuel Oliden was no slouch and, to provide employment for the inhabitants, he established a cotton plantation and a sugar plantation nearby. Beyond, to the south-west ripe for exploitation, lay the Santiago saltpans, known to the Jesuits and to the Zamuco Indians a century earlier. Food and work were available, the auguries were good. All that remained was to verify the claim that the Otuquis reached the Paraguay.

Anxious to lose no time, Oliden sent his son, José León, to explore the route. His first task was to examine the place on the main river – Bahía Negra – where the Otuquis river was supposed to flow out. Would it be suitable for a port? The success of the entire Oliden enterprise depended on what he would find.

Rather than try to go from Oliden straight through the swamp to Bahía Negra, José León planned to go on the known route to the Paraguay, through Brazilian territory to the north. He set off from his father's house at Florída in August 1836, and took the track to Santo Corazón. From there he travelled north-east, cross-country and over the Paraguay river to the Brazilian town of Cuiabá.

Leaving Cuiabá in October 1836 and travelling by boat down the São Lourenço river past Lake Mandiore, he eventually arrived at Corumbá. Finding the town almost deserted, he went on to Albuquerque, then a Brazilian military post with some fifty families living there.

He continued downstream, stopping briefly at Coimbra before reaching the impressive inlet known as Bahía Negra. Here he steered into the Rio Negro, the river he hoped would connect with the Otuquis.

What followed must have been a depressing experience for the youthful explorer. After a short journey of four leagues, with the river still encouragingly wide, he and his companions found it so clogged with the aguape weed that their canoes could go no further. There was no way through. They were forced to retrace their route to the main river.

In his report about the Rio Negro, José Oliden wrote:

> At its entrance, this river is as deep as the Paraguay, but at the place where we got to, it had already become much shallower. Its banks are low, surrounded by groves of palm trees that are flooded in the rainy season.

Its entrance was guarded by "barbarian Indians from the Potorera [Zamuco] nation, divided into small settlements each with their own names".[18]

Travelling back to Corumbá, José Oliden climbed the hill above the river. Looking to the west, he saw the end of the Serranía de Sunsas, the range of hills above his father's settlement of Florída. So clear and close did they seem that he thought it would be worth trying to return to Florída from Corumbá by land.

They set off with some implements, rucksacks full of food, and a Guaycuru guide. Passing the Laguna Yacadigo and the hill of the same name, José Oliden got another good view of the range of hills that would lead back home. This should have been the historic route to the west, but to the traveller of the nineteenth century, it proved absolutely impassable. They struggled gamely on, their hands torn by thorns and their bodies attacked by mosquitoes. But eventually, like the conquistadores three centuries earlier, they were forced to return to the Paraguay at Corumbá.[19]

José León's expedition did not return to Florída until February 1837, after a journey that had lasted five months. His report made such depressing reading that no one was prepared to invest in the Otuquis project. Although revived in various forms over the years, the early enthusiasm was never recovered.

Ten years later, in 1845, Manuel Oliden's secretary, Mauricio Bach, was still attempting to find routes through to the Paraguay. The French traveller Francis Castelnau met him at Fort Olimpo, on the Paraguay river below Bahía Negra. The Bolivians had appointed the German adventurer to be the Bolivian consul in Paraguay, and he was waiting at the frontier port to be allowed to travel down the river to Asunción. Both Bach and Castelnau were refused permission.[20]

Lieutenant Lardner Gibbon, a United States traveller in northern Bolivia in the early 1850s, also met Mauricio Bach, and was given José León Oliden's account of his expedition to the Paraguay. Gibbon remained optimistic about a possible route, reporting that neither Bach nor Oliden had been able to examine the Otuquis properly "from the fear their Indians had of the savages, and want of knowledge in the management of canoes, which they did not use like the Brazilian Indians".[21]

Lieutenant Gibbon's compatriot Captain Thomas Page, who travelled up the Paraguay in 1853, took the trouble to survey the inlet at Bahía Negra, and found the fishing "fantastic". Travelling up the Rio Negro for three days in the *Water Witch*, he was impressed by the depth of water. There were times "when the channel was so narrowed by grass that both wheels were in it, and yet we had a depth of twelve feet of water".[22]

When he could go no further, he anchored the *Water Witch* and continued upriver in a small boat for a further six miles. There he found that "the river was entirely closed by camelotes and grass, and yet we still had nine feet of water". Returning to the Paraguay, Captain Page remained singularly impressed by the possibilities. He wrote a glowing account. "So far as my observation enables me to judge, I perceive no insurmountable obstacle to the navigation of this river. I am convinced that a steamer properly constructed could skim over or cut through this sea of grass."

With this experience behind him, Captain Page became an enthusiastic campaigner for Bolivia's right to an outlet onto the Paraguay.

> Possessing but one indifferent port on the Pacific – Cobija – and from this separated by the Cordillera of the Andes, it is only by her rivers that the wealth of her mines and the fruits of her forests, teeming with many of the products of the Indies, can be brought into the trade of the Atlantic.

Nor, in his fertile imagination, would this be a one-way trade.

> From being one of the best populated as well as the richest of the South American states, a field is at once opened for the manufactures of Europe and the United States. At simply a nominal expense, when we look to the vastness of the interest involved, might she effect this outlet into the Paraguay.

To bring the fruits of contemporary capitalism into the Bolivian province of Chiquitos, all that would be required would be to clear the Otuquis river, "now obstructed by a dense growth of grass".[23]

Later, when asked to endorse the proposal to establish a way through to the Paraguay, Page was more cautious:

> As the navigability of the Otuquis is supposed to [have been] established from the high lands of Bolivia for a long distance in its course south-east, and as the expedition under my command examined it for 31 miles above its confluence with the Paraguay, it only remains to determine the connection between the two points.

That connection was never made. Years later, in the 1870s, a road was forced through from Corumbá to Santa Cruz, and in the 1940s a railway line. But the water route proved to be a chimera.[24]

Notes

1. *Ferrocarril Brasil–Bolivia, Informe de la Comision Mixta Boliviano–Brasileña correspondiente a los años 1938 y 1939.*
2. The dispute was about slaves and land, but it took the form of a bitter political struggle between the Jesuits and the Franciscan bishop of Asunción, Bernardino de Cárdenas. The story occupies many pages in the early Jesuit histories of Paraguay, and Cárdenas in the anti-Jesuit histories is sometimes perceived as a forerunner of the independence struggle 150 years later. A good useful account of the controversy can be found in Philip Caraman, *The Lost Paradise: the Jesuit republic in South America*, London 1975, pp. 82–98.
3. Cosme Bueno, "Descripción de las provincias pertenecientes al obispado de Santa Cruz de la Sierra", in *El conocimiento de los tiempos*, Lima 1771.
4. Robert Southey, *History of Brazil*, London 1819, vol. 3, p. 167.
5. Quoted in José Aguirre Acha, *La antigua provincia de Chiquitos*, La Paz 1933, p. 69.

6. Cosme Bueno, *El conocimiento de los tiempos*, Lima 1771.
7. Both Cosme Bueno and Juan Patricio Fernández give a very large number of the names of the many Indian nations of Chiquitos, and it is worth listing some of them, simply to illustrate the magnitude of our loss. This is Cosme Bueno's list of 1771: Piacocas, Punaxicas, Quibuquicas, Quimecas, Guapacas, Baurecas, Payconecas, Guarayos, Anaporecas, Bohococas, Tubacicas, Zibacas, Quimomecas, Yurucaricas, Cucicas, Tapacuracas, Paunacacas, Quitemocas, Napecas, Pizocas, Tanipicas, Xuberecas, Parisicas, Xamanucas, Tapuricas, Taos, Bazorocas, Pequicas, Parabacas, Otuques, Ecorabecas, Curacanecas, Batasicas, Meriponecas, Quidabonecas, Cupiecas, Ubisonecas, Zarabecas, Curiminacas, Chamaros, Penoquicas, Boros, Mataucas, Otures, Veripones, Maramoricas, Morotocas, Caypotorades, Guaycurus.
8. Martín Dobrizhoffer, *An Account of the Abipones: an equestrian people of Paraguay*, London 1822, vol. 1, p. 165. According to Cosme Bueno's estimate, the population of Santa Cruz in the 1760s was 6000, together with 1500 Indian slaves.
9. *Anuas 1766*, Arch. S.J. Rome. Para. Hist. 1710–67. Quoted in Philip Caraman, *The Lost Paradise: the Jesuit Republic in South America*, London 1975, p. 184.
10. Domingo Muriel, *Historia del Paraguay desde 1747 hasta 1767*, Madrid 1918, pp. 218–21.
11. Dobrizhoffer, vol. 3, p. 413.
12. Alcides Dessalines d'Orbigny, *Voyage dans l'Amérique Meridionale*, Paris 1835–47. This magnificent publication consists of nine enormous volumes. Volume 1 contains d'Orbigny's travels in Argentina and Uruguay. Volume 2 is an account of his expedition to Chiquitos. Volume 3 describes his journey through Mojos. Volume 4 deals with the different Indian races he came across. Volume 5 is about reptiles. Volume 6 is concerned with crustaceans and palms. Volume 7 is about stones and minerals. Volume 8 contains maps and topographical drawings and paintings. Volume 9, an atlas of molluscs, contains beautiful colour drawings of birds, animals and shells.
13. D'Orbigny, it should be recorded, sired at least one child in the mission towns of Chiquitos. The French expedition to Bolivia of 1906, that of Georges Crequi-Montfort, came across a man who claimed to be his grandson, still proudly bearing the name of d'Orbigny.
14. D'Orbigny found that there was still a small nucleus of Chiquitos Indians, brought originally by the Jesuits to spread what had been chosen as the hegemonic language of this mission territory. There were some Zamucos (considered to be the same as the Guarañocas of Santiago Apóstol and the Morotocas of San José), who came from the Chaco further to the south. There were 150 Otukes, though only a couple of old men were still able to speak the language. The few remaining Curaves had lost their language.
15. Mauricio Bach, *Descripción de la nueva provincia de Otuquis en Bolivia*, 1842. First published in 1836: republished in 1885 (by Antonio Quijarro); and again in 1929 (after Paraguay had attacked the Vanguardia fort near Bahía Negra).
16. Dobrizhoffer, vol. 1, p. 434.
17. Moritz Bach, *Die Jesuiten und ihre Mission Chiquitos in Sudamerika: eine historisch-ethnographische Schilderung*, Leipzig 1843.
18. José Oliden's report of his journey is printed as an appendix in Mauricio Bach, *Nueva provincia de Otuquis*, La Paz 1929, p. 21.
19. Yet the local people seemed to have had no difficulty in getting through. Back at Corumbá, the explorers visited the small village of Tereno Indians who provided the Brazilian fort at Albuquerque with fruit and vegetables (the village visited twenty years later by Captain Thomas Page and sixty years earlier by Father Sánchez Labrador). The Indians said that some of them had crossed the Chaco and had visited Chuquisaca (Sucre) a couple of years earlier. They were extremely glad to hear about the Otuquis project, they said. They had long dreamed of a road through to Florída that would enable them to obtain salt, the one thing they lacked.
20. Francis Castelnau, *Expédition dans les parties centrales de l'Amérique du sud, histoire du voyage*, Paris 1850.
21. Lardner Gibbon, *Exploration of the Valley of the Amazon*, part 2, Washington 1854, p. 175. Gibbon's report also gave news of the final destination of Manuel Oliden. The owner of the Otuquis Concession finally abandoned Chiquitos, moved to Sucre, and returned eventually to his birthplace of Buenos Aires. He left "his valuable lands and their production to the Indians, who live an easy life, in plenty and in an hospitable climate". Oliden sold his Otuquis Concession to Luis Vernet, once

the governor of the Malvinas/Falkland Islands. Vernet's daughter Malvina (born on the islands on 5 February 1830, though she left the following year) married Greenleaf Cibber, who also made explorations in Chiquitos. There is a modern memorial to Luis and Malvina Vernet, erected in 1981, in the Recoleta cemetery in Buenos Aires.

22. Thomas Page, *La Plata, the Argentine Confederation, and Paraguay*, London 1859. pp. 171–3.

23. Thomas Page, p. 445. Some time later a Spanish hydraulic engineer, Sánchez Núñez, claimed that the Otuquis could be made navigable for 240 leagues if works were carried out to remove the obstacles that Captain Page had identified in 1854. There is a reference to this in Santiago Vaca-Guzmán, *El Chaco Oriental, su conquista y civilización*, Buenos Aires 1887, p. 82.

24. One further attempt was made, in 1879, to rediscover the route from the upper Paraguay to eastern Bolivia, nearly fifty years after the Otuquis Concession had first been granted to Manuel Oliden. Some urgency was attached to this new attempt, for in losing the War of the Pacific against Chile, Bolivia had lost Cobija and her trading outlet onto the Pacific Ocean. Now more than ever, an eastern port on the Paraguay seemed a major priority. A scientific, commercial and military expedition, sponsored by the Bolivian government, left Buenos Aires in March 1879, and steamed up the Paraná and the Paraguay. Its task was to explore the Otuquis area. Its leader was Francisco Brabo. His secretary was Filiberto de Oliveira Cezar, an Argentine writer who has left a fictionalized version of the expedition. The chief engineer was an Englishman long in these parts, John Minchin, who has left an account that reposes in the archives of the Royal Geographical Society (RGS) in London. Their researches proved what Father Sánchez Labrador had discovered a hundred years earlier, that there is no river access from Chiquitos to the Paraguay. Minchin drew a line under the whole affair. On the western (Bolivian) side of the Paraguay, he told a meeting of the RGS in 1881, there are no tributaries north of the Pilcomayo. Fifty miles before reaching the Paraguay, the Otuquis river forms a series of swamps. For part of the year, these are completely dry. See Filiberto de Oliveira Cezar, *La vida en los bosques sudamericanos, viaje al oriente de Bolivia*, Buenos Aires 1893; and J.B. Minchin, "Eastern Bolivia and the Gran Chaco", *Proceedings of the Royal Geographical Society*, volume 3, London 1881.

12

SANTIAGO APÓSTOL

By lorry from Roboré to the mission of Santiago

In Roboré we have found a man who takes a small lorry each day to Santiago Apóstol, carrying passengers and produce. The problem is that he has to wait for the morning train, the chief source of both. The arrival of the train, from Puerto Quijarro or from Santa Cruz, is always an uncertain feast. Today there are rumours of trees on the line. The schedules are always maintained, the relatively quick alternating with the incredibly slow, but the train that comes today at noon may have been meant to arrive yesterday morning. So we have our lorry driver, but no departure time.

The morning ticks by, and we sit waiting in the dusty central square. There is a church and a barracks, a familiar South American combination. A memorial on the church wall records the presence of an Austrian priest here in the 1940s. There are still Austrian priests and nuns in Chiquitos, an almost unbroken thread since the days of the Jesuits in the eighteenth century when Austria provided much of the manpower for the missions.

Roboré is a military town, established in 1916. Some of its otherwise idle soldiers are busy sweeping the streets, others are working on an extension to the barracks, a new one built in the 1970s in General Banzer's time. Even during the Chaco War against Paraguay in the 1930s, Roboré seems to have played an insignificant role, or at least that is what the commanding officer says. We call by at his cool courtyard to get our passports stamped.

Off the square, we find a shop where an old woman sells small rolls with cheese in them. She has just finished baking them. They are so cheap that we have no coins small enough to buy them, so we stock up with a few shrivelled oranges as well. There is little husbandry around here, no drive for improvement, just a bleak sense of survival. If it was not for the soldiers and the railway line, the town would long since have disappeared into the bush.

Eventually a train arrives, the slow train from Puerto Quijarro. Our lorry loads up behind the station with sacks, and we get a privileged seat on the driver's bench at the front. Our destination, the old Jesuit mission of Santiago Apóstol, is about 20 kilometres away, forty minutes in the truck.

Like Santo Corazón, Santiago was one of the later foundations in Chiquitos, first

SAN RAFAEL. Woman standing before the crucified Christ in the old Jesuit mission church of San Rafael, in the Bolivian province of Chiquitos. Set up at the end of the seventeenth century, the San Rafael mission was an important launching pad for Jesuit expeditions to the Paraguay river, to connect with its missions in Paraguay.

CHIQUITOS. Costumes of the Chiquitanos drawn by Alcides d'Orbigny during his travels through the province in 1831.

SAN MIGUEL. "An immense cathedral-size church with a long and lofty nave and a huge golden altarpiece reaching from floor to ceiling." The Jesuit mission was established in 1721, yet in the village today the prosperity of past centuries is hardly a memory.

SAN JOSÉ DE CHIQUITOS. The old Jesuit mission here was founded in 1698, though the present church was built towards the end of the Jesuit era. It is the only one in Chiquitos constructed of stone. San José was also the site of the first settlement of Santa Cruz de la Sierra, established by Nuflo de Chavez in 1561.

SAN JOSÉ DE CHIQUITOS. The Jesuit church drawn by d'Orbigny during his visit to Chiquitos in 1831. "On first arriving at the mission square," he wrote, "I was hardly prepared for the buildings that surround it. One would not have imagined that these could have been created by peoples barely emerged from a state of savagery."

SANTA ANA. Virgin "looking like a Latin American madame" with two gift-wrapped angels in modern frilly clothing, at the old Jesuit mission church.

SANTIAGO APOSTOL. Gold-leafed eighteenth-century sculpture of Saint James in the mission church. Carved by the Chiquitanos, it is prudishly covered by a contemporary cloak of red velvet.

SAN MIGUEL. "A baroque and angelic San Miguel, carved with great virtuosity, flies out of the centre of the altarpiece."

SAN IGNACIO. A three-day annual festival in the old mission town in which the world is turned upside down "with the Indians making fun of the conquistadores."

SAN IGNACIO. The masks give them "an extremely doleful appearance."

SAN IGNACIO. Four small boys wind ribbons round the maypole and then unwind them again. "We were watching exactly the same routine observed and written about by d'Orbigny, on exactly the same spot, on 30th July 1831."

CONCEPCIÓN. The exterior of the Jesuit church of a mission that was founded in 1709. "Garish as it seems, the restored church is a telling reminder of the wealth and ostentation of these buildings in the eighteenth century, and yet another example of the dramatic decline which the region has suffered in the subsequent two hundred years."

CONCEPCIÓN. The interior of the mission church "drips with gold leaf, administered with a trowel. The roof is held up by sixteen gigantic carved wooden pillars, each hewn from a single tree."

SANTA ANA. The exterior of the church at the Jesuit mission, founded in 1755. In the early nineteenth century, Santa Ana was the capital of Chiquitos. Today it is "in an advanced state of decay".

SAN JAVIER. "The old Jesuit complex at San Javier is the most agreeable" of all the Chiquitos missions.

SAN RAFAEL. Here there is a stone sundial with the date 1765, just two years before the Jesuit missionaries were expelled from South America.

SAN JAVIER. "The scale is less gargantuan than in the other churches, and there is an intimate feel to it."

SANTA CRUZ DE LA SIERRA. Costumes of the Cruceños, drawn by d'Orbigny, 1831.

YURACARES. A nation living between Santa Cruz and Mojos, drawn by d'Orbigny, 1831.

established in the 1740s some ten leagues to the east of the present site, at the end of the Santiago chain of hills. From the very beginning, it had a military function: "it was necessary to use force against the attacking barbarians", a Jesuit apologist of the time wrote. "I confess that the mission has a military appearance," the Father Superior, Domingo Muriel, wrote in his history of the last years of the missions. "But let's examine the kernel of the problem. As a result of the attacks on the Indians, many who had lived in darkness were brought into the light, to enter into the path of true peace."[1]

The newly founded mission was not short of enemies. To the south lived the Zamucos (later called the Guarañocas or the Ayoreo), an untamed Indian nation that the Jesuits never succeeded in dominating, although they struggled to do so for more than forty years. To the east were the intransigent Guaycurus. Even when a few individuals were corralled into a mission, the ones that remained outside continually attacked the mission lands. The security problem became so great at Santiago that the priests were eventually forced to move the mission, in 1754, to a safer position higher up the hillside.

Set up by Fathers Gaspar Troncoso and Gaspar Campos, the mission initially had 410 families, and a total population of 1614. Here they built a church and a college, and by the time of the expulsion of the Jesuits it was a thriving community. When Spanish soldiers arrived in 1767 to take its two Jesuit priests away, there was a moving scene when the entire town turned out to greet the soldiers, the children in single file and the adults in their feathered plumage.[2]

With the Jesuits gone, the town soon decayed. In 1801, the college was burnt down; it was never rebuilt. Isolated, and in a frontier area, the mission at Santiago continued to be much molested by the untamed Zamucos. The Spanish governors of Chiquitos tried to achieve by force of arms what the Jesuits had done through guile, but military expeditions against the Zamucos were unsuccessful in their aim, only fostering a new and enduring Indian hatred of the whites. The Indians became implacable enemies, attacking anyone who came near the saltpans of Santiago and San José – an important source of revenue for the mission town. For many years in the early nineteenth century, no outsiders were able to venture into their territory.

When Alcides d'Orbigny came here in September 1831, he found the town was still surviving, though "of the buildings of the Jesuits, only the church remains, in very poor condition". But he was "much impressed by the satisfied air and the good looks of the natives. Without doubt they are the happiest people in the province."[3]

D'Orbigny had travelled here from San José, climbing the Chochiis mountain on the way. He spent a week in the town, staying in an Indian house on the square. He was particularly impressed by the talent of the villagers for dancing.

> They perform nearly all the national dances, a fact of which I became convinced by the variety I saw each day after our arrival. For the most part somewhat imitative, these dances are accompanied by music that, though lacking variety, is quite lively. During

the course of the dances, the Indians create numerous different patterns, some of which impressed me by their originality.

But even in his day, Santiago was decaying, and the energetic dancing of the Zamucos (Guarañocas) had its darker side. The population had declined to 1234 inhabitants.

I have to say, though, that the culture of these cheerful Guarañocas has been wholly corrupted. These things did not go on, it seems, during the time of the Jesuits. After their expulsion and during the wars of independence, when Santiago was a garrison town, the soldiers introduced dissolute habits. The people have no shame and are cynical to the ultimate degree.[4]

Other nineteenth-century writers had written about Santiago in similar vein. Soon we would be there, to discover what it looks like at the end of the twentieth century.

The missionary tradition at Santiago de Apóstol

The road to Santiago is a rough sandy track, crossing a river on a wooden bridge and then winding upwards into the hills. The old mission village is quite high up, about 800 metres, and is itself surrounded by low cliffs.

At the entrance to the village is the cemetery, much used it seems, with many gaudy ribbons on display. Then, inevitably, there is the barracks – for Chiquitos has been a military zone since the eighteenth century – and finally the main square.

Unusually, the square is on a gentle slope, with the old mission church on the left at the top. It looks quite old, and was roughly repaired in 1954. At the bottom of the square is a small evangelical chapel, dating from 1940.

Outside the church, under the overhanging roof, hang four large old bells, three from the nineteenth century and one, very cracked, from the eighteenth. "Ano 1769, Santiago Ora Pro Nobis". It must have arrived here just as the Jesuits left. The bells were all taken down when the tower could no longer support their weight. Leaning up against the church wall is an old barleysugar wooden column, to show what there once used to be.

Inside you get something of the flavour of the old missions. Fourteen square wooden pillars march down the nave, seven on each side, holding up the roof. A red brick floor, unglazed, slopes gently up to the altar. Here at least is something of the old style of the Jesuits of the eighteenth century: an elaborate carved altarpiece. Two bearded and painted saints guard the entrance to a cupboard, with two cherubs on either side above a lily. This too is flanked by barleysugar columns.

To the right of the altar is a splendid carved statue of Santiago the Apostle, Saint James, sporting a tricorn hat, trousers tricked out in gold leaf, a red jerkin and brown sandals. As often in these parts, the statue is prudishly covered with material, a great cloak of red velvet. For the benefit of the camera, we tried to move it aside to show the gold carved folds of the undergarments beneath.

These carved images remain from Jesuit times, but there is a more modern memorial too, a war memorial. "EL PUEBLO DE SANTIAGO A SUS HIJOS Y HEROES MUERTOS EN LA CAMPANA DE 1932". The village remembers its thirty sons and heroes killed in the campaign of 1932 during the Chaco War.

On the carved wooden board are many Indian surnames; four are called Yospi, four Paraba, four Tejaya. But the first names are more familiar: Sebastián, Salomón, Nemesio, and Carmelo. They left here for the south to fight against Paraguay for the sake of a line on the map. But they were fighting a battle that had been fought for centuries. The memorial records the war of 1932, but it might have been 1832 against the Brazilians, or 1732 against the Chiriguanos, or 1632 against the Portuguese, or 1542 against the conquistadores.

Eventually a priest emerges from the adjoining cloister. A large gloomy man with a heart complaint, he says he has been transferred here from San Ignacio for a quieter life. Born in San Matías, on the Brazilian frontier, he only arrived in Santiago six months ago. He is looked after by a rosy-faced nun from Santa Cruz, also a recent arrival.

"This is not the old church," he says, "though the contents come from the Jesuit time." He takes us out by a side door to an open space used as a football pitch. Beyond are some shallow grass steps. "There," he says, "that's where the church used to stand. It had a roof of straw in the old days and was burnt down three times."

The village now has a population of only 1500, half of whom belong to the military battalion, camped permanently off the square. There are some advantages to this. Because of the military presence, the village has electric light and the telephone. There is also piped water.[5]

For years, though, dynamic leadership of the village has been provided not by the Catholic successors to the Jesuits or by the military, but by the evangelical church at the bottom of the square. Just the day before we arrived, the old evangelical teacher had been buried, in the cemetery we had passed. A North American woman by the name of Haight, she had died aged ninety. Her husband had died four years earlier.

These two American missionaries had come together to Santiago Apóstol in 1930 and set up a boarding school. In 1940 they built the tiny evangelical church on the corner of the square. The school gave work to the villagers, getting them to grow vegetables to feed the students.

They faced exactly the same problems as their Jesuit predecessors two centuries earlier: war, disease, and conflict with other Indian nations. The Chaco War against the Paraguayans, in which so many villagers were killed, was followed by a great smallpox epidemic. The evangelists worked hard to save them, just as the Jesuits would have done, in an isolation hut set up outside the settlement. And even in the

1930s there were attacks on Santiago Apóstol from "bárbaros" living the other side of the hills.

"They did good work for the village," our Catholic priest says, reflecting on the lives of the two Protestants. "But they caused a lot of trouble with regard to religion." The previous day the evangelical congregation had asked for the mission bells to be rung as the old woman's coffin passed the Catholic church on its way to the cemetery. The same request had been made when her husband died, and it had been granted.

Yesterday the priest had again given permission, but it clearly went against the grain. "The village", he says, "is divided."

As so often in the past, all this good work has run into the sand. Both Catholics and evangelicals used to have boarding schools (there is still a college building next to the church). Now they are both closed. Only the schools still function, just for the village children.

There are still "bárbaros" over the hills, the Ayoreo, though they are controlled by a fresh generation of North American missionaries from the New Tribes Mission. The Ayoreo of today are the descendants of the Zamucos and the Guarañocas encountered by the Jesuits in the eighteenth century.[6]

"The 1930s were a good time for the village," the priest says, "in spite of everything. But now there is nothing for anyone to do. There are just old people here – and they do live to be very old – and the very young, and of course the soldiers." We found a small girl in the square, hitching a lift to Roboré to see her sister. She said her father made beds and mattresses and sold them in Roboré. It sounded a precarious living.

So after 250 years of Catholic evangelism, not much is left to show for it. "The 'indígenas' don't come to church at all," the priest says, "they resist it. Of course there are now very few left. Culturally they become mestizos. Ellos sobreviven porque Dios es grande. They survive because God is benevolent."

And with this brief survey of the hopeless situation of his flock, he turns back into the church that is filled with ancient mementoes of an earlier more hopeful time. We take the lorry back to Roboré and enquire at the station about the train to the next mission along the railway line, San José de Chiquitos. It is scheduled to leave tonight.

Notes

1. Domingo Muriel, *Historia del Paraguay desde 1747 hasta 1767*, Madrid 1918, p. 211.
2. Pablo Hernández, *El extranamiento de los Jesuitas del Rio de la Plata y de las misiones de Paraguay*, Madrid 1908.
3. Alcides Dessalines d'Orbigny, *Voyages dans l'Amérique Méridionale*, Paris 1845.
4. According to d'Orbigny's account, the Santiago mission was formed from Guarañocas (Zamucos) and Tapiis. The Jesuits, as usual, had added a few Chiquitos for the purpose of creating a dominant

language. The Tapiis had entirely lost their language, but the Guarañocas, being the most numerous, had still managed to keep theirs.

5. Apparently Cordecruz, the state development agency based in Santa Cruz, had declared there was not enough water available around here to be worth piping into the village. But the previous priest, knowing that a Jesuit mission would have been built in a suitable place, worked with the villagers to join together three small tributaries coursing down a neighbouring hill. Soon they had a mighty stream, producing water all the year round. Seeing that there was a sufficient supply and one so pure that it did not need a purification plant, Cordecruz was persuaded to provide the pipes and install them.

6. In 1944, a group of five North American missionaries based in Roboré disappeared on their way to make contact with the Indians between the Tucabaca river and Santo Corazón. George Haight led a search party from Santiago and they eventually found an Indian camp, which contained articles that had belonged to the five men. Collins, one of the members of the search party interviewed four years later, said that "there has always been great mutual hatred and fear in this region between the Bolivians and the Indians. Every contact made with the Indians has been considered, under great provocation, an opportunity to kill them, and the Indians have retaliated. They have made surprise raids on the villages, killing the men and women and dashing out the children's brains on the doorposts, and so on, and then dashing back into the forest. The same thing goes on today. No Bolivian will travel the forest trails alone and unarmed. The Indians hate and mistrust white men and resist every attempt the Government makes to correct their primitive life. The white people are as brutal as the Indians, with notable exceptions, and it's almost impossible anywhere to make peaceful contact" (quoted in Peter Grieve, *The Wilderness Voyage*, Jonathan Cape, London 1952, p. 175).

13

SAN JOSÉ DE CHIQUITOS

By train from Roboré to San José

It is dawn on the train from Roboré. We are frozen by the cold. It has been an arctic night, and it is now a chilly morning. With the early light, we catch a glimpse of an extraordinary hill formation, great cliffs and escarpments popping out of the surrounding scrub and swamp. This is the Chochiis mountain, halfway between the Paraguay and the Rio Grande. It must also, I think, be Tapuaguazú, the great hill that the first Europeans were told about, from whose summit a greatly peopled plain could be discerned.

Apart from the single railway track, bravely pressing through the swamp and forest, the land looks almost impenetrable. Occasionally, from the carriage window we glimpse a clearing, with a few huts and some grey smoke. One such is Taperas, a tidy village with a church surrounded by low hills; an attractive spot. Here was one of the many resting places of the Jesuit mission of San Juan Bautista, never safe from attack and constantly on the move. *Tapera*, in Spanish, means an abandoned village.[1]

At about half past eight, we draw slowly into the station of San José de Chiquitos, a mission town that was not abandoned. Founded by the Jesuits in 1698, it has a history that goes back even further. The train is too long for the meagre platform. It has to stop twice to let the passengers off. Most people do not bother to wait for the second stop. They clamber down cheerfully into the long grass, stooping under their sacks of luggage. We follow gingerly, getting out on the south side where there seems to be a track through into the town.

An ancient taxi, not wishing to miss our lucrative custom, takes us on a trip into the central square. Here we find lodgings at the Hotel Raquelito, an airy single-storeyed building that is modern, pleasant and clean. Opposite, on the other side of the square, stands the old mission church.

What a sight! A stone façade of four linked ecclesiastical buildings spreads along the entire east side of the plaza. These are the only stone Jesuit mission buildings this side of the Paraguay. All the others are constructed of wood and adobe. Even at San José, stone was in short supply, and only the façade is made of this rare material.

First, from the left, is the parroquia, the headquarters of the clergy. In the old days, it would have been the Casa de los Muertos, the chapel for the dead. Then comes the church itself, then the bell tower, and finally the Jesuit college. In the bright morning sunshine, this is a splendid display, an impressive and grandiose scene.

Alcides d'Orbigny, who came here in September 1831, more than sixty years after the expulsion of the Jesuits, was equally impressed with this astonishing place. He had come riding down from San Rafael, further to the north.

> After travelling in the forests for some time, almost any construction produces a strong impression. Yet on first arriving at the mission square, I was hardly prepared for the buildings that surround it. One would not have imagined that these could have been created by people barely emerged from a state of savagery. I examined the stone structures with real pleasure. They were in Moorish style with their original façades.[2]

D'Orbigny took out his pencil and settled down to sketch them.

> These monuments consist first of a tower of three stories, with a gallery running around the top floor. This is the main entrance to the college. To the left is the main front of the church, simply designed, and crowned (as is the tower) with small pilasters and crosses of stone. Only this façade existed when the Jesuits were expelled in 1767. . . .
>
> Further to the left is the Chapel of the Dead, where the dead are laid for twenty-four hours before burial. And on the right is the government house or college. This entire group of buildings have arched ceilings, providing a certain coolness in this otherwise torrid climate. The college has three courtyards surrounded with living quarters and workshops. The main square is huge, decorated in the centre with a great stone cross surrounded with palm trees.

Today the cross has gone, but the palm trees (or their lineal descendants) remain. Before the Sunday congregation assembles, we walk inside the church. Two sets of nine whitewashed wooden pillars run up the nave, holding up the roof. Those nearest the west door are being replaced with modern ones of fluted wood. Large wooden frame windows let in light from either side.

It is generally believed, as d'Orbigny suggested, that the Jesuits had only just finished the stone façade when they were expelled in 1767. San José itself suffered badly from fire in 1781. But the vaulting by the altar looks as if it dates back to the eighteenth century, and it may well have been done at the same time as the façade.

Behind the impressive front on the square, the buildings are uninteresting. The façade of the parroquia hides nothing but a mud construction with a tin roof. The college at the other end still looks solid enough, but the central cloister has lost its sense of quiet contemplation and has a new life as a handball court.

Within the church, however, many intriguing relics of the Jesuit era survive. There are several splendid carved wooden statues and, on the right side, a magnificent baroque altarpiece, in white, gold and blue. It contains a recessed

Madonna framed on either side by two great doric pillars. Below is a triptych cupboard adorned with seraphim.

On the flanks of the choir stand two extravagant archangels with silver wings: one carries a fish in his right hand, the other a sword. Two framed and painted recesses, with a floral motif and what looks like the original colours of white and orange, contain statues in such bad repair that they have been given clothes. Close up, they look faintly comic, like the kind of modern doll that is sold to be dressed up by its owner.

Behind the altar half a dozen silver frames hang, filled with a hodgepodge of religious motifs as though this were some kind of provincial iconostasis. The church is gradually being repaired, and the side chapels are piled up with old wooden statuary.

We walk around as the two bells in the tower are tolling for the nine o'clock mass. There were few takers at eight-thirty, but by nine there must have been about 130 people in the church. The citizens of San José do not seem to be overly devout, unlike the people in the mountain regions of Bolivia. They come to church for social, secular reasons, to see and be seen.

Several of the great cathedral churches of Chiquitos were built to the designs of a single architect, Father Martin Schmid. Born in Switzerland in 1694, he crossed the Atlantic to Buenos Aires in 1728 and worked for thirty-seven years in the mission towns of Chiquitos, mostly in San Javier, San Rafael and Concepción. He formed part of that great flood of German-speaking Jesuits who came out to South America in the eighteenth century and helped to transform mission life. It is this central European background that gives many of the mission churches their pronounced Bavarian or Bohemian feel.

From the same origin comes the extraordinary emphasis on music. Father Schmid built organs as well as cathedrals. He ordered an organ to be made for one of the Chiquitos missions, the first to arrive, in 1730. It was built in Potosí and brought down to the tropical lowlands on muleback. He then taught the Chiquitos Indians how to build the instruments. A decade or so later, he was able to write that "all the mission towns now resound to the music of my organs. I've also made large numbers of many kinds of instrument, and taught the Indians to play them."[3]

Although the churches have a German flavour, particularly in their decorative style, they can also be seen as extensions of "the long hut" that many Indian nations – particularly the Guaraní – constructed in their pre-Conquest towns, immense and airy buildings in which two or three thousand people could gather. Mission government, which depended to such a large extent on the rule of the Indian caciques, was perceived by many Indians as a continuation – and doubtless an improvement – of what they had known before.

There was also an important mystical and ceremonial element in the mission churches. Father Charlevoix, writing in the middle of the eighteenth century, gives a rosy picture of the churches established earlier by the Jesuits working among the Guaraní of Paraguay. These, though built of stone, were the models for the wood and adobe cathedrals of Chiquitos.

> The first missionaries immediately perceived that in order to inspire the new converts with a great respect for the holy place, and for the worship peculiar to it, it was proper to employ some exterior pomp and ceremony; and nothing has been spared to make use of this observation.
>
> All the churches are large, with three and often five naves, somewhat too low, indeed, for their length and breadth, because the roof is supported by columns of one piece. In the largest churches there are at least five very neat altars. In the middle is the great altar which has always something august and striking in it. The Spaniards themselves are surprised to see them so magnificent, and so rich in plate, linen and ornaments.[4]

Building churches, and decorating them, almost became an end in itself:

> It is the only subject of emulation between the reductions, some of whom have been known to rebuild their churches from the very foundations, merely to put them on a level with others; and even deprive themselves of the necessaries of life to effect it. . . .
>
> All the churches are adorned with paintings which represent the principal mysteries of our holy religion, and the most heroic actions of the saints of the Old and New Testament. These paintings are separated by festoons and compartments of an everlasting verdure, interspersed with the most beautiful flowers, and the whole church sprinkled with sweet waters which perfume the air.

Today the pictures have gone. Even in the nineteenth century, travellers reported that they were rotting in their frames.

Alcides d'Orbigny and his retinue of twenty, including the Bolivian governor of Chiquitos, Marcelino de la Peña, were to spend a week at San José. As was the usual custom, dating back to the pre-Conquest era, they had been ceremoniously received at the entrance to the town: by the administrator, the priest, and the Indian authorities. Then, under triumphal arches, they walked through to the main square, "and once there to the college building, preceded by young Indians of both sexes who sang and danced".

D'Orbigny noted that San José had once, in the time of the Jesuits, had a population of 5000. But the civil wars that marked the period of independence, and more recently "seven years of famine and smallpox" had caused many deaths. He reckoned that there were only about 1800 people when he was there, in 1831.

Hunger and disease had dogged the Chiquitos settlements from the very beginning. But d'Orbigny detected a fresh reason for the backwardness of San José: the disappearance of the forest. Now a theme of the late twentieth century, this was also the concern of travellers in the early nineteenth. The demoralized inhabitants of the area, with their slash-and-burn technique, were gradually destroying their habitat. D'Orbigny wrote of "the disagreeable custom people here have" of burning off their fields every year to renew the pasture.

> If the places where they have been doing this for some time have not already lost their great trees, they are now well on the way to so doing. Only a few remain, far apart and stunted, lacking almost entirely their stout trunks and shade-giving branches.
> This policy of deforestation has given rise, in some places, to droughts that were hitherto unknown. These have intensified year by year in a most alarming fashion. San José has had to survive a calamity of this kind over a period of seven years, during which the inhabitants have not been able to harvest a single crop. Many of them died as a result of the administrator's lack of foresight.

The effect of the fires had been dramatic:

> Instead of the really huge trees that you can still find in places far from the mission town, you can only see a few isolated examples close by, covered with miserable greenery that gets daily more impoverished. There is no doubt that if the administrator does not take severe measures to repress this practice, with a policy of conservation, a catastrophe is being stored up for the future.

Today the land around San José is dry scrub. A territory that had provided sustenance to thousands of Indians before the Europeans arrived, was close to being a desert two hundred years after the Conquest.

Nor was it only Indians who had lived at San José. After various trips outside San José, d'Orbigny had one more site to visit, "a place whose interest lies in the historical links that bind it". He was referring to the ruins of the old city of Santa Cruz de la Sierra. These lie some two kilometres to the west of San José, in woods quite close to the hills.

> In spite of its proximity to the hills and the abundance of construction material, this town was built of mud. It was about a kilometre wide, and you can still see, from the raised lines of earth, that it was laid out in lines and in squares. The outline of the main square and the church can still be seen beneath the trees. . . .
> For a long time I walked its streets, returning in my mind to the time of the conquistadors, when men almost without weapons dared to cross the continent through places where no one would risk going today.

Even before the Jesuits arrived, this magnificent spot had been a sixteenth-century Spanish town, the first in the centre of South America.

Nuflo de Chávez and the establishment at San José in 1561 of the city of Santa Cruz de la Sierra

The Spanish town in the outskirts of San José de Chiquitos, over whose ruins d'Orbigny found himself walking in 1831, had been founded nearly three hundred years earlier, in April 1561. Its construction had been ordered by the Spanish conquistador Nuflo de Chávez, who had marched here from the Paraguay. He called it Santa Cruz de la Sierra, after a place in Spain, between Cáceres and Trujillo, where he had spent some period of his childhood.

The land around the settlement was fertile, with much fruit and fish, and great fields tilled by the Corocotoquis Indians. According to Chávez's optimistic report, there were 80,000 Indian households in the surrounding countryside.[5]

Nuflo de Chávez belonged to the second generation of conquistadores on the Paraguay. The first had come with Pedro de Mendoza in 1535, a group that included Juan de Ayolas and Domingo de Irala. The second had come with Alvar Núñez Cabeza de Vaca in 1540. Nuflo de Chávez was to be the most important Spanish figure in Paraguay's sixteenth-century history after Irala – and in Bolivia's too.

Born in Spain in 1516, he was an upper-class Spaniard with extremely good connections.[6] A skilled politician and an indefatigable explorer, Nuflo de Chávez was based initially in Asunción. He had taken part in Cabeza de Vaca's famous expedition into Chiquitos in 1543, and had subsequently led a number of small, probing journeys into the Chaco, in 1545 and 1547.[7]

Then, in 1547–48, Nuflo de Chávez formed part of the disastrous expedition organized by Domingo de Irala that crossed Chiquitos and discovered other Spaniards on the western side of the Chaco (see pages 91–3). Seeking new lands, the conquistadores from the Paraguay had been forestalled by those from Peru. Since Chávez had such good contacts with the Spanish ruling class, Irala sent him over the Andes to Lima, to negotiate for assistance from the viceroy.

Almost every year, it seems, through the 1540s and 1550s, large Spanish expeditions, accompanied by hundreds – sometimes thousands – of Indians, crossed Chiquitos from the upper Paraguay to the Rio Grande. Initially in search of a route through to the silver of the Andes, these adventures had gradually deteriorated into slaving expeditions, looking for the cheap labour that would enable their Paraguay settlements to survive. As internecine conflicts developed among the conquistadores themselves, these extraordinary journeys developed into searches for new lands in which to settle, away from the bitter political divisions among the colons in Asunción.

Such was the aim of Nuflo de Chávez in the 1550s. Deprived of the leadership of Paraguay, which might have been his when Domingo de Irala died in 1556, he set off again for Chiquitos. He clearly hoped to carve out a fresh fiefdom for himself in this still largely unexplored zone. He left Asunción in February 1558, taking the usual route up the Paraguay. This was another gigantic expedition. Some 220 Spanish soldiers travelled in 23 brigantines, accompanied by 3500 Indians in 250 canoes.

Chávez went first to the Xarayes lake to the north of Lake Uberaba and spent much of the year exploring the land and rivers beyond. Finding his way through the upper reaches of the Paraguay blocked by waterfalls and rapids, he returned downriver to Lake Gaiba – the by now familiar entrance to the route across Chiquitos and the northern Chaco.

Making his way through Chiquitos, he crossed the watershed between the Paraguay and the Amazon, and arrived on the banks of the San Miguel river, some way to the north of the Bañados de Izozog. Running parallel to the Rio Grande, the San Miguel eventually joins the Madeira and the Amazon.[8]

The San Miguel river was of considerable significance in the plans of Nuflo de Chávez. It opened a way through to the north: to the mysterious territory of Mojos and to the Amazon. By the 1550s, access to the Amazon meant not only new lands, but the possibility of a new route back to Spain, avoiding the hazards of the south Atlantic.

Finding fertile ground by the river's edge, Nuflo de Chávez and his expeditionary force rested for four months. He needed fresh provisions for his army, and in this time a harvest of maize could be sown and reaped. But the territory was densely populated. The Spanish soldiers had occupied someone else's land, and soon it became clear that they had outstayed their welcome. In May 1559, they were threatened by a large and hostile force of twenty thousand Chiquitos Indians.

Chávez seems to have thought that if he gave the Indians no trouble they would leave him in peace. Twenty years earlier this might have been possible, but after nearly a dozen European expeditions had come thundering through Chiquitos like murdering locusts, the local inhabitants can have had few illusions about the intentions of the most recent visitors. Father Charlevoix writes:

> When he thought he had least to fear from those brave Indians, who had given so much uneasiness to the conquerors of Peru, he found them before him, armed with pikes, darts and arrows, defended by a strong pallisado surrounded with ditches and trenches; and the whole with pointed stakes of a very hard wood driven into the earth.[9]

Chávez sent messengers to the Indian settlement to discover if the Indians were prepared to agree terms of peace. The reply of the Indians was to kill the messengers.

> Finding that the Chiquitos were resolving in good earnest not to let him proceed any further, Chavez hesitated no longer to attack them; and, at last, obliged them to give way and take to their heels, though not without the loss of many good men who were killed on the spot, and a great many others, who, though very slightly wounded in

appearance, died in a few days after, the Chiquitos, it seems, having made use of poisoned arrows to defend themselves.

The battle was a major disaster for the Spaniards. According to a contemporary account, "more than forty Spaniards were wounded, and more than one hundred or so horses, and seven hundred friendly Indians. Of these, nineteen Spaniards died of the poisonous herb within twelve days, as well as three hundred Indians and forty horses."[10]

The defeat was also a political disaster for Chávez. In its wake came a mutiny in the expeditionary force. The mutineers had a powerful case. They argued that they were in a heavily populated area, and the Indians were clearly not friendly. To establish a Spanish settlement in this area would be a daunting, if not impossible, task. They should return to the Paraguay.

Having delivered an ultimatum, the mutineers called for a vote. Those in favour of a retreat won the day. Seventy-three Spanish soldiers, rather more than half the surviving force, together with 1500 of their friendly Guaraní Indians, set off on the return journey in June 1559. They marched back across Chiquitos to Lake Gaiba, recovered their boats and sailed down the river to Asunción.

Nuflo de Chávez was left with forty-five Spaniards and a few hundred Guaraní. Up till that point, these had proved faithful supporters of the Spaniards. But the quarrel between the whites had left them in a rebellious mood. They were severely disciplined by Chávez, but their continuing loyalty was now in doubt.

His visionary purpose undimmed, Chávez crossed the San Miguel river and continued on to the west. Reaching the banks of the Rio Grande, in August 1559 he founded a town and called it Nueva Asunción de la Barranca, "the new town of Asunción on the cliff". Here he divided up the available land and gave plots to his remaining Spanish soldiers – with a supply of Indians to do the work. Since they were still, as always, short of provisions, he ordered them to prepare the ground for crops.

From this settlement at La Barranca, Chávez sent out his deputy commander, Diego de Mendoza, to make contact with the neighbouring Indians, a group of Chiriguanos.

From its bases in the Chaco, this impressive Indian nation was to provide the toughest opposition the Spaniards ever faced in the centre of South America. "There is no nation in the inland of South America", Nicholas del Techo wrote, "more terrible to the Spaniards, or more destructive to the Indians, than these Chiriguanos." Unlike the Guaycurus in the eastern Chaco, or the Payaguas on the Paraguay, the Chiriguanos were never bought off or suborned. They maintained a fierce sense of independence until the end of the nineteenth century.

According to the earliest accounts, the Chiriguanos had their origin in a migration of Guaraní peoples from the lands to the east of the Paraguay river. Among the first to go in search of the Land Without Evil, they had moved westward across the

Chaco in the fifteenth century.[11] Later, from their base in the Chaco, they reached the lower slopes of the Andes east of Sucre and Cochabamba. There they had already come into contact with Spanish forces before the arrival of Nuflo de Chávez. They had encountered soldiers advancing from Peru, and had resisted these encroachments into their territory from the very beginning.

Faced with such determined resistance, and perceiving the need for a military solution, the Spanish viceroy in Lima, Andrés Hurtado de Mendoza, the marquis of Cañete, had sent an expedition down to the Chaco from Lima in 1556. It was led by Captain Andrés Manso, a trusted soldier who had fought in the Peruvian wars.

''This officer advanced, without meeting any resistance, as far as the extensive plains between the Pilcomayo and the Red River [the Bermejo]; and had even begun to build a town.''[12] Initially, Captain Manso found Chiriguano caciques who were prepared to collaborate, notably one called Vitapue.

These were the Indians with whom Diego de Mendoza, the lieutenant of Chávez, was about to make contact. But advancing from the new Spanish base at Nueva Asunción de la Barranca, he suddenly heard the voice of another Spanish-speaker. He knew nothing of the exploits of Andrés Manso and the sound came to him with the same sense of shock that had affected the expedition to the west of Domingo de Irala ten years earlier (see pages 91–3). A Spanish speaker did not mean the presence of a friend or comrade. It meant a rival for control of the land.

Diego de Mendoza had indeed bumped into Andrés Manso, who was travelling with fifty-two Spanish soldiers and the usual sizeable Indian retinue. Manso's force was small, but unlike Chávez he had written orders from the viceroy to occupy the land. Once again, the two halves of the Spanish empire were on a collision course in the heart of the continent.

You cannot help feeling rather sorry for Captain Manso. He had travelled from Lima, with a goodly company of Spanish soldiers, with a commission from the viceroy to defeat the Chiriguanos. He was all set to occupy the territory east of the Bolivian Andes, the area to the south of what is now the modern city of Santa Cruz de la Sierra.[13] Happily ensconced in his newly occupied territory, he was suddenly made aware of the arrival on his borders, coming from the east, of Nuflo de Chávez and his (admittedly reduced) cohorts from the Paraguay.

When the two men met, they had a furious argument. Both claimed the territory on which they stood. Who had the right to settle? The soldiers from Paraguay operating on their own account, or the soldiers from Lima with the viceroy's commission in their leader's pocket?

The two groups of quarrelling Spaniards could hardly decide their quarrel by battle since they were surrounded by great numbers of hostile Indians. If the whites fell out, the Indians would surely win.

Eventually the viceroy in Lima made a north–south divide. Manso was to move to the south of the Bañados de Izozog into the Chiriguano territory controlled by the cacique Vitapue, with whom he had already made a tentative alliance. Chávez was to keep the route open to the northern Paraguay and was in addition given what he really wanted: the unexplored territory to the north, known as Mojos.

This was the fabulous land that Hernando de Ribera had heard about on his journey to the north of Lake Xarayes in 1543, the land of the Gran Paitití, the Celestial Jaguar. In recognition of his rights, Chávez was awarded the title of Governor of Mojos. This new territory was to be separate from both Peru and Paraguay.

Manso undoubtedly had the worst part of the bargain. Since he had already explored into the waterless Chaco, he must have been well aware of his raw deal. Initially, he refused to accept the viceroy's judgment. In the rough justice of the time, Chávez had him arrested and packed off to Sucre.

Having disposed of his rival, Chávez went in search of a site for the capital city of his new province. Leaving Hernando de Salazar in charge at La Barranca, he marched some way to the west. On 26 February 1561, halfway between the Rio Grande and the Paraguay river, he paused at the place now occupied by San José de Chiquitos, and ordered a town to be built. He called it Santa Cruz de la Sierra.

Not only was it very fertile, there was also abundant labour. The figure of 80,000 households that Chávez reported meant a population of about half a million.[14] But Chávez was to take no chances. He relied for his own security on a group of 3000 Itatines, brought from across the Paraguay. Reasonably well disposed to the Spanish cause, they were settled some 30 leagues to the south-east of his new town, ready to be called on in emergencies.

Andrés Manso, meanwhile, had been released from detention in Sucre. From there "he went to a Chiriguano settlement called Zapirin, and in the plains of Tarinqui, near a stream, some 12 leagues away, he created another settlement, establishing peaceful relations with the neighbouring Indians". The new town of Andrés Manso was called Santo Domingo de la Nueva Rioja. For a while, his Spanish settlers lived there unmolested. It was only a momentary lull.

The Guaraní revolt in Asunción, and the expedition across Chiquitos by the bishop and the governor in 1564

Before Nuflo de Chávez established himself in the settlement of which the ruins can still be found outside San José de Chiquitos, the majority of the soldiers with whom he had first travelled across Chiquitos had mutinied and returned to Asunción. Hardly had they got back before they were faced by a major rebellion of their hitherto loyal Guaraní Indians.

The Spanish invaders thought that they had maintained reasonably friendly relations with these Indians, ever since they had first arrived on the Paraguay twenty years earlier. But now Asunción itself, their home base, was under threat.

The Guaraní revolt, Father Charlevoix wrote two centuries later, was caused by the historic antagonism between Europeans and Indians that the Spanish had preferred to ignore. It was designed "to shake off a yoke, the weight of which grew from day to day more intolerable".[15]

The revolt had an additional and immediate cause. The divisions between the whites that had taken place on the trans-Chiquitos trip had left them vulnerable. Almost as an inexorable rule, whenever the Spaniards quarrelled among themselves, the Indians took advantage of these quarrels to rebel. On this occasion, the Guaraní Indians accompanying the expedition of Nuflo de Chávez had discovered something to their advantage. They had learnt about a weapon that was capable of causing great havoc in the ranks of the European invader. "Having seen the effects of the poisonous arrows of the Chiquitos, they had brought home a great quantity of them."

The Guaraní thought, with some justification, that if they had some of these arrows themselves, "they might soon be able to exterminate part of the Spaniards, and oblige the rest to abandon the country". It was an irresistible perspective.

The Guaraní revolt at Asunción began on a small scale, but it "soon became a much more serious affair than it was at first thought to be; and the governor had occasion for all his forces to suppress it". At the start, it looked as if the powerful position of the Spaniards in Paraguay, built up over the previous two decades, was in jeopardy.

It was too much to hope for. The Guaraní had overlooked one important matter. The poisoned arrows of the Chiquitos had passed their sell-by date. They could wound, but they did not kill. Over time, they lost their all-important function. "The Guaranís had the advantage in the first skirmishes, and, if the poison of their arrows had not lost a great deal of its activity, might possibly have accomplished their design."

The Spaniards managed to put down the rebellion, but they had had a very great scare, and were obliged to negotiate a ceasefire:

> The Spaniards found it requisite to treat with great gentleness those who first discovered a desire of peace, for fear the whole nation, which was very numerous, should conspire together; and supply with despair, the place of poison, now no longer of any service to them.

For a few years, there was an uneasy peace on the Paraguay. Some years later, in 1564, after the revolt at Asunción had been crushed, Nuflo de Chávez left his new settlement at Santa Cruz and returned to collect his wife and family.

He found the inhabitants of Asunción still unnerved by the recollection of the revolt. Many of them were attracted by his suggestion that they should return with him to his new settlement. He organized yet another extraordinary expedition to the west across Chiquitos. The governor, Francisco Ortiz de Vergara, and the bishop, Fray Pedro Fernández de la Torre, the two most important political figures in the town, decided to leave too, and joined him on the journey back to Santa Cruz de la Sierra.

They set off in October 1564 with 120 Spaniards, plus 30 mestizos and the usual army of one thousand Guaraní Indians. Part of the expedition travelled up the Paraguay river, loaded onto 21 boats and 80 canoes. Another group, of 30 Spaniards and 800 horses, journeyed north by land. Assembling the two groups at Puerto Itatín (Albuquerque), the expedition set off once again, through the swamps and forests of Chiquitos, to the west.

As they started their march, thankful to leave the rebellious Guaraní behind them, they heard disquieting news of the situation ahead. On the south-western frontiers of Chiquitos, a revolt by the Chiriguanos was under way. The settlement at Nueva Asunción de la Barranca, on the banks of the Rio Grande, had been destroyed.

Almost the entire garrison was wiped out. One of Chávez's lieutenants, Anton Cabrera was killed, and only two Spaniards survived the onslaught to tell the tale. Because of the floods, they were unable to get the news through to Santa Cruz for several weeks.

No isolated incident, this was the start of the first major Chiriguano rebellion against the European invasion. Its leader, the cacique Vitapue, was the erstwhile friend and ally of Andrés Manso. He destroyed La Barranca and Manso's settlement at Santo Domingo de la Nueva Rioja in a single night.

At Santo Domingo, the Chiriguanos surrounded the town in the dark. Standing guard at the gates, they put the town to the torch, and then, as the Spaniards emerged from their houses to put out the flames, the Chiriguanos shot them down with a hail of arrows. Andrés Manso himself was killed and only one European – a Portuguese – survived, to escape to Sucre. Nothing remains of the settlement except the name of the surrounding plains, called to this day "los llanos de Manso".

While Nuflo de Chávez was in Asunción, Hernando de Ribera had been left in charge at Santa Cruz de la Sierra. Hearing of the destruction of the other two settlements, he launched a campaign of bloody reprisals against the Chiriguano.

Later, when Madrid got to hear of these disasters, the king declared that a state of war now existed with this resolute nation. He accused the Chiriguanos of being "rebels, assassins, and cannibals". The war, fought without quarter, was to last for more than three hundred years.

Nuflo de Chávez meanwhile, with Governor Ortiz de Vergara and Bishop Fernández de la Torre in tow, was in receipt of this news as he travelled westwards across Chiquitos. Hardly had his party digested it before they were themselves attacked. Asunción, Chiquitos and the Chaco, the whole area was now aflame, up in arms against the Europeans.

The expedition from Asunción survived this sudden onslaught, but the Indians secured some useful booty from the baggage train. One trunk they stole contained the robes of the bishop. The chronicler could hardly hold back a chuckle. One Indian "wore the cassock, another the surplice, and a third took the mitre. Standing on top of a hill, dressed in such a way, we could not – in spite of all our misfortunes – help laughing.''

The Spanish expedition continued unscathed, losing nothing more serious than their dignity. They arrived safely at Santa Cruz, today San José de Chiquitos, in May 1565.

In spite of what they had been through, and the lessons they had learnt, the Spaniards again quarrelled among themselves. On their arrival, Chávez ordered the arrest of Governor Ortiz de Vergara.

He was held in detention for a year, then released and allowed to set off for Sucre. On the way, he passed the ruins of Manso's settlement of Santo Domingo de la Nueva Rioja. He paused there to bury the bones of the dead. When he eventually got to Lima, he was disavowed by the viceroy, who sent him back as a prisoner to Spain.

The leaders of the colony at Santa Cruz were anxious to explore to the north. Nuflo de Chávez had permission to do so from the viceroy, and with him was Hernando de Ribera, the man who had travelled north of Lake Gaiba in 1543 and brought back news of a ''tierra rica'' in the land called Mojos. But there was a dearth of European soldiers and colonists in the town. Those there, the chronicler records, were happy to sit around. They displayed no enthusiasm either for fighting or for exploring.

These were not the only problems the chronicler mentions. Too many of the hitherto friendly Indians had been enslaved, leaving the survivors uncooperative. The hostile Chiriguanos had remained a permanent threat, forcing the settlement to remain forever on its guard. And the lack of any facilities on the Paraguay at Lake Gaiba had made transshipment difficult. The settlement remained isolated and alone.[16]

Disaster soon struck again. In 1568, Bishop Fernández de la Torre began the return journey to Asunción, accompanied by the new interim governor, Felipe de Cáceres. Nuflo de Chávez agreed to accompany them across Chiquitos, to show them the way through to the Paraguay. He was looking for gold mines.

Some way ahead of the main expedition, with a small group of a dozen men, Chávez lay resting one evening in his hammock. He and his men were suddenly set upon by a few Itatines, who had hitherto been loyal, and killed. Only one of the Spaniards escaped to tell the tale.

The surviving leaders in Santa Cruz, Diego de Mendoza and Hernando de Salazar, launched massive reprisal raids. They waged war against the guilty and the innocent alike. It was, Ruy Diaz de Guzmán wrote, ''a cruel punishment unequalled in the history of the kingdom''. Neither women nor children were spared.[17]

The governor and the bishop, meanwhile, continued their journey back to Asunción. Yet once in Paraguay, they too were forced to remain on the defensive. What had once been a mere revolt now resembled something more like a permanent rebellion. Thirty years after the Spaniards had first travelled up the Paraguay, the prospects for settlement in both Paraguay and Chiquitos seemed extraordinarily bleak.

Until the end of the century, the settlement of Santa Cruz was isolated and unsafe. The only solution was to move it to somewhere more easily defended. In 1590, a new and ambitious governor. Lorenzo Suárez de Figueroa, founded a new town to the west of the Rio Grande. He called it San Lorenzo de la Frontera. Four years later, Santa Cruz was transferred to a new site west of the Rio Grande, at Cocotá, close to San Lorenzo. Later, it joined forces with San Lorenzo, the site of the modern city of Santa Cruz de la Sierra.[18]

Not everyone supported the move. Some of the settlers remained, hanging on grimly and making their individual peace with the local Indians. Others, despairing of a future there or indeed in South America, decided to risk the dangers of a journey back to Spain down the Amazon. Theirs was an amazing journey. They built a boat and journeyed down the San Miguel to the Itenes, the Mamoré and the Amazon. Coming out to the Atlantic at Belém, they eventually returned to Cadiz.[19]

They left a large extent of territory that had been despoiled, its inhabitants decimated. "This province", Ruy Diaz de Guzmán wrote in 1612, some fifty years after the first settlement of Santa Cruz, "was once much peopled with the native inhabitants, though now it seems they have been largely destroyed".[20]

Guzmán, himself a mestizo, apportioned the blame equally. The decline in population, he wrote, "occurred partly as a result of the continuous attacks made upon them by the Spaniards who enslaved them, and partly through the cruel and bloody wars of the Chiriguanos, who with their thirst for human blood have destroyed several nations of this province".

For the next hundred years, throughout most of the seventeenth century, the Chiriguanos in the Chaco and the Chiquitos Indians further north survived in an independent territory beyond Spanish control. But they were not left alone. They suffered all the time from slave-raiding expeditions, both from the Portuguese moving westwards across the upper Paraguay and from the Spaniards in Santa Cruz crossing to the east of the Rio Grande. By the 1690s, unable to stand this ruthless persecution any longer, the Indians of Chiquitos were ready to make a deal with the Spaniards.

The battle against the Portuguese on the San Miguel river in 1692

North-west of San José de Chiquitos, on the banks of the San Miguel river, a battle of considerable significance took place early in 1692. This was not a fight between Spanish settlers and Indians, but a fresh episode in the long struggle between the Spaniards and the Portuguese. It entailed the first involvement of the Jesuits in the military defence of Chiquitos. Close to a large Indian settlement earmarked by the Jesuits for a mission town, a joint force of five hundred Chiquitos Indians and thirty Spanish soldiers from Santa Cruz defeated a troop of Mameluke slave-raiders.

According to a triumphalist Spanish chronicler, the Mamelukes were massacred: out of 150 men, only six remained alive. Both the Portuguese commander, Antonio Ferraez, and his lieutenant, Manuel de Frias, were killed. Of the six survivors, three were captured and three escaped – to warn another Portuguese raiding party in the neighbourhood of the dangers they faced. (This party had already assembled fifteen hundred Penoquis Indians to be sent back to São Paulo as slaves.)[21]

The significance of this battle was the presence at it of Father José de Arce, one of the most redoubtable Jesuit fathers in Paraguay at the end of the seventeenth century. Described as "a philosopher", he had arrived in South America in 1672 from the Canary Islands, at the age of twenty-one.[22]

The large Indian settlement near the San Miguel river had been selected by Father Arce as a suitable place to organize a Jesuit mission town – the first in Chiquitos. He had set out to the east from Santa Cruz on 9 December 1691, in the general direction of Chiquitos and the Paraguay river. He had considerable difficulty in finding a guide, but eventually came across two men who claimed they were familiar with the route. Travelling east, they soon crossed the Rio Grande (the Guapay), and arrived at this large settlement, close to the San Miguel.

Since it was late in the year, and the rainy season and the floods had already begun, there was no hope of getting through to the Paraguay that year. Father Arce himself had already fallen ill. So, finding the Indians friendly, he called a halt to the exploration. He decided to set up his first mission town where he was. He called it San Javier.

This, of course, was territory that had for long been threatened by the slave-traders from São Paulo as well as by those from Santa Cruz. Father Arce had achieved the neutralization of the second, but the first were soon to materialize. An Indian arrived at the town bringing news of an impending Mameluke attack. He had escaped from their clutches some weeks earlier when they had crossed the Paraguay.

Father Arce went out on a scouting expedition a long way to the east with three Indian guides. He wanted to try to locate the Portuguese troop, to discover its size. Eventually they found it, and it proved to be large. There was nothing that a priest and a handful of Indians could do to stop it. So Arce left the Indians behind and hurried back to Santa Cruz. (They were hidden in a place called Caposo that was later to be the site of the mission of San Rafael.)

Arce needed to warn the authorities of the imminent Portuguese invasion. Jesuit missionaries might be a nuisance as critics of slavery, but as the eyes and ears of the white settlers in hostile country they were invaluable.

Father Arce got what he needed: military help. He returned from Santa Cruz to his new mission of San Javier with thirty Spanish soldiers. This was all that the Cruceño authorities could spare. But with their assistance he gathered together an army of five hundred Chiquitos Indians from the settlement, armed with their speciality – poisoned arrows – which had caused so much havoc in the Spanish ranks a century earlier.

Expecting the Portuguese to attack the town, Father Arce withdrew his army to the banks of the neighbouring San Miguel river. The Portuguese found a largely unoccupied town, but the following day they were lured out, and the battle took place on the river bank.

The battle was a triumph for both the Cruceños and the Indians – and indeed for the Jesuits. The Spaniards lost six men, the Indians only two. And the Jesuits were able to show the Indians that they had temporal as well as spiritual power. But although initially impressive, their luck did not continue. After the battle, the surviving Spanish soldiers withdrew to Santa Cruz. The embryonic Jesuit mission was left defenceless against further Portuguese attack.

The Mameluke slave-raiding expeditions remained an ever-present threat.[23] One of the captured Portuguese prisoners, Gabriel Antonio Maciel, gave the Jesuits details. He explained how they had entered Chiquitos through Lake Mandiore, the most southerly of the three lakes on the upper Paraguay, and had taken six weeks to get to San Javier. He also told of the earlier Mameluke slaving expeditions that he knew of. One had gone through Chiquitos three years previously (in 1689) without trouble. But on another, the Mameluke leader, Juan Borallo de Almada, had been killed by the Peñoquis, the very group of Indians he had been trying to enslave.

It was clear from this information that the Indian settlement chosen to be the Jesuit mission town of San Javier was placed directly on the route the Mamelukes were accustomed to follow to the west. One way of protecting the Indians would be to move the town off the east–west road and closer to Santa Cruz.

Yet this in turn was to create fresh problems. Many Cruceños were just as keen as the Mamelukes on capturing Indians to sell into slavery. So the new Chiquitos mission was soon vulnerable on both fronts: from the Portuguese and from the Spaniards.

When the Jesuits went to Santa Cruz to argue their case against the slavers, they were roughly treated. They concluded that the site of the mission would have to be moved yet again. It was hardly an auspicious start.

"These removals," Father Lucas Caballero commented, "and the general lack of everything, and the frequent onset of illness, resulted in a marked diminution in the number of neophytes. Some retired to the hills, others died of hunger or poverty." The work of the missionaries was not easy.

Notes

1. The Jesuit mission of San Juan Bautista, first established in 1699 by Juan Bautista Zea and Patricio Fernández, occupied at least three different sites during the time of the Jesuits. The town started near

the banks of the upper reach of the Tucabaca river, on the northern slopes of the Serranía de Santiago. Then the Jesuits moved to the south, near San José; and then they shifted further to the east. Taperas still has the feel of a Jesuit town. One of the reasons for the frequent removals was the proximity of the Chaco frontier to the south, still replete with hostile Indians. Another was the water supply. Too often it came out from the hillside hot. And the sandy soil, typical of the northern Chaco, made agriculture difficult.

The first mission at San Juan had a population of nearly two thousand, made up from the neighbouring nations of Chiquitos, Boros and Parayacas. Sixty years later, the population had risen to seven thousand. It was "one of the largest and richest villages" in Chiquitos. One of the reasons for its wealth was the nearby Chochiis mountain, where there was a silver mine, of which Mauricio Bach claimed to have seen traces in the 1830s.

By the time Bach and d'Orbigny got there, San Juan Bautista was in dramatic decline. Bach says it was now "the smallest and the poorest" mission in the region, with a population of barely six hundred. The church and chapel were only thatched with straw, and it was the only mission in Chiquitos with no organ.

2. Alcides Dessalines d'Orbigny, *Voyages dans l'Amérique Méridionale*, Paris 1845.

3. Quoted in Hans Roth, "Las misiones jesuiticas en Sudamerica", in Antonio Bosl, *Una joya en la selva boliviana*, Vicariato Apostolico de Nuflo de Chávez, Concepción 1988.

4. Pierre François Charlevoix, *The History of Paraguay*, London 1769, vol. 2, pp. 279–80. Father Charlevoix noted that "the Christian Republick of the Chiquitos . . . differs in nothing from that of the Guaranis, upon which it has been modelled, but that it was sooner brought to perfection, because the Chiquites are more laborious than the Guaranis; and supported their missionaries for some years, during which they received no pension from court" (vol. 2, p. 199).

5. Julio Cesar Cháves, *Descubrimiento y conquista del Rio de la Plata y el Paraguay*, Asunción 1968, p. 267, quoting the "Relacion de Nuflo de Chávez del ano 1561". This relacion, and that for 1559, is printed in Blas Garay (ed.), *Colección de documentos relativos a la historia de America y particularmente a la historia del Paraguay*, Asunción 1899.

6. His brother, Diego de Chávez, had entered the Church and had become the confessor of King Philip II. His wife, Elvira, came from the influential Mendoza family.

7. The 1547 expedition was the first Spanish exploration of the Pilcomayo, the potentially important river that crosses through the middle of the Chaco from the Andes to the Paraguay. Chávez's report revealed for the first time that the river could not serve as a transit route across the continent. Swamps and rapids made parts of it unpassable at all times of the year, as they still do today. But his report, and the memory of it, was lost. As a result, innumerable expeditions tried to go that way for the next three hundred years, until the end of the nineteenth century. Many of them ended in disaster.

8. One of the historic and little-known rivers of South America, the San Miguel lies to the east of San José de Chiquitos. Rising in the Andes near Sucre, it starts life in the same area as the Pilcomayo and the Rio Grande. Here it is called the Parapeti. Then, curling down into the lowlands past the town of Camiri and into the Chaco, it disappears into the Bañados de Izozog, the great and impenetrable – and unnavigable – marsh just south of a line from Santa Cruz to San José. Emerging from this foetid swamp, and renamed the Quimome (the Arrow), it passes near San José and there forms the large Concepción lagoon. San José marks the watershed. To the west, the waters drain to the Amazon; to the east, the sluggish streams eventually emerge into the Paraguay. The Quimome soon changes name again – becoming the San Miguel – and moves to the north-west, close to the Jesuit mission town of San Javier. Further north, at Magdalena, it becomes the Itonamas. This then flows into the Guaporé (sometimes called the Itenes), which flows into the Madeira, which flows into the Amazon – a lineage of almost biblical dimensions.

9. Charlevoix, *History of Paraguay*.

10. Ruy Diaz de Guzmán, *Anales del descubrimiento, población y conquista del Rio de la Plata*, Ediciones Comuneros, Asunción 1980, p. 230.

11. Initially they were few. "What is most to be admired," Father Del Techo wrote, "only four thousand of them transplanted themselves at first; but in process of time, having brought some prisoners to follow their course, and increased by procreation, they spread abroad beyond their mountains, and

scattered the terror of their name far and near'' (Nicolás del Techo, *The History of the Provinces of Paraguay, Tucumán, Rio de la Plata, Paraná, Guaíra, and Uruaica*, London 1746, p. 93.

12. Charlevoix, *The History of Paraguay*, vol. 1. p. 201.

13. Enrique de Gandia, *Historia de Santa Cruz de la Sierra*, Buenos Aires 1935.

14. Placido Molina, *Historia de la gobernación e intendencia de Santa Cruz de la Sierra*, Sucre 1936, p. 8.

15. Charlevoix, vol. 1, p. 156.

16. ''Relación verdadera del asiento de Santa Cruz de la Sierra, limites y comarcas, para el Excmo Sr Don Francisco de Toledo, Visorrey del Piru'', in Marcos Jímenez de la Espada, *Relaciones Geograficas de Indias – Peru*, Madrid 1965, vol. 1.

17. Ruy Diaz de Guzmán, *Anales del descubrimiento, población y conquista del Rio de la Plata*, Ediciones Comuneros, Asunción 1980, p. 230.

18. The need to occupy and explore Chiquitos continued after the retreat from San José. The governor and captain-general of Santa Cruz de la Sierra, Beltrán de Otazo y Guevara, ordered his deputy, Fernando de Loma Portocarrero, to march east in 1597, across the northern Chaco to the Paraguay river. Portocarrero made the journey from October to December, and left ample documentation. His purpose was to subdue the nation of the Xarayes, to secure the territory's exit to the upper Paraguay, and to free a way through to the imagined treasures of the north.

    Previous Spanish expeditions had always found the Xarayes to be friendly. They had provided a number of interpreters for successive generations of Spanish adventurers, and even a number of volunteers to guide them through the swamps to the west of the river. But they were a large and powerful nation who could effectively block the road when they chose to do so.

19. Cited in Placido Molina, *Historia de la gobernación e intendencia de Santa Cruz de la Sierra*, Sucre 1936, p. 47.

20. Ruy Diaz de Guzmán, *Anales del descubrimiento*, p. 232.

21. José Aguirre Acha, *La antigua provincia de Chiquitos*, La Paz 1933, pp. 36–7.

22. Emilio Ravignani (ed.), ''Cartas Anuas de la provincia de Paraguay, 1609–1614'', in *Documentos para la Historia Argentina*, vol. 19. Buenos Aires 1927.

23. In May 1692, the desperate settlers of Santa Cruz appealed to the governor of Paraguay in Asunción for help against the Portuguese raiders. Communications, through Tarija and Tucumán, were not easy, and it was not until November that the governor replied, suggesting that the mission Indians should be called up. See Jaime Cortesão, *Jesuitas e bandeirantes no Guaíra, 1549–1640*, volume 1 of *Manuscritos da coleção de Pedro de Angelis*, pp. 302–11.

14

SAN RAFAEL

By lorry from San José de Chiquitos to San Rafael and Santa Ana

We had not meant to move away from San José de Chiquitos quite so soon. Cold and exhausted from travelling in the train from Roboré, we would have preferred to stay where we were. But travel in South America usually means taking your chances when they come – not always at the moment you would choose. So when we heard rumour of a lorry going north that day towards San Ignacio, and a trip that would get us there in time for the start of the annual fiesta, we felt bound to explore the possibility. Brief investigation seemed to indicate that because of the fiesta, there would be no further transport north for several days. We would have to go now, or later, much later.

So that afternoon saw us break away from our prolonged love affair with the trans-continental train, and found us climbing up into the back of a small lorry, a camioneta.

There are ten of us altogether. Two large women and the driver sit in front, while the rest of us are perched on two wooden benches on either side, with a great pile of baggage in between. The camioneta has a canvas covering which proves to be doubly disadvantageous. You cannot see out, except at the back which is just a cloud of dust, and the canvas does not prevent the dust from covering us with a rich veneer of red earth. Still, there is a crack of light at the front and things can occasionally be glimpsed, a few birds, and even something that looks rather like a fox.

At one stage we are stopped by a herd of white cebu cattle, perhaps a thousand of them, guided by six gauchos looking dramatic on their horses, with leather jerkins, red bandanas and a great winding horn. "Pura plata" someone in the lorry says, pointing out that each beast is worth four hundred dollars, and twice that the other side of the Brazilian frontier.

Enrique, our driver, is thirty-five and a bachelor. He lives on his own in San José, and makes the trip to San Ignacio twice a week. He has a girlfriend in the restaurant in San Rafael and another who is an announcer at the San Ignacio television station.

Once he went as far as São Paulo and thought there were too many people. He is worried, he says, about Aids.

His mother comes from San José, but now lives in Santa Cruz. His father is dead, but was once a foreman of a construction gang that helped build the railway in the 1940s. He used to own a property in Santa Cruz, four blocks from the plaza, but somehow they lost it when he died. Enrique has one sister and seven brothers, one of whom works in a bank.

After about two hours, driving very fast along a good straight dirt road, we come to the mission town of San Rafael, with a great open plaza and a splendid, restored church.

The Jesuits first came to San Rafael at the end of 1696. A mission was first set up here by Juan Bautista Zea and Francisco Hervas. The settlement had an initial population of some 3000 people, made up of Indians from the Taos nation. Built on a high and spacious hillside, it was surrounded by forests "filled with wood suitable for any kind of work".

The site was selected in order that the mission might be close to the Paraguay. But as a result, it was always under threat from the Portuguese.

By the end of the Jesuit era, in 1767, its population had more than doubled, to 7000. Then it was an extraordinarily prosperous place. Yet by the 1830s the number of inhabitants was down to a mere 700. According to Mauricio Bach, who travelled here first with d'Orbigny in 1831, it was badly affected by smallpox (as was neighbouring Santa Ana) during the period of the last Spanish governor, Sebastián Ramos.

The people had gone, but much else remained. In Bach's day, it still had a good church, "one of the finest in the land", and "a well-tuned organ".

San Rafael still has the largest old Jesuit church in the area. Its magnificence and grandiosity – the sheer scale of the enterprise – is difficult to describe. Unlike San José, which has a stone façade, San Rafael is made entirely of wood. Outside, with its dramatic long roof presiding over the town square, it is a startling phenomenon. Inside, it is stupendous.

Down a side street, through a hedged entrance to some ancillary buildings, we find an Austrian nun. She takes us into the church through a side door. The roof of the nave is supported by immense carved wooden pillars, nine on either side. The walls are whitewashed and painted with a red geometric design.

Like two or three of the other old Jesuit churches in Chiquitos, the building at San Rafael was restored, in the 1970s, with German money. It was the first in Chiquitos to be done, and even now it shines a bit too brightly. More paintings have survived here than is usual, seemingly from the eighteenth century, but they remain dirty and uncleaned. The nun takes us to see a delightful altarbox with doors that swing open, a lovely piece of carpentry.

Outside, the tower is made entirely of wood with an internal staircase. There is also a stone sundial, inscribed with the date 1765, just two years before the Jesuits were expelled. The nuns here still feel that the expulsion was a disaster, "a tragedy", one says. They are well aware of just how poor their villages now are. "The Jesuits", she says, "did more in one century than anyone else has done in two."

I ask what has happened to the musical tradition here that is so often commented on by earlier travellers. She says that no trace of it now remains.

San Rafael is more prosperous than its close neighbours San Miguel and Santa Ana, but today's population is little more than one thousand, not much more than in d'Orbigny's time. The nuns teach religion in school, and one of them runs the kindergarten.

We have a Pepsi Cola here, in a low room on the street, a block from the church, looking over a well-swept courtyard. It is unusual to find a café in these mission villages, but the occasional bus from San José to San Ignacio stops here to feed its passengers. The owner says that the old languages have all gone. Even Chiquitano, the common language that the Jesuits imposed on a variety of nations, is now only spoken by a few old people in the village. Many of the peasants are ashamed to use it. Those who went to the altiplano in search of work found the old language served their purpose ill. They could only communicate to Quechua-speakers in Spanish.

Soon we are travelling on to Santa Ana, a forty-minute drive from San Rafael along a bumpy road. We arrive late in the afternoon, the shadows already lengthening across the unkempt central square. We turn into the plaza, uncared for and filled with long grass and a couple of bottle trees. To left and right a few old houses survive upright, but only just. The whole place seems in an advanced state of decay, though not without charm. Nothing but crumbling adobe and thatch, and not much sign of plaster or paint.

Enrique, the driver, claims that people here only earn enough money to get drunk – a traditional slur against the Indians, but one with more than a grain of truth in Santa Ana.

Across the plaza is the church, long and low and unreconstructed, with a prevailing impression of faded green. There is a separate wooden tower and a college building, but it is on a much smaller scale than San Rafael.

We get the key to the church from a woman in a hut nearby. She accompanies us around with three small children. We enter from the back, coming in behind the main altar. It is dusty and gloomy and full of cobwebs, but in the robing space is a long and lovely painted chest of drawers, clearly from the Jesuit era.

There is some doubt about the age of this church. When Francis Castelnau came here in the 1840s, he thought that it had been rebuilt after the expulsion of the Jesuits in 1767. Maybe so. There are certainly none of the characteristic IHS signs, though some of the carved wooden sculptures are clearly from the eighteenth century. One is of Saint Ignatius. Nearly all have been gift-wrapped in modern frilly clothing and are rather simpler than those in other mission churches. But there is one splendid figure of Christ with his hands lashed to a post in front of him, very dark with a crown of thorns, too dark to photograph. Near the altar is an equally splendid

Virgin, looking like a Latin American madame, accompanied by two angels and placed on a stretcher ready to be carried round the village.

The entire church is made of wood, even the arches in the chancel which elsewhere usually have plaster over mud brick or adobe. Outside, on the college side, there is a stone sundial, but on the other side where the wooden belltower stands, the long grass and general lack of attention make it almost impossible to penetrate.

The front of the church, which has an external staircase and balcony to the musicians' loft, has been painted up in gaudy colours, pink, yellow and blue, and looks as if it has escaped from a fairground. Yet in d'Orbigny's time, this settlement was the capital of Chiquitos and the seat of the governor's residence.

Its importance was due to its position on the frontier with Brazil. According to a report of 1807, the Spanish authorities were worried about the loyalties of its Indian inhabitants.[1] They were liable to slip over the frontier at any time. This was the reason why the mission had been placed there in the first place, and why the governor of Chiquitos, both in the time of the Spaniards and later when Bolivia was independent, established his headquarters there.

The Santa Ana mission was first established in 1755, by Father Julian Knögler, in the decade before the Jesuits were expelled. Formed principally of Chiquitos Indians, it had an initial community of 367 families, 1787 people in all. In a book Father Knögler wrote years later, in exile in Europe, he explained how the mission system long established in the Guaraní missions of Paraguay was adapted to the requirements of Chiquitos.

First, the Jesuits had to mount an expedition to find Indians to populate a new mission. They would move out into the countryside in pairs, accompanied by friendly Indian guides.

> We were received well by the Indians and loaded with fruit and the produce of the earth. In return the natives were given glass beads, small bells, needles and hammocks. It was our rule to take nothing without returning something of equivalent value.[2]

Father Knögler would follow up this initial exchange with a short speech explaining what his expedition was up to in Indian territory. "It is for your sake, my children, that I have left my parents and brothers who live over there where the sun rises. I learned that you were without hammocks and I have come to bring them to you."

His acolyte would then distribute three hundred hammocks, and Father Knögler would discuss the tribulations of his trip. The hammocks would then be followed up with a second, and yet more significant, offering: of iron axes. "Here are some axes I brought with me. There are enough to make a clearing. . . . I am going to hand them to your cacique so that you can cut down the trees." One historian says that the Jesuits "could have done nothing without the axes" that they distributed.[3]

Having got the Indians hooked with these useful artefacts the missionaries would find a mission site, often one with which the Indians were themselves familiar.

> The first step is to find a suitable site immune from floods. Then the forest is cleared and a large square formed in which the houses are arranged in rows. Three sides are for the Indians, and the fourth is for the church and the houses of the missionaries, as well as the workshops and the school. The houses are poor, made of wood thatched with thick grass, but the church is well-built.

Although the town of Santa Ana seems to have entered a long period of decline in the post-Jesuit period, the neighbouring countryside remained at a higher level of development than the comparable area across the frontier in Brazil. The Count of Castelnau, who arrived in Santa Ana from Brazil in June 1845, was impressed by how much more prosperous Chiquitos was than the Brazilian province of Mato Grosso, which he had just passed through.

In Chiquitos, he wrote, the population was much larger and more "civilized", the roads were infinitely better kept up, and his party was able to sleep each night under cover. The travellers' chief problem was language. Father Knögler had followed the Jesuit practice of teaching and speaking in the Chiquitano language. In 1845, the Indians around Santa Ana still spoke the Chiquitos language and had no knowledge of Spanish. As a result, Castelnau's expedition often had difficulty understanding the directions they were given.[4]

The Jesuit search for the Paraguay route in 1702

The mission at San Rafael had been set up for one purpose. Its position was perceived to be close to a route that might get through to the Paraguay. As soon as the mission was stabilized and its permanent existence assured, expeditions were sent out into the swamps to try to reach the river.

Although the new mission appeared to lie within reach, there were human as well as physical obstacles. At least one unfriendly Indian nation – the Guaycurus – barred the way. "Everywhere," Father Charlevoix wrote, the Jesuits "met with armed Indians who obliged them to turn back."[5]

But the fathers were determined. After a setback in 1701, a fresh expedition was launched from San Rafael in May 1702. It consisted of two priests, Father Francisco Hervas and Father Miguel de Yegros, and forty Chiquitos Indians from the mission.

They took with them a catechist, a youthful recruit from the nation that had effectively prevented them from getting through the previous year. He turned out to be extremely useful, guiding them successfully through the territory of three nations – the Curuminos, the Batafis, and the Xarayes.

Then disaster struck. Before they got to the river, their guide inconveniently got a splinter in his foot and died. It did not bode well for their expedition. One of the chroniclers records that "they travelled through thick woods and over steep mountains, crossing marshes and lagoons, in continual fear of falling into the hands of their enemies".[6]

After a two-month journey, they came to a wide stretch of water. It was, they believed, "the Paraguay river, or at least a tributary". By now it was August, the dry season, and the course of the river should have been obvious to them. They commanded the Indians to construct an immense wooden cross on the river bank, a sign that an expedition coming up the river from Asunción would not miss. Anyone seeing it would get the message that this was the entrance to the route across Chiquitos.

Its task completed, the expedition returned to San Rafael the way it had come. Father Hervas was then sent the long way round to Asunción and the Paraguay missions – via Tarija, Tucumán and Santa Fé – to tell them the good news. A route had been found.

The following year, in June 1703, also in the dry season, Father Hervas and a group of four other priests from the Paraguay missions set off upstream from Asunción to look for the marker cross that he had left on the river bank. Soon, they thought, the northern route through to Chiquitos would be securely established. It was a large expedition, with several boats and many Indians.

The composition of the team is an indication of its importance. Led by the Father Provincial of Paraguay, Bartolomé Xímenes, a powerful and influential priest who had previously been the Society's Procurador in Rome, it included two energetic and charismatic priests from Chiquitos, Father José de Arce and Father Juan Bautista Zea.

By October, after three months on the river, they had reached the southernmost of the lakes on the upper Paraguay, Lake Mandiore. Here they began searching for the cross. Failing to find it, they moved on up to Lake Xarayes or Uberaba. Here too they failed to find any trace of the San Rafael marker.

By December, the rains had begun and the priests – like the conquistadores before them – had to debate whether to stay or return. Father Ximenes, the most senior, voted to return. He argued powerfully that supplies were running low, the porters were reluctant to hang around, the Portuguese danger was ever present, many of the priests were increasingly unwell, and he himself had begun to suspect that their maps were mistaken and that the cross would never be found. Fathers Hervas, Arce and Zea would have preferred to spend the rainy season in the upper Paraguay, and to resume the search when the floods subsided. Father Ximenes won the argument, or imposed his will. The expedition started off downstream, returning to Asunción at the beginning of January 1704.

Later that year, in October 1704, another expedition set out from Chiquitos. Father Patricio Fernández left San Rafael along the route followed by Hervas and Yegros two years earlier. He found that the cross they had erected was still there, but he realized at once that it had not been put up in a suitable place. It was on an inland swamp, not on the banks of the Paraguay. With his Indian companions, he continued to explore, but they were soon stopped by the floods and the onset of the rainy season. They returned to San Rafael at the end of January 1705.

It was another ten years before the Paraguay Jesuits felt confident enough to embark on a new attempt. The indomitable Father Arce, together with Father Bartolomé Blende, set off from Asunción in January 1715. The governor of Paraguay and half the town trooped down to the river to see them off. They carried a large amount of baggage, presents from the Guaraní mission towns to the newly established missions of Chiquitos.

From the start it proved to be a difficult journey. Hostile Indians barred their way. They had immense difficulty getting past the Payaguas, and they had to bribe the Guaycurus with some of the presents intended for the Chiquitos.

As before, the Jesuits embarked on a long search for signs that Father Juan Patricio Fernández had erected on the river bank, signs that would enable them to take the track through to San Rafael. In all, they spent seven months on the river, going up and down until the end of August. Eventually Father Arce became so irritated that he decided to abandon the boats and make the journey inland himself, come what may.

Unlike the situation more than ten years earlier, when he had been forced to return to Asunción by his superior, Father Arce was now, at the age of sixty-four, his own master. He took a dozen Indians with him, leaving Father Blende and the others behind on the river. It was like a repeat of so many of the expeditions across Chiquitos, ever since the days of Juan de Ayolas nearly two hundred years earlier. An account of his journey to San Rafael, written by the Indians who went with him, survives embedded in the history of Chiquitos written by Father Juan Patricio Fernández.[7]

Arce and his troop of Indians left the Paraguay from Lake Mandiore at the beginning of September 1715, travelling through thick forests and swamps. Sometimes they ate fish and turtle, sometimes they ate nothing. Sometimes they saw smoke in the distance.

After a month of this grim journey, with Father Arce becoming increasingly frail and ill, they came to a river with fish. Soon they saw fresh evidence that they might get through to the other side of the swamps. The smoke they saw proved to be that made by a party of Indians led by Father Juan Bautista Zea who had set out from San Rafael to look for them. A few days later they found the track to Chiquitos, and on it they met a couple of Indians who were carrying Father Zea's portable altar. When Father Zea himself was found, it must indeed have been a cheerful moment. They struggled on to San Rafael. The route had been conquered.

Hardly had they got there, however, before Father Arce felt obliged to make the return journey to the Paraguay to see what had happened to Father Blende, left with the boats at the side of the lake. This time they went back along the trail that Father

Fernández had already blazed, but it was none the less another painful journey through forest and swamp. To provide additional assistance, they were followed a little later by the Vice-provincial and by Juan Bautista Zea. This expedition was forced back by the rising floodwaters covering the Pantanal, and returned to San Rafael.

Father Arce's group got through to the Paraguay, but Blende and the boats had disappeared. As had happened so often before, the crew of his boats had become restless. Two Spaniards, the pilot and the captain, were particularly irritated that the pious Jesuit had refused to allow them to buy slaves. After waiting for two months for news of Father Arce, they insisted on being allowed to return downriver. Father Blende was obliged to fall in with their wishes.

On the way back, they met some Payaguas who expressed the desire to be Christianized. Insufficiently on his guard, and ever on the look-out for converts, just as the Spaniards were on the look-out for slaves, Father Blende invited them on board for food. It was a mistake. The Payaguas came with their axes and virtually the entire expedition was hacked to death. A handful of friendly Indians survived to tell the tale. The bodies of the dead were left on an island beach.

Father Arce, coming downstream a little later, found them there. Constructing a boat at the lake on the Paraguay, he had set off with thirteen Christian Indians at the beginning of December. Arriving at the island, they were then themselves killed by the Payaguas.

It was to be another two years before the story got out. Four of the Christian Indians, who had formerly been enslaved by the Payaguas but had then been rescued by Arce on his outward trip and used as interpreters, survived the killings. They were captured but subsequently managed to escape. Setting off upriver, they reached the lake and were able to get through to San Rafael. They brought the news of Father Arce's death.

It was the end of an era, for other possibilities seemed to be opening up. The same year, 1715, the Jesuits from Tarija had successfully established a mission town at Salinas. From there, a fresh possibility dawned of opening a more direct route to Asunción along the Pilcomayo river. In 1721, Father Patiño, Father Rodríguez and Father Niebla set out from Asunción to try to test the viability of the Pilcomayo route.

In 1722, the ever-energetic Father Hervas had explored the Bañados de Izozog, travelling from San Rafael to Charagua (near Camiri). This opened up the possibility of linking Chiquitos with Tarija without having to go through Santa Cruz.

In 1723, the Chiquitos Jesuits had set up their most southerly mission town, at San Ignacio de Zamucos. From here they hoped to make a route through to the Pilcomayo.

All these initiatives proved in the end to be futile. But it was necessary for them to be made. For in 1716, after the deaths of Father Arce and Father Blende, the Real Audiencia in Charcas, at the request of the burghers of Santa Cruz, ordered that the northern Chiquitos route be closed. Throughout the two previous decades, Santa Cruz had continually expressed its concern that the reopening of this route would facilitate the westward drive of the Portuguese. This view had now prevailed.[8]

So two decades of frenetic exploration had left the Jesuits precisely nowhere. Indeed they had overreached themselves. In the 1720s, the two most powerful nations in the Chaco, the Chiriguanos and the Zamucos, began a major rebellion against Spanish encroachment, a rebellion in which the missions were inevitably caught up.

Notes

1. Manuel Ballivián, *Las provincias de Mojos y Chiquitos*, volume 1 of *Documentos para la historia geográfica de la república de Bolivia*, La Paz 1906, p. 90.
2. Jürgen Riester, "Julian Knögler SJ und die Reduktionem der Chiquitano in Ostbolivien", in *Archivum Historicum SJ*, Rome July–December 1970, pp. 268–348.
3. José Chantre y Herrera, *Historia de las misiones en la Marañon Espanol*, Madrid 1901.
4. Francis Laporte, Count of Castelnau, *Expédition dans les parties centrales de l'Amérique du Sud, Histoire du voyage*, Paris 1850.
5. Father Pierre François Charlevoix, *The History of Paraguay*, London 1769, vol. 2, pp. 112–13.
6. Jaime Cortesâo (ed.), *Manuscritos da Coleção de Angelis*, vol. 6, *Antecedentes do Tratado de Madri, Jesuitas e Bandeirantes no Paraguai, 1703–1751*, Rio de Janeiro 1955.
7. Juan Patricio Fernández, *Relación Historial de las Missiones de los Indios, que llaman Chiquitos, que estan a cargo de los padres de la Companía de Jesús de la Provincia de Paraguay*, Madrid 1726.
8. Thierry Saignes, "L'indien, le portugais, et le jésuite: alliances et rivalités aux confins du Chaco au xvii siècle", *Cahiers des Amériques Latines*, Paris, no. 9–10, 1974, pp. 213–45.

15

SAN MIGUEL

The restored church of the Jesuits at San Miguel

The old mission village of San Miguel lies on a rough and stony track, half an hour's ride from both Santa Ana and San Rafael. Most people do not care to do it, says Enrique, our driver. The stones rip up their tyres. We give a lift to a couple of rural schoolteachers whom Enrique takes pity on. He does not charge them as he knows they are badly paid: only 200 bolivianos a month. Then we are stopped by a small group of impoverished Indians. They have no money at all and speak little Spanish, but give us some sugar cane in exchange for the ride. They come from the *comunidades*, the Indian settlements, that exist in the scrub outside the old mission villages. There is no market for anything they grow, and they plant just enough to keep themselves alive. Two hundred years ago they might have been singing in the choir at San Miguel. Today they just survive. They seem very poor.

The church and college at San Miguel stand on a small eminence overlooking the typical Jesuit square. The buildings are immense and overbearing, and they have been so freshly restored that they look almost new. The village seems deserted.

We go through a gate under the painted white belltower, and into a spacious courtyard with the church on one side. We try various doors in the college wall, but everything seems shut up. We surmise that perhaps the priest has headed off to the fiesta in San Ignacio. But there is a school playground next door full of fun, and we ask the teacher where we might obtain a key to the church.

He directs us to the front entrance of the Escuela Teresita, and here we find an Austrian nun, Sister Isabel. She hails from the Tirol, and says she has been in Chiquitos for twenty-five years.

She tells us to wait outside the church and then, with a considerable sense of theatre, she opens from the inside the great west doors. In these impoverished surroundings, we express the amazement that is expected of us. Indeed, even after seeing some of the other Jesuit churches, San Miguel is still an amazing sight. Restored between 1978 and 1984, it is an immense cathedral-size church with a long and lofty nave and a huge golden altarpiece reaching from floor to ceiling. The customary statue of Christ stands on the wall to the left, with a beautifully carved Virgin on the right, and – for the first time that we have seen – a wall of mica.

This phenomenon is referred to in all the travellers' tales and was obtained by the Jesuits from excavations not far away. D'Orbigny in the 1830s went to see where it came from. From one angle, the mica gives a grey and uninteresting impression. From another, it begins to sparkle and dance. By candlelight, it must look spectacular.

A baroque and angelic San Miguel, carved with great virtuosity, flies out of the centre of the altarpiece. There is also a magnificent golden pulpit with a great and ornate canopy hanging from the ceiling.

The mission here was established in 1721 by Father Felipe Suárez. He assembled a group of 295 families, 1473 people altogether, from the neighbouring nations of Bosorocos, Tabicas, and Pequicas. The Chiquitos were the single largest group. "The mission is in a good position," Father Sánchez Labrador noted in 1766, "high up and surrounded by woods." Its people, he wrote, have a reputation for valour.

After the Jesuits were expelled, the town went into decline, but even as late as 1804 there was considerable educational and industrial activity. According to an inventory of that time, there was a carpentry shop in San Miguel, with one carpenter and 18 apprentices; a painter with 25 apprentices; a blacksmith with 12; a school with 43 students, both boys and girls; and a music school with 2 teachers and 50 students.

We walk out of the church and look out over the great sloping square with its characteristic row of half a dozen ancient bottle trees. In a hut on the left is a small workshop where the ancient tradition of wood carving, once encouraged by the Jesuits, has been revived. Two or three young people are turning out sculptures made from cedarwood. Lying on the floor is an excellent Christ on a cross, a good copy that when painted could easily pass for old. They are also making carved doors for cupboards. But San Miguel is miles from any potential market, and visitors are few and far between. To show willing, we purchase a small wooden dish with a tapir carved on it.

Alcides d'Orbigny arrived here in July 1831, with forty Indians carrying his luggage, and fifteen cooks carrying their food. Like Father Sánchez Labrador, he was impressed by the site of the mission: a small hill surrounded by cultivated fields with woods beyond. He was enchanted by the great church, delighted with the flying statue of San Miguel, and made content by "some excellent Italian music that the natives played". He also bore witness to the planting of a new vineyard, something that had been forbidden in the colonial era.

The Spaniards had left Bolivia only six years earlier, and the town of San Miguel had briefly been the headquarters of Gil Toledo, the first Bolivian governor of Chiquitos. A strange visionary figure, and very much of his era, Toledo had decided that the new Bolivian state should adopt the sun worship of its Inca ancestors. This bizarre enthusiasm may well have been the reason why he had been made governor of a distant province where he could freely practise his cult.

Every morning at daybreak, d'Orbigny records, Governor Toledo required the

Indian population of San Miguel to bow down before the sun. They were obliged to do the same at sunset. Since the Chiquitos Indians were not remotely related to the Inca Indians of the Andes, and indeed had been brought up by the Jesuits to be extremely devout Catholics, they were outraged by the introduction of this new religion. Toledo was forced to withdraw from San Miguel to Santa Ana, and eventually, so unsuccessful was his period as governor, he was obliged to leave Chiquitos altogether.

Some fifteen years later in 1845, when another French traveller, Francis Castelnau, came here, the situation had deteriorated. Many of the mission houses were in ruins, and Castelnau thought that San Miguel was in a worse condition than Santa Ana or San Ignacio. In the 1880s, Gabriel René-Moreno reported that the village was extremely poor and abandoned.

Today, as elsewhere in Chiquitos, the situation in San Miguel remains precarious and despairing. Perhaps fifteen hundred people still live in the village, with another thousand in the surrounding *comunidades*. Rebuilding the church briefly gave people a little work, but that brief flurry of activity has not sparked off a wider revival. There is a sawmill outside the village, but good wood is now hard to find, and the markets are far away. The prosperity of past centuries is not even a memory.

The enrolment of the Chiquitos Indians from the Jesuit missions to fight the Spanish war against the Chiriguanos, 1727–35

The principal purpose of establishing Jesuit missions in Chiquitos had been to stabilize the Spanish frontier area against hostile Indians and marauding Portuguese. In the 1760s, the mission Indians of Santiago and Santo Corazón were used to wage war against the Guaycurus on the Paraguay. Forty years earlier, in the 1720s, they had been deployed against the Chiriguanos, in the area south of Santa Cruz.

The principal threat to the Spanish settlement at Santa Cruz, both in its first incarnation at San José de Chiquitos in the sixteenth century and later at its present site west of the Rio Grande, came from the Chiriguanos. The problem they posed to Spanish power was very similar to that caused by the Guaycurus.[1] A state of war existed between European and Indian for three hundred years, until the end of the nineteenth century.

Like the Guaycurus, the Chiriguanos had rebelled against the Spaniards from the very start. It was the Chiriguanos who had destroyed the ambitions of Andrés Manso in 1564. In 1568, a royal cédula, or decree, was issued declaring war on the Chiriguanos, and giving the job of pacifying them to the governor of Santa Cruz.[2] Then the viceroy in Lima took a hand. In 1574, Viceroy Toledo organized, and personally led, a military expedition against the Chiriguanos. He went with five hundred Spanish soldiers and one thousand friendly Indians. Advancing east of Cuevo, near Camiri, his troops were eventually forced to retreat, defeated as much by the climate as by the Chiriguanos. The Indians, for their part, cleverly withdrew when faced with a frontal attack.[3]

A decade later, in 1584–85, the Spaniards launched no less than four military expeditions against the Chiriguanos simultaneously – from Potosí, Tarija, Pojo, and Santa Cruz. This was a war of extermination, and although it did not end the Chiriguano threat, it succeeded in terrorizing the Indians for a generation. They were left militarily weak and politically divided, unable to take the initiative. Their subsequent sporadic attacks against Spanish centres – Santa Cruz, Tarija, and Tomina – became increasingly easy for the Spaniards to repel.

In the first twenty years of the seventeenth century, the Spaniards sought to reinforce their advantage through a number of fresh terror expeditions into Chiriguano lands, but for much of the rest of that century, there was a virtual truce. In practice, Spanish settlement in the Andean lowlands of eastern Bolivia was slow; the early trade routes across to the Paraguay had withered, and the Chiriguanos, in vast tracts of the Chaco, were left wholly undisturbed. Indeed some writers believe, contrary to the usual notion about the decline of the South American Indians, that the Chiriguano population notably expanded in this period.[4]

When the Jesuits first became active in Paraguay and what is now Bolivia, early in the seventeenth century, representatives of the Chiriguanos approached the Jesuits in Sucre to request assistance. Faced with continuing Spanish repression, they may have perceived the Jesuits to be the lesser evil. One Jesuit was told by the Chiriguanos that their people "would easily be brought to embrace the faith if some fathers that understood the Guaraní language were sent to them". Although Chiriguano is a separate language, its Guaraní origin makes it easy for a Guaraní-speaker to understand it.

A preliminary expedition by Jesuit fathers into Chiriguano territory suggested that the establishment of a mission might bear useful fruit. The Provincial of Paraguay, Father Diego Torres, wrote to his superiors in Rome to suggest that "it would be an advancement to Christianity if two fathers, well versed in the mission in Paraguay, were sent into Peru to labour for the salvation of these Chiriguanos".[5]

At that time, missionary personnel were in short supply. The Paraguay missionaries had their hands full in Guaíra and Itatín. It was not possible to do anything until the 1630s. Then Father Ignacio Martínez, one of the most experienced Jesuit missionaries of Paraguay, who had been involved in the mission efforts in Guaíra, Itatín, and Tape, was sent over from Asunción to Tarija. From there, he travelled with Father Pedro Alvárez east into the Chaco, to live among the Chiriguanos. It was uphill work, and "For some years," del Techo comments wryly, "they laboured much without any great success." These first Jesuit missionaries sent to the Chiriguanos were soon withdrawn.

For another hundred years, the Chiriguanos maintained themselves on the borders of the Chaco, fighting a rearguard action as Spanish settlers pressed eastward into the lower folds of the Andes. The Jesuits returned briefly in the 1690s, but they were no more successful than they had been earlier. Caught between the distrust of the Chiriguanos and the hostility of the Spanish landowners, they were once again obliged to withdraw.

Then in the 1720s, to the surprise and dismay of the Spaniards, the Chiriguanos embarked on a great rebellion throughout eastern Bolivia. It was a premeditated and organized effort to push the whites out of Indian territory. Throughout the previous half-century, Spanish landowners, traders and missionaries had gradually been encroaching to the east, from Sucre, Tarija, and Santa Cruz. The Chiriguano now felt strong enough to put a stop to this, and in Juan Bautista Aruma they had a powerful and charismatic leader.

In alliance with the Tobas and the Mocoví, Aruma was able to put seven thousand fighting men into the field. Some of them had firearms. At the end of September 1727, in the area of the Pilcomayo east of Tarija (to the south of Chiquitos), the Chiriguano army attacked mission settlements, Spanish farms and the mule-trains of foreign traders. Some two hundred Spaniards were killed, and many of their women and children were taken prisoner. The financial losses of the settlers were enormous.

The initial success of the Chiriguano attack was soon followed up by an assault on the Spanish town of Sauces (now Monteagudo) in March 1728, with an attacking force of more than nine thousand men. The church was burnt to the ground, and the Chiriguanos took eighty Spanish prisoners.

After six months, during which the Chiriguanos had regained much of what had once been their territory, the Spaniards were in a position to launch a counter-attack. As they had done nearly two hundred years earlier, they sent in military expeditions from three different centres: Tarija, Tomina, and Santa Cruz.

Such an ambitious military plan left them short of men. In Santa Cruz, Governor Francisco Antonio de Argomoza y Zeballos had only twelve hundred soldiers at his disposal. To bolster the Spanish force against the considerably more numerous Chiriguanos, the Real Audiencia in Sucre gave orders that the Jesuit missions in Chiquitos were to provide additional troops for the war.

In San José de Chiquitos, Father Bartolomé Mora assembled a small band of two hundred Chiquitano archers from the surrounding missions. With one other priest, he and his Indian troops joined the governor's army in Santa Cruz.

The campaign against the Chiriguanos lasted from July until October 1728. The Spanish soldiers, with Chiquitano assistance, laid waste to the Chiriguano villages around Camiri. Between two and three hundred Chiriguanos were killed and more than a thousand were taken prisoner.[6] The Spaniards had regained the initiative. But with both sides holding prisoners, there was an obvious need to organize an exchange. Peace talks were scheduled.

The Spaniards in South America often accused the Indian nations of deceit. If the charge was valid the Europeans had nothing to learn from the Indians. When sixty-two Chiriguano caciques, including Juan Bautista Aruma, arrived to discuss ways in which Spaniards and Indians might avoid such conflicts in the future, they were immediately detained. Taken under guard to Tarija, many were sent on to Potosí to work as slaves in the silver mines.[7]

The Chiquitos soldiers who had fought on the Spanish side returned to their Jesuit missions. They complained bitterly at the treatment they had received from the Spaniards during the campaign, and said that they would never participate in such operations again. Their principal complaint was that they were not paid, but they also objected to having to travel on foot. Only the Spaniards had horses to ride.

In spite of the treachery that had led to the capture of Aruma and the other caciques, the spirit of the Chiriguanos had not been crushed. The following year, the Spaniards were forced to make a further expedition. Once again, orders were given to the mission Indians from Chiquitos to turn up. They had become indispensable to the Spanish cause.

According to Father Bartolomé Mora, the Jesuit from San José who travelled with them, the Chiquitos made better soldiers than the Spaniards when faced with the Chiriguanos. They were particularly adept at avoiding arrows. Able to move their bodies extremely quickly, they were such good bowmen that they could use their own weapons to deflect the arrows of the enemy. The Spaniards, weighed down by heavy armour, were not nearly so agile.[8]

During the 1729 expedition, there was an ambush near Cuevo, in which forty-two Spanish soldiers and six Chiquitanos were wounded. The expedition was not as successful as that of the previous year and was eventually obliged to return to Santa Cruz suffering from lack of food. The Chiquitanos once again complained of the treatment they received.

For some years, there was a truce. But the Chiriguano threat remained. In 1735 Chiriguanos arrived at the gates of Santa Cruz. For several months, the city was under siege. Once again the Chiquitos from the Jesuit missions (340 of them this time) were summoned to the rescue of the Spanish settlers.

Over the next 150 years, until the end of the nineteenth century, the Chiriguanos maintained a steady rearguard action, with a major war nearly every twenty years as each new generation came to maturity. In January 1892, the final uprising took place, in exactly the same area south of Santa Cruz where Ernesto Che Guevara was to organize a guerrilla campaign in 1967. With the blessing of the bishop of Santa Cruz, Bolivian troops left the city and moved south towards Lagunillas and Monteagudo. Hundreds of Chiriguanos were killed, the wounded were shot, prisoners were executed, and the caciques were strung up in the central square. This, the final Chiriguano rebellion, was drowned in blood.

Father Ignacio Chomé and the attempt to reach the Pilcomayo from Chiquitos

In 1737, the Spanish governor of Santa Cruz made a great sweep through Chiquitos.

He noted the Jesuit enthusiasm for a fresh push into the Chaco. "They perceive that the main door to this huge province has been closed by the war that these frontier nations have been waging for nigh on seventy years."[9]

After the deaths of Father Arce and Father Blende in trying to discover a route between Chiquitos and the Guaraní missions in Paraguay, Father Patino had investigated the Pilcomayo river, further to the south across the Chaco, but found that it was not navigable to the Andes. Swamps and rapids made it impassable.[10]

But suppose a land route could be discovered, running north across the Chaco from the Pilcomayo to San José de Chiquitos? Apart from the hazards of nature, which were considerable, the only obstacle in the way was a large population of Zamuco Indians. Could these hostile Indians be pacified and converted?

Over the centuries, the Zamucos appear and reappear in this region in various guises. Sometimes today they are called the Ayoreo, sometimes the Chamococas or the Guarañocas. The Jesuits had first made contact with them in 1717, some twenty or thirty years after the establishment of the first mission towns in Chiquitos. Brother Alberto Romero had made contact with them during an exploring trip, in an area of the Chaco that lies to the south of the present-day Corumbá to Santa Cruz railway line.

The Zamucos, it seemed, were interested in a mission being established in their territory. At that time, they were in more or less permanent conflict with two other neighbouring nations, the Ugarones and the Tobas. A little friendly Jesuit assistance and support would certainly have been useful.[11]

Nothing came of these first contacts. In practice, even when the local Jesuits wanted to organize a new mission, they did not always have the wherewithal. A mission could not be conjured up out of a hat. Planning – particularly of food and personnel – was an essential prerequisite. The Zamuco request also coincided with the order forbidding the opening up of the northern Chiquitos–Paraguay route.

Two years later, however, in the dry season of 1719, Brother Romero returned to the place where he had last seen the Zamucos. They were no longer there, and he was told that they had withdrawn to a faraway lake well stocked with fish. On arrival at this lake, Romero and his companions were killed.

Four years later, the Jesuits made another attempt to approach the Zamucos. Better prepared this time, they were able to set up a rudimentary mission, calling it San Ignacio de Zamucos.

From the start, the mission was riven with internal dissensions. As elsewhere in Chiquitos, the Jesuits had tried to set up a mission that would include groups from a variety of different nations: Cucatares, Satienos and Ugarones, as well as Zamucos. The presence in the mission of representatives of these different warring nations seems to have been at the root of the dissension. The Zamucos and the Ugarones were traditional enemies. Both groups soon wanted to leave. As luck would have it, the place chosen seems to have been unsuitable. The crops produced were poor.

So, in 1726, the Jesuits were obliged to abandon the mission. This in itself was not unusual. Many of the Chiquitos missions began at one site and then moved to another. On this occasion, the Jesuit priests were able to take four hundred Zamucos from the abandoned mission and rehouse them in the mission at San José.

The following year, this group returned to the old site. With some help from the Chiquitanos of San José, they set about the task of building a proper mission station, with church and plaza and school. For a while it was reasonably successful. Maize was grown and stored, and salt was collected from the saltpans some 60 leagues away. The basis for a permanent mission had been created.

Some ten years later, in 1738, this embryonic settlement was joined by Father Ignacio Chomé, one of the most extraordinary Jesuit priests to devote his life to the affairs of Chiquitos. A brilliant linguist, born in Belgium, Father Chomé had originally hoped to go to the Jesuit missions in China. While waiting in Spain to go to the east, he spent four years studying theology at Avila. He also learnt Greek, Hebrew, English and Spanish, as well as Chinese.[12] Then, in the late 1720s, desperately short of priests for their ambitious expansion programme of missionary activity, the Jesuit fathers of Paraguay began campaigning in Europe for reinforcements to be sent to their province. Knowing of the language difficulties that the priests were facing there, the Jesuit General decided that young Chomé should be diverted to Paraguay. His language skills would come in useful. He took a boat to South America from Cadiz on 24 December 1729.[13]

After a year in Buenos Aires, the Jesuit Provincial (Jerome Herrán) was so impressed with Chome's linguistic abilities that he decided to send him to the recently established missions of Chiquitos. The missionaries were having greater difficulty with the languages there than they had had in Paraguay.

Travel to Chiquitos from Buenos Aires was not easy. Father Chomé set off for Córdoba, but even the trip as far as Santa Fé was difficult. "The Guaycuru barbarians", he wrote in a letter to his friends in Europe, "have made themselves the masters of the entire country." In one week, there had been alarums three nights running. Had it not been for the armed escort doing the rounds throughout the night, their caravan would have been attacked.

The expedition finally got to Santa Fé, but it was too dangerous to travel beyond the town. To get to Chiquitos that year was out of the question. Father Chomé was diverted to the Guaraní missions east of the Paraguay. That journey was not easy either.

To go from Santa Fé to Corrientes, on the Paraná river, involved crossing eight large rivers and twenty smaller ones. The countryside along the route was controlled by Charrua Indians, considered by the Spaniards to be little better than robbers and highwaymen. Undaunted, as befitted a young missionary, Father Chomé set off on horseback, accompanied by three Indians and three men to look after the baggage mules. In spite of all the alarums, he arrived safely at the Guaraní mission towns some two weeks later.

He was not impressed by what he found. The appeal to Europe for missionary recruits had been a desperate one. Here, there were few, and many were over sixty. "Most of those we have met are so ill and broken down by age that they have to be carried to church in a chair to carry out their priestly duties."

Father Chomé stayed for a while at the missions along the Paraná to lend a helping hand, first at San Ignacio, then at Corpus, and finally at Yapeyu. Learning the language of the Guaraní, he was much impressed by its beauty. "I would never have thought that, in a centre of barbarism like this, they could speak a language which, in my opinion, by its nobility and harmoniousness, cannot be rivalled by those that I have learnt in Europe; it has modulations and delicacies of such a sophisticated kind that it takes years to learn well."

In 1737, Father Chomé was at last transferred to Chiquitos. Based initially at San José de Chiquitos, he spent a year learning the language of the Zamucos. His transfer had a political purpose. Coming from the Guaraní missions, his task was to help in the search for a connecting route between these missions and those of Chiquitos – through the Chaco.

His initial task was to embark on explorations to the south, towards the Pilcomayo. On his first expedition, he set off with a large complement of friendly Indians, both Zamucos and Ugarones.[14] After travelling about 25 leagues into the bush, the Indians turned tail, first the Ugarones, then the Zamucos. Without them, and their survival skills, in the Chaco desert, he was unable to penetrate further, and was forced to return.

Indefatigable, Father Chomé tried again in 1739, with a hundred Indians from the mission, all travelling on foot. This time, on the journey south they were able to travel some 70 leagues into the desert. Then, seeing a lot of fires in the night, Father Chomé was informed by his Indian guides that they were near a large settlement of Tobas, a Chaco nation known for its hostility to the Zamucos. The Tobas were present in numbers far superior to his meagre troop. They also had horses.

Father Chomé feared that if the Tobas discovered his expeditionary force, they would follow it back to the mission at San Ignacio de Zamucos and destroy it. Once again he was obliged to withdraw. The route to the Pilcomayo was proving to be no easier than the route through to the Paraguay.

In 1740, Chomé tried again, with 70 Morotocos sent down from the mission at San Juan Bautista. Hardly had they set off before the cacique of the Ugarones died. Apparently he was poisoned by drinking the juice of the root that the Indians use in the Chaco when there is no water. There was consternation. If the life-giving plant had become a danger, there was no hope of survival in the desert. Once again, the explorers were forced to return to the San Ignacio mission.

Two months later, as Chomé had earlier feared, the Tobas were found to be reconnoitring close to the mission. The following year, they attacked. On this occasion they were beaten off, but hovering in the Chaco beyond the horizon, they remained an ever-present threat.

Father Chomé made two further efforts to get to the Pilcomayo, but with the pervasive, if hidden, presence of the Tobas, very few of his Zamuco Indians could be persuaded to go with him. He did not have sufficient support to travel far.

The danger of the situation was exemplified by the fate of his fellow missionary at San Ignacio, Father Augustín Castanares in 1744. Venturing beyond the mission perimeter, Father Castanares was caught by the Tobas and killed.

At this stage, Father Chomé seems to have decided that the San Ignacio mission could no longer be sustained in such hostile territory. The final straw came in 1745 when the Zamucos and the Ugarones within the mission once again started fighting among themselves, just as the Tobas outside were gearing up for another attack.[15]

Father Chomé took rapid action. He made preparations to leave for San Juan Bautista, burning the oil paintings in the church and burying the silver vessels used for mass. At that moment, a rescue expedition arrived led by Father Antonio Guasp, a youthful missionary fresh from the Jesuit college at Córdoba, with no knowledge of the local languages nor indeed of mission culture.

Father Guasp had travelled from San Juan with a group of Chiquitos Indians, unaware that they were historically hostile to the Ugarones at San Ignacio. His bodyguard insisted on returning to San Juan the following day. Father Chomé sent a desperate message with them, asking for an escort of two hundred armed Chiquitos to be dispatched to take him through territory now controlled by the Tobas.

The Father Superior in San Juan refused to send them, knowing that if he did so there would be a clash between the Chiquitos and the Ugarones. Benignly, since he knew that Father Chomé had buried all his silver vessels, he sent another priest, Father Esponella, to San Ignacio with some fresh ones. They would be able to say mass together with the necessary equipment. Father Esponella had only been in San Juan for a year and did not speak much Zamuco. Father Guasp spoke none.

With Father Esponella's arrival, there were now three missionaries at San Ignacio de Zamucos, all desperate to close the place down and move out. In October 1745, they achieved their ambition. Father Esponella took a group of Ugarones to San Juan, and Father Chomé and Father Guasp went with the remaining Zamucos to San José. In San Juan, the Ugarones found a friend in Father Contreras who had been the chief priest of San Ignacio de Zamucos before Father Chomé. Father Contreras went on subsequently to found San Ignacio de Chiquitos, taking many of the Ugarones with him.

As for Father Chomé, he settled further north in Concepción. There he began the plans for building the cathedral church. Before it was finished, however, he was transferred to San Javier, and there, among other works, he wrote a Zamuco grammar and dictionary. He was living in San Javier when the Jesuits were expelled from South America in 1767.

Notes

1. The parallel between the Guaycurus and the Chiriguanos is an intriguing one. Both had a slave race with whom they were tied by bonds of family and affection, and this race was the same in both cases. The Guaycurus had the Guanas, the Chiriguanos had the Chane. These were effectively the same (Arawak) people. To avoid confusion, Métraux calls this nation the Chane when they are found in the western Chaco, and Guana when they are found on the Paraguay.
2. Placido Molina, *Historia de la gobernación de Santa Cruz de la Sierra*, La Paz 1936.
3. Francisco Pifarré, *Los Guarani-Chiriguano*, vol. 2, *Historia de un pueblo*, Cipca, La Paz 1989.
4. Pifarré, pp. 93–4.
5. Nicholas del Techo, *Historia de Paraguay*, p. 93.
6. Pablo Pastells, *Historia de la Compañía de Jesús en la provincia del Paraguay*, Madrid vol. 6, pp. 578–93.
7. Pifarré, p. 236. Franciscan missionaries met Aruma thirty years later. He had not forgotten the treachery of the Spaniards of which he had been a victim.
8. Thierry Saignes, *Ava y Karai, ensayos sobre la frontera chiriguano (siglos XVI–XX)*, Hisbol, La Paz 1990.
9. Manuel Ballivián (ed.), *Documentos para la historia– geográfica de Bolivia*, La Paz 1906, vol. 1, pp. 119–20.
10. The possibilities of the Pilcomayo were endlessly tested in the second half of the nineteenth century when a stream of explorers tried to advance into the Chaco by the Pilcomayo route:
    1875 A Bolivian expedition led by Colonel Antonio Paradiz
    1882 A French expedition led by Jules Crévaux, who was killed by Tobas
    1883 A French/Bolivian expedition led by Arthur Thouar
    1884 An Argentine expedition led by Colonel Valentín Feilberg concludes definitively that the Pilcomayo is not navigable up to Bolivia
    1885 A Bolivian expedition led by Suárez Arana. It set off from Boca de Riachuelo on 1 June, after President Gregorio Pacheco had decreed that a way through to the Atlantic had to be found.
11. Pifarré, p. 180.
12. Ignacio Chomé was a Belgian by origin, born in Douai on 31 July 1696. His father was a pewtersmith. The details of his early life come from a life published in Douai in 1864 and available on crumbling paper in the British Museum library (L. Dechriste, *Vie du R.P. Ignace Chomé*, Douai 1864).
13. The journey took more than three months. He did not arrive in Montevideo until 9 April 1730. Like all Jesuits he was an indefatigable letter-writer and he tells his story himself. The journey was made with eight hundred men on three ships. One soldier died on the crossing, but as they had taken on a number of pregnant women from the Canary Islands, Chomé notes ruefully that they arrived with a larger complement than they had left with. Crossing the Plate estuary to Buenos Aires, he wrote that "the river Plate is more dangerous than the open sea".

    Thirteen of the new missionaries were sent off to the Guaraní missions, the rest went to Córdoba, but Chomé, in Buenos Aires, found twenty thousand blacks, men and women, lacking religious instruction and with no Spanish. Most had come as slaves from Angola and the Congo. Chomé quickly learnt their languages and within three months was able to take their confessions.
14. Molina, pp. 168–70.
15. The Ugarones had a sub-nation, the Sapios. Their cacique, Santiago Dione, had come to San Ignacio de Zamucos in 1732, but by 1745 he had decided that his group should leave. There was a battle first with the Ugarones then with the Zamucos. There was even a plan to kill Chomé, but Dione dropped dead first.

16

SAN IGNACIO DE VELASCO

The Jesuit church at San Ignacio

We arrive at San Ignacio after dark, on the eve of their annual three-day fiesta. Even in the dark, it seems to be a sizeable town and we stop at six hotels before we find one with an empty room. After a long ride in a lorry, we are exhausted and filthy, but too weary to do anything except walk out into the plaza and find a beer and some empanadas, the ubiquitous South American pasty. Hundreds of people are already assembling for the evening's dancing. I fall asleep in my clothes, still wearing two layers against the cold. And this is the tropics.

In the very early morning there is no electricity, but later it is turned on and we have a lukewarm shower. Very heaven. The cold, everyone says, is most unusual. The hotel is enchanting, a rooming house opening onto a central courtyard. Drying on the concrete floor are the skins of three jaguars, an entire family, father, mother, and child.

When we go out to get some breakfast in the square, we find a group of civic dignitaries assembled in the town hall on the side opposite the church. An official gives a stirring speech saying what wonderful things are being done by the provincial government, and how many roads are being built. He talks of the need to build new settlements on the frontier with Brazil. The dignitaries look well-fed and powerful. In the evening we find them eating at the Restaurant El Cacique.

The magnificent old church built by the Jesuits in the 1750s fell to pieces two hundred years later. No one had the money in the 1950s, or indeed the inclination, to restore it. So they simply pulled it down. Later, they set about rebuilding it, rather more modestly than before: it is considerably shorter than the original church. But they kept what they could, and the interior is dazzling.

It is dominated – as it always must have been – by a massive old eighteenth-century altarpiece the height of the nave. Dripping with gold, it contains eight lifesize carved wooden saints. Each stands in a rounded frame holding his charac-teristic symbols, flanked by sculpted pillars. They stare out as though fixed for ever in a sumptuous box at the opera. Above are four reclining barely clothed angels with prominent white wings. Recumbent in the pediment, they seem intensely secular.

Below is an ornate pulpit and canopy, a bishop's chair, and a wonderful lectern, painted gold, red and blue, with a carved wooden bible on top: Tu palabra me da vida: JHS.

On the right of the chancel is a statue of the Virgin rather larger than lifesize, with a sweet face and long black tresses. She wears a gorgeous embroidered dress, all in wood but tricked out in white and gold. She stands in a recess against a blue fluted sky, with a halo of twelve six-pointed golden stars. On either side are twin vine-girt columns, topped with fleur-de-lis capitals. Above them the cherubim face one another on each side of the pillars, twelve in all.

Above the altar, in the broken pediment, a great oval gilded sun shines out from a central circle, enclosing four red hearts on a golden background surrounding the legend MRA – Maria. The Virgin herself, with a left foot peeping out from beneath an embroidered hem, stands on the many-headed dragon of the Apocalypse. Three heads are visible, their twin bulls' horns sticking out at right angles to the rest of the sculpture.

On the left of the chancel is an altar of comparable splendour, with a statue of an exceptionally wounded Christ, bearded and with long dark hair, crowned with spikes on a coal-black cross. The gashes from the deep cuts on his torso, and on his arms and his legs, bleed profusely. The iron nails in his hands and feet look grimly convincing. Some latter-day prude has placed a white embroidered apron round his midriff, hiding the scanty sculpted towel beneath that performed the same function perfectly well.

In front of the high altar, to the left, on handles ready to be carried through the streets, stands the patron saint of the church and of the town, the man who founded the Society of Jesus, Saint Ignatius himself, carrying as ever a book.

Halfway down the nave, on either side, are two more altars, one with a saint holding a child by the hand, the other with a saint showing his stigmata and holding a crucifix before him with the figure of Christ upon it. Both are framed with two pillars on either side, one gold fluted with a red background, the other with green foliage. Nearer the entrance, on either side, are two confessionals, elaborately carved with pillars and much decoration on top, painted dark red picked out in green.

Of all the churches in Chiquitos, the contents of this one in San Ignacio, though placed in a modern frame, give the greatest sense of the splendour and magnificence that characterized the Jesuit achievement in this remote area two hundred and fifty years ago.

Founded in 1748, the mission town has never failed to draw the admiration of a trail of visitors. D'Orbigny in 1831 admired the sculptures, though he found the Jesuits' wooden organ no longer produced a note. Castelnau in 1845 remarked on the mica shining from the walls. In 1798, the mission had still boasted a great library of sixty-six books, including four Chiquitos dictionaries, a Chiquitos grammar, and a book of six sermons in Chiquitos. There were also grammars in Guaycuru, Lule and Tenecote.[1]

Today, San Ignacio is a pleasant provincial town, with a flourishing market, a grass airstrip, a hospital and a television station. Walking past the church, we stroll down to the lake. On the right, behind the church, is a sawmill and a collection of workshops; on the left a group of soldiers plays football by the water's edge. Three or four girls are drying themselves after bathing, and a couple of others are amusing themselves in a small blue wooden boat.

Here d'Orbigny watched an old Indian experiment with a barbasco plant. Thrown into the water, it had the effect of dynamite, stunning the fish and enabling them to be easily netted. The Jesuits arranged for these lakes to be created by damming small streams. They provided water and fish, and were also a line of defence.

Fiesta time at San Ignacio

Today is the first day of the fiesta of San Ignacio. The festival lasts for three days, and each day is celebrated in turn by a different class in the town. This day, with the smallest crowd, is the day for the Indians.

Outside the church, a crowd has gathered and an energetic priest darts in and out. He is wearing his civilian clothes, as though anxious not to be overly associated with the ceremonies taking place beyond the church door. For the fiesta is an openly pagan affair. Yet his church clearly plays an important role in what now goes on.

When Colonel Fawcett came here in 1913, on his way from Santa Cruz to Vila Bella de Mato Grosso, he suggested bad temperedly that carnival was a permanent feature of life in the town:

> Carnival had not yet finished in San Ignacio – in fact the New Year celebrations had never really ended. In most of the shabby houses we heard the tinkle of guitars to the drone of dismal voices, and the smell of cachaca was thick in the air. Here and there a drunk lay sprawled against a step or wall, or flat on the ground like the victim of a massacre. Not a dog barked or a bird cried; it was as though the place was subsiding into the coma that precedes death.[2]

The colonel was unusually lugubrious. "Neglect and decay brood over the whole region," he noted. "Isolation has killed it." He dismissed San Ignacio as "an impoverished village", with its "largely Indian population of 3000" living "a hand-to-mouth existence".

Today, San Ignacio is no longer an Indian town. The two or three hundred Indians who survive here are assembled in the plaza to celebrate what is left of their traditions. Whether the fiesta has been recreated by antiquarian priests, or whether it has survived intact from year to year is difficult to ascertain. But what we see is a faithful version of what Alcides d'Orbigny observed when he came here in 1831.

Four men in black hats appear first, carrying flags. These have a yellow cross diagonally slashed across a red background. It is the flag of Chiquitos. The black-hatted men give the flags away, and then pick up four staves with hearts on top. Long ribbons hang down from them. To the beat of two drums, the four men set off round the square, one of them carrying an embroidered standard. The crowd follows, the women walking separately from the men. There are perhaps two hundred participants and one hundred onlookers. In 1831, d'Orbigny observed six thousand people participating in the processions.

The church bells keep up a cacophony of sound, echoing the drums. Left behind is a string band, four men with violins of the kind they still make in Chiquitos, made here first in Jesuit times. They have sashes over their shoulders in the Bolivian national colours, red, yellow and green. Set into the sashes, back and front, are tiny mirrors.

After walking round the square two and a half times, all at a fair lick (coming down the centre at the end), the four masters of the dance return to the area outside the church and perform some further rituals with the flags. A pipe now plays to the continued beat of drum. They march up to the church door and the leading participants enter. Inside is the glint of gold, and three women can be observed engaged in the homely task of putting a clean white tablecloth on the altar. They seem part of an altogether separate ceremony.

Meanwhile a dozen men carrying staves stand by the entrance door, six on each side. A man inside begins a loud chant to a continuing drum outside. Then the cofradia, the Indian elders, all of them old men except for one old woman, embrace and shake hands.

The old woman is wearing a modified tipoi, the shift that women wore in the Jesuit towns in the eighteenth century. She has a sculpted bead necklace, large gold earrings, and wears her long black hair parted in the middle. Incongruously she has a blue cardigan. In the shade it is quite cold. She gives an Indian greeting: a handshake, a touch with the right hand to the other person's left shoulder, and then another handshake. She says the people round here speak a dialect, and when pressed further as to its name, she says "Chiquitano".

It seems, in all, a relaxed, informal occasion. The Chiquitos flags are laid out on a table at the church door and people come up to kiss them. Everyone goes off for a parade around the town.

We repair to the local Hotel Palace and, it being about two o'clock in the afternoon, enquire about the possibility of lunch. Eight middle-class ladies, sitting by the window on the square, jump up as one and say "Si!" with such enthusiasm that they all burst out laughing. They appear to be the upper end of the San Ignacio Women's Institute and they (or perhaps their maids) have been cooking wonderful food for the fiesta sufficient for an army: roast pork, chicken with olives, salads and chuño, the frozen black potato from the altiplano. So far, they have had few takers and we have clearly come to their rescue. We have a splendid lunch, a couple of beers, and then return to the fiesta, the parade still marching round the outskirts of town.

Later in the afternoon the maypole was brought out, first carried horizontally by two men with two small babies clinging on at either end. Then it was placed upright into a hole in the ground, with four small boys on either side, each holding a coloured ribbon attached to the top. The boys themselves were dressed in much glitter, with knitted bonnets on their heads. Here too a small mirror was attached. They wound their ribbons round the pole with some intricate footwork and then unwound them again. We were watching exactly the same routine observed and written about by d'Orbigny, on exactly the same spot, on 30th July 1831.

D'Orbigny had travelled here on the eve of the fiesta from Santa Ana, some 12 leagues away. "The track was filled with so many Indian men and women on their way to the fiesta that it seemed like a procession." His party camped outside San Ignacio that night, a great camping site having been prepared for them by the administrator in charge of the town. "An army of cooks" had been sent to prepare the food, and the Frenchman was much struck by the forest of posts that had been driven into the ground to allow the Indians to hang their hammocks. By this time there were some five hundred Indians travelling with them, all on the way to the next morning's fiesta.

> It was an extraordinary scene, everyone preparing for bed in complete silence. The campfires, around which six or seven hammocks were hung together, gave a powerful light, illuminating the entire site. Swinging ghostly white in the blackness of the night, the hammocks gave an unusual and impressive aspect to the picture. I gazed at it for a long time before finally stretching out in the open air on my bed of bamboo canes.[3]

The following morning, the straggling procession continued to San Ignacio. Since d'Orbigny was travelling with the governor of Chiquitos, they entered the town under triumphal arches and were greeted with much music and dancing. D'Orbigny calculated that six thousand people took part in the celebrations, some wearing cloth that looked more than a century old.

In the evening, d'Orbigny witnessed a dance that he had not seen before:

> Three Indians, comically dressed, began clowning. One of them put a large round wooden pole, three metres high, into a hole. A small boy, holding on to sixteen coloured ribbons attached to the top of the pole, handed them out to his companions. These formed a delightful chain, creating a beautiful plait with the ribbons by winding them around the pole until they were all used up. They then did the same thing in the opposite direction. Finally, the plaited ribbons were unwound, floating free as they had done at the start.
>
> They were followed by eight Indian men, in disguise and wearing masks. Their antics provoked considerable amusement among the onlookers.

We saw the same show, later in the day, 160 years later. At sunset, soon after five-thirty, six masked men dressed as conquistadores emerged from the cloister next to the church. They wore red and blue and yellow, and appeared to be a derivation of what d'Orbigny had seen.

Their masks gave them an extremely doleful appearance, and they danced around, at a stately pace, looking extremely silly. This was the world turned upside down, with the Indians making fun of the conquistadores, and the crowd laughed appropriately. Eventually, when the pace had grown too slow, a black demon appeared, chasing the Europeans away. The Indian magic triumphs over the conquerors.

But this was only a fiesta. The reality of the situation was revealed when I saw a jeep drive up behind the crowd and park itself in the road. Two athletic young men wearing jungle shorts leapt out, climbing up onto the back to get a better view. They came with no sinister intent. They were off duty. But on the door of the jeep, in stencilled lettering, a message proclaimed that it belonged to the "INFANTRY BATTALION WARNES". I had noticed the name on the barracks building two blocks away. Its frontage on the street is painted entirely in camouflage green and brown, as though someone had got some paint left over, and the entrance is guarded by two camouflaged turrets. Inside a message to the troops on the wall reads:

GUIDE THE RESPONSIBLE,
CORRECT THE IRRESPONSIBLE,
CAPTURE THE INCORRIGIBLE.

Colonel Warnes was the officer in the independence army who killed one thousand captured Indians south of here, near the mission of San Rafael, in 1815. His shadow still hovers over the province of Chiquitos.

Colonel Ignacio Warnes, the independence struggle and the massacre at Santa Bárbara in 1815

During the guerrilla wars for independence, which affected much of Bolivia off and on between 1810 and 1825, the mission towns of Chiquitos were unable to stand aloof from the struggle. In the mission of San Rafael, prolonged occupation by the military caused much suffering. Armies were garrisoned in the town for extended periods, "sowing disorder", as d'Orbigny put it.

Outside the town, a terrible battle occurred at Santa Bárbara. D'Orbigny recounts how, after spending a few days at the mission town in 1831, his expedition had set off through a thick forest:

I came out of it three leagues further on and emerged into the valley of Santa Bárbara. As we travelled through the valley, the governor showed me the place where, on 7

October 1815, one of the bloodiest battles of the wars of independence had been fought.[4]

"The governor", d'Orbigny's companion on his travels through Chiquitos, was the governor of the province, Marcelino de la Peña. Bolivia in 1831 had been independent for just six years, and many of its officials were men who had been on the Spanish side during the long civil war that had preceded the end of Spanish rule. De la Peña was one of these. Born in Cuzco, he had served for some time in the Spanish army, ending up as a lieutenant-colonel. He had fought in the campaigns across Chiquitos in 1814 and 1815, and had participated in the battle at Santa Bárbara in which the Spanish forces were defeated. He and a few survivors had retreated across the frontier to Brazil, and he had remained there for the next ten years.

In 1825, however, with Bolivia independent, he was able to return. He was employed first as the chief of police in Santa Cruz, and then as the governor of the province of Mojos. When d'Orbigny arrived in the area, he had been appointed governor of Chiquitos. His trip with d'Orbigny was his first as governor, but he knew the province well and was able to tell the French traveller what had happened there during the independence wars.

As in other parts of South America, and especially the Caribbean, the nineteenth-century independence struggle against Spain in the east of Bolivia began as a revolt by black slaves. On 15 August 1809, an incipient rebellion in Santa Cruz was uncovered by the Spanish authorities and crushed. Eleven blacks were sent for trial to Charcas (Sucre), accused of planning to kill the bishop and other prominent figures in the town.[5]

The following year, after a successful revolt against Spain in Buenos Aires on 25 May, Argentine soldiers came north to Santa Cruz to give a helping hand to the anti-Spanish "patriot" forces there. Independence was declared on 24 September.

The declaration in Santa Cruz was a trifle premature. For the next five years, armies loyal to the Spanish Crown and the liberation forces seeking independence from Spain – with their attendant Indian troops – marched backwards and forwards across eastern Bolivia. Neither side was able to gain a permanent advantage.

At the end of 1810, the anti-Spanish faction in Santa Cruz appointed one of their number, Juan Manuel Lemoine, to be the new governor of Chiquitos. But the following year his Spanish predecessor, Colonel José Miguel Becerra, marched back into Chiquitos from Brazil where he had taken refuge. Colonel Becerra knew the territory well. He had been involved in a two-year campaign against the Chiriguanos between 1806 and 1808. Now, with the aid of Portuguese troops led by Commander Albuquerque, he recaptured Santa Cruz from the "patriots". He even got as far as Cochabamba, recovering it for the Spanish crown.

Two years later, in March 1813, the patriot forces had recovered the initiative. Colonel Becerra was forced to retreat again over the Brazilian frontier. General

Belgrano, the Argentine commander in charge of the patriot forces in Potosí, sent one of his colonels, Ignacio Warnes, to be the new governor of Santa Cruz.

Colonel Warnes was to play an important role in Chiquitos. A rough soldier, he was an Argentine who had taken part in the defence of Buenos Aires in 1807 and had subsequently fought with General Belgrano in the battles against the Spanish in Salta and Tucumán. As governor, it is claimed that "he ruled despotically and arbitrarily, losing the goodwill of the inhabitants both for himself and for his cause".[6]

By the end of 1813, Belgrano himself had been defeated, Spain was once again in the ascendant. A Spanish colonel, Manuel Joaquín Blanco, marched on Santa Cruz and captured it in May 1814.

Colonel Warnes managed to escape, and joined a patriot troop outside the town. Since this troop controlled the lifeline from Santa Cruz to the other Spanish forces in the mountains, Colonel Blanco was obliged to leave the city to fight it. At a celebrated battle at Florída, south of Santa Cruz, on 25 May 1814, the Spanish forces were routed. Colonel Blanco himself was killed, as were some 270 of his Spanish soldiers.

After the battle, Colonel Warnes marched on Santa Cruz. There he found Colonel Blanco's second-in-command, Colonel Francisco Udaeta, entrenched with a garrison of three hundred men. Warnes drove him out of the town, across the Rio Grande and into Chiquitos.

There the Spanish forces managed to reorganize themselves, controlling the province of Chiquitos but not the town of Santa Cruz. They assembled a great army of Chiquitos troops from the old mission towns, led by the Spanish governor, Altolaguirre, with Marcelino de la Peña as his second-in-command. Colonel Udaeta was also there.

A year later, in October 1815, the patriot forces led by Colonel Warnes marched out from Santa Cruz to do battle with Altolaguirre's Spanish army. They clashed at Santa Bárbara in the neighbourhood of San Rafael.

Colonel Warnes won, the Spanish lost. Altolaguirre was killed. De la Peña and Udaeta managed to escape across the frontier to Brazil. Some three hundred Spanish soldiers were left dead on the field. Hundreds of Indians lay wounded.

D'Orbigny records what happened, as he had been told by de la Peña, a participant observer in these events:

> The Spanish troops, commanded by Altolaguirre (whose second-in-command was Marcelino de la Peña), had formed an ambush behind a trench in the bottom of the valley. They had three thousand Chiquitos Indians guarding their flank. But they were then attacked from the side by Warnes, the general commanding the independence troops. The patriot army, consisting of five hundred horse and fifteen hundred footsoldiers, fell on the Indians with fiercesome war cries. These fled in some disorder, creating such

havoc among the Spanish troops that the latter were all killed, with the exception of thirty men – among them four officers – who managed to escape.

It was then that the massacre organized by Colonel Warnes occurred:

> The butchery was horrific. Dead and wounded covered the plain. Tired of the killing, Warnes thought that the quickest way of getting rid of the wounded would be to set fire to the scrub and the fields of hay, thereby burning up the unfortunate survivors still able to breathe.

Colonel Warnes is one of the heroes of independent Bolivia, honoured with the name of a town outside Santa Cruz, and the name of a regiment that keeps the peace to this day in the mission towns.

D'Orbigny noted dryly that "this kind of performance by the political leaders took place rather too frequently, though the fanaticism of their partisan spirit goes some way to explain such inhumanity. On this single occasion, more than a thousand Indians perished."

Marcelino de la Peña managed to escape from the butchery and found sanctuary in the safety of the forest. He then set off for Santa Ana, the last mission town before the Brazilian frontier. On the road, he met a fourteen-year-old Indian girl who had been what d'Orbigny optimistically describes as his protégée. She warned him that Santa Ana was now occupied by patriot troops, and offered to guide him to the frontier by a roundabout route. He accepted her offer gladly. When they reached the border, she would have accompanied him further, but he would not allow her to do so. She gave him her silver cross so that he might survive in exile.

Such a gesture was, d'Orbigny noted sententiously, "a dramatic contrast to the atrocious conduct of Warnes".

These were not gentle times. The following year, 1816, Colonel Warnes received his deserts. The colonel in charge of the royalist troops in Cochabamba, Francisco Javier de Aguilera, marched on Santa Cruz and fought a battle outside the town. Colonel Warnes was defeated and killed. He had no monopoly on atrocities. General Aguilera put Warnes's head on a pikestaff, and ordered nine hundred patriots in Santa Cruz to be shot.

Aguilera kept Santa Cruz in royalist hands for nearly another decade. Independence was not declared there until 14 February 1825.

Notes

1. Gabriel René-Moreno, *Biblioteca Boliviana, Catálogo del archivo de Mojos y Chiquitos*, Santiago 1888, p. 599.
2. Percy Harrison Fawcett, *Exploration Fawcett*, Hutchinson, London 1953, p. 194. On this expedition, Colonel Fawcett bumped into the Swedish explorer Baron Nordenskjold at a German rubber barraca on the Guaporé river. Nordenskjold "with his plucky wife was engaged in investigating the more

accessible Indian tribes of the Guaporé. It says a lot for this attractive young Swedish lady that she was ready to tramp in the forests with her husband and wade swamps for days together in order to meet some distant tribe." Fawcett, of course, was investigating the more inaccessible tribes.

3. Alcides d'Orbigny, *Voyage dans l'Amérique méridionale, 1826–1833*, Paris 1835–1847.

4. Ibid.

5. Enrique de Gandia, *Historia de Santa Cruz de la Sierra, una nueva república en Sud America*, Buenos Aires 1935, p. 161.

6. José Evaristo Uriburu, *Historia del General Arenales 1770–1831*, London 1924.

7. In Chiquitos there was a bizarre state of affairs in 1825.

14 February	Independence is declared in Santa Cruz.
15 April	The (Portuguese) provisional governor of Mato Grosso informs Emperor Dom Pedro that he has annexed Chiquitos to Brazil.
6 August	Bolivia declares its independence in Sucre, without representatives from Chiquitos.
13 August	Portuguese emperor tells the governor of Mato Grosso to abandon his claim to Chiquitos. The new republic of Bolivia annexes Chiquitos.

17

SAN JAVIER

By bus from San Ignacio to Concepción and San Javier

The journey from San Ignacio to Concepción takes six hours in a crowded bus. This is the largest distance between any of the dozen Jesuit missions in this area, except for Santo Corazón, out on a limb on the Brazilian border. The country round here is more open than the territory further east or south, and presumably there was no mission here because the area was "safe" – from the Portuguese or the Chiriguanos – though it may also have been too swampy.

Much of the forest has been cleared, and there are some large haciendas, a lot of cattle and some quite pretty villages: groups of huts with a green sloping down to the water, with fruit trees, hens, pigs and horses, each house with its little patch of land, and sometimes a rural school.

There is an atmosphere of arcadia, but it does not bear much examination. There is no electricity or running water, and the huts are made of adobe and palm thatch. In the rainy season the idyll would soon be over. Theoretically on a main road from Santa Cruz to Brazil, the track is often narrow and boggy. Much of the way we were skirting or crossing swampland. Near Concepción, where the scrub gives way to rather noble palm trees, we found tractors and graders at work, building a new dirt road on this uncertain soil courtesy of a German aid programme. It will be some time before it reaches San Ignacio.

For the moment, the existing sandy track has to suffice. We met several broken-down vehicles, their drivers trying to find somewhere in the shade to keep cool in the middle of the day. Our bus, too, found the going hard, slowing down to a crawl in order to avoid ploughing into a mound of loose sand. At one stage we halted in a narrow stretch to allow a thousand head of cattle to go by, heading, as we had seen them before, for illegal sale in Brazil. They had half a dozen cowboys with them, one armed with a winding horn almost as large as a tuba.

At one stage we passed some very tiny straw dwellings huts, with their roofs almost touching the ground. Wood-felling was going on and the occupants appeared to be woodcutters. Could these have been the original *chiquitos* huts, the tiny dwellings that gave their name to the Chiquitos nation?

We left San Ignacio at nine in the morning. Indeed, we were quite lucky to get away. In the aftermath of the fiesta, many people were seeking to travel. An extra bus had been put on, one at seven, one at eight, and ours at nine.

We arrived at Concepción at three o'clock on a hot afternoon, stopping outside a bar on the main square. We found lodgings in the Sede Ganadero, a block away. This is the kind of clean and simple place that the local landowners have clubbed together to build: half a dozen rooms round a courtyard looked after by a family. Here they can stay when caught in town, through rain or lack of a truck or a plane. Government officials stay here too on their peregrinations around the country. Visiting military, of course, stay in the local barracks, as present here as everywhere else we have visited.

The Jesuit mission at Concepción is one of the earlier missions in Chiquitos, founded by Father Lucas Caballero in 1709. But its church is now the most restored of all the mission churches, and the most vulgar. Its brashness is still shocking more than a decade after the restoration was completed. The West Germans, in Bolivia as in Paraguay, had faint qualms about giving aid money to military dictators, and poured their largesse into the restoration of the legacy of the Jesuits.

Garish as it seems, the restored church is a telling reminder of the wealth and ostentation of these buildings in the eighteenth century, and by its magnificence provides yet another example of the dramatic decline which the region has suffered in the subsequent two hundred years.

We came late in the afternoon, entering through the cloister and an entrance on the side. The interior drips with gold leaf, administered with a trowel. Here as elsewhere the roof is held up by sixteen gigantic carved wooden pillars, each hewn from a single tree. The main altar background consists of six alcoves with barley-sugar columns on either side, gold on orange. The top three spaces contain paintings of no merit, the bottom three display poorly repainted statues, dressed in modern material and arranged so that it is impossible to see the state of the sculpture underneath.

The actual altar cupboard has a more intricate design and is both more intimate and more convincing. But elsewhere the gold leaf has been laid in such a voluptuous manner as to leave one feeling almost revolted by the opulence.

As in the other Jesuit mission churches of the area, there is a Virgin at the head of the right hand nave, encased in double gold pillars, and a Christ on the right, here accompanied by two women carved so crudely that they appear to be modern. Along either side of the nave stands an eighteenth-century confessional, glittering with the same gold and orange that illuminates the high altar.

In the evening, there was a service in the church, and it suddenly became a more friendly place, filled with villagers. Two small children howled miserably and had to be taken out by their elder sisters.

The next morning, we took breakfast at the Sede Ganadero, in the airy front room between the street and the courtyard. Two government officials were sitting at the table drinking coffee and they greeted us as fellow members of a class alliance. They work for the Fondo Social de Emergencia and wander round the Bolivian oriente in a jeep, checking on development projects. A very nice job. The Fondo Social, which depends directly on the president's office, gets money from the World Bank and other international agencies.

Designed to alleviate the severe poverty visited on the country by the policies of the World Bank's alter ego, the International Monetary Fund, the Fondo Social has little more than a cosmetic impact. Every project – here a small school, there a new bridge – is clearly labelled "President of the Republic". He may get a little local credit, and his party may perhaps win the next elections.

The military dictators of the past used to do exactly the same, particularly in this area – once (in the seventeenth century) the Military Government of Chiquitos – and they were often rewarded with a small bronze bust in the main square. There is one here in Concepción of General Hugo Banzer Suárez, one of the bloodiest dictators in his time but now a respected father of the nation.

The two officials were young and energetic, doing their bit. The chief priority here has been the construction of silos, in the comunidades far from the main track, and feeder roads to get to them. They emphasized the extraordinary poverty of Chiquitos, saying that it was as bad as the altiplano and much worse than in the nineteenth century. They praised the work that the Franciscans are doing in the area of Ascención de Guarayos, on the way from Chiquitos to Mojos.

The religion industry is still powerful in this part of the world. Given the existence of sorcerers and shamans before the arrival of the Spaniards, it clearly has a long pedigree. Here in Concepción, in addition to the great rebuilt Jesuit mission church , there are two evangelical churches, one a bible school run by North Americans just across the street from the Sede Ganadero, the other a Seventh Day Adventist tin tabernacle.

Uncertain how we are to get transport on to San Javier, we pack up and wander down to the main square, parking ourselves in the Club Social to wait for a possible bus. Outside, the adolescents of the town fiddle with the amplifiers of a tape recorder all morning. According to the cook at the Club Social, who makes us some lunch of soup and a milanesa, the old people of Concepción still speak the Chiquitos language, but not the young ones. There is another language spoken in the town, she says, but she does not know its name. She herself works as a cook in the club, helped by her two teenage daughters. She has seven children altogether and one of her sons is doing his military service at the camp at San Ignacio. Her husband and the other boys work on their piece of land in the country far away. She worked for a year as a maid in Santa Cruz.

A bus does come eventually, yesterday's scheduled bus from San Ignacio. We climb on, and it does a ceremonial tour around the town touting for passengers. It finally stops at a café near the bypass where we wait for another half-hour for the famished passengers to have lunch. At three o'clock in the afternoon, we set off for San Javier.

The road to the west goes through steep hills, and the country here is more jungly than anything we have seen before. Where the land is flat, it has been cleared and turned into fertile meadows interspersed with palm trees. It is a short run to San Javier and we arrive about four-thirty. The bus unloads in the central square.

San Javier was the first mission to be established in Chiquitos, in 1692. Surrounded by hills and woods, it occupies an enchanting site. The Jesuits found gold nearby, but were never able to exploit it commercially.

We are led off by a youth to a singularly unprepossessing lodging house two blocks away, with no water and no electric light, but we accept the room for fear of finding something worse. Subsequently, of course, we find a delightful place meant for upmarket travellers, but by then we cannot be bothered to move.

Unusually for a Jesuit mission town, there is not much water around here. A huge new concrete circular water tank has been built on top of a tall tower a block away from the square, a symbolic triumph, the twentieth-century equivalent of the mission church. Unlike God's love, the water is not inexhaustible. It is turned off at five every afternoon, and not turned on again until eight the next morning.

We are quickly drawn back to the plaza by the sound of drums beating. Moving towards the great Jesuit church we find six girl drummers, six girl cymbalists, and a majorette with a swagger stick. They are marching very very slowly. Behind them come about three hundred children, class by class, marching up the hill along a road between the houses. They drill around the square and then pause to sing the national anthem, ''Morir Antes Esclavos Vivir'' (Better to die than to live as slaves), and other patriotic songs.

Here the military dictator remembered in the square is Germán Busch, the hero of the Chaco Wars of the 1930s, and the forerunner of subsequent progressive nationalist regimes. The children are rehearsing for Bolivia's national day, 6 August, when there will be a big parade. This group is only the afternoon school. The morning school is of the same size. Six hundred children in a poverty-stricken village.

Then, with the light fading, we go to look at the old Jesuit church and the mission compound, where Father Ignacio Chomé once worked on his Zamuco grammar. In the process of being restored, but without the grotesque sums of money that have been made available from foreign sources to rebuild the churches at Concepción, San Rafael and San Miguel, the old Jesuit complex at San Javier is the most agreeable of them all.

The church and its associated buildings – tower and cloisters – take up the entire west side of the square. Four great wooden pillars hold up the roof, and another eight run along in front of the cloister wall. Eight of the old bells hang in front of the entrance porch, and above it is the familiar legend in Latin: DOMUS DEI PORTA COELI. (In Concepción they have rendered it in Spanish.)

Inside, a dozen workmen are draped about the scaffolding, two of them repainting the elaborate patterns on the roof. The scale is less gargantuan than in the other churches, and there is an intimate feel to it. Two original recessed confessionals remain, similar to those at San Miguel, and there is a little side chapel off the left aisle of a kind that we have not seen before. Few statues are on show – a dusty Christ near the door and a couple stacked together in the sacristy – but the rest may have been put away. The chief joy is the cloister on the north side of the church, a charming sanctuary enclosing the old tower, with a palm tree growing in its garden.

We had supper in a pleasant courtyard off the square, next to a college that runs university courses in cattle genetics. We ate chicken and tallarines with rice, consuming three bottles of Paceña beer to prepare us for the ordeal of our lodgings. We watched a snatch of television which showed a sycophantic journalist praising President Jaime Paz Zamora and General Banzer for having jointly ruled the country so well for a year, and I could not help recalling that Banzer, a great survivor, had actually run the country for nearly twenty years. We also saw a brief glimpse of film that seemed to suggest that Iraq had invaded Kuwait or something like that. The Middle East seems a long way away from this lovely place.

The arrest of the Jesuits in Chiquitos in 1767, and the expulsion of the Society of Jesus from South America

Outside the mission town of San Javier, on the night of 31 August 1767, a troop of Spanish soldiers commanded by Lieutenant-Colonel Diego Antonio Martínez de la Torre had made an overnight bivouac. Before dawn, the cavalry troop of eighty men moved silently into the great central square and surrounded the Jesuit college. At the sound of the morning bell ringing in the belfry in the patio, the priests emerged from their sleeping quarters and made their way into the church for prayer. The colonel was waiting for them.

Captain of the Mallorca infantry regiment stationed in Santa Cruz de la Sierra, Colonel Martínez had spent much of previous years keeping an eye on Portuguese troop movements along the frontiers of Chiquitos. It was a task in which the Santa Cruz settlers had been involved for close on two centuries. During the war scare of 1766, the colonel had passed through San Javier on his way to San Rafael and Santa Ana. Those were the two missions closest to the frontier. On that occasion, the priests at San Javier had been extremely welcoming and helpful to his officers and his men. Now Colonel Martínez had orders to arrest them. They were to be detained, sent into exile and forbidden to return. The penalty for disobedience was death.

The expulsion of the Jesuits from San Javier, from Chiquitos, from Paraguay and from Latin America was not exactly unexpected. It had its roots both in Europe and in South America.

In the 1750s, the Jesuits of Paraguay had defended the rights of their mission Indians to the east of the Uruguay river. The territories of seven well-established missions were, under the terms of the Treaty of Madrid of 1750, to be transferred to Portuguese jurisdiction.[1] Having fought against the Portuguese for a hundred and fifty years, the Indians of the Guaraní missions – heirs to the struggles of Ruiz de Montoya – could hardly agree to see their ancestral settlements handed over to their enemies as the result of a European fiat. Instinctively, they rebelled.

Like nearly all such rebellions, the revolt of the seven Indian towns was snuffed out by the colonial powers, acting on this occasion in concert. It was tough for the Indians, and also for the Jesuits, their erstwhile protectors. Whether or not some Jesuits were involved in supporting the rebellion, their defence of the Indians' rights caused problems for the Society of Jesus in Europe, at a time when it was already under serious attack.[2]

Terminal trouble for the Jesuits began in 1758 in Portugal. They were accused of involvement in a conspiracy to kill the king. In 1759, all Jesuits were expelled from Portugal and from all Portuguese territories, including, of course, Brazil. Three years later, the anti-Jesuit contagion had reached France. In 1762, all Jesuits were expelled from France.

Then, in March 1766, there were riots in the streets of Madrid. It was instantly alleged that the Jesuits were involved. A year later, in April 1767, all Jesuits in Spain were rounded up. In June, the order of expulsion arrived in Mexico; in August, it reached Paraguay and Peru – and Chiquitos.

Tales of conspiracies and riots were merely the excuse. The Society of Jesus was the first victim of the new mood in Europe, the rising tide of free-thinking and free-masonry that characterized the mid-eighteenth century and was eventually to find political expression in the French events of 1789. The faith that had sustained millions for so long, and had penetrated into the remoter corners of the world, was to be cut off at its taproot. As so often in imperial history, events in a faraway province were essentially a by-product of more dramatic changes in Europe, over which the local people had little inkling and no control. Few Europeans were interested in the fate of the Jesuit missions of South America.

In San Javier de Chiquitos on that night in August 1767, there were, unusually, four resident Jesuit priests. The superior of their order in Chiquitos, Father José Rodríguez was also staying in the college. It seems fairly clear that they knew what was going to happen. The previous day, hearing news that Colonel Martínez had camped outside the town, they had sent messengers to invite him and his officers to lodge in the college. The colonel refused the offer. He said that he was on active duty and should remain with his troops.

The following morning, establishing himself in a college room, he summoned the priests to give them the news. Entering with a candle, the Father Procurator of the mission, Antonio Priego, asked the question to which he already knew the answer:

"Is this about the expulsion of the Jesuits from the territories of the king? We know about it, and are ready to obey."[3]

That was the response that the colonel wished to hear. The chief fear of the Spanish authorities was the prospect that the expulsion of the Jesuits might lead to an Indian uprising. The trouble ten years earlier, in southern Paraguay, when the resiting of the Spanish–Portuguese border had led to just such a rebellion – in which the local Jesuits had played an ambiguous role – was still fresh in their minds.

The authorities were right to be wary. Ten years later, the entire chain of the Andes was to explode. The revolutionary uprising of Tupac Amaru, from 1780 to 1781, was a struggle for freedom by the indigenous population on a scale without precedent in the history of the Conquest. It reached from the mountains into the plains, and into every town. In November 1780 it erupted in Cuzco, Arequipa, Huamanga and Puno. By March 1781 it had reached La Paz, Oruro, Cochabamba and Chuquisaca. The Europeans drowned the rebellion in blood, repression on such a scale that it delegitimized whatever legitimacy the Spaniards might have claimed for themselves after more than two centuries of occupation.[4]

But this still lay more than ten years in the future. In San Javier de Chiquitos, in 1767, all was peaceful. The priests were kept under house arrest in their college, and went meekly about their daily tasks. But in the eastern mission of Santiago, there was a great tumult when one of Martínez's officers arrived to arrest the priests. He was forced to move quickly on to Santo Corazón. In both those missions, and in San Juan Bautista, it needed the skill and diplomacy of the Jesuits themselves to calm the anger of their Indian flock.

The orders from Spain were to bring out the priests immediately, but Colonel Martínez allowed them to stay for six months, using the seasonal floods as an excuse. They could not be removed and sent into exile until the waters had subsided.

Taking advantage of the shaky resolve of the friendly colonel, the Jesuit superior in San Javier suggested that perhaps the more ancient priests might be allowed to stay. Many of them were old and frail, and had devoted their lives to the peoples of Chiquitos. They had no other home.

Colonel Martínez was initially inclined to grant the request. Half the Chiquitos missionaries were over sixty. Were they really a threat to the Spanish crown? Would they not be more useful looking after the Indians? It was an attractive solution, but it was not to be. Fresh orders came swiftly from Santa Cruz, forbidding any such thing.

By the end of October, Colonel Martínez's men had managed to round up thirteen priests from the more westerly mission towns. At the beginning of November, they were sent off to Santa Cruz, escorted by an officer and a handful of soldiers. Two months later, at the end of December, a further six priests were packed off, together with the main body of the troops that had come to Chiquitos in August. Not until

April 1768, when the Pantanal floods had gone down, were the last four Jesuits in Chiquitos, based in Santiago and Santo Corazón, despatched to Santa Cruz.

From there, they began the long journey over the Andes to Lima. From Lima, they went on to Panama and Spain. Father Ignacio Chomé and Father Juan Messner died in the Andes, Father Esteban Palozzi died in Portobelo, Father Juan Rodríguez in Cartagena. Twenty of the twenty-four missionaries of Chiquitos, including the great architect Father Martín Schmid, survived to make the Atlantic crossing to Spain.[5] Then, after many privations, most of them settled with the other priests from Paraguay in the Italian town of Faenza, with a minuscule Spanish pension. In July 1773, the Pope dissolved the Society of Jesus altogether, and confiscated all its property.

Six thousand Jesuits were expelled from Spain and from the Spanish empire in this dramatic exodus. It was difficult and tragic for the individual priests. It was a disaster for the Indians they had left behind.

When the Jesuits were expelled from Chiquitos, they had just finished a census of their province. The ten mission towns contained a total population of nearly 24,000. Someone now had to accept responsibility for policing these settlements. For his part, Colonel Martínez asked repeatedly to be relieved of his post. He knew that, without the Jesuits, the province would become ungovernable. The twin threat – from the Indians and from the Portuguese – would become ever more difficult to deal with.

The Spanish authorities assumed initially that the Jesuits could simply be replaced with other priests. If they considered the matter at all, they thought that life in the missions would go on as before. The tough and worldly bishop of Santa Cruz, Francisco Ramón de Herboso y Figueroa, was given the task of finding priests to send to Chiquitos. It was a tall order. The bishop was short of priests for his own town and district. Now, he had to find an additional fifty, for both Chiquitos and the more northerly Jesuit province of Mojos.

The Jesuit priests in Paraguay and Chiquitos, for the most part, had been educated Europeans, with practical experience as well as notable linguistic and philosophical skills. There was a sprinkling of creole priests among them who were also men of considerable accomplishment. The ordinary priests or curas of South America were, almost to a man, corrupt, ill-educated locals. A career in the Church, for them, was little more than a disguised form of unemployment. The opportunity to man the missions of Chiquitos gave them an unequalled chance to enrich themselves, to rape and to pillage.

Evidence of the scale of degradation of their activities comes from all the reports of the governors of the province in the years after the Jesuits were expelled. The curas were still behaving badly when d'Orbigny travelled through Chiquitos in 1831. Visiting the mission at Santa Ana, he was present when a deputation of Indian caciques from San Juan Bautista appeared before the governor. They were there to complain about the behaviour of the cura. They said that he had slept with so many of the wives and daughters of the community that they were obliged to go elsewhere for confession. Nineteen girls were presented to the governor, all victims of the cura. The eldest, d'Orbigny noted, was barely eleven.[6]

When the ecclesiastical scrapings of the province of Santa Cruz were sprinkled around Chiquitos in 1768, the Indians rose up to reject them. There was an uprising in Concepción in February, another in Santa Ana in March. In the east, the Guaycurus simply regained their old territory west of the Paraguay that had been so successfully usurped by the Jesuits. In 1773, a military expedition, with five hundred Chiquitos archers and fifteen soldiers from Santa Cruz, had to be sent to reopen the road to Santo Corazón. In 1781, San José was sacked and burnt down. It was a tragic end to a century of development.

Bishop Herboso toured the area in 1768 to see what was happening and what was needed. He arrived first at San Javier in August, and went on to Concepción, Santa Ana, San Rafael, and San Ignacio. An ignorant, opinionated, Church-bound prelate, he seems to have been wholly uninformed about the development of the mission towns in the time of the Jesuits. He had no notion of their economic and social progress, nor of the skills of the Indians. He was surprised and impressed by the Jesuit organs he found in the churches of Chiquitos, commanding that one should be made for his cathedral in Santa Cruz.

He was amazed, a contemporary chronicler wrote, "that a few Indians, who only know their own barbarian language, can manage a compass, understand proportions and numbers, and apply the rules of music to construct such works".[7]

Bishop Herboso stayed in Chiquitos until May 1769. He returned to Santa Cruz depressed and daunted by the magnitude of the problems ahead.[8] But with his hand-picked priests now occupying the Chiquitos towns, owing their position and their allegiance to the bishopric of Santa Cruz, he had reason to be satisfied by the growth of his political influence.

But the scandal caused by the curas in Chiquitos became so great that the secular authorities were eventually obliged to intervene. In the 1770s, a new Spanish governor of Chiquitos, Juan Bartolomé Verdugo, arrived to try to clean up the Augean stables created during the curas' rule. Verdugo knew both Chiquitos and Mojos well. He had participated in the military expeditions sent to the Baures and the Itenes between 1763 and 1766.

In 1774, he presented a report to the viceroy on the economic needs of the former mission towns. It took the form of a plan "to relieve the decadence and ruin that now threatens them as a result of the abuses committed in them".[9] Verdugo proposed the creation of politico-military governors for Chiquitos and Mojos, to be dependent militarily on Santa Cruz and politically on Charcas. These men would take over the role of the corrupt curas.

For the next forty years or so, an administrative battle was waged between servants of the Spanish state as to who should control the old towns of Chiquitos, corrupt priests or secular administrators. The advocates of secular control eventually won, but they found that the administrators could be just as corrupt as the curas. The Indians of Chiquitos were then faced with a dual oppression, from the Church and the State.

In comparison with other parts of the European empire in South America in the eighteenth century, and indeed with many parts of Europe at that time, the mission towns of Chiquitos had once been models of utopian socialism, presided over by the benign dictatorship of a handful of well-meaning Jesuits. Then, with the stroke of a pen in Europe, and the speed of a thunderclap, the whole splendid edifice came tumbling down.

The Jesuits had come first to the old settlement of Santa Cruz (at San José de Chiquitos) in the sixteenth century. The missions came a century later, but by the time of the expulsion, some of the mission towns were nearly eighty years old. In that time, the Jesuit missionaries had introduced several generations of Indian people to the bizarre cults and practices of the Europeans. In the process, they had persuaded many of their neophytes of the advantages of their system.

The Jesuit missions gave the impression of being self-contained, self-sufficient, almost autarchic entities, capable of surviving on their own. Yet nothing could have been further from the case. They were utterly dependent on the ideological control of the Jesuit priests, and these priests – the supermen of their age – were themselves wholly dependent on the Spanish Crown.

The crown in Madrid was theoretically all-powerful. Yet it too was under pressure. It could not isolate itself from the winds of change sweeping through eighteenth-century Europe. When it decided that the archaic force that the Jesuits had come to represent in Europe was now a possible barrier to the survival of the monarchy itself, it swiftly ordered its destruction. In doing so, it probably did not even notice – it certainly did not care – what the effect would be in South America. In the 1750s, it had casually reorganized frontiers without any care for the people on the spot, and the same lack of attention to detail was evident in the 1760s. The withdrawal of the Jesuits was to leave large tracts of the frontier area of their empire in a state of chaos and anarchy, leading to a long period of decadence – a decline that has continued for more than two hundred years.

The crown was oblivious to all this, and was in any case to lose these territories – and much, much more – within the next half-century. Europe had picked up South America in the fifteenth century like a child's ball, played around with it for three hundred years, experimented with its peoples, destroyed its individual nations, pillaged its forests and mines, and then tossed it away as though it were a useless, discarded toy. Perhaps Asia and Africa – the "discovery" of the nineteenth century – would prove more amusing.

Notes

1. When Portugal and Spain came to delimit their South American frontier, under the terms of the Treaty of Madrid, Spain wished to have Sacramento (Colon), on the northern shore of the entrance to the River Plate. It had been a constant bone of contention between the two empires. Portugal, for its part, believing that there was gold in the seven Uruguay missions, was prepared to do a swap: Spain would get Colon, Portugal would get the missions. Spain, knowing that there was no gold, agreed to the deal. On paper, in Europe, it was easy. On the ground, in South America, it took no account of the Indians who lived in the missions. It led to a war.

2. The Guaraní War of the 1750s falls out of the scope of this book, but there is an interesting insight into the Jesuit involvement in Felix Becker, *Die politische Machtstellung der Jesuiten in Sudamerika im 18 Jahrhundert. Zur Kontroverse um den ''Jesuitenkonig'' Nikolaus 1 von Paraguay*, Bohlau Verlag, Cologne–Vienna 1980 (Spanish version, *Un mito jesuitico, Nicolas 1, rey del Paraguay*, Carlos Schauman, Asunción 1987). Becker suggests that the Jesuits were more involved in the Indian resistance than their historians have usually admitted.

3. Gabriel René-Moreno, *Biblioteca Boliviano, Catálogo del archivo de Mojos y Chiquitos*, Santiago 1888, p. 317. Pablo Pastells gives a slightly different version.

4. The Indian rebellion of 1781 was fiercely repressed in every Spanish town in the Andes. In Sucre, on 17 March, 17 Indian rebels were hanged in the Prado in the morning, and 14 were whipped and mutilated in the main square in the afternoon. A month later, 5 were hanged in the morning, and one hanged and quartered as the cathedral clock struck seven. In May, 7 were hanged, drawn, and quartered. Two centuries later, the Indian rebellion of Sendero Luminoso is being repressed on a similar scale. See Gabriel René-Moreno, *Ultimos dias coloniales en el Alto-Perú*, Santiago de Chile 1896, pp. 55–6.

5. José Manuel Peramas, *De vita et moribus tredecim virorum Paraguaycorum*, Faenza 1793.

6. Alcides d'Orbigny, *Voyage dans l'Amérique Méridionale*, Paris 1835–1847.

7. Cosme Bueno, *El conocimiento de los tiempos*, Lima 1771.

8. Gabriel René-Moreno, *Biblioteca Boliviana*, p. 570. Bishop Herboso came up with one concrete idea. In order to deal with the Portuguese threat, he suggested that Spanish settlements should be established close to the three lakes on the Paraguay, Mandiore, Uberaba, and Gaiba. These would be able to rival the Portuguese towns of Cuiabá and Mato Grosso, and would also help to consolidate Spanish power in an area where the Indians were in the great majority. It was the birth of the idea that brought British settlers to Lake Gaiba in the 1920s. After scrutiny by the Council of the Indies in March 1772, the idea was approved by the king in September. But nothing came of it. There was no spare money for colonial development – there never had been – and white settlers, like trained priests, were in short supply.

    Twenty years later, in 1793, the Spanish surveyor Felix de Azara was writing to the viceroy from Asunción with the same suggestion ''that from Santa Cruz and Asunción should go Spaniards to form a settlement on the banks of the lagoon joined to the river Paraguay, west of it, just north of Albuquerque, giving to its settlers the nearby lands that once belonged to the former settlement of Santiago''. Azara wanted ''a point of contact'' with Chiquitos that would enable the Spanish in Asunción ''to keep an eye on the Portuguese mines'', and to safeguard communications ''between Paraguay and Chiquitos and Peru'' (letter from Azara to the viceroy, 17 September 1793, in Pedro de Angelis, *Colección de obras*, Buenos Aires 1836, vol. 3, p. 49.

9. ''Proceso de la gobernación militar de Chiquitos'', in Ricardo Mujia, *Bolivia–Paraguay: Exposición de los titulos que consagran el derecho territorial de Bolivia sobre la zona comprendida entre los rios Pilcomayo y Paraguay*, La Paz 1914, vol. 2, part 4, chapter 24, p. 541.

PART IV

The Missions of Mojos

By the mission of the Mojos is understood an assemblage of heathen American nations . . . These nations inhabit a country of a vast extent, which is discovered in proportion as, leaving Santa Cruz de la Sierra, we travel along a vast chain of steep mountains, running from north to south . . .

This vast extent of country seems to be a pretty even plain; but 'tis commonly overflowed for want of drains to carry off the waters. These waters proceed from the abundant rains, from the floods which rush from the mountains, and from the overflowing of rivers. During above four months in the year, these nations can have no communication with one another; for being obliged to retire to the high grounds, to secure themselves from the inundations, their huts are at a great distance from one another.

Some Account of the Country Inhabited by the Mojos, printed in *Lockman's Travels of the Jesuits*, London 1762

On the campos or prairies of eastern Bolivia, between the Beni, the Mamoré, the Itonama, and the Guaporé, about 30,000 real unmixed Indians – the Mojos – still exist in the former Jesuit missions, fifteen large regularly planned villages.

Totally cut off from the outside world – on one side by the ice-covered Cordillera de los Andes; and, on the other, by pathless wastes of forest, together with scarcely explored rivers full of rapids and cataracts – and deprived, moreover, of their leaders and teachers, they live in a state of disheartening depression and bondage little removed from absolute slavery.

Franz Keller, *The Amazon and Madeira Rivers*, London 1874

18

SANTA CRUZ DE LA SIERRA

By bus from San Javier to Santa Cruz

Like Colonel Diego Martínez in 1767, we get up before dawn and watch the sun slowly illuminate the façade of the great Jesuit church at San Javier. While we are packing up in leisurely fashion, a messenger arrives to say that the bus is already waiting in the main square and raring to go. The bus is small, with only a few passengers, and after an hour's drive we stop at San Ramón for breakfast. This is a junction settlement, where two major roads meet, and the roadside is lined with small huts selling food. Rickety wooden tables balanced on petrol cans are laid out under makeshift cotton shelters, and dogs sniff around for scraps. The smell is delicious, a mixture of cooking oil and kerosene and wood smoke. In the early morning light, this delightful settlement has the appearance of a peaceful yet bustling oasis.

We have reached the main road that runs from Santa Cruz de la Sierra to the north, to the Franciscan missions of Guarayos, to the town of Trinidad, the capital of the Beni, once the great province of Mojos. This was the route taken by the early Spanish conquistadores, pressing into unknown territory. Soon we shall go in that direction too, but for the moment our destination is Santa Cruz, so we leave the lorries rumbling off to the north, and take the left-hand turn to the south.

First we take a straight well-made dirt road that goes through a colonization area. Here tracks lead off into the scrub on either side, to settlements where Indians from the altiplano have been brought down to make the jungle bloom. Everything is planned and regular; on the map the area looks like the precise surgeon's sewing of a wound. The struggle between the settlers and the jungle is evenly matched. After twenty years or so, the settlers have not made much of a dent.

Further along, however, is the territory of the Mennonites. These fearsome religious maniacs with limitless funds have got hold of immense bulldozers with which they are destroying great tracts of forest. These new prairies are put down to maize and soya, giving these foreign colonists an unshakeable grip on the agricultural economy of the region. They already supply Santa Cruz with all its milk and vegetables. Against this competition, the Bolivian Indian settlers have no chance.

The tractors and machinery are new, and maybe they employ the equivalent of a sabbath goy to clear the land. For the typical Mennonite is still the farmer in dungarees, driving his horse and buggy along the track as though he was in Oklahoma. His fat wife in flowing dress and bonnet sits at his side, keeping an eye on their two small children, fair-haired and blue-eyed. Among themselves, they speak German.

Funny people, these Mennonites. I met a progressive one who had been born in Siberia, his family having gone to Russia from Danzig in the eighteenth century, in the time of Catherine the Great. Hostile to war and revolution and military conscription, he had travelled to Moscow from Siberia in 1929 and had arrived in Paraguay in 1932, just when the Chaco War was about to break out. He had meant to go to Canada, but the Canadians would only take immigrants who were fit. Many of the Russian Mennonites in those days suffered from trachoma. The Paraguayans were not so choosy. He was bitterly opposed to the conservative Mennonites of Bolivia, who had earlier been settled in Mexico. Their religious observation was so bizarre that they would take the rubber wheels off their John Deere tractors and replace them with metal spikes. He said they were very ignorant and badly educated. Many of them couldn't read, and they couldn't really understand the words of the Bible when it was read to them.

Past the territory of the Mennonites, we come eventually to the railway line and follow it to the Rio Grande. The road crosses the river on a long box-girder bridge that it shares with the railway. The river here is very wide and shallow, full of mudbanks. The bridge stretches far over the flood plain on either side. West of the river is the small station of Pailón, once the Jesuit port of Pailas, and the sole point of entry into the mission territory of Chiquitos. Here were the warehouses and port installations that served both Chiquitos and the province of Mojos in the eighteenth century. Nothing now remains.

When I first came to Santa Cruz twenty-five years ago, it was just a hot dusty town with whitewashed one-storey houses, a typical forgotten spot in the heart of the continent. There were some nice touches: the roofs extended over the pavements, providing protection in wet weather, and the pavements themselves were lifted high above the prevailing mud. But it was essentially a one-horse town, though by that time the horses had given way to Toyota jeep taxis. For three and a half centuries, endowed with so much hope and opportunity, Santa Cruz de la Sierra was a frontier town on the way to nowhere. Its Spanish governors and bishops grumbled endlessly about its lack of facilities and food. The bishops preferred to live up in the hills at Mizque.

Then, in 1971, a man from Santa Cruz seized power in La Paz. Suddenly, a Cruceño was president of Bolivia. Not for nothing has the main road from the airport been named Avenida Banzer, after General Hugo Banzer Suárez. Under his aegis, Santa Cruz has rapidly become the most important town in the country, living off the oil royalties that accrue to it from the oilfields of the Bolivian Chaco, and from the drug money that flows in from the Beni. The old town is now almost unrecognizable; modest skyscrapers and ring roads characterize the new city.

We go in search of friends, Cecilia and Javier, and eat out in the best Italian restaurant in South America, and talk about the past. Tomorrow we shall fly off to the Beni, to the old Jesuit province of Mojos, the legendary plains that the Incas once tried to conquer.

The expedition to Mojos ordered by the Inca Yupanqui in the fifteenth century

In the great waterlogged territory of Mojos that lies to the north-west of Santa Cruz de la Sierra, innumerable Indian nations have lived for thousands of years. In more recent times, it has been "discovered" by a steady stream of European explorers. Most of these have entered the territory from the south, from the east, or from the north. But the first outsiders to come here of whom we have a record "discovered" it from the west. They were not Europeans, but soldiers of the Inca. They travelled down the most difficult route of all, from the mountains east of Cuzco in Peru. They came through the great rainforest that skirts the eastern edge of the Andes, and into the fast and broad rivers of the upper Amazon basin, rivers that sluice up and down according to the seasons, like the lock of a canal.

Long before the Spaniards arrived in South America, the Incas in the Andean highlands possessed an ancient account, handed down by their ancestors, of a civilization to the east of their great mountain range. According to this antique tradition, the nations on the far side of the mountains "were populous and the land fruitful". Part of their land, however, was uninhabited, "being nothing but mountains, lakes, bogs and marshy ground".[1]

The first Cuzco ruler to investigate this story was the Inca Yupanqui, ruler of Peru in the middle of the fifteenth century. When he took control of the Inca empire, he went – as was the custom of his predecessors – on a prolonged three-year visit to his existing realm. Then, according to the account of Garcilasso de la Vega, he decided on expansion. His people needed new lands. He would send a military expedition into fresh territory to the east.

The dream of moving Indians from the cold and overcrowded Andean plateau onto the hot and deserted Amazonian plains has lasted from that day to this. Presidents talk about it, development economists draw up plans for it, road builders profit from it, and a few thousand settlers struggle down from their ancient haunts every year to find a new kind of misery in the tropics.

The Inca Yupanqui was the first to advocate population transfer, and the first to encounter its inherent difficulties. He was aware that people already lived in the tropical plains. He knew, for example, that "the greatest and most considerable" of the nations in these eastern territories were called the "Musu". Later, the Spaniards were to call them, and their entire region, "Mojos".

The Incas also knew, from the historical account they had inherited, that it would be possible to get to Mojos from the Andes through "a passage by a great river". The Inca Yupanqui ordered a large military expedition to be prepared.

> It being impossible to find a way into Musu over the inaccessible mountains and through the lakes and bogs, the King Yupanqui resolved to follow the course of the river, though as yet not known or discovered. In pursuance of which, order was given to cut down timber and make boats, or floats, for transporting ten thousand men, with provision sufficient for them, the which were two years in preparing.
>
> All which being built and made ready, and the soldiers raised and armed, and the victuals and ammunition provided, and the generals and officers named – all which were Incas of the royal blood – they embarked in their boats, made capable to carry thirty or forty or fifty men apiece.
>
> Their provisions they laid in the middle of the boats, raised about half a yard from the bottom to keep them from wet. With this force and preparations, they sculled down the stream.

This delightful expedition set off from a river near Cuzco and travelled east towards Mojos. The river was most probably the Madre de Dios, which starts in the Andes, runs into Bolivia and joins the Beni before meeting the Mamoré and forming the Madeira.

The Inca's armada soon ran into opposition from an Indian nation, the Chunchu, living along the river's banks, but it was not held up for long. The Andean troops were powerful enough to overpower them, and the Chunchu gave presents to the Inca as a sign of their submission: "parrots, monkeys, drills, honey, wax, and other fruits which their country yielded".

The expedition then continued "to other countries and nations until they came to the province of Musu", calculated to lie about two hundred leagues from Cuzco. This land, says Garcilasso de la Vega's account, was inhabited "by a numerous and warlike nation, having all things plentiful of their own product".

By the time they got there, the great expedition that had left the Andes "was reduced to a very small number". The defeat of the Chunchu, the rigours of the journey, and the difficulty of adapting to the tropical climate, had taken their toll. The Inca army was clearly not capable of defeating the "numerous and warlike" Indians of Mojos.

In these circumstances, there appears to have been something resembling a truce. Garcilasso de la Vega suggests that the Mojos, impressed by the Inca religion, agreed to acknowledge the Sun as their principal god. This sounds perfectly possible since, a century or so later, the Mojos were also happy to pay lip service to the god of the Spaniards, changing their allegiance almost overnight.

The Mojos were not, however, prepared to be vassals of the Inca. They had been visited by his soldiers, perhaps a little intimidated, but they had not been conquered. They said they would be proud to be accounted as his "allies, friends and confederates".

The Mojos also agreed to allow the surviving Inca soldiers "to live and inhabit in their country, for there not remaining above a thousand of them, they did not apprehend any danger of being subdued or enslaved by them, and therefore freely gave them liberty to take their daughters and kindred for their wives".

To confirm this new alliance, the Mojos sent ambassadors to Cuzco, "taking a great compass in their way thither to avoid the high mountains, marshy grounds and bogs, which were not passable in the direct line".

This extraordinary tale suggests that, in the Mojos, the Incas felt that they were faced with a comparable civilization, with whom they had to bargain and negotiate, rather than fight and subdue. This tale was one of the origins of the tales of El Dorado, a belief that there was, somewhere in the Amazonian jungle, a hidden society of great power and wealth.

It may also be that the influx of Inca soldiers, who had stayed behind, helped to bring the existing Mojos civilization to fresh heights of achievement, so that the wonders of Mojos, about which the early Spanish conquistadores were told, were in fact the result of a combination of two great societies, one in the mountains, the other in the plains.

Many years after the expedition sent by the Inca Yupanqui, the children of the Inca soldiers that had stayed behind conceived "the natural desire of visiting the country of their forefathers". From their homes in the plains, they decided to visit the distant Andean city of Cuzco.

They received news on the way that the Inca Huayna Capac was dead, "and that the Spaniards possessed the land". The old empire of the Incas had been "subverted and utterly destroyed".

So the children of the Incas returned to Mojos, without ever having reached Cuzco or having met the Spaniards. On their return, "they were ever afterwards highly esteemed and held in veneration, and all matters both of war and peace [were] committed to their management".

This entire story hovers on the borders between history and myth, yet it became an important element in the subsequent history of Mojos. Garcilasso de la Vega is often considered to be an unreliable chronicler, but this particular tale seems to have the ring of authenticity.

The first Spanish expedition into Mojos from Upper Peru, undertaken by Diego Alemán in 1564

We are on firmer ground with the first Spanish expeditions into Mojos in the sixteenth century. They had a similar purpose to the great journeys across Chiquitos at the same time – to open up new territory in search of silver and gold. But whereas the early conquistadores on the upper Paraguay already knew about the existence of treasure to the west in Peru – since Francisco Pizarro had brought Atahualpa's treasure back to Spain before they left – the explorers of Mojos had no such concrete information to go on.

The first Spanish expedition into Mojos, of which there exists an elementary record, was made in 1564 by Diego Alemán, a Spanish captain based in La Paz. He travelled with twelve Spaniards on what was meant to be a reconnoitring expedition, "to see and observe how the land lay". The idea was to return later "with great force" to make a proper conquest.[2]

Alemán's soldiers went "on foot, both for privacy, the better to surprise the natives, and because the way was mountainous and not passable on horseback". They made their entry into Mojos through Cochabamba, travelling north over the mountains.

For four weeks they travelled "through mountains and thickets and unfrequented places", coming at last "to a view of the first province of that people". They had arrived at the beginning of the great plains of Mojos, "where there are swamps to the level of the knee and even the waist". This "first province" of the plains was called Machari.

Beyond it, according to one contemporary account, was the far more important region of Paitití, later to become the source of the El Dorado legend. This was,

> . . . a very extensive province where the Indians say that there is a large lake, and in the lake is an island with a temple where the Indians of all these provinces go to sacrifice to their gods. Since they have the Sun as their god, they call this the House of the Sun.[3]

The cacique of this province was considered to be "as powerful as were the Incas of Peru".

Beyond Paitití was a yet more legendary province, called Peneca. Here we are on familiar territory, for this is the story in all the accounts of El Dorado: the presence of the Amazons. Here "the women are said to be great warriors".

The existence of the Amazons is an intriguing area for speculation. What seems less controversial is that the contemporary chroniclers were undoubtedly impressed by the size and extent of the civilization that lay on the frontiers of Mojos. In all these provinces, the chronicles agree, "there is a greater number of people than in New Spain (Mexico) and in Peru. The Indians that have seen them say that there are settlements so large that they stretch for half a league."

The expedition of Diego Alemán, we are led to suppose, had glimpsed the promised land. Then disaster struck. In spite of their efforts to travel unobserved, they were soon discovered by the Mojos Indians. Late one evening they were ambushed, and ten Spaniards were killed. Diego Alemán himself was captured. Only two people managed to escape from the battlefield. One of them, a mestizo from Cochabamba, Francisco de Araya ("El Moreno"), was wounded. The next day, with the Indian curaca who had been their guide, these survivors were able to observe the scene from a hidden vantage point:

> So soon as it was day, the two Spaniards and the curaca could from the top of the hill discover a great number of Indians, with lances and pikes and breastplates, which glittered against the sun, all which, as the guide assured them, were made of gold, and that they had no silver in their country, but that only which they procured from Peru in exchange for their gold. And to describe the greatness of that country, he told them, that as the list [border] was to that mantle, so was all Peru in comparison with that country; but, to let pass his cosmography, there is no doubt that this province was both wide and long.[4]

According to Garcilasso de la Vega's colourful account, the captured Alemán subsequently became a chief of the Mojos and led them in battle against a nation the other side of the Amarumayu river (the Madre de Dios).

Francisco from Cochabamba died soon after getting back over the mountains to his home town. But before he died, he left a journal of the expedition which is presumably the basis of the chroniclers' tales. His journal was so stirring that it "moved many others to undertake this design". The thirst for Mojos, and for El Dorado and Paitití, had been aroused.

One of those so moved was "a young and brisk gentleman" called Gómez de Tordoya. He was keen that a fresh expedition should be sent to Mojos, but the viceroy in Lima, the Count of Nieva, "fearing a mutiny or some combustion", forbade it to take place.[5] The viceroy was faced with the usual problem during the first century of the Conquest: there were too many adventurous young men seeking to explore new territory. Their freelance armies posed a considerable threat to the stability of the lands already occupied.

Two years later, a new governor of Peru, Lope García de Castro, gave the commission to explore Mojos to someone else. This man, Gaspar de Sotelo, made an agreement with the Inca Tupac Amaru to supply him with boats. This expedition was planning to enter Mojos from the old route down the Madre de Dios taken by the Inca Yupanqui's army, rather than by the southern route attempted by Diego Alemán. For some unexplained reason, Governor García de Castro withdrew the commission from Gaspar de Sotelo and gave it to a third aspirant instead, a man called Juan Alvarez Maldonado.

In the event, two Spanish expeditions set out for Mojos. One, led by Alvarez Maldonado, went by river. The other, led by Gómez de Tordoya – who still thought he had an entitlement to go granted him by the Count of Nieva – went over the mountains.

Gómez de Tordoya, who had only sixty men, seems to have got to the western edge of the Mojos plains before Alvarez Maldonado, who was caught up in the territory of the Chunchu. Just as the viceroy had feared, there was strife between the Spaniards. Gómez de Tordoya decided to deal with his Spanish rival before taking on the Indians, and waited to ambush Alvarez Maldonado as he paddled down the river. Alvarez Maldonado's expedition was much larger than that of Gómez de Tordoya. He had two hundred and fifty foot soldiers and one hundred cavalry, all shipped on the flat-bottomed boats provided by the Inca Tupac Amaru. Gómez de Tordoya had the advantage of surprise. The two armies seem to have been reasonably matched:

> They fought that whole day, as also the second and third, with that spite and rage, and with such little consideration, that they were almost all killed; and as such as did escape with their lives,were yet so wounded that they were disabled and unfit for service.

At this stage the Chunchu Indians, who had presumably been observing this long battle without much grief, "fell in upon those that remained alive and utterly destroyed them, amongst which Gómez de Tordoya was also slain".

The Chunchu had made quite a haul. Alvarez Maldonado they captured alive, and they also held Simón López, a gunsmith, and Diego Martín, a Portuguese friar. Alvarez Maldonado, "considering that he was wounded and a man in years" was soon released. But a man who made guns and a European religious sorcerer were too important to let go.

> The friar and the gunsmith they kept above two years afterwards, during which time they employed the gunsmith solely in making them hatchets and pick-axes of copper, and the friar they held in great veneration because he was a priest.

Two years later, these two men were also released, and returned to Cuzco. Describing their recent experiences, they were also the first to give details of an even older piece of history, the story of the original Inca involvement in Mojos – the expedition ordered by the Inca Yupanqui – before the arrival of the Spaniards in Peru. It was from their account that Garcilasso de la Vega was able to weave his tale.

The early military expeditions into Mojos from Santa Cruz

For the first fifty years after the Spanish Conquest, there were frequent clashes in the heart of the continent between rival white groups. The battle between Alvarez Maldonado and Gómez de Tordoya on the frontiers of Mojos was typical, as was the stand-off between Nuflo de Chávez and Andrés Manso on the borders of Chiquitos. These divisions between the colonial forces endangered the entire enterprise. The Europeans were still a tiny minority in a hostile continent.

In the case of the unexplored territory of Mojos, the Spanish viceroy in Lima in the

1570s, Francisco de Toledo, decided that there were to be no more fruitless expeditions cutting their way through the jungle from the Andes. To prevent further rivalry, he issued an order in 1573 that in future the surviving settlers in Santa Cruz de la Sierra – men who had come from the Paraguay – were to be given the sole right to explore into this largely untouched region.

The settlers in Santa Cruz were not in fact able to organize a successful expedition into Mojos until some twenty years later, in 1595. This was nearly forty years after Nuflo de Chávez had first settled in Chiquitos with that express purpose in mind: a reflection of the immense difficulties that beset the settlement from the very start. Their uncertain friendship with the Chiquitos Indians, and the constant threat posed by the Chiriguanos to the south, meant that the tiny band of Spanish settlers based at Santa Cruz was forced to hone its survival skills rather than embark on fresh expeditions of conquest. However alluring the land of Paitití might be, soldiers could not be spared to undertake the journey.

In the 1580s, a new and dynamic governor of Santa Cruz, Lorenzo Suárez de Figueroa, decided that the time was ripe to tackle Mojos. We have important information about Mojos, he wrote in 1586. ''There are a large number of well-dressed people there, rich in gold and silver and cattle, with fertile lands.'' The governor was keen to explain why Santa Cruz was the best starting point for an expedition. ''It would be much easier to explore and populate that territory from this city than from anywhere else, because the track goes through regions that are already inhabited, and there are no sierras or mountains to be crossed.''[6]

Without more ado, Suárez de Figueroa organized an exploratory land expedition, through Chiquitos, to Mojos. This proved unable to penetrate very far, encountering resistance from two Indian nations, the Tapacuras and the Timbues.

A second, larger expedition from Santa Cruz, travelling this time by land and by boat on the Rio Grande (or Guapay), was sent out by Suárez de Figueroa in 1595, led by Juan de Torres Palomino. It was accompanied by a Jesuit priest, Hierónimo de Andión, whose letters sent back to his mission superiors form the basis of our knowledge of the trip.[7]

Lorenzo Suárez de Figueroa was himself responsible for bringing the Jesuits to Santa Cruz. But the decision to send one of their fathers on what was bound to be a tough military expedition, in which men would kill and be killed, must have been a difficult one for the Jesuits. The Provincial was forced to justify everything in his Annual Letter to Rome.

> In the month of July of the year 1595 the military expedition and conquest of the Mojos was begun. This is a large province, inhabited by decently clothed and intelligent people about whom we have heard for a long time. They possess, and use, silver. The Spaniards who originally came to Santa Cruz did not stay there because they wanted to settle, but because the town was seen as a staging post on the way to the discovery that they intended to make.

Eventually, this year, they set off, accompanied by Father Hierónimo de Andión. He went with them to extend the flag of Christ's cross into areas where it had never before been unfurled. Although, in truth, the Company has never sought to participate in this kind of military expedition, because of the troubles that can occur to those involved, there seemed to be a number of good reasons to go on this one. After discussing the matter with all the fathers in Santa Cruz, it was decided that it would be not just convenient but also important for Father Hierónimo to go with the soldiers.

Father Hierónimo initially had some doubts himself. When already on the way, he wrote a letter to the Provincial, on 17 July 1595, explaining to them:

There is one drawback, and it is not small, and it is that I am travelling with the soldiers. Yet anyone familiar with the ferocity and inhumanity of these [Indian] nations, who have never seen Spaniards before, would have to concede that there is really no other way to proceed.

So the expedition set out from Santa Cruz to San Lorenzo de la Barranca, on the shores of the River Guapay, and began its journey towards the north. Father Hierónomo chronicled the difficulties that arose.

To go to examine the lie of the land a little lower down the river, the governor sent a captain with eighteen soldiers in a small boat, accompanied by about forty Indians. They went for several days without seeing anyone, or signs of anyone, and then entering another great river that joins the Guapay, they came across two canoes. There were fourteen Indians on the beach, roasting great quantities of the meat of pig that they had hunted.

The friendly Indians of the Spaniards promptly killed thirteen of these beach-combers, capturing one, who subsequently died. "It was a pity," Father Hierónimo wrote, "as he would have made an excellent guide. Even though no one understood his language, he made signs giving news of the nations that lay ahead."
The saintly father reflected hard on the meaning of these developments:

The Lord who spilt his own blood for these souls will be well served by the opening of this gateway, so that these nations can enter through that of the Gospel. For more than forty years [since 1555] the Spaniards have hoped to embark on this military expedition, and only now have they been able to do so. Thanks to the Lord, we are now on the road, and, if he does not call me to account before, I hope, with his divine favour, to see myself in Paitití, that destination that is so famous and so sought after.

In a second letter, written on 14 September 1595, Father Hierónimo gives further details of the trip down the Guapay. Although there were some boats, the bulk of the expedition – they had three hundred horses – seems to have gone by land, close to the river bank but opening up a path with machetes and axes. "This took longer than we had expected, and soon we ran short of food."

A boat was then sent down the river with twenty-five soldiers, to see what the route looked like ahead. Encountering a group of Indians and some food, they were almost immediately set upon by some three hundred Indian bowmen. Their arrows, like those of the Chiquitos, were tipped with poison. But the crossbows of the Spaniards proved more than a match for the Indians, who fled into the hills.

The Spaniards then came to seven towns where the Indians were friendly, but they had no means of communication, "even though we had brought interpreters from several different nations".

Father Hierónimo was impressed with what they found:

There is much food in this province, for they are splendid farmers and the land is extremely fertile. Their houses are well made, and their household goods and utensils the same, in fact the best we have seen so far. All the houses are large, holding up to six people in each one. They are all placed around a single great square, with their doors opening out onto it. In the middle of the square is a great covered hut where they eat and drink, and at the entrance to the town is another smaller hut, closed on one side, which serves as a gateway.

At this stage, they heard news of the death of Lorenzo Suárez de Figueroa. His death, in August that year, only a month after the expedition had set out, seems to have brought it to a premature end.

At the beginning of the seventeenth century, the province of Mojos was still effectively undiscovered by the Spaniards. Small probing expeditions had taken place, but nothing on the scale of the great trans-Chiquitos expeditions of the mid-sixteenth century. Then, in 1602, a new governor of Santa Cruz, Juan Mendoza Mate de Luna, advanced down the Guapay with an expedition of 150 men. Royal permission had been granted to establish two towns in Mojos. Madrid had suddenly become interested in the area again because the authorities had been shown "a map made by an Englishman who had sailed up the Marañón and had seen huge settlements with many Indians".[8]

Mate de Luna's expedition did indeed found a new town, somewhere between the mountains and the swamps, and they called it Trinidad. But the expeditionaries fell out among themselves, partly, it seems, because the place chosen was so unsuitable for settlement. A mutiny was put down with much brutality, and most of the surviving settlers fled away into the swamps and were never seen again.

In 1617, another expedition was organized by Mate de Luna's successor as governor, Gonzalo de Solís Holguín. A force of seventy-five Spaniards, accompanied by two hundred friendly Chiquitos Indians, was sent north through Chiquitos to the eastern parts of Mojos. A Jesuit priest, Father Hierónimo de Villarnão, went with them. They found a number of Indian villages, killed some Indians, and returned. A further expedition was sent out in 1624, accompanied by a Jesuit priest, Father Juan Navarro, but it too ended badly, with mutiny and rebellion among the troops. Governor Solís Holguín died shortly afterwards.

The result of all these expeditions should perhaps have suggested to the Spaniards that there was no El Dorado waiting round the corner. But the lure or temptation of Mojos was still strong. The president of the Audiencia of Charcas, Juan de Lizarazú, planned a fresh expedition in 1636, and took exceptional measures to ensure that it would be a success. He asked all the surviving members of Solís Holguín's journey of 1617 to write an account of what they had seen and found (these are the source of much interesting material about Mojos in the early seventeenth century).[9] But the expedition never materialized.

There is a pause in the records for nearly forty years. The inhabitants of Mojos remained largely unmolested by European conquerors, though there was clearly some contact between the Spanish inhabitants of Santa Cruz and the Mojos Indians, a trade both in food and slaves.

In 1667, the Mojenos apparently requested assistance from the Spaniards in order to fight their enemies, the Canacures. A fresh expedition, led by Juan de la Hoz, went north, again accompanied by a Jesuit brother, Juan de Soto. He was the first to report on the possibility of establishing mission towns in Mojos.

Brother de Soto returned to Mojos the following year with a companion, but they were eventually forced to abandon their explorations. Alarmed by the possibility that the establishment of missions would merely be a prelude to slavery, the Indians threatened to kill them.

The Jesuits in this early period had had no better luck than the military. They had been granted the right to establish missions in Chiquitos and Mojos in 1597, but the first religious pioneers were killed by Indians, Miguel de Arrea in 1597 and Bernardo Reus in 1629. Individual priests had gone on the military expeditions of the early seventeenth century, but none of these had led to permanent settlement. Yet the memory of a settlement at a place named Trinidad remained; at the end of the seventeenth century, it became a reality again.

Notes

1. Garcilasso de la Vega, *The Royal Commentaries of Peru* (translated by Sir Paul Rycaut), London 1688, p. 272.
2. According to one version, Alemán embarked on a march across the mountains to Mojos having been commissioned to do so by the viceroy in Lima, the Conde de Nieva ("Entrada de la jornada de los Mojos y descubrimiento de la tierra de Los Llanos", in Marcos Jiménez de la Espada, *Relaciones geográficas de Indias – Peru –* Biblioteca de Autores Espanoles, vol. 185, Madrid 1965, vol. 3, pp. 276–80). According to another account, Alemán had been persuaded to go by an Indian curaca (or cacique) who told him that there was "much gold" to be found there, and offered to be his guide. Garcilasso de la Vega, pp. 175–6.
3. "Memoria de la tierra de Los Llanos segun se pudo saber por indios que habian estado alla", in Marcos Jiménez de la Espada, vol. 3, p. 277.
4. Garcilasso de la Vega, pp. 275–6.
5. Viceroy Nieva had arrived in Lima in April 1561 (taking over from Andrés Hurtado de Mendoza, Marqués de Cañete, who was viceroy from June 1556 to September 1560) and died in February 1564, which hardly gives him time to have ordered this further expedition not to take place. He was succeeded, as an interim ruler, by Lope García de Castro. (The next viceroy, Francisco de Toledo, did not arrive until November 1569.)
6. "Relación de la ciudad de Santa Cruz de la Sierra por su gobernador don Lorenzo Suárez de Figueroa, June 2, 1586", in Jiménez de la Espada, vol. 1, p. 403.
7. The letters are quoted in the "Annua de la Companía de Jesús, Tucumán y Peru, 1596, (Misión o residencia de Santa Cruz de la Sierra)", printed in Jiménez de la Espada, vol. 2, p. 93. The Annual Letter explained that the company had been working out of Santa Cruz for about eleven years (that is, since 1587) with seven fathers and two brothers. They had been extremely active among the Chiriguanos. They had been summoned to work in Santa Cruz by the governor, Lorenzo Suárez de Figueroa, who had been educated at the Jesuit college in Córdoba in Spain.
8. Victor Maurtua, *Juicio de limites entre el Perú y Bolivia*, Madrid 1906.
9. Juan de Lizarazú, "Informaciones hechas por Don Juan de Lizarazú sobre el descubrimiento de los Mojos, 1638", printed in Maurtua, vol. 9, pp. 124–6. *Juicio de limites entre el Perú y Bolivia.*

19

TRINIDAD

From Santa Cruz de la Sierra to Trinidad

Buses are wonderful in South America, trains are nearly as good. Aeroplanes –
though sometimes necessary – are definitely a third choice. It is to do with
expectations. Airports and airlines often give an impression of First World efficiency, and consequently disappoint more when they fail. It is also partly a question
of class. Buses are for the great mass of humanity, a necessary and vital form of
transport. The bus always gets through, even if the passengers have to get out and
dig through the landslide. Aeroplanes are for the South American bourgeois class,
politicians visiting their power base, small traders making a deal, professionals on a
per diem, ineffable wealthy women who would not like to be seen on a bus. Maids
travel by bus.

In Bolivia, there is an excellent air service that runs several times a day from La
Paz, through Cochabamba, to Santa Cruz and back. Linking the three most important cities, it runs in a straight line across the middle of the country, like Orion's Belt,
always on time and always full.

The trouble begins when you try to deviate from this central axis. If you want to go
somewhere else, it is better by bus. So it proved when – behind schedule as always –
we tried to fly to Trinidad.

The old Jesuit mission town of Trinidad, north-west of Santa Cruz, is now the
capital of the Beni, the great cattle and drugs region of northern Bolivia which in
former centuries was called Mojos. We are going in search of the old missions,
stretched out along the Mamoré, one of the great tributaries of the Amazon.

If we can get there. We wait all afternoon at the huge empty airport of Santa Cruz.
The plane was supposed to have departed at half past one, but one informant tells
us that it has mechanical problems and is grounded in Cochabamba. At five o'clock
they announce that the flight is cancelled. A wonderful scene ensues, enraged
middle-class women berating the wretched airline official. All to no avail. Will there
be a flight in the morning? No one knows. Some passengers decide to take the all-
night bus: a twelve- or fourteen-hour ride and they will be in Trinidad in the
morning. We take the risk and stay in Santa Cruz for the night. The airline provides
us with transport back to town, and we stay at the Residencial Bolívar in Calle Sucre,

a perfect backpackers' retreat, complete with a young man in a hammock listening to his Walkman.

The next morning we slip away at six, and miraculously the plane is there, waiting for take-off. The flight to Trinidad, high above the Rio Grande, takes about forty minutes. The Rio Grande runs into the Mamoré, and soon after we are skimming over the Trinidad church and landing on the flat plain beyond. Here it is sunny, and the climate is hot and damp.

Taking a taxi into the town, we put up at the Hotel Ganadero, a modern block near the centre. The lobby is filled with North American military, for this is one of the centres of the US anti-drug crusade in Bolivia. A black soldier is wearing a tee-shirt with the proud message: "Operation Just Cause, Panama, December 31, 1989". There is a swimming pool and a bar on the roof, and much of the crusade takes place up there.

Once past the central square, Trinidad is a pretty decrepit place. The low plastered houses and the unpaved alleys belong to village rather than town life. Cows and donkeys amble about.

The church is not the old Jesuit one, but dates from the early twentieth century. A few pieces of Jesuit silver are on display, with the telltale IHS mark, but there are no sculptures to speak of.

In the evening we had supper in a Chinese restaurant, the Dragon. It had red-painted columns on the outside, and its Chinese owner had moved here from São Paulo. We ate steaks of an exquisite river fish, covered in honey and chillies. Later we walked round the square and watched the Indians listening to the band playing in the centre. The local Mojos Indians are short, with dramatic, almost ugly faces, quite different from the rounded soft curves of the Indians of Chiquitos.

The establishment of a Jesuit mission in Trinidad in 1686

The Jesuits first established a mission town beside the Mamoré and called it Trinidad in 1686. Its founder was Father Cyprián Baraza, a Jesuit from Pamplona. He was a member of an energetic group of priests who pressed into Mojos in the last twenty years of the seventeenth century. Trinidad was not the first mission in Mojos. A town had been set up at Loreto, upriver to the south, a couple of years earlier. But Trinidad, because of its central position, became one of the most important.

The Jesuit conquest of Mojos began in 1675 with an expedition from Santa Cruz by three priests famous in Jesuit annals: Cyprián Baraza, Pedro Marbán, and José Castillo. They explored for many years and were to establish a number of mission settlements along the Mamoré.[1] These settlements were to last for just one hundred years. In English, their story has rarely been told.[2]

In the course of a century of mission endeavour in Mojos, the Jesuits created twenty-one mission towns. Some moved from their original site, sometimes several times, and not all of them survived more than a few years. But by 1767, when the Jesuits were expelled from South America, there were still fifteen flourishing missions. A dozen still exist today as significant settlements in the Mojos area of the Beni: Trinidad, Loreto, San Javier, San Pedro, Baures, Magdalena, San Joaquín, Exaltación, Santa Ana, Reyes, San Borja, and San Ignacio.

As with the mission area of Chiquitos, this was a zone in which the Jesuits were completely alone with the various Indian nations that they "reduced". There were no Spanish settlements in the area, although towards the end of the Jesuit period, Spanish soldiers were involved in helping to protect the frontier area against the Portuguese. As in the mission towns of Chiquitos, and as earlier in Guaíra and Itatín, plague and epidemic became a regular occurrence in Mojos. Yet this was not an area of European settlement. One is forced to conclude that mission life itself promoted illness and disease. An enclosed urban environment, involving discipline and work, was not the same as a society where people wandered freely in the swamp and scrub.

To keep up the numbers in their missions, decimated by disease, the Jesuits were obliged to go on expeditions into the jungle, little different from those of the slavers they so abhorred. Most towns only contained about two thousand Indians, and the total population of the Mojos towns never went much above thirty thousand. But in the eighteenth century, they became stable, wealthy communities. In addition to staples like yucca, the Indians had formerly cultivated sugar cane and bananas. Now, the Jesuits introduced rice, coffee and cacao, and planted orange trees. They also organized a steady trade with Santa Cruz via their closed port on the Rio Grande at Pailas. Some trade was done by land in the dry season, by ox-drawn cart. But since all mission towns were close to the river system, most of the commerce of the province was carried by water.

The Jesuits established themselves in Mojos at the end of rather more than a hundred years of rather indifferent missionary endeavour. To what extent did they know what they were doing when they plunged so eagerly into the conversion of new Indian nations?

In the early years of the European conquest of South America, the conversion of the native inhabitants to Christianity was of little interest to the white settlers, whose chief concern was their need for cheap labour. Enthusiasm for the conversion of the Indians was more or less a private matter of the monarchs of Spain and Portugal. They funded it to some extent, and gave it verbal encouragement, yet it was hardly at the top of their political agenda. In any case, the task that they had so lightly taken on, the conversion of nations far more numerous than their own, was not one that they could actually carry out with any hope of success. They had neither the money nor the priests to enforce the extension of their Christian ideology.

At the beginning of the seventeenth century, perceiving the difficulties faced by the Christian monarchs, the Catholic Church in Rome had begun to take a more direct interest in schemes to assist the ideological penetration of areas of European expansion. The Society of Jesus had proved to be a useful pilot scheme, providing Rome with an intelligence service in the colonial world second to none. It had also, in its embryonic missions in Brazil and Paraguay, constructed neat blueprints for ideological induction centres that appeared both cheap and effective. But the Jesuits were inevitably tied to the white settler community and the local military elite. Given the global challenge, something more grandiose was clearly necessary.

In 1622 Pope Gregory XV set up the Sacred Congregation for the Propagation of the Faith, an institution that sought to give Christianity in the imperial world an indigenous feel. If the Church of God was to survive, it would have to do so independently of the secular power that had helped to give it a global reach. Indigenous cultures must be respected and indigenous clergy recruited.

The stern instruction sent out in 1659 from the office of the Sacred Congregation for Propagation of the Faith in Rome was an indication of the new winds blowing:

> Do not regard it as your task, and do not bring any pressure to bear on the peoples, to change their manners, customs, and uses, unless they are evidently contrary to religion and sound morals. What could be more absurd than to transport France, Spain, Italy, or some other European country, to China? Do not introduce all that to them, but only the faith which does not despise or destroy the manners and custom of any people, always supposing they are not evil, but rather wishes to see them preserved unharmed.
>
> It is the nature of men to love and treasure above everything else their own country and that which belongs to it; in consequence there is no stronger cause for alienation and hate than an attack on local customs, especially when these go back to a venerable antiquity. This is more especially the case, when an attempt is made to introduce the customs of another people in the place of those which have been abolished. Do not draw invidious contrasts between the customs of the peoples and those of Europe; do your utmost to adapt yourselves to them.[3]

Even more perceptive were the authors of the founding document of the Société des Missions Etrangères in Paris in 1663. They declared that proclaiming the Gospel was not sufficient, and called for an indigenous clergy to be set up:

> This is the only way in which true religion can be established on a permanent footing; . . . it will be difficult for Europe to go on forever supplying priests, who take a long time to learn the language, and in time of persecution are easily recognised, arrested, driven out, or put to death, while priests of the country are able more easily to remain in concealment, and in the end will be able to bring their countries to the point to which they will no longer need help from abroad.[4]

When the first generation of Jesuits arrived permanently in Mojos in the 1680s, this was the nature of their ideological preparation. They were ready to adapt themselves to the places in which they found themselves.

When Father Cyprián Baraza first rowed down the Mamoré from Loreto to Trinidad, his contemporary biographer notes that he settled down in an Indian hut, imitating the Indians' every act. "He made himself a barbarian with these barbarians, the easier to lead them into the paths of salvation." He might have had a low opinion of them – he thought that the inhabitants of Mojos "seemed lost to all sensations of humanity or religion" – but he knew where his duty lay.[5]

He had many inducements up his sleeve "to win the esteem and affection of these nations". With skills in "physic and surgery", he set up a health clinic, and "when any of them fell sick, twas he prepared their medicines, washed and dressed their wounds, and cleaned their huts".

Father Baraza was killed some years later, when exploring among the Baures Indians to the north. As a result of his violent death, the accounts of his life are all infused with a high degree of religiosity, appropriate to one about to receive the martyr's crown. Whereas in 1600, most Jesuits were more like soldiers than priests, by 1700 they had evolved into boy scouts, with a highly developed sense of religious mission. Fifty years later, on the verge of expulsion, they were to become more agnostic, cynical aid workers on development projects with a strong sense of the limitations of their role.

From his base in a hut in Trinidad, Father Baraza had managed to assemble within a year some two thousand scattered Indians. With this raw material, he formed a large town, "and 'twas called the Blessed Trinity". Soon a church had been built, and cattle brought from Santa Cruz. This ability of the Jesuits to organize the physical as well as the spiritual needs of their flocks was one of the keys to their success.

One of Father Baraza's other achievements was to explore a route from Mojos to Lima that did not involve travelling through the Spanish cities of Santa Cruz, Cochabamba, or La Paz. He found a way that cut directly west across the plains of Mojos to the Andes. This enabled the Jesuits' mission colony to maintain contact with their power base in Lima, and with the viceroy, avoiding the centres of white settler power in Santa Cruz and Cochabamba.

The go-ahead for the establishment of missions in Mojos had originally been given by the Jesuits in Lima. Unlike the Chiquitos missions which, though close to Santa Cruz, were controlled from Paraguay, the Mojos missions came within the jurisdiction of Lima. The initiative had come from a Jesuit brother in Santa Cruz, José del Castillo. Involved with Spaniards there who had a trading relationship with the Indians of Mojos, Brother Castillo had been on one of their expeditions, and advanced a considerable way into their country. "He won the affection of the chief persons of these nations, who promised him an abode among them. Overjoyed, he set out for Lima, to inform his brethren of the hopes he entertained of winning over these barbarians to Christ."

That was in 1675. When in Lima, Brother Castillo was introduced to Father

Cyprián Baraza, then aged thirty-three, who "had long besought his superiors to allot him the most painful missions"; the Jesuit superiors agreed to allow the two priests to try to set up missions in Mojos. The two men returned to Santa Cruz, and prepared for this new adventure.

> They embarked on the River Guapay in a small canoe, made by the heathens of that country, who served them as guides. They did not arrive among the Mojos till after sailing, with great trouble and fatigue, for twelve days, during which they were frequently in danger of losing their lives.

They survived, partly because of "the sweetness and modesty of this apostolical Father", and partly no doubt because of "some inconsiderable presents he made the Indians, of fish-hooks, needles, glass beads, and such like". These, the chronicler writes, "made them bear, insensibly, with his presence".

Cyprián Baraza and José Castillo spent four years wandering around Mojos, "sometimes through fens lying almost under water, and at other times through lands scorched with heat, and ever in danger of being sacrificed to the fury of barbarians".

Eventually Father Baraza fell so ill, with a "quartan ague", that he was obliged to return to Santa Cruz to recover. When he got better, the Santa Cruz governor thought that he might be usefully deployed among the Chiriguanos, the principal threat to the settler colony at that time.

Baraza seems at first to have agreed to cooperate. He learnt the Chiriguano language and set off to the south of Santa Cruz. But he had no more luck with the Chiriguanos than had the Chiquitos Jesuits. "The unworthy manner in which they received the Blessed Word he preached to them, obliged him to abandon this corrupt people." Father Baraza was not the first nor the last of those who found the Chiriguanos too much for them.

So he was allowed to return to Mojos. There, "after eight years and a half's toil", he established the first mission at Loreto, with six hundred Indians gathered in.

In the first few years, there was considerable toing and froing, from Santa Cruz to Mojos and from Lima to Santa Cruz. The initial expedition of the Jesuit fathers was in the nature of an exploration, of putting a toe in the water. Subsequently, official approval was required, and a lot more priests. The first mission town was not formally established until the early 1680s, and even then it moved several times during the first three years.

One place that they chose turned out to be the spot where Governor Mate de Luna's expedition had camped in 1602, and where his son had sought to establish a Spanish town. Although this had happened eighty years earlier, the events of that expedition were still fresh in the minds of the Indians. They remembered how the Spanish mutineers had been punished, and how, after an ambush, many Indians had been killed.

After some five years' work, Loreto had about five thousand inhabitants. With "a fresh supply of missionaries", Baraza was able to move on to create the mission town at Trinidad.

After many years in and around the waters of the upper Mamoré, Father Baraza was allowed to go exploring to the north-east, to the territory of the Baures:

> The most important discovery, and which gave Father Cyprián the highest pleasure, was that of the Baures. These people are more civilized than the Mojos. They have a great number of villages, in which are streets and a sort of square where the soldiers exercise. Every village is surrounded with a strong palisade which secures it from the weapons of war employed in that country. They set up a kind of trap in the highways which stop their enemies on a sudden. They use in battle a kind of shield made of canes interwoven one with the other, which are proof against arrows, and covered with cotton and feathers of various colours.

This was an exciting new territory, and Father Cyprián visited a great many of these villages, "all whose inhabitants seemed to be of a tractable disposition and to approve of the new law he preached". This is land to the east of the Mamoré, towards the Guaporé, in the area of the present-day mission town of Magdalena.

> This success gave him great joy, but it was soon damped. Two converts, his companions, heard a great noise of drums in the night-time in a village he had not yet visited. Now seized with a panic, they besought the missionary to fly with all possible speed before it was too late, assuring him, they were so well acquainted with the customs of the country, and the levity and inconstancy of the people, that they were certain this sound of drums and the tumultuous motion of the Indians, who were armed, might prove fatal to them.

But Father Baraza, intent on martyrdom, stood his ground. He was confronted with "a troop of Baures, armed with hatchets, bows and arrows".

> One of these barbarians, forcing away the cross he held in his hand, struck him a violent blow on the head with an axe, which killed him.
>   Thus died Father Cyprián Baraze, the 16th September 1702, in the 61st year of his age, of which he had spent 27 years, two months and a half, in converting the Mojos.

Although the Jesuits did not like being involved with the Spaniards of Santa Cruz, there were occasions when they seem to have tacitly agreed that a show of force by the colonial power was necessary. The Indians could not be allowed to murder missionaries with impunity. So the Spaniards were allowed to use the death of Father Baraza to teach the Baures a lesson. The governor of Santa Cruz, Benito de Ribera y Quiroga, sent out a large military expedition of Spanish soldiers and one thousand Christian Indians, commanded by General Félix Cortés, to the Baures villages. The Mojos Jesuits supported this expedition and sent two priests with it, doing so, they said, to try to mitigate the acts of repression that were bound to occur.

They did not have much luck. A number of those Indians deemed to have been responsible for the death of Father Baraza were hanged. A further 250 were captured and taken to Santa Cruz as slaves. Some of them died on the journey. One of these Baures captives had been living in the mission town of San Ignacio, where he had been taken by the Jesuits so that he might learn the Mojos language and serve as an interpreter. He managed to escape, but drowned when crossing a lake.[6]

In practice, whenever the Jesuits moved into new areas to try to force the Indians into mission towns, the Indians almost invariably put up a tough opposition. While there were always some Indians who perceived the potential benefit in the new scheme of things that the missionaries would propose, there were always others who raised the alarm or who spoke out against what they saw as a most dangerous development.

In the early years, when Father Baraza and Brother Castillo had first advanced into Mojos, their efforts had been halted by "a Mojo fugitive from Santa Cruz". This man, familiar with the Spanish town, warned the rural Indians that being nice to the missionaries would lead them to be handed over to the Spanish. The missionaries rejected this notion angrily, and they managed to bribe a cacique, Yucu, to argue the case on their side. He seems to have won the day, for the Mojo "fugitive" died rather suddenly. It was "a kind of miracle", concludes the chronicler without further comment.[7]

The Indians were certainly right to believe that the missionaries were but a foretaste of what was to come. Slaving expeditions remained a real danger. So delighted were the Santa Cruz Spaniards on the occasion of the murder of Father Baraza, by the opportunity they had been given to go on a slaving expedition, that they repeated the experiment a few years later in the same area. Hearing of the advance of the Spanish soldiers into their territory, the Indians came to the Mojos Jesuits and asked for protection. The priests told them not to be worried. The soldiers were friendly. The governor of Santa Cruz, José Cayetano Hurtado de Avila, had told the Jesuits that his soldiers were only moving into Indian territory in order to protect the frontier with Brazil. The priests naively repeated this information to the Indians. Finding the Indians friendly, the Spaniards promptly captured two thousand of them and dragged them back to Santa Cruz, to the mortification of the Jesuit priests who saw the work of years rendered useless.[8]

Notes

1. The chief source for details of their expeditions comes from Antonio de Orellana, "Carta sobre el origen de las misiones de Mojos, 1687", printed in Victor Maurtua, *Juicio de límites entre el Perú y Bolivia,*

Madrid 1906, vol. 10, pp. 1–24. (It seems that Orellana was probably the author of the "Extract of a Spanish Relation, containing the life and death of Father Cyprián Baraza, c.1703", printed in John Lockman, *Travels of the Jesuits*, London 1743, vol. 11.) In addition, there is an account of these early expeditions by José del Castillo, "Relación de la provincia de Mojos", printed in Manuel Ballivián, *Documentos para la historia geográfica de la República de Bolivia*, La Paz 1906, vol. 1, pp. 294–395; and another one by Pedro Marbán, "Relación de la provincia de la Virgen del Pilar de Mojos", in the *Boletín de la Sociedad Geográfica de La Paz*, 1898, vol. 1, pp. 120–67. See also, Diego Francisco Altamirano, "Breve Historia de las Misiones de Infieles que tiene la Compania de Jesus en esta Provincia del Peru, en las Provincias de los Mojos, c.1710", in Manuel Ballivián, *Documentos historicos de Bolivia: Historia de la Misión de los Mojos*, La Paz 1891.

2. See Fred J. Rippy and J.T. Nelson, *Crusaders of the Jungle*, Chapel Hill, North Carolina 1936.
3. Stephen Neill, *A History of Christian Missions*, Penguin Books, 2nd edn, London 1986, p. 153.
4. Neill, pp. 153–4. The actual date of the document is 1700, but is claimed to represent the views of an earlier generation.
5. The story of the first Jesuits in Mojos has been told by various hands (see note 1): This one probably comes from Orellana, and was reprinted in Lockman's *Travels of the Jesuits* in 1743.
6. José Chávez Suárez, *Historia de Moxos*, 2nd edn, La Paz 1986, p. 240.
7. Chávez Suárez, p. 217.
8. Chávez Suárez, pp. 229–30.

20

MAGDALENA

The Jesuit mission at Magdalena

Flying in eastern Bolivia is like taking a country bus. The plane may or may not come – and if it comes it may not go. The military have an airline of their own, Transportes Aéreos Militares, an attempt to cut costs or to line someone's pocket. Fee-paying passengers, however, have priority over servicemen on leave. To cheer up the out-of-the-way places, like the old mission stations of Mojos, the military are accustomed to run weekly flights with their old propeller aircraft. But in the current economic crisis – and current means forever – even these flights have been stopped.

There is, however, the national line, Lloyd Aéreo Boliviano, and this flies twice a week to Magdalena. What is more, in Trinidad they do bookings on a computer. Enquiries suggest that there will indeed be room on the flight.

The small, two-engined Fokker holds about twenty-five people. The flight to Magdalena lasts only about half an hour, but since it is cloudy, little is visible below.

At Magdalena's grass airstrip, a great crowd comes out to greet the plane. We walk more or less straight out of the plane into the village. Magdalena seems very much the back of beyond, yet is much more prosperous than almost anywhere else we have seen, with four schools and a population of six thousand.

It is a typical Jesuit settlement, with a great plaza filled with palm trees, and a grid of streets stretching out on all four sides. Founded in 1720, it has clearly never recovered the prosperity of its first fifty years of existence.

Strolling through to the central square through the fierce afternoon heat, we find lodgings in the front room of the Alojamiento Sildana, a low one-storey building on the corner. Once the election headquarters of Max Fernández, the beer-baron-turned-politico who has been spreading his largesse around the country, it has recently been repainted. All the houses that front onto the square are painted in shades of blue and pink as though someone had paid the inhabitants to do it. Perhaps it was Max Fernández. Our room is absolutely bare, but large and airy, with hooks for hammocks.

The church across the square is, alas, new. Nor does it have much old inside it. There is said to be some Jesuit silver, but a robbery a couple of years ago has caused what remains to be locked away. The priest here comes from Spain. He is an habitué of Mojos, for his previous posting was the old mission town of Concepción de Baures. His brother lives at Bella Vista.

Here, we are near the Brazilian frontier, and the priest says that the old Portuguese fort at Príncipe da Beira can still be found down the river, on the banks of the Guaporé. The area across the border remains a Brazilian military zone. In Magdalena, as in all the other mission towns we have been to, there is a small Bolivian garrison, twenty-five soldiers and a commanding officer.

We walk through the town down to the landing stage on the River Itonamas, an arcadian spot. Small boys are riding their horses, cattle are being driven home, and a herd of bulls has gathered on the further shore. The river is not wide, but deep, with steep banks. It is a tributary of the Guaporé (and hence of the Madeira and the Amazon). Upstream, it reaches through Mojos to the missions of Chiquitos and becomes the San Miguel. This is the famous San Miguel that springs from the Bañados del Izozog near San José de Chiquitos, known to the early conquistadores. In the eighteenth century it was a major highway, an important communication link between the mission towns. Today, two large ferries lie grounded on a mudbank, and a few dugout canoes are drawn up on the beach.

This used to be the main entrance to the village. Alcides d'Orbigny arrived here by boat, in the pouring rain, on 1 March 1832.

> A pier some 500 metres long took me straight into the mission, where the administrator and his family, consisting of his wife and daughters, gave me a warm welcome. They were the first white women that I had seen since leaving Santa Cruz, some nine months earlier.[1]

It was still the rainy season, and d'Orbigny found that the surroundings of the mission were flooded; "the torrential rain fell ever more violently". Obliged to remain indoors, he concentrated on his "statistical and linguistic researches".

After travelling through Chiquitos, d'Orbigny had been rowed down the San Miguel and the Itonamas, and in his day the journey was still perfectly possible. Sixty years later, in the 1890s, when the Spanish explorer Ciro Bayo came to Magdalena, having made the same journey, the route was effectively unnavigable. Bayo found the stream narrow, weedy, and overhung with trees. The Bolivian government of his day, anxious to assist the rubber trade, had offered a prize to whoever would open it up to traffic.[2]

The old church built by the Jesuits, with its thick walls of adobe, was still standing when Bayo came to Magdalena.

> Inside there are three aisles, with brick columns, a ceiling of cane, and a wooden floor. The stoups of holy water are made from marble, and the huge pulpit, with gilded mouldings, is of considerable merit. In the confessionals, immense constructions of

cedar and mahogany, you can still see those great leather seats that our grandparents used to have, once used by the Jesuits when sitting in judgement on the penitent.

Much was in a sorry state. The presbytery still had its paving of tiled brick, and the high altar had a gilded altarpiece, but the paintings were on the verge of ruin:

> Clamped to the walls of the church are a number of immense canvases, oil paintings whose subject matter is difficult to discern, so filthy are they, torn, and covered in dust. The same fate has overcome the statues on the altars, nearly all are damaged and lacking paint, or absurdly clothed.

But the treasures of the church – "great candlesticks, lecterns and holy vessels made from rich and well-worked silver" – had been preserved intact.

D'Orbigny, who had many wonderful descriptive gifts, was never at his best when looking at architecture, getting his centuries muddled up and confusing baroque with gothic. "The church is very broad, built in the gothic style, notable for its wooden sculptures in the most florid style of the Middle Ages."

He was on surer ground with the old Jesuit college, "a square block with an upper storey divided into three great halls". He found it "more beautiful than cosy".

The journey to Magdalena of Manoel Felix de Lima in 1742

In the eighteenth century, the mission town of Magdalena lay close to the Spanish–Portuguese frontier. It was often visited by the Portuguese. The gold rush to Cuiabá of the 1720s had already penetrated through to the Portuguese settlement of Mato Grosso by the 1730s, a town that stood on the far side of the Guaporé from Magdalena.

"Gold was so plentiful," Robert Southey wrote in his history of Brazil, that "it lay upon the surface of the ground."[3] The gold rush brought slavers, traders and adventurers to the waters of the upper Guaporé, and inevitably made an impact on the self-sufficient world of the Mojos missions.

One early seeker after gold in the neighbourhood of Mato Grosso was Manoel Felix de Lima, a Portuguese adventurer from Lisbon. Finding that the gold there was becoming more scarce, he decided to organize a great expedition on the river, to seek his fortune downstream. These exploratory expeditions along the Guaporé were becoming increasingly frequent. Some were engaged in the old task of collecting Indian slaves, some were looking for gold. Others began to look longingly at the vast herds of cattle held by the Jesuit missions of Mojos.

Felix de Lima's expedition set off from Mato Grosso in 1742. He took with him about a dozen whites and forty black slaves and Indians. "Some were mere vagabonds, without character or means; the others, young raw men, unprincipled and deeply in debt, some of whom had already fled from Cuiabá to Mato Grosso to avoid their creditors." Coming across the camp of a slaving expedition soon after they had started, half his team decided to join it. The slaver they joined, Antônio de Almeida Morães, was soon to acquire a reputation in the area comparable to that of Raposo Tavares on the Paraguay a century earlier.

Once past the slaver's camp, Felix de Lima's reduced expedition stopped on its way west at the first Spanish mission they came to. This settlement, the mission of San Miguel, was in the hands of an old Spanish Jesuit, Gaspar de Prado. He received them politely, and directed them on to Magdalena.

The best description of Magdalena, some twenty years after it was first established in 1720, comes from an account of Felix de Lima's journey. He left a manuscript which found its way to Portugal and, eventually, into the hands of Robert Southey. This is Southey's version.

Nearing the Magdalena mission, "a canoe came from the reduction with two Indians on board, one of whom addressed the commander in Spanish, and, in the Jesuit's name, presented him with two dozen fowls, some pigeons, beef, fruit, and sugar". Felix de Lima sent back a message saying that he would arrive at the mission the following day to say mass.

Disembarking at the Magdalena landing stage on the Itonamas, the Portuguese adventurers found that "Indian archers were drawn up in a double row to see them land". Felix de Lima was not overawed by such a display. He had prepared one of his own.

> From the extraordinary wardrobe which he carried with him on this wild voyage, he attired himself in pearl-colour silk stockings, a waistcoat and breeches of embroidered dove colour velvet, and a coat of red barbarisco, lined with white silk, and with cuffs of rose colour velvet; the wig, the gold-laced hat, and the Indian cane completed his costume, and his arms were a pocket-pistol, a silver-hilted sword, and the formidable faça de ponte, or knife of all work, inlaid with gold and silver.

Felix de Lima was welcomed by the two Jesuit priests in charge of the mission, Father Joseph Reiter, a Hungarian, and Father Athanasio Theodoro, an Italian. The Portuguese visitor then presented Father Joseph with two pieces of blue taffeta "of the richest brocade which had ever reached the mines of Mato Grosso".

Father Reiter, anxious that the Portuguese should not think that they were country bumpkins, opened up the sacristy of the church. Inside he showed him an array of "thirty hangings of tissue and brocade . . . sent from Potosí and Lima". The Portuguese had little to teach the Spaniards when it came to conspicuous display.

Southey reports that Felix de Lima was suitably impressed by what he found at Magdalena:

> The whole settlement was enclosed with a square wall, which being probably of clay,

like the church, was covered to preserve it from the weather; and this covering projected so far that there was a dry walk at all times round the Reduction. The great square, according to the usual style of these Jesuit establishments, had a cross at each corner, and a large one on its pedestal in the centre; but in other respects the ground plan appears to have been traced by some whimsical architect; for Manoel Felix says that in whatever direction the houses were seen they appeared in regular order, like the chequers of a chess board; and the country was laid out in farms after the same fashion, with paths of white sand.

A considerable space was enclosed within the walls, so as to afford room for folds and gardens; and the settlement bore many marks of civilisation; there were shops for weavers, carpenters, and carvers; an engenho where rum as well as sugar was made; public kitchens, and stocks for the enforcement of wholesome discipline. The plantations of bananas, mamoens, and cotton were numerous, and the cultivation extended many leagues along the river.

The children were instructed in Spanish, and taught to read; and there was a school of music. Horse and kine were very numerous, and two beasts were slaughtered every day for the various artificers who were employed in the service of the mission. The Indians who had been chiefs before their conversion held the rank of alcaldes.[4]

The mission church, dedicated to Santa Maria Magdalena was, in particular, a most splendid sight:

The church was a spacious building of three aisles, the columns, as in Paraguay, being each the trunk of a tall tree; the walls were well made of clay, and the roof tiled. A calvary stood in the middle; there were three altars richly ornamented, an organ, four stringed instruments which are called harps, and four trumpets, which though made of canes, are said to have been as finely toned as if they had been of metal.

Some Indians who were expert in the art of carving had been brought from another mission; they were employed upon a pulpit, and the Portuguese were astonished at the beauty of their work; it was covered with foliage and the figures of various birds, and was to be gilt when finished. A golden pix [a coffer for consecrated bread] had been sent from Lima as the offering of some devout persons; its value was three thousand five hundred pieces of silver.[5]

Although the two priests were perfectly polite to the visiting Portuguese expedition, "they were not desirous that such visits should be repeated". This was a frontier mission, and Portuguese visitors – after the history of the previous 150 years – could easily be considered to be spies. So, anxious to show that this was Spanish territory that would be defended, the priests decided to provide their visitors with a display of the mission's military strength:

On the second morning, therefore, after the guests had breakfasted upon chocolate and sponge cake, and after mass had been performed, four score horsemen were exercised in the great square before the church. They were dressed in cotton shirts which had been ornamented with some labour, and large trousers of blue baize; their weapon was the macana; they had cotton horse-cloths, and many small bells fastened to the poitral and saddle. . . .

When they had concluded their exercise, both sides of the square were presently filled with archers, naked, their bodies stained red as if for battle, stamping with their feet and setting up the war-whoop. They discharged their arrows into the air skilfully, so as they should fall in the middle of the square; and the great cross was bristled with them as they fell. Both sides then drew nearer each other; and when they were within point blank shot, they raised so terrible a shout that Manoel Felix ordered his people to stand upon their defence, and made some of his negroes gather about him, because he perceived that the natives were more afraid of them than of the whites.[6]

It had of course occurred to the Portuguese adventurers that the information they had obtained about these missions might be of some political importance to the authorities at home. They had another thought. If they could buy some cattle from the missionaries at Magdalena, and drive the beasts back to Mato Grosso, they would not be out of pocket.

Father Reiter said that, for himself, he would be happy to provide them with cattle. First, however, he would have to get permission from his father superior at the mission on the Mamoré of Exaltación de la Cruz.

Part of the Portuguese group set off for Exaltación by boat. Felix de Lima wanted to try making the journey by land, and he stayed at Magdalena for a further three weeks to await a favourable reply. He was to be disappointed. When a message finally came from the Jesuit Superior in Exaltación, it rebuked Father Reiter for having entertained the Portuguese travellers in the first place. It said that the Spanish governor in Santa Cruz would be most displeased when he heard of the incident. Father Reiter was ordered to get rid of the Portuguese as soon as possible, "giving them all necessary assistance for their return".

Felix de Lima was forced to abandon his land journey to Exaltación. He set off instead downriver – down the Itonamas and into the Guaporé – hoping to catch up with the rest of his expedition. But he never found them, and after many adventurous chapters, he made his way down the Madeira to the Amazon and the Atlantic.

When he rowed away from Magdalena, he had left part of his team on its way to Exaltación. Well received there by Father Leonardo de Valdivia, they had been unable to persuade him to provide them with cattle. They stayed for nearly three weeks.

When they departed they gave some trifles to the Indians, but they could only prevail on the Jesuit to receive a piece of silk for the altar, while he liberally presented them with loaves of salt and of sugar, wax, soap, wine, wheaten bread, biscuit, rum, calico, and books of devotion . . . in so flourishing a state were the Moxo missions.

On returning to Magdalena, the group found that Felix de Lima had already left.

Rather than following him downstream, they decided to return upstream to Mato Grosso.

Once back at their base, they prepared for a fresh expedition the following year. They set off in two groups, one led by Francisco de Leme, the other by José Barbosa da Sa. But the situation on the Guaporé had changed dramatically. The slaver Antônio de Almeida had been actively seizing Indians on the river:

> The numerous Indian habitations which they had seen upon their former voyage were now forsaken; the landing places had been filled up, and the houses burnt by the natives themselves; for Antonio de Almeida, with whom the comrades of Manoel Felix had joined company, had made such havoc, and taken so many slaves, that these poor people thought it better to lay their own country waste, and fly into the interior, lest they should be assailed by the same enemies.

As a result of Almeida's activities, the Jesuits were no longer so well-disposed to the Portuguese as they had been the year before. When the group captained by Barbosa da Sa came to a new Spanish mission settlement, it was frostily received.

The Jesuit in charge was Father Athanasio Theodoro, the priest who had greeted Felix de Lima's expedition to Magdalena the previous year. "With as much courtesy as was compatible with such a communication, he informed them that they were a set of runaways, robbers, and pirates."

What Father Theodosio told them was in effect an outline of a new Spanish policy:

> The governor of Santa Cruz had instructed all the missionaries to be upon their guard, and draw out the Indians to oppose them, while he prepared forces to destroy the settlements in Mato Grosso, and erect forts for the purpose of excluding the Portuguese from the navigation of the river.

Father Theodoro's mission settlement, called Santa Rosa, was to be the forerunner of these forts. Settled on the right, northern, bank of the Guaporé, it commanded an important and strategic stretch of the river close to the entrance of the Itonamas.

A century earlier, the Jesuit priests had tried to stand their ground in Guaíra and Itatín against the westerly push of the Paulista slave-traders. They were determined to ensure that history should not repeat itself.

Yet it was to do so a century later. By the middle of the eighteenth century, the attitudes of the missionaries were ambivalent. They were certainly hostile to the Portuguese slave trade. It undermined their relationship with the Indians whom they had promised to protect. Yet they were not averse to enjoying the benefits of ordinary trade and commerce across the frontier. Life in the missions would become much easier if they could do business with the Portuguese settlements across the river.

The missionaries were also lonely in their remote towns. They liked to see the occasional European face. Robert Southey tells the story of Father Theodoro's assistant priest. He was a young Irishman called John Brand. Though a Jesuit, he "seemed not to enter into the political feelings of his superior, and wished to enjoy the company of these visitors as long as he could".

Recently established, Santa Rosa was a bleak outpost, as the report of another Portuguese expedition in 1749 made clear:

> The poverty of the Indians is sufficiently manifested in the humble construction of the dwellings. Few of them are built of mud and straw, and the greater part of the latter material alone, which is woven in such a manner as to form the walls and roof. To this outer poverty corresponds the penury within, because, without any distinction of grade among the Indians, they huddle together in a miserable hammock to sleep, and they have a set of several earthen pots in which they prepare the maize in many forms, all as insipid to the taste as disagreeable to the sight.[7]

Father Theodoro was made of sterner stuff than Father Brand. He was used to the sometimes harsh and lonely life of the missionary. When the second group of Portuguese explorers arrived off Santa Rosa a few days later, the one led by Francisco de Leme, he refused to allow it to land. The group of Barbosa da Sa, meanwhile, had left Santa Rosa and rowed up the Itonamas. When they arrived at Magdalena, they faced a similar hostile reception. The old Hungarian, Father Reiter, told them that they must leave the next day:

> If they came thither in consequence of the good treatment which the first visitors experienced, they would find themselves greatly disappointed: that treatment was bestowed in Christian compassion, upon persons who were supposed to have lost their way in a wild country; had it been suspected that they came on purpose, they would have been very differently received.

The Jesuit allowed them to stay two days, but they were treated roughly:

> The Portuguese were kept in one house, and their [black] slaves in another; and they were not permitted to go out for a moment, except when they went to church. Their fare was coarse and unceremonious . . . maize cakes and boiled beef with a little salt to savour it, served upon the bare table.

Southey, a man of his free-trading time, suggests that the strict orders to have no communication with the Portuguese may not have been altogether to the liking of the Indians:

> The poor Indians, who would gladly have had a regular intercourse established, and a better market opened, both for the supply of their wants, and the disposal of their

TRINIDAD. A Mojos Indian performing the dance of the macheteros in the old Jesuit mission church. Drawn by Franz Keller, 1867. This was, wrote José Aguirre Acha in 1899, ''a vivid portrayal of the struggles of the Mojos against Spanish rule.'' The dance also has a flavour of a civilization that goes back long before the Spaniards arrived.

Trinidad. Musicians inside the mission church, drawn by Franz Keller, 1867.

Trinidad. Musicians at the mission church, drawn by Alcides d'Orbigny, 1832.

TRINIDAD. The Indian council at Trinidad encountered by Lieutenant Lardner Gibbon of the US Navy. From left to right: Maria Nosa, Casemira Nacopearu, Jose Vicente, Cayuba, Juana Jua. Drawn by Lardner Gibbon, 1852.

SAN PEDRO. Dance of the macheteros performed by a Canichana at the San Pedro mission. Drawn circa 1790, probably by Pablo de Oquendo, the head of the art school set up in the mission by Lázaro de Ribera, the Spanish governor of Mojos.

TRINIDAD. Triumph of the settlers. Celebrating Bolivia's national day.

EXALTACIÓN. Boats on the River Mamoré at Exaltación de la Cruz, drawn by Lardner Gibbon, 1852.

MAGDALENA. Boats on the River Itonamas at the Jesuit mission of Magdalena. D'Orbigny landed here in 1832: "a pier some 500 metres long took me straight into the mission."

CANOES. On the Mamoré river at Exaltación. "The jaguar that attacked my canoe", June 1858, from the album of Melchor María Mercado.

CANOES. Drawn by Alcides d'Orbigny, 1832.

CANOES. Descending the Mamoré. Drawn by Lieutenant Lardner Gibbon, 1852.

MAGDALENA. The modern church. A hundred years ago its treasures – "great candlesticks, lecterns and holy vessels made from rich and well-worked silver" – were still intact.

SAN PEDRO. All that remains of the eighteenth-century Jesuit silver, pinned on the church wall above the altar. "For the plates of silver that decorated its altars," wrote d'Orbigny in 1832, "San Pedro could rival not just the cathedrals of Europe, but the richest churches of Peru."

SAN PEDRO. The modern church, with an old Jesuit bell from 1750. In the eighteenth century, San Pedro had its own foundry.

Exaltación. "The central plaza, with its great palm trees, its church buildings, and its houses for the civil authorities", drawn by Franz Keller in 1867.

Exaltación. The mission church today. According to Edward Mathews, who came here in 1874, "the deserted houses and lines of old streets now in ruins give a sad and desolate look to Exaltación."

Mojos Indians. Drawn by d'Orbigny in 1832.

Exaltación. Cayubaba children today. "Enthusiastic and enterprising," wrote d'Orbigny in 1832, the Cayubabas of Exaltación are also "prudent and respectful, uncomplaining and affable."

produce, were much disappointed at this determination, and came in secret to purchase knives, needles, and axes, from their visitors.

Father Reiter finally got rid of his unwelcome guests, requesting them "for the love of God never to return, seeing that the only end of such visits would be to create vexation and mischief".

United again, the two Portuguese groups made their way back to Mato Grosso. Momentarily chastened, the injunctions against them had little effect. Many of them were to return to the Mojos missions in the 1740s and 1750s.

Meanwhile their predecessor, Manoel Felix de Lima, had made his way to Portugal. The governor of Rio de Janeiro, João de Abreu Castello Branco, had sent him to Lisbon to give an account of his great pioneering expedition to the king. He was in for a surprise:

> He sailed for Lisbon with exaggerated notions of the service which he had performed, and in full expectation of receiving magnificent rewards. On his arrival he was put in confinement, and detained a week without cause or pretext, his two negroes and his baggage being kept on board the whole time.

When he was eventually examined by the king's ministers, he recommended that several forts should be built along the Guaporé at the key points where the large rivers from the south flowed into it. "For himself, he required the appointment of Guarda Mor of all the country which he had thus added to the Portuguese dominions, a suitable grant of land, and such other favours as his Majesty might be pleased to bestow."

The ministers pointed out, perfectly correctly, that the lands which Felix de Lima thought that he had discovered for Portugal were "by the right of possession as well as of discovery" vested in Spain. Poor Felix de Lima insisted on claiming what he thought was his due reward. "So strongly was he possessed with this notion that he continued to haunt the court as a miserable suitor till the whole of his substance was expended, and he was reduced to extreme poverty and wretchedness."[8]

It was an inglorious end for a pioneer.

Mojos at war: the struggle between Spain and Portugal on the Guaporé in the 1760s

Some ten years later, at three o'clock on the afternoon of 25 September 1760, the Spanish governor of Santa Cruz came ashore at the landing stage of the Magdalena mission. Alonso Verdugo had been rowed up the Itonamas river from the Guaporé after a lengthy tour through the Mojos missions. With war looming between Spain

and Portugal in Europe, he was on a military reconnaissance expedition, examining the frailties of the frontier.

Delighted with the town like all visitors, he described it as "the largest in the province, not just physically but in the ever-increasing number of new converts". Like Felix de Lima before him, he was duly impressed by "the spacious and beautiful church with its three naves":

> The high altar, the side altars and the pulpit, as well as the medallions that decorate the nave, on which from the brush of a good painter the life of the patron saint is displayed, are most notable; in their skilful execution, their sense of proportion, and their beauty, it would be difficult to find their equal in the entire kingdom.[9]

In the adjacent two-storeyed college, he was welcomed by the three Jesuit priests who controlled the town. The old Hungarian, Father José Reiter, was still there, but the others were more recent arrivals: Father Nicolas Sussich, an Italian: and Father Francisco Espi, from Valencia.

Magdalena was one of the Jesuit missions that lay closest to the Portuguese frontier, but Governor Verdugo was concerned with a particular problem further north: the mission settlement that the Jesuits had established in 1743 at Santa Rosa. A familiar port of call for Portuguese traders and explorers, it had recently moved to the other side of the river. According to the terms of the Treaty of Madrid of 1750, surveyors from Spain and Portugal were supposed to map the South America frontier on the ground. To avoid trouble, the Jesuit General, Ignacio Visconti, had given orders that all missions on the Portuguese side of the border were to be withdrawn before the surveyors arrived.

In Paraguay, famously, this decision caused immense problems and led to war. In Mojos, the withdrawal from Santa Rosa occurred more smoothly, though not without difficulty. The mission was shifted south across the river in the 1750s and renamed Santa Rosa la Nueva. It was easy to construct fresh makeshift buildings, less simple to encourage the Indian population to move. Many remained on the northern side.

For a variety of reasons connected with the inaccessibility of the area, the binational survey team failed to arrive in Mojos until decades later. So the Portuguese governor of Mato Grosso, Antônio Rollín de Moura, took advantage of their absence to move into the vacuum caused by the Jesuits' unilateral withdrawal. In February 1760 he occupied Santa Rosa la Vieja and began the construction of a Portuguese fort overlooking the river. It was this event that precipitated Alonso Verdugo's study tour of his province.

His first act was to send an ultimatum to Rollín de Moura, in October, ordering him to withdraw his forces from Santa Rosa la Vieja. The order was rejected, and Alonso Verdugo began planning a military expedition to dislodge the Portuguese by force.

The Spaniards were not in a strong strategic position. Mojos was a frontier province, run for the previous seventy years solely by the Jesuits on behalf of the Indians. There were no Spanish towns or Spanish settlers in the area. It was notably difficult to get to. The route over the mountains from Cochabamba was perilous, and that down the Rio Grande from Santa Cruz was slow. For half the year, the province was waterlogged.

The Portuguese were much better placed. For them, the Guaporé had become a highway. They were well established in Cuiabá and Mato Grosso. They had sent innumerable explorers down the Guaporé. The Spaniards considered that all this was Spanish territory, but they had never been able to occupy it. Now the land of Mojos, which they had had and held for nearly a hundred years, was under serious threat.

Alonso Verdugo did what he could. He sent small military detachments to fortify and garrison three key installations on the Guaporé: one at Santa Rosa la Nueva, one at the junction of the Guaporé with the Mamoré, and one on the Baures close to the mission of San Miguel. It was well to be prepared, for in 1762, in the wider world, Spain and Portugal were at war.

The Spaniards now began planning a major military expedition that would dislodge the Portuguese not just from their new fortress at Santa Rosa – renamed the Príncipe da Beira – but from Mato Grosso and Cuiabá as well. These wider ambitions were much discouraged by the Jesuit Superior in San Pedro, Father Juan de Beingolea. He pointed out that if the invasion of Mato Grosso was contemplated, it would be more sensible to attack through Chiquitos than through Mojos.

This advice seems to have been heard, for the military authorities in Santa Cruz began preparing a more limited expedition – to regain Santa Rosa. Alonso Verdugo requested the Audiencia in Charcas (Sucre) to send 1400 soldiers to Santa Cruz, to be ready by May 1763. At the same time, he ordered that the Jesuits' bell foundry at San Pedro should be turned over to weapons manufacture.

The Jesuits were given a special role in preparing for the expedition. In addition to manufacturing moulds for making cannon, Father Beingolea agreed that the mission Indians would grow extra maize, rice, maní (nuts) and beans to feed the troops. Fifteen hundred head of cattle would be specially fattened and then taken to high ground above the Guaporé to avoid the floods. Large numbers of extra canoes would be constructed to transport food and munitions.[10]

Finding soldiers and sufficient weapons proved to be much more difficult. Alonso Verdugo was delayed a month, and was unable to leave Santa Cruz with an army until June 1763. Lacking weapons, he set off with only 450 men. Of these, 180 were unarmed. He hoped to find 150 men waiting for him in San Pedro, making a total of 600 soldiers.

His tiny army, carried on a flotilla of canoes, arrived at San Pedro on 22 June 1763. They were greeted with bad news. Antonio Rollín de Moura had not waited to be attacked but had gone on the offensive. With reinforcements from Cuiabá, he had attacked the Jesuit mission at San Miguel. Here, everything of value had been stolen. The place had been burnt down, the Indians had been captured, and the two Jesuit priests, Father Francisco Espi and Father Francisco Rodríguez, had been detained and sent to Mato Grosso.

Worse news soon followed. Crossing the Guaporé from his new base at Príncipe da Beira at three o'clock on the morning of 26 June, the Portuguese commander fell on the makeshift settlement at Santa Rosa la Nueva. The Portuguese army had three hundred men, the Spanish defenders barely a hundred. Of these, most were ill, for they came from the Andean altiplano and were unaccustomed to the heat and low altitude of Mojos. A Spaniard who arrived a week later found them ''all like skeletons, with not a well man among them''.

In spite of their weakness and lack of numbers, the defenders won the day. The Portuguese were forced back across the river. But it was a pyrrhic victory. Arriving there a few days later, Alonso Verdugo was dismayed to find his men prostrate, their officers dead or dying.

Clearly in no shape to prosecute a war, Verdugo was saved by the news from the outside world, arriving belatedly in this remote province. Spain and Portugal were, it seemed, no longer at war. Peace had been signed in Paris. The news came too late to save San Miguel and Santa Rosa, and Rollín da Moura, his immediate ambitions achieved, was happy to offer a truce. Demoralized, with his troops peeling away, Governor Verdugo retreated to Santa Cruz.

Fresh preparations were made in the following two years to dislodge the Portuguese from their advance positions. In April 1766, a much larger expedition left Santa Cruz. Commanded this time by Brigadier Juan de Pestaña, the president of the Audiencia of Charcas, and made up of 2500 men, with rifles sent from Lima and Buenos Aires, it was potentially a powerful force. By the time it arrived at San Pedro in August, however, many of the troops had succumbed to the diseases of the tropics. The officer in charge of armaments, Colonel Antonio Aymerich, had not had much luck with the foundry producing weapons. According to one report, the workers were Indians and only worked when they felt like it. With delays caused by illness and lack of cannon, it was September before Pestaña's army was able to move out of San Pedro. Their destination was the Portuguese fort at Príncipe da Beira.

Once again, as in 1763, the Portuguese were saved by outside events. News arrived that a Spanish boat with a valuable cargo had been detained in the harbour of Rio de Janeiro. If the Spanish troops in Mojos attacked the Portuguese fort, the ship would be confiscated. Given the state of their troops, the Spaniards decided to withdraw without a shot being fired.

Colonel Aymerich was left behind with a small detachment at San Pedro. Brigadier Pestaña returned to Santa Cruz where he died shortly afterwards. The following year, 1767, there were other priorities. An entirely fresh issue was to reach the top of the political agenda in Mojos: the expulsion of the Jesuits.

D'Orbigny's assessment of Magdalena in 1832

Alcides d'Orbigny came to Magdalena some sixty years after the expulsion of the Jesuit priests from the mission. His homework on the Indians there was, as always, extremely thorough:

> The population – of 2781 people in 1832 – is made up entirely of Itonamas Indians, whose guttural language, through its harsh tones, most resembles that of the Quechua and the Aymara, though it is quite different. They are quite tall, and their rather thin legs do not prevent them from being easily the most attractive in the province. As a rule they are good people, though they have a reputation as the most terrible thieves, which might be explained by their state of poverty.

D'Orbigny, in 1832, was able to detect the powerful undertone of hostility that the Indians felt towards the whites after decades of repression and semi-slavery during the post-Jesuit period. "My conversations with the priests and administrators of Magdalena made me feel that the Itonamas have returned under this regime to all the old superstitions and customs of their primitive state." D'Orbigny clearly felt uncomfortable. "I have no personal complaint to make of them. They are docile, even servile, towards whites, who they obviously detest, not without reason."

He expressed his satisfaction with their obvious accomplishments in the field of weaving. He was impressed with the state of their agriculture "which spoke well for the administrator". He saw "huge fields of sugar cane, cotton, and tamarind, and a lot of new cocoa bushes". But he noted that these were only for the benefit of the administrators living in the old Jesuit college and of the Bolivian state. The Indians themselves seemed to receive little in return for their work:

> The allotments of the Indians are four days' walk away, down the Itonamas river, near to where it joins the Machupo. As the poor natives are forever at the disposition of the administrator, they only have two weeks a year in which to sow and two to harvest. Yet since the period of private harvesting is the same as for harvesting and transporting the commercial crops, it often happens that the Itonamas, unable to visit their allotments, lose much of their crop. They live for the rest of the year in the most abject poverty.

D'Orbigny observed that there was a notable lack of harmony between the two outsiders who ruled the former mission, the priest and the administrator. The latter frequently feared for his life. After a week's stay in this atmosphere, the French explorer was clearly pleased to be able to move on.

Earlier, while passing through the neighbouring mission of Concepción de Baures, he had reflected on why the province of Mojos seemed so very different from the Chiquitos region which he had found so agreeable:

I thought that I would find the wretched Indians rather freer in Mojos than in Chiquitos. But I was mistaken. In Mojos they have only one day free for themselves, except for Sundays and feast days which are entirely taken up with religious festivals. For the rest of the year, they are supposed to be working for the benefit of the state. What actually happens is that they are exploited, both by the administrators and by the priests, who do not allow them a moment's rest. They have even less consideration for the women than for the men, which does nothing for the population increase.

D'Orbigny was writing partly for the President of Bolivia and other government ministers who had approved his journey, and he did not mince his words:

Never have I seen such slavery and despotism under a free government. It is worth adding that before my journey, the political leaders of the country had little idea what was going on in these provinces remote from the centre, assuming that they were in some way a possession of the inhabitants of Santa Cruz, who had powerful reasons for hiding the extent to which they had enslaved the native population.

All that was left from the benevolent era of the Jesuits was the consolation of religion and ceremonial, which the Itonamas Indians took refuge in to an obsessive degree:

In the Mojos missions, the Indians spend much more time in church than in those of Chiquitos. The young go both in the morning and the evening to learn the catechism, and at eight at night they all pray together. On Saturdays, following a custom established by the Jesuits, they make a procession round the square in honour of the Virgin, with feather-decked Indians dancing in front.

After gazing at the sunset from the banks of the Itonamas river, we wandered back into town, passing the church's open door. About sixty people had gathered for evensong. There was some singing, but it was rather moderate – a marked decline in fervour since D'Orbigny's time.

On the furthest corner from the church, half a dozen tables were laid out on the roadside. Food was being served by the light of an oil lamp. We sat down and were made most welcome. We had rissoles and rice and yucca, washed down with a fruit drink. Three bolivianos for the two of us. We went to bed well content.

We got up the next morning before sunrise. We had been promised by an ageing ne'er-do-well we had met the night before that he would take us for a walk to some grapefruit groves. He wanted us to go before the heat of the sun was upon them. He failed to show up, so after half an hour's wait on a bench in the plaza, we went for a walk on our own beside the river.

At that hour, it is fresh and delightful, but by eight-thirty the heat has already become insupportable. We returned to the square and found our friend of the night before. He took us to a house in a side street. Here the priest, the army captain, the schoolteacher and a local landowner were having a hearty breakfast of steak and eggs. We were easily satisfied with a cup of chocolate and two buns, happy to have tracked down the town's ruling class to its own private café.

The priest told us that he had lived in Concepción de Baures for sixteen years. He thought that the church there had been rebuilt at least three times since the Jesuits had been expelled. Nothing old was left and he did not think it was worth a visit, especially as it is so difficult to get there. It was, he said, the oldest settlement in these parts.

We then got on to discussing TAM, the military airline, and its current failure to fly to Magdalena. This turned out to be not for economic reasons but because one of its engines had failed. "They are the brides of death," said the priest. "One day they will marry."

Finally we had a lively discussion about Iraq and Kuwait, everyone having heard on the radio that the United States had sent troops to Saudi Arabia. The priest practised his one-upmanship by saying that he had been listening to the French international news programme.

The local landowner turned out to be a man called Ford, the son of an Englishman who had come to Santa Cruz after the First World War. After working in the United States, he had come here to retire with his pension. He had an estancia near Magdalena with eight hundred head of cattle. His wife and children, who were English, had preferred to go and live in Warminster. He remained happily in Magdalena, spending most of the day reading in his hammock.

Notes

1. Alcides d'Orbigny, *Voyage dans l'Amérique méridionale*, Paris 1835–47.
2. Ciro Bayo, *El Peregrino en Indias, en el corazón de la América del Sur*, Madrid 1911. Ciro Bayo, teacher, explorer and adventurer, came to Magdalena in 1896. Working as a schoolteacher in the province of Buenos Aires in 1889, he had conceived the idea of riding up the continent to Chicago, to attend the exhibition in 1892 to mark the four-hundredth anniversary of the Columbus landing. Embarking on this ambitious trip, he got no further than Bolivia. Here he spent several years teaching and working in rubber plantations, mostly in the Beni. He travelled through the Guarayos missions to Magdalena. On the way, he visited Huacaraje, known as the Calzada de los Jesuítas, which had once been the port 004for the mission of Concepción de Baures. He found it "completely abandoned and almost unusable in the rainy season, when it is most needed".
3. Robert Southey, *The History of Brazil*, London 1819, vol. 3, p. 329. The suggestion that the Indian children were taught Spanish seems unlikely, since it was the custom in most missions for Indian languages to be used by priests and congregation alike. Indeed Southey tells us that Father Athanasio Theodoro "was learning the language of the wild Indians that he might preach the faith to them".
4. Southey, vol. 3, p. 328.
5. Southey, vol. 3, p. 330.
6. Southey, vol. 3, p. 331.
7. José Gonsalves de Fonseca, *Voyage made from the city of the Gram Para to the mouth of the river Madeira by the expedition which ascended this river to the mines of Mato Grosso by special order of His Majesty in the year*

1749, Lisbon 1826 (printed in George Earl Church, *Explorations made in the Valley of the River Madeira*, London 1875).

8. "In that condition," Southey writes, "after sixteen years obstinate attendance, and in the sixty-sixth year of his age, Manoel Felix found a melancholy solace in recording his services and his complaints, little thinking that the very writing which then beguiled his hopeless hours would one day find its way to the mountains of Cumberland, and that from that writing, the story of his adventures would be incorporated, by an Englishman, in the history of Brazil" (Southey, vol. 3, pp. 342-3).

9. "Diario del viaje hecho por el gobernador de Santa Cruz de la Sierra a la fortaleza de los Portugueses establecida en el pueblo de Santa Rosa el Viejo por el gobernador de Mato Grosso, November 19, 1760", in Pablo Pastells, *Historia de la Companía de Jesús en la provincia de Paraguay*, Madrid 1949, vol. 8, part 2, pp. 738–49.

10. Pastells, vol. 8, part 2, p. 868.

21

SAN PEDRO DE MOJOS

The Jesuit mission at San Pedro de Mojos

Moving about the great floodplains of Mojos was never easy. That is one of the charms of this obscure region. The conquistadores found it difficult to travel here in the sixteenth century; it was no easier for the Jesuit missionaries in the eighteenth; and the travellers of the nineteenth century were always short of oarsmen for their canoes. Today, everything is simpler. Small private aeroplanes can be used to fly in and out of the old mission towns and land at the homesteads of the great cattle ranches, with few questions asked. It is a paradise for drug traffickers.

Short of time like all modern travellers, we followed the trend, and made the twentieth-century choice. There are still difficulties. It's expensive, it's not always good flying weather, and if you arrive somewhere you can never be sure when you will return. And of course a perspex screen separates you from the stench of the bog and the whine of the mosquito. The chief thing to be said for the aeroplane is that you get a wonderful view, something that all those early explorers were never able to have.

We came to San Pedro de Mojos in a small Italian plane, flying there from a mission further north, Exaltación de la Cruz, in barely half an hour – a journey up the River Mamoré that took nineteenth-century travellers more than half a week. Leaving the Mamoré some way to our right, we flew over flat swampy land with a couple of estancias below. We passed above Puerto Ballivián on the River Ibare, and then, finally, circled over San Pedro a couple of times before coming in to land.

The pilot does not much like the look of the landing strip. His caution is well judged. The ground is very bumpy – "more of a track for horse races than for aeroplanes" – and one of the landing wheels is damaged and can be seen bleeding brake fluid. The pilot shrugs and claims not to be unduly worried. He thinks we will be able to take off again.

About a dozen small children are waiting for us when we finally taxi to a halt. Aeroplanes may be the means of travel for the privileged, but they are still very unusual in San Pedro. We walk with the children, past the cemetery, along a track – perhaps half a mile – into the centre of the village, a few single-storey houses round a central square.

We had seen the church from the air, colour-washed a garish blue, and certainly not old. No Jesuit memories here. Tucked in beside the church, we found a sheltered terrace. A grey-haired Spanish priest got up to greet us. We explained the purpose of our visit. We were looking for Jesuit churches. He smiled.

"None of the old churches in Mojos have survived," he tells us, "and this one is quite new." We knew this really, but it was sad to have it confirmed.

The mission town of San Pedro was first established by the Jesuits in 1696, among the Canichana Indians. They built it close to the river bank, but it was moved to its present site, a few kilometres inland, in the 1820s, more than half a century after the Jesuits had been expelled. It was moved from its often flooded position near the Mamoré to higher ground. The surviving village is still laid out to the familiar Jesuit plan – with a great central square.

Alcides d'Orbigny came to San Pedro de Mojos more than a hundred and fifty years ago, one Palm Sunday in April 1832. The mission town had only been settled into its new site some ten years earlier. Travelling up the Mamoré from Exaltación by boat, the French explorer caught a severe bout of marsh fever on the way, and on arrival he was forced to endure the usual welcoming ceremonies:

> The bells gave notice of my arrival, and, accompanied by musicians, the administrators came out to welcome me, with all the honours imaginable – which I could well have done without, not feeling at all well. I had to stay sitting for two hours without even being able to change my clothes.

D'Orbigny found himself caught up in the preparations for the ceremonies of Holy Week:

> I felt a frisson of horror on seeing no less than twenty groups of statues, almost life-size, representing the scenes of the Passion. These painted groups filled up half the church. Here was the flagellation, the crown of thorns, the way of the cross, and finally the crucifixion.

Then, after vespers, a troop of Indians, dressed in comic fashion and wearing red and other bright colours, processed slowly through the mission.

> They were playing the role of Jews looking for Jesus Christ. They divided into groups, and the people bowed low in front of them as they passed. At night the troop returned, processing around and accompanied by the saddest music imaginable.

The drear sounds of the drums and flutes and bajones were too much for d'Orbigny, and seem to have contributed to the onset of fever. The cura told him that the drums represented the rage of the people against Jesus, the flutes were their cries, and the noise of the great canes was designed to imitate an earthquake.

Before he reached the new town, d'Orbigny had passed the deserted ruins of the old mission near the bank of the river, and he reflected nostalgically on its former splendour.

> In the place that I saw the ruins, the Jesuits had established their San Pedro mission. Its central position soon turned it into the capital of the province. In it was concentrated all its wealth, all its splendour.
>
> Indeed for its monuments, for the number of its statues of saints, for the jewels that adorned the figures of the Virgin and the Baby Jesus, for the plates of silver that decorated its altars, and, perhaps more than anything, for the beautiful wooden sculptures of its church, San Pedro could rival not just the cathedrals of Europe, but the richest churches of Peru.[1]

When the Jesuits were expelled from the mission in 1767, and when the town was handed over to a regime of curas from Santa Cruz, an inventory revealed – according to d'Orbigny – that the church "contained 80 arrobas (1000 kilos) of beaten silver, with a value of approximately 170,000 francs".

The wealth of these old mission churches in the eighteenth century was phenomenal. Lázaro de Ribera, the Spanish governor of Mojos forty years before d'Orbigny's visit, made an inventory of all the Mojos churches in the 1780s:

> With the ornaments that have recently been recovered in the old mission towns, these churches now possess 622 ornaments, with other vestiduras, furniture and liturgical vestments worthy of note. The sacred vessels and silverware that decorate the altars are worth some 14,799 marcos, with 368 ounces of gold. Here I do not include the jewels on the sculptures, nor many other pieces of silver, which because they are embedded in the wood or the ivory, cannot be calculated exactly.
>
> In the warehouse at the Puerto de Paylas [on the Rio Grande near Santa Cruz], there are eight crates of silver belonging to the churches of San Ignacio and La Trinidad, which weigh (including the crate and the leather lining) 2,828 marcos. And in this provincial capital [San Pedro] there exists (from San Ignacio, San Borja, Reyes, Santa Ana, and Santa Rosa) a number of old pieces of silver weighing 446 marcos, and five ounces.[2]

Little now remains of this great treasure. Outside the modern church, a broken bell stands on the ground, in pristine condition apart from the crack. According to legend, it was struck by lightning. "Sancto Ignatio ora pro nobis" says the lettering around it, with the date 1750. Saint Ignatius pray for us. There is the familiar Jesuit stamp upon it: IHS.

In colonial times, the mission of San Pedro had a major industry denied the other missions of Mojos, a foundry. Church bells were distributed throughout the province. Our Spanish priest knows this, though he does not know where the iron was brought from. We are told that the site of the foundry lies down a track beyond the church. Three or four more of the old bells still hang in the church tower. In d'Orbigny's day, the foundry still existed, and much else beside.

> When wandering round the bell foundry, I looked into a shed and found all the old sculptures of the Jesuits, piled up on top of each other. I noted especially a pulpit and a confessional that were still intact, which, because of the profusion of carvings covering the surface, would have been an ornament in one of our own churches today. I was so amazed that I took away a piece that I found on the floor (and I still have it in my collection of americana).

Inside today's modern church, a simple single nave construction, little of the old treasure remains, just a few pieces of Jesuit silver plate still pinned to the wall. Until recently there was a good deal more. Six years ago, there was a robbery and much was stolen. The nails left on the wall that had once pinned the plate, and there are many of them, reveal how much there once was.

Apart from the silver, there is now nothing, not even a statue – of which San Pedro once had an enormous store. Only a little eighteenth-century medallion remains, hanging from a pillar, a reminder of past splendours.

When d'Orbigny visited this church's predecessor, recently built, he found it to be "poorly constructed" but "stuffed with statues of saints and silver ornaments". These had been rescued from the old mission site on the Mamoré ten years earlier.

Among the statues, d'Orbigny claimed to recognize "various wooden sculptures made in Italy by the best sculptors of the last century". These may have been the models from which the Indians worked, but it seems more likely that they were the work of the Indians themselves, for San Pedro was one of the great centres of art and craft training in Mojos in the late eighteenth century, even after the Jesuits had left. Governor Ribera had set up an art school in San Pedro, and brought some of the best artists to the town from Potosí. He wrote in 1792:

> If you exclude drawing, it is true to say that the Indians of Moxos are skilled in all the arts and crafts. In every settlement there are good musicians, and in some of them there are to be found composers, sculptors, architects, organ-makers, metal workers, carpenters, turners, blacksmiths, weavers, tailors, and embroiderers.[3]

Governor Ribera felt that the Indians did not have "a gift for invention, and sometimes their works are not finished off with much taste":

> This defect, it seems to me, comes from their ignorance of design, of having seen nothing of the world beyond the confines of their village, and to have had no examples with which to stimulate their imagination.

The governor set about remedying this obvious lack.

> Two and a half years ago [ie at the beginning of 1790], a school of creative arts was set up in this provincial capital, with a teacher who, after six months, could do nothing more for his students. They had already learnt all he had to teach. They were left with nothing more as a guide than a few prints of Le Brun and Annibal Caracholo [Carraciolo] and other famous painters.

In the central plaza, outside the church, our pilot has made friends with the local schoolteacher, a pretty woman called Claudia wearing a denim skirt. She has only been in the village a few months and comes from Trinidad, to the south. She says she has only sixteen children in her school, and the population of the village is barely five hundred. In d'Orbigny's day there were more than fifteen hundred. A new road has been built through the swamps to Trinidad, which is now only two hours' journey away, and many people have moved there.

Claudia does not yet know much about the history of the mission, though she is familiar with the story about the bell foundry. She says she is trying to compile a dictionary of Canichana, the local language, and is asking the old people to recall their ancient traditions. She is a lone beacon in an otherwise gloomy scene.

D'Orbigny had not been overly impressed with the Canichanas. "Entering San Pedro, I was struck by the repellent aspect of the Canichana Indians who live there." He found that "with their piggy eyes and prominent cheekbones," they were less attractive than other Indian nations. Even the women seemed to lack charm. Though "strong and quite tall, they are not very sociable".

Forty years after d'Orbigny's visit, the Canichanas of San Pedro were to be found all over the Mamoré and the Madeira, as far north as Manaus. Edward Mathews, in 1874, had a high opinion of them. "These Indians are the most desirable of any of the tribes of the Beni. They are excellent workmen with the axe, and are, I think, less addicted to the use of ardent spirits than the Cayubabas or the Trinitarios."[4]

Franz Keller, in 1867, had a similar opinion, having encountered "these broad-shouldered sons of the plains of the Mamoré and Itonama" in the streets of Manaus. "They were about the only persons we saw working in the streets, carrying turtles and fuel from the shore to the houses, or lending a hand at new buildings."[5]

These were men who had travelled down to Brazil from Bolivia, emptying San Pedro of its young men during the rubber boom. They never returned, for obvious reasons. In Manaus, Keller wrote, they would gain "about ten times as much as they could in their own country, where they live in great misery".

The rubber boom brought a brief moment of prosperity to San Pedro's two ports on the Mamoré. Edward Mathews, in 1874, gave a favourable report:

> The sheds at these ports are large and well built, an Indian always living at them, who is

termed the sentinel, and whose duty is to take care of the canoes of the villagers or traders, who leave their craft at the port while they visit the pueblo.

Mathews was impressed by "the style of the work, the quality of the timber, and the tidiness of the place".

Twenty years later, the irreversible decline of the area was once more manifest. When two Franciscans came through San Pedro in 1893, they were unable to hide their gloom. They had considerable difficulty getting there at all.

Francisco Pifferi and Zacarias Ducci came to San Pedro neither by air nor by boat, but by the most difficult route of all – by land:

> The guide became confused and we went round and round these great pampas in circles, causing us great suffering from the fiercesome rays of a sun that is hot as an oven. It is impossible to travel through these pampas without a decent guide. The floods rub out all traces of the track, and everyone goes wherever they think the road to be best. When you are least expecting it, an immense swamp or bog appears ahead, with no solid ground in any direction. You then have to go back the same way that you came – and that is exactly what happened to us. We finally arrived at San Pedro, absolutely exhausted, at one in the afternoon.[6]

The two visiting priests found a village with only forty families ruled over by an administrator from Santa Cruz, with a handful of Canichana alcaldes.

> The corregidor assured us that some twenty years ago the settlement had about eight hundred families. But where are they? Where did they go? To the same question, the same answer, all over Mojos. They were taken off for the benefit of a tiny few, to the great disadvantage – indeed the complete ruin – of the society and the state.

The church, Ducci wrote, was modern but already in ruins. "If it wasn't for a few 'abadesas' who ensure that it is kept clean every day, it would soon be converted into a dung heap for bats." But there were still, in 1893, "many valuable silver treasures, more perhaps than in the other churches we have seen. But they say that much has disappeared already. In fact it is only thanks to the Indian sacristans that more has not gone already."

Ducci noted the great bells that still survived, as did the religious enthusiasms of the Indians who "tenaciously hold on to the customs to which they were introduced by the Jesuits".

We say goodbye to Claudia and return to the airstrip and our wounded plane, and fly off back to Trinidad. On the way, the pilot flies extra low over the Mamoré, first to let us see the luxurious hacienda house that once belonged to Nicolás Suárez, the rubber baron (now of course an officers' club), and then to show us a little tower, just north of Puerto Almacén, that was once the leprosarium of the Jesuits, situated with its own tiny landing stage on the banks of the River Ibare.

Colonel Aymerich and the expulsion of the Jesuits from Mojos in 1767

In the eighteenth century, the mission town of San Pedro de Mojos was the nerve centre of Spanish rule in the province. Far enough from the Brazilian frontier to be under no direct military threat, supported by the friendly and hardworking Canichana Indians and enjoying the benefits of more than half a century of benevolent Jesuit administration, San Pedro was a prosperous and wealthy settlement, connected by river and road with most of the farflung towns of the province.

In August 1767, the senior Spanish officer encamped in the town was Colonel Antonio Aymerich. The ban on Spaniards entering the Jesuit province, officially the rule since the beginning of the century, was no longer enforced. It had always been pretty much a dead letter as far as the military were concerned. There were frontiers to protect, and Mojos was a frontier province.

That was why Colonel Aymerich was in town. He had come over the mountains from Cochabamba the previous year to check on the fortifications that the Portuguese were building to the north, on the site of the old mission of Santa Rosa. He had participated in Brigadier Pestaña's disastrous expedition to the Guaporé, and remained behind in San Pedro when the brigadier withdrew to Santa Cruz to die.

One day, late in August, Colonel Aymerich was handed a letter that had arrived from Charcas. It came from the President of the Audiencia who had just taken over after the death of Pestaña. The message from the new man, Juan Victoriano Martínez de Tineo, was brief. All Jesuit priests, throughout the Mojos province, were to be arrested at dawn on 4 September.

It was a devastating instruction, in Mojos as it had been in Chiquitos (see pages 202–8). If the handful of Spanish soldiers in Mojos provided some much-needed military muscle to keep the Portuguese at bay and the Indians suitably cowed, the Jesuits and their missions were the eyes and ears of Spanish rule. The missionaries knew everything that went on in the province. They controlled and educated the potentially hostile Indians, and they had proved capable of operating an admirable early-warning system, alerting the Spanish authorities over the previous thirty years to the comings and goings of the Portuguese on the Guaporé.

Colonel Aymerich was faced with a daunting task. There were only twenty-three Jesuits in the Mojos area, but they were spread over many mission towns. Some of these were far away and inaccessible. There was no guarantee that the Indians would take the removal of their spiritual and temporal leaders lying down. In the Paraguay missions, in the 1750s, barely ten years earlier, there had been resistance and war when the frontier was moved. Soldiers would clearly have to be sent to the mission towns to winkle out the priests. Yet Colonel Aymerich had few troops at his disposal. After the humiliations of the previous year (see page 244) his primary task was to ward off the Portuguese threat across the border. Few soldiers could be spared. The previous year, trained men had simply gone off, voting with their feet to return home. If past experience was anything to go on, his Indian auxiliaries were likely to desert to the Portuguese at the first opportunity. Many of his usually reliable soldiers from Santa Cruz had already slipped off home, upriver, for some rest and recuperation. Throughout the 1760s, there had been alarums and excursions in the province of Mojos and Chiquitos. The Treaty of Madrid in 1750 and the subsequent fighting south of Paraguay – the Guaraní War – had made everyone nervous. The Portuguese now held a lot of territory that had been Spanish fifty years before. They might even take advantage of this trouble with the Jesuits to grab a bit more. Last, there was the weather to think of. If the priests were to be shifted, it would have to be done before the November rains. After that date, the area would be impassable for six months.[7]

The Jesuit priests in the mission towns of Mojos were jittery too. They knew that the king of Portugal had ordered the entire Society of Jesus out of Brazil. They must have feared that this anti-Jesuit feeling might spread to Spain. In their Mojos missions, the twenty-three priests were responsible for the well-being of nearly twenty thousand Indians. What would happen if they were thrown out? Would their Indians rebel as they had done in Paraguay?

The Jesuit province of Mojos was divided into three parts: the missions along the River Mamoré, those near the River Baures, and those on the plains to the west, La Pampa. The mission at San Pedro, with a population of more than two thousand, was the headquarters for the whole area. The news that the Jesuit fathers were to be expelled spread quickly through the province, and immediately caused trouble.

In the main square of San Pedro, Indians young and old assembled, armed with arrows and machetes. Colonel Aymerich was forced to rely on the Jesuit Superior – the man he was arresting – to calm them down. This was done, but only with considerable difficulty.

Faced with the possibility of more widespread opposition from the local Indians, Colonel Aymerich perceived that he would be wise to withdraw from San Pedro. He went south, up the Mamoré, to the Loreto mission. This was the oldest settlement in these parts and, more important, the closest to Santa Cruz. From there, military reinforcements might be obtained if necessary.

On 3 October 1767, a month after all the Jesuits were supposed to have been evacuated from Mojos, some military reinforcements arrived to assist Colonel Aymerich's beleaguered troops. Lieutenant-Colonel Joaquín Espinosa arrived at Loreto from Santa Cruz with a company of cavalry and six priests. His company consisted of ten officers (some Europeans, some criollos), and 246 men. Colonel Aymerich immediately despatched half the soldiers to Baures to keep an eye on the Portuguese frontier.[8]

Of the six priests sent from Santa Cruz to replace the Jesuits, one stayed in Loreto while the other five went to Trinidad, San Pedro, San Ignacio, Exaltación and Concepción de Baures. There was just one priest to each mission where previously there had been two. Unskilled, corrupt, and wholly without experience, these men were told to don the mantle of the Jesuits. The task was beyond them.

When Colonel Aymerich saw these replacement priests, the best that the Santa Cruz bishop could produce, he said: "Estos monigotillos serán tan inutiles como perniciosos" – these grotesque figures will be both useless and dangerous. He was right. And of course not one of them spoke any of the seven Indian languages of Mojos that the Jesuits had been accustomed to use.

Some understanding of the extraordinary linguistic problems that faced the new regime in the missions of Mojos can be gleaned from the report of a later governor of Mojos, Lázaro de Ribera, who lived here in the 1780s:

> When I first arrived in the province in 1786, I could hardly find an interpreter to explain what I wanted. I suddenly found myself in a land of Babel from which I could only escape with much effort. The Spanish spoken by the few interpreters that could be found was almost as incomprehensible to me as the languages of the Indians. It was necessary to learn this gibberish first in order not to misunderstand the ideas that were being translated from eight different languages.

Good interpreters, Governor Ribera wrote, are absolutely vital. They must have a good knowledge both of their own language and of the other.

> This can only be achieved through prolonged and attentive study. The Indians themselves can hardly aspire to this, and a governor should make an effort to learn some phrases lest his orders are poorly translated. If the announcement is of considerable importance, he should not rely on only one interpreter. One can be bought off, or prejudiced in favour of the administrators, the priests, or anyone who does not want the governor to know what is going on.[9]

By the beginning of October 1767, eleven Jesuits from the Mamoré missions had been detained. As in Chiquitos, it was to be another six months before the priests in the outlying missions could be arrested and evacuated from the province: seven priests from the missions of Baures in the east, and five from the La Pampa missions in the west.

Colonel Aymerich was now in effect the military governor of Mojos. He soon found that Loreto was too far from the middle of the province to be an adequate administrative centre. San Pedro was still potentially rebellious. A war council was eventually set up at Trinidad, made up of a captain, a lieutenant and a handful of carefully selected soldiers from Santa Cruz.

Colonel Aymerich himself was an ill man, not cut out to be a governor. Hoping to give himself something of the aura of the Jesuits, he gave himself the title of

"Reverendo Padre Grande Gobernador". He requested the Spanish authorities in Charcas to provide further instructions about his future role, and they sent him four huge folio volumes of the *Leyes de Indias*, the civil service manual of the Spanish Empire. Not knowing what to do with them, he used them to sit on.

Some decisions were taken. The rebellious Canichana Indians of San Pedro were given permission to form two companies of bowmen, with a uniform and a Canichana officer. They were allowed to parade in the mission square every Sunday after the religious procession.[10]

Colonel Aymerich seems to have enjoyed some personal popularity in the Indian towns, simply because his period in Mojos had overlapped with that of the Jesuits and he had been in their confidence. But inevitably his regime was an interregnum. He died in Loreto, in 1772. Then, as in Chiquitos, the province of Mojos was subjected to a whole series of administrative experiments, with corrupt priests and secular rulers, that lasted long into the nineteenth century.

The reports from Mojos of Tadeo Haenke in the 1790s

Something of the post-Jesuit depression into which the province of Mojos fell in the years after 1767 can be gleaned from the writings of Tadeo Haenke, a Bohemian botanist. Haenke spent two weeks in San Pedro de Mojos in November 1794, some twenty-five years after the expulsion of the Jesuits.

His contribution to the history of Mojos comes chiefly from the report he wrote for the Spanish governor of the province, in which he outlined the results of his visit, emphasizing the disastrous impact made by the Franciscan priests who had replaced the Jesuits.[11] It had been a mistake, he wrote, "one which has caused much mischief", to think that "any friar whatsoever is fit to engage in the work of converting infidels and preaching the gospel".

Haenke had travelled through all the Mojos missions that year, but his devastating report about their condition seems to have had little effect. Haenke is often considered (particularly in Bolivia) a precursor of Alexander Humboldt, but his legacy – like that of so many South American travellers – was never fully exploited. Many of his notes still lie unedited in the library of the Jardín Botánico in Madrid.[12]

Born in Chribska (Kreibitz) in the north of Bohemia in 1761, Tadeo Haenke was a chorister in the Jesuit seminary in Prague in 1772. An enthusiastic botanist, he produced a book of Bohemian flowers in 1786, and in 1789 he secured a place on the Spanish scientific expedition to South America and the Philippines led by Alejandro Malaspina.

Haenke himself, and the expedition as a whole, had its share of disasters. When he arrived at the quayside at Cadiz, he found that Malaspina's ships had sailed without him. He had been delayed in Paris on his way from Prague to Madrid, passing through the city just a few days before the storming of the Bastille. He managed to get on a later boat to Buenos Aires, but was shipwrecked off Montevideo. Travelling by land to Valparaíso in Chile, he finally managed to catch up with the expedition of which he was supposed to be a member.[13]

Haenke seems to have travelled with the Malaspina expedition up the Pacific coast to Mexico and then to the Philippines. But when the ships returned to Peru, on the way back to Spain, he decided to stay in South America. In September 1793, he left Lima and travelled up to the Andes, passing through Huancavelica, Cuzco, Puno and Arequipa.

His canoe was shipwrecked on Lake Titicaca, but he finally reached the Andean city of La Paz. From there, in 1794, he descended to the plains of Mojos, visiting the old mission towns of Reyes, San Ignacio, Santa Ana, San Pedro, and Loreto. Early in January 1795, he arrived at Santa Cruz, and the following year he made his permanent home in Cochabamba.

For twenty years, Haenke travelled through Bolivia, studying the plants and geological formations of the country.[14] He died in Cochabamba in 1816.

In his report to Francisco de Viedma, the governor of Santa Cruz, he drew on the Jesuit training of his youth. He reflected on the qualities needed for missionary work in the mission towns of South America:

> The scrupulous and successful discharge of the duties of the ministry unquestionably requires men of superior talent and education, great firmness of character, and extraordinary prudence. They should be men unmistakeably destined by Providence for this work, men blessed with a constitution of uniform strength, so as to withstand the heat of the torrid zone, the stings of insects, and the immoderate rains of the season; and a good memory, in order to acquire with ease the multifarious dialects of the Indians.

None of these qualities, Haenke went on, "shine forth even in the most earnest of the religious brethren of San Francisco". He concluded with a devastating indictment of their work:

> They persuade themselves that they have fulfilled all their obligations in hurriedly reading the customary prayers every day. The love of riches makes them forget all the striking rules as to poverty which their order prescribes. They derive incredible benefits from the simplicity and hard work of the converts, whom they fetter with tasks which they could not perform if they were beasts of burden.

The work of these priests, Haenke suggested, was carried out "at an immense expense to the state". It created nothing but trouble. "In their temporal government, they rule despotically, being ignorant of all knowledge which appertains to economy and industry." Referring to "the deplorable state of the missions in charge of these evangelisers", Haenke accused the Franciscans of being the cause of their decline. "Since the expulsion of the Jesuits, not only has nothing advanced, but also very many of the missions have ceased to exist. Instead of advancing they have fallen off."

The inevitable result, he warned, was Portuguese expansion. "The Portuguese proceed, step by step, occupying more territory, and approaching nearer every day to the Spanish dominions."

The plan for Mojos of Lázaro de Ribera, 1784–92, and the rebellion of cacique Maraza in San Pedro in 1822

In the 1780s, after more than a decade of decline in the former mission towns of Mojos, and after a whole series of absentee governors, a new man appeared in San Pedro de Mojos, an administrator with considerable skill and talent – and vision.

Lázaro de Ribera y Espinoza was one of the most extraordinary and far-sighted of the Spanish governors of Mojos in the post-Jesuit era. Seeking to build on the work of the Jesuits, already in disrepair after their fifteen-year absence, he worked for an improvement in the condition of the Indians. Inevitably he was to come into conflict with the settlers in Santa Cruz, represented by their civil and religious authorities.

Ribera made his headquarters at San Pedro de Mojos in July 1786. He had travelled over the mountains from Cochabamba and the Chapare. Stopping first at Loreto, he was paddled down the Mamoré to San Pedro. From there, he embarked on a visit to the farflung mission towns of his province. He was in Trinidad in September 1786, and in Magdalena and Concepción de Baures the following year. He also visited Exaltación, San Borja, Reyes, San Ignacio and Santa Ana.

Some years later, in September 1792, he wrote an account of the missions for the benefit of his successor as governor. His report on San Pedro explains some of its natural disadvantages.

> This settlement is the capital of the province. It is not in a very satisfactory position, only two short leagues from the Mamoré river in rather exposed country. Winds from north and south, the most usual direction, lash it with considerable violence for much of the year. Fresh water is not good and is found far away.[15]

With such a difficult climate, agriculture and husbandry inevitably involved a complicated seasonal routine and much travelling:

> The soil, when dry, hardens like a rock and is resistant to cultivation. In the months of June, July, August and September, there is usually little water, and the cattle suffer a lot. They are obliged to leave their traditional lands to find food and grazing far away. Cultivated land is often so far distant that it may take the Indians ten, twelve, or fifteen, days to get there and back. Some of this land is only two, three, or four, leagues away,

and some is nearby on the banks of the Mamoré. But here the crops run the risk of being carried away or submerged beneath the rising waters of the river.

In spite of these problems, living in San Pedro was agreeable and people lived to a ripe old age.

> The climate is dry rather than humid. . . . From September to March, the rays of the sun can be quite trying, but the heat of the day is usually compensated by the fresh airs of the evening. In few settlements do you see so many old people, and some are over ninety.

Apart from appreciating their longevity, Governor Ribera had a very positive view of the other characteristics of the Canichana. "The Indians are extremely capable, the boldest and most energetic in the province. Their weaving and woodwork, and their carving and joinery, is excellent."

Lázaro de Ribera is an interesting figure in the history of Spanish colonial administration. He belonged to what was to be the last generation of administrators before the empire collapsed into anarchy, civil war and independence. Like many such people, in all empires at all times, he believed that the *ancien régime* could be saved and made to work. He was governor of Mojos when the French Revolution occurred, and although the implications of that event took time to percolate through to South America, he was fighting for both administrative and economic reform. He wanted to introduce trade from the outside world into his distant province. Agricultural and industrial production for the market was his ambition.

Born in Malaga in 1756, Ribera came to South America in 1775, at the age of nineteen, as a page to the Spanish viceroy in Lima. He studied there with Cosme Bueno, the famous astronomer and mathematician, who was also the author of several works on South American geography, one of which includes material on the province of Mojos.

Ribera's first governmental task, in 1779, had been in Chile where he was employed in mapping the island of Chiloe. In 1783, while on furlough in Buenos Aires, he received news of his appointment as governor of Mojos, at the age of twenty-eight. He was to take over from General Ignacio Flores, a man who had never actually visited the province over which he was supposed to govern.

In an intriguing quarrel with his predecessor over missing funds, Ribera was arrested by Flores in Charcas before he had had time to get to Mojos. He escaped from prison by jumping down from a balcony and arrived at Buenos Aires twenty-five days later in order to speak to the viceroy. Rebuked and pardoned, after some correspondence with Madrid, he was eventually allowed to return to his job as governor, and made his way back from Buenos Aires to Sucre.

Arriving at San Pedro his first task – the priority in this region throughout the eighteenth century – was to deal with the situation on the Brazil frontier. The specific need was to secure the junction of the Guaporé and the Mamoré against the Portuguese. There was an additional problem in that the curas in the Baures missions were reported to be engaged in smuggling across the border. Ribera requested an additional sixty soldiers to help guard the border.

Ribera soon became a fierce critic of the situation he had inherited in the old missions. He was well aware of the catastrophic decline they had experienced. As he pointed out in June 1788:

At the time of the expulsion of the Jesuits, they had left fifteen towns that were both happy and rich, with a population of some thirty thousand people. Now they are reduced to only eleven, without money or cattle and in an extreme state of decline, with a population of barely twenty thousand.[16]

To remedy the situation, Ribera proposed to confine the curas to their churches. They should not be involved in secular affairs. It was useless, he argued, to continue the Jesuit way of doing things if the curas did not have the capacity or the morality to perform the Jesuit role. The solution was to establish a secular administrator in each mission town. He pointed out that "the inhabitants of Mojos have no idea of private property and live in communities similar to those of the Christians in the first centuries of the Church".[17]

The Ribera plan for the secularization of the administration of the mission towns was introduced with considerable difficulty. It had a major drawback. The new secular administrators soon proved themselves to be just as hopeless and corrupt as the curas had been. Nor was the Spanish state able to provide them with any financial or administrative back-up. Some of them died, some crossed over the frontier to Brazil.[18]

In addition, the priests who had had their temporal power removed were still very much in evidence in the mission towns. As the Jesuits had known well, spiritual control was at least half the battle, and some of the less corrupt priests retained a good deal of power and influence. As the civilian administrators became increasingly unpopular, the priests turned into spokesmen of dissent. In some cases they were instrumental in creating conditions favourable to Indian rebellion.[19]

Under the regime of the next governor of Mojos, Colonel Miguel Zamora y Trivino, such a rebellion did in fact occur in San Pedro – in 1801 – organized by Maraza, the principal Canichana cacique in the town. The Indians simply packed up the governor's goods and chattels into fifty packing cases and asked him to leave.

Maraza was to spark off another rebellion twenty years later, on the eve of independence. The province of Mojos was reasonably free from the civil wars that affected much of what was to become Bolivia in the years from 1810 to 1820. But in November 1819, one of the toughest Spanish military commanders arrived in San Pedro as governor. Colonel Francisco Javier Velasco had played an important part in the battle of Samaipata in 1814 between the royalists and the liberation forces.

Once installed in San Pedro, Colonel Velasco soon found that his authority was under challenge from the aged Maraza. Eventually, in April 1822, the colonel sought to depose Maraza, removing the symbol of his staff of office. In the ensuing commotion, there was shooting in the main square. Maraza himself was shot and killed.

Maraza's son, and the entire Indian council of the town, marched into the central square to recover the body of their cacique. His death was the spark that touched off a rebellion against the Spanish occupying force. Colonel Velasco and his soldiers, together with a few Spaniards, managed to hole up briefly in the ancient college of the Jesuits next to the church. It was a momentary respite.

On 26 April 1822, San Pedro de Mojos was put to the torch; it burnt merrily with animal fat taken from the warehouse. The larger houses of the mission town were all burnt down. So too was the provincial library and archive. All the books and papers that had been kept in the mission towns of Mojos for a century before 1767 had been brought to San Pedro after the expulsion of the Jesuits. Now, the entire collection went up in flames. Colonel Velasco and most of his entourage perished with it.

The Canichana Indians of San Pedro had hoped by their action to provoke a rising throughout the province. Messengers were sent out to all the other mission towns of Mojos. Indian troops were despatched to guard the upper waters of the Mamoré to prevent Spanish reinforcements arriving from Santa Cruz or Cochabamba. Spanish control over Mojos seemed as though it might be at an end.

But the Spanish governor in Santa Cruz, Brigadier Francisco Javier de Aguilera, had a strategy up his sleeve with which to outwit the Indians. Instead of sending Spanish soldiers down the Rio Grande (Guapay) to the Mamoré, he sent them down the San Miguel river instead, towards Magdalena. Cutting across by land, from El Carmen to San Ramón, his troops were able to approach San Pedro from the north.

Warned of the plan, the Canichana decided not to resist. In reality, they were no military match for the Spanish army. In December 1822, Brigadier Aguilera entered San Pedro unopposed. The town had been under Indian control for eight months.

The Canichana had taken one precaution. They hid the Christ figure of the Jesuits, made of solid silver, which was normally on display in the church. It was a wise move. Brigadier Aguilera's first action was to collect the Jesuit silver from all the churches in the province. He needed the money to pay his troops. From San Pedro alone, he took 704 pounds of silver. Fifty years after the expulsion of the Jesuits, Mojos was still a richly endowed province.

Brigadier Aguilera did not enjoy his triumph for long. In 1825, he was captured by the anti-royalist forces that swept into Bolivia. In 1828 he was executed.

Notes

1. Alcides Dessalines d'Orbigny, *Voyage dans l'Amérique Méridionale*, Paris 1835–47.
2. Lázaro de Ribera, *Moxos descripciones exactas e historia fiel de los indios, animales e plantas de la provincia de Moxos en el virreinato del Peru por Lázaro de Ribera, 1786–1794*, Ediciones El Viso, Madrid 1989, p. 213.
3. Ibid. p. 211.
4. Edward Mathews, *Up the Amazon and Madeira Rivers, Through Bolivia and Peru*, London 1879.
5. Franz Keller, *The Amazon and Madeira Rivers: sketches and descriptions from the notebook of an explorer*, London 1874.
6. Zacarias Ducci, *Diario de la visita a todas las misiones existentes en república de Bolivia*, Assisi 1895, p. 95.
7. Gabriel René-Moreno, *Biblioteca Boliviana, Catálogo del archivo de Mojos y Chiquitos*, Santiago 1888, p. 11.
8. Some of them took the instruction too literally. A couple of Cruceño soldiers slipped across the river to the Portuguese fort, taking with them two Indian girls. When they got there, the Portuguese captain took their women, offering them black slave girls in exchange. The Cruceños, mortified, returned across the river.
9. Lázaro de Ribera, p. 209.
10. José Chávez Suárez, *Historia de Moxos*, second edn, La Paz 1986 p. 342.
11. This was a report to the governor of Santa Cruz, Francisco de Viedma, sent from Cochabamba in April 1799, entitled "On the navigable rivers which flow into the Marañon, rising in the cordilleras of Peru and Bolivia". The Spanish version is published in Guillermo Ovando-Sanz (ed.), *Tadeo Haenke: su obra en los Andes y la selva Boliviana*, La Paz 1974. An English translation is in George Church, *Explorations Made in the Valley of the River Madeira*, London 1875.
12. Much material is also to be found in Czechoslovakia. A sumptuous volume, *La botánica en la expedición Malaspina, 1789–1794*, was published in Madrid in 1989, under the auspices of the Real Jardín Botánico, which outlines many of the areas of work still to be done on Haenke. See also Josef Kuehnel, *Thaddaeus Haenke, Leben und Wirken eines Forschers*, Munich 1960.
13. Captain Malaspina fared little better. After a six-year expedition, he returned to Spain and was promptly arrested. The results of his researches were confiscated, though a diary of his travels eventually ended up in St Petersburg. He was released from gaol by Napoleon in 1803, and died in Italy in 1810.
14. In 1800, Haenke travelled through Chiquitos: Santa Cruz– San Javier–Concepción–San Ignacio–Santa Ana–San José–San Juan–Taperas–Rio Tucabaca–Santiago–Santo Corazón–San José–Santa Cruz. Later, during the wars of independence, he retreated from Cochabamba to Mojos, between 1811 and 1813, and kept a low profile. In 1811 he observed a comet from San Ignacio de Mojos, and he did some drawings of the area. He eventually returned to his Elicona Hacienda, outside Cochabamba, where he died.
15. Lázaro de Ribera, p. 219.
16. Chávez Suárez, p. 398.
17. Chávez Suárez, p. 413.
18. Chávez Suárez, p. 427.
19. Ribera subsequently became governor of Paraguay, from 1795 to 1807. In 1801, he led an expedition upriver to Coimbra, then held by the Portuguese, and attempted to dislodge the Portuguese garrison. He failed. Later he was governor of Huancavelica, in Peru, from around 1809 to 1819. He died in Lima in 1824.

22

RETURN TO TRINIDAD

From San Pedro to Trinidad

Flying back into Trinidad from San Pedro, we caught a glimpse of the military lined up in the plaza below. Today is Bolivia's National Day and the formal celebrations have already begun.

There is much excitement in the streets, and we push through the crowds to the plaza, to watch the parade go by. On one side of the square, between the church and the town hall, a shaded saluting base has been erected, filled with local dignitaries: the bishop, the battalion commander and the mayor. These three figures have ruled here for two hundred years, ever since the Jesuits were thrown out.

First come the local schools, with their bands and uniforms and majorettes, and the students themselves in their Sunday best. Then come the professional associa-tions and the trade unions and all the workplace organizations: the banks, the water board, the electricity company, the airport staff, the insurance firm. All are given an exuberant welcome by a sycophantic cheerleader. Loudly over the loudspeaker, he explains just what each group has been doing to make Bolivia great.

Then come the peasants and the Indian organizations, all that is left of the original population. They are shy and unnerved, knowing their place. They last organized a rebellion here in 1887, and have kept a low profile ever since.

Finally, as a reminder of who has the last word in this society, come the serried ranks of the armed forces. First the army, then the navy, then the airforce. And after that the military police, and the civil police. And then their bands. The army band, the navy band, and the airforce band. And the military police band and the civil police band.

It is a huge display for a small provincial town and it goes on for the best part of two hours. We eventually retire to an icecream parlour on the corner of the plaza.

Visitors to Trinidad in the late nineteenth century

In the second half of the nineteenth century, a steady stream of foreign travellers passed through Trinidad and the old mission settlements of the Mamoré. Many of them were connected with a project to build a railway cross a short stretch of land in the middle of the continent. As with the utopian schemes to open up the upper Paraguay to European trade and commerce, and immigration, so there were imaginative proposals to create new opportunities on the great tributaries of the Amazon. The Americans and the British were particularly active.

Unfortunately for the success of such plans, river access from the Atlantic to the fertile plains of northern Bolivia – up the Amazon and the Madeira to the Mamoré and the Beni – was blocked by a series of dramatic rapids on the Madeira, in Brazil just to the north of the Bolivian border. No modern steamer could hope to negotiate them. So for more than fifty years, in London, Washington, La Paz and Rio de Janeiro, a project was discussed and endlessly revived to build a railway round the rapids, to ensnare this distant province into the new world of global trade. Like the Panama Canal, the Madeira–Mamoré railway was one of those typically ambitious nineteenth-century engineering projects that seized the imagination of thousands of people far from the scene.

One visitor to Trinidad, in 1867, was Franz Keller, a German engineer resident in Brazil. He was one of the first. He had been commissioned, with his father, "to explore the Madeira River and to project a railroad along its bank".[1] After visiting the Madeira rapids, the two men and their entourage travelled on into Mojos. Franz Keller was later to write a book describing his experiences. He emphasized the region's essential obscurity:

> Though in a few years puffing locomotives will be speeding through them, the districts we explored have till now been so detached from communication with the rest of the world, and have, notwithstanding their natural wealth, partaken so little of the influence exercised by commerce over the course of universal history, that it is likely more than one of our readers has had to refer to the map.

One man who did not have to look at the map was a United States engineer, George Earl Church, who had first come exploring in South America in 1858 and later became an ardent promoter of the railway scheme. Taking time off to serve as a colonel during the US civil war in the 1860s, Church returned to the Amazon in 1868 as the chairman of the Madeira and Mamoré Railway Company, entrusted with raising money to build the line around the Madeira rapids.[2] He travelled to Trinidad from Santa Cruz in September 1871, in canoes manned by thirty-seven boatmen. From there, he went on down the Mamoré, past Exaltación, to the Madeira.

The resident engineer on Colonel Church's Madeira project was Edward Mathews, another visitor to Trinidad (in 1874). For various reasons, Mathews wrote, "the prosecution of the enterprise fell into abeyance for some considerable time". Money had not been forthcoming, as Colonel Church had hoped, and the engineering difficulties – and the struggle with the forest – proved to be much harder than the original entrepreneurial optimists had imagined. So Mathews, obliged to return home, decided to travel through Bolivia and Peru. He turned the diary of his journey into a book. In it, he describes his journey up the Amazon in 1874, travelling from Para to the Madeira rapids, and from there to the Mamoré.

Like Franz Keller, Mathews thought that his readers might be interested in an unfamiliar area of the world. Since "the Eastern trip to India, China, Japan, and home via San Francisco and New York, has been done by so many", he wrote, he hoped that the story of a rather different journey might attract readers: those suffering from ennui at the thought of yet another hackneyed account of an expedition across North America.

> There may be adventurous spirits in search of new worlds to conquer, who would be pleased to know of a journey offering the combined attractions of canoeing on the magnificent affluents of the Amazon and a journey in the saddle across the Andes.[3]

He clearly had little inkling that he was travelling in the footsteps of hundreds of others, or that his own journey would itself become a beaten track for adventurers in the twentieth century.

Even before the construction of the railway around the rapids, trade and commerce had already begun to penetrate the old Jesuit towns of Mojos by the 1870s, in marked contrast to the situation a hundred years earlier when the entire area had been virtually self-sufficient.

For those who participated in this new development, it was often adventurous and dangerous work, but for those who controlled it, the rewards were considerable. Mathews travelled up the Madeira and the Mamoré from Brazil with a Bolivian merchant who expected to sell goods to the value of 3400 pounds sterling in the old mission town of Exaltación. The trader to whom he sold them would then send canoes "up the affluents of the Mamoré or the Itenez to the various pueblos of the department of the Beni".

Trinidad seemed at first sight to be a beneficiary of this opening up to trade. Mathews noted that although it was but "a small town", some of the houses were "well built, of brick or adobe walls", and all had tiled roofs. But the trade came from the south and the east, not from the north. For that, his railway would be necessary.

> There are a few merchants and storekeepers of considerable position and resources, whose principal trade appears to be the export of cocoa to Cochabamba and Santa Cruz, receiving in return flour and potatoes from Cochabamba, and dry goods from Santa Cruz, these latter being brought thither from the Brazilian town of Corumbá on the river Paraguay.

But as the products of European factories slowly percolated through, into the smallest tributaries of the great Amazonian system, little benefit came to the mission Indians. Franz Keller wrote:

> In the present state of things, the Indians are entirely in the hands of a horde of lawless adventurers, intent upon their own gains; from the vain but crafty Bolivian, and the fugitive defaulter from Rio de Janeiro, to the ignorant Polish pedlar, and the dirty Neapolitan tinker. Under pretext of trading, these cheat and defraud the artless redskins in the most shameful way.

Cheating traders were not the only problem. Mathews had found the shopkeepers of Trinidad doing well, but everyone agreed that the place was a shadow of its former self. The town "did not display a very animated appearance". Part of the reason for this was the return of an old, all too familiar tragedy.

> Smallpox was very prevalent at the time, and numbers of people, both old and young, appeared to have suffered greatly. This disease almost decimates the Indians at frequently recurring intervals, for the authorities have no idea of isolating the sick, and vaccination is but partially enforced; the Indians, in ignorance of its benefits, being naturally averse to it.

But there was something else. A new and yet more alarming problem was slowly to destroy the mission towns of Mojos. The global demand for rubber had struck the Amazon basin, and there was always a shortage of labour. Many of the Indians from Trinidad and the other missions of the Mamoré were dragged off to work in the rubber fields further to the north. It was work akin to slavery, and the mission Indians were dragged off by slaving entrepreneurs much as their forefathers had been. Mathews reported that "the people complained bitterly of the great emigration to the rubber-grounds of Brazil". They "spoke of Trinidad as depopulated". Many houses seemed to be left "empty and uncared for".

Like many of his age and class, Mathews was not predisposed to look benevolently on the Indians. But he was impressed by the skills and achievements of the survivors he met. "The bulk of the population is formed of Mojeno or Trinitario Indians who appear to me to be the most intelligent, as they certainly are the best-looking, of all the tribes of the Beni."[4] He found that although the Indians would acknowledge a white and mestizo Bolivian as their "patron" or employer, each different group still had its own cacique or headman with "authority over the whole tribe". This authority was not always well used, since the cacique was "generally in the pay of the prefect or corregidor", the servant of the Bolivian state.

While Mathews found the Mojeno Indians intelligent "and naturally active and hard working", he regretted the fact that they were "much given to habits of drinking, which render them very uncertain and little to be depended on". But he was impressed with their craftsmanship:

> The Indians of Trinidad, Santa Cruz, and other towns of the department of the Beni, though, like most men of the Indian race, fond of the dolce far niente, "swing in a

hammock", "smoke cigarette" kind of existence, are very clever in their specialities. Some of the produce of their handlooms will compare very favourably with the fabrics of civilised countries, if not for texture, at least for strength and durability. . . . The hammocks they weave from the native cotton are handsome and strong, whilst the "cascaras" or bark shirts that they beat out of the inner skin of several trees, are marvels of patience and ingenuity.

Yet it was this charming if low-level economic activity that was now threatened by the developments that Mathews and Keller were hoping to bring to Mojos by building a railway.

Mathews was also amazed by the Indians' writing skills:

All of them who had done service in the churches as sacristans and choristers are able to write; they can also read music, for which they use the ordinary five-line system. There are small schools in all the principal Indian villages in which reading, writing, and Catholic prayers are taught in the Castilian language; and I was rather surprised to see the amount of rudimentary knowledge that is drilled into the Indians.

Franz Keller gives a similarly optimistic account of what he perceived to be the civilization of the Indians.

The Government pays – it is startling to record the fact – a schoolmaster in every pueblo; and, poor as the teaching may be, yet one occasionally finds an Indian able not only to speak but also to read and write Spanish. Among our eighty paddlers there were two who could read Portuguese almost fluently, and who accepted with the greatest pleasure some "books for the young" I had with me. Now, as the whole library at the the disposal of the Indians in the pueblos consists of a few written prayers, which have descended from father to son, from the time of the Holy Fathers, we may conclude that with proper help they would become tolerably good scholars.

Echoing the attitudes of his time, Mathews argued that the Indians were "as a race" not at all "deficient in natural intellect". He believed them to be "of a much higher grade than the Brazilian negroes of African descent".

Yet if Trinidad was losing its Indian population, these foreign visitors did not mourn. They considered that a solution was already in sight. Here, as on the Paraguay, the theme of the times was European immigration.

Just as the early Spanish and Portuguese settlers in South America had got little joy from the Indians and had been forced to import African slaves on an immense scale, so after independence the ruling elites sought to bolster their power with white immigration from Europe. This was a much simpler strategy than that of trying to develop their countries for the benefit of the peoples who actually lived there.

This Latin American desire for white immigrants coincided with much nineteenth-century propaganda in Europe in favour of sending its apparently surplus population – for which the contemporary expansion of capitalism could provide no jobs – to occupy the lands of others in distant parts of the globe. Travelling up the Mamoré from Exaltación to Trinidad, Mathews could not help observing that this land of flat beach and pampa, free from "barbaros", would be "very valuable for emigration". It had, he perceived, a splendid climate, and "land of excellent quality for the production of crops of sugar-cane, rice, maize, plantains, and every other description of tropical produce, together with capital pampas for cattle rearing". Franz Keller, travelling up the same river a few years earlier, had a similar view:

> These countries do indeed demand attention, if it be only on the ground that they offer the fair prospect of some day becoming outlets for those fermenting elements which, with increased seriousness, have lately menaced social order in over-peopled Europe.

Keller was writing in 1874, just a few years after the Paris Commune had been drowned in blood.

For both Keller and Mathews, all that was needed to facilitate immigration and the expansion of trade was the means of transport. "Nowhere in the whole continent, a hundred miles from the coast," Keller noted petulantly, "is there a regular carriage-road to be found; and the mule, or at best the creaking ox-cart, with its enormous wooden wheels fixed on the axletrees, are the indispensable vehicles."

Yet in Mojos, roads and ox-carts were not so necessary. Its great network of rivers, large and small, was in place already, just waiting for something less labour-intensive than a canoe. The Beni, wrote Mathews, was "a department whose roads are laid out by nature in the stupendous network of riverine canals with which it is favoured, and upon which the villages are built".

At Cerrito, just below Exaltación, he had seen what he perceived to be the shape of the future. Moored at the river bank, he found a small steamer, the *Explorador*, that had been portaged over the Madeira rapids in 1871. About forty feet in length, it had been built especially for the Mamoré by Messrs Yarrow and Co. of Poplar. It would, thought Mathews, "be able to carry on a good business, trading amongst the towns of the Beni".

To get to Exaltación, the *Explorador* had been brought up the Amazon and round the Madeira rapids:

> This was no trifling feat to accomplish, and involved dragging the iron launch for miles on land over rocks and through dense tropical forests in the rainy season and at times when fevers were most prevalent and virulent. The machinery of the launch was very much impaired by the strain to which it had been subjected, but the hull was still in serviceable condition.[5]

Neither Keller nor Mathews, of course, was a wholly disinterested witness. Both were drumming up support for the Madeira–Mamoré railway line. Mathews wrote:

> The construction of the Madeira and Mamoré Railway is the only event that can save the once flourishing department of the Beni from becoming again the hunting-grounds of the savage Siriono.
> The opening up of the route past the rapids would arrest entirely the decay of these fertile provinces, by affording a ready means of transit to a good market for the chocolate, sugar, tobacco, oxen, hides, tallow, skins, and other produce for which the inhabitants are now only able to realise but a small amount in value compared with what they will be able to when the route is open.

This was wishful thinking. By the time the floodgates were opened to foreign trade, the Indian population of Mojos had been swept away in the feverish activity caused by the rubber boom.

The great Indian rebellion of Santos Ñoco in 1887

The old Jesuit church at Trinidad survived until the last quarter of the nineteenth century. All the travellers of that period bear witness to its surviving splendour. Lardner Gibbon, a lieutenant in the United States Navy, spent two months in Trinidad in 1852 during an exploration of the upper waters of the Amazon. Like Captain Page on the Paraguay during the same decade, he was opening up the interior waterways of South America for the benefit of United States trade. But his report does not contain the same lyrical passages extolling the merits of free trade that characterize the work of Page. Lieutenant Gibbon was more interested in the Indians, and he was impressed by the mixture of the secular and the profane that characterized life in the old missions:

> After mass, we witnessed a grand procession, headed by the prefect and clergy, followed by the whole population dressed in white gowns, "camecitas" as they are called here. Whenever the Indians are performing church service, the women unplait their hair, and allow it to hang gracefully loose behind their white dresses. The hair of the men is cut short.[6]

The procession then paraded round the central square.

> At each corner of the plaza was an arbour, constructed of green foliage and flowers, with plantain trees and palm leaves. As they marched round to music and singing, the scene was beautiful and interesting. The red race dressed in white cotton cloth, following the Catholic clergy in rich costume, bearing wooden images on their shoulders; three thousand savages, half-civilised, were singing church music, and

living under the laws of quasi white men. The few creoles who walked by the side of the prefect and clergy were but a drop in the plate.

Fifteen years later, in 1867, Franz Keller, the German engineer, attended a similar event. The high mass, he wrote, "was executed with a precision and correctness that did not show the least trace of decline", and "reflected credit on the musical capacity of the red race".

Sunday morning in the old Trinidad church was one of his favourite memories of his expedition, though he recorded his experience in his sometimes rather sneering style:

> At early morning I left the house of my kind host, and walked leisurely through the streets of the pueblo to the square in which the church is situated. The rising sun was gilding the clay walls of the edifice, which, though devoid of all architectural beauty, yet contrasted effectively with the low mud-houses in its vicinity; sparkling dew-drops clothed the grass and flowers; and a refreshing cool wind swept in from the campos. Again I contemplated the naively conceived frescoes on its front, of St Francisco and St Luis de Gonzaga, albeit they were not executed by artists great in colours and lines, and the masterpiece of the tympanum, the mystic device representing the Holy Trinity.[7]

Keller was soon joined in contemplation in the Trinidad church by two Indians who turned out to be the bellringers, and "almost immediately the bells of the campanile summoned the villagers to prayers". The bells were not rung in a European manner, Keller noted, but rather in the style that he was accustomed to in Brazil where:

> . . . several well-tuned ones are hammered on at the same time after a peculiar, usually very quick, rhythm. It does not sound very solemn; but the lively melody of the peals harmonises well with the blue sky, the bright sun, and the gaudily dressed congregation, which goes to church rather for diversion and for society than for devotion.

That was the custom in the more secular society of urban Brazil with which Keller was familiar.

> It is far otherwise, however, in the old missions of the Mamoré; where both men and women approached silently and seriously; the former, without exception, clad in the classical camiseta of home manufacture; the latter already luxuriating in chemises of the gaudy, large-flowered cottons of Europe, with their long black hair flowing loose over the shoulders, sometimes down to the knees. Even the children, most of them lovely little creatures, walked as demurely as their elders, with rosaries in their chubby brown hands. For this auditory at least, church and divine service had retained all the glory and holiness wherewith the Jesuits of old had surrounded them.

Keller watched the service from the musicians' gallery, and like Lieutenant Gibbon, he was amazed that this was almost entirely an Indian occasion:

> Facing the altar, I could easily watch the filling of the wide hall below, wrapped at first in a mystic twilight. In the first row, close to the choir, squatted the women on mats, after saying a short prayer on their knees; and behind them were the men. The few white faces, the secretary of the prefect, and two or three merchants, were completely lost in the crowd of Indians; and I almost fancied I was hearing mass in the time of Montoya or of one of his successors.

Father Ruiz de Montoya, of course, had been active in Paraguay rather than in Mojos, but Herr Keller's sentiments were on the right track. Keller was also intrigued by the fact that the musical tradition of the Jesuit era had survived so well:

> In this gallery, which showed two small organs in richly carved cases with painted panels, presently assembled the musicians with their fiddles, harps, and bajones, under the leadership of the master of the chapel, a venerable-looking Indian, with large spectacles adjusted by a cord, with little round pieces of lead, passing over the crown of his head; and the singers, with a small red flag, had taken their post close to the solid wooden balustrade, to help the choir below in case of need.
>
> The priest now appeared before the altar, and the solemn tones of a fine old missa swept through the spacious aisle. It was the festival of some saint; and the altar exhibited its richest silver adornments, while slender palms, waving their graceful boughs from the pillars of the aisle and from the music tribune, added the charm of tropical vegetation to the fairy-like picture.

Keller was impressed by the scene, seeking to explain its meaning in the general deprivation and sense of loss that faced the Indians in their daily life:

> The zeal with which the Indians of former Missions in Bolivia cling to the present day to the rites of the Catholic Church, may partly have its source in their childish taste for outward pomp and gaudy shows; but certainly a good deal of it arises from their striving to gain some equivalent for their lost nationality.

Although he had the usual views, typical of his time and class, about "the indolent character of the Indians", Keller also possessed a rare insight into the reason for their apparent slothfulness.

> If a nation is bereft at once of everything which till then it cherished – its gods, its chiefs, and all its peculiar ways of life – and if it is brought into contact with European corruption; in the state of moral destitution consequent on the loss of all national and religious support, the worst results are unavoidable.

And for the whites and the mestizos in Trinidad, worse was to come. For some twenty years later, in May 1887, these "swing in the hammock" Indians, driven beyond endurance, were to organize a general uprising, the last of the great rebellions in Mojos.

Lieutenant Gibbon, in 1852, had been rather more perceptive. The Indians were not merely suffering from a sense of loss, they were simply suffering. There were few whites or creoles present in Trinidad, but those that were there made it their business to keep the Indians in a permanent state of terror. One weapon at the command of the authorities was strong drink. Edward Mathews had noted that the Indians "were much given to the habits of drinking". But it was the state authorities that provided the means. Gibbon described the scene during a bullfight on Trinity Sunday:

> Great jars of chicha had been provided by the authorities of the town, and passed around among those who wanted to drink. There were few who declined, and as soon as the bull was let out, baskets of bread, made of corn and yucca meal, were emptied from the balcony over the heads of the people, who scrambled after it.

Something of the racist attitude of the officials can be gleaned from Gibbon's description.

> The manner in which this bread was presented to Indians from the government store was the same as throwing corn to poultry elsewhere. They scrambled for it, amidst the dust that had just been torn up by the hoofs of the enraged bull.

As his investigations progressed, Gibbon made the acquaintance of an Indian cacique called Mariano Cayuba, a man in his seventies who was the Indian second-in-command in the town:

> Cayuba often came to see me. He spoke a little Spanish, and was so anxious to know all about my country that we became great friends. I asked him whether the people were happy. He said "Yes; but we are all slaves to the white man; we used to have plenty of cattle and fine horses. The white man comes from Santa Cruz and drives them all away."[8]

Lieutenant Gibbon made further enquiries.

> By the laws of the land, Indians are punished by whipping on the bare back with a raw-hide rope – twelve stripes for insubordination, drunkenness or idleness. The custom among the authorities has been to punish whenever they deem it proper, with as many lashes as they please, though there is less punishment now than in former times.

Sometimes the Indians were powerful enough to complain successfully to higher authority, and sometimes they were able to get their revenge.

One prefect, who was exceedingly tyrannical in his behaviour to these people, was recalled, as the Indians signed a petition against him to the President. He was displaced and afterwards banished to Brazil. On the voyage down the Mamoré river, the crew filled the boat with water at midnight while the ex-prefect was sleeping. They swam to the bank, and he was drowned.

Gibbon was writing in the 1850s. Thirty years later, the economic situation of the Indians had deteriorated, and there had been no let-up in the racist repression by the whites. In May 1887, there was a great explosion. The leader of the Mojos Indians in Trinidad at that time was called Guayocho. He was regarded by the whites as a "choquihua" or "brujo", a sorcerer. He was said to be an excellent ventriloquist. Among the Indians, the rumour had spread that he was Jesus Christ, a Christ returned to give them back their land.

According to one version, by Ciro Bayo, an Argentine schoolteacher who came here in 1896, the uprising was planned for 19 May, Ascension Day. It was scheduled to start while the whites were all safely at prayer in the great Trinidad church. But the night before, someone discovered that something was up. On Ascension Day morning, the whites were prepared. Just before mass was about to begin, the church doors were locked. All the Indians in the town were rounded up and detained by the militia.[9]

Many of them were tortured. Núñez, the principal cacique, was beaten to death. His wife was given 200 lashes, but refused to speak. Guayocho himself, the Christ figure of Trinidad, was captured outside the town and shot.

His lieutenant, Santos Ñoco, who seems to have been the secular leader of the rebellion, managed to escape. With a number of others, he withdrew to the west across the Mamoré. There they stayed, creating a small settlement on the banks of the Securé river. They were still holding out a decade later.

According to another version, by an Italian naturalist, Luigi Balzan, who came through Trinidad four years after the rebellion, in 1891, most of the Indians had already left the town before Ascension Day. At the height of the rubber boom, they had taken refuge the other side of the Mamoré in order to avoid being pressganged into working in the rubber fields:

An expedition sent to track them down was wiped out, but after various traps and ambushes, the Indians were surprised and surrounded during mass at the church in Trinidad. A good fifteen lost their lives under the lash, some of them receiving as many as 1200 blows. What a fine thing to take these wretches by surprise in church when they had only been acting in self-defence – against the practices that we white civilizers had imposed upon them! And what morality on the part of certain priests, what Christian charity!

The survivors still live in small villages, many miles from the left bank of the Mamoré. They have built little chapels and busy themselves, free and happy, with agriculture and stock-rearing.[10]

Balzan explained why the Indians had been so anxious to escape from Trinidad:

Just before my arrival in Trinidad, the prefect – indeed a saintly man, who never missed a mass or a procession (of which there were more than forty in four months) and who said that no civilization was possible outside the Catholic religion – had ''sold'' a hundred of his citizens to a Beni rubber producer for a tidy sum, roughly equivalent to 80,000 Italian lire. Then, when one of these poor devils did not want to leave, the prefect had the church surrounded with his law-enforcement troops, seizing those who could provide him with a good profit. I saw this for myself a few days after I arrived.

Balzan gives a bleak picture of the decline of Trinidad:

The town which now has barely a thousand inhabitants is fairly wretched in appearance: two or three houses with three floors and timber passages, and many tiendas, or shops, selling cotton goods and ribbons etc. – too many, in fact, for local needs.

Trade and commerce had reaped a deadly reward. The once-remarkable church was no longer worthy of consideration: ''On one side of the square, flanking the prefect's house, stands the church, with the usual little belltower beside it. It is a church with little ornamentation, rather worn by time.''[11]

Like many other European travellers of the time, Balzan had a secular eye, and had little sympathy for the intermingling of Church and State:

I do not speak of the clergy in these lands, since an entire volume would be needed. Suffice it to say that even the current President of Bolivia, a clericalist of the first water, went so far as to ask Rome to abolish some of the priests' prerogatives. He gave as his reason their immense and almost unbelievable corruption.

The few remaining survivors of the Santos Ñoco rebellion were visited a couple of years after Balzan's expedition, in 1893, by two other Italians. These were not naturalists but Franciscan missionaries, Sebastian Pifferi and Zacarias Ducci.

Not all priests in Bolivia were as corrupt as Luigi Balzan alleged. Yet as politics there grew increasingly anti-clerical in the late nineteenth century, few were spared. The Franciscans, in particular, who ran many missions throughout the country and who had to some extent taken over the role that the Jesuits had made their own in the eighteenth century, came under attack. Like the Jesuits before them, the Franciscans were often less than sympathetic to the demands of Bolivia's settler communities. These usually wanted the Indians to be killed off, or at the very least packed off to the rubber fields – whence they never returned.

Father Pifferi was in charge of all the Franciscan schools in Bolivia, based at the college of his order in Tarija. In 1893, faced with political attacks that aimed to close all the Franciscan missions down, he went on a long expedition through the eastern and northern parts of the country to assess what was going on at first hand. He took Father Zacarias Ducci with him as a secretary and note-taker.

The two priests travelled through the country for six months on horseback. Ducci's account of their travels provides a unique picture of the state of decline into which the old mission towns had fallen by the end of the nineteenth century.[12] They rode into Trinidad in September 1893, six years after the Indian rebellion. "The town is decaying," Ducci wrote in his diary, "like all the settlements in Mojos, as a result of the flight of the indigenous peoples." Only two thousand people still lived there. The church, once so impressive just a decade before, was almost in ruins.

> The splendid altarpiece, the work of so much skill and patience, is about to collapse into fragments. Its silver adornments, like flowers in bloom, and a large number of other pieces, indicate that it was once an antique of considerable grandeur and magnificence.

Father Ducci noted that the surviving Indians were still very religious, tenaciously preserving the practices and customs that had once been established by the Jesuits. Venturing over the Mamoré, the two priests came to the settlement, called San Lorenzo, to which the Indians had fled after leaving Trinidad in 1887. When it was suggested to these Indians that they might now return to Trinidad, one of them replied: "Why should we go in search of death?"

In the last year of the century, more than a decade after the Trinidad rebellion, another visitor passed through the town. He had nothing more cheerful to report. José Aguirre Acha, a Bolivian explorer who travelled through the Beni during the rubber boom, found Trinidad in a lamentable state. The town appears, he wrote, "like the immense skeleton of a settlement that was once important. Many buildings have simply fallen in, leaving irregular open spaces in the blocks they occupy."[13]

A few Indians were still to be found in the town, and they performed a dance in his honour. It was the famous dance of the cane-cutters, once popular throughout Mojos. Acha found it an interesting spectacle:

> The macheteros (cane-cutters) – for that is what they called them – wore tipoyes in many colours, long stockings and high-heeled shoes. On their heads, like a great crest, they wore an immense outcrop of plumage, blue and red, which they waved from one side to the other like a fan, to the monotonous rhythm of a drum, swiftly followed by the noise of castanets that were shaken as they leapt about.

Luigi Balzan gave a similar, though more detailed, account of the dance.

The only thing worth seeing in these festivities is the so-called Dance of the Macheteros – from the (in this case) wooden machete used in the dance. The clothing of the dancers is the usual white tipoi, quite wide at the bottom but narrowing at the hips and slightly raised by means of a waistband. They often wear cascabeles, jingling bands, on the ankle.

They also have a very fine ornament on their heads, a halo of red arara feathers mounted on a woven reed frame. The plumage is fixed behind the head, and the part in front of the frame is covered with green parrot feathers, or yellow ones from the arara. A tail of toucan feathers hangs down behind from where the red plumes forming the halo begin to rise.

The dancing is done during the course of a procession, which is preceded by the images of saints or the portraits of national figures. The old women from the locality, called abadesas, walk in small groups in front of the individual saints, strewing flowers along their path. The drum strikes up with a sharp beat, continually quickening until it falls in with the actual rhythm of the dancing: tan, tan, tan, tan, tan, tan, and so on. At each refrain, the dancers pirouette backwards or forwards, always keeping the machete in their clenched hand. It is, in fact, a religious-military dance. When the procession is over, the dancing continues for hours in front of the closed door of the church.[14]

This was no ordinary dance. It was, José Aguirre Acha wrote without irony, "a vivid portrayal of the struggles of the Mojos against Spanish rule". In spite of the arrival of unregulated trade, of the rubber boom and its consequent depopulation of their towns, the spirit of the Mojos Indians had still not been entirely quenched. In their church services and in their dance, they retained something of their old traditions. A hundred years later, even that has gone.

Notes

1. Franz Keller, *The Amazon and Madeira Rivers: sketches and descriptions from the notebook of an explorer*, London 1874, p. 158.
2. George Earl Church, *Explorations Made in the Valley of the River Madeira*, London 1875; and *The Route to Bolivia via the River Amazon*, London 1877.
3. Edward Mathews, *Up the Amazon and Madeira Rivers, Through Bolivia and Peru*, London 1879.
4. Passing through the lands of the Parententin Indians earlier on his expedition, Mathews complained that "no settler dares to set up a hut on their territory, although it contains very rich growths of rubber trees. The Brazilian government does not allow the improvement of these savage races by the only practical method, namely extermination, but trusts to the efforts of the few missionary friars to whom is entrusted the work of proselytising the untamed tribes of the interior of the empire."
5. Neville Craig, *Recollections of an Ill-fated Expedition to the Headwaters of the Madeira River in Brazil*, Philadelphia 1907, p. 55.
6. Lardner Gibbon, *Exploration of the Valley of the Amazon*, part II, Washington 1854, p. 242.
7. Franz Keller, *The Amazon and Madeira Rivers: sketches and descriptions from the notebook of an explorer*, London 1874. The Jesuits' depiction of the Trinity is a not infrequent sight in the old missions. It shows a three-headed priest holding a curious tricorn device. In his right hand is a large circle with

the word "Father". In his left hand is a similar circle with the word "Son". And at his feet is a third circle with the words "Holy Ghost". Between each circle runs a signboard with the words "Is Not", so that the message as a whole reads: "The Father Is Not The Son Is Not the Holy Ghost Is Not The Father."

But this is not all. In front of the three-headed priest's stomach is a fourth circle with the one word "God". And this circle is joined to the other circles with another signboard with the word "Is". And the completed message reads "God is the Father; God is the Son; God is the Holy Ghost."

In a mission consecrated to such a mystery, Franz Keller wrote, "such an explanation, if we may be permitted so to call it, was rendered all the more necessary by the fact that the red neophytes more than once perplexed the Fathers with unanswerable questions".

8. Gibbon, p. 246.
9. Ciro Bayo, *El Peregrino en Indias*, Madrid 1911, p. 383.
10. Luigi Balzan, *Viaggio di esplorazione nelle regioni centrali del Sud America*, Milano 1931.
11. Luigi Balzan was quite unlike the other European travellers who came up the Mamoré in the late nineteenth century. By origin an Italian naturalist from Padua, he had gone to Argentina in the 1880s and secured a job in the Museo de la Plata, in the town of La Plata. From there he went, in 1887, to Paraguay. In Asunción, he joined a small group of European and Paraguayan intellectuals who were intrigued by the history and geography of that country, notably his compatriot Guido Boggiani, the ethnologist who explored in the upper Paraguay, and Blas Garay, the Paraguayan historian who explored in the archives of Seville. (Tragically, they all died young. Bayo was shot in Villa Hayes, Boggiani was killed in the Chaco, Balzan died shortly after returning to Italy.) At the end of 1890, financed from Italy, Balzan went off on a great two-year expedition through Argentina, Chile, southern Peru, Bolivia and Paraguay. Travelling from La Paz over the Andes, he canoed down the Beni to Riberalta, and then came up the Mamoré, past Exaltación to Trinidad. He stayed there for four months before travelling on to Santa Cruz, across Chiquitos to the Paraguay, and then back to Asunción. After his trip, he returned to Rome to report to his benefactors, and there, in 1893, he died. He had contracted malaria on the expedition. He was only twenty-eight. The account of his travels was not published until many decades later, in 1931.
12. Zacarias Ducci, *Diario de la visita a todas las misiones existentes en la república de Bolivia*, Assisi 1895.
13. José Aguirre Acha, *De los Andes al Amazonas, recuerdos de la campaña del Acre*, second edn, La Paz 1927, p. 126.
14. Balzan.

23

EXALTACIÓN

The Jesuit mission at Exaltación de la Cruz

The most favoured form of urban transport in the Bolivian Beni, giving you rather more intimate contact with your taxi-driver than is normal, is the motor-scooter taxi. Sitting on the pillion and driving over the mixture of sand and paving, and the inevitable bumps between the two, the need to clutch tightly to the driver in front is an essential part of the trip. Initially nervous, we soon got used to it.

In Trinidad, we took two of these taxis to the airport, about five minutes' drive out of town – so close to the town in fact that the planes come in to land close over the central plaza. The airport is little more than an open-sided shed with a couple of stalls and a café. Locating a friendly pilot, we said we would like to fly to Exaltación.

He took us out to see his plane, an Italian twin-engined four-seater. He said it would cost us 250 dollars for an hour's flight. As Exaltación is about an hour away, the journey would cost 500 dollars there and back. No wonder he was friendly.

We took the scooters back to town to get some more money from the (also very friendly) money changer outside our hotel, and returned to the airport. The scooter drivers were pretty cheerful by this time too. We took off about midday, Vivien in front beside the pilot. His name was Jorge Velardo. He learnt to fly, not in the Bolivian airforce as I had imagined, but on a private flying course in Santa Cruz. He had North American instructors, he said, and the course took a year and a half. It cost him 10,000 dollars.

Jorge told us that the drugs trade, and the fight against it, is proving to be very bad for aviators. They always have to say where they are going, and they have to file accurate flight plans. Although there is still quite a lot of flying to isolated haciendas, there is no longer much casual trade of the kind we are usefully providing. He thinks that the United States' actions have been quite effective, and indeed they are one of the causes of the current drastic recession – there is no longer as much drug money in the national exchequer as there used to be. But a lot of smuggling still goes on. The old Jesuit mission town of Santa Ana is now the centre of the trade – "the Medellín of Bolivia", Jorge calls it – and the Americans raid it from time to time.

Our journey took us over the curves of the River Mamoré. Flying low, we had a good view of the river's twists and turns. Even in the dry season there is a vast amount of swampland, and one can trace the many different courses that the river takes. The land is flat, and the country open. A narrow strip of jungle fringes the river bank, but most of this area to the horizon is swamp and savannah and palm trees. And many herds of cattle.

After a flight north of some fifty minutes, we could see Exaltación from the air – a typical Jesuit square with the church in the usual place – a mile or so from the river bank. Even from the air one can see that this church is not even nineteenth century, let alone eighteenth. The decay affecting the entire area of Mojos has not spared Exaltación.

Exaltación was the most northerly of the missions established by the Jesuits in Mojos, founded in the last decade of the seventeenth century. Because it occupied an important strategic spot on the Mamoré, not far from its junction with the Guaporé, from the first it had rather more than its share of visitors. Some came from Peru, down the Madre de Dios or the Beni. Some came from Mato Grosso, down the Guaporé. And some came from the Amazon, travelling up the Madeira, past the great rapids, to the Mamoré.

Robert Southey gives details of a Portuguese expedition that used this latter route in 1723. It arrived at Exaltación from Pará, now Belém, on the lower Amazon.

> The governor of Pará, Joâo da Maya, received information from persons who traded with the natives upon the Madeira, that there were European settlements above the falls, but whether of the Portuguese or Spaniards was uncertain. Upon this he dispatched a party under Francisco de Mello Pacheco to explore the river.[1]

This expedition was accompanied for some of the way by Father Joâo de Sampaio, a Jesuit priest at a mission of Tupinambarana Indians on the Madeira river. He provided the expedition with two hundred oarsmen from his mission, as well as food and canoes.[2]

> They ascended as far as the mouth of the Mamoré, and there fell in with a mestizo who guided them to Exaltación. Pacheco then ascertained that these settlements were made by the Jesuits from Peru; and after an uncourteous correspondence with the governor of Santa Cruz, who forbade him to advance into the country, he returned without any satisfactory account even of what he had explored.[3]

A frequent occurrence in these frontier areas was the arrival of runaway black slaves from Brazil. Exaltación had a visit from "a party of runaways from Bahía, with a priest in company, who frankly avowed that they had fled their own country in consequence of having committed certain acts, which rendered it impossible for them to continue in it with safety". They asked permission to take refuge, but this was refused. "It is not known what became of the adventurers."

Sometimes the visitors seem quite simply to have been spies, or unofficial peace-makers. A Carmelite friar came upriver from the Madeira falls to issue a warning:

> The purport of his coming was to ascertain the distance to the Spanish settlements, and to require that the Spaniards would keep on their own side of the river, and not form any establishments on the right bank, nor collect any Indians from thence, because all the country on that side belonged to the King of Portugal, the natives were his Indians, and his missionaries were employed there.

When the Jesuits were expelled in 1767, the mission's proximity to the Portuguese frontier left it vulnerable to attack. During the rule of the post-Jesuit curas, much of the population found the Portuguese to be the lesser evil, as Lazaro de Ribera reported in 1794:

> This was for many years the scene of innumerable crimes and misdemeanours. The evil conduct of the priests turned the Portuguese into the owners of its production, its cattle, and even of its Indians, who fled in a mad rush to those places where they could seek help, to shelter from the assaults that they had been obliged to sustain.[4]

Alcides d'Orbigny came here some forty years later, arriving at the port on the Mamoré on 1 April 1832. He had spent a week on the river, travelling from the Portuguese fort of Príncipe da Beira on the Guaporé, the old Jesuit mission of Santa Rosa. He was not much pleased by his reception. Lázaro de Ribera had recommended that the corrupt curas should be replaced by secular administrators. When d'Orbigny arrived, this was now independent Bolivia, but in this remote spot, little had changed. The administrators had proved to be as bad as the curas.

> In the bay, Indians boys and girls were bathing. I walked along the path towards the mission, where I could hardly have been less hospitably received by the administrator. In spite of the precise instructions that he had received, he found a thousand ways to irritate me during my week's stay. Luckily the priest did not behave in the same way.
>
> I worked with extreme diligence because I wanted to leave as soon as possible from this most disagreeable residence. But I had to put my notes and my itineraries in order, to collect objects of natural history from the surroundings, to study the history of the mission and its archives, and above all to write the vocabularies of the languages of the Cayubabas, the Pacaguaras, and the Itenes.[5]

D'Orbigny considered Exaltación to be one of the richest missions in Mojos. He thought the Indian weaving was "very attractive", and he liked the cacao.

> Set in a flat plain, in the middle of marshy land, the mission is protected from the floods of the Mamoré by a raised trench that the Jesuits constructed. The central plaza, with its great palm trees, its church buildings, and its houses for the civil authorities, is similar

to that of the other missions. Built according to the style of the Middle Ages, the church is filled with ornaments and sculptures in good taste; its earth walls are decorated with mural paintings. The college is well planned.

A caprice of the administrator has meant the loss of a precious treasure; on the walls the Jesuits had sketched out a detailed map of the province, with which they must have been extremely familiar; then, a few years ago, this administrator had ordered it to be scrubbed out and replaced by gross caricatures and pictures of hunting scenes in the style of European engravings.

D'Orbigny had the usual difficulty in leaving Exaltación, faced by all nineteenth-century travellers – a lack of oarsmen. In his case, the matter was made worse by the much-disliked administrator who apparently hid the best boats. D'Orbigny was given canoes that leaked like sieves, and was lucky to escape shipwreck.

We land on a bumpy grass strip about 800 metres from the village. Hardly have we arrived before two small boys materialize, followed by two girls on a motor scooter, and an older man with a motorbike. These turn out to be the only motor vehicles in the village – there is no motor road to Exaltación – and we take it in turns to be ferried down the track to the village.

The church is rather sweet, with white plastered walls, a wooden front and porch, and with pillars running along the side. The doors are quite pretty, with blue-painted diamond panels. These, when closed, reveal the outline of a great black cross. Attractive enough, the church is less than a hundred years old. This is no longer the magnificent building about which so many nineteenth-century travellers left a record.

The villagers we talk to think that the building is basically the old one. Only the roof and the pillars have been renewed, they say. One new external pillar, they proudly tell us, has just been put in that week. A chunk of the old tree trunk, with its spreading foot, is still on show beside the church.

As elsewhere, there are two or three old bells on display, hanging to the side of the entrance porch. The only one with lettering gives a date of 1830; it was made two years before d'Orbigny arrived on his tour of inspection.

The man with the motorbike, who seems to be some kind of cacique, invites us to take a Coke while we wait for the enfermera, the local nurse. She has the key to the church. Small children come out to greet us, scrambling onto a splendid ox-cart with solid wooden wheels to get a better view.

Edward Mathews, the British engineer on the Madeira railway, came here in 1874 and wrote an account of the state of the original church as he found it.

The church is a very old edifice built of adobes, and was constructed by the Jesuits more than 200 years ago [a slight exaggeration], the "cura" of the town informing me that there were ecclesiastical records belonging to it which vouched for its age.

The façade facing onto the central square of the village is highly ornamented with figures in cement handsomely painted; the columns are made in a twisted pattern, and there are, on either side of the principal door, images of Christ and a Virgin, about eight feet in height, elaborately moulded and painted. The interior has been highly decorated with relievo ornamentation in mud cement, but has now become much decayed, all the pictures, of which there were a great many, having fallen out of their frames.[6]

No "ecclesiastical records" now survive in Exaltación. Everything old has been filched over the years. André Bresson , a French engineer who came here three years after Mathews, in 1877, records that he stole a prayerbook manuscript from the time of the Jesuits – and notes that it was stolen from him later in Peru.[7]

When the enfermera comes with the key, we are able to get a glimpse of the inside of the church. There is even less left of the old Jesuit splendour than there was in Mathews' day. Six silver plates are still fixed to the altar wall, but in a group of carved wooden statues, only one looks old. A Christ figure, in agony, lashed to a post, stands near the entrance, and this at least looks as though it has survived from the eighteenth century. In a side chapel, several old statues are lying about, including, propped up in a corner, a figure of Christ on an immense cross, wrapped in bandages like an Egyptian mummy. It is the pride of the village, brought out once a year. Nearby is another huge and heavy cross. The date on its base is 1831. We see no sign of the objects that Luigi Balzan, the Italian naturalist, had marvelled at when he came here a hundred years ago in 1891:

> The one thing of beauty at Exaltación, which would well merit being in other hands, is the wooden engraving and sculpture on the high altar, and indeed throughout the church. This was work that the Jesuits got the Indians to do. I also saw two large chests with images of the Birth of Jesus and the Massacre of the Innocents: a miracle of perseverance crowded with small figurines.[8]

The Indian population assembled at the Exaltación mission by the Jesuits were Cayubabas. We are told that some of the old people still speak the language. There were about two thousand there in d'Orbigny's day. They are beyond any doubt, he wrote, "the best people in the province: for their openness and their lack of vices". He was impressed by their willingness to work:

> They are naturally strong, with regular features. For a long time I had men with me from this nation, and I have nothing but praise for their character. Indefatigable paddlers, their pilots are very experienced. Enthusiastic and enterprising, they are also prudent and respectful, uncomplaining and affable.[9]

Luigi Balzan had a similar view. "Though not very tall, the Cayubabas are a strong and robust people, with an excellent disposition."

Their reputation as reliable and steadfast oarsmen lasted throughout the nineteenth century. They paddled the boat that brought Edward Mathews here in 1874, to the landing stage "situated at the apex of a large bend in the river, each arm being at least a league in length". Here there is a fifty-foot difference between high and low water.[10]

There is a track from the river to the village, "across a pampa, with a few isolated trees and a rough grass three or four feet in height, which at certain seasons is burnt, so that new grass fit for the cattle may spring up".

The burning, Mathews noted, had to be done "when the wind is quiet, and can only be done in patches, for if the fires were not kept under control, the villages and plantations would be greatly endangered".

When he got to the village, it was in better shape than today. Built on the flat pampa, it consisted of "about a hundred houses, built of adobe walls, with tiled roofs, arranged in square blocks in the usual South American fashion".

Mathews had to stay in Exaltación for ten days. Like d'Orbigny, he had trouble with the crew of his canoe. They were local and did not wish to continue the upriver journey with him to Trinidad. He had to find fresh oarsmen. The available Indians were decreasing in number, he noted:

> . . . and the deserted houses and lines of old streets now in ruins give a sad and desolate look to Exaltación. The present population cannot be more than 1500, and I should judge that less than fifty years ago [in 1824] there would have been nearly 4000 Indians at the mission.

Mathews traced the decline to "the baneful effects" of the rubber-collecting trade along the Madeira and the Purus, a trade that was depopulating all the towns of the Beni. The previous year, he noted, forty-three canoes had descended the rapids from Bolivia with cargoes of rubber and cinchona bark. Only thirteen had returned upriver.

With ten Indians for each canoe, there was a net loss that year of three hundred men. Mathews thought that was probably an underestimate. In the decade from 1862 to 1872, Bolivia had been losing men from the mission towns at the rate of one thousand a year.

Twenty years later, Luigi Balzan was to record his belief that, unlike the people of the other mission towns, not many of the inhabitants of Exaltación had been induced to work the rubber. He thought that "as they are the best rowers on the river, they are nearly always away from home on trips – from Villa Bella to the Madeira or to Trinidad".

Edward Mathews had a gloomier, and probably more correct analysis. The fate of these Bolivians, he wrote, was to suffer "a form of slavery" far worse than that experienced by the Brazilian blacks. They were effectively pressganged into work as seringueiros, or rubber-tappers, further down the river, on the Madeira in Brazil. Mathews, who knew the river well, outlined what happened to them:

> At most of the barracas on the Madeira River where the seringueiros live, the Sundays are passed in perfect orgies of drunkenness, for it is on that day that the peon delivers over to the patron the rubber that he has collected during the week. The patron is also a shopkeeper, and therefore treats his peon liberally to white rum (called cachaca on the river), and when, under the influence of this liquor, the poor peon is induced to buy trinkets, calicoes, ribbons, and other articles that he could do very well without. These are charged to him at enormous prices, whilst his rubber is credited to him at inversely corresponding low ones, and thus he is kept under a heavy load of debt, and cannot, under the Brazilian laws, leave his patron until it is worked off, which happy event the patron takes care shall not happen.

Mathews thought that one of the worst features of the disastrous emigration was "the fact that rubber speculators and merchants descending the rapids will not allow the Indians to take any of the females with them". It was always argued that there was no room on the boats. "Thus it arises that in every town in the Beni the females are in a majority of perhaps five to one over the males, and the populations are decreasing." Quoting a Portuguese estimate of 1749 that there had been twenty-six thousand Indians in the fifteen Jesuit missions of the Beni, Mathews reckoned that in the 1870s probably "not more than eight thousand would be found".

Mathews also outlined a way in which the former lands of the Cayubabas had simply been taken away from them over the years. Coming up the river before reaching Exaltación, he had passed a cacoa plantation – chocolatales – that, he said, had been created in the eighteenth century as a dependency of the Jesuit mission. These, he wrote, are "very extensive and are now claimed as government properties". The government authorities at Exaltación and Trinidad farmed out these plantations "to speculators who make good profits, as there is no labour, or very little, expended in clearing".

All the speculators needed was cheap labour at harvest time, and this was provided for them by the local Cayubabas:

> At the proper season, which is during the months when the river is in flood, from February to March, the Cayubaba Indians from Exaltación descend to these plantations, and collecting the cocoa pods which are then ripe, clear the trees somewhat of the dead leaves and rubbish that has fallen during the year, leaving the chocolatales to the savages and wild animals until the collecting time again comes round.

The speculators took the profit, perhaps reflecting that "close to the plantations there was often a clearing, with a hut and a small plot of land for fruit and vegetables". Here the visiting Cayubabas would stay for the harvest season and, if they were lucky, would grow enough food to see them through the rest of the year.

Yet even these small plots were not sacred. Mathews rowed past when the Cayubabas were not in residence, and he was surprised when his boatmen helped themselves to the produce of the small plots. ''I was told that it was an understood custom that all travellers should help themselves as freely as they wished at these plantations, which are the first that parties ascending the rapids into Bolivia can arrive at.''

Was this the custom established by the Portuguese in the eighteenth century, or was it a tradition that stretched back rather further in time, to an era of prosperity before the Europeans ever set foot in Mojos?

The search for the Gran Paitití, the land of the Celestial Jaguar

This territory of Mojos – the watery plain to the north-east of the western curve of the Andes in Bolivia – was regarded by the first Spanish conquistadores, long before they got here, as one of the possible sites of El Dorado. They had heard a lot about it. In Peru, there had been tales of a legendary country to the east of Cuzco, once investigated by the Incas. In Paraguay, there had been similar stories of a great civilization lying in the swamps somewhere to the north-west.

Later, in their multifaceted search for this land of wealth and plenty, the Spaniards from Santa Cruz were to hunt for many years in these flatlands north of Trinidad, an area now called the Beni. They were looking for the land of a great leader called the Great Moxo, sometimes known as Paitití, the Celestial Jaguar. Sometimes this name was thought to be that of a man, sometimes it was perceived to refer to a large lake, and sometimes to a high metal-bearing mountain. For the Spaniards, Paitití was a name that symbolized a territory with an advanced and wealthy civilization, one that they had not yet found and one that they wished to conquer.

In the twentieth century, the man most associated with the search for an El Dorado in the swamps and jungles of the upper Amazon is Colonel Fawcett, whose disappearance in the 1920s sparked off a rash of expeditions and travel books.[11] Fawcett had glimpsed a Portuguese manuscript of a journey in 1743 which appeared to reveal the existence of a great pre-Conquest city. After a lifetime spent in the area fixing the frontiers between Bolivia and Brazil, he disappeared on an expedition that went to look for it.

For most of the twentieth century, historians have argued that this Amazonian El Dorado, like the others elsewhere in South America, was a mirage. According to this unromantic version, the conquistadores up the Paraguay – who first heard the story in the 1540s – were getting a jumbled account of the wonders of the Inca empire in the mountains of Peru, which lost nothing in the telling. The ''large lake'' was Lake Titicaca on the frontiers of Bolivia and Peru, and ''the metal-bearing mountain'' was merely one of the great peaks of the Andean chain. Only the Quechua and the

Aymara of the Andes, ruled and controlled by the Incas, had a civilization capable of generating that kind of legend.[12]

This has been the traditional wisdom. Then it began to dawn on people that the Incas themselves knew of something rather interesting going on in the lands to their east. The Incas had heard these rumours of a great civilization. Indeed the Inca Yupanqui – before the arrival of the Spaniards – had sent an expedition to examine what went on in those parts, travelling down from Cuzco on the Andean plateau into the plains of the Amazon basin (see pages 213–15).

Recent archaeological research by William Denevan has revealed that what are now the flat cattle lands (and drug trails) of northern Bolivia may well have been an El Dorado in its own right, a prosperous and organized society sustaining a huge population infinitely larger than the meagre settlements of today. One authority suggests the population could be counted in the hundreds of thousands in the pre-Columbian era, but declined to 50,000 in the middle of the eighteenth century, ending up with about 15,000 today.[13]

Although in the colonial period there was little sign of gold, in the late twentieth century modern dredging techniques have produced a small-scale gold rush to the rivers of the northern Beni. The Jesuits are known to have exploited the mine at San Simón, their most easterly mission, and the Portuguese were also familiar with its possibilities.

Long before the Spaniards, or even the Incas, arrived here, the Gran Moxo ruled over an extraordinary civilization, a society with little gold or silver but with a large settled and wealthy population that engaged in the building of astonishing earthworks. These constructions, of which tens of thousands survive, were used to grow food – in an area that was flooded annually. These artificial hills, canals, ditches and terraces survive throughout the region.

An early reference to this civilization comes from a Jesuit writer in Lima, José de Acosta. Writing in 1590 that the Europeans were still somewhat ignorant about "the greater part of America", the part that lies between Peru and Brazil, he revealed what he had heard:

> There are many opinions about it; some say it is only swamp, filled with nothing but lakes and bogs; but others say that in those parts there exist great and flourishing kingdoms, and from it they have concocted these tales of Paitití, of El Dorado, and of the land of the Caesars, and say that there are wonderful things. From one member of our Company, a trustworthy man, I have myself heard that he had seen great settlements and roads as wide and well-trodden as those of Salamanca and Valladolid.[14]

A souped-up version of the same story, at much the same time, gives more macabre detail.

> This great lord held sway over large subject provinces, whose people served him with considerable affection for they were a docile and loyal nation. He possessed immense

treasure, and what he had was displayed in great buildings, like temples, under a strong guard. He would visit his idols once a month, to whom, at the time of the new moon, he would offer a two-year-old child that he would himself put to the sword, retaining the blood of the innocent one. In the same way he would kill the most excellent sheep, and, mixing its fat with the blood of the innocent one, would sprinkle the mixture in honour of the sun, from whence it came, and then over those who witnessed the event.[15]

This version places the legendary land of Paitití along the banks of the Guaporé.

In search of it, a number of expeditions were launched by the Spaniards in the thirty years after 1540, both from their Andean settlements in Peru and Bolivia, and from their base on the upper Paraguay. The expeditions from the west stumbled across the headwaters of the Beni and the Madre de Dios, but were effectively blocked from getting into Mojos proper by the great belt of forest that lies along the eastern slopes of the Andes.[16] Their fate has been graphically depicted in the late twentieth century in Werner Herzog's film *Aguirre, Wrath of God*.

Those coming from the east suffered less from hostile geography than from human failings. These were the followers of Nuflo de Chávez based at the early settlement of Santa Cruz de la Sierra (at its original site at what is now San José de Chiquitos). In 1560, Nuflo de Chávez was appointed by the viceroy to be governor of Mojos, though he was killed before he had time to explore the region with which he had been presented. Indian hostility was to prevent further exploration for nearly half a century.

There was, however, an earlier expedition – in 1543 – which produced a text whose surface miracles have rather tended to obscure the detail beneath. Towards the end of the famous expedition into Chiquitos from Lake Gaiba, led by Alvar Núñez Cabeza de Vaca, a small scouting party was sent north from the lake. Led by Captain Hernando de Ribera, the party of fifty-two soldiers travelled up the Paraguay in a small brigantine called *El Golondrino* (The Swallow). Arriving at the land of the Xarayes, they abandoned the boat and marched to the west with a guide from the Xarayes. Ribera was then told many apparently fabulous tales: of a land of "female warriors", of a nation "of very small Indians who make war upon the women", and of "large nations of black people . . . eagle-faced with pointed beards like the Moors".[17]

These stories are not, on the face of it, unbelievable. In a densely inhabited area of an immense size, there were many nations, with different characteristics. In descriptions, these characteristics take an exaggerated form; nations with dominating women become Amazons, small Indians become dwarves, sallow, bearded people become blacks or Arabs. The Guatos on the upper Paraguay, drawn by the Count of Castelnau in the 1840s, could easily have filled the description of this latter group.

So in spite of its apparently fabulous feel, the report of Hernando de Ribera is clearly not without value. Further on, he gives a description of an area which sounds very like the kind of place that William Denevan's archaeological researches in Mojos have revealed.

> Farther to the west there is a large lake, so wide that it is impossible to see from shore to shore, and by its side dwells a nation who wear clothes, and possess much metal and brilliant stones, which they work into the borders of their dress; and they find these stones in the lake. They have large villages, are agriculturalists, and have stores of provisions, besides an abundance of geese and other birds. From the place where I was, they said I might reach the lake and its settlements in fifteen days, always travelling through inhabited country, abounding in metal, and by good roads. They offered to show us the way thither when the floods subsided.

The lake was said to be only a fortnight's journey away from the upper Paraguay, so this can hardly be a reference to Lake Titicaca. Some now claim that it was Lake Rogo-aguado, not far from Exaltación. Ribera's Indian informants were clearly capable of distinguishing between the civilizations of the Amazon swamp and those of the Andean highlands beyond. He was told of "high mountains" – the Andes – of "great waterless deserts of sand" – the Atacama desert of northern Chile – and of a land beyond where "lay the salt water and the great ships" – the Pacific.

Ribera's expedition from Lake Gaiba only lasted six weeks, there and back, so it is unlikely that he himself penetrated as far as Mojos. He may have crossed the watershed and reached the waters of the upper Guaporé, where information about the civilizations existing downstream would have been readily available. His report, written down in Asunción in 1545, a year after his expedition's return, was to become the bible of all subsequent Spanish explorations to the west of the upper Paraguay.

So where was this wonderful land, the land of Paitití? The Jesuits believed that it was the territory around their mission at Exaltación de la Cruz. Their arguments were quite simple.

One of their priests in Mojos, Father Agustín Zapata, had advanced down the Mamoré from Trinidad in 1693 into the land of the Canichana Indians, in the area of San Pedro. There he heard news of another nation downstream, further to the north, called the Cayubabas.

He set off to find them, carrying the usual gifts of knives, axes and machetes, as well as maize and yucca. Returning some time later, he reported that he had visited seven villages. Each had a population of some 1800 people. They were governed by a bearded cacique called Paitití.[18]

He returned two years later, and subsequently reported entering a large village with a central square, a house of worship, and several streets. The people there wore feathers and shawls. An immense fire burned day and night, and on it deer and rabbits and birds were sacrificed.

Here, Father Zapata established the mission of Exaltación de la Cruz, at the heart of what had once been a great civilization. Three hundred years later, there is almost nothing to remind us of its past glories. When William Denevan came here in 1962, he met "only a handful of people in the settlement who spoke Cayubaba", though "a few more lived nearby, in scattered hamlets". He found that they had preserved little or none of the traditions and legends that went back before the Jesuit era.[19]

Yet in the accounts by nineteenth-century travellers of the rituals played out within and outside the great Jesuit church at Exaltación, there is a flavour of a civilization that goes back long before the Spaniards. As in Trinidad, all visitors who witnessed the spectacle were entranced by the dance of the macheteros, an antique celebration that the Jesuits had somehow managed to harness to their cause.

Edward Mathews, the British engineer who came here in 1874 and observed the celebrations to mark the feast of John the Baptist, noted how the worshippers moved seamlessly from the Christian to the pagan. Much of the day was spent throwing water at everyone – a Spanish custom – in a kind of symbolic mass baptism. But before mass was celebrated – "with great beating of drums and blowing of horns" – the water play was abandoned, and something different began.

"The service of the mass was of a most barbarous character, and has evidently been adapted to the customs of the aborigines of these parts by the Jesuits." Mathews watched while two dancers began to gyrate, first at the altar, then at the church door.

> There were two Indians with head-dresses of macaw's feathers arranged so as to form a circle at the back of the head, and attached thereto is a long appendage, reaching to the ground and made of the breast feathers of the toucan, terminating with a real tiger's tail. These men have a species of bell-anklets to their feet, and a large wooden machete, or cutlass, in their right hands.

Mathews assumed that the macheteros were intended to typify "the soldiers of the Church, fighting and conquering its enemies", but the dance clearly had an earlier origin.[20] Franz Keller, the German engineer from Brazil who came here two years later in 1876, also observed the celebration.

> A dozen of the sword dancers . . . went singing and dancing and brandishing their broad knives and wooden swords, from cross to cross, headed by their chieftain, who carried a heavy silver cross, and followed by the whole tribe. They wore dazzling white camisetas, rattling stag's claws on their knuckles, and a fanciful head-gear composed of the head-feathers of the araras and of yellow and red toucan's breasts.[21]

Keller noted that several high wooden crosses were erected in different parts of the town, perhaps in honour of the town's name. When the dancers emerged from the church, they continued their mystic celebration:

> At every cross, and before the altars of the church, they performed a sort of allegorical dance, with a great show of brandishing their inoffensive weapons, which they at last,

breathless and perspiring, laid down together with their savage diadems at the foot of the crucifix; the whole evidently representing the submission of the Indians and their conversion to Christianity.

When Luigi Balzan, the Italian naturalist, came here in Holy Week in 1891, he missed the dance of the macheteros, but in church on Good Friday, during the sermon, he observed "a curious spectacle".

The priest went up into the pulpit and started to speak. Then, at a certain point in his sermon, he commanded a number of old Indians to remove the crown and the nails from the figure of Christ. They laid him out on a bed. Each of these items was formally presented to the statue of the Madonna which stood, decorated with banana leaves, next to the great crucifix. As each object was displayed before her, all the Indians, especially the women, beat themselves in the face and began to cry out loud.[22]

What began as a simple display of Christian enthusiasm on a European model soon developed into something much more pagan and aboriginal, to the intense irritation of the priest:

When he had had enough of this bawling and wanted to continue with his sermon, the priest made a sign for them to be silent. But his gesture was misunderstood, setting off a yet more desperate outburst of wailing. Rebuking them in foul language, he strode back into the sacristy.

The Cayubaba Indians then went out of the church to process round the square. Here they re-established their secular priorities:

It was a much-coveted honour to carry the church's banner, and on this occasion it was granted to the official local candidate in the forthcoming elections. The provincial subprefect walked in the procession with the key to the Holy Sacrament hanging from his neck.

Luigi Balzan, an Italian anti-clerical, was anxious to depict the corruption of the clergy and the tragedy of the Indians held in thrall to the archaic rituals of the Catholic Church. But the Cayubaba were clearly celebrating something that went much further back in time, as Franz Keller had noted when watching the sword dancers. The dance was an essential part of their culture that the caciques tenaciously preserved:

Old Bolivians have told me that these dances used to be executed by dozens of macheteros, and that they would probably have ceased altogether if the chieftains did not exert the full weight of their authority in behalf of keeping them up, even forcing the young men, in case of need, to take part in them.

Little of this rich tradition has survived into the twentieth century. Exaltación today is a poor and depopulated village. Only the houses sprinkled round the central square have survived. Beyond are a few simple huts. There might perhaps be 1500 inhabitants, probably less. The former school buildings, on the corner by the church, are largely in ruins, though a couple of classrooms have been done up and made habitable. No priest now lives in the village, and most of the men are obliged to work far beyond its boundaries.

There has been no improvement since Balzan's visit, a hundred years ago. He was depressed, even then, by the prevailing sense of decline. "This is the most wretched little town," he wrote in 1891, "with poor thatched huts – many falling into ruin." Even the old tamarisk trees had been cut down. José Aguirre Acha, who came in 1899, also found it "a complete ruin". The population, he reckoned, had declined to barely three hundred people.[23]

Leaving the church, we took the track down to the Mamoré which lies about a mile away. Riding pillion on the village's two motor scooters, we passed an ox-cart laden with grapefruit, pulled by two oxen. That was the way visitors came in the last century.

A small settlement of bamboo houses, with a large outside clay oven, stands on the crest of the river bank. Below, at the foot of a great cliff, flows the great river itself, an immense and mighty stream. Two men on the beach are loading heavy planks onto a small boat.

Even now in the dry season, the river here is very wide, making a great sweep round from left to right. Great sandbanks emerge on the further shore. There are two large canoes on the river, one being paddled fore and aft, the other with an outboard motor. Neither is the size of the great boats that paddled past here in the eighteenth and nineteenth centuries.

This is all the traffic now to be seen on what was once one of the great waterways of South America. The explosion caused by the rubber trade at the turn of the twentieth century was the last time that European prosperity brushed Exaltación's sleeve, and caused it to lose its inhabitants. What may have been the centre of the prosperous civilization of Paitití is now a ghost village. We took the motor scooters back to the airstrip, and flew away.

Notes

1. Robert Southey, *History of Brazil*, vol. 3, London 1819, p. 341.
2. John Hemming, *Indian Gold*, London 1978, p. 431.
3. Southey, vol. 3, p. 341.
4. Lázaro de Ribera, *Moxos, descripciones exactas, e historica fiel de los indios, animales e plantas de la provincia de Moxos en el virreinato del Peru por Lázaro de Ribera, 1786–1794*, Ediciones El Viso, Madrid 1989.
5. Alcides Dessalines d'Orbigny, *Voyage dans l'Amérique méridionale*, Paris 1845.

6. Edward Mathews, *Up the Amazon and Madeira Rivers, Through Bolivia and Peru*, London 1879.

While waiting in Exaltación, Edward Mathews made some effort to study the Cayubaba language. He learnt to count in it – carata, mitia, curapa, chata, mitaru, tariduboi. On his travels through this territory, he also learnt a bit of Mojeno (the language of Trinidad) and of Canichana (that of San Pedro). The last two, he noted, "do not appear to be able to count beyond three; arriving at that they commence again, and have to arrange all their calculations in sets of threes, which seems to be a most complicated proceeding".

There was, however, a way round the problem. "As most of the Indians have learnt the Spanish numerals, I observed that they invariably counted the first three numbers in their own language and then went off into cuatro, cinco, etc. I managed to get the Cayubabas up to "tariduboi", or six, and then they would go on with siete, ocho, nueve, etc."

7. André Bresson, *Sept années d'explorations, de voyages et de séjours dans l'Amérique australe*, Paris 1886, p. xiv.

André Bresson travelled through northern Bolivia in the 1870s. He was a French engineer, and described himself as a consul of Bolivia. He dedicated his book of travels to Ferdinand de Lesseps. It was, he wrote, the result of seven years' exploration and study, and it was written with a purpose. "France has forgotten its colonizing traditions. They must be revived. . . . Bolivia and the country of the Amazon offer us territories and horizons without limit."

He tells how in the first few days of 1870 ("de si douloureuse mémoire") he was appointed to take part in a commission that was to study the guano deposits and the metal-bearing reefs in South America generally and Bolivia in particular. He did indeed travel all over the country, coming up with a wonderful idea to build a canal from Reyes to Exaltación, via Lake Rogo-aguado.

In February 1877 he travelled down from La Paz to the Beni. Travelling down the Beni to the mouth of the Mamoré he then went up the Mamoré to Exaltación to collect some boats in order to descend the Amazon. He reported that as well as the corregidor and the padre, there was also a teacher in the town. When he finally left and set off downstream, he took three boats, thirty-two Mojos Indians, and three months' provisions. Before leaving, he gave the assembled company on shore a taste of fishing with dynamite. They were much amazed.

8. Luigi Balzan, *Viaggio di esplorazione nelle regioni centrali del sud America*, Milano 1931.

9. D'Orbigny wrote that the Cayubabas "still subscribe to a number of superstitions that clearly go back to primitive times. They are most marked among those who look after the cattle. When a Cayubaba knows that his wife is not well, he will never mount on horseback, for fear of falling and thus causing his wife to become more ill."

10. Mathews.

11. P.H. Fawcett, *Exploration Fawcett*, London 1953; Peter Fleming, *Brazilian Adventure*, London 1933. G.M. Dyott, *Man-hunting in the Jungle*, New York 1930.

12. This was for long the thesis upheld by Erland Nordenskjold, Enrique de Gandia, and Alfred Métraux.

13. William M. Denevan, *La geografia cultural aborigen de los Llanos de Mojos*, La Paz 1980 (originally published as *The Aboriginal Cultural Geography of the Llanos de Mojos of Bolivia*, University of California Press, Berkeley 1966).

14. José de Acosta, *Historia natural y moral las Indias, 1590*, Hakluyt Society, London 1880.

15. "Relación de Diego Felipe de Alcaya, Cura de Mataca". This was written by Diego's father, Martín Sánchez de Alcaya, one of the founders of Santa Cruz de la Sierra. He sent it, via his son, to the viceroy, Marqués de Monte Claros, and to the president of the Audiencia of Charcas, Juan de Lizarazú, with a view to getting permission to explore Mojos. The text of this remarkable document is in Ricardo Mujia, *Bolivia–Paraguay*, La Paz 1914, vol. 1: *Epoca colonial anexos*. See also Thierry Saignes, *Los Andes orientales, historia de un olvido*, Cochabamba 1985.

16. Among these early expeditions into Mojos from the west was that of Captain Pedro de Candia, a Greek from Crete, in 1538. Trapped in the jungle with eight hundred men, advancing barely a league a day, he was forced to return with his expedition. Another attempt was made the following year, in 1539, by Captain Pedro Anzures Enríquez de Campo Redondo. This failed too, though Peranzures (as he is sometimes called) went on to found the city of Charcas (Sucre), arriving in eastern Bolivia before

the men who came up the Paraguay. The details of these and other expeditions are in José Chávez Suárez, *Historia de Moxos*, second edn, La Paz 1986, pp. 55–75.

17. "The narrative of Hernando de Ribera", in Luis Domínguez (ed.), *The Conquest of the River Plate*, Hakluyt Society, London 1891, pp. 263–8.

18. Agustín Zapata, "Carta del Padre Agustín Zapata al Padre José de Buendia en la que da noticias del Paitití, 1695", in Victor Maurtua, *Juicio de límites entre el Perú y Bolivia*, Madrid 1906, vol. 10, pp. 25–8. See also Diego de Eguiluz, *Historia de la misión de Mojos*, Lima 1696.

19. William Denevan, *La geografía*.

20. Mathews.

21. Franz Keller, *The Amazon and Madeira Rivers: sketches and descriptions from the notebook of an explorer*, London 1874.

22. Balzan.

23. José Aguirre Acha, *De los Andes al Amazonas, recuerdos de la campaña de Acre*, second edn, La Paz 1927, p. 137.

BIBLIOGRAPHICAL NOTE

Five hundred years after Columbus, no comprehensive history of the swamp regions of Paraguay, Bolivia, and Brazil has been written in any language. The great Indian civilizations of Chiquitos and Mojos, the extraordinary mission culture of the Jesuits in the eighteenth century, the long frontier struggles between Spain and Portugal, and even the secular, white settler rule of the nineteenth century, has gone largely unrecorded and ignored, both in South America itself and beyond.

Sometimes I think it is the fault of William Prescott. For more than a hundred years, the works of that great nineteenth-century American historian have influenced the Anglo-Saxon view of the Latin American past. He was read by every schoolteacher, and by many students too. Yet Prescott only tackled the Spanish conquest of Mexico and Peru. Brazil was ignored, and a history of the third leg of the great Spanish tripod construction in South America – Paraguay – was never written.

Yet the material is not lacking. The archives of the sixteenth century are replete with reports from the conquistadores themselves, justifying and often embellishing their activities. Many of these documents have been printed in Spain in the last one hundred and fifty years. These great modern collections, as John Hemming points out, are not always easy to use; they "sometimes run to over a hundred volumes, but have no sequence or index." But once mastered, they form a rich vein of historical evidence.

From the seventeenth and eighteenth centuries, many of the regular letters of the Jesuit provincials now exist in print. Long and detailed, and written nearly every year, they describe the problems and vicissitudes of their missions, and their struggles with both the Indians and the Spanish colons. In the course of the eighteenth century, the Jesuits began to produce their own histories of their mission endeavours, so packed with information that they have had a lasting influence on all subsequent historians. It has proved almost impossible to break out from beneath their spell.

At the end of the eighteenth century and the turn of the nineteenth, fresh accounts began to come in from Portuguese and Spanish surveyors, the men involved in mapping the frontier areas between Portugal and Spain. From that time, too, come the first independent travellers' tales.

Then, in the early period of independence, reports were published as a result of the great scientific expeditions from Europe – naturalists and explorers, full of wide-eyed curiosity and the spirit of scientific enquiry.

Later in the century came travellers with an economic and commercial bent, seeking out opportunities for business and trade, and often obsessively interested in steamer traffic and the construction of railways.

Toward 1900, nationalist academics began pouring over the archives in Seville and Madrid and Rome, searching for the material that would defend the frontiers of Bolivia against Peru, of Paraguay against Argentina, of Bolivia against Paraguay. Innumerable volumes of historical documents were published that sought to lay prior claims to pieces of the old Spanish empire.

At the same time, the early ethnologists – mostly from Germany, and then from Sweden and Italy – started to take an interest in what was left of the original Indian population.

Finally, in the twentieth century, national (and nationalist) histories of individual countries began to appear, produced from the document volumes published by the academic researchers. These histories, written for the national curriculum of an embryonic national school system, justify and eulogize the emergence of a Bolivian, or Paraguayan, or Argentine "race" or "people" or "nation", who are alleged to have created a country in the early nineteenth century from the amalgam of Spanish, Indian, mestizo and black.

And that is the sum total of what is available. There is not much hope that a fresh appraisal of the Latin American past is imminent. The poor countries of South America cannot provide the resources to rewrite their history more than once every century. In the rich world, the tendency of historians in the late twentieth century has been to write detailed monographs rather than to contemplate the panoramic sweep that was the hallmark of an earlier generation. And this way of doing things has begun to filter through to South America. There has been some brilliant work in Bolivia on the history of the Chiriguanos, and in Paraguay on the social and economic impact of the conquistadores on the Guaraní, and in Rio Grande do Sul on the economies of the early Jesuit missions. But these are grains of sand on a very large beach. The Argentines, for example, are still too close to the killing fields of the 1880s to be able to do much to reappraise their Indian past without national trauma.

Only these most recent researches have begun to ask questions about the Indian population of the territories between the Paraguay and the Amazon. When I began this book I did not think it would be possible today to recreate an Indian history of this part of the world, a history written by the conquered. Nor have I tried to write such a book. But now I believe that it could be done. There is enough material in archives, and from the investigations of anthropologists, to give us a clear picture of the lowland swamp and forest civilizations that existed before the Europeans arrived, and of the extraordinary struggles waged for three centuries to maintain the local culture against the alien invader.

John Hemming has already sketched out, on the gigantic canvas of Brazil, the various avenues of potential research. His magnificent volumes are an indication of what can be done by a single dedicated individual. What is needed is not so much the discovery of new material as the new eye that will refocus the information that already exists – an eye that will absorb the work of historians, demographers, musicologists, economists, naturalists and anthropologists, to recreate a fresh version of the past to replace the archaic and racist view of South American history that has prevailed for so long, both in the continent itself and outside.

Out of the celebrations and jamborees that mark the 500th anniversary of the Columbus landing, it would be suitable if some great European state were to see fit to finance a research project – an international institute of historical Indian studies – that would attempt to undertake this fresh version. For the colonization and destruction of South America is part of Europe's history too. As today's Europeans gaze back with ill-concealed pride, congratulating themselves on the achievements of hundreds of years of European art and culture, they should from time to time be able to remind themselves that there has been a darker and altogether more negative side to their story.

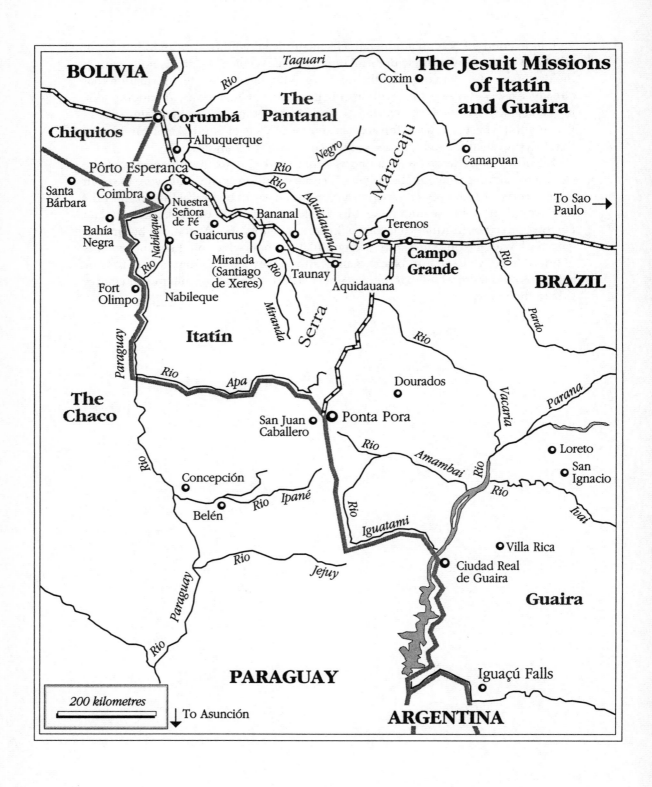

**The Jesuit Missions
of Itatín
and Guaira**

BOLIVIA

Taquari

Rio

Coxim

**The
Pantanal**

Corumbá

Chiquitos

Albuquerque

Camapuan

Pôrto Esperanca

Rio

Negro

Santa
Bárbara

Coimbra

Nuestra
Señora
de Fé

Rio

Rio

Aquidauana

do

Maracaju

To Sao
Paulo →

Bananal

Bahía
Negra

Guaicurus

Terenos

Rio Nabileque

Miranda
(Santiago
de Xeres)

Taunay

**Campo
Grande**

Fort
Olimpo

Rio

Miranda

Serra

Aquidauana

BRAZIL

Nabileque

Itatín

Pardo

Paraguay

Rio

Apa

Rio

Dourados

**The
Chaco**

San Juan
Caballero

Ponta Pora

Vacaria

Loreto

San
Ignacio

Rio

Amambai

Rio

Concepción

Rio

Rio Ipané

Rio

Iguatami

Rio

Parana

Belén

Villa Rica

Rio

Jejuy

Ciudad Real
de Guaira

Guaira

Paraguay

Rio

PARAGUAY

Iguaçú Falls

200 kilometres

↓ To Asunción

ARGENTINA

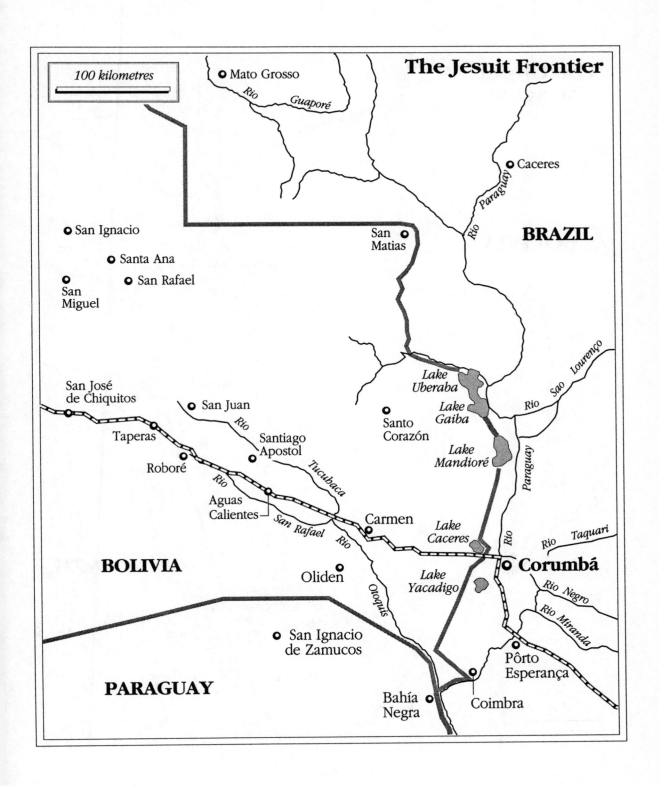

The Jesuit Frontier

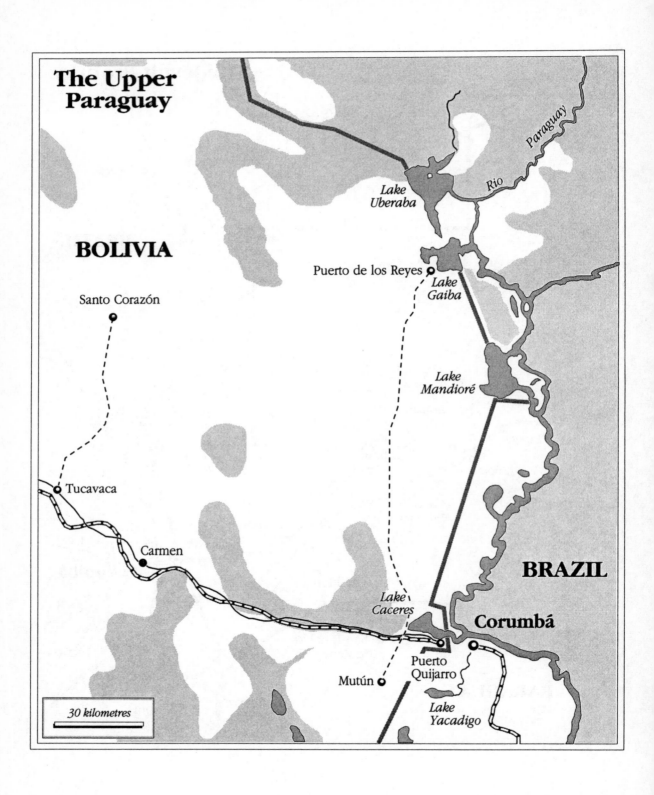

The Upper Paraguay

BOLIVIA

BRAZIL

Paraguay

Rio

Lake Uberaba

Puerto de los Reyes

Lake Gaiba

Lake Mandioré

Santo Corazón

Tucavaca

Carmen

Lake Caceres

Corumbá

Puerto Quijarro

Mutún

Lake Yacadigo

30 kilometres

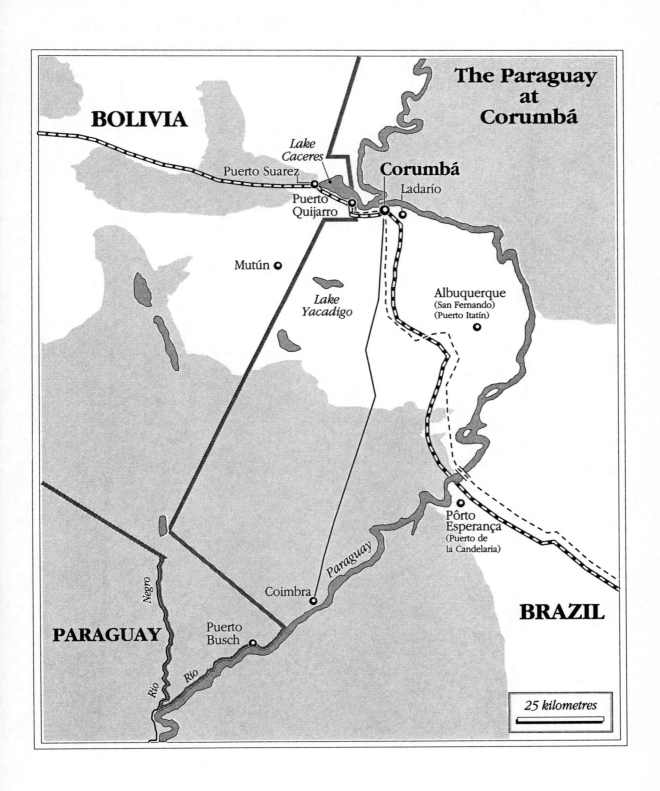

The Paraguay at Corumbá

BOLIVIA

Lake Caceres

Puerto Suarez

Corumbá

Ladarío

Puerto Quijarro

Mutún

Lake Yacadigo

Albuquerque
(San Fernando)
(Puerto Itatín)

Pôrto Esperança
(Puerto de la Candelaria)

Coimbra

Paraguay

BRAZIL

PARAGUAY

Negro

Puerto Busch

Rio

Rio

25 kilometres

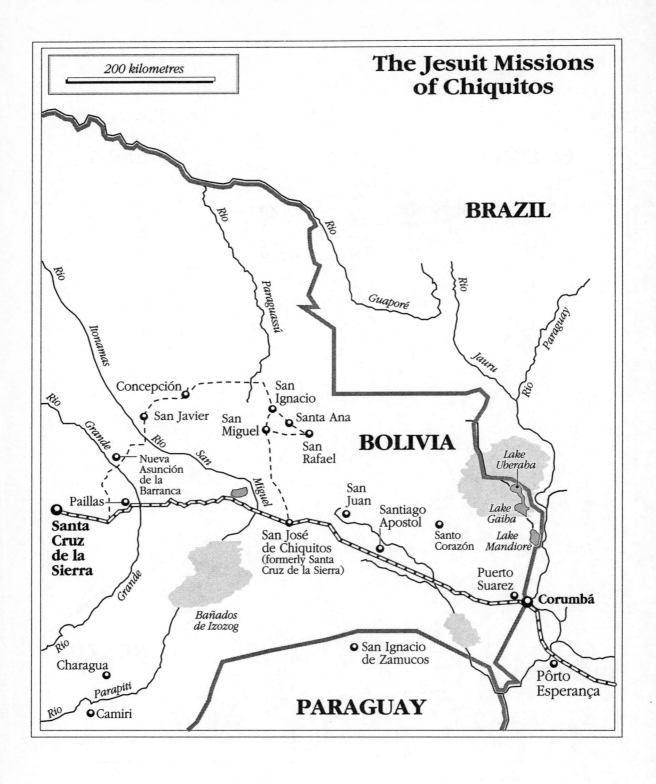

The Jesuit Missions of Chiquitos

200 kilometres

BRAZIL

BOLIVIA

PARAGUAY

Rio

Rio

Rio

Guaporé

Jauru

Rio

Paraguay

Itonamas

Rio

Paraguassú

Concepción

San Javier

San Ignacio

San Miguel

Santa Ana

San Rafael

Rio

Grande

Rio San

Nueva
Asunción
de la
Barranca

Paillas

Santa
Cruz
de la
Sierra

Miguel

San José
de Chiquitos
(formerly Santa
Cruz de la Sierra)

San
Juan

Santiago
Apostol

Santo
Corazón

Lake
Uberaba

Lake
Gaiba

Lake
Mandioré

Puerto
Suarez

Corumbá

Grande

Bañados
de Izozog

San Ignacio
de Zamucos

Pôrto
Esperança

Rio

Charagua

Parapiti

Rio

Camiri

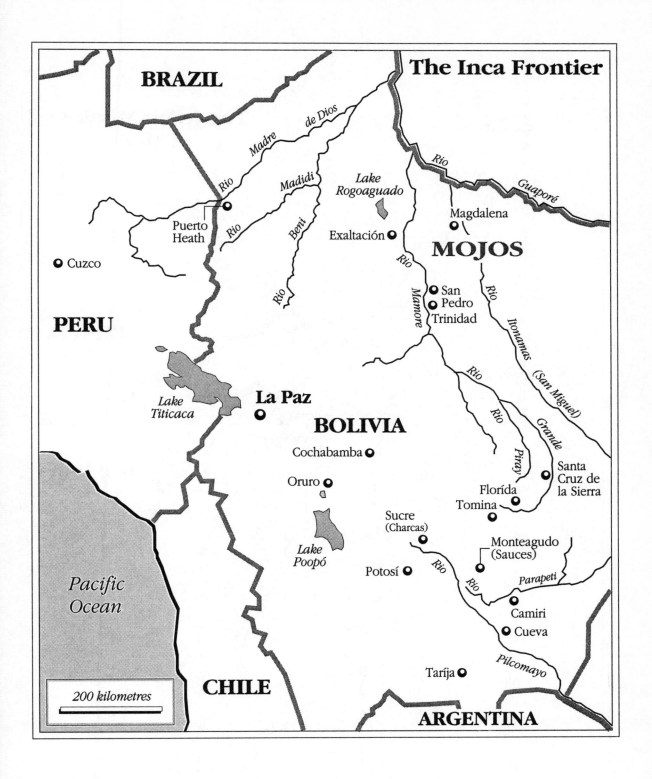

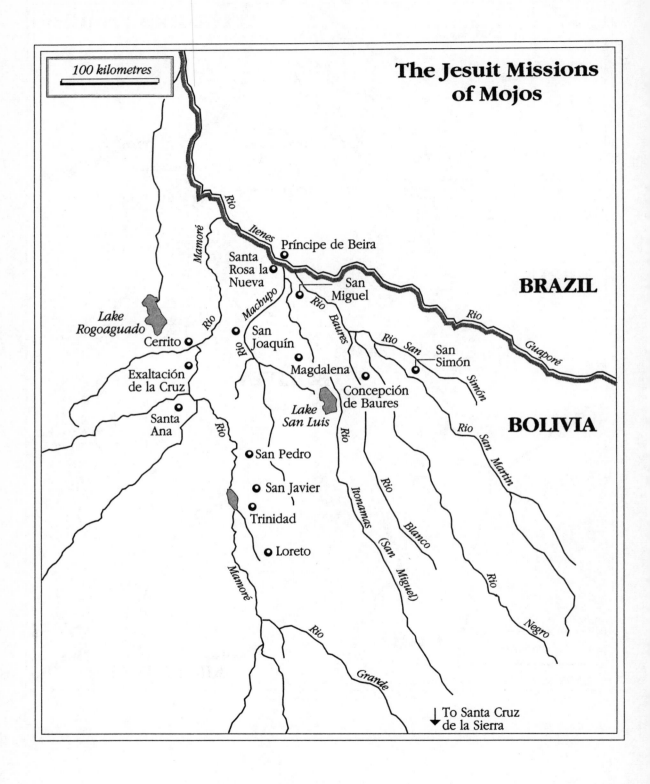

The Jesuit Missions of Mojos

100 kilometres

BRAZIL

BOLIVIA

Lake Rogoaguado

Cerrito

Exaltación de la Cruz

Santa Ana

Rio Mamoré

Rio Machupo

San Joaquín

Magdalena

Lake San Luis

San Pedro

San Javier

Trinidad

Loreto

Rio Itenes

Príncipe de Beira

Santa Rosa la Nueva

San Miguel

Rio Baures

Rio San

San Simón

Rio Guaporé

Rio Simón

Concepción de Baures

Rio San Martín

Rio Itonamas (San Miguel)

Rio Blanco

Rio Negro

Rio Grande

Mamoré

To Santa Cruz de la Sierra

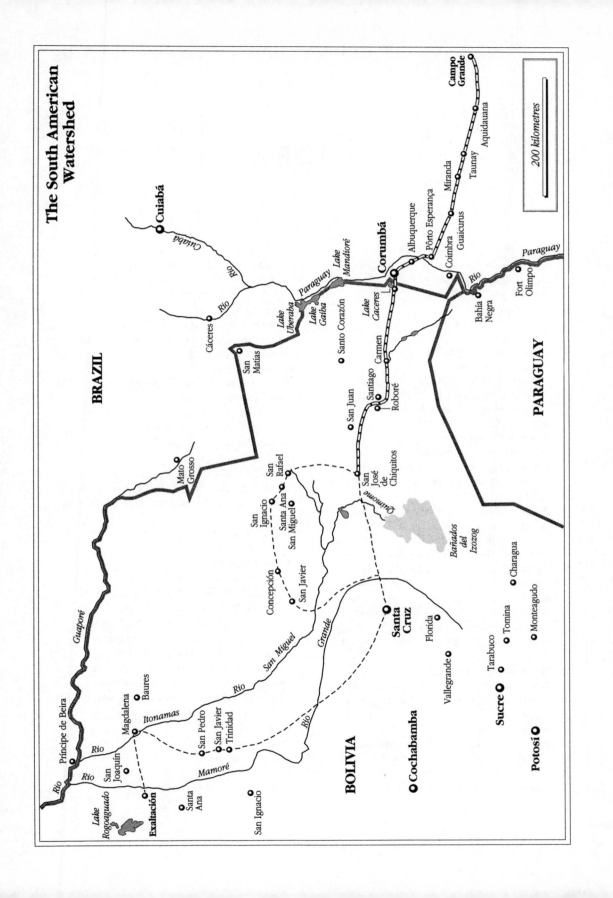

The South American Watershed

Cuiabá

Rio Cuiabá

Cáceres

Rio

BRAZIL

San Matías

Lake Uberaba

Lake Gaiba

Lake Paraguay

Lake Mandioré

Santo Corazón

Lake Cáceres

Corumbá

Albuquerque

Pôrto Esperança

Coimbra

Guaicurus

Rio

Bahía Negra

Fort Olimpo

Paraguay

Campo Grande

Aquidauana

Taunay

Miranda

Carmen

Santiago

San Juan

Roboré

San José de Chiquitos

Quitunine

PARAGUAY

Mato Grosso

San Rafael

San Ignacio

Santa Ana

San Miguel

Concepción

San Javier

San Miguel

Grande

Bañados del Izozog

Charagua

Tomina

Monteagudo

Tarabuco

Santa Cruz

Florida

Vallegrande

Sucre

Potosí

Cochabamba

BOLIVIA

Rio Grande

Guaporé

Príncipe de Beira

Rio

San Joaquín

Rio

Lake Rogoaguado

Exaltación

Santa Ana

San Ignacio

Mamoré

Magdalena

Baures

Itonamas

Rio

San Pedro

San Javier

Trinidad

200 kilometres

INDEX

PROV. DES MOXOS

de Matto Grosso

S. Fr. Xavier

R. Mamore

R. Grande de la Plata

R. Itai de la Magdelena

R. Piray

PR. DES CHIQUITOS

L. Xa

R. chapare

GOUV. DE S.ᴬ

GO UVERN

✝ S.ᵃ Cruz de la Sierra

CRUZ DE LA SIERRA *

les Morotocos

CHACO *

R. de Pilcomayo

les Zamucos

R. de Paraguay

S. Bernardo de Tarija

R. de Tarija

LLANOS DE MANSO ou PR.ᴱ DE YAPIZLAGA

les Lenguas

S. Salvador

les Chiriguanos

les Guaycurus

Juguy *

les Paraguas

R.

I. de Pilcomayo

SALTA *

Va

R. Guachipas

les Mocobis

✝ As

Villa

R.

les Frentones

R. Vermejo

PROVINCE

S.ᵉ Ro

S. Miguel de Tucuman

DE

Corrientes

S. Fernando

S. Yago del Etero

Se

THE LINCOLNSHIRE
COLOURING BOOK

THE LINCOLNSHIRE
COLOURING BOOK

PAST AND PRESENT

Take some time out of your busy life to relax and unwind with this feel-good colouring book designed for everyone who loves Lincolnshire.

Absorb yourself in the simple action of colouring in the scenes and settings from around the county, past and present. From iconic architecture to picturesque vistas, you are sure to find some of your favourite locations waiting to be transformed with a splash of colour.

There are no rules – choose any page and any choice of colouring pens or pencils you like to create your own unique, colourful and creative illustrations.

Blue Court, Grantham ▸

Ellis Windmill, Lincoln ▸

St Botolph's church, popularly
known as the Boston Stump ▶

Buckets and spades at Skegness ▸

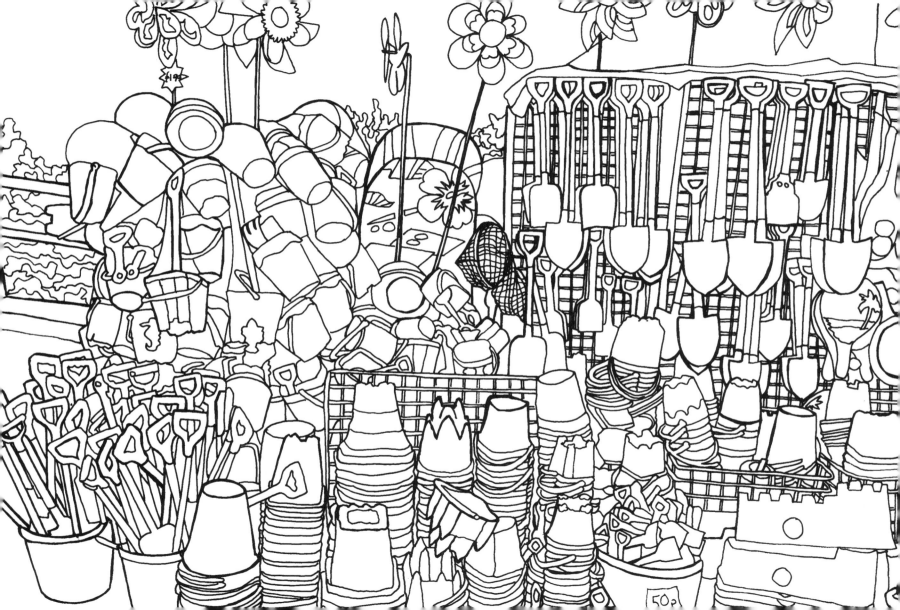

A horse and trap on Cleethorpes seafront, 1920 ▸

Beach huts on Mablethorpe seafront ▸

Burghley House, Stamford – one of
England's greatest Elizabethan houses ▶

Cows heading for market in Boston, 1945 ▸

Cadwell Park racing circuit
in the Lincolnshire Wolds ▸

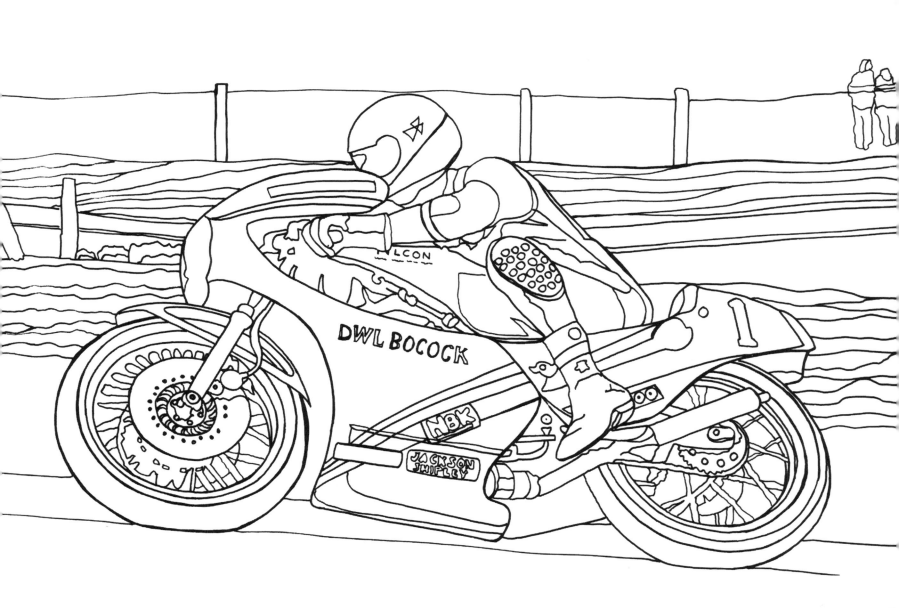

A Design student's balloon-filled window
display at Thomas Parker House, Lincoln ▶

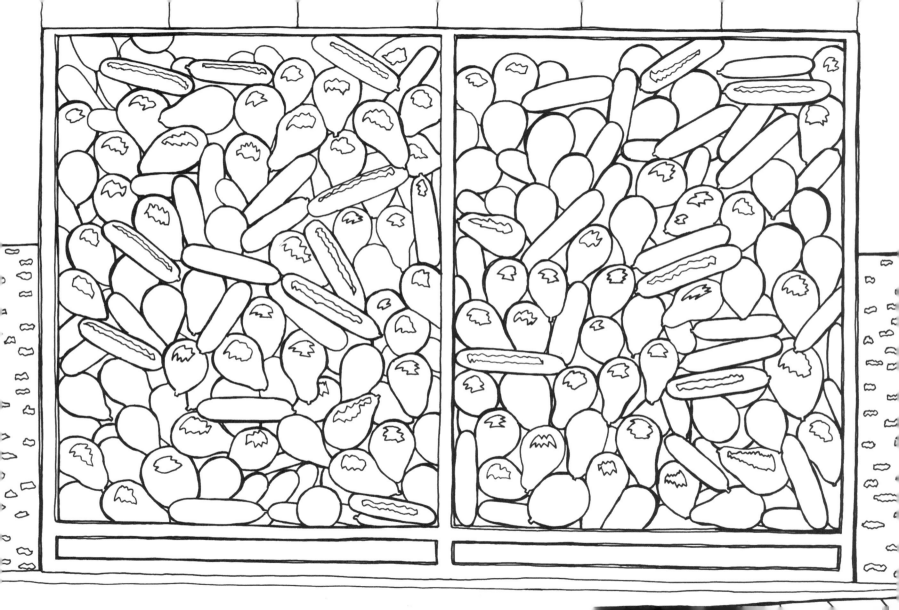

Donkey rides on Skegness beach, pre-war ▸

Edwardian strollers on Cleethorpes pier, *c.* 1910 ▸

Fairground rides on Cleethorpes seafront ▶

TOKENS Sold Here!
...FOR ALL RIDES! ...

Avro Lancaster B.VII NX611 at
Lincolnshire Aviation Heritage Centre ▸

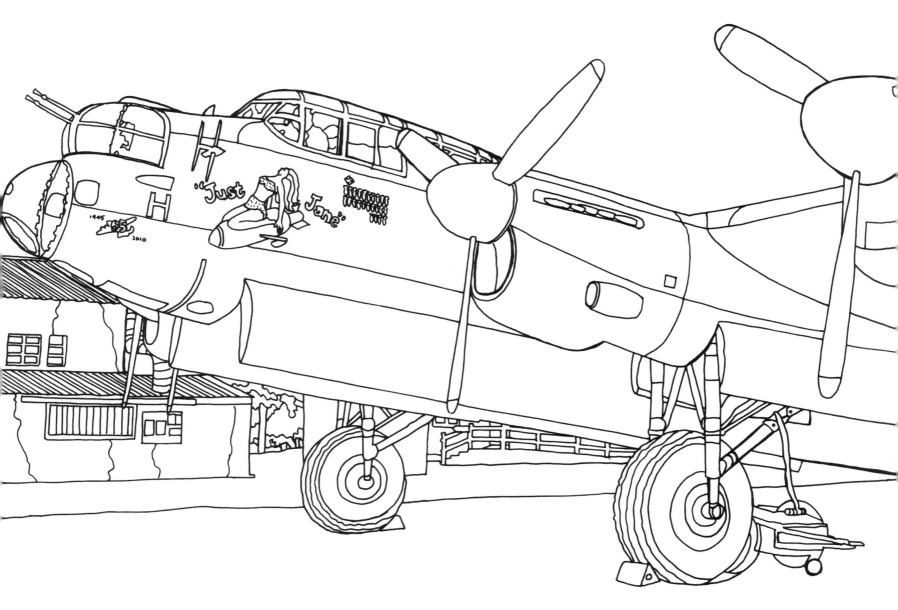

Gainsborough Old Hall — one of the best
preserved medieval manor houses in England ▸

Stamford High Street with St Martin's
church in the background ▶

Fashionable swimsuits at
Sutton-on-Sea in the 1890s ▶

Horncastle town sign ▸

The Odyssey roller coaster at
Fantasy Island, Ingoldmells ▸

Ingoldmells post office, *c.* 1910 ▶

Jews' Court, Lincoln ▶

Lincoln Castle ▶

Lincoln longwool sheep ▶

Lincoln Farmers' Market, with Lincoln Visitor
Information Centre in the Tudor building ▸

The beautiful Lincolnshire Wolds ▸

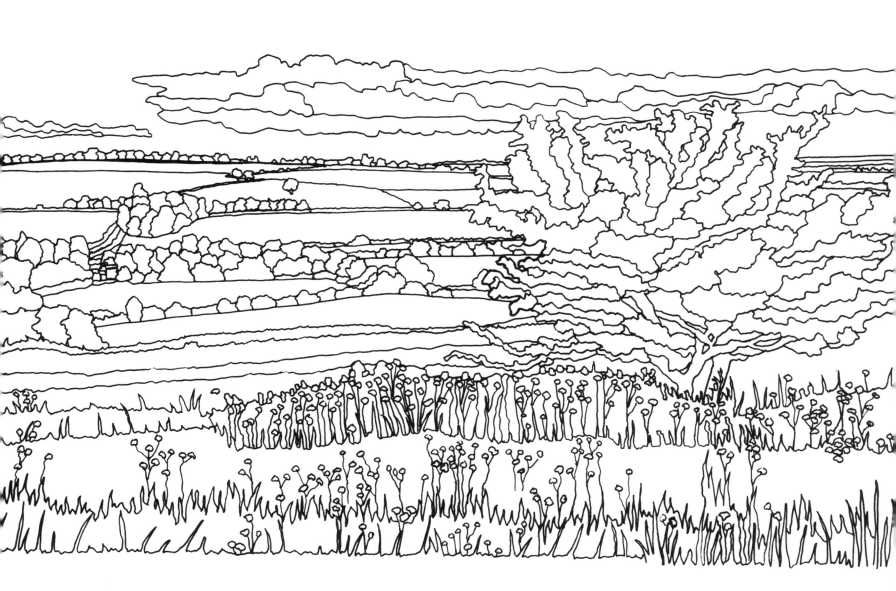

Lincolnshire Road Transport Museum, Lincoln ▸

Lincoln Cathedral ▶

Steam train from Lincolnshire
Wolds Railway at Ludborough ▸

Market Rasen ▸

A meerkat at Lincolnshire Wildlife Park ▸

An old shop display at the Museum
of Lincolnshire Life, Lincoln ▸

The River Welland, Spalding ▶

Sincil Bank Stadium, home of Lincoln City FC ▸

St Denys' church, Sleaford ▸

Seals at Donna Nook National Nature Reserve ▶

Stamford Ladies' Cycling Club
at the turn of the century ▶

A butterfly at the Butterfly &
Wildlife Park, Long Sutton ▸

Scunthorpe Sports Academy ▸

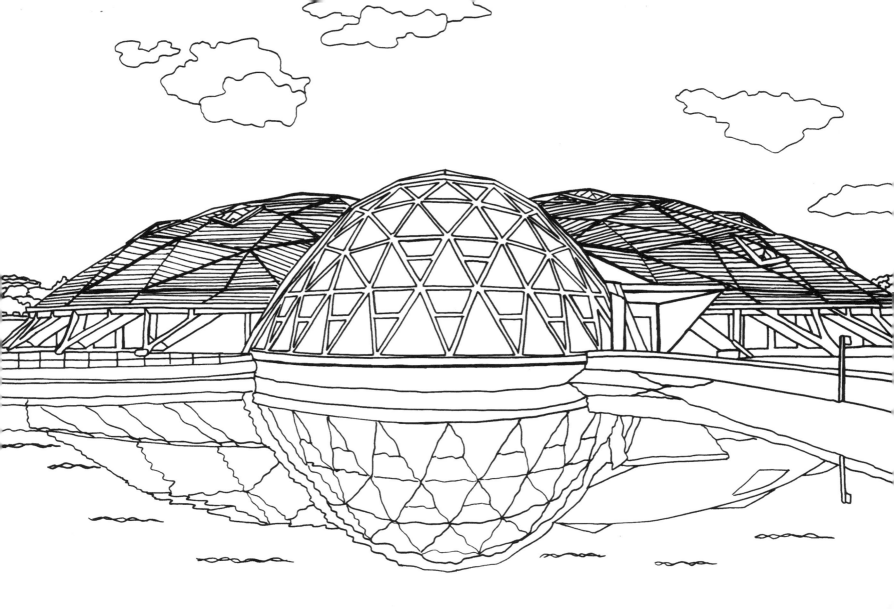

Tractor at Old Bolingbroke ▸

A Typhoon takes off from RAF Coningsby ▸

Donkey rides in Skegness, early 1900s ▸

Model railway at Mablethorpe, *c.* 1930s ▸

Louth Market Place, 1928 ▶

Paddle tug SS *Privateer* at Packhorse Quay,
Boston, at the turn of the century ▸

Also from The History Press

ADVANCED PLACEMENT EXAMINATION IN ENGLISH: COMPOSITION AND LITERATURE

Laurie Rozakis, Ph.D.

Assistant Professor of English
Suny College of Technology at Farmingdale

ARCO

New York   London   Toronto   Sydney   Tokyo   Singapore

Second Edition

 ARCO

Simon & Schuster, Inc.
15 Columbus Circle
New York, NY 10023

DISTRIBUTED BY PRENTICE HALL TRADE SALES

Manufactured in the United States of America

2   3   4   5   6   7   8   9   10

Library of Congress Cataloging-in-Publication Data

Rozakis, Laurie.
    Advanced placement examination in English : composition and
literature / Laurie Rozakis. — 2nd ed.
        p.   cm.
    Includes bibliographical references.
    ISBN 0-13-011629-7
    1. English philology—Examinations—Study guides. I. Title.
PE66.R64   1990
807.6—dc20
                                                                90-30149
                                                                CIP

Contents

PART 5. ANALYZING DRAMA

PART 6. THREE SAMPLE EXAMINATIONS IN ENGLISH COMPOSITION AND LITERATURE

Preface

This revised edition retains all the original features that made the first edition of this text unique among Advanced Placement study guides. First, it includes a separate Writing section—not in any other guide to the Advanced Placement exam in English and Language—that takes students step by step through the writing process. Beginning with outlining skills, it continues with different methods of organization and provides specific lessons and worksheets on detailing and style. It also covers punctuation and grammar and usage—areas vital to a successful finished product. Next, many works of literature are reprinted in full—again, unique with regard to longer works—eliminating the necessity of using several different texts and time-consuming research. The plot summaries that accompany each work also provide quick review and clarification of chronology and character. This, in turn, makes teaching easier, since all the material required is in one book. Where possible, there are clear and concise review sheets designed for quick study. This is especially handy in an area such as drama, where there is a great deal of material for the student to organize. The enormous selection of excerpts from well-known works of American, English, and World literature gives students the greatest possible exposure to important material. It also encourages outside reading and exploration. The copious examples greatly clarify difficult concepts, especially those in the Poetry section. The Essay section is also unique among Advanced Placement study guides, providing further examples of fine writing.

But there's been a great deal added that makes this guide even more useful. We've included an entire new section designed to help you get started writing your essays. You'll find "Generating Your Thoughts" at the beginning of Part 2, "Essay Writing Guide." Complete with three different methods of getting started as well as a handy reference chart, it is designed to help you quickly begin getting ideas down on paper. Along with this is a new section on "Revising and Editing Your Essay," structured to show you how to rework your composition quickly. It includes a chart on standard proofreader's symbols to aid you in making neat, universally accepted corrections. Also new to this edition is a section that explains how the Advanced Placement essays are graded. This section clearly defines the criteria used to rate your paper and explains the "holistic" scoring method. You'll find *Scoring* at the end of the *Introduction*. In addition, the section on *Sentence Variety* has been greatly expanded, including several new ways to improve your writing style. Finally, in response to requests from students and teachers, a section on perhaps the two most frequently confused grammatical points—*Case and Apostrophes*—has been added. You'll find this new section in *The Elements of Writing Style*.

Acknowledgments

"Among School Children" and "Sailing to Byzantium" reprinted with permission of Macmillan Publishing Company from *The Poems* by W. B. Yeats, edited by Richard J. Finneran. Copyright 1928 by Macmillan Publishing Company, renewed 1956 by Georgia Yeats.

"Design" and "Fire and Ice" from *The Poetry of Robert Frost* edited by Edward Connery Lathem. Copyright 1923, 1930, 1939, © 1969 by Holt, Rinehart and Winston. Copyright 1936, 1951, © 1958 by Robert Frost. Copyright © 1967 by Lesley Frost Ballantine. Reprinted by permission of Holt, Rinehart and Winston, Publishers.

Note on Reading Lists: Suggested reading lists are provided for short stories, novels, satire, essays, poetry, and drama. The works included on these lists offer a wide range of literature of recognized literary merit. Any of these works would be suitable for discussion and analysis on the Advanced Placement exam. All of them will help to increase your appreciation for and understanding of our literary heritage.

Introduction

The Advanced Placement program administered by the College Entrance Examination Board has grown remarkably over the past two decades. From an original 104 schools sending Advanced Placement candidates to 130 colleges, the program has expanded to include some 3,500 secondary schools and 1,500 colleges (*Beginning an Advanced Placement English Course,* by the Advanced Placement English Development Committee, Edition Y. Princeton: College Entrance Examination Board, 1976, p.3). More than 80,000 examinations a year are taken in English alone. This growth suggests that more and more secondary schools are offering Advanced Placement courses. Aside from the obvious pleasure inherent in studying more challenging material, the Advanced Placement courses represent a very significant savings in college tuition. A student can also save a great deal of time by earning college credits during high school, affording him/her the opportunity to graduate early from college, enter graduate school earlier, or begin a career more quickly. Because of Advanced Placement credit, a student may also be able to take additional courses, exploring areas of interest that would not otherwise fit into a busy schedule.

The Advanced Placement program now offers two courses and examinations in English: English Composition and Literature, and English Language and Composition. The two different Advanced Placement courses are designed to represent the two types of freshman English courses generally offered in colleges and universities, but either course may substitute for a year's worth of English credit. Consequently, students may take either examination, but not both. The English Composition and Literature course is designed for those who have trained in literary study; it is still the more popular course, almost 92,000 examinations being administered in 1988. The English Language and Composition course is for those students who have attained the reading and writing skills generally expected at the end of the freshman year of college but who have not necessarily studied literary analysis. Approximately 30,000 students took this examination last year.

Both examinations are three hours in duration and are graded according to the same scale:

5	extremely well qualified
4	well qualified
3	qualified
2	possibly qualified
1	no recommendation

"5" papers demonstrate	originality and imagination, and are clearly focused discussions made up of coherent arguments of exceptional clarity. They leave the reader convinced of the soundness of the discussion, impressed with the quality of the writing style, and stimulated by the intelligence and insight of the writer.
"4" papers demonstrate	a solid, logical, and persuasive discussion, but lack the originality or insight of the "5" papers. The development lacks the grace and style of the "5" papers, and may seem a bit predictable and plodding.
"3" papers demonstrate	a thorough but not totally convincing discussion of the topic, marked by the sense that the writer has not com-

	pletely thought out the issues. There are writing errors; some are distracting.
"2" papers demonstrate	an attempt made to organize the essay, but the structure is flawed and the supporting detail is weak. There may be serious problems with the mechanics of correct written English.
"1" papers demonstrate	a lack of understanding; they either do not address the topic directly or fail to answer the question. They draw obscure, irrelevant, bizarre conclusions and are seriously deficient in the conventions of standard written English.

The English Composition and Literature examination tests both your writing ability and knowledge of literature. Ordinarily, the examination consists of one hour of multiple choice questions followed by two hours of essay questions. The essay section is weighed twice as heavily as the multiple-choice questions. Examinations can be divided in a number of ways. Some typical examinations may look like this:

A. 55 minutes devoted to multiple-choice questions on a poem
    20 minutes devoted to an essay about a prose passage
    25 minutes devoted to an essay about a poem
    45 minutes devoted to a general essay
    45 minutes devoted to a general essay

B. 25 minutes devoted to multiple-choice questions on a poem
    25 minutes devoted to an essay about the poem questioned above
    45 minutes devoted to a general essay
    45 minutes devoted to an essay on a prose passage
    40 minutes devoted to a general essay

C. 45 minutes devoted to multiple-choice questions on two poems
    30 minutes devoted to an essay comparing the two poems
    60 minutes devoted to a general essay
    45 minutes devoted to a general essay

The multiple-choice section tests your ability to read poetry and/or prose sections carefully to discern meaning and identify specific literary techniques. You will be expected to be familiar with such terms as connotation, denotation, metaphor, simile, irony, syntax, tone, etc. The essay section stresses your skill in organizing your thoughts coherently, developing ideas fully, responding to general questions with specific evidence, and writing clearly and vividly. The Advanced Placement Grading Committee will look especially for your ability to mold language, to utilize and recognize imagery and symbolism, point of view, audience, mood, and tone. But a knowledge of literary convention alone by no means guarantees success in either examination. You must have a knowledge of the various modes of writing—narrative, descriptive, expositive, and persuasive—and an ability to use them properly. A close study of sample essays in this text will assist you in developing a clear and well-organized essay style.

The English Language and Composition examination, like the English Composition and Literature exam, is made up of multiple-choice and essay questions. In this test, however, the multiple-choice questions test your ability to rework sentences and analyze the language of prose passages. The essays require you to demonstrate your skill in using various rhetorical styles. Usually, the test consists of one hour of multiple-choice questions followed by two hours of essay writing. The essay section is given twice as much weight as the multiple-choice portion.

SCORING

The short answer questions on both the English Composition and Literature exam and the English Language and Composition exam are machine-scored, as per Educational Testing Service standard practice. The essays, however, are read individually by specially trained high school and college teachers who gather for five days during the late spring. Your paper will be evaluated on the basis of a single, overall impression. This method of grading is called "holistic scoring," as it concentrates more on a single, overall effect than focusing on individual errors. Holistic scoring assumes that error count alone cannot accurately reflect competency levels. In other words, the whole of a piece of writing is greater than the sum of its parts. On the positive side, *minor* writing errors that do not seriously affect the content of your paper will be overlooked. The reader will concentrate on the total or "holistic" effect of your argument. On the negative side, although ETS has a high level of reliability, your paper will only be read once. This places more emphasis on effective introductions, conclusions, and clear, specific detail.

List of Works

Work	Author	Work	Author
"When I was One-and-Twenty"	A.E. Housman	"The Sun Rising"	John Donne
"With Rue My Heart is Laden"	A.E. Housman	"There Was a Child Went Forth"	Walt Whitman
"Upon a Spider Catching a Fly"	Edward Taylor		
"The Last Leaf"	Oliver Wendell Holmes	"Meeting at Night"	Robert Browning
		"Annabel Lee"	Edgar Allan Poe
"Terminus"	Ralph Waldo Emerson	"To Helen"	
from *The American Crisis*	Thomas Paine	"Crossing the Bar"	Alfred, Lord Tennyson
"Speech in the Convention, at the Conclusion of its Deliberations, September 17, 1787"	Benjamin Franklin	"One Dignity Delays for All"	Emily Dickinson
		"Pied Beauty"	Gerard Manley Hopkins
"Thanatopsis"	William Cullen Bryant	"My Last Duchess"	Robert Browning
from *Of Time and the River*	Thomas Wolfe	from "Crossing Brooklyn Ferry"	Walt Whitman
from *To Kill a Mockingbird*	Harper Lee	"Intimations of Immortality from Recollections of Early Childhood"	William Wordsworth
Sonnet 10	John Donne		
"Dover Beach"	Matthew Arnold	Sonnet 116	William Shakespeare
"A Man Adrift on a Slim Spar"	Stephen Crane	Sonnet 73	
"On His Blindness"	John Milton	Sonnet	Henry Wadsworth Longfellow
Sonnet 130	William Shakespeare		
"The Black Cat"	Edgar Allan Poe	Sonnet 14	Elizabeth Barrett Browning
"The Birthmark"	Nathaniel Hawthorne		
"The Blanket"	Floyd Dell	Sonnet 43	
summary: *The Scarlet Letter*	Nathaniel Hawthorne	"How Soon Hath Time"	John Milton
summary: *Pride and Prejudice*	Jane Austen	"Design"	Robert Frost
summary: *Portrait of the Artist as a Young Man*	James Joyce	"Fire and Ice"	Robert Frost
		summary: *Hamlet*	William Shakespeare
"A Modest Proposal"	Jonathan Swift	summary: *Medea*	Euripides
summary: *1984*	George Orwell	summary: *Othello*	William Shakespeare
"Man Thinking" "Reliance on Property" "Traveling"	Ralph Waldo Emerson	summary: *Death of a Salesman*	Arthur Miller
"Second Inaugural Address, March 4, 1865"	Abraham Lincoln	summary: *Mourning Becomes Electra*	Eugene O'Neill
		summary: *Our Town*	Thorton Wilder
"Sailing to Byzantium"	William Butler Yeats	summary: *The Frogs*	Aristophanes
"Among School Children"	William Butler Yeats	summary: *Tartuffe*	Molière
"The Dalliance of the Eagles"	Walt Whitman	"Nature"	Henry W. Longfellow
"The Eagle"	Alfred, Lord Tennyson	"Captain John Smith Among the Indians"	John Smith
"On First Looking Into Chapman's Homer"	John Keats	from "Sinners in the Hands of an Angry God"	Jonathan Edwards
from "A Pindaric Ode"	Ben Jonson		
"Composed Upon Westminster Bridge, September 3, 1802"	William Wordsworth	"Upon the Burning of our House"	Anne Bradstreet
"The Tyger"	William Blake	"What is an American?"	Hector St. John de Crevecoèur
"Ozymandias"	Percy Bysshe Shelley		
"The Lamb"	William Blake	"To S.M., A Young African Painter on Seeing his Works"	Phillis Wheatley
"Hymn to God My God, in My Sickness"	John Donne	"His Excellency, General Washington"	
from *Amoretti*, Sonnet 15	Edmund Spenser		
Sonnet 18	William Shakespeare	preface to the *House of the Seven Gables*	Nathaniel Hawthorne

Part 1

Diagnostic Test and Analysis

General Directions for the Diagnostic Test

This test was constructed to be representative of what you will encounter on the Advanced Placement exam. Take the test in a quiet room without distractions, following all directions carefully and observing all time limits. Try to get as close as possible to actual test conditions, and take the test in one sitting. The more carefully you match test conditions, the more accurate your results will be, and the better able you will be to evaluate your strengths and weaknesses.

CONTENT OF THE TEST

There will most likely be a poem with questions that require you to be aware of the following things:

Figures of speech	These can include such terms as metaphor, simile, analogy, personification, hyperbole, etc. You will have to know what each figure of speech is and be able to recognize examples found in the body of the verse.
Poetic types	These can include the sonnet, ode, narrative verse, ballad, dramatic monologue, hudibrastic verse, doggerel, etc. You will have to know one type from the other and be able to tell what type a particular selection represents and why.
Poetic style	This includes the choice of language and figures of speech, the arrangement of words, such as inversion, and the reason for the poet's specific choice. You may be asked to explain how the techniques used fit in with the theme and reinforce it.
Poetic movements	There are a variety of poetic trends and movements, such as the Symbolists, the Metaphysical poets, or the Realists. You will have to know the characteristics of each group and be able to tell with which school the poem you are looking at is most closely allied. Of course, there are a great many poets who are not linked to any formal "school" of poetry.
Meter, rhyme, rhythm	You will have to be able to distinguish such basic poetic metric patterns as iambic pentameter, and be able to establish the rhyme scheme of a poem. You will also have to know how to "scan" a poem to discover its rhythm.
Author	While there is no way you will be able to give a full biography of any author, you will be required in some instances to establish something about the author from his/her verse. Thus, you may be asked what the author's attitude is toward something based on a poem, or when he/she may have lived, or what his/her attitude toward a certain subject matter may be.

Tone and mood   You will be able to tell the prevailing mood or tone of a work from its word choice and arrangement. The mood could be elevated and lofty, or depressing and bitter.

Meaning   Probably the single most important aspect of poetic interpretation is discovering the meaning—the theme—of the poem. What is it that the author is saying? Why did the author write this poem? What is the author telling us? What lines or phrases help you to arrive at this conclusion? You will be expected to do a close textual analysis, isolating specific words and phrases to prove your points.

For prose passages, you will most likely have to be aware of:

Tone   Again, the prevailing mood of the piece, established through word choice and arrangement.

Theme   What is the author's meaning? Why did the author write this passage? What, if anything, did he/she hope to accomplish?

Speaker   Do not confuse the *speaker* of the work with the *author;* they are rarely the same. Often the author adopts a *mask* to present a specific theme.

Technique   Word choice, sentence variety and length, punctuation, figurative language, etc. all combine to form the *style* of a piece.

You may be asked to do any and all of the following: Compare two poems; compare two prose passages; respond to a prose passage or a poem; explain the author's theme in a prose or poetic passage; or answer a series of questions on poetry or prose and then write an essay.

LITERARY ESSAY

There is also the Literary Essay, in which you are given a selection of works of "recognized literary merit" with which to answer a question. If no list is provided, you are expected to select a work of value suitable to your education and the question. This usually eliminates all books that are classified as "best-sellers," and relies instead on what we call "classics." You will have to give *clear, specific examples* drawn from the text of the book(s) you use and you will be expected to show evidence of a firm grasp of grammar and usage, as well as vocabulary and writing technique. See unit 2, Essay Writing Guide, for specific details and examples.

Diagnostic AP Examination

SECTION 1

Part A: Time—20 minutes

Directions: Read the following poem and answer the questions that follow it.

UPON A SPIDER CATCHING A FLY

Thou sorrow, venom elf.
  Is this thy play,
To spin a web out of thyself
  To catch a fly?
5   For why?

I saw a pettish wasp
  Fall foul therein:
Whom yet thy whorl pins[1] did not clasp
  Lest he should fling
10   His sting.

But as afraid, remote
  Didst stand hereat,
And with thy little fingers stroke
  And gently tap
15   His back.

Thus gently him didst treat
  Lest he should pet,[2]
And in a froppish,[3] waspish heat
  Should greatly fret[4]
20   Thy net.

Whereas the silly fly,
  Caught by its leg,
Thou by the throat took'st hastily,
  And 'hind the head
25   Bite dead.

This goes to pot, that not
  Nature doth call.[5]
Strive not above what strength hath got,
  Lest in the brawl
30   Thou fall.

This fray seems thus to us:
  Hell's Spider gets
His entrails spun to whip cords thus,
  And wove to nets,
35   And sets.

To tangle Adam's race
  In's[6] stratagems
To their destructions, spoil'd, made base
  By venom things,
40   Damn'd sins.

But mighty, Gracious Lord,
  Communicate
Thy Grace to break the cord; afford
  Us glory's gate
45   And state.

We'll nightingale sing like,
  When perched on high
In glory's cage, Thy glory, bright:
  Yea, thankfully,
50   For joy.

                —Edward Taylor

1. *whorl pins* are used to hold thread on a spindle.
2. *pet* means irritable.
3. *froppish* means cranky, irritable.
4. *fret* means break, rupture.
5. *that not/Nature doth call* means those who do not rely on a person's inborn ability to distinguish good from evil.
6. *In's* means in his.

1. What is the analogy in the sixth stanza?
   (A) The spider bit the fly's head off. In a similar manner, "Hell's Spider" (line 32) is poised to bite off the venom elf's head.
   (B) The venom elf (line 1) calls man to brawl, but "Hell's Spider" comes between them.
   (C) Man will go to ruin if he does not follow natural reason. The spider "bags" his victim, just as Satan catches his victim, man.
   (D) Man must allow himself to be called by Nature. If he fails to respond to this natural summons, Satan will "bag" him.
   (E) Man "flies" as the insect does; nonetheless, Satan is ready to "bag" him.

2. Who is "Hell's Spider" in line 32?
   (A) Satan
   (B) Man
   (C) The black widow spider
   (D) The venom elf
   (E) A representative of Adam's race

3. What are the "venom things" in line 39?
   (A) Base metals that poison man
   (B) "Damn'd sins" that sting man to death and destruction
   (C) Strands of the web that entangle man
   (D) The entrails of "Hell's Spider"
   (E) The spider's poison

4. What is the "cord" in line 43?
   (A) The cord that guards Heaven's gate. The poet wants to break it and be allowed to enter Heaven.
   (B) The cord that connects the child to his mother
   (C) The whip cord the spider uses to trap the fly
   (D) The cord that the devil uses to trap man
   (E) The cord that the venom elf uses to entrap man

5. What is the figure of speech in the seventh stanza?
   (A) A metaphor
   (B) A simile
   (C) An analogy
   (D) Personification
   (E) Hyperbole

6. What does that figure of speech in the seventh stanza mean?
   (A) The activity of the spider is similar to man's fall from grace.
   (B) The activity of the fly is similar to man's fall from grace.
   (C) The activity of the nightingale is similar to man's fall from grace.
   (D) Entrails are compared to the venom elf and the spider's whip cords.
   (E) God's grace is personified in the spider.

7. What is the figure of speech in the last stanza?
   (A) Metonymy
   (B) Synocdoche
   (C) Metaphor
   (D) Simile
   (E) Mixed metaphor

8. In the final stanza, the nightingale symbolizes
   (A) the spider
   (B) the fly
   (C) man
   (D) God
   (E) the sweet bird of youth

9. How is the entire poem an analogy?
   (A) Fly : spider :: man: devil
   (B) Spider : fly :: man : devil
   (C) Venom elf : spider :: devil : man
   (D) Venom elf : nightingale :: spider : fly
   (E) God : man :: spider : venom elf

10. This poem would be described as metaphysical because
    (A) it is witty, subtle, highly intellectual
    (B) it uses many elaborate and surprising figures of speech
    (C) it compares two very dissimilar things
    (D) it uses an extended conceit
    (E) all of the above

11. The poem is an example of a(n)
    (A) sonnet
    (B) ode
    (C) hudibrastic verse
    (D) doggerel
    (E) none of the above

12. The author is most likely
    (A) an atheist
    (B) an agnostic

(C) religious
(D) irreligious
(E) a biologist

13. The rhyme scheme here is best described as
    (A) *abbaa*
    (B) *ababb*
    (C) *aabaa*
    (D) *aabca*
    (E) *ababa*

14. The tone of this poem is
    (A) intense and agitated
    (B) thoughtful and morose
    (C) witty and light
    (D) resigned and pessimistic
    (E) irreligious

15. Which of the following statements is *not* true about the poem?
    (A) The poem compares two very dissimilar things.
    (B) The poet is a very learned man.
    (C) The poet believes Satan is ready to catch his victims at any moment.
    (D) Man is silly, vulnerable, and easily destroyed by Satan's traps.
    (E) The poet is little concerned with religion; he is actually dealing with the material world of insects.

16. The poet switches topics to make his comparison in line
    (A) 31
    (B) 15
    (C) 36
    (D) 20
    (E) 46

Part B: Time—25 minutes

Directions: Read the two poems that follow and discuss each of the following:
1. How the two authors view old age and how their views differ from one another
2. What effect this difference in view has on the *tone* of each poem
3. Differences in *style* between the two poems

Cite specific lines from each poem to make your point clearly.

THE LAST LEAF

I saw him once before,
As he passed by the door,
  And again
The pavement stones resound,
5 As he totters o'er the ground
  With his cane.

They say that in his prime,
Ere the pruning-knife of Time
  Cut him down,
10 Not a better man was found
By the Crier on his round
  Through the town.

But now he walks the streets,
And he looks at all he meets
15 Sad and wan,
And he shakes his feeble head,
That it seems as if he said,
  "They are gone."

  The mossy marbles rest
20 On the lips that he has pressed
  In their bloom,
And the names he loved to hear
Have been carved for many a year
  On the tomb.

25 My grandmamma has said—
Poor old lady, she is dead
  Long ago—
That he had a Roman nose,
And his cheek was like a rose
30 In the snow.

But now his nose is thin,
And it rests upon his chin
  Like a staff,
And a crook is in his back,
35 And a melancholy crack
  In his laugh.

I know it is a sin
For me to sit and grin
   At him here;
40 But the old three-cornered hat,
And the breeches, and all that,
   Are so queer!

And if I should live to be
The last leaf upon the tree
45   In the spring,
Let them smile, as I do now,
At the old forsaken bough
   Where I cling.

          —*Oliver Wendell Holmes*

TERMINUS

It is time to be old,
To take in sail:—
The god of bounds,
Who sets to seas a shore,
5 Came to me in his fatal rounds,
And said: 'No more!
No farther shoot
Thy broad ambitious branches, and thy root.
Fancy departs: no more invent;
10 Contract thy firmament
To compass of a tent.
There's not enough for this and that,
Make thy option which of two;
Economize the failing river,
15 Not the less revere the Giver,
Leave the many and hold the few.
Timely wise accept the terms,
Soften the fall with wary foot;
A little while
20 Still plan and smile,
And,—fault of novel germs,—

Mature the unfallen fruit.
Curse, if thou wilt, thy sires,
Bad husbands of their fires,
25 Who, when they gave thee breath,
Failed to bequeath
The needful sinew stark as once,
The Baresark marrow to thy bones,
But left a legacy of ebbing veins,
30 Inconstant heat and nerveless reins,—
Amid the Muses, left thee deaf and dumb,
Amid the gladiators, halt and numb.'

   As the bird trims her to the gale,
I trim myself to the storm of time,
35 I man the rudder, reef the sail,
Obey the voice at eve obeyed at prime:
'Lowly faithful, banish fear,
Right onward drive unharmed;
The port, well worth the cruise, is near,
40 And every wave is charmed.'

          —*Ralph Waldo Emerson*

SECTION 2

Part A: Time—45 minutes

Directions: Read the two selections that follow. Then write an essay comparing and contrasting the *tone* of the first selection with that of the second. Use specific examples from each selection to make your points clearly. The first excerpt is from *The American Crisis* by Thomas Paine; the second, *Speech in the Convention, at the Conclusion of its Deliberations, September 17, 1787,* by Benjamin Franklin.

SELECTION 1

These are the times that try men's souls: The summer soldier and the sunshine patriot will in this crisis, shrink from the service of his country; but he that stands it NOW, deserves the love and thanks of man and woman. Tyranny, like hell, is not easily conquered; yet we have this consolation with us, that the harder the conflict, the more glorious the triumph. What we obtain too cheap, we esteem too lightly:—'Tis dearness only that gives everything its value. Heaven knows how to put a proper price upon its goods; and it would be strange indeed, if so celestial an article as FREEDOM should not be highly rated. Britain, with an army to enforce her tyranny, has declared that she has a right (*not only to*) TAX but "to BIND *us in* ALL CASES WHATSOEVER," and if being *bound in that manner,* is not slavery, then is there not such a thing as slavery upon earth. Even the expression is impious, for so unlimited a power can belong only to GOD . . . .

I have as little superstition in me as any man living, but my secret opinion has ever been, and still is, that God Almighty will not give up a people to military destruction, or leave them unsupportedly to perish, who have so earnestly and so repeatedly sought to avoid the calamities of war, by every decent method which wisdom could invent. Neither have I so much of the infidel in me, as to suppose that he has relinquished the government of the world, and given us up to the care of devils; and as I do not, I cannot see on what grounds the king of Britain can look up to Heaven for help against us: a common murderer, a highwayman, or a house-breaker, has as good a pretence as he . . . .

I once felt all that kind of anger, which a man ought to feel against the mean principles that are held by the tories: A noted one, who kept a tavern at Amboy, was standing at his door, with as pretty a child in his hand, about eight or nine years old, as I ever saw, and after speaking his mind as freely as he thought was prudent, finished with this unfatherly expression, *"Well! give me peace in my day."* Not a man lives on the continent but fully believes that a separation must some time or other finally take place, and a generous parent should have said, *"If there must be trouble, let it be in my day, that my child may have peace,"* and this single reflection, well applied, is sufficient to awaken every man to duty. Not a place upon earth might be so happy as America. Her situation is remote from all the wrangling world, and she has nothing to do but to trade with them. A man

can distinguish himself between temper and principle, and I am as confident, as I am that GOD governs the world, that America will never be happy till she gets clear of foreign dominion. Wars, without ceasing, will break out till that period arrives, and the continent must in the end be conqueror; for though the flame of liberty may sometimes cease to shine, the coal can never expire. . . .

The heart that feels not now is dead; the blood of his children will curse his cowardice, who shrinks back at a time when a little might have saved the whole, and made *them* happy. I love the man that can smile in trouble, that can gather strength from distress, and grow brave by reflection. 'Tis the business of little minds to shrink; but he whose heart is firm, and whose conscience approves his conduct, will pursue his principles unto death. My own line of reasoning is to myself as straight and clear as a ray of light. Not all the treasures of the world, so far as I believe, could have induced me to support an offensive war, for I think it murder; but if a thief breaks into my house, burns and destroys my property, and kills or threatens to kill me, or those that are in it, and to *"bind me in all cases whatsoever"* to his absolute will, am I to suffer it? What signifies it to me, whether he who does it is a king or a common man; my countryman or not my countryman; whether it be done by an individual villain, or an army of them? If we reason to the root of things we shall find no difference; neither can any just cause be assigned why we should punish in the one case and pardon in the other.

SELECTION 2

Mr. President,

I confess, that I do not entirely approve of this Constitution at present; but, Sir, I am not sure I shall never approve it; for, having lived long, I have experienced many instances of being obliged, by better information or fuller consideration, to change opinions even on important subjects, which I once thought right, but found to be otherwise. It is therefore that, the older I grow, the more apt am I to doubt my own judgment of others. Most men, indeed, as well as most sects in religion, think themselves in possession of all truth, and that wherever others differ from them it is so far error. Steele,[1] a Protestant, in a dedication, tells the Pope, that the only difference between our two churches in their opinions of the certainty of their doctrine, is, the Romish Church is *infallible,* and the Church of England is *never in the wrong.* But, though many private persons think almost as highly of their own infallibility as of that of their sect, few express it so naturally as a certain French lady, who, in a little

dispute with her sister, said, "But I meet with nobody but myself that is always in the right." *"Je ne trouve que moi qui aie toujours raison."*

In these sentiments, Sir, I agree to this Constitution, with all its faults—if they are such, because I think a general government necessary for us, and there is no *form* of government but what may be a blessing to the people, if well administered; and I believe, further, that this is likely to be well administered for a course of years, and can only end in despotism, as other forms have done before it, when the people shall become so corrupted as to need despotic government, being incapable of any other. I doubt, too, whether any other convention we can obtain, may be able to make a better constitution; for, when you assemble a number of men, to have the advantage of their joint wisdom, you inevitably assemble with those men all their prejudices, their passions, their errors of opinion, their local interests, and their selfish views. From such an assembly can a *perfect* production be expected? It therefore

1. *Steele* most likely refers to Richard Steele, the English essayist.

astonishes me, Sir, to find this system approaching so near to perfection as it does; and I think it will astonish our enemies, who are waiting with confidence to hear that our counsels are confounded like those of the builders of Babel, and that our States are on the point of separation, only to meet hereafter for the purpose of cutting one another's throats. Thus I consent, Sir, to this Constitution, because I expect no better, and because I am not sure that it is not the best. The opinions I have had of its *errors* I sacrifice to the public good. I have never whispered a syllable of them abroad. Within these walls they were born, and here they will die. If every one of us, in returning to our constituents, were to report the objections he has had to it, and endeavor to gain partisans in support of them, we might prevent its being generally received, and thereby lose all the salutary effects and great advantages resulting naturally in our favor among foreign nations, as well as among ourselves, from any real or apparent unanimity. Much of the strength and efficiency of any government, in procuring and securing happiness to the people, depends on *opinion,* on the general opinion of the goodness of that government, as well as of the wisdom and integrity of its governors. I hope, therefore, for our own sakes, as a part of the people, and for the sake of our posterity, that we shall act heartily and unanimously in recommending this Constitution, wherever our influence may extend, and turn our future thoughts and endeavors to the means of having it *well administered.*

On the whole, Sir, I cannot help expressing a wish, that every member of the convention who may still have objections to it, would with me on this occasion doubt a little of his own infallibility, and, to make *manifest* our *unanimity,* put his name to this instrument.

Part B: Time—30 minutes

Questions 1–22 refer to the following poem.

THANATOPSIS

To him who in the love of Nature holds
Communion with her visible forms, she speaks
A various language; for his gayer hours
She has a voice of gladness, and a smile
5 And eloquence of beauty, and she glides
Into his darker musings with a mild
And healing sympathy that steals away
Their sharpness ere he is aware. When thoughts
Of the last bitter hour come like a blight
10 Over thy spirit, and sad images
Of the stern agony, and shroud, and pall,
And breathless darkness, and the narrow house
Make thee to shudder and grow sick at heart—
Go forth, under the open sky, and list
15 To Nature's teachings, while from all around—
Earth and her waters, and the depths of air—
Comes a still voice—
        Yet a few days, and thee
The all-beholding sun shall see no more
In all his course; nor yet in the cold ground,
20 Where thy pale form was laid with many tears,
Nor in the embrace of ocean shall exist
Thy image. Earth, that nourished thee, shall claim
Thy growth, to be resolved to earth again,
And, lost each human trace, surrendering up
25 Thine individual being, shalt thou go
To mix forever with the elements,
To be a brother to the insensible rock
And to the sluggish clod which the rude swain
Turns with his share and treads upon. The oak
30 Shall send his roots abroad and pierce thy mold.

Yet not to thine eternal resting place
Shalt thou retire alone; nor couldst thou wish
Couch more magnificent. Thou shalt lie down
With patriarchs of the infant world—with kings,
35 The powerful of the earth—the wise, the good.
Fair forms, and hoary seers of ages past,
All in one mighty sepulcher. The hills
Rock-ribbed and ancient as the sun; the vales
Stretching in pensive quietness between;
40 The venerable woods; rivers that move
In majesty; and the complaining brooks
That make the meadows green; and, poured
    round all
Old Ocean's gray and melancholy waste—
Are but the solemn decorations all
45 Of the great tomb of man. The golden sun,
The planets, all the infinite host of heaven,
Are shining on the sad abodes of death
Through the still lapse of ages. All that tread
The globe are but a handful to the tribes
50 That slumber in its bosom. Take the wings
Of morning, pierce the Barcan wilderness,
Or lose thyself in the continuous woods
Where rolls the Oregon, and hears no sound
Save his own dashings—yet the dead are there;
55 And millions in those solitudes, since first
The flight of years began, have laid them down
In their last sleep—the dead reign there alone.
So shalt thou rest, and what if thou withdraw
In silence from the living, and no friend
60 Take note of thy departure? All that breathe

Will share thy destiny. The gay will laugh
When thou art gone, the solemn brood of care
Plod on, and each one as before will chase
His favorite phantom; yet all these shall leave
Their mirth and their employments, and shall
65   come
And make their bed with thee. As the long train
Of ages glides away, the sons of men,
The youth in life's green spring, and he who goes
In the full strength of years, matron and maid,
70 The speechless babe, and the gray-headed man—
Shall one by one be gathered to thy side,

By those who in their turn shall follow them.
So live, that when thy summons comes to join
The innumerable caravan which moves
75 To that mysterious realm, where each shall take
His chamber in the silent halls of death,
Thou go not, like the quarry slave at night,
Scourged to his dungeon, but, sustained and
    soothed
By an unfaltering trust, approach thy grave
80 Like one who wraps the drapery of his couch
About him, and lies down to pleasant dreams.

—*William Cullen Bryant*

1. In lines 1–17, what does the poet say man should do when torn by thoughts of death?
   (A) Seek diversion.
   (B) Think instead of "darker musings" and the "eloquence of beauty."
   (C) Listen to Nature.
   (D) Ignore Nature's promptings, for they offer false hopes.
   (E) Continue his daily routine and push such thoughts firmly aside.

2. What will Nature be able to offer man, according to the poet?
   (A) The sluggish clod
   (B) The insensible rock
   (C) Healing sympathy
   (D) The magnificent oak
   (E) The company of fascinating people

3. In lines 17–57, what comfort does the poet believe Nature offers man when he is facing death?
   (A) The beauty of the open sky and still waters
   (B) A "magnificent couch" decorated with glories
   (C) The warm embrace of the ocean
   (D) Old friends and fond memories
   (E) None at all; it is cold and unyielding.

4. Who has shared Nature's "magnificent couch"?
   (A) The patriarchs of the infant world
   (B) Good people
   (C) Wise men
   (D) Kings
   (E) All of the above

5. In lines 57–72, why is dying without being mourned not important?
   (A) Since you are already dead, you have little use for what the living say.
   (B) It is actually very important, for it determines your fate.
   (C) Mourning customs are hypocritical at best, for few of us are really concerned about anyone else's mortality.
   (D) Mourning is unnecessary, for all who are unaware of the person's passing will be joining him soon enough.
   (E) It offers little comfort to the survivors.

6. In lines 73–81, what *is* important to the poet and the poem's meaning?
   (A) That man will live in continuing trust with Nature
   (B) That man set his affairs in order before his death
   (C) That man make his peace with his neighbors
   (D) That man summon his friends and relatives to his side before his passing
   (E) That man fight death to the last, not surrendering his will to Nature's

7. Why must man base his faith in Nature?
   (A) There is nothing else to comfort him.
   (B) So that when he faces death, he can be secure in the knowledge that Nature will sustain him and make him a part of the natural order.
   (C) Nature will reward him with riches beyond his wildest dreams.
   (D) There is no Supreme Being for Man to seek.
   (E) There is no reason.

8. What does the "mighty sepulcher" in line 37 most nearly mean?
   (A) The tomb
   (B) Clay
   (C) Nature
   (D) Earth
   (E) The individual grave

9. To what does the above term refer?
   (A) The final resting place of the wicked
   (B) The mighty grave of all
   (C) The mighty grave of the worthy
   (D) The afterlife
   (E) The process by which man is forgotten

10. What is the "destiny" spoken of in lines 60–61?
    (A) Rebirth
    (B) Death
    (C) Joining with the Supreme Being
    (D) Mourning
    (E) Accepting Nature

11. What poetic technique does the author use in the final two lines?
    (A) Simile
    (B) Personification
    (C) Alliteration
    (D) Apostrophe
    (E) Inversion

12. What is death compared to in these final two lines?
    (A) Mourning
    (B) Nature
    (C) Rebirth
    (D) Sleep
    (E) The ocean

13. When the author published this poem in a new edition, he added lines 1–17, up to "Yet a few days, . . .". What purpose did this serve?
    (A) It explained the *theme* more fully.
    (B) It established the *tone* more firmly.
    (C) It framed the poem by clearly defining the subject matter.
    (D) It made the poem conform to an established literary form.
    (E) It introduced Nature and offered a bit of hope.

14. At the same time as the above additions were made, he also added the final 16 lines, beginning with "As the long train." Why did he do this?
    (A) They allow him more room for additional figures of speech.
    (B) They offer hope and consolation.
    (C) They establish the poem as a ballad.
    (D) They ask man to fear death as a worthy opponent.
    (E) They complete the rhyme pattern.

15. The view expressed in this poem most clearly shows the influence of
    (A) the Realistic school
    (B) the Naturalist school
    (C) the Imagist movement
    (D) the Symbolist movement
    (E) the Romantic movement

16. The poem presents a movement from
    (A) life to death
    (B) death to rebirth
    (C) doubt to hope to doubt
    (D) ecstasy to joy to sorrow
    (E) faith to rebirth

17. The poem is a(n)
    (A) villanelle
    (B) dramatic monologue
    (C) sonnet
    (D) ballad
    (E) none of the above

18. All of the following are true about the language of the poem EXCEPT:
    (A) The poet uses poetic contraction such as "list" for "listen."
    (B) Sentences and phrases are inverted for poetic effect.
    (C) The words are selected to call for two different levels of interpretation.
    (D) The words are not unusual or difficult to define.
    (E) The poet makes frequent references to Nature.

19. The language of the poem can best be described as
    (A) labored
    (B) economical
    (C) extravagant
    (D) awkward
    (E) ill suited to the subject matter

20. The speaker of the poem is
    (A) nature
    (B) the dead
    (C) the "powerful of the earth"
    (D) the poet
    (E) different in different stanzas

21. The following line is an example of what poetic technique? "Yet a few days, and the all-beholding sun shall see no more in all his course."
    (A) Oxymoron
    (B) Conceit
    (C) Inversion
    (D) Personification
    (E) Synecdoche

22. The *tone* here is intended to be
    (A) comforting
    (B) frightening
    (C) neutral
    (D) passive
    (E) excited

SECTION 3

Time—60 minutes

Directions: Select a major character from any work of recognized literary merit and show how that character is human in that he or she possesses both good and bad traits. It is this balance between the two extremes that makes us "human," and this is true in literature as well as life. Be sure to include specific examples from the work under discussion to make your point. If you wish, you may select from the following list:

Madame Bovary   *The Scarlet Letter*

Ethan Frome   *The Adventures of Huckleberry Finn*

Vanity Fair   *Moby Dick*

The Red Badge of Courage   *Lord Jim*

Hamlet   *Catch-22*

The Portrait of a Lady   *The Turn of the Screw*

ANSWERS AND EXPLANATIONS FOR DIAGNOSTIC TEST

Section 1, Part A

1. **(C)** The poem is using the analogy of a spider and a fly to show how Hell's spider—Satan—traps Adam's race—man. (A) is partly correct, for the spider did indeed bite the fly's head off, as the lines "Whereas the silly fly,/Caught by its leg,/Thou by the throat took'st hastily,/And 'hind the head/Bite dead" (stanza 5) tell us. The rest of the question is not correct, though, for the "venom elf" mentioned in the first line does not refer to the *fly*, as the answer choice implies, but rather to the spider. (B) is not correct, for again, the "venom elf" refers to the spider, not the fly. (D) is not correct for the poem does not say that man must allow himself to be called by Nature. Rather, the sixth stanza explains that man must listen to his inborn ability to tell right from wrong. This choice is far too general and thus fails to answer the question. (E) is wrong, for the poem does not say that man flies. An ability to fly would have nothing to do with Satan's power to ensnare man.

2. **(A)** As mentioned in the first answer above, "Hell's Spider" is Satan, the devil. We can tell this is so by the eighth stanza, specifically in the phrase "Adam's race," in line 36, referring to mankind. Only the devil would be able to entrap man. Thus (B), Man, cannot be correct. (C) is equally wrong, for nowhere in the poem is a black widow spider mentioned. (D) The "venom elf" mentioned in the first line refers to a spider spinning a net to catch a fly, not to the devil himself, and (E) the representative of "Adam's race" is the one being trapped, not the one doing the trapping.

3. **(B)** In keeping with the analogy between the spider (Satan) and the fly (man) set up above, it follows that the "venom things" that trap man would be his sins. (A) cannot be correct, for base metals have nothing to do with spiders and flies and the battle between Satan and man. (C) is partly correct, for man is indeed tangled in a web, but the comparison is more fully expressed in answer (B). (D) and (E) may appear to be correct, but a closer examination reveals that nowhere is poison considered.

4. **(D)** The cord is the devil's way to trap man. (A) makes no sense, for the poet would not beg God's grace to break the cord. God's grace is awarded to man to ease sins. (B) There is no mother-child discussion here, and so this choice is incorrect. (C) looks like a correct answer at first glance, but by this point in the poem, we are beyond the spider-fly analogy, and so an answer with the devil and man is more suitable. The same is true for answer choice (E).

5. **(C)** The figure of speech here is an analogy, as a comparison is constructed between the spider of the beginning of the poem and the devil. Each sets traps to ensnare its prey. (A) is wrong, for a metaphor is a comparison between two objects in a *brief* and *succinct* manner. Unless it is an "extended metaphor," it would rarely stretch more than a line, and certainly not through a whole poem. (B) A simile is a kind of metaphor that uses either "like" or "as" to make the comparison, as in "He eats like a horse." (D) Personification gives human attributes to objects, and (E) hyperbole is exaggeration for literary effect.

6. **(A)** The spider traps the fly as the devil traps man: Each constructs clever snares for its unsuspecting prey. (B) appears to be a correct answer, but the analogy between the fly and man is not close enough to select this as a better answer than (A). A fly cannot reason and escape from a trap; a fly cannot stop himself from sinning. (C) is wrong, for nowhere in stanza 7 is a nightingale mentioned. (D) is wrong, for entrails are not *compared* to the spider. (E) We cannot see God's grace in the spider, for the spider is identified with the devil.

7. **(D)** As mentioned in answer 5, a simile is a brief comparison using "like" or "as." The line in the last stanza, "We'll nightingale sing *like* . . . ," as man in heaven is likened to a bird singing with joy, is the correct choice here. (A) means using the name of one object for that of another of which it is a part or related, such as "scepter" for "sovereignty." (B) is a figure of speech in which part is used for the whole, as when modern poet and dramatist T.S. Eliot says a "pair of ragged claws" in referring to crab in his poem "The Love Song of J. Alfred Prufrock." (E) is a metaphor that has portions that do not fit together, as in "sailing to the crosswalk of life," for a crosswalk would not be found on the ocean.

8. **(C)** Man, washed free of his sins, will sing gloriously in heaven, says the poet. Lines 43–44, "Thy Grace to break the cord; afford/Us glory's gate" is a clue to this, especially the word "Us."

9. **(A)** The fly is caught by the spider in the same way as man is caught by the devil, the poet claims. None of the other answers correctly expresses this relationship.

10. **(E)** To answer this question correctly, you would have to know what the metaphysical poets, a group who wrote during the seventeenth century in England, believed in and practiced. All of the choices listed in the question are characteristic of this movement. You will be expected to have a knowledge of the main poetic and literary movements, and be able to distinguish between them. Study the material in the Poetry Unit and the Novel Unit concerning this aspect of the exam.

11. **(E)** Again, a knowledge of basic poetic *forms* is required to correctly answer this. A sonnet, for example, is a poem that has 14 lines, either an English (Shakespearean) or an Italian (Petrarchian) rhyme scheme, and iambic pentameter rhythm. An ode, (B), is a lyric poem that expresses a great deal of emotion, usually concern-

ing exalted figures. Originally, it was sung rather than recited. (C) Hudibrastic verse is mock-heroic verse in tetrameter couplets, and doggerel, (D), is poorly-written and -regarded verse. All of these are discussed in the Poetry Unit.

12. **(C)** The final two couplets tell us that the author is most likely a very religious person, as the poem concludes with the wish that God will wash away the devil's traps and afford us all His grace. In this light, choices (A), (B), and (D) would not fit. Choice (E), a biologist, has little to do with the poem, as it does not focus on what we would consider "natural" or "nature" phenomena.

13. **(B)** We figure rhyme scheme by assigning a letter to each word that rhymes. For example, Cat (A)/ Bat (A)/ Mat (A)/ would all be assigned the same letter as they all rhyme. The next word that does not rhyme, such as "like," would be assigned the letter "B".

This continues for the length of the poem. (B) is the correct choice, as

elf	A	wasp	A
play	B	therein	B
thyself	A	clasp	A
fly	B	fling	B
why	B	sting	B

is how we would assign the letters for the rhyme scheme.

14. **(C)** "Witty and light" best expresses the *tone* of the poem. The tone of a work of literature is the particular manner or style, the mood of a piece of writing. It is determined through the author's choice of words and their placement. Here, the very comparison between Satan and the spider and a fly and man establishes the general tone, for were the author to be (A), intense and agitated, or (D), resigned and pessimistic, we would have had a different choice of analogy. The ending also, with its vision of redemption, would not fit in with selections (A) and (D). The very subject of the work—God's grace and man's acceptance or rejection of the devil's snares—contradicts choice (E).

15. **(E)** As established in previous answers, the poet is very much concerned with religion. Thus, the only answer that is *not* true would be (E). The questions that have the word *not* or *only,* or any other qualifier, must be read very carefully; they are often answered incorrectly because they are read too quickly and the *not* is ignored.

16. **(A)** The switch is made in line 31, where the poet says "This fray seems thus to us . . ." and ties the spider to the devil and the fly to man to make his point.

Section 1, Part B

"Terminus" is a calm, dignified, realistic statement of an old man accepting his age and fast-approaching death. The first line—"It is time to be old"—can be cited to support this. Lines 39–40—"The port, well worth the cruise, is near,/And every wave is charmed."—also illustrate this. It is a poem of serious and deep contemplation, whereas, in contrast, "The Last Leaf" is light and playful in tone. The majority of the figures of speech in "The Last Leaf" are comic, with the exception of those used in the final verse. Images such as "the pruning-knife of Time" (line 8) has "Cut him down" (line 9) and "his nose . . . rests upon his chin/Like a staff" (lines 31–33) are examples of the comic tone of "The Last Leaf" which show how it differs from "Terminus." But the figure in the final stanza is sad and lonely, for the last leaf upon the tree in the spring is even sadder than the last leaf in autumn. This leaf has been able to survive the winter, and surrounded by the new leaves bursting forth, must now wither away and die. Also, in the final stanza, the poet, who has maintained his distance from his subject, now identifies with him, looking forward to the time when *he* will be "the last leaf upon the tree/In the spring."

Section 2, Part A

The first speech has an emotional tone, trying to incite the audience into a frenzy of fighting. It can be called inflammatory or incendiary, as phrases such as "I cannot see on what grounds the king of Britain can look up to Heaven for help against us; a common murderer, a highwayman, or a house-breaker, has as good a pretence as he . . ." illustrate. He is calling the king names, trying (with great success, as it turned out) to incite the people to revolution. The second speech, in contrast, is far more deliberate and reasoned in tone with far fewer quotable, incisive phrases. The first speech strives for a soapbox approach, to reach the common man, the general audience, while the second has a more rational tone for a more elevated and educated audience.

Section 2, Part B

1. **(C)** The poet feels that man should listen to Nature when thoughts of death obsess him. Lines 2–3 tell us that "she speaks/A various language" and line 7 explains Nature's "healing sympathy." Lines 8–15 specifically instruct man to shake off his thoughts of the "last bitter hour" by going forth to Nature, under the open sky, and "list" (listen) to what the Earth and waters and air can tell.

2. **(C)** This is a direct quote from the poem (line 7), as mentioned in question 1.

3. **(B)** The phrase "Couch more magnificent" is found in line 33. The author is saying that nothing could be more majestic than to share eternity with the most powerful the earth has known—kings, the wise, the good.

4. **(E)** Lines 34–37 list all those who are buried in the earth.

5. **(D)** The line "All that breathe/Will share thy destiny" (lines 60–61) explains that mourning is not necessary, for in time all will pass on to Nature's bed.

6. **(A)** The poet is very concerned that man live in trust with Nature. The lines "Thou go not, like the quarry slave at night,/Scourged to his dungeon, but, sustained and soothed/By an unfaltering trust, approach thy grave . . . and lies down to pleasant dreams" (lines 77–81) tell us this.

7. **(B)** The entire poem is concerned with man's acceptance of the natural order, that man will live and die according to Nature's rules and thus all will work in a great cosmic harmony.

None of the other choices fit with the poem's meaning.

8. **(D)** A "sepulcher" is a tomb, and "mighty" means grand. Here, the earth is the grandest tomb of all, for it is the largest and holds all the great, wise, and mighty from all time.

9. **(B)** See the answer for question 8 for an explanation.

10. **(B)** The "destiny" is death, what all people, no matter how great or small, hold in common. None of the other choices are always true, for we have no assurance that all will have to mourn, (D), or accept Nature, (E).

11. **(A)** A simile is a comparison using "like" or "as," and here we have "*Like* one who wraps the drapery of his couch/About him. . . ," comparing sleep with a warm and comfortable blanket to the grave's shroud. Both, the poet claims, should be approached calmly and with trust. (B), personification, is giving human qualities to inanimate objects, and (C), alliteration, is the repetition of the initial letter, as in "Peter Piper picked a peck of pickled peppers." (D), apostrophe, is addressing someone who is not present, as if the author here were to say, "Dear Nature . . ." Inversion, (E), occurs when portions of the sentence are switched around for literary effect.

12. **(D)** Death is compared to sleep, as the reader is instructed to approach death as if it were but sleep on a warm couch.

13. **(E)** The new lines offer more hope, speaking as they do of "gayer hours" (line 3), "voice of

gladness" (line 4), and "healing sympathy" (line 7). The poet had come under fire for what many saw as a bleak picture of death, although he intended it to offer great comfort.

14. **(B)** Again, these lines offer a bit of hope and unify the beginning and the end of the poem. Rarely will an author add anything simply to allow room for more figures of speech, (A); the poetic devices add to the meaning, not substitute for it. The poem is not a ballad, (C), and nowhere is death to be feared or battled. See the final lines.

15. **(E)** The major influence on "Thanatopsis" by William Cullen Bryant is a movement called Romanticism, which flourished during the nineteenth century. Some of the ideas of the movement reflected in this poem include a belief in the changeable, variable state of the physical world (often called "mutability") and the feeling that all is prey to decline and decay. The Romantics also felt that even though everything changes and declines, God remains absolute and reveals Himself through His greatest, though changeable, creation—Nature. Bryant also used many of the writing techniques of the Romantic school. There is a great reliance on artificially inflated diction and syntax. The Romantics felt that old-fashioned, out-of-date word order and choice could be used to establish a serious and philosophical tone. Thus we find words like "thou," "thy," and "shalt," as well as contractions such as "list" for "listen." Even in the nineteenth century, which seems so long ago, no one was speaking in this manner. Inversion, discussed previously, was also a Romantic technique. Also referred to as anastrophe, it is the movement of a word or phrase from its normal and expected position in the sentence for poetic effect or emphasis. It can also be used to maintain poetic rhythm and rhyme. As shown above, Bryant made extensive use of this technique.

16. **(A)** The poet speaks of life in the beginning, and concludes with a discussion of the way in which a person should approach death—calmly, and with trust in Nature.

17. **(E)** (A) A villanelle is a short poem of fixed form, five tercets followed by a final quatrain, having rhyme and refrains. This is not the case with "Thanatopsis." (B) A dramatic monologue is a poem that has one person telling a dramatic story, such as Robert Browning's "My Last Duchess." There is no story, no narrative, here. (C) A sonnet is a poem of 14 lines having a very specific rhyme and rhythm, which is not the case here either, and (D), a ballad, is a simple narrative poem, usually having a romantic theme and able to be set to music and sung. "Thanatopsis" is none of these.

18. **(C)** There is only one level of interpretation here, the poet's belief that Nature will welcome man and comfort him and that man's death will unite him firmly with the universe and the natural order of life. Be careful with questions that have the word EXCEPT in them, for they can be tricky to read.

19. **(A)** The inversions and poetic contractions, such as "list" for "listen," make the poem difficult to read. In no way would the language be economical (B), for there are a great many words here, and a case could be made that this would have been a better, more effective poem, if the author had used fewer. The language is not *best* described by either (C) or (D), although a case could be made for both, as well as (E). Remember to select the answer that *best* completes the question, even though there will be choices that appear to be correct. There is always one that is most accurate.

20. **(D)** The speaker makes no pretensions to be Nature or the "powerful of the earth," choices (A) and (C). The voice remains the same throughout the poem, and thus choice (E) is not correct.

21. **(C)** This is an inversion, as the words are switched out of their expected order. The sentence would most usually read, "Yet a few days, and the all-beholding sun shall not see any more in all his course." (A) An oxymoron is a seeming contradiction, such as "cruel kindness." (B) A conceit is an elaborate metaphor or extended comparison, and (D), personification, is giving human qualities to inanimate objects. (E) A synecdoche is the use of a part for a whole or a whole for a part, such as "five sails" for five ships.

22. **(A)** The poet intends to comfort man about death. We can see this especially in the final lines.

Section 3

The essay asks that you show both the good and bad traits a character possesses to conclude that the character is "human" like all of us. Briefly, a chart could be used to show these character traits. In *The Adventures of Huckleberry Finn,* for example, we see that Huck, the main character, is "human" because he has the following balance of good and bad traits:

Good

Risks eternal damnation ("All right, then, I'll go to hell") to rescue Jim after he is sold to the slave traders for "forty dirty dollars."

Works hard at school and tries to learn; initially does try to stop Tom from the worst of the plans to "rescue" Jim at the end of the book.

Bad

Plays three progressively dangerous and humiliating tricks on Jim—the nickel/hat trick, the snake trick where Jim gets bitten, and worst of all, the "trash" incident.

Goes along with Tom on the escape plans at the end of the book, which are very dangerous. Tom is shot and wounded. Abandons his studies with ease when his father kidnaps him from cabin.

The same can be done for Shakespeare's *Hamlet:*

Good

Wrestles with his conscience before he will kill Claudius—he must have proof.

Well loved by the common people, shown especially in Act V with the gravediggers—he had the "common touch"

Honest, decent, kind, possessor of a keen conscience (scenes with Horatio).

Bad

When he does have proof—Claudius's confession in his private room—does not act and compounds the tragedy.

Treats Ophelia very shabbily when he feels she has thrown him over; treats his mother as poorly when he comes close to killing her in the "closet" scene. Ghost stops him.

Indecisive and too much given to brooding—see Act I with his mother's comments.

HOW TO USE THE DIAGNOSTIC TEST

1. Take a look back at each section and see where you did well and where you did poorly. Did you find the poem very hard to analyze or the essay difficult to organize? Did the prose passages and essay stump you? On a sheet of paper, note which sections were hard for you and which questions you could not answer.

2. You will have a list that will look something like this:
   Simile?
   Metaphor?
   How to organize essay?
   What's *tone*?

3. Now, go through this book and write down the page numbers of the sections that explain what you need to know.
   Simile?   p. ——
   Metaphor?   p. ——
   How to Organize essay? p. ——

4. Do not spend much time on those sections you understood. Rather, to make the best use of this book and the time allowed, focus on the sections that you found most difficult. Make sure all your questions are answered.

5. When you have finished all your study, take the three simulated exams at the end of this book. After each exam, make note of the questions you missed and the concepts that gave you trouble. Go back to the study sections for additional help in your own personal troublespots before attempting the next exam.

Part 2

Essay Writing Guide

Step by Step to High-Scoring AP Essays

1. Before you do anything else, make sure that you understand exactly what is required of you. Ask yourself the following questions:

   • What must I prove?

   • How much time do I have to complete the essay?

   • What form—novel, short story, poem, drama—am I required to use?

   • How many works or characters or aspects must I consider? One? Two?

   • Is the work or are the works that I have selected of "recognized literary value"? It is usually best to select works that you have covered in class or that have come from the AP reading list. Avoid works that have been made into recent popular movies and stick with something that you are sure will be acceptable. This is not the time to experiment with outside reading.

   • Who are they asking me to select? A main character? A supporting player? The narrator? Is the person that I have selected the proper one?

   • Do I know the work well enough to be sure of the details? Do I have the chronology straight: Do I recall the actual order of events? Do I know the characters? Can I spell their names? Can I recall their various relationships? This is crucial, for the success of your thesis will directly depend on the strength of your *detail*, and major errors in this area can seriously weaken your essay. Make sure you know the work. Before you finalize your choice, make a list of all the important and relevant details from the works you are considering.

2. After you have thought out all of the above, rephrase the thesis statement in your own words to make sure that you understand what you will have to do. Try several different variations and double-check selection of characters, etc. Again, be sure you have the correct and necessary information from the works.

3. Construct an outline, either jotted or topic (see Organizing Your Thoughts, page 25). Make sure that you have included all the correct details in the correct order. Check that you have included all you need to make your point. Do not be afraid to include dialogue and specific quotes, if you can recall them. You will find that if you know a book or play well, many important interchanges will come to mind. These might include such crucial details as Hamlet's "To be or not to be" speech; Huck Finn's famous denial of public conscience, "All right, then, I'll go to hell," or his last lines, as he "lights out for the territory ahead of the rest;" Macbeth's "Lay on Macduff" speech, just to name a few. These are the *specific details* that can make the difference between a *good* paper and a *great* one. It is a good idea to prepare several books and poems, noting details and lines that impressed you. **This does not mean that you will insert lines wherever you can to impress the reader; they must, of course, directly prove your point or they are valueless.** But if you have carefully outlined several different works, the specific details will come to mind.

4. Write the introduction. This is a very important part of your paper, as we will discuss later in detail. It establishes your thesis and captures your reader's attention. If the thesis is incorrect, the paper will not prove the point; if the introduction is dull and lifeless, the reader's attention will drift, and he may miss some of your points. Make sure you rephrase the question, include title and author, and establish what you will prove.

5. Write the first draft. Of course, it is always best to write more than one draft of a paper, but you may not have the time to do so. Thus, it is important that you follow the outline to make sure that you have included all your salient points. Do not count on having the time to complete two drafts, but keep in mind that if you are so fortunate, your paper will be the better for it. Never leave extra time at the end; use every minute that you are allowed.

6. Make sure that you *proofread* very carefully. This can be one of the most important steps in any paper, for no matter how valid your points, how clear your examples, if you have made a great many careless writing errors, you will lose credit. While your essay will be evaluated holistically (on the total impression it makes), errors can distract your reader and reduce the effectiveness of your arguments. Try to leave your paper for a few moments, perhaps look over the short answers or another essay, and then go back to it refreshed. *Always* make sure that you have time to proofread, and be as careful as you can to read what is there, not what you *think* is there.

Generating Your Thoughts

It is always difficult to begin writing—especially so on a pressured exam, where you have precious little time to map out your ideas. There are few things as disheartening as staring at a blank sheet of paper, wondering where to start. You don't have the luxury of sitting and thinking for awhile, musing on the various aspects your topic presents. You are not allowed to bounce your ideas off others; you have no recourse to primary or secondary texts. There will most likely be no opportunity for a second draft or extensive revision. Your first draft will have to stand as your final effort.

How do you begin? Is it best to just take a few deep breaths and plunge right in? Or are you perhaps better off planning for a few moments, even though it seems like everyone around you is already writing? Almost all writers agree that planning results in a better finished product, especially when there is little or no time for revision. Planning helps your ideas flow with greater logic and order. It also guarantees that all important details will be included in their proper places.

Therefore, even though it might appear that everyone else has already begun writing, *always* try to set aside some time to plan what you are going to say and how you are going to say it. Naturally, the time you spend planning depends on how much time you have to write your essay. Use the chart that follows to determine how much time you should allocate to planning your essay:

If you have 20 minutes for your essay	plan for 3–5 minutes
If you have 25 minutes for your essay	plan for 5 minutes
If you have 30 minutes for your essay	plan for 5 minutes
If you have 40 minutes for your essay	plan for 5–7 minutes
If you have 45 minutes for your essay	plan for 7 minutes
If you have 60 minutes for your essay	plan for 7–10 minutes

Now that you know approximately how much time to set aside for planning your essay, let's look at ways to best use that time.

Writers all have their own ways of generating ideas, but what works well for one person may be ineffective for another. Below are three different ways to get your thoughts flowing. Try all three with the simulated AP essay questions in this text. Experiment to discover which method works best for you. Then, use that method or a combination of methods on the actual test.

One possible way to begin is to *brainstorm*. First, re-read the question. Then, put your pen on the paper—and don't lift it up again until you have finished brainstorming! Now, allowing yourself about 2 minutes, write down all the ideas that you can concerning the question. These can be single words or phrases. You can abbreviate or use dashes (—) or slashes (/) to save time. The most important thing about successful brainstorming is to continue writing, as quickly as you can. Don't worry if a few of your ideas seem irrelevant to the topic, or if you write the same idea twice, or if you misspell some words. If you can't think of anything to write but still have time left, continue writing, even if you write your name or the date. You should be able to generate a list of about 15 different ideas within the 2 minute time frame. For example, let's brainstorm with this simulated AP essay question:

"... show how the main character is unwilling or unable to accept members of his or her community or family and is thus isolated and alone. Also explain how the author prepares the reader for this rejection of human companionship. Consider at least two elements of fiction such as theme, setting, characterization, or any other aspect of the writer's craft in your discussion."

Brainstorming sample

—Hamlet	—father dead
—mother remarried/uncle/2 months	—R & G spies
—Ophelia cut off	—ghost
—distrusts Claudius	—distrusts mother
—contemplates suicide	—"to be or not to be"
—Claudius/murder plot/England	—has only Horatio
—play within a play	—black cloak
—madness	—battlements at night

Now you have a list of ideas you can use to begin writing. While not every idea will fit, you should have enough to begin arranging your ideas into a coherent whole, a topic discussed at length in the next section, "Organizing Your Thoughts." But first, let's look at a second way to generate ideas, freewriting.

Some writers find it easier to think in sentences rather than words or phrases. When they begin brainstorming, they find themselves writing down very long phrases that grow into sentences, even brief paragraphs. If this description fits your writing style, you might find it easier to generate ideas through *freewriting*. With brainstorming, you write down *words or phrases*; with freewriting, you write down *sentences*.

Allowing about 3 to 4 minutes, or about twice as long as you set aside for brainstorming, write down all the ideas you have concerning the test question in complete sentences, tying your ideas together in a loose, off-the-top-of-your-head paragraph. By no means will this be a finished composition; rather, it is a very brief paragraph designed to get you thinking. By nature it will be somewhat rambling, poorly-organized, and perhaps even confusing in places—but it will serve to get your ideas flowing and establish a starting place for your composition. Let's freewrite the same simulated AP question:

"... show how the main character is unwilling or unable to accept members of his or her community or family and is thus isolated and alone. Also explain how the author prepares the reader for this rejection of human companionship. Consider at least two elements of fiction such as theme, setting, characterization, or any other aspect of the writer's craft in your discussion."

Freewriting sample

Even though he tries to establish meaningful contact with people in his family (Gertrude/Claudius) and community (Laertes, Ophelia, Rosencrantz and Guildenstern), he fails and is alone. Shakespeare prepares the reader for this by using characterization and theme. He comes back to his home Denmark because he thinks that he is going to attend his father's funeral. Imagine his surprise when he discovers that he is also witnessing his mother's marriage (funeral baked meats/irony). He is isolated because he is unable to talk to his mother after she has remarried (Act I, and later scene in her room), and he really does not trust his uncle. Later we find out how perceptive this is. His girlfriend cuts him off; his friends R & G are disloyal.

There is a lot missing from this brief paragraph (including the main character's name!), yet it serves well as a springboard for a focused, well-developed essay. Notice how this freewriting establishes the primary points to be discussed, lists the main characters, and begins introducing some specific detail. Although there is little here that directly addresses the second half of the question: "Consider at least two elements of fiction such as theme, setting, characterization, or any other aspect of the writer's craft in your discussion," we do have enough generated to begin arranging a formal response.

The third method of generating your thoughts involves *asking questions*. There are two different ways to do this. One frequently used method is called *QAD* (Questions, Answers, Details); the second method involves asking yourself the traditional journalistic questions. Let's take a look at QAD first.

As with brainstorming and freewriting, the QAD method of generating ideas is designed to take only a few moments. Consult the chart on page 25 to best pace your time on each individual AP essay question. QAD is especially useful on a factual literature essay. Here is a sample pertaining to tragedy and *Macbeth*:

Question	Answer	Details
What is tragedy?	representations of serious actions which turn out disastrously for the main character(s)	1. involves a character for whom we have sympathy 2. serious occurrence 3. circumstances beyond one's control 4. results in hero's death

This should take a few moments to briefly outline. Next, zero in on the question, and fill in the chart with details pertaining to it. The following is an example from *Macbeth*.

QUESTION	ANSWER	DETAILS					
		WHAT HAPPENS?	WHERE?	WHEN?	WHY?	HOW?	WHO?
What is a situation involving a serious or calamitous occurrence?	Macbeth goes to the cave of the witches.	He sees three visions.	Appearing from the cauldron.	After seeing Banquo's ghost at the feast.	Because of his uncertainty and fear regarding his position as King.	He reacts by deciding to continue his killing.	Macduff's family.

Another way of asking questions to generate ideas focuses on the 5 W's and H: Who? What? When? Where? Why? and How?

Again, working within the time frame outlined on the chart for generating ideas, select whichever variations on these questions apply to your topic. Here are some suggestions:

Who
—was involved?
—does this concern?
—does this affect?

What
—happened?
—was the cause?
—were the results?
—does this mean to the plot or theme as a whole?

When
—did it happen? (try to narrow your response down to a specific time or page
    number)
—will the results be apparent?

Where
—did it happen?

Why
—did it happen?

How
—did it happen?

You will most likely find this method of generating ideas even more useful if you narrow down your questions to best suit your specific topic—the more specific the question, the more focused your response. Consider again the simulated AP question with which we have been working:

"... show how the main character is unwilling or unable to accept members of his or her community or family and is thus isolated and alone. Also explain how the author prepares the reader for this rejection of human companionship. Consider at least two elements of fiction such as theme, setting, characterization, or any other aspect of the writer's craft in your discussion."

Here are some questions to consider:

- What work will I use?
- Is it a work of recognized literary value?
- Who is the main character?
- What in the book tells me that this character is unwilling or unable to accept people?
- How does the author use theme to anticipate the character's rejection of people?
- How does the author use symbolism to anticipate the character's rejection of people?

To summarize, there are many different ways to generate ideas; we have discussed but three of the most common. Select the method—or combination of methods—that best suits your individual style of composition. Also consider the nature of the specific AP question you are being asked—different methods work better with different questions—and the amount of time you have. Regardless of the method(s) you ultimately adopt, successful prewriting techniques can greatly improve the quality of organization and detail in your composition. These techniques can make it easier for you to begin writing, and help to ensure that you will make the best use of your time.

Exercises: Generate ideas for each of the following simulated AP questions by using *brainstorming, freewriting,* and *asking questions.* You can try all three methods on each question, but make sure to try each method at least once.

1. Read the two poems that follow. Then compare the mood of the first with the mood of the second, showing how the mood of each poem serves to define and reinforce the theme. Use specific lines from both poems to support your discussion. Time—45 minutes.

WHEN I WAS ONE-AND-TWENTY

When I was one-and-twenty
   I heard a wise man say,
"Give crowns and pounds and guineas
   But not your heart away;
Give pearls away and rubies
   But keep your fancy free."
But I was one-and-twenty,
   No use to talk to me.

When I was one-and-twenty
   I heard him say again,
"The heart out of the bosom
   Was never given in vain;
'Tis paid with sighs a plenty
   And sold for endless rue."
And I am two-and-twenty,
   And oh, 'tis true, 'tis true.

       —A.E. Housman

WITH RUE MY HEART IS LADEN

With rue my heart is laden
   For golden friends I had,
For many a rose-lipt maiden
   And many a lightfoot lad.

By brooks too broad for leaping.
   The lightfoot boys are laid;
The rose-lipt girls are sleeping
   In fields where roses fade.

       —A.E. Housman

2. Explain how any three poetic devices Gerard Manley Hopkins uses in "Pied Beauty" contribute to the poem's theme. You may select from the following list: alliteration, sound devices, meter, rhythm, rhyme, figurative language, vocabulary, word use, color use. Time—45 minutes.

PIED BEAUTY[1]

Glory be to God for dappled things—
   For skies of couple-colour as a brindled cow;
      For rose-moles all in stipple upon trout that swim;
Fresh-firecoal chestnut-falls; finches' wings;
   Landscape plotted and pieced—fold, fallow, and plough;
      And all trades, their gear and tackle and trim.

All things counter, original, spare, strange;
   Whatever is fickle, freckled (who knows how?)
      With swift, slow; sweet, sour; adazzle, dim;
He fathers-forth whose beauty is past change:
      Praise him.

       —Gerard Manley Hopkins

3. Select a major character from any work of recognized literary merit and show how that character is unable to adjust successfully to his or her environment. Be sure to include specific examples from the work to make your point. Time—60 minutes.

---

[1]*Pied* means of two or more colors, variegated.

Organizing Your Thoughts

One of the best ways to organize material you have generated through brainstorming, freewriting, asking questions, or a combination of these methods is to use an *outline*. Outlines are especially effective in literary essays where you must be sure to include all the necessary details in the correct order. There are four main kinds of outlines: jotted, topic, sentence, and paragraph. Each one is useful in certain circumstances, depending on the subject, the time allotted, and how secure you feel with the material.

THE JOTTED OUTLINE

The jotted outline is the simplest way to quickly organize the material you have generated through brainstorming or freewriting. When using the asking questions method, an outline is not usually required as the basis of the composition is already established. Like most writers, you are apt to find the jotted outline especially useful if you are pressed for time, which is certainly the case on the AP exam.

With the jotted outline, you arrange the brief phrases you have gathered into a logical whole. At the same time, you must delete any words or phrases from your original list that are irrelevant to the topic as well as add any new material you require to fully flesh out your thesis. Use parallel phrasing to keep your thinking straight. Here's a jotted outline for a typical AP essay on literature:

Question
"A sharp insight can change a person's life for better or worse. Select a character from a recognized work of literary value and show how this is true."
Outline
Thesis: Huckleberry Finn has a sharp insight which changes his life for the better.

1. Huck—typical upbringing for child in 1830s—taught blacks inferior to whites
2. Meets Jim/Jackson's Island/strike up closer friendship/travel down Mississippi
3. Begins to see Jim as person/story of Jim's daughter's deafness/Jim's aim to buy wife and children
4. Huck/sharp insight/Cairo/lies to slave traders; gets $40/"All right, then, I'll go to hell"—letter to Miss Watson/rescue of Jim

Now you have a chronological list of items you will consider to make your point. You can refer to your outline to make sure you discuss all your points clearly.

THE TOPIC OUTLINE

If time permits, the topic outline will usually help you organize your thoughts more throughly than the jotted outline. The topic outline takes the jotted outline one step further. The jotted outline *lists* words or phrases that represent main ideas; the topic outline, in contrast, *arranges* these brief phrases in a highly formalized structure. Again, keep these phrases parallel to further encourage logical thinking. Your thoughts will thus be ordered in an *inductive* manner, as your major points are set upward in tiers of ascending importance, and *deductive*, as your major headings are divided into smaller and smaller subheads. You mark headings and subheadings by alternating numbers and letters as you proceed downward from Roman numeral I through captial A to Arabic 1 and little a, until you reach, if you need them, parenthesized (1) and (a). You indent equal headings equally, so that they fall into the same column, Roman under Roman, capital under capital, and so on, in this manner:

I. _____
   A. _____
      1. _____
      2. _____
   B. _____
      1. _____
         a. _____
            (1) _____
               (a) _____
               (b) _____
            (2) _____
         b. _____
      2. _____
II. _____
   A. _____
   B. _____
   C. _____
   D. _____
      1. _____
      2. _____
      3. _____
         a. _____
         b. _____

Headings always come in pairs; you cannot have a I without a II, an A without a B, a 1 without a 2, etc. This is because an unpaired heading suggests a detail is too small for separate treatment, and should really be part of a larger heading directly above. Let's take another look at the question on "sharp insight":

I. Topic paragraph
   A. Topic sentence—title, author, thesis statement
   B. Material that will be covered in PP2—first events leading up to sharp insight
   C. Material that will be covered in PP3—conclusion on sharp insight
   D. transition into PP2

II. Beginning of proof
   A. Topic sentence—restatement of thesis
   B. Huck's upbringing/attitude toward slaves
   C. Huck meets Jim on Jackson's Island/begin down Mississippi
   D. Scene with Jim's tale of daughter's deafness/Huck begins to realize Jim a person with feelings
   E. Scene right before Cairo—Jim reminds Huck how good Huck has been to him

  F. Huck has beginning of insight with slave traders at Cairo—lies for Jim to slave traders/accepts $40

  G. Thesis statement—Huck begins to accept Jim as a person, has insight that Jim is "white inside"

III. Climax of insight

  A. Topic sentence—brief recounting of events leading up to selling of Jim

  B. King sells Jim for "40 dirty dollars." Huck decides to write letter to Miss Watson/letter itself

  C. Huck rips up letter/says, "All right, then, I'll go to hell!" Decides to risk eternal damnation (refer to II B) to save his friend. Sudden realization

  D. Huck and Tom rescue Jim

  E. Concluding sentence

IV. Conclusion

  A. Topic sentence—Huck experiences sudden insight/realizes that Jim a human being, despite all he has been taught about blacks

  B. Summarize PP2

  C. Climax of sudden realization—Huck risks eternal damnation to save Jim

  D. Conclusion—scene at Cairo: Huck begins to accept Jim

This is the type of outline that you will use most frequently on the AP examination, for it is well worth the time to clearly organize your thoughts before you begin to write. In this manner, you can make sure that you have included clear details (Cairo, quotes, etc. as shown) and made your point.

THE SENTENCE OUTLINE

The sentence outline requires more time than either of the previous two methods, but it can be very helpful if you tend to think in longer phrases or you find it useful to plan even more tightly before you begin to write. Because it forces you to think out your plan so carefully beforehand, it can greatly speed up your writing time. Few outlines will be as complete as the one that follows, but you can see how easy writing an essay will be with an outline this full.

> Thesis: Holden Caulfield, the main character in J. D. Salinger's *The Catcher in the Rye,* is removed from the mainstream of society for a variety of reasons and is more independent than the person who must rely upon others. One critic has linked him to other characters in American literature who live alone, and dubbed this kind of character "the American Adam." Compare Holden's isolation with the isolation of any other character in American literature.*

 I. Holden is isolated from society, even though he attempts to make contact with others.

  A. Holden first visits his old history teacher from Pencey Prep, Mr. Spencer.

   1. Although Holden admires Spencer, they fail to make contact as Spencer reads Holden's failing examination paper to him.

---

*See R.W.B. Lewis, *The American Adam: Innocence, Tragedy and Tradition in the Nineteenth Century.* Chicago: The University of Chicago Press, 1955.

      2. Things get even worse as the teacher forces Holden to listen to the pathetic note Holden had added to his paper.

      3. Even though Holden sees that Spencer is trying to help him end his isolation, the older man fails to establish a link, symbolized by the magazine he throws failing to reach the bed.

  B. Holden next has a conversation with his roommate, Ward Stradlater, and again we see his isolation.

      1. Stradlater, whom Holden considers a "phony," has Holden writing his essays for him.

      2. Stradlater ignores what Holden has to say about Jane Gallagher, Holden's friend, more intent on her physical appearance than her basic humanity.

      3. Although Stradlater invites Holden to join them on the date, he is unable to bring himself to establish a bond.

II. Huckleberry Finn, from *The Adventures of Huckleberry Finn* by Mark Twain, is also isolated from society.

  A. Huck has no family.

      1. His mother died when Huck was born.

      2. His father, a drunken bum, abuses Huck by locking him in a cabin alone for three days.

      3. Although his guardians, the Widow Douglas and Miss Watson, mean well, neither is able to become "family" to him.

  B. Huck's actions set him off from society.

      1. Huck runs away to Jackson's Island to escape his abusive Pap.

      2. Huck sails down the Mississippi River with a runaway slave, Jim, surviving by "borrowing" food.

      3. Huck risks what he considers eternal damnation to save Jim from a return to slavery.

      4. At the end of the book, Huck "lights out for the territory ahead of the rest," running away once again.

An outline this complete might not be possible in the time allowed on the exam, but some students find it a useful method for their particular writing styles. There is one final method of outlining, more useful for summaries of reading than for preparation of essays, and that is the paragraph outline.

THE PARAGRAPH OUTLINE

The paragraph outline strengthens your ability to organize your paragraphs by topic sentences, since in this type of outline you write a topic sentence for each and every one of your paragraphs. Since your paragraphs are many and your divisions few, it is most convenient to use a combination of Roman and Arabic numerals. A paragraph outline could look like this:

I. Holden seems unable to maintain even the most tenuous link with others.

    1. As he is having breakfast in a cheap cafeteria, Holden meets two nuns, and is filled with pity for them.

    2. He gives them ten dollars, even though he is running out of money himself, and tries to buy them breakfast, which they refuse.

    3. Holden and the nuns have a long conversation about literature and it appears that the meeting will go well after all.

4. But as they part, Holden blows smoke at the nuns, which disturbs him a great deal.

5. He feels as though he has behaved very badly and wonders if he should have given them more money. Even in this seemingly innocent meeting, Holden is unable to establish a link with others.

This type of outline is generally too detailed to be useful in a literature essay for a timed examination, but it will be handy for extended reading assignments, term papers, or any untimed and extensive essay.

To outline your reading, you first summarize the essay into one sentence. Then you go back through the essay, writing down a series of sentences that summarize the main ideas as they come along. You may use the author's own words, but it is generally easier to summarize with your own briefer statements. Then you arrange the statements into major and minor importance, and rearrange them in the proper order.

OUTLINING TECHNIQUES

The following points will make your outlines clearer and more helpful in structuring your essays:

1. **Title.** Set the title off from the text of the outline. Do not underline it or place it in quotes. Make it as specific as you can, even if your essay will not be as specific as your title. This will help focus your thoughts more clearly.

2. **Capitalization.** Capitalize only the first word of each heading (and other words that would normally be capitalized).

3. **Punctuation.** Put periods after headings that are complete sentences, but not after phrases.

4. **Headings.** Whenever possible, make headings grammatically parallel. Try not to mix headings—some nouns, some sentences, some fragments. This may not always be possible, of course, if you are rushed for time, but it will make the actual writing of the essay easier if the headings are parallel.

Outlining Exercise

Directions: Construct a topic outline on the following simulated AP question using the form provided below. Try to be as specific as possible and keep your headings and subheadings as parallel as possible.

"Failure in human relationships results when one shirks the normal responsibilities of one's position in life." Show how this is true with one character from a recognized work of literary value.

I.

    A.

    B.

    C.

    D.

II.

    A.

    B.

        1.

        2.

    C.

        1.

        2.

    D.

III.

    A.

    B.

        1.

        2.

    C.

        1.

        2.

    D.

IV.

    A.

    B.

    C.

    D.

Possible Answers: (Using *The Scarlet Letter* by Nathaniel Hawthorne)

I. Topic paragraph
  A. Topic sentence—rephrase question/Arthur Dimmesdale avoids his responsibilities.
  B. Material in PP2—Arthur's involvement with Hester Prynne
  C. Material in PP3—Arthur's involvement with Chillingworth and the town
  D. Lead-in PP2

II. Beginning of thesis
  A. Topic sentence—rephrase question and answer
  B. Arthur's affair with Hester/birth of Pearl/scene with Arthur beseeching Hester to reveal her lover/irony/denial of responsibility
    1. Detail on Arthur's role
    2. Detail on Arthur's normal responsibility
  C. Hester, disgraced, has to support Pearl alone/psychological and physical
    1. Economic—seamstress—because of Arthur's failure to support them
    2. Problems with Pearl—no father
  D. Summary of above

III. Conclusion of thesis
  A. Topic sentence—Arthur's responsibility extended beyond Hester to Chillingworth and the town.
  B. Responsibility to Hester's husband, Chillingworth
    1. Chillingworth "leech"
    2. Ripping aside of vestments
  C. Responsibility to town
    1. Secret guilt—bloody scourge in closet
    2. Town worships him, the more the guilt increases

IV. Conclusion
  A. Summary of thesis
  B. Summary of PP 2
  C. summary of PP 3
  D. General conclusion

The Elements of Writing Style

Style is the manner in which you express yourself, your choice of words and their arrangement. One of the most important elements of style is *sentence variety*. A difference in sentences, short or long, loose or periodic, can alert your reader to a change in thought, to an important point. It makes the difference between a dull paragraph or essay and one that catches the reader's attention and keeps it. There are a great many ways to vary sentences. The following chart is a quick review of the many different ways to start a sentence:

INTRODUCTORY SENTENCE ELEMENTS

Introductory Element	Job—Acts as— Does the Work of	Ends With or Begins With	"Clue"	Sample
1 ADVERB	Will modify the verb which follows close by	*-ly*	Will have a comma following it	QUIETLY
2 PREPOSITIONAL PHRASE	Acts as a modifier Adjective or Adverb	A noun or pronoun as its last word	Begins with a preposition	UNDER THE TABLE
3 DEPENDENT CLAUSE	Has a subject and a verb	Begins with a subordinate conjunction followed by a comma	cannot stand alone	WHEN MY FRIEND ARRIVES,
4 MAIN CLAUSE	Has a subject and a verb	May be joined by a coordinate conjunction to another main clause	May stand alone as a sentence	WE CAN ALL LEAVE FOR THE DANCE
5 VERBAL	Used as a noun, adjective, or adverb in a sentence	Is a word derived from a verb	Has a "hint" of action	SINGING, BROKEN, WOUNDED TO DREAM
6 INFINITIVE	A *verbal* used as a noun, adjective, or adverb	Begins with the word *to*	Can be changed into a gerund	TO SEE
7 PARTICIPLE	A *verbal* used as an adjective— will modify a noun or pronoun	Ends in *-ing*, *-ed, -en, -t*	Followed by a comma	SINGING IN THE RAIN,
8 GERUND	A *verbal* used as a noun	Ends in *-ing*	Can put "the act of" in front of it	MAKING FUNNY NOISES
9 ADJECTIVE	Will modify a noun or pronoun	Generally comes in front of the word it modifies	Can also be a predicate adjective	YOUNG, GREEN

37

Introductory Element	Job—Acts as—Does the Work of	Ends With or Begins With	"Clue"	Sample
10 ADVERB	Modifies a verb, adjective, or adverb	Usually ends in *-ly* and answers the question: When? Where? How? Why?	Usually ends in *-ly*	VERY, SINCERELY
11 NOUN	Is used in a sentence as a subject, direct object, indirect object, predicate nominative, or object of the preposition	The words *the* or *a* can be put in front	Made plural by adding *-s* or *-es*	WISDOM, PIZZA, COURAGE
12 APPOSITIVE	Will give additional information (make you positive) of the noun	Comes after a noun	Set off by commas	,OUR MAILMAN,

SENTENCE VARIETY

A sentence is a group of words that expresses one complete thought. Essentially, it tells us that:

someone (or something) *did* something

Example: Harry ran for a mile.

or

someone (or something) *is* something

Example: Harry is president.

Every sentence has a subject (the someone or something) and a verb. Therefore, the shortest possible sentence would be

Stop! (Subject understood to be "You" Verb is "Stop!" or any other command)

There are three main kinds of sentences:

Simple: a single subject and verb group, although either may be plural

> *Examples:*   Last July was unusually warm.
> Mary and John went to the beach and the park. (plural subject)

Compound: two or more simple sentences joined together in one of the three ways described below. A compound sentence unites two ideas, but it does not necessarily show the relationship between them. Compound sentences can be formed in the following ways:

1. semicolon (;)

   Example: The sun scorched the land; the lack of rain made it untillable.

2. comma + coordinating conjunction (and, but, or, for, so, yet, nor)

   Example: The sun scorched the land, and the lack of rain made it untillable.

3. semicolon + conjunctive adverb (accordingly, nevertheless, consequently, otherwise, furthermore, then, hence, therefore, however, thus, moreover)

   Example: The sun scorched the land; moreover the lack of rain made it untillable.

There are many different ways to vary your sentences. Always select the method that will make your point clearer and hold the reader's attention. Let's look at some of the most effective ways to create vigorous, concise sentences.

1. Compound Sentence Elements

Sections of sentences may be compounded, eliminating wordiness. Elements that may be compounded include subjects, verbs, direct objects, predicate nouns and adjectives, other adjectives, and entire predicates. When more than two elements are compounded, they become a series.

Examples:

Compound predicate adjective:	My sister is *obstinate, obsessed,* and *zealous.*
Compound verb:	She *cheers, coaxes,* and *curses* the players.
Compound predicate:	He *stares at the plays, yells at the pitcher in anger,* and *raises his fist.*

2. Appositives

An appositive (a noun) renames the noun it is placed immediately after. It also eliminates wordiness. It is especially useful on a literature essay when identifying characters.

Example:

Subject first:	The President of the Board of Education, *a frequent visitor to the schools,* is well known to all the students.
Appositive first:	*A frequent visitor to the schools,* the President of the Board of Education is well known to all the students.

3. Adverbs

An adverb may be placed at the beginning of a sentence. It adds variety to your writing by allowing the sentence to begin with something other than its subject.

Example:

Frequently, he praises the teacher and commends her teaching style.

4. Subordinate clauses

Using subordinate clauses creates complex sentences. Recall that a complex sentence shows the relationship between clauses and emphasizes one (the "independent" clause) over the other (the "subordinate" clause.) The independent clause can stand alone as a complete sentence; the subordinate clause cannot. There are four types of clauses, each with its own list of subordinate conjunctions.

An adverbial clause. The adverbial clause describes by telling how, where, why, when, or under what condition. It can be placed in many positions within the sentence, adding great variety to your writing. If such a clause is placed at the beginning of the sentence, it must be set off by a comma. Look for these words:

How	Where	When	Why	Under what condition
as if	where	while	because	if
as though	wherever	when	since	unless
		whenever	as	though
		as	so that	although
		before		
		after		
		since		
		until		

Examples:

While he stares at the television, he speaks to his sister.

He speaks to his sister *while he stares at the television.*

An adjective clause. The adjective clause describes a noun by telling which, what kind of, or how many. It cannot be moved within the sentence and is most often placed after the noun it describes. If it is surrounded by commas, it can be removed from the sentence. It is not set off by commas, it is essential to the sentence and cannot be removed. Look for these words:

which	what kind of	how many
who	what	which
whom	whatever	whichever
whomever		
whoever		
that		

Examples:

My grandfather, *who is a sports enthusiast*, watches ballgames every weekend. (Because it is surrounded by commas, the clause can be removed from the sentence.)

He gets a big bowl of popcorn *which he eats in front of the television*. (Because it is not surrounded by commas, this clause cannot be removed from the sentence.)

A noun clause. The noun clause may be used in the same ways that a noun can be used: as a subject, direct object, indirect object, predicate noun, or object of a preposition. Look for these words:

what	who	how	that
whatever	whoever	however	whether
whomever	where	why	whom
wherever			

Examples:

As the subject of the sentence: *What he does* every weekend seems ridiculous to me.

As the direct object: He really loves *what he does on the weekend.*

Elliptical clause. The elliptical clause is any of the three types discussed above with some of the unnecessary words omitted in order to eliminate wordiness.

Example:

While he stares at the plays, he yells at the television.

becomes

While staring at plays, he yells at the television.

Note how "he" and "the" have been removed, and "stares" is replaced by "staring." Be very careful not to remove necessary words and create a confusing sentence.

5. Prepositional phrases

A prepositional phrase contains a preposition + either a noun or a pronoun. It can function either as a adjective or an adverb. If it is functioning as an adjective, it cannot be moved and must be placed next to the noun it describes or after a linking verb. If it is functioning as an adverb, it may be placed in several different positions within the sentence.

Commonly Used Prepositions

about	besides	in spite of	since
above	between	in regard to	through
according to	beyond	inside	throughout
across	by	instead of	till
after	by way of	into	to
against	despite	like	toward
along	down	near	towards
around	during	of	under
at	except	off	until
because of	for	on	up
before	from	on account of	up to
behind	in	out	upon
below	in addition to	out of	with
beneath	in place of	outside	within
beside	in front of	over	without

Examples:

Adjective: A computer nut *like my father* spends all Sunday at the terminal.

Adverb: *During the winter*, he works far into the night.

6. Gerund and Infinitive Phrases

Gerunds and infinitives are verbs used as nouns. An infinitive is the "base" (unconjugated) form of a verb; it is always in the form of *to + the verb*. Gerunds always end in "-ing." Gerunds, which cannot serve as a sentence's main verb, are always used as nouns. Gerund or infinitive phrases begin with a gerund or infinitve. They function within a sentence in the same way as any of the five noun functions (as a subject, direct object, indirect object, predicate noun, or object of a preposition). Use such phrases sparingly, since they can create awkward and wordy sentences.

Examples:

Infinitive phrase as a subject: *To be a musician* is my friend's goal.

Infinitive phrase as a direct object: She wants *to practice the drums all day long.*

Gerund phrase as a subject: *Having us all listen* is an essential part of her practice.

Gerund phrase as a predicate noun: Her goal is *watching us all writhe in agony.*

7. Present and Past Participial Phrases

Present and past participles are verbs used as adjectives. A present participle is the -ing form, and a past participle is the -ed form. Present and past participial phrases begin with present or past participles. They function as any other adjective or adjective phrase. Sophisticated and concise, a participial phrase must be placed carefully next to the noun it describes. If it is not, the meaning of the sentence can be confused.

Examples:

Present participial phrases: *Staring at the screen,* he cheers the team.

Past participial phrase: *Surrounded by bowls of food,* he munches in front of the TV.

Notice how switching the order of the two phrases in the last example would confuse the meaning of the sentence. "He munches in front of the TV surrounded by big bowls of food" implies that the TV—not the man—is surrounded by food.

Remember that the "best" sentence is not the longest or the shortest, the simplest or most intricate. The most effective sentence is that which expresses your thought most clearly, concisely, and gracefully. This means that no one sentence style is better than another; complex sentences are not "better" than compound sentences, and so forth. Select the sentence style that best expresses what you have to say. The most effective writing styles are usually a mixture of different sentences, including simple, compound, and complex.

Practice Sentence Variety

Exercise 1: Rewrite the following paragraph to vary the sentences. You may combine sentences, reduce sentences to clauses, or rephrase as needed, but you must not change the meaning of the original paragraph.

Uncle Sam was my Aunt Helen's husband. Uncle Sam did nothing for a living. He appeared to have no past. He came from Blackheart, Indiana. This one fact was known about him. Nobody seemed to know anything else about him. A picture of Blackheart emerged for me. The picture was reconstructed from Uncle Sam's conversation. The reconstructed picture showed that Blackheart consisted mainly of ball parks, pool rooms, and hardware stores. Aunt Helen came from Medford. Medford consisted of shopping malls, movie theatres, and food stores. What could have brought my Uncle Sam and Aunt Helen together? The other members of our family spoke freely of their relations. Some of these relations were real. Some of these relations were imaginary. Uncle Sam spoke of no one. Uncle Sam did not even speak of a parent.

One possible revision (remember that there are many possible and equally correct ways to revise any essay to vary sentences and create interest):

Uncle Sam, my Aunt Helen's husband, did nothing for a living and appeared to have no past. We knew only that he came from Blackheart, Indiana, and from his conversations about his childhood home, I was able to reconstruct what it must have been like. A picture emerged of a small town consisting chiefly of ball parks, pool rooms, and hardware stores. Aunt Helen, in contrast, came from Medford, which was made up of shopping malls, movie theatres, and food stores. We all wondered what could have brought these two together. The family spoke of their past, discussing real and imaginary relations, but Uncle Sam spoke of no one, not even a parent.

Exercise 2: Shift the sentence elements in each of the following examples for greater sentence variety and better writing style. Then decide which version of each sentence is best suited to your subject, audience, and style.

1. A bowling team was formed this winter for the first time in the history of the school.
2. A mysterious figure stepped cautiously into the darkened room.
3. Sally, a voracious reader, keeps the librarian busy supplying her with books.
4. Candidates for a driver's license must take the written examination to prove their knowledge of traffic regulations.
5. The children, when their mothers are working, are cared for in nursery schools.
6. The audience, tired and hot, soon became impatient.
7. We were frightened by the explosion and dared not move from our places.
8. More than half the 90,000 acres under cultivation had not been ruined by the recent drought.
9. Accept the plan we have proposed if you have nothing better to offer.
10. There will never be a real compromise between such stubborn adversaries.
11. Sorters stand around the village store and chat with one another while waiting for the afternoon mail to be sorted.
12. A small boy, sobbing bitterly, ran toward me.

Possible Answers

Individual writing style, purpose, and audience will dictate which version of each revised sentence you select. Choose the sentence that is the most concise and graceful. This will generally be the one with the most succinct phrasing. Below are some suggested responses, although you may prefer the original sentences to the revised versions because they better reflect your personal writing style.

1. For the first time in the history of the school, a bowling team was formed this winter.
2. Cautiously, a mysterious figure stepped into the room.
3. A voracious reader, Sally keeps the librarian busy supplying her with books.
4. To prove their knowledge of traffic regulations, candidates for a driver's license must take the written examination.
5. When their mothers are working, the children are cared for in nursery schools.
6. Tired and hot, the audience soon became impatient.
7. Frightened by the explosion, we dared not move from our places.
8. The recent drought had not ruined more than half the 90,000 acres under cultivation.
9. If you have nothing better to offer, accept the plan we have proposed.
10. Between such stubborn adversaries there will never be any real compromise.
11. While waiting for the afternoon mail to be sorted, sorters stand around the village store and chat with one another.
12. Sobbing bitterly, a small boy ran toward me.

LOOSE AND PERIODIC SENTENCES

English sentences can be classified according to the form they take: simple, compound, complex. They can also be grouped according to style: loose and periodic.

In the loose sentence, the subject and predicate often come near the beginning of the sentence, and subordinate parts follow. The sentence is grammatically complete before its conclusion. For example:

Then, having reached the dingy, grimy, and rickety depot station, we would get out, walk rapidly across the tracks of the station yard where we could see great flares and steamings from the engines, and hear the crash and bump of freight cars shifting, the tolling of bells, and the sounds of great trains on the rails.

Grammatically and logically, the sentence above could have ended after the word "out." It could also end after "yard" and "engines."

Another kind of sentence, much less frequently used, is the periodic. Here, the writer withholds his meaning until the very end and the reader is held in suspense. The sentence cannot end early either grammatically or logically. Here is an example:

And to all those familiar sounds, filled with their exultant prophecies of flight, the voyage, morning, and the shining cities—to all the sharp and thrilling odors of trains—the smell of cinders, acrid smoke, and of musty, rusty freight cars, the clean pineboard of crated produce, and the smells of fresh stored food—oranges, coffee, tangerines, and bacon—there would be added now all the strange sights and smells of the coming circus.

It is impossible to end this sentence before the phrase at the end, for the full meaning is withheld until that point and the sentence would be a fragment without its final portion.

Practice Writing Loose and Periodic Sentences.

Exercise

1. If we wish to remain free, if we wish to maintain justice, if we hope to be esteemed throughout the world, we must be prepared to defend, whenever it is threatened, the liberty of each individual citizen.
2. With the trumpets blaring, the drums booming, and the children screaming their wild delight, the marchers passed in review.
3. We have done our best, although our dreams have now faded, our efforts have proved fruitless, and we have tasted the bitterness of defeat.

Possible Answers

1. This is a periodic sentence, as the meaning is at the end. A loose version would read as follows:
   We must be prepared to defend, whenever it is threatened, the liberty of each individual citizen, if we wish to remain free, if we wish to maintain justice, if we hope to be esteemed throughout the world.

2. This is also a periodic sentence, as the meaning is at the end. A loose version would read as follows:
   The marchers passed in review, with trumpets blaring, drums booming, and children screaming their wild delight.

3. This is a loose sentence, and a periodic version would be:
   Although our dreams have now faded, our efforts have proved fruitless, and we have tasted the bitterness of defeat, we have done our best.

SUPPLYING DETAILS

The most effective way to get your point across to your reader is through the use of detail: sharp, specific words selected to appeal to the senses and make the reader experience what you are describing. In a literary essay, the details are drawn from the work under discussion, and must be as specific as you can possibly make them. This means that quotes or paraphrases that directly make your point would be especially effective. In this way, your reader will understand your point while becoming convinced that you have read the book carefully.

The following passage from Thomas Wolfe's *Of Time and the River* illustrates effective use of detail. Read it and answer the questions that follow.

October is the richest of seasons. The fields are cut, the granaries are full, the bins are loaded to the brim with fatness and from the cider press the rich brown oozings of the York Imperials run. The bee bares to the belly of the yellow corn, the fly gets old and fat and blue, he buzzes loud, crawls slow, creeps heavily to death on a sill and ceiling, the sun goes down in blood and passion across the bronzed and mown fields of Old October.

Questions

1. What is the main impression here?
2. List the details that create the impression.
3. How is the paragraph organized?
4. Describe the sentences—variety, length, etc.
5. What letter or sound predominates?

Answers

1. The main impression is of fullness and richness as autumn closes.
2. There are a great many details to select: "rich brown oozings," "bronzed and mown fields," "bins loaded to the brim," etc.
3. The action of the poem moves from outside (the fields) to the inside (bins, cider press) back to the outside (sun goes down in blood). It can also be viewed as top to bottom: fields cut down, sun setting, standing for the closing of a season.
4. The sentences are very long and flowing, mainly compound and simple.
5. "M" and "O," suggesting richness and fullness, are the main letters.

Now do the same with this passage from Harper Lee's *To Kill a Mockingbird:*

Maycomb was an old town, but it was a tired old town when I first knew it. In rainy weather the streets turned to red slop, grass grew on the sidewalks, the courthouse sagged in the square. Somehow, it was hotter then: a black dog suffered on a summer's day; bony mules hitched to Hoover carts licked flies in the sweltering shade of the live oaks on the square. Men's stiff collars wilted by nine in the morning. Ladies bathed before noon, after their three o'clock naps, and by nightfall were like soft teacakes with the frosting of sweat and sweet talcum.

People moved slowly then. They ambled across the square, shuffled in and out of the stores around it, and took their time about everything. The day was twenty-four hours long but seemed longer.

Questions

1. What is the main impression here?
2. What details add to this impression?
3. What sound is used over and over?
4. Describe the sentences.

Answers

1. The main impression is heat and slowness.
2. The details include words such as "sagged," "wilted," and "ambled."
3. "S" is used to suggest heat and slowness.
4. The sentences are long, again suggesting exhaustion, and include all three types: simple, compound, and complex.

WORD CHOICE

Another important element of writing style is word choice. Saying exactly what you mean in a way that is fresh, clear, and correct can make your writing both interesting and effective. Following are some examples of poor word choice that can result in low scores on the AP exam:

Clichés

Clichés are phrases that have become stale and overused. They are to be avoided in your writing because they show a lack of imagination and an inability to convey exactly what you mean.

Clichés include such commonplace phrases as:

sweet as sugar	slow but sure	raining cats and dogs
tried and true	sick and tired	hard as nails

Wordiness

A tendency to ramble on or to bury your point in excess verbiage may cause readers to lose patience with your essay and to award you an unacceptably low score for your work. Get to your point quickly, with a lot of relevant detail but no unnecessary words.

Practice Eliminating Wordiness

Eliminate unnecessary words by striking out every unessential word in the sentences that follow:

Exercise

1. We watched the big, massive, black cloud rising up from the level prairie and covering over the sun.
2. Far away in the distance, as far as anything was visible to the eye, the small, diminutive shapes of the settlers' huts were outlined in silhouette against the dark sky.
3. Modern cars of today, unlike old cars of yesteryear, can be driven faster without danger than old ones.
4. When what the speaker was saying was not audible to our ears, I asked him to repeat again what he had said.
5. It was in this mountain vastness that the explorers found there the examples of the wildlife for which they had sought for.

Possible Answers

1. Eliminate: big, up, level, over
2. Eliminate: Far away, as far as anything was visible to the eye, small, in silhouette
3. Eliminate: of today, of yesteryear, than old ones
4. Eliminate: what, was saying, to our ears, again
5. Eliminate: It was, that, there the examples of, for which, had, for

Ambiguity

Ambiguity occurs when the reader is unsure of the meaning of your sentences. There are several different ways it can occur:

1. *Misplaced Modifiers.* When a phrase, clause, or word is placed too far from the word that it describes, the sentence fails to convey the exact meaning and may produce confusion or amusement.

Examples:

Misplaced phrase: Francis caught sight of the bus passing through the kitchen door.

Obviously the bus did not pass through the kitchen door. The phrase "through the kitchen door" modifies "caught sight of" and should be placed nearer to it, rather than next to "passing." The sentence should read: "Through the kitchen door, Francis caught sight of the bus passing."

Misplaced clause: They bought a cat for my brother that they call Spot.
    The clause "that they call Spot" describes "cat," not "brother." The sentence should read: "They bought a cat that they call Spot for my brother."

Misplaced word: To get to the pool we nearly traveled three miles.
    The word "nearly" describes "three." The sentence should read: "To get to the pool we traveled nearly three miles."

Practice Eliminating Misplaced Modifiers

Correct misplaced modifiers by revising the sentences that follow. Some of the sentences may be correct as given.

Exercise

1. We came upon a hospital rounding the corner.
2. The shrub was given to us by a relative that was supposed to flower in the spring.
3. The qualified doctor can only prescribe medicine.
4. Occurring in May, we were astonished by the event.
5. Reserve a room for the lady with a bath.

Possible Answers

1. Rounding the corner, we came upon a hospital.
2. The shrub that was supposed to flower in the spring was given to us by a relative.
3. Only a qualified doctor can prescribe medicine.
4. The event that occurred in May astonished us.
5. Reserve a room with a bath for the lady.

2. *Dangling Constructions.* When the noun or pronoun to which a phrase or clause refers is missing or in the wrong place, you have an unattached, or dangling, phrase or clause. (A *phrase* is two or more words having neither a subject nor a predicate. A *clause* is a group of words having both a subject and a predicate.) An example of a dangling construction that could result in ambiguity follows:

While driving along the highway, a fatal head-on collision was seen.

This is incorrect because it lacks a noun or pronoun—*who* saw the collision? The correct version would read: "While driving along the highway, *we* saw a fatal head-on collision."

Practice Eliminating Dangling Constructions

Correct dangling constructions by choosing the correct word or group of words for each of the sentences that follow on page 49.

Exercise

1. All the next week, (driving, while driving, as I drove) back and forth to school, the scene remained clear in my mind.
2. Though (we were troubled, troubled) by many worries, the results were better than we could have hoped.
3. The tomb of the Egyptian pharaoh commanded attention (as we came, coming) into the hall.
4. (Rushing, As she rushed) down the hall, her hat fell off.
5. (After failing, Since they had failed) the test, the teacher advised them to study more.

Answers

1. as I drove
2. we were troubled
3. as we came
4. As she rushed
5. Since they had failed

3. *Faulty Pronoun Reference.* When you are not sure what a pronoun is referring to, you have an ambiguous sentence. For example:

> Because my children had so many toys, I gave *them* to the local charity. (What was given away? The children or the toys?)

> Mr. Smith operated a wheat farm, and his daughter hopes to become *one.* (She hopes to become a farm?)

Frequently Misused Words or Word Pairs

There are a great many English words that are often confused. Here are just a few examples of words whose meaning every AP student should know.

Advise, Advice. *Advise* is a verb (people advise students); *advice* is a noun. (The teacher gave us good advice.)

Altogether, All Together. *Altogether* means "completely," while *all together* means "all at one time," as in "We repeat the motto all together at each meeting."

Effect, Affect. *Effect* is most often used as a noun meaning "result" as in "The effect of the war was felt for years afterward." *Affect* is most often used as a verb meaning "to influence," as in "Alcohol affects the brain."

Have, Of. *Have* is a verb; *of* is a preposition. Never write something like "He might *of* helped him."

Its, It's. *Its* is the possessive form, meaning "belonging to it." *It's* is a contraction for *it is.*

Lead, Led. *Lead* is a noun, a metal (as in "The pipe was made of lead."). *Led* is the past tense of the verb "to lead."

Loose, Lose. *Loose* is an adjective that means "free, unattached," while *lose* is a verb meaning "to part with unintentionally."

Passed, Past. *Passed* is the past tense of "to pass," a verb that means "to go by." *Past* has three possible uses:
   1) as an adjective meaning "having taken place at a prior time" as in "He was in charge at past meetings."
   2) as a noun meaning "time gone by" as in "Let the past go!"
   3) as a preposition meaning "beyond" as in "We missed the turn and drove past the train station."

Principle, Principal. *Principle* means "rule, or general truth," while *principal* means "main," as in "main teacher."

Respectfully, Respectively. *Respectfully* means "with proper respect," and *respectively* "in the order stated," as in "The yellow, purple, and orange boxes belong to Harry, Sam, and John, respectively."

Than, Then. *Than* is a conjunction used in comparisons; *then* means "at that time."

Their, They're, There.
   Their means "belonging to them," and shows ownership.
   They're is a contraction for "they are."
   There means "in that place."

Who's, Whose *Who's* is a contraction for "who is"; *whose* is a possessive, showing "belonging to whom."

Your, You're. *Your* means "belonging to you"; *you're* is a contraction for "you are."

Practice Using Word Pairs

Choose the correct word by completing each of the sentences that follow.

Exercise
   1. Did you see that bus as it (passed, past) the intersection?
   2. How will the new tax (affect, effect) your home?
   3. My American history teacher had a lot of time to make up for (past, passed) errors.
   4. On his doctor's (advice, advise), he returned to work.
   5. He is taller (then, than) his sister, (who's, whose) younger (than, then) he is.

Answers
   1. passed
   2. affect
   3. past
   4. advice
   5. than, who's, than.

Verbs Often Confused

Just as there are pairs of words that get confused and result in loss of credit on your AP essays, so there are verbs that are frequently misused. Study the following groups of verbs and make sure you know how to use them correctly.

Accept, Except *Accept* means "to receive"; *except,* "to leave out."

Affect, Effect *Affect* means "to influence"; *effect,* "to bring about."

Borrow, Lend *Borrow* means "to take with the intention of returning"; *lend,* "to give with the intention of getting back."

Bring, Take *Bring* means, "to carry toward the speaker"; *take,* "to carry away from the speaker."

To Lie means to "recline"
present: The cat lies (is lying).
future: The cat will lie.
past: The cat lay.
perfect: The cat has lain, will have lain.

To Lay means to "put" or "put down."
present: The player lays (is laying) his dice down.
future: The player will lay his dice down.
past: The player laid his dice down.
perfect: The player has laid, had laid, will have laid his dice down.

Precede, Proceed. *Precede* means "to go before in rank and time"; *proceed,* "to move forward, advance."

Practice Using Verbs Often Confused

Choose the correct word by completing each of the sentences that follow.

Exercise

1. I had (lain, laid) awake all night, worried about the exam.
2. (Bring, Take) this paper to the nurse.
3. Where did you (lie, lay) the book I was reading?
4. If anyone wants that book, tell him it (lays, lies) on the table.
5. At first people were not allowed to leave the ship, women and children (accepted, excepted).

Answers

1. lain
2. take
3. lay
4. lays
5. excepted

Incorrect Expressions

The following chart summarizes the most commonly misused expressions.

Incorrect	Correct
1. Don't *aggravate* me	Don't *annoy* me
2. Try *and* do better	Try *to* do better
3. The reason is *because*	The reason *is that*
4. *Being that*	*Since*
5. *This here* place	*This* place

Incorrect	Correct
6. Give me *them* books	Give me *those* books
7. *That there* dog	*That* dog
8. Different *than*	Different *from*
9. He (she, it) *don't*	He (she, it) *doesn't*
10. *Due to* sickness	*Because* of sickness
11. Five *foot* tall	Five *feet* tall
12. He (She) swims *good*	He (She) swims *well*
13. They *had ought* to	They *ought* to
14. My *mother, she says*	My *mother says*
15. *This here* rabbit	*This* rabbit
16. *In "Poe" it* tells about	*"Poe"* tells about
17. *Irregardless*	*Regardless*
18. Kind of *a*	*Kind of*
19. *Like* he told you	*As* he told you
20. *Me and my friend* went	*My friend and I* went
21. *Most* always	*Almost* always
22. *Off of*	*Off*
23. A *real* good dinner	A *really* good dinner

Agreement

The elements of a sentence must "match." This refers especially to subjects and verbs, or pronouns and antecedents (the word to which a pronoun refers). Here are a few rules to keep in mind:

1. A singular verb requires a singular subject. A plural verb requires a plural subject.
   EXAMPLE: Too many commas in a paragraph often (cause, causes) confusion.
   The correct answer is *cause,* for the plural subject requires a plural verb. Remember that a great many verbs in English that are singular end in *s.*

2. Subjects that are singular in meaning but plural in form (such as measles, news) require a singular verb.

3. Singular subjects connected by or, nor, either . . . or, neither . . . nor require a singular verb.
   EXAMPLE: Either the witness or the defendant (is, are) lying.
   The correct answer is *is,* for the subjects are connected by either . . . or.

4. A compound subject connected by *and* requires a plural verb.
   Exception to this rule: A compound subject that is considered as one unit is paired with a singular verb.
   EXAMPLE: The long and short of the matter (is, are) that we lost the race.
   The answer is *is* because "long and short" is considered as one unit.

5. If a subject is made up of two or more nouns or pronouns connected by *or* or *nor,* the verb agrees with the nearer noun or pronoun.
   EXAMPLE: Neither Mary nor my aunts (is, are) arriving for the winter.
   The answer is *are,* for *aunts* are plural.
   EXAMPLE: Either you or she (is, are) to blame.
   The answer is *is* to agree with the closer pronoun.

6. A pronoun agrees with its antecedent. The antecedent is the word to which the pronoun refers.

EXAMPLE: If anyone questions the safety of the journey, refer (him, them) to me.
The answer is *him* to agree with the singular pronoun *anyone*.
Common singular pronouns include:

anyone	everyone	someone
no one	one	each
either	neither	anybody
everybody	somebody	every (person, etc.)
many a (person, etc.)		

Practice Agreement

Choose the correct word by completing each of the following sentences.

Exercise

1. There, hiding in the tall reeds, (was, were) six bandits.
2. There (was, were) a dog and a mouse in the chair.
3. The books they read (shows, show) they are advanced students.
4. Each of the women (observes, observe) all the rules.
5. Everybody (was, were) asked to remain standing.

Answers

1. *were* to agree with the plural subjects *bandits*
2. *were* to agree with the compound subject connected by *and*
3. *show* to agree with the plural subject books
4. *observes* to agree with the singular pronoun *each*
5. *was* to agree with the singular pronoun *everybody*

Case

Pronouns can be confusing because they have different forms for different uses. The following chart reviews pronoun usage:

Pronouns as Subjects (Nominative Case)	**Pronouns as Objects** (Objective Case)	**Possessive** (Possessive Case)
I	me	my, mine
you	you	your, yours
he	him	his
she	her	her, hers
it	it	its
we	us	our, ours
they	them	their, theirs
who	whom	whose
whoever	whomever	whoever

Let's review the rules for correct pronoun usage:

1. A pronoun used as a subject is in the subject (nominative) case.
   EXAMPLES: (Who, Whom) do you believe is the most nervous?
   (*Who* is the subject of the verb *is.*)
   I believe no one is as nervous as (she, her).
   (*She* is the subject of the understood verb *is* (as *she is*).
   Exception: A pronoun used as the subject of an infinitve takes the objective case.
   EXAMPLE: My teacher expects John and (I, me) to pass.
   (*Me*, together with *John*, is the subject of the infinitive phrase *to pass.* The entire phrase *John and me to pass* is the object of *expects.*)
2. A pronoun used as a predicate nominative takes the subject (nominative) case. A noun or pronoun after any form of *to be* (is was, might have been, etc.) is called a predicate nominative.
   EXAMPLE: It was (we, us) students who studied the hardest. (Use *we* as the predicate nominative after the verb *was.*)
3. A pronoun used as the direct object of a verb, object of an infinitive, object of a preposition, or indirect object takes the objective case.
   EXAMPLES: (Who, Whom) will you send to study with us?
   (*Whom* is the direct obejct of the verb *will send.*) Between you and (I, me), there have never been any real problems.
   (*Me* is the object of the preposition *between.*)
4. A pronoun used in apposition with a noun is in the same case as that noun.
   EXAMPLE: Two students, Henry and (he, him), wrote exceptionally well.
   (The pronoun must be in the subject (nominative) case—*he*—because it is in apposition with the noun *students*, which is in the subject case.)
5. A pronoun that expresses ownership is in the possessive case. Remember that nouns that express ownership (mine, yours, his, hers, its, ours, theirs, etc.) never require an apostrophe. Don't confuse possessive pronouns with contractions.

Possessive Pronoun	Contraction
its	it's (it is)
your	you're (you are)
their	they're (they are)
whose	who's (who is)

NOTE: The word "its' " is not a correct form of either "its" or "it's." It has no meaning at all in English and, therefore, has no use.
EXAMPLE: He became an expert on the theater and (its, it's) greatest starts.
(*Its* is the correct spelling of the possessive case, which is needed here to express ownership. The word *it's* is a contraction, meaning "it is.")

Practice Case

Exercise

Write the correct choice in each sentence and state the reason for your answer.

1. He bought the cake for Debbie and (she, her).
2. Bill and (I, me) have been elected to the General Organization.
3. The heroes are (they, them).
4. (We, Us) girls want to study together.
5. Call for Elizabeth and (I, me) later today.
6. The principal is (she, her).
7. The leaders are Bob and (he, him).
8. My mother and (I, me) changed the tire.
9. He asked all of (us, we) boys for our opinion.
10. May I use (your's, yours)?

Answers

1. *her*, object of the preposition "for"
2. *I*, subject of the sentence
3. *they*, predicate nominative (note "are," a form of "to be")
4. *We*, subject of the sentence
5. *me*, object of the preposition "for"
6. *she*, predicate nominative ("is" as a form of "to be")
7. *he*, predicate nominative ("are" as a form of "to be")
8. *I*, subject of the sentence
9. *us*, object of the preposition
10. *yours*, correct possessive form

Parallel Structure

Parallel structure means that ideas of the same rank or significance are in the same grammatical form. A look at the following examples will illustrate this important element of writing style.

EXAMPLE: Mailing a letter a few days too early is better than (to run, running) the risk of its arriving late.
The verbal noun *running* is required to match or parallel the verbal noun *mailing*.

EXAMPLE: You should always eat foods that are nourishing and (tasty, taste good).
The predicate adjective *tasty* parallels the predicate adjective *nourishing*.

EXAMPLE: To do the job required is more difficult than (to plan, planning) heroic actions.
The infinitive *to plan* parallels the infinitive *to do*.

Practice Parallel Structure

Exercise

Complete each of the following sentences.

1. I expected her to be angry and (that she would scold, to scold) him.
2. The modern train has the advantages of strength and (being speedy, speed, moving quickly).
3. To complete a task at once is better than (to fret, fretting) about it.
4. He enjoys dancing, skating, and (to go swimming, going swimming, swimming).
5. He appeared tired and (a disappointed man, disappointed).

Answers

1. to scold
2. speed
3. to fret
4. swimming
5. disappointed

PUNCTUATION

Another essential ingredient of writing style is punctuation. The ability to use different forms of punctuations to express your ideas will give variety, coherence, and strength to your writing. Punctuation also provides a key to the logic of your argument; for example, when a reader sees a colon in your work, he/she knows that you intend to present a series of items or to explain more fully an idea that you have just stated. In the same way, readers know that sentences connected with a semicolon are closely related to each other.

It is assumed that every AP student knows how to use periods and question marks correctly. Here then are some of the less familiar rules of punctuation.

Use Commas . . .

1. To set off words of direct address (words that tell to whom a comment is addressed).
   EXAMPLE: Mr. Smith, that is the reason I was not in class.

2. To set off words in apposition (words that give additional information).
   EXAMPLE: A heavy sleeper, my mother is always the last to awake.

3. To set off a direct quotation.
   EXAMPLE: "Tomorrow I begin my new job," he said.

4. To set off a parenthetic (interrupting) expression.
   EXAMPLE: These prices, Lord help us, are the highest in town.

5. After interrupting words at the beginning of a sentence.
   EXAMPLE: Oh, I am glad to hear that.
   Interjections to be set off by a comma include: Yes, no, well, etc.

6. Before a conjunction (and, but, or, for) in a compound sentence, unless the compound sentence is very brief.
   EXAMPLE: Bill is not in the office today, but he will be here tomorrow.

7. After each item in a series, except, of course, the last.
   EXAMPLE: For dinner we had porkchops, applesauce, peas, and carrots.

8. To set of contrasting expressions.
   EXAMPLE: The boys, not the men, did most of the chores around the farm.

9. After an introductory prepositional phrase.
   EXAMPLE: Along the route from the bus terminal to the hotel, the major was treated to a brass band.

10. After an introductory subordinate clause.
    EXAMPLE: When I received an A in English, my parents were very surprised.

11. After an introductory participial phrase.
    EXAMPLE: Frightened by our approach, the badger fled.

12. To set off nonessential participial phrases.
    EXAMPLE: The child, weakened by loss of fluids, fell asleep.

13. After the opening of an informal letter.
    EXAMPLE: Dear Sue,

14. After the close of any letter.
    EXAMPLE: Sincerely,

NOTE: With closing quotation marks, the comma is always inside.

Use A Semicolon. . .

1. To divide items in a series when the items contain commas.
   EXAMPLE: The following directors were named: Charles Lawrence, president; Robert Aristedes, vice-president; Jennifer Fink, secretary.

2. Between main clauses that contain commas.
   EXAMPLE: Charles Smith, the hero, dotes on Mary Capone; and he eventually gives up his throne to save Harry Capone, Mary's husband.

3. Between main clauses when the conjunction (and, but, or for) has been left out.
   EXAMPLE: We have made several attempts to reach you by telephone; not a single call has been returned.

4. Between main clauses connected by however, moreover, nevertheless, for example, consequently etc.
   EXAMPLE: It was really a lovely car; consequently, she felt no urge to return it.

NOTE: With closing quotation marks, the semicolon is outside.

Use A Colon. . .

1. After the word "following" and any other word that indicates a list or series.
   EXAMPLE: We had the following for lunch: fruit, cheese, broiled chicken, mashed potatoes, green beans, salad, and dessert.

2. Before a quotation of greater than five lines.

3. Before part of a sentence that explains or gives an example of what has just been stated.
   EXAMPLE: We have a firm rule: We will not be undersold.

4. After the opening of a business letter.
   EXAMPLE: Dear Mr. Fuller:

NOTE: With closing quotation marks the colon is outside.

Use A Dash. . .

1. To show a sudden change in thought.
   EXAMPLE: We have a republican student council—of course, we are not allowed to set all the rules—that allows us a voice in governing the school.
   Avoid excessive use of the dash in a formal paper, as it makes for a breathless and casual tone.

2. Before a summary of what has just been stated.
   EXAMPLE: Staying on the football team, maintaining high grades, keeping my part-time job—everything depends on the use of the family car.

Use Parentheses. . .

1. To enclose additional information.
   EXAMPLE: The decline in profits in the past three years has been marked (see chart on page 49).

2. To enclose numbers or letters.
   EXAMPLE: A book owned by a public library is usually catalogued by (1) a title card, (2) an author card, (3) a subject card.

Use Brackets. . .

1. To enclose information that interrupts a direct quotation.
   EXAMPLE: She said, "I tutored Sam with his math [in fact, she saved him from failing] when he had Mr. Smith as a teacher."

Use Quotation Marks. . .

1. To set off titles of short works (essays, short stories, etc.).
2. To set off definitions.
3. To set off direct quotations.

Use Apostrophes. . .

1. To indicate ownership.
   To form the possessive of singular nouns and indefinite pronouns, add *'s*. Use only an apostrophe, without an *s*, when the noun already ends in *s*.
   EXAMPLES: "The Mon*k's* Tale" is one of Chauce*r's Canterbury Tales*.
   When he would arrive at Mar*y's* home was anyon*e's* guess.
   For goodnes*s'* sake, the bos*s'* son got fired!

   To form the possessive of a plural noun (those ending in *s* or *es*) add only the apostrophe.
   EXAMPLES: Two week*s'* sick leave and three month*s'* medical allowance are available to those who were laid off.
   The Lopeze*s'* children are always ready to add their two cent*s'* worth.

   Use an apostrophe with only the last noun in a compound word or to show joint possession.
   EXAMPLES: My brother-in-la*w's* book was left in Debbie and Barr*y's* apartment.
   The editor-in-chie*f's* responsibility ended on Tuesday.

2. Use an apostrophe to show that letters have been omitted in contractions or to show that numbers have been left out of dates.
   EXAMPLES: I should*n't* have, but it could*n't* have been avoided.
   The *'85* champions were better than the *'86* winners.

3. Use an apostrophe and add an *s* to form the plural of numbers, letters, or words used as words.
   EXAMPLES: When you write, make sure your *1's* and *7's* can be easily read.
   Too many ver*y's* can decrease the effectiveness of your speech.

Practice Punctuation

Exercise 1: Insert all necessary punctuation in each of the following sentences.

1. All the people who have not presented proper identification will be excluded from the train.
2. Yes I have been there
3. How often do you consider Mr Smith said how exciting it is to visit foreign lands
4. Huntington High is the only school that beat us last year but we fully expect to beat them in a rematch
5. At the start of the walk through the city everyone was in a good mood
6. For these reasons my fellow citizens I need your vote
7. The first moon walk was July 20 1972
8. Paul Parker the head of the debating team is in my science class
9. The results I am not at all pleased to say took us by surprise
10. Don't you agree that parents not small children should be held responsible

Exercise 2: Change each word and phrase in parentheses to its possessive form.

1. The (college library) holdings are extensive.
2. My (sister-in-law) car is new and shiny.
3. (Lerner and Loewe) play *My Fair Lady* was based on (George Bernard Shaw) play *Pygmalion.*
4. (Harold Robbins) and (Stephen King) novels are best sellers.

Answers—Exercise 1

1. No punctuation need be added.
2. Yes, I have been there.
3. "How often do you consider," Mr. Smith said, "how exciting it is to visit foreign lands?"
4. Huntington High is the only school that beat us last year, but we fully expect to beat them in a rematch.
5. At the start of the walk through the city, everyone was in a good mood.
6. For these reasons, my fellow citizens, I need your vote.
7. The first moon walk was July 20, 1972.
8. Paul Parker, the head of the debating team, is in my science class.
9. The results, I am not at all pleased to say, took us by surprise.
10. Don't you agree that parents, not small children, should be held responsible?

Answers—Exercise 2

1. college library's
2. sister-in-law's
3. Lerner and Loewe's, George Bernard Shaw's
4. Harold Robbins', Stephen King's

CAPITALIZATION

In the same way that careless mistakes with punctuation can lose you points—as well as confuse the points you are trying to make—so errors in capitalization can mar an otherwise fine essay. Review the rules that follow to make sure that your essays are as correct as possible.

1. Capitalize the opening word of a sentence and of a direct quotation. Do not capitalize the second half of a divided quotation, unless it begins a new sentence. EXAMPLE: "*If* you go three blocks south," the man explained, "*you* will see the library."

2. Capitalize the first word of a line of poetry, unless the poet did not do so.

3. Capitalize the salutation of a letter, as well as the noun or title in the salutation. EXAMPLE: Dear Pat, Dear Uncle Sam,

4. Capitalize only the opening word of the complimentary close of a letter. EXAMPLE: Very truly yours,

5. Capitalize the first word of each item in an outline.
   EXAMPLE: I. Driver training
           A. In the classroom
           B. Behind the wheel

6. Capitalize proper nouns and proper adjectives.
   EXAMPLES: Shakespeare, Shakespearean play
   Do not capitalize the second part of hyphenated numbers.
   EXAMPLE: Forty-second Street
   Do not capitalize north, south, east, west when used to indicate direction.
   Do not capitalize seasons.

7. Capitalize names of historical events, eras, documents, organizations, institutions, names of languages, nationalities, races, religions, references to the Supreme Being.

8. Capitalize titles before a person's name.
   EXAMPLE: Captain Smith
   Do not capitalize titles used alone, except for very high government officials.

9. Capitalize titles of parents and relatives not preceded by a possessive word (your, mine, etc.).
   EXAMPLE: I saw Father with Uncle Harry.
   Exception: If a name follows a title, capitalize the title, even when preceded by a possessive word.
   EXAMPLE: My Uncle George plays racketball.

10. Capitalize titles of books, plays, etc. but do not capitalize articles (a, an, the), conjunctions, or short prepositions in titles.
    EXAMPLE: *The Old Man and the Sea*

11. Capitalize titles of newspapers and magazines, but do not capitalize the word *the* before the title unless it begins the sentence.
    EXAMPLE: the *New York Times*.

12. Capitalize titles of courses.
    EXAMPLE: Psychology 101, Mathematics 212
    Do not capitalize school subjects, except languages.
    EXAMPLE: I am taking psychology, mathematics, history, and English.

13. Capitalize brand names, but not the product.

14. Capitalize the words *I* and *O,* but not *oh,* unless it begins the sentence.

15. Capitalize personifications.
    EXAMPLE: O Liberty! O Liberty!

Practice Capitalization

Exercise

Correct the capitalization in each of the following sentences.

1. go one mile South then turn East and you will come to the Empire state building.
2. He said that spring came late this year, but we were all looking forward to Summer, for we were to visit the pacific ocean and yellowstone national park.
3. "If you go to New england," the man said, "Be sure to visit the Doctor and my uncle George."

Answers

1. Go one mile south then turn east and you will come to the Empire State Building. (Capitalize the first word of a sentence; do not capitalize "south" and "east" when used to give directions; capitalize proper names such as the "Empire State Building.")
2. He said that spring came late this year, but we were all looking forward to summer, for we were to visit the Pacific Ocean and Yellowstone National Park. (Do not capitalize the seasons; capitalize proper names.)
3. "If you go to New England," the man said, "be sure to visit the doctor and my Uncle Sam." (Capitalize the names of geographic locations; do not capitalize the continuation of a quote; do not capitalize common nouns such as "doctor"; capitalize a title if it follows a name, even if it is preceded by a possessive word.)

Revising and Editing Your Essay

Revising involves revamping thesis statements and supporting details to more closely answer the question. It also includes adding additional examples and reworking existing material. *Editing* entails eliminating redundancy and correcting grammar, usage, spelling, and punctuation.

Ideally, you would have ample time to completely redraft your essay. But, this is rarely possible on the AP test. Most often, your first draft stands as your final draft, with perhaps some minor attention paid to surface errors. Even if you do have time to revise and edit, you might be unwilling to mark up your carefully written paper. You might decide to let a few errors slide by rather than turn in a sloppy-looking final copy.

It's *always* best to correct any errors and do whatever editing and revising you can. Consider writing on every other line and printing, especially if your handwriting is difficult to read. Make your correction marks clear and simple—avoid big X's. Cross out words with a single line and write the correction neatly. If you need to move blocks of copy, make sure your reader understands what you intend. Use the following proofreader's symbols to clarify your corrections:

delete (remove)

new paragraph

no new paragraph

insert a letter, word, sentence

insert a space

transpose a letter, word, sentence

close up

rewrite as a capital letter   *cap*

rewrite as a lower case letter   *lc*

Pace yourself carefully to ensure you will have time to correct the most damaging errors in composition and style. The following chart can help you plan your time most effectively:

If you have 20 minutes for your essay	revise for 3–5 minutes
If you have 25 minutes for your essay	revise for 5 minutes
If you have 30 minutes for your essay	revise for 5 minutes
If you have 40 minutes for your essay	revise for 5–7 minutes
If you have 45 minutes for your essay	revise for 7 minutes
If you have 60 minutes for your essay	revise for 7–10 minutes

Writing an Essay on Prose

The AP essay question takes many different forms. Following are descriptions of the kinds of essay questions you are likely to encounter on your exam.

SAMPLE QUESTIONS

1. Two works will be presented, perhaps two essays, two speeches, or two poems. You will be asked to read both selections and write an essay in which you explain what qualities in the first work make it superior to the second work. You will be expected to be conversant with the conventions of that genre. Thus, if the works are prose, you will be expected to discuss descriptive language, tone, and theme. If the selections are poems, you will discuss figurative language, tone, mood, irony, and various poetic devices. In either case, you will be expected to isolate *specific examples* from each work to construct your comparison/contrast essay.

2. Again, two selections of the same genre will be presented. You will be expected to isolate the *themes* of each and compare them. This may take the form of a question that reads: "Write an essay based on the works above in which you discuss how the author's conception (or description or portrait or portrayal, etc.) of the theme differs from one work to the other." You will be expected to select specific details from the works to support your conclusion. The themes may be the same or they may be radically different, or there may be subtle shades of difference in how each author's *tone* or mood colors the definition of the subject under discussion.

3. You will be asked to select a character from a work of recognized literary value and discuss one aspect of this character or the character in relation to the theme of the work under discussion. There may be a list of authors or works below the question, but you are usually free to select from any work of comparable excellence. Because you must choose a work that you are sure is valued by the literary community, you should stick to works that you have treated in class. You may be asked why the character is good and worthy of your admiration, or why the character is a villain and deserves the treatment he is accorded. In all cases, you will be expected to place the character in the novel and discuss his actions in relation to other characters in the work in order to prove your point. Thus, if you were trying to show that the King from Mark Twain's *The Adventures of Huckleberry Finn* was a villain, you would discuss how he sold Jim for "forty dirty dollars" into slavery, just when it appeared that Jim would be able to rejoin his family. You could also discuss his various "scams"—The Royal Nonesuch, the temperance revivals, the swindle of the Wilkes sisters.

4. You will be asked to read a prose selection and discuss how the author's *style* reveals the *theme* of the work. You will be expected to consider various elements of style such as tone, diction, figurative language, sentence length and variety, detail, and so forth. This means that you will have to take the passage "apart" and look at each section very carefully, then put it back together and reconsider the meaning.

5. There is occasionally an essay that is not based on literature. In this case, you may be asked to respond to a brief passage and show how you agree or disagree. You

may be presented with a definition of a certain item, place, or feeling and be asked to write your own version of a definition. If they give you a passage on "love," for instance, you will be expected to write your own definition of love, drawing from your own experience *specific examples* to support your claims. You may, of course, use literary examples if they fit and serve to back up your thesis.

6. The final portion of a play, a novel, an essay, or a narrative poem may be considered either very important or simply as a gathering up of the loose ends of the plot. You will be asked to evaluate the final portion of a work, discussing its importance to the rest of the work. Obviously, you will have to demonstrate a clear knowledge of the rest of the work and prove how the ending relates to the body as a whole. This will again call for specific examples, names, dates, and places to back up your thesis.

STUDENT RESPONSES WITH EVALUATIONS

Analyze the following examples of student essays and explain why each one does or does not fulfill the AP requirements. Use the questions below as guidelines for your evaluations.

1. Does the essay answer the question?
2. Are the examples specific and well-selected?
3. Is the writing clear? Does it reflect all the elements of writing style: grammar and usage, spelling and punctuation, parallel structure and placement of modifiers, word choice and sentence variety?
4. What specifically can be done to improve this essay? For example, rewrite sentences that are dull or incorrect, rearrange portions of the essay, and add specific examples where needed.

Questions for Essays A–E:

"Failure in human relationships results when one avoids the normal responsibilities of one's position in life." Show how this is true for any one character from any work of recognized literary value that you have read. Time—30 minutes.

Essay A

FAILURE IN HUMAN RELATIONSHIPS

People fail in their relationships when they avoid the responsibilities of their particular position in life. In *The Glass Menagerie*, Tom Wingfield, a young man frustrated by life and its difficulties, gives us a perfect example of this unfortunate situation.

Tom's expected responsibility is to support his mother and sister because his father deserted the family. In the thirties, when this story takes place, women had little chance of finding work outside the home. Amanda, the mother, had tried to obtain work selling magazine subscriptions over the telephone, and the little that she was able to make went to send her handicapped daughter to secretarial school. Tom had a job in a warehouse and did the best he could to sustain the family. The problem began when Amanda began to criticize everything Tom did, including his eating habits, his smoking, and his movie-going. Her constant carping created a great deal of friction between them, as he began to resent her and their relationship deteriorated. Amanda told Tom that he was responsible for the family until his sister Laura was married, but Tom wanted no part in finding his sister a suitable husband. He avoided fulfilling his responsibilities by deserting the family and joining the Merchant Marines.

While it is obvious that Amanda's nature did not help her relationship with her son, if Tom would have attempted to resolve their difficulties, perhaps things could have turned out differently. However, as a result of not providing for the family and fulfilling his expected responsibilities, Tom's relationship with his mother failed.

Analysis of Essay A

Introduction. The use of a title is good, for it helps the writer as well as the reader to focus on the topic. Note that the title is correct as written, since it is not underlined or set in quotes. Note also that the title is not ornate or overly clever; something that zeroes in on the topic is all that is necessary. Do not waste time fashioning a clever title. You are better off devoting that time to the essay itself.

The first sentence is well-written, a clear restatement of the thesis. While it could be made more interesting through the use of a quote or a brief anecdote from the work, it nonetheless gets to the point and alerts the reader to the topic.

The second sentence can be improved: The author's name is missing, and the description of Tom is too general. Be specific in describing the topic of your AP essay. In this instance, the writer should have mentioned Tom's desire for freedom versus the necessity of supporting his mother and sister.

The topic paragraph needs *at least* one more sentence to flesh it out. As a rule of thumb, the topic paragraph (or any paragraph, for that matter) needs at least three sentences to be complete. These include a topic sentence, a body sentence, and a clincher sentence, for a paragraph is an essay in miniature. Naturally, a body paragraph needs more than three sentences in order to provide specific examples of the points you wish to make. One possible solution for this topic paragraph is to move up the first sentence of paragraph 2 ("Tom's expected responsibility. . .") and write a new topic sentence for paragraph 2.

Body. If the first sentence is going to remain in the paragraph, it has to be more closely related to the sentence that follows. As it stands the style is choppy and weak.

The third sentence of paragraph 2 has a lot of good specific detail, but it could be improved by adding the name of the daughter, Laura, to parallel the inclusion of the name of the mother, Amanda.

Sentence 4 ("Tom had a job in a warehouse. . .") can be improved. Where did he work? How much did he make? Did he really do his best to support the family? A great deal more detail can be added here.

Sentence 5 ("The problem began. . .") is not totally correct. Actually, the problem began much earlier, when Tom's desire to be a poet was thwarted by the family's need. There is no doubt that Amanda's constant carping created a rift between them, but Tom already bitterly resented the lot he had been appointed in life. To suggest otherwise is to miss the nuances in the play.

The remainder of paragraph 2 is too vague and partially incorrect. It is not true that "Tom wanted no part in finding his sister a suitable husband," for Tom did indeed bring home his friend, Jim (ironically a young man Laura had long admired), as a possible suitor. Again, the writer overlooks the play's nuances.

Conclusion. The first sentence of paragraph 3 must be rewritten, for its meaning is not proven in the essay. The writer offers no proof that either of the characters could have healed the breach. The last sentence is fine.

This paper would receive a grade in the range of C+ to B−, a 3 on the Advanced Placement grading scale. The basic outline is good, but the essay lacks specific details and includes some inaccurate statements.

Essay B

In *The Glass Menagerie*, by Tennessee Williams, Tom Wingfield fails in human relationships by avoiding his normal responsibilities. After his father left the family to pursue his own pleasures, Tom, the son, was left to support the family, his mother, Amanda, and his sister, Laura, who lived together in a run-down tenement house. But he found himself unable to take his mother's constant criticism, and desperate to salve what remained of his future, Tom deserted the family to seek his own life.

When Tom's father, a telephone man in love with long distances, deserted the family, Tom had to abrogate his dream of becoming a poet and secure a job that offered immediate financial remuneration. He accepted sixty-five dollars a month as a worker in the Continental Shoemaker's Warehouse, a job he loathed. His nights were his only times of "freedom," when he could escape to the movies and enter a world of wonderful dreams. There was also a stage show, and the magician Malvolio would escape from a nailed-shut coffin. Obviously, this is a symbol for Tom's condition, nailed into a coffin by the circumstances of his life. But after awhile Tom realized that he could not escape forever into the dream world of the movies. As he told his friend Jim, "It's our turn now to go to the South Sea Island. . .I'm tired of movies and I am about to move!" When Jim asks him where he is going to move, he replies, "I'm starting to boil inside. Whenever I pick up a shoe, I shudder a little thinking how short life is and what I am doing." Rather than paying the light bill that month, Tom joined the Merchant Seamen Union, clearly announcing his intention to follow in his father's path and desert the family.

Tom fails in human relationships—especially his relationship with his mother, Amanda—when he fails to fulfill his normal responsibility of supporting the family. He feels that the family is stifling his ambition to be a poet, and that he has done enough to support them. He leaves to find his own destiny.

Analysis of Essay B

Introduction. This introduction is more fully expanded than the one that we first looked at, as each character is mentioned and relationships are briefly explained. Pay close attention to the thesis as it is stated: Tom found himself unable to withstand his mother's constant criticism, and so he left the family. Also change "salve" to either "save" or "salvage."

Body. The first sentence begins quite well, with the line "a telephone man in love with long distances" a most specific detail drawn directly from the play. The rest of the sentence, though, can be greatly improved by the removal of the "abrogate" and "remuneration." Both are used simply to impress the reader, and simpler words would be more effective in their places. Always choose the words best suited to the tone and style of your essay. Readers are impressed by the way you *use* the words you select.

The rest of the paragraph provides a wealth of specific detail, from the size of Tom's salary, to the name of the factory, to the description of the stage show. This shows that the writer knows the play well and can draw on very specific details to prove the point.

Conclusion. Here is where we become aware of the problem with this paper. Recall that in the introduction the writer carefully made the point that Tom found himself unable to withstand his mother's constant criticism and so he left to seek his own way. In the conclusion the writer states that the family is stifling Tom's ambition to be a poet. The problem is that the writer fails to prove either of these points in the essay. We get specific descriptions of how Tom feels nailed down and shut in, but we do not get any proof of the thesis stated in the introduction.

Thus, though this essay is far richer in detail than Essay A, it is actually a weaker paper, for the thesis is not proven. Essay B would receive a grade lower than a C, or a 2.5 on the AP scale.

Essay C

When one avoids the normal responsibilities of one's position in life, failure in human relationships will surely develop. This is true of Macbeth in William Shakespeare's play, *Macbeth*. In the beginning of the play, Macbeth is a loyal warrior to his king, Duncan, but as the play progresses he shuns his responsibilities and thus fails in human relationships.

As King Duncan's kinsman, Macbeth is one of the most trusted generals. His reputation was also achieved by his many loyal and brave acts during battle. Macbeth, already in possession of the title Thane of Glamis, is given the leadership of the armies in the war against the traitorous Thane of Cawdor. He upholds his reputation by fighting bravely for the king, and is rewarded by the good King with the title of the defeated Thane of Cawdor. This shows how Duncan is a fair and decent King, rewarding his men justly and generously for their bravery, and how Macbeth fights with distinction in the beginning of the play, fulfilling his normal responsibilities as a loyal thane. But all this changes right after the battle, when Macbeth encounters three witches.

Macbeth and his friend Banquo come upon three weird sisters as they journey home from battle. The witches tell Macbeth that he shall have a glorious future as Thane of Cawdor (he does not yet know he is to receive the title) and eventually King. Intrigued, Macbeth continues on his journey home to learn that he has indeed been given the title of the disloyal thane. This sparks his ambition and he first begins thinking about killing the King to hasten any chance he may have to become King himself. He tells his wife what has happened and she adds to his ambition, planning the ways to kill Duncan. They accomplish the heinous deed that night, stabbing the good and generous King and planting the daggers on his guards. It is at this point that he has deviated from his normal responsibilities as a loyal servant to his King, for killing one's king is one of the very worst deeds anyone could ever execute. From this point on, the play describes the destruction of all of Macbeth's relationships.

Anyone he viewed as a threat to his shaky power base was killed. He murders Banquo, for the witches had prophesized that Banquo's heirs would become king. He had intended to kill both Banquo and his son, Fleance, but Fleance escaped the murderers during the fray. He also murders Macduff's family in act IV, scene 2, for the loyal Macduff, another of Duncan's original soldiers, organized the rebellion against the now power-crazed Macbeth. The scene where Macbeth's soldiers murder Macduff's family—all the little "chickens"—shows us again how far Macbeth has moved away from his responsibility, how fully he has failed in human relationships.

Macbeth's denial of his normal responsibilities as a loyal soldier to the good King Duncan result in the destruction of all human relationships. By the end of the play he has become a murderous tyrant, devoid of all humanness.

Analysis of Essay C

Introduction. The introduction divides the answer into two parts: Macbeth's loyalty to the good King Duncan in the beginning of the play, and his later denial of his proper role as kinsman and thane. Check to make sure paragraph 2 discusses the first point; paragraph 3, the second.

The writing is adequate, but can be made more interesting by varying sentences or trying to catch the reader's attention with a quote or a brief anecdote.

Body. As mentioned above, the first part of the body should, if it is going to follow the outline suggested by the introduction, discuss Macbeth's fulfillment of his normal responsibilities in the beginning of the play. This it does, and very well, with a lot of specific details. The author discusses Macbeth's behavior during battle, and how the good King rewards him. This is crucial, for it must be shown that Macbeth is slaying a *good* king and thus committing a heinous deed. The setting aside of normal responsibilities would make no sense if Macbeth were killing an evil person—witness Macduff's actions in the end of the play. The final part of this paragraph is especially good, as the writer specifically says "This shows how. . ." These are key words and phrases that will help you keep your writing in focus, as you are forced by phrases such as "This proves. . .," "This illustrates," "This is an example of. . .," to keep on the topic.

Paragraph 3 is supposed to show that Macbeth fails in the execution of his normal responsibilities as a loyal thane and subject of the good king. Despite some syntax errors ("Macbeth and his friend Banquo come upon three weird sisters as they journey home from battle." Who is doing the traveling? The sentence is unclear as it stands.), the writer does a very good job of showing that in killing the king, Macbeth has violated the duties of any subject, much less a sworn supporter. The sentence "It is at this point that he has deviated from his normal responsibilities as a loyal servant to his king. . ." is especially good, for it ties up the rest of the paragraph and makes the point. The final sentence explains that the rest of the essay will show how all of Macbeth's relationships are destroyed.

The author does indeed prove the rest of his point, as he shows how Macbeth's relationships with Banquo, Fleance, and Macduff were destroyed when Macbeth set aside his normal and expected human responsibilities. The reference to "chickens"—recalling Macduff's impassioned speech upon hearing of the murder of his family—is good, for it is a moving and effective specific detail. The final sentence restates the topic and makes the point clear.

Conclusion. This is inadequate, recalling our discussion of a minimum of three sentences per paragraph. By recalling some of the specific details covered in the essay thus far, the author could easily expand upon the somewhat skimpy concluding paragraph.

This is a good essay, well organized and supported with specific detail. It would be in the A range, a 5 on the AP scale.

Essay D

Achilles, a character in Homer's *Iliad,* avoids his responsibilities and thus fails in human relationships. Achilles' duty was to lead the Achaeans into battle against the Trojans, but he let his personal feelings interfere with his duty as a soldier.

Achilles withdraws from the battlefield in anger, furious with Commander-in-Chief of the Achaean army, the greedy Agamemnon, who has threatened to take his mistress, Briseis, away from him. Achilles is maddened by Agamemnon's insolence, and despite his reverence for honor, retires from the battlefield. To placate Achilles' wounded pride, Agamemnon offers an apology, but Achilles will not accept it. Achilles' wounded pride and deep frustration with Agamemnon lead him to avoid his responsibility to the Achaean Army and lead to his failure in human relationships. He has an obligation to his fellow Achaeans, who greatly respect him and would honor him if he would return to battle. But he refuses to honor his responsibilities as a leader of men, and remains apart from his fellows.

One consequence of his withdrawal is the death of his dearest friend, Patroclus. Watching the enemy advance, standing on the sidelines, Achilles asks Patroclus to fight in his place, but Patroclus was not a warrior—he is Achilles' squire. Although he is inexperienced as a warrior, he feels it is his duty to honor Achilles' request. He goes to war in Achilles' armor and in the heat of battle is slain by Hector, a Trojan hero. This shows a failure on Achilles' part, for he had set aside his duty and forced another to take his place.

After Patroclus is killed, there is even greater fighting and vast destruction. There is an especially fierce battle around Patroclus' corpse, for the Trojans have taken it and the Achaeans are determined to recover it themselves. The Achaeans want Achilles to join in the Trojan War to recover Patroclus' corpse, which they hope will in some way alleviate Achilles' guilt for causing the death of his best friend. Hector instructs his Trojan allies to enter the conflict over the body, and the Trojans force back the Achaeans. Hippothus, a respected Achaean warrior, is slain. The ground runs red with blood.

Death and destruction follow Achilles' refusal to honor his responsibility to serve in battle. When he does finally join the battle, much destruction has already ensued, and his closest friend has been killed.

Analysis of Essay D

This response is a 5, an A, because it clearly proves the thesis that Achilles avoids responsibility and thus fails in human relationships. There is a good deal of clear, specific detail, and the style is mature and graceful. Note the variety of sentences, from the simple "Death and destruction follow Achilles' refusal to honor his responsibility to serve in battle" (5th paragraph) to two compound sentences in the first paragraph. Note how artfully the complex sentences have been crafted, with a variety of punctuation and stylistic devices. The writer has been especially successful in compressing a great deal of information into each sentence while retaining clarity and stylistic variation. We see this in the beginning of the second paragraph, where Agamemnon is both identified and characterized as the writer makes her point. The sentences exhibit an elegant agility as well. The dash in the second sentence of the third paragraph, for example, effectively shows a dramatic change in thought. The images are vivid, such as the startlingly effective, "The ground runs red with blood" in the fourth paragraph. It is also impressive to see how thoroughly the writer has studied and understood the work, keeping the characters and their relationships clear.

Essay E

When one abandons his normal responsibilities, failure in human relationships develops. Such is the case with Jason in Euripides' tragedy, *Medea*. Jason abandons his role as husband and father in order to marry a princess and raise his social status. In so doing, his relationship with his wife, Medea, is destroyed. In the ensuing carnage, he also loses his family and all that he held dear.

Jason's relationship with Medea, indeed his entire life, is destroyed when he neglects his normal responsibilities. Jason leaves his wife to marry the daughter of the King of Corinth, an action that will enable him to become King. He tells his wife that this will also benefit her, for it will enable their children to become royal. Although he attempts to rationalize his act, Medea believes that it is nothing other than abandonment, and her revenge leads to Jason's new wife's death. His abandonment of his normal responsibilities is at the root of this failure in human relationships.

As Jason neglects his responsibilities as a husband, he also sets aside his duties as a father. One of the main reasons he leaves Medea is to father more children, showing us that he seems to feel that families are replaceable. He soon learns otherwise, when Medea murders their children to spite him. Jason has lost his princess, his new family, his children by Medea. Because he leaves his children and neglects his paternal duties to them, Jason destroys his paternal relationships.

Jason's neglect of his responsibilities is all the more disturbing when one considers Medea's initial sacrifices. Herself once a princess in Colchis, Medea killed her own father to protect Jason in battle. She gives up her family and royal status to marry him. For Jason then to desert her, knowing all that she has done for him, makes his setting aside of human responsibilities all the more despicable.

Jason is a clear example of one who abandons his normal responsibilities and suffers for it. His relationship with his wife and children is destroyed. Because he places a higher social position above his family, he loses the most important relationship in his life. Euripedes' *Medea* shows Jason's mistake and the tragic price he must pay.

Analysis of Essay E

Again, this essay would receive a grade in the 5, or A range because it thoroughly proves the statement that rejecting one's responsibilities leads to failure in human relationships. Here, the writer shows through pertinent detail that Jason abandons his role as a husband and father to further his social ambition. In so doing, he destroys all that he once held dear, shattering relationships. As with Essay D, the writer's choice of words and images prove his point and provide sentence variety. Note how the level of syntax and diction combine to create a mature, effective style. Also notice how thoroughly the point is made, usually repeated at the end of each paragraph for emphasis and closure.

Question for Essay F and G

"A sharp insight can change a person's life for better or worse." Using any one recognized work of literary merit, show how this is true. Time—30 minutes.

Essay F

ONCE UPON A NIGHTMARE

In certain novels, there are characters who experience a sharp insight into the world around them which can alter their lives for better or worse. In Erich Maria Remarque's *All Quiet on the Western Front,* Paul Baumer is hurled into harsh surroundings and experiences just such an insight. Paul is a 19-year-old boy who enlists in the German Army during World War I and is immediately aware of the devastation war engenders. Paul's experiences lead him to realize many important things that will alter his life.

Paul's first insight occurred after a few months of feeling cold, hungry, and afraid. He began to wonder what he would do with his life should peace be declared that very day. He understands the fact that the education he has received in high school was trivial; it has left him unprepared for life. By being subjected to the nightmares associated with war, Paul suddenly realizes that he is too mature to re-enter school, and too old to become apprenticed in any skill. He characterizes himself, and others like him, as a lost generation. We can see from Paul's sudden realization that he is in a precarious position. He has missed all the fun and excitement associated with a normal high school life. He feels alienated and worried because the war has destroyed all his aspirations. Associated with this first sudden realization are several other moments of related awareness.

Paul experiences another insight when he returned home for 17 days. While on leave, he becomes aware of the fact that he no longer feels comfortable in his own home. He has an awkward feeling about himself; he is aware that it is he, not the home, that has changed drastically. The hastened maturity that he has undergone has caused him to drift away from his former way of life, and he has unwillingly become isolated from all that he was because of these changes.

There is another instance when he realizes a sudden change. He is temporarily stationed at a prison camp where he takes a long look at the other prisoners, Russians. He realizes that these men are really human beings just like his countrymen, his friends, and due to the decisions of their leaders, these people so like him have become enemies. Paul realizes that they could just as easily have become friends if the leaders had so decreed. This insight shows how confused Paul is, for he does not understand why he is fighting a war. He can see no difference between himself and the Russian prisoners, and is baffled that a simple word of command could set up barriers between people.

Paul Baumer has several sharp realizations during his experiences in World War I, all related to the changes he undergoes and the horrors that he witnesses. He was forced to mature too soon in order to cope with the blood, death, and constant bombardment. He feels lost, alienated from all that he once loved—friends, family, home. He has suddenly realized that he is a member of a confused, frightened, and wandering society, living out an unthinkable nightmare.

Analysis of Essay F

Introduction. The topic sentence is fine, a restatement of the thesis, but the rest of the paragraph can use improvement. The second sentence needs to be combined with the third, so that Paul is clearly identified. Also, the sentences could be better stated; this is an ideal place to work in sentence variety.

The most important problem with the opening, however, is the fact that the thesis is not answered. Was Paul's life changed for better or worse? What is it that he realizes? What is the *one* clear insight that he has that alters his life? Without this clear statement of purpose, the rest of the paper skirts around the issue, ending up showing a handful of insights, but not answering the question.

Body. The first sentence here again underscores the problem of the introduction: The question does not call for a "first insight"; rather, it asks that the author focus on *a* sharp insight. The next part of the body evinces the same problem, as does the final paragraph. Each of the several realizations is well proven, but unless they are all tied together into one, the thesis remains unproven.

Conclusion. The final sentence of the essay is what we have been looking for all along—as all the "little" things that Paul realizes come together into one sharp moment of awareness. The problem is that this is too slender a thread to tie an entire essay together; this must be stated at the end of each paragraph to fit the response to the question.

The paper would be in the low B range, a 3.5 on the AP scale.

Essay G

Sometimes a character in a story experiences a sharp insight which changes his life. This is true in *All Quiet on the Western Front,* by Erich Maria Remarque. In this novel, a young German soldier named Paul Baumer recounts the barbaric chaos he suffered through in the desperate days of the First World War.

Paul is not at all prepared for the hardships and extreme hatred of the enemy which is necessary for a soldier to possess in order to kill. After a few weeks on the battlefield, Paul realizes that his life as a child has come to an end, and he suddenly wishes that he could return to the simple life he had previously experienced. He expresses this as he says, "I am little more than a child; in my wardrobe still hangs short, boy's trousers—it is such a little time ago, why is it over?" Paul realizes suddenly that war has robbed him of his childhood.

After intentionally killing someone for the first time, the complete desolation of his situation comes forth as he whispers to the dead soldier, "I will fight against this war which has struck us both down; from you, taken life—and from me—? Life also. There is no hope of ever getting out of this." This sharp insight causes Paul to lose sight of his dreams of fame and glory, and he no longer wants to be involved in fighting and death. But he is compelled to continue—"We are insensible, dead men who through some trick, some dreadful magic, are still able to run and kill." Paul felt his life no longer had worth, and it is this last dreadful sharp insight which causes his death on a day "so quiet and still on the Western Front."

Paul Baumer experienced the sharp insight that war has robbed him of any hope for a normal life. He learns fear, despair, hoplessness, and finally death.

Analysis of Essay G

Introduction. This paper has the same fault as the one before; the thesis is not clearly answered. What is it that Paul realizes? How does this change his life?

Body. The first sentence is awkward, and despite the quote from the book, the point remains inconclusive. We are not convinced on the basis of the single quote that Paul has indeed been robbed of his childhood. More must be shown to clearly prove the thesis.

Again, it is a very good idea to use as many specific quotes and details as possible, but they have to be drawn to the thesis to be of any value. Here, we have the statement that "There is no hope of ever getting out of this," and are told that this is Paul's insight, yet a little further down we are told that he felt that his life no longer had worth. The question calls for a single insight, and these various ideas are not drawn together into a cohesive whole to make a single point. The final sentence is especially perplexing—how did the insight cause his death? What happened? Is it a real death or symbolic? All this must be shown through specific example, to make the point and receive maximum credit.

Conclusion. The conclusion, though far too short, provides a thesis that can be the basis of the paper—that war has robbed Paul of any hope for a normal life. If this were rephrased in the topic paragraph, the essay would far more easily prove the thesis.

The paper is in the low B, high C range, a 3 on the AP scale. Compare these two essays with Essays D and E on pages 70 and 71. Note especially how competently those writers proved the thesis.

Writing an Essay on Poetry

Following are some Advanced Placement questions on poetry. None are exact replicas of exam questions, but all are very much like what you will be asked. You will have the poem or poems in front of you as you answer the question. You will be expected to make close reference to the poems and quote specific lines and words to make your point clearly.

SAMPLE QUESTIONS

1. Often in poems the final lines resolve the situation presented in the rest of the work. This is especially true in Elizabethan (English) sonnets, where the final two lines, called the couplet, serve to sum up the situation and present the speaker's position. They have a different rhyme from the rest of the poem and are usually indented to set off their position more firmly. You will be asked to show how the final lines of a poem resolve the situation presented in the beginning. Thus, you will have to describe what happened in the beginning, what happens in the end, and how the two fit together. Time—15 minutes.

2. You will be required to strip a poem down to its basic elements and analyze how those elements work together to establish the theme, tone, or mood of the work. You will have to be aware of rhythm, rhyme, the speaker's attitude (not to confused with the poet's attitude; the speaker and the poet are not the same, as poets often assume masks to present their views), the elements of language, grammar, diction, etc. One of the most effective ways of discovering how all the elements interrelate is to rewrite the poem into a paragraph in your own words to help you make sure you understand what the speaker is saying. Then you can use this paragraph as a basis for your essay. You may also be asked to relate two poems to each other in this manner, and show how they are the same or different. Time—45–60 minutes.

3. Often poems, like prose works, present different views of people or events. You will be asked to break the poem down to its elements (to help you better understand it as well as demonstrate a knowledge of the parts of a poem) and then analyze how the different parts affect the theme or the tone. You can also be asked to show how the different parts relate to one another, how they fit together to produce a unified whole. You may also be asked to isolate one specific element, such as language or symbolism, and show how it operates within the whole. Time—45–60 minutes.

4. You may be asked to explain a poem's theme, its meaning, its "message." Why did the author write this poem? Was he/she trying to effect social change? Make a personal statement? Sway a specific group of people? Often, you will have to consider the elements of poetry in your analysis. These can include figurative language, metrical devices, etc. Time—30–45 minutes.

5. You may be required to analyze the tone or mood of a poem, or to compare the tones or moods of two different poems presented side by side. You will have to be aware of specific different tones, such as sarcastic, hopeful, depressed, etc. and how the elements of a poem contribute to the tone. See the sample responses to this question in the pages that follow. Time—45 minutes.

6. You may be required to "scan" a poem to determine its meter (the poetry section explains how to determine meter). Then, you may be asked how the meter and metrical devices relate to the theme and contribute to the total effect of the poem. Time—45 minutes.

7. You may be asked how any of the specific poetic elements, such as rhyme, figurative language, symbolism, etc. contribute to the author's desired end. Time—30 minutes.

8. You will be asked to trace and identify the poem's allusions, references to established works of literature, or well-known events or people outside the structure of the poem. Thus, you will have to be familiar with established works such as those of Shakespeare and Milton, works such as the Bible and ancient classical writings such as mythology. The best way to accomplish this is through wide reading of a variety of sources. You should also keep up with current events and be aware of well-known historical events and people. Time—45 minutes.

9. Read the poem below and then answer the questions that follow it. Time—30 minutes.

SONNET 10

Death, be not proud, though some have callèd thee
Mighty and dreadful, for thou art not so;
For those whom thou think'st thou dost overthrow
Die not, poor Death, nor yet canst thou kill me.
5 From rest and sleep, which but thy pictures be,
Much pleasure; then from thee much more must flow;
And soonest our best men with thee do go,
Rest of their bones and souls' delivery.
Thou'rt slave to fate, chance, kings, and desperate men,
10 And dost with poison, war, and sickness dwell;
And poppy or charms can make us sleep as well
And better than thy stroke. Why swell'st thou then?
One short sleep past, we wake eternally,
And Death shall be no more: Death, thou shalt die.
                                        —*John Donne*

1. Who is the speaker addressing? What is the speaker's attitude toward that which/who he is addressing? How does this affect the meaning of the poem?
2. What is the *form* of this poem? How is this specific form suited to the content of the poem? Specifically, how do the final two lines of the poem explain the theme and author's attitude?
3. According to the speaker, what different things affect the subject of the poem? What effect do these various things have on the poem's subject?
4. What do you think moved the poet to write this poem?

Suggested Responses

1. The speaker is addressing Death, which is personified as a living being. The speaker's attitude is defiant and bold, as he attack's Death's supposed invulnerability. The speaker's attitude reinforces the poem's meaning, that Death is not to be feared, for Death is but a brief passage to an eternal life.

2. The poem is a sonnet, as the title indicates. The final two lines indicate the sonnet's "turn," summing up the speaker's point, explained in #1.

3. The speaker charges that Death's supposed power is undercut (and finally destroyed) by the following realities: 1) We derive much pleasure from rest and sleep, which mirror Death; 2) Death is at the mercy of fate, chance, kings, desperate men; 3) Death lives with poison, war, and sickness; 4) Drugs ("poppy") and magic spells ("charms") induce sleep as well as Death; 5) Death is but a brief passage into eternal existence.

4. While answers will vary, mention that the author most likely lost a loved one or fears his own death.

10. Read the poem below and then answer the questions that follow it. Time—45 minutes.

DOVER BEACH

The sea is calm tonight.
The tide is full, the moon lies fair
Upon the straits;—on the French coast the light
Gleams and is gone; the cliffs of England stand,
5 Glimmering and vast, out in the tranquil bay.
Come to the window, sweet is the night-air!
Only, from the long line of spray
Where the sea meets the moon-blanched land,
Listen! you hear the grating roar
10 Of pebbles which the waves draw back, and fling,
At their return, up the high strand,
Begin, and cease, and then again begin,
With tremulous cadence slow, and bring
The eternal note of sadness in.

15 Sophocles long ago
Heard it on the Aegean, and it brought
Into his mind the turbid ebb and flow
Of human misery; we
Find also in the sound a thought,
20 Hearing it by this distant northern sea.

The Sea of Faith
Was once, too, at the full, and round earth's shore
Lay like the folds of a bright girdle furled.
But now I only hear
25 Its melancholy, long, withdrawing roar,
Retreating, to the breath
Of the night-wind, down the vast edges drear
And naked shingles of the world.

Ah, love, let us be true
30 To one another! for the world, which seems
To lie before us like a land of dreams,
So various, so beautiful, so new,
Hath really neither joy, nor love, nor light,
Nor certitude, nor peace, nor help for pain;
35 And we are here as on a darkling plain
Swept with confused alarms of struggle and flight,
Where ignorant armies clash by night.
—*Matthew Arnold*

1. Who is the speaker here? Who is he addressing?
2. What is the speaker's *mood*? Show what elements contribute to this mood.
3. Identify the elements of figurative language and show how they contribute to the tone and theme.
4. What is the *tone* of this poem? What details—specific words and events—contribute to the establishment of the tone?

5. What is the theme of this poem? What details contribute to this?
6. Which stanza sums up the meaning of the poem? How is this accomplished?
7. Write an essay in which you explain how the sights and sounds of the beach evoke a specific mood in the speaker. Identify the mood and show what elements contribute to its establishment.

Suggested Responses

1. The speaker is a man standing at a window. He is addressing the woman by his side.
2. The speaker is sad, melancholy. Note the sea's "eternal note of sadness" (line 14); "turbid ebb and flow/Of human misery" (17–18); and "It's melancholy, long. . ." (25).
3. Note especially the alliteration; internal as well as external rhyme; metaphors (ocean's sound compared to human misery, ocean's tides compared to ebb and flow of man's religious belief); similes ("Like the folds of a bright girdle furled"); and vivid imagery ("moon-blanched," "naked shingles of the world," "armies clash").
4. The tone is melancholy, almost bitter in the final stanza. See #2.
5. The theme is the need for human companionship to counter the world's bleakness and seeming hopelessness.
6. See the final stanza.
7. Answers will vary.

STUDENT RESPONSES WITH EVALUATIONS

Read the student essays on poetry that follow and explain why they do or do not fulfill the Advanced Placement requirements. Use the questions below as guidelines for your evaluations. Then read the critical analysis that follows each essay.

1. Does each essay answer the question? If there is more than one part to the question, are *all* parts answered?
2. Are there clear and specific examples drawn from the text itself to back up the points? Are the examples tied into the answer? In other words, does the writer use phrases like, "This shows that. . ." or "This proves that. . ." to make the point clearly?

3. Is the writing clear? Do the sentences flow smoothly? Are all portions of each paragraph and each essay logically connected? If there is a point made in the introduction, for example, is that point carried through the body to the conclusion?

4. Does the essay exhibit command of writing skill? Is it clear that the work has been proofread for careless errors? Does the work demonstrate knowledge of grammar and usage, spelling and punctuation, parallel structure, and placement of modifiers?

5. What about *style?* Is there variety in sentence structure? Are the words carefully selected for their specific nature and suitability to the essay?

Question for Essays A–C

Read the two poems that follow. Then, compare the *tone* of the first with the *tone* of the second. Show how they are the same and different. Use specific lines from each work to support your points. Time—45 minutes.

A MAN ADRIFT ON A SLIM SPAR

A man adrift on a slim spar
A horizon smaller than the rim of a bottle
Tented waves rearing lashy dark points
The near whine of froth in circles.
5   God is cold.

The incessant raise and swing of the sea
And growl after growl of crest
The sinkings, green, seething, endless
The upheaval half-completed.
10   God is cold.

The seas are in the hollow of The Hand;
Oceans may be turned to a spray
Raining down through the stars
Because of a gesture of pity toward a babe.
15 Oceans may become gray ashes,

Die with a long moan and a roar
Amid the tumult of the fishes
And the cries of the ships.
Because The Hand beckons the mice.

20 A horizon smaller than a doomed assassin's cap,
Inky, surging tumults
A reeling, drunken sky and no sky
A pale hand sliding from a polished spar.
      God is cold.

25 The puff of a coat imprisoning air:
A face kissing the water-death
A weary slow sway of a lost hand
And the sea, the moving sea, the sea.
      God is cold.
                    —Stephen Crane

ON HIS BLINDNESS

When I consider how my light is spent,
Ere half my days, in this dark world and wide,
And that one talent which is death to hide
Lodged with me useless, though my soul more bent
5 To serve therewith my Maker, and present
My true account, lest he returning chide,
"Doth God exact day labor, light denied?"
I fondly ask: but Patience, to prevent
That murmur, soon replies: "God doth not need
10 Either man's work or his own gifts; who best
Bear his mild yoke, they serve him best. His state
Is kingly: thousands at his bidding speed
And post o'er land and ocean without rest.
They also serve who only stand and wait."
                    —John Milton

Essay A

In "A Man Adrift on a Slim Spar," the author states "God is cold." The author feels that God does not care one way or the other if the man at sea lives or dies. The dying man is in a natural setting—the ocean. In this setting, the man is helpless and it is God, who created the ocean, who has the ability to rescue or take the life of the lost man. In line 26, "A face kissing the water-death," we realize that the man at sea will die. The author again states that "God is cold."

In John Milton's "On His Blindness," we read of a blind man who despite his handicap, asks God how he should serve Him. Patience replies in line 9, "God doth not need either man's work or his own gift's; who best bears his mild yoke, they serve him best." Here, the man seems to be deeply religious and devoted to serving God. God, appreciating the man's devotion despite his handicap, simply states those who bear what has been put upon them are serving God.

In the first poem, the speaker is angry with God. He resents that God allows a man to suffer at sea. In the second poem, however, the speaker is devoted to serving God and does not get angry at God because of the handicap of blindness, inflicted upon him by God. The second speaker has served God while the first has failed.

Evaluation of Essay A

The main problem with the student's treatment of "A Man Adrift on a Slim Spar" is that he does not address himself directly to the question of *tone;* rather, he provides a summary of the plot. While such summaries are necessary in many instances to establish the tone and answer the question, they cannot substitute for an answer that addresses itself to the question. The line "God is cold," repeated twice, does not explain the tone.

The problem persists into the second paragraph where the writer treats Milton's sonnet. Again, the question of tone is not resolved. While the writer correctly summarizes the plot, he does not answer the question.

As in paragraphs 1 and 2, the conclusion contrasts the plots of the two poems, but fails to explain the differences in tone.

This essay would receive a below-average grade, a D or a 1 on the AP scale, since it does not answer the question.

Essay B

"A Man Adrift on a Slim Spar" and "On His Blindness" have very different tones. The first poem depicts God as an unfeeling being who allows man to die needlessly. In this case, the man is drowning in the ocean. "The puff of a coat imprisoning air: A face kissing the water-death . . . God is cold." These lines show the poet's view that man is isolated and untouched by God. He is left alone on Earth in his fight for survival.

In contrast, "On His Blindness" views God as a power beyond question. Milton wonders why God has taken away his sight, robbing him of his ability to write. Patience's reply, "They also serve who stand and wait," signifies God's purpose that seemingly cruel and tragic things on earth have a meaning. Even though Milton has tragically lost his power to serve God, this writing ability, he is still serving God by keeping the faith.

In conclusion, "A Man Adrift on a Slim Spar" views God as unfeeling while Milton's "On His Blindness" sees God as caring. Both poems depict a tragic occurrence, a drowning and blindness. The difference between the two lies in the first poet's belief that God inflicts tragedy without a purpose while Milton views God's actions as purposeful. The difference in the two poems' tone lies in their view of God.

Evaluation of Essay B

This example, in sharp contrast to the one before it, addresses itself to the question of *tone* right from the start. The writer directly answers the question by telling us how the speaker feels about God. While there could be more examples more fully explained, the question is directly addressed.

There is a good transition—"in contrast"—between the first and second paragraphs. Here, however, the question of tone is not directly answered, even though it is alluded to in plot summary. Furthermore, the student should not assume that the speaker *is* the author. This may be true but it is still not an assumption we can safely make. This holds true for all literature.

The conclusion does serve to tie the essay together and answer the question, especially in the first line and the last one.

This is a better essay than Essay A, and would receive a grade in the B range, a 4 on the AP scale. Paragraph 2 needs to address itself more directly to the question, and more examples throughout the entire essay would be a significant improvement.

Essay C

The tone of the first poem, "A Man Adrift on a Slim Spar," differs markedly from the tone of the second, "On His Blindness." While each poet describes an omnipotent God, the first Supreme Being is cold and indifferent; the second, warm and compassionate.

On a literal level, the first poem describes a man vainly clinging to a slender scrap of wood in the middle of the fierce ocean. The poet carefully stacks the odds against the drowning man: the spar is "slim" (line 1), the "horizon smaller than the rim of a bottle" (line 2), the ocean endlessly "rearing lashy dark points" (line 3). God is all-powerful, the poet says, able to control the seas in the hollow of His hand, to make of them what He wishes. The ocean may be transformed into a gentle "spray/Raining down through the stars" because God feels compassion toward a child, or it may become a merciless storm that brings fishes and sailors alike to their brutal ruin—all at His whim. The man adrift in the ocean is doomed, his "pale hand sliding from a polished spar" as his face kisses "the water-death" and he sinks from sight. God is not actively against this man—or any man, for that matter—the poet says; rather, He is merely "cold," indifferent to the man's suffering and torment in the bitter cold ocean of life. The tone reflects this view of God, and so "A Man Adrift on a Slim Spar" is bitter and harsh. The second poem, however, is in a very different vein.

"On His Blindness" has a much more traditional view of God and His relationship to man, echoed in its more traditional form. A sonnet written with an abba/abba/cde/cde rhyme scheme, this poem depicts God as every bit as powerful as in the first example but a great deal more compassionate. The speaker begins by lamenting the loss of his vision, which renders his one talent, the ability to write, virtually useless. He is distraught because he desires above all else to serve God through his one talent, to be able to represent himself fully and glorify God through his prose and verse. God will not force him to perform tasks beyond his ability, he knows, such as compose verse in His honor without sight, but nevertheless he wishes to contribute to God's glorification. This is in marked contrast to the first poet's attitude, for he has no desire whatsoever to serve God in any capacity. God has allowed him but a slim spar and turned His back. The first speaker, then, never even discusses the notion of dedicating himself to God. In the Milton sonnet, on the other hand, God, in the form of Patience, reassures the speaker that those also serve who "stand and wait." God is King, the second poem states, and has thousands to actively carry out His bidding. The speaker need not worry that he has failed to properly honor his God.

The two situations are very different, as are the attitudes of the speakers. In the first, the speaker sees God as cold and indifferent and thus the tone emerges as bitter and harsh. In the second, the speaker sees God as compassionate and understanding, and thus the tone is gentle and reassuring.

Evaluation of Essay C

The introduction gets right to the point and answers the question clearly. While mentioning each poem by name so there will be no confusion, the writer specifically indicates what the *tone* is for each.

The plot summary provided in the second paragraph clearly contributes to answering the question, for it focuses on the theme. There is good sentence variety, especially in the varied use of punctuation. In the same way, the writer uses a great many carefully selected adjectives, such as "vainly," "slender" and "fierce," in the first sentence of the second paragraph alone. There are many clear examples drawn from the text, and each is used to make the point. From the line "God is not actively against this man. . ." to the end of the paragraph, the point is clearly stated and well supported by good specific examples.

The third paragraph on Milton's sonnet also addresses itself to the question. The two paragraphs are tied together with the last line of the second paragraph, lending unity to the whole. The first line of the third paragraph could perhaps be revised, for while the author justifies the inclusion of the rhyme scheme in the word "traditional," it is not germane to the discussion here. But the specific examples clearly state the tone, and the last portion of this paragraph makes a clear comparison between the two poems.

The conclusion sums up all that has been stated before and makes the point well.

This is a superior essay, well in the A range, a 5 on the AP scale. It makes the points carefully, with well-selected examples, and its style, with sentence variety and good word choice, contributes to the effectiveness of the answer.

Question for Essays D–H

Read the following poem and discuss the author's theme. 1) What is the *tone* of the first 12 lines of the poem? 2) What is the *tone* of the final two lines? 3) How are they different? 4) How is the form of the sonnet suited to this method of development? Time—30 minutes.

SONNET 130

My mistress' eyes are nothing like the sun;
Coral is far more red than her lips' red;
If snow be white, why then her breasts are dun;   3
If hairs be wires, black wires grow on her head.
I have seen roses damasked, red and white,
But no such roses see I in her cheeks;   6
And in some perfumes is there more delight
Than in the breath that from my mistress reeks.
I love to hear her speak; yet well I know   9
That music hath a far more pleasing sound:
I grant I never saw a goddess go;
My mistress, when she walks, treads on the ground. 12
   And yet, by heaven, I think my love as rare
   As any she belied with false compare.
                  —William Shakespeare

Essay D

In Sonnet 130, by William Shakespeare, two different tones are expressed. The first, which makes up the first 12 lines of the sonnet, is sarcastic and witty. The second, which concludes the work, is more serious.

In the first 12 lines of the poem, the speaker describes his mistress in a sarcastic manner. He creates a visual representation through such phrases as "My mistress' eyes are nothing like the sun" and "coral is far more red than her lips red." But these descriptions in no way indicate that he does not love her, as the second part of the poem reveals.

In the final two lines we see the speaker's true feelings for his mistress. Although this woman does not have any of the traditional attributes mentioned in the Elizabethan love sonnet, she has something that he obviously values more—something in her manner and personality which he finds attractive.

The tone changes from sarcastic to serious as the poem progresses, although his feelings for his mistress remain the same throughout. Love is not always based on physical attraction; it goes deeper, within the heart, mind, and soul.

Evaluation of Essay D

The topic paragraph gets right to the point and clearly states the *tones* involved here. What is missing is a clear evaluation of the *theme* and a mention of how the sonnet form is suited to the poet's purpose. All these elements must appear in the topic paragraph in order to answer the question completely.

The second paragraph begins to establish the writer's meaning, but a great deal more can be done with examples to make that meaning clear. The writer should take us, step by step, through the poem to show clearly how the tone is sarcastic. There is a good transition in the final line of the second paragraph, leading logically into paragraph 3.

Paragraph 3, like paragraph 2, needs more specific examples to make the author's point. Again, examples must be taken from the poem and fully explained to show how the tone changes. This must be tied in with theme in this specific instance to make the author's point.

The concluding lines do establish the tone of the work, but the author failed to prove his conclusion clearly in the body of the essay.

This essay would be in the low B to high C range, a 3 on the AP scale. Although the writer obviously understood the poem, he did not provide enough specific examples to thoroughly prove his point.

Essay E

The tone of the first 12 lines of Shakespeare's Sonnet 130 are very different in meaning from the couplet at the end of the poem. While both parts of this work are concerned with love, the first part is much more sarcastic and even degrading, whereas the second part is much more flattering and compassionate.

In lines 1–12, the speaker insults his mistress by saying such things as "her eyes are nothing like the sun" and "If hairs be wires, black wires grow on her head." In all the traditional comparisons, she falls short.

The final two lines are much more loving. The poet states that although his mistress may have her faults—chief among them being her appearance—he loves her. There is much more to love than surface appearance and the poet wants to make this clear. This is stated in the final two lines.

Evaluation of Essay E

This introduction appears to be better than the one before it, for the author clearly states the *tone* of the poem. The *theme* can be inferred from the line "both parts of the work are concerned with love," but the question of the role of the sonnet in the tone and theme is not addressed.

The rest of the essay is not well written, however, as the examples provided (and there are far too few) are in no way tied into the author's point. This must be done to answer the question. The essay needs two or three times the number of examples given to fully answer the question.

This essay would be in the D range, a 1 on the AP scale, as it lacks clear examples and fails to make the point.

Essay F

The surprisingly sarcastic tone of Shakespeare's Sonnet 130 illustrates his strong feelings toward comparing love to beautiful images in life. Shakespeare uses lines 1–12 of the sonnet to create a picture of his mistress, and the reader learns that she does not measure up to the ideal of Elizabethan beauty. The woman is depicted as homely, pale, and awkward, with a shrill voice and bad breath. Even though her attributes cannot be expressed as the traditional comparisons to the sun or roses, she does possess qualities that make the speaker love her. This is evident in the last two lines, when the tone shifts from sarcastic and humorous to serious. The speaker states that he does indeed love her, and this love need not be compared to anything to make it stronger. His love for his mistress is true and can stand on its own. The sonnet form is suitable for this change in tone for the body illustrates the speaker's distaste for silly comparisons and the last two lines reinforce his point in a serious manner.

Evaluation of Essay F

The first line leads us right into the question, and while the writer does not tie in all five parts of the original assignment, she does answer this portion partially. There should be some specific lines drawn from the poem to back up her assertions that the woman is "homely, pale, and awkward." She also shows some knowledge of the traditions of Elizabethan love verse, referring to the sun and roses as traditional metaphors in the 16th century. There is a good transition to the question of the tone in the final two lines, but again it would be better were she to allude to the specific lines and quote those parts more germane to her argument. The final comment on the sonnet form can be enlarged to make the point clearer.

This essay is in the B– range, a 3.5 on the AP scale.

Essay G

The author's theme in Sonnet 130 is that beauty is not the most important priority in a relationship. Although the woman in the poem doesn't measure up to the traditional symbols of beauty such as the sun, coral, and a rose, she does possess other qualities which make him think that their love is very rare indeed. The tone of the first 12 lines of the poem is sarcastic and somewhat teasing, but in the final two lines the sarcasm is dropped, replaced by the author's feeling of genuine love for his mistress. Their love is truer than any "she belied with false compare." There is nothing phony about her—she is not a rose or a goddess, or any of the stereotypical love symbols—and he loves her all the more. The form of the sonnet is ideal for conveying this message, as the last two lines, with their specific rhyme, allow the speaker to clearly establish his theme.

Evaluation of Essay G

The writer's conclusion that beauty is not the most important aspect of a relationship is partly true here, but Shakespeare is also saying that the relationship he has with his mistress is such that it is diminished through false comparison, a point that should be made in the first few sentences. If the writer is going to say that Shakespeare feels that the woman has other qualities more valuable than beauty, he must be able to document those qualities, through specific examples drawn from the poem. The question is answered in the line that begins "The tone of the first twelve lines. . .," but this is not backed up with specific examples from the text. The same is true throughout the rest of the paragraph, especially in the final line, where the "specific rhyme" alluded to is not explained with examples.

The question is not fully answered and there are not enough examples to make the point clearly. The paper is in the C– range, a 2 on the AP scale.

Essay H

The tone of the first 12 lines of Shakespeare's Sonnet 130 contrast sharply to the tone of the final two, and this difference establishes the theme of the entire work. The first twelve lines of the poem parody the form and content of the typical love verse, as the woman fails to measure up to any of the traditional emblems of love and devotion. Thus, her eyes, the time-honored windows of the soul, lack the clear radiance of the sun, and her lips, the deep, rosy tint of coral. Her skin is mottled and dark; her hair, coarse wires. The tone is playful and mocking, as Shakespeare inverts all the accepted tools of the love sonneteer's trade to construct a series of false analogies. The tone of the final two lines, however, differs sharply. Frequently the final two lines of an Elizabethan sonnet, called the couplet, serve to sum up the meaning of the preceeding 12 lines and establish the author's tone. Such is the case here, for the couplet's tone and meaning differ markedly from the rest of the poem. These two lines are serious, not light and playful, as the author declares his love for the lady he has just pilloried at the stake of false comparison. He wrote this poem, he says here, to parody her tendency to compare their love to objects and in so doing, establish false analogies. Their love is a rare and serious thing, he states, not to be diminished through "false compare." The sonnet is well suited to this difference in tone, as the couplet in the end allows the author the opportunity to sum up the first 12 lines and establish the theme. Here, he abjures the parody of the first 12 lines to firmly and seriously declares his love.

Evaluation of Essay H

This example clearly answers the question fully, with style and grace. The first line ties in all the possible threads, tone, and theme, as well as alluding to the question of sonnet form by mentioning the last two lines. The next sentence follows logically, and the ones after that provide clear examples of the speaker's point. Next, the writer moves to the final two lines, and displays a knowledge of the conventions of the Elizabethan sonnet. The writer then shows, through specific example, how the final two lines differ in tone from the first twelve, and finally shows how the sonnet form is well suited to the theme of the poem.

This is a well-written essay, with clear examples and good word choice and sentence variety. It fully answers the question and would be in the A range, a 5 on the AP scale.

SUGGESTED READING LIST

The following books discuss the writing process, grammar and usage, and general rules of composition. These books are intended to supplement—not replace—actual writing practice.

Baker, Sheridan. *The Practical Stylist*. 3rd edition. New York: Thomas Y. Crowell, 1969.

Brooks, Cleanth and Robert Penn Warren. *Modern Rhetoric*. 3rd ed. New York: Harcourt Brace Jovanovich, 1970.

Cohen, Benjamin. *Writing about Literature*. Glenville, IL: Scott, Foresman, 1973.

Follet, Wilson. *Modern American Usage*. ed. Jacques Barzun. New York: Warner Publishing Company, 1987.

Hodges, John C. and Mary E. Whitman. *Harbrace College Handbook*. New York: Harcourt Brace Jovanovich, 1987.

Kane, Thomas and Leonard Peters. *Writing Prose*. 3rd edition. New York: Oxford, 1969.

Kirzner, Laurie and Stephen Mandell. *The Holt Handbook*. New York: Holt, Rinehart and Winston, 1987.

McCrimmon, James. *Writing with a Purpose*. Boston: Houghton Mifflin, 1973.

Perrin, Robert. *The Beacon Handbook*. Boston: Houghton Mifflin Company, 1987.

Roberts, Edgar. *Writing Themes about Literature*. 3rd edition. New York: Prentice-Hall, 1973.

Strumpf, Michael and Auriel Douglas. *Painless, Perfect Grammar*. New York: Arco, 1985.

Strunk, E. and E.B. White. *The Elements of Style*. New York: Macmillan, 1972.

Warriner, John E. *Advanced Composition*. New York: Harcourt Brace Jovanovich, 1968.

Part 3

All About Prose

The Short Story

The actual definition of the short story has been subject to much discussion. It is impossible to distinguish a short story from a novel on any single basis other than length, and neither has a formally established length. As a general rule, the short story is narrative prose fiction shorter than a novel, usually not exceeding 15,000 words. It usually has fewer characters than a novel and a less involved plot—one main line of action rather than interwoven stories—but these rules are not hard and fast. Many works that cannot be classified are called "long stories" or "short novels" to illustrate the difficulty critics have had in pinning down this genre. One cannot say that a good short story has more unity than a novel, for frequently unity has no relation to the situation at all. A short story may deal with a briefer period of time, but again this may not always be the case. What happens most frequently is that a short story is, by nature of its length, less complex than a novel, and rather than tracing the development of a character, which is frequently the case with a novel, it focuses on a particular moment in that character's life and development. As Poe phrased it, the author of a short story strives to achieve a "single effect" in the pages allotted to him. While the short story has a rich and detailed history, it has frequently been eclipsed by its showier cousin, the novel.

BRIEF HISTORY OF THE SHORT STORY

The earliest known short stories date from the year 3000 B.C., Egyptian tales inscribed on papyrus and found entombed with other Egyptian effects.

The short story next appeared as an outgrowth of the oral tradition. The Anglo-Saxon epic *Beowulf,* ballads, and German folk tales, called *märchen* (the source of modern-day fairy tales) had their roots in the oral tradition, as did *The Iliad* and Hesiod's *Theogony,* a collection of Greek myths.

Other countries also contributed to the short story's rich legacy. From India came the *Jatakas,* the teachings of Buddha, around the year 500 B.C., and the *Panchatantra,* Hindu beast fables. In these fables, animals talked like human beings to make moral points. Aesop, the Greek slave who lived in the sixth century B.C., originated similar fables that were written down in the first and second century A.D. By the Middle Ages, animal fables, like "The Owl and the Nightingale" (1225), were popular.

The Bible contributed also. The Old Testament abounds in examples of short stories: the tales of Ruth, David and Goliath, and Esther are all cases in point. In the New Testament, Christ's parables serve the same literary function.

The Middle Ages saw the appearance of many short narrative forms. The *conte dévot,* in the twelfth and thirteenth centuries, were short religious tales recounting saints' miracles and intended for pious instruction. The *Miracles of Mary* were especially popular, as they glorified the chivalrous devotion to ideal womanhood, as represented by the Virgin Mary. The *fabliaux,* originated in France in the thirteenth century, were short humorous verses that exposed human weaknesses in a bawdy and entertaining manner. Chaucer's *Canterbury Tales,* especially one like "The Miller's Tale," are examples of this genre (1387–1395). The *lai,* a secular short verse tale of romance, which dates from the thirteenth and fourteenth centuries, is also in this mode. The *exemplum,* an illustrated moral tale used in sermons, was intended to instruct, rather than entertain. Chaucer's "Pardoner's Tale" would be an exemplum.

By the early 1500's, prose began to replace verse. The invention of printing stimulated silent reading, displacing the oral tradition. Jest books, with puns and jokes, became popular. *Hundred Mery Tales,* which dates from 1526, is a noteworthy example.

The *novella,* a short prose tale, appeared as early as the fourteenth century in Italy. Boccaccio's *Decameron* and William Painter's later *Palace of Pleasure* (1566) show this trend. Parodies and burlesques also became popular.

In Spain, the picaro, a rogue who engaged in a series of adventures in which he managed to triumph over folly and vice, appeared in tales called *picaresques.* Cervantes' *Don Quixote* (1605) and Le Sage's *Gil Blas* (1715) are picaresques.

Prose sketches appeared in newspapers and magazines in England, depicting brief and realistic stories about middle-class life. These stories were overshadowed by the development of drama during the Renaissance, but achieved real success early in the eighteenth century in such British magazines as *Tatler* and the *Spectator.*

The Arabian Nights, romantic tales, sometimes overlaid with morality, date back to the eighth century, but they were first published in French in 1704. It is with the growth of the mass market and the rise of the commercial magazine in the nineteenth century that the modern short story really begins.

Washington Irving (1783–1859) is regarded by many critics as the father of the modern short story. He saw the purpose of fiction as entertainment, not instruction, and entertain he did by combining American and European history and folklore, social observation and humor.

Lavish gift books appeared in America during this time, richly illustrated and beautifully packaged, but full of banal tales of unrequitted love, ghosts, devils, and mad queens. For example, *The Atlantic Souvenir* (1826–1832) was a popular gift from young men to young women in the nineteenth century, much as candy or flowers are today. In the early part of the nineteenth century, with a few notable exceptions, the quality of popular fiction was low. Poe and Hawthorne stand out as exceptional writers during this time.

Poe Defines the "Well-Made Tale"

Edgar Allan Poe, who lived from 1809 to 1848, clearly established the boundaries and guidelines for the short story and greatly elevated the standards for shorter fiction. In his famous review of Nathaniel Hawthorne's *Twice-Told Tales* (1842), Poe laid down the "rules" for what has come to be called the "well-made tale."

In a skillfully constructed tale, according to Poe, "[the author] has not fashioned his thought to accommodate his incidents; but having conceived, with deliberate care, a certain unique or *single effect* to be wrought out, he then invents such incidents—he then combines such events as may best aid him in establishing this preconceived effect. If his very initial sentence tends not to the outbringing of this effect, then he has failed in his first step. In the whole composition there should be no word written, of which the tendency, direct or indirect, is not to the pre-established design."

Poe's rules were rigid in other regards, too. He felt that for unity of effect the ideal short story should be read without pause. For this reason, he limited the length of the story to one to two hours' reading time. The *effect* that Poe sought to create was terror, passion, or horror—or "a multitude of other such effects."

In his *Philosophy of Composition,* published in 1846, Poe established that the aim of the short story was to include not only *truth,* the satisfaction of the intellect, but *passion,* the excitement of the heart.

While some have ridiculed his theories as rigid, they have had great effect on the development of the short story.

Hawthorne Introduces the Concept of Romance

Nathaniel Hawthorne, who lived from 1804 to 1864, changed the course of the short story by constructing tales that spoke to the human heart and conveyed truths that held for all times.

Hawthorne saw romance as vital to the development of the short story. To this end, he saw the writer's imagination as the starting point and the artist's highest achievement as the faithful reproduction of his own imagination and conception of the world. In "Roger Malvin's Burial," for example, Hawthorne suggests that the imagination changes the outer world by "casting certain circumstances in the shade."

In the preface to his *House of the Seven Gables*, Hawthorne explained his concept of romance:

> When a writer calls his work a Romance, it need hardly be observed that he wishes to claim a certain latitude, both as to its fashion and material, which he would not have felt himself entitled to assume, had he professed to be writing a Novel. The latter form of composition is presumed to aim at *a very minute fidelity,* not merely to the possible, but to the probable and ordinary course of man's experience. The former—while, as a work of art, it must rigidly subject itself to laws, and while it sins unpardonably, so far as it may swerve aside from the truth of the human heart—has fairly a right to present the truth under circumstances, to a great extent, of the *writer's own choosing or creation.* If he think fit, also, he may manage his atmospherical medium as to bring out or mellow the lights and deepen and enrich the shadows of the picture. He will be wise, no doubt, to make very moderate use of the privileges here stated, and, especially, *to mingle the Marvellous rather as a slight, delicate, and evanescent flavor,* than as any portion of the actual substance of the dish offered to the Public (italics mine).

Hawthorne, then, saw the writer of romance as allowed to take a certain latitude with reality, to add details and situations that would not appear in the novel, due to the latter's strict observance of "reality." This is not to say that he was advocating what we would today call a "science-fiction" story; rather, he said that the writer was allowed to take certain liberties to enrich his story, but he must never stray so far from the truth as to make his reader doubt the veracity of the tale. While sometimes ignored or, in the case of Poe, maligned by their contemporaries, Hawthorne and Poe, working independently, helped shape the course of the modern prose tale.

HOW TO EVALUATE A SHORT STORY

1. First, establish the *plot,* the sequence of events in the story. Are they all external, or do some take place in characters' minds? The sequence of events may not be chronological (the order of time). The author may have established a flashback or retrospect, a recounting of an earlier episode than the one that has just been presented. Or the story can open *in medias res*—the middle of the action—and later show how the plot arrived at that point. You will find it helpful to construct a brief outline or a timeline of events to establish the chronology.

2. Next, focus on the *narrator.* Who is he/she? From what point of view is he/she relating the events? Is it one of the following three first-person views:

First-Person Observer "I last met Smith in 1955."

First-Person Participant "I had just gotten my first job and was looking for an apartment."

Innocent Eye Told through a first-person narrator who is naive or unreliable, as when Faulkner has an idiot, Benjy Compson, narrate the first section of *The Sound and the Fury*. Although 33 years old, Benjy has the mind of a three-year-old, and thus the events are told from that point of view.

Or does he/she use a third-person narration?

Omniscient Records the thoughts of all the characters

Selective Omniscient Enters the minds of some characters to record their thoughts

Objective Omniscient Simply records what is plainly visible

Editorial Ominscient Records the characters' thoughts and also comments on them.

Can we trust the narrator or does he/she have an interest in the tale as a participant? Is he/she sane?

3. Then seek out the author's *theme* or main idea. Is the author's purpose simply to entertain or does he/she intend to comment on the human condition in some manner? What details and events contribute to the establishment of the theme?

4. If you have read other stories by the same author, determine how this one is similar, or different. Can you see a connection between this work and others by the same author?

5. Look for any *symbols*. Are there people or objects that stand for something greater than themselves? What do they represent and what was the author's purpose in creating them?

6. Examine the author's *point of view*. Is it evident from the story? Does the author have a specific attitude toward the events or characters he/she has created? Is the author involved or aloof? Does the author's attitude matter to this tale or is it irrelevant?

7. Determine whether you can discern a *time frame* for the story or whether the time is irrelevant to the tale. Does this story fit with others that were written in the same decade, say the 1920s or 1930s? Does it reflect the spirit of the times or does it transcend time to speak for all ages?

Use the techniques outlined to evaluate and analyze the three short stories that follow.

THE BLACK CAT

by Edgar Allan Poe

For the most wild yet most homely narrative which I am about to pen, I neither expect nor solicit belief. Mad indeed would I be to expect it, in a case where my very senses reject their own evidence. Yet, mad am I not—and very surely do I not dream. But tomorrow I die, and to-day I would unburden my soul. My immediate purpose is to place before the world, plainly, succinctly, and without comment, a series of mere household events. In their consequences, these events have terrified—have tortured—have destroyed me. Yet I will not attempt to expound them. To me, they have presented little but horror—to many they will seem less terrible than *baroques*. Hereafter, perhaps some intellect may be found which will reduce my phantasm to the commonplace—some intellect more calm, more logical, and far less excitable than my own, which will perceive, in the circumstances I detail with awe, nothing more than an ordinary succession of very natural causes and effects.

From my infancy I was noted for the docility and humanity of my disposition. My tenderness of heart was even so conspicuous as to make me the jest of my companions. I was especially fond of animals, and was indulged by my parents with a great variety of pets. With these I spent most of my time, and never was so happy as when feeding and caressing them. This peculiarity of character grew with my growth, and, in my manhood, I derived from it one of my principal sources of pleasure. To those who have cherished an affection for a faithful and sagacious dog, I need hardly to be at the trouble of explaining the nature or the intensity of the gratification thus derivable. There is something in the unselfish and self-sacrificing love of a brute, which goes directly to the heart of him who had had the frequent occasion to test the paltry friendship and gossamer fidelity of mere *Man*.

I married early, and was happy to find in my wife a disposition not uncongenial with my own. Observing my partiality for domestic pets, she lost no opportunity of procuring those of the most agreeable kind. We had birds, gold-fish, a fine dog, rabbits, a small monkey, and a *cat*.

This latter was a remarkably large and beautiful animal, entirely black, and sagacious to an astonishing degree. In speaking of his intelligence, my wife, who at heart was not a little tinctured with superstition, made frequent allusion to the ancient popular notion, which regarded all black cats as witches in disguise. Not that she was ever *serious* upon this point—and I mention the matter at all for no better reason than that it happens, just now, to be remembered.

Pluto—this was the cat's name—was my favorite pet and playmate. I alone fed him, and he attended me wherever I went about the house. It was even with difficulty that I could prevent him from following me through the streets.

Our friendship lasted, in this manner, for several years, during which my general temperament and character—through the instrumentality of the Fiend Intemperance—had (I blush to confess it) experienced a radical alteration for the worse. I grew, day by day, more moody, more irritable, more regardless of the feelings of others. I suffered myself to use intemperate language to my wife. At length, I even offered her personal violence. My pets, of course, were made to feel the change in my disposition. I not only neglected, but ill-used them. For Pluto, however, I still retained sufficient regard to restrain me from maltreating him, as I made no scruple of maltreating the rabbits, the monkey, or even the dog, when, by accident, or through affection, they came in my way. But my disease grew upon me—for what disease is like Alcohol!—and at length even Pluto, who was now becoming old, and

consequently somewhat peevish—even Pluto began to experience the effects of my ill temper.

One night, returning home, much intoxicated, from one of my haunts about town, I fancied that the cat avoided my presence. I seized him; when, in his fright at my violence, he inflicted a slight wound upon my hand with his teeth. The fury of a demon instantly possessed me. I knew myself no longer. My original soul seemed, at once, to take its flight from my body; and a more than fiendish malevolence, gin-nurtured, thrilled every fibre of my frame. I took from my waistcoat-pocket a penknife, opened it, grasped the poor beast by the throat, and deliberately cut one of its eyes from the socket! I blush, I burn, I shudder, while I pen the damnable atrocity.

When reason returned with the morning—when I had slept off the fumes of the night's debauch—I experienced a sentiment half of horror, half of remorse, for the crime of which I had been guilty; but it was, at best, a feeble and equivocal feeling, and the soul remained untouched. I again plunged into excess, and soon drowned in wine all memory of the deed.

In the meantime the cat slowly recovered. The socket of the lost eye presented, it is true, a frightful appearance, but he no longer appeared to suffer any pain. He went about the house as usual, but, as might be expected, fled in extreme terror at my approach. I had so much of my old heart left, as to be at first grieved by this evident dislike on the part of a creature which had once so loved me. But this feeling soon gave place to irritation. And then came, as if to my final and irrevocable overthrow the spirit of PERVERSENESS. Of this spirit philosophy takes no account. Yet I am not more sure that my soul lives, than I am that perverseness is one of the primitive impulses of the human heart—one of the indivisible primary faculties, or sentiments, which give direction to the character of Man. Who has not, a hundred times, found himself committing a vile or a stupid action, for no other reason than because he knows he should *not*? Have we not a perpetual inclination, in the teeth of our best judgment, to violate that which is *Law*, merely because we understand it to be such? This spirit of perverseness, I say, came to my final overthrow. It was this unfathomable longing of the soul *to vex itself*—to offer violence to its won nature—to do wrong for the wrong's sake only—that urged me to continue and finally to consummate the injury I had inflicted upon the unoffending brute. One morning, in cold blood, I slipped a noose about its neck with the tears streaming from my eyes, and with the bitterest remorse at my heart;—hung it *because* I knew that it had loved me, and *because* I felt it had given me no reason of offence;—hung it *because* I knew that in so doing I was committing a sin—a deadly sin that would so jeopardize my immortal soul as to place it—if such a thing were possible—even beyond the reach of the infinite mercy of the Most Merciful and Most Terrible God.

On the night of the day on which this most cruel deed was done, I was aroused from sleep by the cry of fire. The curtains of my bed were in flames. The whole house was blazing. It was with great difficulty that my wife, a servant, and myself, made our escape from the conflagration. The destruction was complete. My entire worldly wealth was swallowed up, and I resigned myself thenceforward to despair.

I am above the weakness of seeking to establish a sequence of cause and effect, between the disaster and the atrocity. But I am detailing a chain of facts—and wish not to leave even a possible link imperfect. On the day succeeding the fire, I visited the ruins. The walls, with one exception, had fallen in. This exception was found in a compartment wall, not very thick, which stood about the middle of the house, and against which had rested the head of my bed. The plastering had here, in great measure, resisted the action of the fire—a fact which I attributed to its having been recently spread. About this wall a dense crowd were collected, and many persons seemed to be examining a particular portion of it with very minute and eager attention. The words, "strange!" "singular!" and other similar expressions, excited my curiosity. I approached and saw, as if graven in *bas-relief* upon the white surface, the figure of a gigantic *cat*. The impression was given with an accuracy truly marvelous. There was a rope about the animal's neck.

When I first beheld this apparition—for I could scarcely regard it as less—my wonder and my terror were extreme. But at length reflection came to my aid. The cat, I remembered, had been hung in a garden adjacent to the house. Upon the alarm of fire, this garden had been immediately filled by the crowd—by some one of whom the animal must have been cut from the tree and thrown, through an open window, into my chamber. This had probably been done with the view of arousing me from sleep. The falling of other walls had compressed the victim of my cruelty into the substance of the freshly-spread plaster; the lime of which, with the flames, and *ammonia* from the carcass, had then accomplished the portraiture as I saw it.

Although I thus readily accounted to my reason, if not altogether to my conscience, for the startling fact just detailed, it did not the less fail to make a deep impression upon my fancy. For months I could not rid myself of the phantasm of the cat; and, during this period, there came back into my spirit a half-sentiment that seemed, but was not, remorse. I went so far as to regret the loss of the animal, and to look about me, among the vile haunts which I now habitually frequented, for another pet of the same species, and of somewhat similar appearance, with which to supply its place.

One night as I sat, half stupefied, in a den of more than infamy, my attention was suddenly drawn to some black object, reposing upon the head of one of the immense hogsheads of gin, or of rum, which constituted the chief furniture of the apartment. I had been looking steadily at the top of this hogshead for some minutes, and what now caused me surprise was the fact that I had not sooner perceived the object thereupon. I approached it, and touched it with my hand. It was a black cat—a very large one—fully as large as Pluto, and closely resembling him in every respect but one. Pluto had not a white hair upon any portion of his body; but his cat had a large, although indefinite splotch of white, covering nearly the whole region of the breast.

Upon my touching him, he immediately arose, purred loudly, rubbed against my hand, and appeared delighted with my notice. This, then, was the very creature of which I was in search. I at once offered to purchase it of the landlord; but this person made no claim to it—knew nothing of it—had never seen it before.

I continued my caresses, and when I prepared to go home, the animal evinced a disposition to accompany me. I permitted it to do so; occasionally stopping and patting it as I proceeded. When it reached the house it domesticated itself at once, and became immediately a great favorite of my wife.

For my own part, I soon found a dislike to it arising within me. This was just the reverse of what I had anticipated; but—I know not how or why it was—its evident fondness for myself rather disgusted and annoyed me. By slow degrees these feelings of disgust and annoyance rose into the bitterness of hatred. I avoided the creature; a certain sense of shame, and the remembrance of my former deed of cruelty, preventing me from physically abusing it. I did not, for some weeks, strike or otherwise violently ill use it; but gradually—very gradually—I came to look upon it with unutterable loathing, and to flee silently from its odious presence, as from the breath of a pestilence.

What added, no doubt, to my hatred of the beast, was the discovery, on the morning after I brought it home, that, like Pluto, it also had been deprived of one of its eyes. The circumstance, however, only endeared it to my wife, who, as I have already said, possessed, in a high degree, that humanity of feeling which had once been my distinguishing trait, and the source of many of my simplest and purest pleasures.

With my aversion to this cat, however, its partiality for myself seemed to increase. It followed my footsteps with a pertinacity which it would be difficult to make the reader comprehend. Whenever I sat, it would crouch beneath my chair, or spring upon my knees, covering me with its loathsome caresses. If I arose to walk it would get between my feet and thus nearly throw me down, or, fastening its long and sharp claws in my dress, clamber, in this manner, to my breast. At such times, although I longed to destroy it with a blow, I was yet withheld from so doing, partly by a memory of my former crime, but chiefly—let me confess it at once—by absolute *dread* of

This dread was not exactly a dread of physical evil—and yet I should be at a loss how otherwise to define it. I am almost ashamed to own—yes, even in this felon's cell, I am almost ashamed to own—that the terror and horror with which the animal inspired me, had been heightened by one of the merest chimeras it would be possible to conceive. My wife had called my attention, more than once, to the character of the mark of white hair, of which I have spoken, and which constituted the sole visible difference between the strange beast and the one I had destroyed. The reader will remember that his mark, although large, had been originally very indefinite; but, by slow degrees—degrees nearly imperceptible, and which for a long time my reason struggled to reject as fanciful—it had, at length, assumed a rigorous distinctness of outline. It was now the representation of an object that I shudder to name—and for this, above all, I loathed, and dreaded, and would have rid myself of the monster had I dared—it was now, I say, the image of a hideous—of a ghastly thing—of the GALLOWS!—oh, mournful and terrible engine of Horror and of Crime—of Agony and of Death!

And now was I indeed wretched beyond the wretchedness of mere Humanity. And *a brute beast*—whose fellow I had contemptuously destroyed—*a brute beast* to work out for *me*—for me, a man fashioned in the image of the High God—so much of insufferable woe! Alas! neither by day nor by night knew I the blessing of rest any more! During the former the creature left me no moment alone, and in the latter I started hourly from dreams of unutterable fear to find the hot breath of *the thing* upon my face, and its vast weight—an incarnate nightmare that I had no power to shake off—incumbent eternally upon my *heart*!

Beneath the pressure of torments such as these the feeble remnant of the good within me succumbed. Evil thoughts became my sole intimates—the darkest and most evil thoughts. The moodiness of my usual temper increased to hatred of all things and of all mankind; while from the sudden, frequent, and ungovernable outbursts of a fury to which I now blindly abandoned myself, my uncomplaining wife, alas, was the most usual and the most patient of sufferers.

One day she accompanied me, upon some household errand, into the cellar of the old building which our poverty compelled us to inhabit. The cat followed me down the steep stairs, and, nearly throwing me headlong, exasperated me to madness. Uplifting an axe, and forgetting in my wrath the childish dread which had hitherto stayed my hand, I aimed a blow at the animal, which, of course, would have proved instantly fatal had it descended as I wished. But this blow was arrested by the hand of my wife. Goaded by the interference into a rage more than demoniacal, I withdrew my arm from her grasp and buried the axe in her brain. She fell dead upon the spot without a groan.

This hideous murder accomplished, I set myself forthwith, and with entire deliberation, to the task of concealing the body. I knew that I could not remove it from the house, either by day or by night, without the risk of being observed by the neighbors. Many projects entered my mind. At one period I thought of cutting the corpse into minute fragments, and destroying them by fire. At another, I resolved to dig a grave for it in the floor of the cellar. Again, I deliberated about casting it in the well in the yard—about packing it in a box, as if merchandise, with the usual arrangements, and so getting a porter to take it from the house. Finally I hit upon what I considered a far better expedient than either of these. I determined to wall it up in the cellar, as the monks of the Middle Ages are recorded to have walled up their victims.

For a purpose such as this the cellar was well adapted. Its walls were loosely constructed, and had lately been plastered throughout with a rough plaster, which the dampness of the atmosphere had prevented from hardening. Moreover, in one of the walls was a projection, caused by a false chimney, or fireplace, that had been filled up and made to resemble the rest of the cellar. I made no doubt that I could readily displace the bricks at this point, insert the corpse, and wall the whole up as before, so that no eye could detect any thing suspicious.

And in this calculation I was not deceived. By means of a crowbar I easily dislodged the bricks, and, having carefully deposited the body against the inner wall, I propped it in that position, while with little trouble I relaid the whole structure as it originally stood. Having procured mortar, sand, and hair, with every possible precaution, I prepared a plaster which could not be distinguished from the old, and with this I very carefully went over the new brick-work. When I had finished, I felt satisfied that all was right. The wall did not present the slightest appearance of having been disturbed. The rubbish on the floor was picked up with the minutest care. I looked around triumphantly, and said to myself: "Here at least, then, my labor has not been in vain."

My next step was to look for the beast which had been the cause of so much wretchedness; for I had, at length, firmly resolved to put it to death. Had I been able to meet with it at the moment, there could have been no doubt of its fate; but it appeared that the crafty animal had been alarmed at the violence of my previous anger, and forbore to present itself in my present mood. It is impossible to describe or to imagine the deep, the blissful sense of relief which the absence of the detested creature occasioned in my bosom. It did not make its appearance during the night; and thus for one night, at least, since its introduction into the house, I soundly and tranquilly slept; aye, *slept* even with the burden of murder upon my soul.

The second and the third day passed, and still my tormentor came not. Once again I breathed as a freeman. The monster, in terror, had fled the premises for ever! I should behold it no more! My happiness was supreme! The guilt of my dark deed disturbed me but little. Some few inquiries had been made, but these had been readily answered. Even a search had been instituted—but of course nothing was to be discovered. I looked upon my future felicity as secured.

Upon the fourth day of the assassination, a party of the police came, very unexpectedly, into the house, and proceeded again to make rigorous investigation of the premises. Secure, however, in the inscrutability of my place of concealment, I felt no embarrassment whatever. The officers bade me accompany them in their search. They left no nook or corner unexplored. At length, for the third or fourth time, they descended to the cellar. I quivered not in a muscle. My heart beat calmly as that of one who slumbers in innocence. I walked the cellar from end to end. I folded my arms upon my bosom, and roamed easily to and fro. The police were thoroughly satisfied and prepared to depart. The glee at my heart was too strong to be restrained. I burned to say if but one word, by way of triumph, and to render doubly sure their assurance of my guiltlessness.

"Gentlemen," I said at last, as the party ascended the steps, "I delight to have allayed your suspicions. I wish you all health and a little more courtesy. By the bye, gentlemen, this—this is a very well-constructed house," (in the rabid desire to say something easily, I scarcely knew what I uttered at all),—"I may say an *excellently* well-constructed house. These walls—are you going, gentlemen?—these walls are solidly put together"; and here, through the mere frenzy of bravado, I rapped heavily with a cane which I held in my hand, upon that very portion of the brickwork behind which stood the corpse of the wife of my bosom.

But may God shield and deliver me from the fangs of the Arch-Fiend! No sooner had the reverberation of my blows sunk into silence, than I was answered by a voice from within the tomb!—by a cry, at first muffled and broken, like the sobbing of a child, and then quickly swelling into one long, loud, and continuous scream, utterly anomalous and inhuman—a howl—a wailing shriek, half of horror and half of triumph, such as might have arisen only out of hell, conjointly from the throats of the damned in their agony and of the demons that exult in the damnation.

Of my own thoughts it is folly to speak. Swooning, I staggered to the opposite wall. For one instant the party on the stairs remained motionless, through extremity of terror and awe. In the next a dozen stout arms were toiling at the wall. It fell bodily. The corpse, already greatly decayed and clotted with gore, stood erect before the eyes of the spectators. Upon its head, with red extended mouth and solitary eye of fire, sat the hideous beast whose craft had seduced me into murder, and whose informing voice had consigned me to the hangman. I had walled the monster up within the tomb.

Questions on "The Black Cat"

1. What is the sequence of events in this story? Are they external or internal?
2. Who is the narrator? What is the point of view used by the author?
3. Can we trust the narrator? Is he sane?
4. What is the author's purpose in writing this story?
5. If you have read any other stories by Poe, in what ways is this one similar or different?
6. What is the author's point of view here?
7. What is the "single effect" the author wishes to create in this tale? Isolate words from the first paragraph that contribute to that effect. Why did Poe use so many words in the first paragraph to build to an effect?
8. Where is the narrator in the first paragraph? Why? What will happen to him tomorrow?
9. Explain perverseness and discuss why the narrator feels these impulses.
10. Isolate and explain the purpose of the symbols used here.
11. What is the tone and mood of this tale?

Sample Essay Questions

1. How does "The Black Cat" illustrate Poe's theory of the "well-made tale"? Time—30 minutes.

2. Many twentieth-century short story writers, while acknowledging the importance of Poe's theories, have derided the "well-made tale" as artificial and contrived. Support or attack this point of view, using "The Black Cat" as proof. Time—45 minutes.

Answers to Questions on "The Black Cat"

1. The main character, driven mad by drink, has undergone a complete change of character. Previously docile and even-tempered, drink has transformed him into a madman who tortures animals and finally kills his wife. He is sentenced to die on the morrow. The events are internal, and we follow his thoughts in a flashback.
2. The narrator is not to be confused with the author—Poe did not kill anyone or torture small animals; even his highly-publicized drinking has been recently thought to be undiagnosed diabetes. The point of view is first-person participant.
3. The narrator is insane when under the influence of drink, but sane when he recounts the events here.
4. Using the conventional nineteenth-century notions of the effects of drink—it was widely believed that excessive drinking would drive men mad—Poe is entertaining us for a few hours. This is not a temperance tract.
5. Poe wrote three main "types" of stories: horror, detective, and "arabesques and grotesques," which were tales of weird and fantastic events. This story follows the pattern of his horror tales.
6. He is not entering into the morality of the character's action, for this is a tale to entice you through horror and entertain you for a few hours.
7. The effect is horror and terror, and words such as "wild," "terrified," "torture," and "horror" contribute to it. Poe felt that it was vital to establish the effect in the very first paragraph, and all words he used had to contribute to the effect.
8. The narrator is in jail for the murder of his wife, and he will be killed tomorrow.
9. Perverseness is the desire or the compulsion to do that which you know is wrong and destructive. The narrator acts this way because of drink.
10. Gallows, the bas-relief of the cat, the murder of the wife, all contribute to the horror.
11. The tone/mood is one of horror and terror.

Suggestions for Essay Answers

1. The "well-made tale" has a clear beginning, middle, and end. Discuss the divisions within this tale, showing how each is clearly defined. Then, consider the "single effect" he so highly prized—"terror, passion, or horror." This story is rich in terror and horror, and a good focal point would be the scene where the narrator sinks the ax into his wife's skull and then buries her in the wall. The mutilation of the cat, carving out its eyeball, would also establish this point. Finally, you could discuss how the topic paragraph immediately establishes the "single effect" and isolate the words and phrases that do so.
2. Your answer here will depend on your point of view concerning the "well-made tale."

If you like it . . .	If you dislike it . . .
Single effect of horror entertaining Story can easily be read within one sitting Unified, with beginning, middle, end; you know what's happening to each of the characters and can follow the plot	Single effect of horror is dull, need additional themes. You prefer longer less compressed tales. Predictable, with beginning, middle, and end; you prefer "slice of life" tales *you* have have to piece together to fully understand.

Let's examine a tale from Nathaniel Hawthorne in the same manner. Use specific details drawn from the tale to support your point of view.

THE BIRTHMARK

by Nathaniel Hawthorne

In the latter part of the last century there lived a man of science, an eminent proficient in every branch of natural philosophy, who not long before our story opens had made experience of a spiritual affinity more attractive than any chemical one. He had left his laboratory to the care of an assistant, cleared his fine countenance from the furnace smoke, washed the stain of acids from his fingers, and persuaded a beautiful woman to become his wife. In those days when the comparatively recent discovery of electricity and other kindred mysteries of Nature seemed to open paths into the region of miracle, it was not unusual for the love of science to rival the love of woman in its depth and absorbing energy. The higher intellect, the imagination, the spirit, and even the heart might all find their congenial aliment in pursuits which, as some of their ardent votaries believed, would ascend from one step of powerful intelligence to another, until the philosopher should lay his hand on the secret of creative force and perhaps make new worlds for himself. We know not whether Aylmer possessed this degree of faith in man's ultimate control over Nature. He had devoted himself, however, too unreservedly to scientific studies ever to be weaned from them by any second passion. His love for his young wife might prove the stronger of the two; but it could only be by interwining itself with his love of science, and uniting the strength of the latter to his own.

Such a union accordingly took place, and was attended with truly remarkable consequences and a deeply impressive moral. One day, very soon after their marriage, Aylmer sat gazing at his wife with a trouble in his countenance that grew stronger until he spoke.

"Georgiana," said he, "has it never occurred to you that the mark upon your cheek might be removed?"

"No, indeed," said she, smiling; but perceiving the seriousness of his manner, she blushed deeply. "To tell you the truth it has been so often called a charm that I was simple enough to imagine it might be so."

"Ah, upon another face perhaps it might," replied her husband; "but never on yours. No, dearest Georgiana, you came so nearly perfect from the hand of Nature that this slightest possible defect, which we hesitate whether to term a defect or a beauty, shocks me, as being the visible mark of earthly imperfection."

"Shocks you, my husband!" cried Georgiana, deeply hurt; at first reddening with momentary anger, but then bursting into tears. "Then why did you take me from my mother's side? You cannot love what shocks you!"

To explain this conversation it must be mentioned that in the center of Georgiana's left cheek there was a singular mark, deeply interwoven, as it were, with the texture and substance of her face. In the usual state of her complexion—a healthy though delicate bloom—the mark wore a tint of deeper crimson, which imperfectly defined its shape amid the surrounding rosiness. When she blushed it gradually became more indistinct, and finally vanished amid the triumphant rush of blood that bathed the whole cheek with its brilliant glow. But if any shifting motion caused her to turn pale there was the mark again, a crimson stain upon the snow, in what Aylmer sometimes deemed an almost fearful distinctness. Its shape bore not a little similarity to the human hand, though of the smallest pygmy size. Georgiana's lovers were wont to say that some fairy at her birth hour had laid her tiny hand upon the infant's cheek, and left this impress there in token of the magic endowments that were to give her such sway over all hearts. Many a desperate swain would have risked life for the privilege of pressing his lips to the mysterious hand. It must not be concealed, however, that the impression wrought by this fairy sign manual varied exceedingly, according to the difference of temperament in the beholders. Some fastidious persons—but they were exclusively of her own sex—affirmed that the bloody hand, as they chose to call it, quite destroyed the effect of Georgiana's beauty, and rendered her countenance even hideous. But it would be as reasonable to say that one of those small blue stains which sometimes occur in the purest statuary marble would convert the Eve of Powers to a monster. Masculine observers, if the birthmark did not heighten their admiration, contented themselves with wishing it away, that the world might possess one living specimen of ideal loveliness without the semblance of a flaw. After his marriage,—for he thought little or nothing of the matter before,—Aylmer discovered that this was the case with himself.

Had she been less beautiful,—if Envy's self could have found aught else to sneer at,—he might have felt his affection heightened by the prettiness of this mimic hand, now vaguely portrayed, now lost, now stealing forth again and glimmering to and fro with every pulse of emotion that throbbed within her heart; but seeing her otherwise so perfect, he found this one defect grow more and more intolerable with every moment of their united lives. It was the fatal flaw of humanity which Nature, in one shape or another, stamps ineffaceably on all her productions, either to imply that they are temporary and finite, or that their perfection must be wrought by toil and pain. The crimson hand expressed the ineludible grip in which mortality clutches the highest and purest of earthly mould, degrading them into kindred with the lowest, and even with the very brutes, like whom their visible frames return to dust. In this manner, selecting it as the symbol of his wife's liability to sin, sorrow, decay, and death, Aylmer's sombre imagination was not long in rendering the birthmark a frightful object, causing him more trouble and horror than ever Georgiana's beauty, whether of soul or sense, had given him delight.

At all the seasons which should have been their happiest, he invariably and without intending it, nay, in spite of a purpose to the contrary, reverted to this one disastrous topic. Trifling as it at first appeared, it so connected itself with innumerable trains of thought and models of feeling that it became the central point of all. With the morning twilight Aylmer opened his eyes upon his wife's face and recognized the symbol of imperfection; and when they sat together at the evening hearth his eyes wandered stealthily to her cheek, and beheld, flickering with the blaze of the wood fire, the spectral hand that wrote mortality where he would fain have worshipped. Georgiana soon learned to shudder at his gaze. It needed but a glance with the peculiar expression that his face often wore to change the roses of her cheek into a deathlike paleness, amid which the crimson hand was brought strongly out, like a bas-relief of ruby on the whitest marble.

Late one night when the lights were growing dim, so as hardly to betray the stain on the poor wife's cheek, she herself, for the first time, voluntarily took up the subject.

"Do you remember, my dear Aylmer," said she, with a feeble attempt at a smile, "have you any recollection of a dream last night about this odious hand?"

"None! none whatever!" replied Aylmer, starting; but then he added, in a dry, cold tone, affected for the sake of concealing the real depth of his emotion, "I might well dream of it; for before I fell asleep it had taken a pretty firm hold of my fancy."

"And did you dream of it?" continued Georgiana, hastily; for she dreaded lest a gush of tears should interrupt what she had to say. "A terrible dream! I should wonder that you can forget it. Is it possible to forget this one expression?—'It is in her heart now; we must have it out!' Reflect, my husband; for by all means I would have you recall that dream."

The mind is in a sad state when Sleep, the all-involving, cannot confine her spectres within the dim region of her sway, but suffers them to break forth, affrighting this actual life with secrets that perchance belong to a deeper one. Aylmer now remembered his dream. He had fancied himself with his servant Aminadab, attempting an operation for the removal of the birthmark; but the deeper went the knife, the deeper sank the hand, until at length its tiny grasp appeared to have caught hold of Georgiana's heart; whence, however,

her husband was inexorably resolved to cut or wrench it away.

When the dream had shaped itself perfectly in his memory, Aylmer sat in his wife's presence with a guilty feeling. Truth often finds its way to the mind close muffled in robes of sleep, and then speaks with uncompromising directness of matters in regard to which we practise an unconscious self-deception during our waking moments. Until now he had not been aware of the tyrannizing influence acquired by one idea over his mind, and of the lengths which he might find in his heart to go for the sake of giving himself peace.

"Aylmer," resumed Georgiana, solemnly, "I know not what may be the cost to both of us to rid me of this fatal birthmark. Perhaps its removal may cause cureless deformity; or it may be the stain goes as deep as life itself. Again: do we know that there is a possibility, on any terms, of unclasping the firm gripe of this little hand which was laid upon me before I came into the world?"

"Dearest Georgiana, I have spent much thought upon the subject," hastily interrupted Aylmer. "I am convinced of the perfect practicability of its removal."

"If there be the remotest possibility of it," continued Georgiana, "let the attempt be made at whatever risk. Danger is nothing to me; for life, while this hateful mark makes me the object of your horror and disgust—life is a burden which I would fling down with joy. Either remove this dreadful hand, or take my wretched life! You have deep science. All the world bears witness of it. You have achieved great wonders. Cannot you remove this little, little mark, which I cover with the tips of two small fingers? Is this beyond your power, for the sake of your own peace, and to save your poor wife from madness?"

"Noblest, dearest, tenderest wife," cried Aylmer, rapturously, "doubt not my power. I have already given this matter the deepest thought—thought which might almost have enlightened me to create a being less perfect than yourself. Georgiana, you have led me deeper than ever into the heart of science. I feel myself fully competent to render this dear cheek as faultless as its fellow; and then, most beloved, what will be my triumph when I shall have corrected what Nature left imperfect in her fairest work! Even Pygmalion, when his sculptured woman assumed life, felt no greater ecstasy than mine will be."

"It is resolved then," said Georgiana, faintly smiling. "And, Aylmer, spare me not, though you should find the birthmark take refuge in my heart at last."

Her husband tenderly kissed her cheek—her right cheek—not that which bore the impress of the crimson hand.

The next day Alymer apprised his wife of a plan that he had formed whereby he might have opportunity for the intense thought and constant watchfulness which the proposed operation would require; while Georgiana, likewise, would enjoy the perfect repose essential to its success. They were to seclude themselves in the extensive apartments occupied by Aylmer as a laboratory, and where, during his toilsome youth, he had made discoveries in the elemental powers of Nature that had roused the admiration of all the learned societies in Europe. Seated calmly in this laboratory, the pale philosopher had investigated the secrets of the highest cloud region and of the profoundest mines; he had satisfied himself of the causes that kindled and kept alive the fires of the volcano; and had explained the mystery of fountains, and how it is that they gush forth, some so bright and pure, and others with such rich medicinal virtues, from the dark bosom of the earth. Here, too, at an earlier period, he had studied the wonders of the human frame, and attempted to fathom the very process by which Nature assimilates all her precious influences from earth and air, and from the spiritual world, to create and foster man, her masterpiece. The latter pursuit, however, Aylmer had long laid aside to unwilling recognition of the truth—that our great creative Mother, while she amuses us with apparently working in the broadest sunshine, is yet severely careful to keep her own secrets, and, in spite of her pretended openness, shows us nothing but results. She permits us, indeed, to mar, but seldom to mend, and, like a jealous patentee, on no account to make. Now, however, Aylmer resumed these half-forgotten investigations; not, of course, with such hopes or wishes as first suggested them; but because they involved much physiological truth and lay in the path of his proposed scheme for the treatment of Georgiana.

As he led her over the threshold of the laboratory, Georgiana was cold and tremulous. Aylmer looked cheerfully into her face, with intent to reassure her, but was so startled with the intense glow of the birthmark upon the whiteness of her cheek that he could not restrain a strong convulsive shudder. His wife fainted.

"Aminadab! Aminadab!" shouted Aylmer, stamping violently on the floor.

Forthwith there issued from an inner apartment a man of low stature, but bulky frame, with shaggy hair hanging about his visage, which was grimed with the vapors of the furnace. This personage had been Aylmer's underworker during his whole scientific career, and was admirably fitted for that office by his great mechanical readiness, and the skill with which, while incapable of comprehending a single principle, he executed all the details of his master's experiments. With his vast strength, his shaggy hair, his smoky aspect, and the indescribable earthiness that incrusted him, he seemed to represent man's physical nature; while Aylmer's slender figure, and pale, intellectual face, were no less apt a type of the spiritual element.

"Throw open the door of the boudoir, Aminadab," said Aylmer, "burn a pastil."

"Yes, master," answered Aminadab, looking intently at the lifeless form of Georgiana; and then he muttered to himself, "If she were my wife, I'd never part with that birthmark."

When Georgiana recovered consciousness she found herself breathing an atmosphere of penetrating fragrance, the gentle potency of which had recalled her from her deathlike faintness. The scene around her looked like enchantment. Aylmer had converted those smoky, dingy, sombre rooms, where he had spent his brightest years in recondite pursuits, into a series of beautiful apartments not unfit to be the secluded abode of a lovely woman. The walls were hung with gorgeous curtains, which imparted the combination of grandeur and grace that no other species of adornment can achieve; and as they fell from the ceiling to the floor, their rich and ponderous folds, concealing all angles and straight lines, appeared to shut in the scene from infinite space. For aught Georgiana knew, it might be a pavilion among the clouds. And Aylmer, excluding the sunshine, which would have interfered with his chemical processes, had supplied its place with perfumed lamps, emitting flames of various hue, but all uniting in a soft, impurpled radiance. He now knelt by his wife's side, watching her earnestly, but without alarm; for he was confident in his science, and felt that he could draw a magic circle round her within which no evil might intrude.

"Where am I? Ah, I remember," said Georgiana, faintly; and she placed her hand over her cheek to hide the terrible mark from her husband's eyes.

"Fear not, dearest!" exclaimed he. "Do not shrink from me! Believe me, Georgiana, I even rejoice in this single imperfection, since it will be such a rapture to remove it."

"Oh, spare me!" sadly replied his wife. "Pray do not look at it again. I never can forget that convulsive shudder."

In order to soothe Georgiana, and, as it were to release her mind from the burden of actual things, Aylmer now put in practice some of the light and playful secrets which science had taught him among its profounder lore. Airy figures, absolutely bodiless ideas, and forms of unsubstantial beauty came and danced before her, imprinting their momentary footsteps on beams of light. Though she had some indistinct idea of the method of these optical phenomena, still the illusion was almost perfect enough to warrant the belief that her husband possessed sway over the spiritual world. Then again, when she felt a wish to look forth from her seclusion, immediately, as if her thoughts were answered, the procession of external existence flitted across a screen. The scenery and the figures of actual life were perfectly represented, but with that bewitching, yet indescribable difference which always makes a picture, an image, or a shadow so much more attractive than the original. When wearied of this, Aylmer bade her cast her eyes upon a vessel containing a quantity of earth. She did so, with little interest at first; but was soon startled to perceive the germ of a plant shooting upward from the soil. Then came the slender stalk; the leaves gradually unfolded themselves; and amid them was a perfect and lovely flower.

"It is magical!" cried Georgiana. "I dare not touch it."

"Nay, pluck it," answered Aylmer,—"pluck it, and inhale its brief perfume while you may. The flower will wither in a few moments and leave nothing save its brown seed vessels; but thence may be perpetuated a race as ephemeral as itself."

But Georgiana had no sooner touched the flower than the whole plant suffered a blight, its leaves turning coal-black as if by the agency of fire.

To make up for this abortive experiment, he proposed to take her portrait by a scientific process of his own invention. It was to be effected by rays of light striking upon a polished plate of metal. Georgiana assented; but, on looking at the result, was affrighted to find the features of the portrait blurred and indefinable; while the minute figure of a hand appeared where the cheek should have been. Aylmer snatched the metallic plate and threw it into a jar of corrosive acid.

Soon, however, he forgot these mortifying failures. In the intervals of study and chemical experiment he came to her flushed and exhausted, but seemed invigorated by her presence, and spoke in glowing language of the resources of his art. He gave a history of the long dynasty of the alchemists, who spent so many ages in quest of the universal solvent by which the golden principle might be elicted from all things vile and base. Aylmer appeared to believe that, by the plainest scientific logic, it was altogether within the limits of possibility to discover this long-sought medium; "but," he added, "a philospher who should go deep enough to acquire the power would attain too lofty a wisdom to stoop to the exercise of it." Not less singular were his opinions in regard to the elixir vitæ. He more than intimated that it was at his option to concoct a liquid that should prolong life for years, perhaps interminably; but that it would produce a discord in Nature which all the world, and chiefly the quaffer of the immortal nostrum, would find cause to curse.

"Aylmer, are you in earnest?" asked Georgiana, looking at him with amazement and fear. "It is terrible to possess such power, or even to dream of possessing it."

"Oh, do not tremble, my love," said her husband. "I would not wrong either you or myself by working such inharmonious effects upon our lives; but I would have you consider how trifling, in comparison, is the skill requisite to remove this little hand."

At the mention of the birthmark, Georgiana, as usual, shrank as if a redhot iron had touched her cheek.

Again Aylmer applied himself to his labors. She could hear his voice in the distant furnace room giving directions to Aminadab, whose harsh, uncouth, misshapen tones were audible in response, more likely the grunt or growl of a brute than human speech. After long hours of absence, Aylmer reappeared and proposed that she should now examine his cabinet of chemical products and natural treasures of the earth. Among the former he showed her a small vial, in which, he remarked, was contained a gentle yet most powerful fragrance, capable of impregnating all the breezes that blow across a kingdom. They were of inestimable value, the contents of that little vial; and, as he said so, he threw some of the perfume into the air and filled the room with piercing and invigorating delight.

"And what is this?" asked Georgiana, pointing to a small crystal globe containing a gold-colored liquid. "It is so beautiful to the eye that I could imagine it the elixir of life."

"In one sense it is," replied Aylmer; "or, rather, the elixir of immortality. It is the most precious poison that ever was concocted in this world. By its aid I could apportion the lifetime of any mortal at whom you might point your finger. The strength of the dose would determine whether he were to linger out years, or drop dead in the midst of a breath. No king on his guarded throne could keep his life if I, in my private station, should deem that the welfare of millions justified me in depriving him of it."

"Why do you keep such a terrific drug?" inquired Georgiana in horror.

"Do not mistrust me, dearest," said her husband, smiling; "its virtuous potency is yet greater than its harmful one. But see! here is a powerful cosmetic. With a few drops of this in a vase of water, freckles may be washed away as easily as the hands are cleansed. A stronger infusion would take the blood out of the cheek, and leave the rosiest beauty a pale ghost."

"Is it with this lotion that you intend to bathe my cheek?" asked Georgiana, anxiously.

"Oh, no," hastily replied her husband; "this is merely superficial. Your case demands a remedy that shall go deeper."

In his interviews with Georgiana, Aylmer generally made minute inquiries as to her sensations and whether the confinement of the rooms and the temperature of the atmosphere agreed with her. These questions had such a particular drift that Georgiana began to conjecture that she was already subjected to certain physical influences, either breathed in with the fragrant air or taken with her food. She fancied likewise, but it might be altogether fancy, that there was a stirring up of her system—a strange, indefinite sensation creeping through her veins, and tingling, half painfully, half pleasurably, at her heart. Still, whenever she dared to look into the mirror, there she beheld herself pale as a white rose and with the crimson birthmark stamped upon her cheek. Not even Alymer now hated it so much as she.

To dispel the tedium of the hours which her husband found it necessary to devote to the process of combination and analysis, Georgiana turned over the volumes of his scientific library. In many dark old tomes she met with chapters full of romance and poetry. They were the works of the philosophers of the middle ages, such as Albertus Magnus, Cornelius Agrippa, Paracelsus, and the famous friar who created the prophetic Brazen Head. All these antique naturalists stood in advance of their centuries, yet were imbued with some of their credulity, and therefore were believed, and perhaps imagined themselves to have acquired from the investigation of Nature a power above Nature, and from physics a sway over the spiritual world. Hardly less curious and imaginative were the early volumes of the Transactions of the Royal Society, in which the members, knowing little of the limits of natural possibility, were continually recording wonders or proposing methods whereby wonders might be wrought.

But to Georgiana the most engrossing volume was a large folio from her husband's own hand, in which he had recorded every experiment of his scientific career, its original aim, the methods adopted for its development, and its final success or failure, with the circumstances to which either event was attributable. The book, in truth, was both the history and emblem of his ardent, ambitious, imaginative, yet practical and laborious life. He handled physical details as if there were nothing beyond them; yet spiritualized them all, and redeemed himself from materialism by his strong and eager aspiration towards the infinite. In his grasp the veriest clod of earth assumed a soul. Georgiana, as she read, reverenced Aylmer and loved him more profoundly than ever, but with a less entire dependence on his judgment than heretofore. Much as he had accomplished, she could not but observe that his most splendid successes were almost invariably failures, if compared with the ideal at which he aimed. His brightest diamonds were the merest pebbles, and felt to be so by himself, in comparison with the inestimable gems which lay hidden beyond his reach. The volume, rich with achievements that had won renown for its author, was yet as melancholy a record as ever mortal hand had penned. It was the sad confession and continual exemplification of the shortcomings of the composite man, the spirit burdened with clay and working in matter, and of the despair that assails the higher nature at finding itself so miserably thwarted by the earthly part. Perhaps every man of genius in whatever sphere might recognize the image of his own experience in Aylmer's journal.

So deeply did these reflections affect Georgiana that she laid her face upon the open volume and burst into tears. In this situation she was found by her husband.

"It is dangerous to read in a sorcerer's books," said he, with a smile, though his countenance was uneasy and displeased. "Georgiana, there are pages in that volume which I can scarcely glance over and keep my senses. Take heed lest it prove as detrimental to you."

"It has made me worship you more than ever," said she.

"Ah, wait for this one sucess," rejoined he, "then worship me if you will. I shall deem myself hardly unworthy of it. But come, I have sought you for the luxury of your voice. Sing to me, dearest."

So she poured out the liquid music of her voice to quench the thirst of his spirit. He then took his leave with a boyish exuberance of gayety, assuring her that her seclusion would endure but a little longer, and that the result was already certain. Scarcely had he departed when Georgiana felt irresistibly impelled to follow him. She had forgotten to inform Aylmer of a symptom which for two or three hours past had begun to excite her attention. It was a sensation in the fatal birthmark, not painful, but which induced a restlessness throughout her system. Hastening after her husband, she intruded for the first time into the laboratory.

The first thing that struck her eye was the furnace, that hot and feverish worker, with the intense glow of its fire, which by the quanities of soot clustered above it seemed to have been burning for ages. There was a distilling apparatus in full operation. Around the room were retorts, tubes, cylinders, crucibles, and other apparatus of chemical research. An electrical machine stood ready for immediate use. The atmosphere felt oppressively close, and was tainted with gaseous odors which had been tormented forth by the processes of science. The severe and homely simplicitiy of the apartment, with its naked walls and brick pavement, looked strange, accustomed as Georgiana had become to the fantastic elegance of her boudoir. But what chiefly, indeed almost solely, drew her attention, was the aspect of Aylmer himself.

He was pale as death, anxious and absorbed, and hung over the furnace as it depended upon his utmost watchfulness whether the liquid which it was distilling should be the draught of immortal happiness or misery. How different from the sanguine and joyous mien that he had assumed for Georgiana's encouragement!

"Carefully now, Aminadab; carefully, thou human machine; carefully, thou man of clay!" muttered Aylmer, more to himself than his assistant. "Now, if there be a thought too much or too little, it is all over."

"Ho! ho!" mumbled Aminadab. "Look, master! look!"

Aylmer raised his eyes hastily, and at first reddened, then grew paler than ever, on beholding Georgiana. He rushed towards her arm with a gripe that left the print of his fingers and seized her fingers upon it.

"Why do you come hither? Have you no trust in your

husband?" cried he, impetuously. "Would you throw the blight of that fatal birthmark over my labors? It is not well done. Go, prying woman, go!"

"Nay, Aylmer," said Georgiana with the firmness of which she possessed no stinted endowment, "it is not you that have a right to complain. You mistrust your wife; you have concealed the anxiety with which you watch the development of this experiment. Think not so unworthily of me, my husband. Tell me all the risk we run, and fear not that I shall shrink; for my share in it is far less than your own."

"No, no, Georgiana!" said Alymer, impatiently; "it must not be."

"I submit," replied she calmly. "And, Alymer, I shall quaff whatever draught you bring me; but it will be on the same principle that would induce me to take a dose of poison if offered by your hand."

"My noble wife," said Aylmer, deeply moved, "I knew not the height and depth of your nature until now. Nothing shall be concealed. Know, then, that this crimson hand, superficial as it seems, has clutched its grasp into your being with a strength of which I had no previous conception. I have already administered agents powerful enough to do aught except to change your entire physical system. Only one thing remains to be tried. If that fail us we are ruined."

"Why did you hesitate to tell me this?" asked she.

"Because, Georgiana," said Aylmer, in a low voice, "there is danger."

"Danger? There is but one danger—that this horrible stigma shall be left upon my cheek!" cried Georgiana. "Remove it, remove it, whatever be the cost, or we shall both go mad!"

"Heaven knows your words are too true," said Aylmer, sadly. "And now, dearest, return to your boudoir. In a little while all will be tested."

He conducted her back and took leave of her with a solemn tenderness which spoke far more than his words how much was now at stake. After his departure Georgiana became rapt in musings. She considered the character of Aylmer, and did it completer justice than at any previous moment. Her heart exulted, while it trembled, at his honorable love—so pure and lofty that it would accept nothing less than perfection nor miserably make itself contented with an earthlier nature than he had dreamed of. She felt how much more precious was such a sentiment than that meaner kind which would have borne with the imperfection for her sake, and have been guilty of treason to holy love by degrading its perfect idea to the level of the actual; and with her whole spirit she prayed that, for a single moment, she might satisfy his highest and deepest conception. Longer than one moment she well knew it could not be; for his spirit was ever on the march, ever ascending, and each instant required something that was beyond the scope of the instant before.

The sound of her husband's footsteps aroused her. He bore a crystal goblet containing a liquor colorless as water, but bright enough to be the draught of immortality. Aylmer was pale; but it seemed rather the consequence of a highly-wrought state of mind and tension of spirit than of fear or doubt.

"The concoction of the draught has been perfect," said he, in answer to Georgiana's look. "Unless all my science have deceived me, it cannot fail."

"Save on your account, my dearest Aylmer," observed his wife, "I might wish to put off this birthmark of mortality by relinquishing mortality itself in preference to any other mode. Life is but a sad possession to those who have attained precisely the degree of moral advancement at which I stand. Were I weaker and blinder it might be happiness. Were I stronger, it might be endured hopefully. But, being what I find myself, methinks I am of all mortals the most fit to die."

"You are fit for heaven without tasting death!" replied her husband. "But why do we speak of dying? The draught cannot fail. Behold its effect upon this plant."

On the window seat there stood a geranium diseased with yellow blotches, which had overspread all its leaves. Aylmer poured a small quantity of the liquid upon the soil in which it grew. In a little time, when the roots of the plant had taken up the moisture, the unsightly blotches began to be extinguished in a living verdure.

"There needed no proof," said Georgiana, quietly. "Give me the goblet. I joyfully stake all upon your word."

"Drink, then, thou lofty creature!" exclaimed Aylmer, with fervid admiration. "There is no taint of imperfection on thy spirit. Thy sensible frame, too, shall soon be all perfect."

She quaffed the liquid and returned the goblet to his hand.

"It is grateful," said she with a placid smile. "Methinks it is like water from a heavenly fountain; for it contains I know not what of unobtrusive fragrance and deliciousness. It allays a feverish thirst that had parched me for many days. Now, dearest, let me sleep. My earthly senses are closing over my spirit like the leaves around the heart of a rose at sunset."

She spoke the last words with a gentle reluctance, as if it required almost more energy than she could command to pronounce the faint and lingering syllables. Scarcely had they loitered through her lips ere she was lost in slumber. Aylmer sat by her side, watching her aspect with the emotions proper to a man the whole value of whose existence was involved in the process now to be tested. Mingled with this mood, however, was the philosophic investigation characteristic of the man of science. Not the minutest symptom escaped him. A heightened flush of the cheek, a slight irregularity of breath, a quiver of the eyelid, a hardly perceptible tremor through the frame,—such were the details which, as the moments passed, he wrote down in his folio volume. Intense thought had set its stamp upon every previous page of that volume, but the thoughts of years were all concentrated upon the last.

While thus employed, he failed not to gaze often at the fatal hand, and not without a shudder. Yet once, by a strange and unaccountable impulse, he pressed it with his lips. His spirit recoiled, however, in the very act; and Georgiana, out of the midst of her deep sleep, moved uneasily and murmured as if in remonstrance. Again Aylmer resumed his watch. Nor was it without avail. The crimson hand, which at first had been strongly visible upon the marble paleness of Georgiana's cheek, now grew more faintly outlined. She remained not less pale than ever; but the birthmark, with every breath that came and went, lost somewhat of its former distinctness. Its presence had been awful; its departure was more awful still. Watch the stain of the rainbow fading out of the sky, and you will know how that mysterious symbol passed away.

"By Heaven! it is well-nigh gone!" said Aylmer to himself, in almost irrepressible ectasy. "I can scarcely trace it now. Success! success! And now it is like the faintest rose color. The lightest flush of the blood across her cheek would overcome it. But she is so pale!"

He drew aside the window curtain and suffered the light of the natural day to fall into the room and rest upon her cheek. At the same time he heard a gross, hoarse chuckle, which he had long known as his servant Aminadab's expression of delight.

"Ah, clod! ah, earthly mass!" cried Aylmer, laughing in a sort of frenzy, "you have served me well! Matter and spirit—earth and heaven—have both done their part in this! Laugh, thing of the senses! You have earned the right to laugh!"

These exclamations broke Georgiana's sleep. She slowly unclosed her eyes and gazed into the mirror which her husband had arranged for that purpose. A faint smile flitted over her lips when she recognized how barely perceptible was now that crimson hand which had once blazed forth with such disastrous brilliancy as to scare away all their happiness. But then her eyes sought Aylmer's face with a trouble and anxiety that he could by no means account for.

"My poor Aylmer!" murmured she.

"Poor? Nay, richest, happiest, most favored!" exclaimed he. "My peerless bride, it is successful! You are perfect!"

"My poor Aylmer," she repeated, with a more than human tenderness, "you have aimed loftily; you have done nobly. Do not repent that with so high and pure a feeling, you have rejected the best the earth could offer. Aylmer, dearest Aylmer, I am dying!"

Alas! it was too true! The fatal hand had grappled with the mystery of life, and was the bond by which an angelic spirit kept itself in union with a mortal frame. As the last crimson tint of the birthmark—that sole token of human imperfection—faded from her cheek, the parting breath of the now perfect woman passed into the atmosphere, and her soul, lingering a moment near her husband, took its heavenward flight. Then a hoarse, chuckling laugh was heard again! Thus ever does the gross fatality of earth exult in its invariable triumph over the immortal essence which, in this dim sphere of half development, demands the completeness of a higher state. Yet, had Aylmer reached a profounder wisdom, he need not thus have flung away the happiness which would have woven his mortal life of the selfsame texture with the celestial. The momentary circumstance was too strong for him; he failed to look beyond the shadowy scope of time, and, living once for all in eternity, to find the perfect future in the present.

Questions on "The Birthmark"

1. Describe the tone of the story. What words and situations contribute to its creation?
2. All the characters can be described as "types." Indicate what these "types" might be and show how this stereotyping helps or hinders the story.
3. In the beginning of the story, Aylmer is depicted as a man with an all-consuming love for science. How, then, does his love for his wife fit into his life?
4. What is the theme here? What is Hawthorne saying to the reader?
5. At the time this tale was written, in the middle 1800's, Hawthorne was very close to many people who characterized themselves as Transcendentalists. Although his wife was an ardent Transcendentalist, Hawthorne never fully adopted the philosophy. The Transcendentalists held that there was some knowledge of reality that man could grasp through his intuition rather than his reason, that man and espe-

cially nature were inherently good, and that if left to his own devices, man would work things out in the best possible way for himself and his neighbors and friends. They felt that since man was good, no government was necessary (Thoreau's famous "that government is best which governs not at all"), and thus man needed no rules to control him. Hawthorne, in contrast, was drawn to the Puritan past of his ancestors, and felt that the past had a very real effect on man in the present. Show how Hawthorne was affected by Transcendentalism and then by his Puritan past. Use this story to make your case.

6. This tale can be considered an allegory, a narrative in which characters, action, and sometimes setting represent abstract concepts or moral qualities. Show how this statement is true.

7. Why do Aylmer's attempts to perfect his wife fail?

8. In what ways is this tale an example of the "well-made tale"? Consider plot, characters, unity of effect, setting, etc.

Answers to Questions on "The Birthmark"

1. The tone is heavy and somber, and there is a creepy Gothic atmosphere to the tale. The ill-omened dream, the Quasimodo-like appearance of Aminadab, Aylmer's unsuccessful experiments, and Georgiana's intrusion into the furnace room all foreshadow evil and failure. Hawthorne's old-fashioned language, such as "I shall quaff whatever draught you bring me" lends an air of strangeness to the setting. Hawthorne deliberately chose this ornate, almost archaic style to reinforce the story's eerie mood.

2. Aylmer is the mad scientist, his wife the beautiful and agreeable young lady, Aminadab the half-human lab assistant. The use of "types" helps the reader quickly recognize the character's role in the tale and allows the reader to focus on the theme rather than lengthy character identification.

3. See the last sentence of the first paragraph. Georgiana, a symbol of spirituality, ironically leads her husband deeper than ever into the mystery of science. In the end, she becomes the victim of his scientific attempts.

4. Hawthorne is telling the reader that we cannot attempt to control creation, that man is unable to attain perfection. In this he is allied to his Puritan heritage (one of his ancestors was the famous hanging judge in the Salem witchcraft trials of 1692) and its belief in God's firm control. Georgiana's tiny flaw was the hand of God, the mark that He stamps on all his creations to link them to Him. If she were to become perfect, she would be an angel, not a mortal.

5. Aylmer does not transcend or go beyond reality; rather, he looks at reality too closely. "He failed to look beyond the shadowy scope of time . . . to find the perfect future in the present." The Transcendentalists, such as Emerson and Thoreau, left no room for the darker, less cheerful view of man we find in Hawthorne's work.

6. Aylmer might stand for the higher intellect, the imagination that attempts to attain human perfection. Georgiana would stand for spiritual beauty, the earth's home for the spirit of the angels. Aminadab would be the purely physical side of man.

7. Only the Creator has the right to attempt to establish perfection, and anything that is perfect is, by definition, unsuitable for this world.

8. There is a clear beginning, middle, and end, and a "single-effect." In this case the effect is of terror and horror at what one person, acting out of love, can do to another.

Let's examine a modern tale.

THE BLANKET

by Floyd Dell

Petey hadn't really believed that Dad would be doing it—sending Granddad away. "Away" was what they were calling it. Not until now could he believe it of Dad.

But here was the blanket that Dad had that day bought for him, and in the morning he'd be going away. And this was the last evening they'd be having together. Dad was off seeing that girl he was to marry. He'd not be back till late, and they could sit up and talk.

It was a fine September night, with a silver moon riding high over the gully. When they'd washed up the supper dishes they went out on the shanty porch, the old man and the bit of a boy, taking their chairs. "I'll get me fiddle," said the old man," and play ye some of the old tunes." But instead of the fiddle he brought out the blanket. It was a big, double blanket, red, with black cross stripes.

"Now, isn't that a fine blanket!" said the old man, smoothing it over his knees. "And isn't your father a kind man to be giving the old fellow a blanket like that to go away with? It cost something, it did—look at the wool of it! And warm it will be these cold winter nights to come. There'll be few blankets there the equal to this one!"

It was like Granddad to be saying that. He was trying to make it easier. He'd pretended all along it was he that was wanting to go away to the great brick building—the government place, where he'd be with so many other old fellows having the best of everything. . . . But Petey hadn't believed Dad would really do it, until this night when he brought home the blanket.

"Oh, yes it's a fine blanket," said Petey, and got up and went into the shanty. He wasn't the kind to cry, and, besides, he was too old for that, being eleven. He'd just come in to fetch Granddad's fiddle.

The blanket slid to the floor as the old man took the fiddle and stood up. It was the last night they'd be having together. There wasn't any need to say, "Play all the old tunes." Granddad tuned up for a minute, and then said, "This one you'll like to remember."

The silver moon was high overhead, and there was a gentle breeze playing down the gully. He'd never be hearing Granddad play like this again. It was as well Dad was moving into that new house, away from here. He'd not want, Petey wouldn't, to sit here on the old porch of fine evenings, with Granddad gone.

The tune changed. "Here's something gayer." Petey sat and stared out over the gully. Dad would marry that girl. Yes, that girl who'd kissed him and slobbered over him, saying she'd try to be a good mother to him, and all. . . . His chair creaked as he involuntarily gave his body a painful twist.

The tune stopped suddenly, and Granddad said: "It's a poor tune, except to be dancing to." And then: "It's a fine girl your father's going to marry. He'll be feeling young again, with a pretty wife like that. And what would an old fellow like me be doing around their house, getting in the way, an old nuisance, what with my talk of aches and pains! And then there'll be babies coming, and I'd not want to be there to hear them crying at all hours. It's best that I take myself off, like I'm doing. One more tune or two, and then we'll be going to bed to get some sleep against the morning, when I'll pack up my fine blanket and take my leave. Listen to this, will you? It's a bit sad, but a fine tune for a night like this."

They didn't hear the two people coming down the gully path, Dad and the pretty girl with the hard, bright face like a china doll's. But they heard her laugh, right by the porch, and the tune stopped on a wrong, high, startled note. Dad didn't say anything, but the girl came forward and spoke to Granddad prettily: "I'll not be seeing you leave in the morning, so I came over to say good-by."

"It's kind of you," said Granddad, with his eyes cast down; and then, seeing the blanket at his feet, he stopped to pick it up. "And will you look at this," he said in embarassment, "the fine blanket my son has given me to go away with!"

"Yes, she said, "it's a fine blanket." She felt of the wool, and repeated in surprise, "A fine blanket—I'll say it is!" She turned to Dad, and said to him coldly, "It cost something, that."

He cleared his throat, and said defensively, "I wanted him to have the best. . . ."

The girl stood there, still intent on the blanket. "It's double, too," she said reproachfully to Dad.

"Yes," said Granddad, "it's double—a fine blanket for an old fellow to be going away with."

The boy went abruptly into the shanty. He was looking for something. He could hear that girl reproaching Dad, and Dad becoming angry in his slow way. And now she was suddenly going away in a huff. . . . As Petey came out, she turned and called back, "All the same, he doesn't need a double blanket!" And she ran up the gully path.

Dad was looking after her uncertainly.

"Oh, she's right," said the boy coldly. "Here, Dad"—and he held out a pair of scissors. "Cut the blanket in two."

Both of them stared at the boy, startled. "Cut it in two, I tell you, Dad!" he cried out. "And keep the other half!"

"That's not a bad idea," said Granddad gently. "I don't need so much of a blanket."

"Yes," said the boy harshly, "a single blanket's enough for an old man when he's sent away. We'll save the other half, Dad; it will come in handy later."

"Now, what do you mean by that?" asked Dad.

"I mean," said the boy slowly, "that I'll give it to you, Dad—when you're old and I'm sending you—away."

There was a silence, and then Dad went over to Granddad and stood before him, not speaking. But Granddad understood, for he put out a hand and laid it on Dad's shoulder. Petey was watching them. And he heard Granddad whisper, "It's all right, son—I knew you didn't mean it. . . . " And then Petey cried.

But it didn't matter—because they were all three crying together.

Questions on "The Blanket"

1. What is the predominant symbol in this tale?
   (A) The fiddle
   (B) The blanket
   (C) The china doll
   (D) The moon
   (E) The scissors

2. What does that main symbol represent?
   (A) The problems of the aged in America
   (B) The enormous rise in divorce and remarriage with all its attendant problems
   (C) The father's attempt to assuage his guilt
   (D) The difficulty of life in rural America
   (E) The importance of cutting bonds and knowing when to let go

3. What is the theme of this story?
   (A) Things were rough for this family, and however unpleasant it may be, it was necessary to hold on to good items like blankets.
   (B) The old man got exactly what was his due.
   (C) Unintentionally, we all do cruel and unpleasant things.
   (D) It can be very difficult having old people around, especially if there is a remarriage.
   (E) Things have changed greatly over the past fifty years.

4. What is the author saying about old age and the difference between generations?
   (A) There really is an enormous difference between the three generations.
   (B) Old age is a golden time.
   (C) It is better to be young than old.
   (D) There is no real "generation gap": we will all be old someday.
   (E) The old are very poorly treated as a general rule.

5. What is the overall tone of this story?
   (A) Melancholic
   (B) Cheerful
   (C) Uplifting
   (D) Sardonic
   (E) Sarcastic

6. The girl is described as a "china doll"
   (A) to show how callow she was
   (B) to show how pretty she was
   (C) to indicate her concern for Granddad, however muted it may appear on the surface
   (D) to indicate what a good wife she would be
   (E) to indicate what a suitable wife she would be

7. The term "china doll" was selected to describe the girl because
   (A) she is very, very pretty and uses cosmetics to the best advantage
   (B) her "hard, bright face" reveals her true nature
   (C) it explains why Petey and Granddad admire her
   (D) she has very fine manners, revealed when she says goodbye to Granddad
   (E) she is like a doll

8. What is the tone of paragraphs 7 to 9?
   (A) Revulsion
   (B) Quiet happiness
   (C) Peaceful contentment
   (D) Bitter resentment
   (E) Sadness and pain

9. How is Granddad's tone in paragraph 10 different from Petey's tone in paragraphs 19–24?
   (A) Brave resignation to bitter sarcasm

(B) Clever subterfuge to childlike solemnity
(C) Disguised sarcasm to cold fear
(D) Melancholy gaiety to bewildered confusion
(E) Open bitterness to bitter sarcasm

10. The "blanket" connotes
(A) death
(B) suffocation
(C) warmth
(D) marriage
(E) old age

11. The word "shanty" suggests
(A) a broad, expansive country estate
(B) a well-to-do-family
(C) an historic old home
(D) a family living a lower-middle-class existence
(E) abject poverty

12. The "scissors" best represent
(A) severing the bonds of love, duty, respect
(B) severing the bonds of unpleasant duty
(C) cutting loose from that which is holding you back

(D) cutting dead weight
(E) assuming new freedoms and human possibility

13. The point of view in this story is most closely
(A) first-person observer
(B) first-person participant
(C) omniscient
(D) editorial omniscient
(E) limited omniscient

14. The story is most closely related to the literary movement known as
(A) Realism
(B) Surrealism
(C) Symbolism
(D) Naturalism
(E) Graveyard school

15. Granddad's attitude can best be described as
(A) considerate and understanding
(B) carefully controlled resentment toward his son's financée
(C) anxious and worried
(D) bitter but resigned to the treatment he is receiving
(E) understandably very upset

Answers to Questions on "The Blanket"

1. (B) A blanket is a symbol of warmth, comfort, home. Obviously, the symbol is being used here in an ironic manner, as that is what is being denied to Granddad.
2. (C) The father feels that by giving his father the best blanket he can buy, he will somehow feel better about sending the old man to the government home.
3. (C) The father did not really mean to be cruel, as evidenced by the ending which shows his love for his father.
4. (D) Petey's line about saving the other half of the blanket for *his* father when he sends *him* away tells us this.
5. (A) This is a melancholy, sad story, as we feel the sad music and lonely times bred by misunderstanding and conflict.
6. (A) "Callow" means shallow and superficial.
7. (B) "Hard and bright" are used to show that she is a cold and unfeeling person; she begrudges the double blanket for the old man, feeling a single would have been more than enough.
8. (E) Petey is sad that he will never hear his grandfather play again, and that his father's wife will "slobber" all over him in her insincere attempts to be a mother to him.
9. (A) Granddad is putting on a brave front about the situation; Petey is being cold and sarcastic when he offers to cut the blanket in two to save the cost of another to send *his* father away with.
10. (C) The good wool blanket is intended to comfort Granddad in his old age.
11. (E) A shanty is a poor hovel.

12. (A) By offering to cut the blanket, Petey is saying that if that is the way you, Dad, treat your father, you can expect me to treat you that way too.
13. (C) The narrator is all-knowing.
14. (A) This is a realistic view of the problems many families face with aged parents and remarriage. See definitions of all other literary movements.
15. (A) We must understand that Granddad is not being sarcastic in what he says; he honestly attempts to see his son's point of view.

ESSAY QUESTIONS ON THE SHORT STORY

Directions: Allow yourself 45 minutes to organize, write, and correct an essay on each of the following topics. Follow the directions for generating and organizing your thoughts as described in **Part 2: Essay Writing Guide**. Be sure to leave time to revise and edit your essay at the end. Suggestions for answers follow the questions.

1. Compare the use of language in any two short stories by different authors. Establish the level of diction (elevated, conversational, colloquial, etc.) and sentence structure (simple, compound, complex) as well as punctuation. Then, cite specific examples to prove the difference between the stories.

2. Discuss how James Joyce uses symbols to convey his theme in any two stories from *Dubliners*.

3. Although he lived during the 1850's, Hawthorne often drew from the Puritan past of the 1600's for his themes of guilt and sin. Show how this is evident in any one of his short stories, drawing specific examples from the tale under discussion.

4. Some collections of short stories are so structured that the stories can be read either individually or as a unit. Individually, they have all the elements that we have come to expect from a short story, but when taken as a whole, the collection works as a novel, with each story, functioning as a chapter, adding something incremental to the plot. Discuss how this is true for one of the following: Joyce's *Dubliners*, Anderson's *Winesburg, Ohio*, or the short stories of F. Scott Fitzgerald or Ernest Hemingway.

5. There are many ways an author can convey his meaning to his audience, but the short story writer, because of the limitations of space, often must telescope his message. Thus we find that some short story writers rely a great deal on the use of symbols to compress a lot of meaning into a short space. Select any one of the short story writers from the list below, or any other writer of equal stature, and show how he/she uses symbols to convey theme effectively in a short story.

Hawthorne	Conrad	James, Henry
Joyce	Lawrence	Mann
Porter, K.A.	Anderson	Hemingway

6. Discuss how the personality of a main character from a short story is established through the use of dialogue. Include as many specific examples as possible.

7. Show how the images from any one short story are consistent, drawn from the same source. These sources may include nature, animals, etc. Then, show how the images determine the theme of the tale.

8. Some authors focus on particular symbols in their tales: One of the most striking is the use of color. Show how any of the following short story writers, or any

others of the same stature, use color symbols in any one of their tales.

Joyce   Lawrence   Porter   Anderson

9. Some short story writers focus on the psychological aspect of man's life to create tales that probe the unconscious. Select any one tale and show how the author uncovers the inner workings of a character's mind.

10. The setting of a short story can often be a pivotal factor in the development of theme. Show how this is true in any one tale.

11. Select any short story and describe how the author's specific choice of words establishes the tone.

12. Show how the ending of any short story is foreshadowed by the beginning. Discuss symbol, image, characterization, and so forth to establish your thesis.

13. Select any short story from the "modern school" (Chekhov, Mansfield, James, Joyce, etc.) and contrast it to any story from the "traditional school" (Poe, Dickens, O. Henry, etc.). Using symbol, image, characterization, tone, mood, etc., show how the tales are different and the same.

Suggestions for Answering Essay Questions on the Short Story

1. Differences in the use of language are especially clear between Edgar Allan Poe and Anton Chekhov, or Daniel Defoe and Katherine Mansfield, or Ernest Hemingway and Charles Dickens. Hemingway, for example, uses simple sentences, commas rather than semicolons, and conversational or colloquial diction. Dickens uses complex sentences and, by twentieth-century standards, far more elevated diction.

2. "Clay" uses the symbol of clay to describe Maria's life, while "The Dead" uses the symbol of snow to show what happened to Gabriel's feelings. None of Joyce's stories is discussed here because of space limitations, but the work bears looking into on your own.

3. In "Roger Malvin's Burial," for example, we see how Reuben Borne must bear the guilt for leaving his father-in-law to die alone, even though Roger Malvin had asked him to leave to save his own life. This sin colors the rest of Reuben's life, affecting his marriage and career. The sin and guilt are not erased until the symbolic murder of his son, Cyrus, who stands for all that was best in Reuben.

4. In *Winesburg, Ohio,* for example, the main character, George Willard, appears in most of the stories as a unifying factor. Even when he is not in the story, however, his presence is felt, as in the story concerning his mother. The entire work shows us *why* George would feel compelled to leave Winesburg, by describing the stultifying lives of its inhabitants.

5. In Hawthorne's "Roger Malvin's Burial," the tree stands for the blight that has descended on Reuben Borne's life. In Anderson's "Paper Pills," the small rolls of paper that Dr. Reefy compresses in his pockets represent his thoughts, crammed into small spaces, no longer expressed to anyone, symbolic of the compression of his life.

6. See the main characters in Mansfield's "The Dill Pickle."

7. See Hawthorne, whose images, usually drawn from nature, illustrate the theme of the effect of sin and guilt on the human heart.

8. The color brown is carried through *Dubliners,* from the clay in the story of the same name to the final stories.

9. Henry James, D. H. Lawrence, Conrad Aiken and Edgar Allan Poe would all be

appropriate choices. In Aiken's "Silent Snow, Secret Snow," for example, we see how a boy retreats from the problems of his environment, escaping into his mind, turning inward like a flower becoming a seed again.

10. Lawrence's "Rocking Horse Winner," for example, describes how a young boy obtains funds to enable his parents to continue to live in the style they covet. Had the tale been set in a different environment, it would not have illustrated the same theme, the parents'—especially the mother's—greed for the more they have become accustomed to, captured in the phrase, "We must have more money, we must have more money."

11. In any of Poe's horror tales, we find that each word is selected to establish the tone of horror and terror. Thus, in the first paragraph of "The Black Cat," we find the words "terrified," "horror," and "torture," to select a few. This technique continues throughout the tale. See "The Philosophy of Composition."

12. In Poe, for example, we see that the character's personality, established in the first paragraph of "The Black Cat," predisposes him to the tragedy that is to follow, for his good nature is destroyed by drink.

13. We find a far greater concern for the "well-made tale" in those tales from the "traditional" school. These "traditional" stories have a clear beginning, middle, and end, and the narration is in the first or third person. They are concerned with a clear "single effect" and the clear transmission of plot. In the "modern" school, in contrast, we find more of a "slice of life" approach, a greater concern for the creation of a specific image than the transmission of a traditional plot. These modern tales usually try to capture the inner workings of the mind rather than employing a third-person or first-person narration; they favor the "stream of consciousness" and compression of detail.

SUGGESTED READING LIST

The following critical analyses and collections of short stories contain introductions and commentaries that are useful for studying the short story:

Bloom, Edward A. and Lillian Bloom, eds. *The Variety of Fiction: A Critical Anthology.* Indianapolis: Odyssey Press, 1969.

Brooks, Cleanth and Robert Penn Warren. *Understanding Fiction.* New York: Appleton-Century-Crofts, 1959.

Lesser, M.X., and J.N. Morris. *Modern Short Stories: The Fiction of Experience.* New York: McGraw-Hill, 1962.

MacKenzie, Barbara. *The Process of Fiction.* 2nd ed. New York: Harcourt Brace Jovanovich, 1974.

West, Ray and Stallman, Robert. *Art of Modern Fiction.* New York: Holt, Rinehart and Winston, 1956.

Aiken, Conrad	"Silent Snow, Secret Snow"
Aleichem, Sholom	"Teyve Wins a Fortune"
Andersen, Hans C.	"The Emperor's New Clothes"
Anderson, Sherwood	*Winesburg, Ohio*
	"The Egg"
Babel, Isaac	"The Story of my Dovecot"
Barthelme, Donald	"Report"
Benet, Stephen Vincent	"The Devil and Daniel Webster"
Böll, Heinrich	"Christmas Every Day"
Borges, Jorge Luis	"Deutsches Requiem"
Bradbury, Ray	"I Sing the Body Electric"
	"A Medicine for Melancholy"
Camus, Albert	"The Funeral"
Capek, Karel	"Money"
Cather, Willa	"Paul's Case"
Cheever, John	"The Enormous Radio"
	The World of Apples
Chekhov, Anton	"The Bet"
	"Gooseberries"
	"Gusev"
	"Misery"
	"A Father"
	"The Kiss"
	"A Problem"
	"Ward No. 6"
	"In Exile"
	"My Life"
	"Peasants"
	"The Darling"
Connell, Richard	"The Most Dangerous Game"
Conrad, Joseph	"Heart of Darkness"
	"The Secret Sharer"
Crane, Stephen	"The Blue Hotel"
	"The Open Boat"
	"The Bride Comes to Yellow Sky"

Daly, Maureen	"Sixteen"
Defoe, Daniel	"The True Relation of the Apparition of One Mrs. Veal"
Dell, Floyd	"The Blanket"
de Maupassant, Guy	"The Diamond Necklace"
	"Useless Beauty"
	"A Normandy Joke"
	"Ball-of-Fat"
	"A Piece of String"
	"Mlle. Fifi"
	"A Fishing Excursion"
	"The Little Cask"
	"The False Gems"
Dickens, Charles	"A Christmas Carol"
Irving, Washington	*The Sketch Book*
	"Rip Van Winkle"
	"The Legend of Sleepy Hollow"
	"The Spectre Bridegroom"
	"The Broken Heart"
	Tales of a Traveller
	"Adventures of the German Student"
	"The Devil and Tom Walker"
Jackson, Shirley	"The Lottery"
	"Charles"
Jacobs, W. W.	"The Monkey's Paw"
James, Henry	"The Jolly Corner"
	"The Beast in the Jungle"
	"The Tree of Knowledge"
	"The Turn of the Screw"
Joyce, James	*Dubliners*
Kafka, Franz	*The Penal Colony*
	"The Metamorphosis"
	"A Country Doctor"
	"A Little Fable"
	"A Hunger Artist"
Kipling, Rudyard	"The Gardener"
Lardner, Ring	"Haircut"
	"The Golden Honeymoon"
Lawrence, D. H.	"The Rocking Horse Winner"
	"The Man Who Loved Islands"
Lessing, Doris	"To Room Nineteen"
	Stories
Malamud, Bernard	*The Magic Barrel*
	"Angel Levine"
Mann, Thomas	"Little Herr Friedmann"
Mansfield, Katherine	"Garden Party"
	"The Dill Pickle"
	"Bliss"
Melville, Herman	"Bartelby the Scrivener"
O'Connor, Flannery	*The Collected Stories*
O'Flaherty, Liam	"The Sniper"
O'Hara, John	*The O'Hara Generation*

Parker, Dorothy	"Standard of Living"
	"The Waltz"
Pirandello, Luigi	"The Cat, A Goldfinch, and the Stars"
Porter, K. A.	"The Jilting of Granny Weatherall"
	"Noon Wine"
Poe, Edgar Allan	*The Complete Stories and Poems of Edgar Allan Poe*
	"The Murders in the Rue Morgue"
	"The Black Cat"
	"The Gold Bug"
	"The Descent into the Maelstrom"
	"The Tell-Tale Heart"
	"The Purloined Letter"
	"MS Found in a Bottle"
	"William Wilson"
	"The Fall of the House of Usher"
	"The Cask of Amontillado"
	"The Pit and the Pendulum"
	"The Masque of the Red Death"
Proust, Marcel	"Overture"
Roth, Philip	"Defender of the Faith"
Saki	"The Open Window"
Salinger, J. D.	*9 Stories*
Sartre, J. P.	"The Wall"
Steinbeck, John	"Chrysanthemums"
Stevenson, R. L.	"The Bottle Imp"
Stockton, Frank	"The Lady, or the Tiger?"
Taylor, Elizabeth	"Spry Old Character"
Taylor Peter	*The Complete Stories*
Thurber, James	"The Catbird Seat"
	"The Secret Life of Walter Mitty"
Trilling, Lionel	"Of This Time, of That Place"
Twain, Mark	*The Great Short Works of Mark Twain*
	"The Celebrated Jumping Frog of Calaveras County"
	"The Facts Concerning the Recent Carnival of Crime in Connecticut"
	"Jim Baker's Blue Jay"
	"Letter to the Earth"
	"The Man That Corrupted Hadleyburg"
	"The Mysterious Stranger"
Updike, John	"A & P"
Wells, H. G.	"The Time Machine"
Welty, Eudora	*The Complete Stories of Eudora Welty*
Wharton, Edith	"Roman Fever"
White, E. B.	"The Door"
Williams, W. C.	"Use of Force"
Wright, Richard	"Bright and Morning Star"
Vonnegut, Kurt	"Report on the Barnhouse Effect"

The Novel

A *novel* is a fictional prose narrative of substantial length. As mentioned in the short story chapter, there is no specific length that distinguishes the two genres, but the terms *short novel* or *novelette* are sometimes applied to narratives of fewer than one hundred pages that seem too short to be considered novels. This is an arbitrary rule at best.

DEVELOPMENT OF THE NOVEL

The novel is related to the epic because it is not limited to historical facts, but allows for the creation of fictional worlds and people. But in the epic, the characters are usually gods and men of supernatural abilities, whereas in the novel, the characters are usually ordinary mortals living in a world closer to the one we inhabit.

A more direct cousin of the novel is the *romance*. As discussed in the short story chapter, such tales described exciting adventures in strange and wonderful lands. The authors felt free to range from the everyday reality and were seldom interested in the details of ordinary, middle-class life. One of the earliest examples, the anonymous *Sir Gawain and the Green Knight,* for instance, includes the story of a green man who neatly survives decapitation. For the romance, then, adventure was far more important than character development.

In Italy, during the Middle Ages and the Renaissance, a prose tale was called a *novella,* meaning a "new short thing," or "news."

The *picaresque novel,* which presents the adventures of *rogue,* (called a *picaro* in Spanish), is usually a detailed satiric picture of middle-class life, describing the shrewd manner in which the rogue triumphs over the less-clever members of the middle and upper classes he encounters on his travels. Because the form originated as a burlesque of the sixteenth-century Spanish tales of chivalric adventures, the picaro wins one encounter after another, and the novel has a very episodic structure. *The Adventures of Huckleberry Finn* by Mark Twain is a more modern version of the picaresque novel.

If a novel includes historical settings or people drawn in such detail that the reader feels that the historical period as well as the characters are the subject, then the whole may be termed an *historical novel.* Dickens' *A Tale of Two Cities,* even though it has no real historical figure developed in the narrative, can be called an historical novel because of its emphasis on the setting—France during the Revolution—but usually there is some historical figure present. In recent years, historical figures have played larger roles in novels, but these have been termed "fictional biographies," because of the depth of character development.

The *roman à clef* (French for "novel with a key") uses as its main characters contemporary figures disguised with false names. For example, D. H. Lawrence appears as Mark Rampion in Aldous Huxley's *Point Counter Point.*

The *bildungsroman* or *erziehungrsroman* (German for "novel of development") deals with growing up, whereby the hero becomes aware of himself as he relates to the world outside his subjective consciousness. Thomas Mann's *The Magic Mountain* is a well-known example of this genre. When the *bildungsroman* is concerned with the development of the artist, as is James Joyce's *A Portrait of the Artist as a Young Man,* it may be termed a *kunstlerroman* (German for "novel of the artist"). This type of work pays great attention to the mental attitudes of its characters, and may also be called a psychological novel. Although this genre dates back at least as far as the Russian novelist Dostoevski, it has been greatly commented upon in the twentieth century. An especially important kind of psychological novel is the *stream-of-consciousness novel*. By means of the *interior monologue,* the stream-of-consciousness novel attempts to look into the minds of its characters, recording their mental activity complete with all apparent irrelevancies. Usually there is little punctuation, few logical transitions, and few author's interventions in these interior monologues, which, while they serve to represent the mind, can be very difficult to read and understand. James Joyce's *Ulysses* is a stream-of-consciousness novel, and its final chapter, the thoughts of Molly Bloom, represent an interior monologue. The entire section, almost fifty pages long, contains only three conventional sentences.

The novel has changed greatly in the twentieth century, largely through the efforts of Henry James (especially in *The Ambassadors*), Marcel Proust (*Remembrance of Things Past*), and James Joyce (*Ulysses* and *Finnegan's Wake*). While these novelists were not personal friends, their works contain similar characteristics and techniques that effected a change in the novel as we have traditionally come to define it.

The traditional novel, something like *Tale of Two Cities* by Charles Dickens, presents a series of events worked out on the stage of external reality that generally is very close to what we have come to expect of everyday life. The *modern novel,* in contrast, presents a series of events enacted on the stage of *internal reality,* and the reader is required to enter into the internal world the writer has created, rather than the external world to which he is accustomed. Further, the artist creates a *special language* to convey this reality. Thus, he does not speak *about* the mind, as in the traditional novel, but rather seeks to *enter* the mind, and make the reader see events through the character's eyes. He may even try to simulate the actual thoughts of a character as they flow through his mind, called "stream of consciousness." At other times, he may try to distill a moment of time and reduce it to exact language, to capture the moment as it has happened. This attempt to find in language the exact equivalent of experience itself allies the modern novelist with the modern poet and makes the modern novel distinctly different from its predecessors.

Another major difference between the traditional novel and the modern version lies in the notion of *plot*. In the traditional novel, such as *David Copperfield,* the reader enters into the action through the plot, the story. But modern novels such as *Ulysses* have no plot as such, and the reader must gather the story for himself, putting together the pieces as he can. Sometimes the events are very discontinuous, as in the final chapter of *Ulysses,* Molly Bloom's interior monologue, and the reader must translate the author's rendition of the complex inner workings of the mind. The result is what Henry James called the "atmosphere of the mind."

LITERARY MOVEMENTS

Existentialism

The writings of this movement stress the loneliness, insecurity, and irrevocability of man's experience and the dangerous situations in which these qualities are most prominent. It also focuses on the serious and anxious attempts of serious people to face these situations and the evasive or desperate and ultimately useless attempts of weak people to escape them. Most followers of this movement think that the future is undetermined and that man is free, but that he has neither fixed potentials nor fixed values to aid him. Our free choice of actions asserts our actions as valid: In Jean-Paul Sartre's own words, "man makes himself." Man must himself form his own character. Existentialist criticism approached literature by asking how well it depicts these complexities of man's situation.

Expressionism

This school presents life as the author (or his character) passionately feels it to be, not as it appears on the surface to the dispassionate eye. Thus the Expressionist's work often consciously distorts the external appearance of an object in order to picture the object as he feels it really is. Scenery in an Expressionist drama, for example, would not be photographically accurate, but would be distorted so that, for instance, the wall of a courtroom may tilt at a weird angle to reveal the accused's state of mind. The movement was especially dominant in German painting during the decade following World War I.

Naturalism

This movement attempted to portray a scientifically accurate, detached picture of life, including everything and selecting nothing for particular emphasis. This is often called the "slice of life" technique when focused on a narrow bit of scientific realism. Many of the Naturalists were very much influenced by evolutionary thought, and regarded man as devoid of free will and soul, a creature whose fate was determined by the twin pulls of environment and heredity. The movement was represented in the works of Emile Zola, Theodore Dreiser, Frank Norris, Stephen Crane, and others to a lesser extent. The emphasis on scientific determinism, heredity, and environment—Social Darwinism—differentiates Naturalism from Realism, and the two should not be confused.

Realism

In contrast to Naturalism, Realism is the detailed presentation of appearances of everyday life. William Dean Howells, a notable Realist, said that the movement "sought to front the every-day world and catch the charm of its work-worn, care-worn, brave, kindly faces." This movement is closely linked to the Local Color school, which concentrated on picturesque details—scenery, customs, language—characteristic of a certain region. Though often sentimental, local color could go beyond externals and delve into character, and thus is an important part of realism. In its humble, everyday subject matter, Realism has its roots in Romanticism, but Realism generally shuns the Romantic interest in the exotic and mysterious. After the Civil War, American Realism showed a note of disillusionment not present in Howells, painting little people who had their share of petty vices. This can be found in the work of Mark Twain, Stephen Crane, and Hamlin Garland. Realism is not the same as Naturalism, which usually paints a picture of life determined by the twin forces of heredity and environment.

Romance

The Romance describes strange lands and wonderful adventures. It allows the writer greater latitude to "mingle the Marvelous . . . as a slight, delicate, and evanescent flavor," in Nathaniel Hawthorne's words (in his preface to *The House of the Seven Gables*). A novel, in contrast to a romance, assumes the writer will aim at a very minute fidelity to facts, but here the writer may, as Hawthorne again remarks, "swerve aside from the truth of the human heart." The romance may include the traditional hero with the white hat on the white horse; the evil villain with the long black mustache; the lovely young woman in need of rescue, and the hairbreadth rescue itself.

Surrealism

The Surrealist aims to go beyond what is usually considered "real" to the "super real," which would include the world of dreams and the unconscious. Surrealists especially shun middle-class ideals and artistic traditions, believing that all these deform the creations of the artist's unconscious. With its emphasis on spontaneity, feeling, and sincerity, Surrealism is linked to Romanticism. The movement was especially strong in France in the 1920s and 1930s.

Symbolist Movement

The Symbolist movement arose in France in the second half of the nineteenth century and included writers Mallarmé and Valéry. W. B. Yeats, the Irish writer, was influenced by the movement. Some Symbolists believed in an invisible world beyond that of concrete events—Yeats, for example, experimented with automatic writing—but other Symbolists found the concrete world functioned to stimulate their writings. Such Symbolists believed that an object was neither a real thing nor the holder of divine essence; it simply called forth emotions, which were communicated by words whose sounds would be able, they thought, to call forth the same emotion in the reader. Extreme followers of the Symbolist movement believed that poetry was sound with associations rather than words with meanings.

Private Symbol. This is a symbol that is not commonly held by a great many people. It is unique to its inventer and user. Thus, for Yeats, a heron came to symbolize subjectivity.

Conventional Symbol. This is a symbol that is widely accepted and used by other writers. It is able to arouse deep feelings and possess properties beyond what the eye alone can see.

ANALYSIS AND INTERPRETATION OF *THE SCARLET LETTER*

Author: Nathaniel Hawthorne
Date of Publication: 1850

Plot Analysis

The Custom-House. This essay was originally published with the book and thus was intended to accompany it. It serves several purposes:

- It tells how the narrator discovered a faded scarlet A and sheets of manuscript that tell the story that follows. (This is not true, for although Hawthorne did indeed work in the Salem Custom House, where he claims the discovery took place, the story is all his invention. The plot actually appeared some nine years previously in one of Hawthorne's short stories.)
- It sets the mood and the feeling for the tale, by gradually placing us back in the seventeenth century.
- It serves as a form of revenge, for Hawthorne had lost his position in the Custom House because of the Whig victory in the 1849 elections. The election of Zachary

Taylor occasioned a shift in personnel and the loss of Hawthorne's political clout. Hawthorne used this essay to sketch biting portraits of his former Whig colleagues, sketches so sharp as to draw immediate fire from the local newspapers.

Chapter 1—The Prison-Door. This chapter serves to establish the *setting*, seventeenth-century Boston, through detailed description: drab, weather-beaten wooden prison; colorless people; unsightly plot of weeds. These descriptions combine to give the reader the impression of a dreary, decayed, miserable piece of land and group of people. A great deal is also accomplished through the use of *symbols:*

rust, decay, ugliness	=	the *mood* of the people, setting, novel
prison	=	*theme* of punishment
cemetery	=	*theme* of death
rose bush	=	love Hester and Dimmesdale share
		invitation to find "sweet moral blossom"
		Hester herself, the one beautiful element

Chapter 2—The Market-Place As the Puritans await Hester Prynne's public punishment, they discuss her sins in a very uncharitable manner. The people who deride her most are the most physically unattractive, and the ugliest woman goes so far as to declare that Hester ought to be killed outright for her sins. Hester's sin, it emerges, is adultery, the proof evident in her little daughter, Pearl. Hester is brought out before the crowd to undergo public punishment, and she is an exceedingly beautiful and impressive young woman. She thinks of her former life.

This chapter serves to introduce us to the main character as well as to establish the smug, self-righteous nature of Puritan society. This is shown in the holier-than-thou attitude of the women who criticize Hester so freely and cruelly.

Chapter 3—The Recognition. Hester, still on the scaffold to be publically humiliated, catches sight of a small, misshapen man on the outskirts of the crowd. He, seeing her, is equally taken aback. We learn that this is her husband, who had sent her ahead to America some two years earlier. She had assumed that he had been lost, and because of these unusual circumstances, she is not being executed for her sin, but instead must wear the Scarlet Letter and withstand public punishment. The stranger, whom no one realizes is her husband, reveals that he has been held by the "heathen-folk." The Reverend Arthur Dimmesdale is called upon to plead with Hester to reveal her lover's name. Despite his pleas, she refuses to name her partner. This is a highly ironic scene as we later realize, for the Reverend himself is Hester's lover, and were this fact known, his career would be ended in humiliation.

This chapter reveals Hester's strength of will, as she undergoes this punishment alone.

Chapter 4—The Interview. After seeing her husband and withstanding the public display, Hester and her child, Pearl, are in a frenzy. Ironically, Hester's husband, who is a physician, is brought in to minister to them. He calms them both with potions. We learn that her husband, who will go under the name of Roger Chillingworth, bears little ill-will against Hester. He had fallen in love with her, and thought that his gentle nature would win her heart. But he is quite old and she never came to love him, nor ever lied and told him that she did. He is determined to discover the man who has violated his marriage and probe his soul. To this end, he makes Hester swear that she will keep his indentity secret.

Chapter 5—Hester at Her Needle. Hester is released from jail and free to go wherever she desires, but her love for Dimmesdale keeps her in Boston, and she rents a small cottage on the outskirts of the town. She supports herself and her infant daughter through her skill at needlework—the same skill evident on the Scarlet A that so inflamed the women of the town in the first chapter—and her work is in great demand for every occasion but weddings. Despite the popularity of her needlework, Hester and her daughter are complete social outcasts. While she shows her penance for her sin by wearing the coarsest clothing and taking the abuse of the Puritans, Hester inwardly rebels at the injustice of the situation, for she did not sin alone.

Chapter 6—Pearl. Pearl, Hester and Dimmesdale's daughter, is an exceptionally beautiful child, which Hester accentuates by dressing her in the most gorgeous clothing, so that Pearl appears as a miniature of the A, so stunning as to cast a circle of light about her. But Pearl will not bend to rules, possessing a character "whose elements are perhaps beautiful and brilliant—but all in disorder." Her fiery passion, love of mischief, and disrespect for authority remind Hester of her own sin of passion. Pearl adds to Hester's sorrow rather than soothing it, for the deep love Hester feels for her daughter is tempered by fear of her wildness. Pearl is also a living reminder of her sin, and in a perverse way, Pearl delights in taunting her mother about the Scarlet A, pelting it with flowers, asking endless questions about it.

This portrayal of Pearl shows us one level of Hawthorne's genius, for it is entirely possible that a child living isolated from society would become wild and disrespectful of rules. It is also logical that she would focus on the A, shining against Hester's somber clothing, as it would appear a wonderful plaything. On the other hand, this functions well as a symbol, a living A juxtaposed against the cloth A Hester wears. Both remind her of her sin; both are inescapable.

Chapter 7—The Governor's Hall. Hester hears that certain influential citizens, feeling it would be better for both mother and child, plan to remove Pearl from her care. Alarmed, she goes to the Governor's mansion to plead to keep her child. Pearl is dressed in scarlet and gold, a perfect representation of the A. When they enter the mansion, the A on Hester's chest is reflected in a suit of armour to such an extent that she seems hidden behind it. Hester's proud and defiant acceptance of her punishment is demonstrated by the way she dressed Pearl as a miniature of the A.

Chapter 8—The Elf-Child and the Minister. The Governor, shocked by Pearl's immodest dress, challenges Hester's fitness to raise her child. To test her, they question Pearl on her knowledge of catechim. Although Hester has taught her much about religion, much more than most three-year-olds would be expected to know, Pearl deliberately pretends ignorance. Horrified, the Governor and the Reverend are ready to take Pearl from Hester at once. Hester protests, and appeals to Dimmesdale for help. Holding his hand over his heart, he speaks so persuasively that they allow Hester to keep Pearl. This is the first hint that we have that there is something in, on, or about Dimmesdale's heart that causes him discomfort.

Chapter 9—The Leech. Chillingworth has been well received in the town, the people believe that he has been helping their beloved minister, Dimmesdale. Dimmesdale entrusts his health to Chillingworth and they spend much time together, even moving into the same house. Gradually some of the townspeople come to suspect that Chillingworth is not what he appears, that he is secretly evil. Finally, the townspeople come to believe that Dimmesdale is in the hands of the devil. All have faith, though, that he will triumph over evil.

Chapter 10—The Leech and His Patient. The title of this chapter is a pun, for a leech refers to the small bloodsucking worm doctors used to remove what they thought to be toxic substances from their patient's bodies. Thus, doctors were also called Leeches. In this instance, though, the pun has greater depth, for Chillingworth is trying to suck the life from his patient in his efforts to plumb Dimmesdale's soul. Chillingworth has become obsessed with his search for Dimmesdale's guilt. One day he finds the minister asleep in his chair, and seizing the opportunity, pulls aside the minister's vestments. What he sees causes him to "turn away with a wild look of wonder, joy, and horror" and do a little dance of joy. The reader is never told what Chillingworth actually sees. Perhaps, indeed, there is nothing there at all, and what Chillingworth perceives is simply that which he wishes to perceive. This motif is picked up again in the very end of the book, as Dimmesdale reveals his chest to the entire community.

Chapter 11—The Interior of a Heart. Now in possession of what he takes to be proof of Dimmesdale's guilt, Chillingworth begins his unrelenting torture of the minister. Ironically, as Dimmesdale's suffering grows greater and his guilt increases, he grows more popular among the congregation. Church members, not knowing of his secret sin, build him up as "a miracle of holiness." Incapable at this point of publically admitting his guilt, Dimmesdale substitutes self-punishment, often beating himself bloody.

This is a very *ironic* situation, for the more Dimmesdale tries to assert his guilt and rid himself of his sin, the more the people believe him to be innocent. In an interesting twist, Chillingworth is "more wretched than his victim," as he tortures the poor minister.

Chapter 12—The Minister's Vigil. Dimmesdale leaves his house one night and walks to the scaffold where Hester stood clutching Pearl seven years ago. He shrieks aloud at the mockery of his position—revered by the townspeople, but really a secret sinner, unable to share in his lover's public humiliation and pain. Laughing at the vision of himself frozen upon the scaffold, he hears Pearl's answering laugh. Hester and Pearl mount the scaffold, and the two adults stand linked by Pearl, the living symbol of their guilt. Dimmesdale promises to speak from the scaffold of his guilt on the great judgment day. At that moment, he looks up, and sees the sky illuminated by a dull red light in the shape of an A. At the same instance he sees that Pearl is pointing toward Chillingworth, who stands nearby, staring at the three on the scaffold. Overcome with terror, Dimmesdale asks Hester who Chillingworth really is. Hester, remembering her promise, remains silent, but Pearl pretends to answer the minister by whispering some nonsense in his ear. Chillingworth leaves. The next day, Dimmesdale ironically preaches one of his finest sermons. Later, the Sexton returns one of Dimmesdale's gloves that was found on the scaffold, and they speak of the red A that appeared in the sky. They suggest that it signified the death of a local dignitary, showing he was an "angel" and is ascending to heaven.

This is the midpoint of the book, structured so that there is a scaffold in the very beginning, in the very middle, and the very end. The scaffold stands for death and public punishment, and the three observers can be said to represent the state, church, and evil. This chapter also plays with variations on the A, with Hester, Pearl, and Dimmesdale forming an A, the A in the sky, etc.

Chapter 13—Another View of Hester. Hester is shocked at Dimmesdale's appearance, for he has greatly withered under Chillingworth's unrelenting torture. But many things have happened in seven years. Hester's quiet duty to the sick and the poor have won her great respect among the townspeople who once hated her. The A is now seen as a positive sign, said to stand for "able," and is greatly welcomed by those in need. Hester, too, has changed physically. The warmth, passion, and charm have been replaced by a coldness and severity. Her once-luxuriant hair is covered by a tight cap, and she resembles a nun. She is determined to speak with Chillingworth and have him cease torturing the minister.

Chapter 14—Hester and the Physician. Hester meets with Chillingworth, and is shocked by the change in his appearance. The visage of the gentle scholar has been replaced by the dark, evil face of the devil, complete with glowing red eyes. She pleads with him to stop plunging into Dimmesdale's soul, but he says that the *situation,* not his character, has created the necessity for his actions. We can see that Chillingworth is evil for violating the sanctity of the human heart, but that he is not a devil. It is the role of fate.

Chapter 15—Hester and Pearl. Pearl asks Hester why she wears the A and why the minister holds his hands over his heart, for by now this has become his way. Hester does not answer, and here we see her loneliness and misery, with only a rather perverse child as her companion. Despite the change in the townspeople's attitude, she has no real friends among them.

Chapter 16—A Forest Walk. Hester arranges to meet with Dimmesdale to discuss Chillingworth's true indentity. They meet in the forest, and the narrow path they trod can be said to symbolize the narrow moral path that Hester has followed for the past seven years. The forest can stand for the moral wildnerness itself, the brook for the current of life.

Chapter 17—The Pastor and His Parishioner. Hester and Dimmesdale meet, and he explains the misery of his position, a minister idolized by his flock but carrying a dark sin in his heart. She reveals to him that Chillingworth is her husband, and they decide that Chillingworth's sin is greater than theirs, for he has "violated the sanctity of the human heart." Dimmesdale's terror of Chillingworth increases, to the point where he sees death as the only possible escape. He appeals to Hester to think for him, and though appalled by his weakness, she advises him to leave Boston with her and Pearl. He makes a reference to a Scarlet Letter, saying his "burns in secret." We do not know, however, if he has an actual letter somehow imprinted on his breast, or guilt eating at his soul.

Chapter 18—A Flood of Sunshine. Hester and Dimmesdale agree to leave Boston. In joy, she throws off the Scarlet Letter, and lets her beautiful hair down. Her youth and beauty return. Symbolically, the sun breaks through the clouds and shines down upon them. In Nature, the two have yielded to their natural impulses (love), and it appears that Nature approves and that all will be well.

Chapter 19—The Child at the Brook-side. Dimmesdale wishes to speak with Pearl but she won't cross the brook. She gazes at ther mother's chest without the A and screams. She won't stop screaming until Hester pins the A back on. Dimmesdale kisses Pearl but she washes it off, and stands alone as Hester and Dimmesdale make their final plans for escape.

The living A (Pearl) forces Hester to take up the cloth A once again. This chapter works well on several levels, for it is entirely possible that a small child would be upset by a radical change in her mother's appearance and be unwilling to have a stranger kiss her. It also works well on a symbolic level, for Pearl is unwilling to accept a change in Hester until Dimmesdale has made public penance for his sin; she is equally unwilling to accept him until he has done what is right.

Chapter 20—Minister in a Maze. Dimmesdale goes over the escape plans in his mind. Hester will book passage for them in four days. On the way home he feels wicked impulses, which can be viewed as the subconscious effects of his decision to run away rather than admit his guilt to the townspeople.

Chapter 21—The New England Holiday. Hester and Pearl go to the market-place on Election Day, a very important holiday for the Puritans. We learn that Chillingworth has discovered their plans and has booked passage on the same ship.

Chapter 22—The Procession. Dimmesdale looks strong walking in the Election Day procession. All the strangers in town stare at the A on Hester's chest as though she were a freak. Dimmesdale, in sharp contrast, is treated as though he were a saint by the townspeople. The author comments, "What imagination would have been irreverent enough to surmise that the same scorching stigma was on them both," that they share the same sin, despite the difference in treatment they are accorded. There is some literary foreshadowing, as the Mistress Hibbins (taken as a witch) reveals to Hester that the "saint on earth" (Dimmesdale) carries the Black Man's mark on his chest (an A?) that will soon be revealed.

This chapter shows the wide gulf between Hester (the sinner) and Dimmesdale (the saint), although we know that the definition of "sinner" and "saint" can be applied equally in the reverse. It is all up to Dimmesdale now—he must bridge the gap, reveal his guilt, and show himself for what he really is.

Chapter 23—The Revelation of the Scarlet Letter. This is the most brilliant and triumphant moment of Dimmesdale's life, as the crowd emerges awed by the power of his speech. They shout out a tribute, but it fades as he totters and his face turns ashen. He joins Hester and Pearl on the scaffold, and Chillingworth appears and tries to stop him, for if Dimmesdale reveals the truth, Chillingworth will have been robbed of his full revenge. As Dimmesdale, Hester, and Pearl climb to the top of the scaffold together, Dimmesdale tells Hester that he is dying and must acknowledge his guilt. He cries out to the crowd of his guilt, tears the ministerial band from his chest, and stands flushed with triumph before the crowd. Then he sinks down. Pearl kisses him (compare the kiss he tries to give her at the brook-side), he bids Hester farewell, and dies. This is the climax of the book.

Chapter 24—Conclusion. People are not sure what they saw when Dimmesdale ripped open his clothing. Some swear he had the identical image of Hester's A branded in his chest, while others, equally sure, believe that his breast was as naked as that of a newborn infant. It is possible that his enormous guilt caused an A to appear from within, or that he actually burned or carved one on his chest. Part of the power of the book is that we are not sure what *is* on his chest, what people actually *did* see.

Hawthorne did not want to add this part of the book, but the publisher felt that a moral was necessary. This was very common in nineteenth-century novels. Here, the moral is "Be true! Be true! Show freely to the world, if not your worst, yet some trait whereby the worst may be inferred!" The publisher also felt that some of what he saw as loose ends had to be tied. Thus, Hester returns to her cottage after a trip to Europe, having gained wisdom through suffering, and she wears the A for the rest of her life. She was buried next to Dimmesdale, with the same tombstone, with the motto "On a field, sable, the letter A, gules" (On a black shield, the letter A, in red). It is unknown what happened to Pearl, but some believe that she married and lived happily; some say they saw Hester making baby clothes. Chillingworth dies, his reason for living gone.

One Possible Interpretation of Events in *The Scarlet Letter*

Theme: Hawthorne was showing the moral and psychological results of sin. These include isolation and morbidity as well as a distortion of character. Chillingworth, for example, becomes an evil, twisted, satanic figure, in contrast to the gentle scholar Hester married. Dimmesdale becomes progressively more "dim," as his will is sapped by Chillingworth's endless probing. And Hester sets aside her youth and beauty to serve the poor, becoming nun-like in the severity of her dress and manner. All three are drastically changed as a result of sin. Hawthorne felt that Chillingworth's sin was the worst of all—"violating the sanctity of the human heart"—far worse than Hester and Dimmesdale's initial passion, and even Dimmesdale's inability to share in the sin publicly.

Character: Chillingworth and Dimmesdale can be seen as two aspects of the *will*—the active and the inactive. From its inception, Puritanism generated a strong belief in the power of the will to overcome all obstacles in the path of the New Israelites in America, in the path of the individual who strove toward Election. But at the same time the Puritan doctrine of predestination denied the possibility of any will except God's. This created a bind that many found impossible to overcome.

Chillingworth unites the intellect and the will, and coldly, with sinister motives, analyzes Dimmesdale. This is the unpardonable sin.

Dimmesdale is the intellect without the will (recall the chapter where he begs Hester to think for him, and though appalled by his weakness, she plans their abortive escape to England). He is passive, all eloquence, sensitivity, refinement, and moral scruple. He preyed upon himself as Chillingworth preyed on him, beating himself in secret to punish himself for his weakness.

Pearl is intuition, the lawless poetic view of the world. She is the artistic impulse outlawed by Puritan doctrine.

Chillingworth	probing intellect, almost the stereotypical mad scientist
Dimmesdale	moral sensibility, effete New Englander
Pearl	the artist, the unconscious
Hester	fallible human reality, what we all are

Brief Review of Puritanism for *The Scarlet Letter*

To the Puritans, the Bible was a complete body of laws, bringing all the spiritual life into relation not only with theology and ethics but with all knowledge and conduct.

The Puritans claimed the right of the individual to read and interpret the Bible for himself, yet in the fundamentals of their faith they agreed with the teachings of John Calvin, the French Protestant reformer. The main tenets of Calvinism can be summarized as follows:

1. God—and only God—elects the individual to be saved.
2. God designs complete salvation and redemption only for those elect.
3. Fallen man (All men are fallen because of the orginal sin of Adam and Eve.) is in himself incapable of true faith and repentance. Only God can supply that, if He so desires.
4. God's grace is sufficient for the elect.
5. A soul once regenerated is never completely lost.

Thus, all men are born evil, because of the original sin of Adam and Eve. God elects certain ones for salvation and only those will be saved. You do not know if you are one of the elect—that can only be discovered after you have died—and so life was often spent in a constant state of self-examination.

The Puritan faith made life anything but dull. The world was the setting for a great drama, man in relation to God and Satan, heaven and hell. It was also the drama of Christian society, for having voyaged to America, the Puritans thought of themselves as the chosen people, the new Israelites in the New Israel. In this Holy Commonwealth, the Bible was the Constitution, only church members were citizens, and God's ministers ruled the state. The more this corporate blessedness was undermined by Satan—in the form of Indians, witches, dissenters, and internal church conflicts—the more passionately it was believed in and enforced.

Hawthorne's relative, John Hathorne (Nathaniel added the "w"), was a judge at the Salem witch trials of 1692. He was merciless in his devotion to what he saw as his duty, ridding the state of witches, and was given the name "the hanging judge of Salem." This is thought to have sparked Nathaniel's interest in the past, although his family always had an inward turn. They were not a social family, and the early death of Nathaniel's father, a sea captain, is thought to have contributed to this introspection. In any event, Nathaniel had a deep and abiding interest in the Puritan past, unusual in the 1850s, when his contemporaries were exploring the notion of man as divine and capable of his own salvation.

Some select qualities of the Puritan

God is just, not merciful.	God rewards the just and punishes the wicked.
Pleasure is suspect.	Duty is important.
All men are sinners.	Predestination was real.
There is moral value in all.	Against the Roman Catholic Church

REVIEW OF *PRIDE AND PREJUDICE*

Author: Jane Austen
Date of Publication: 1813

Plot Summary

Chapter 1. As the novel opens, Mrs. Bennet is questioning her husband about a "young man of large fortune from the north of England" who has just rented a mansion not far from the Bennet's home. Mrs. Bennet wishes the eligible bachelor to marry one of her five daughters; she is worried that the Lucases, who also have daughters, will get to him first. Mr. Bennet teases his wife and calls his daughters "silly and ignorant," except for Elizabeth. These opening scenes indicate that one of the main themes of the book is the business of getting one's daughters, or oneself, married. The term "business" is just what the author intends, and she uses a great many business terms, such as "property," to indicate the materialistic and coarse nature of this entire preoccupation.

Chapter 2. Despite his teasing, Mr. Bennet does pay a call on Mr. Bingley, the bachelor, and everyone eagerly looks forward to his return call. In this chapter we see Mr. Bennet's intellectual superiority to his wife and three younger daughters. The daughters, in order from eldest to youngest, are Jane, Elizabeth, Mary, Kitty, and Lydia.

Chapter 3. Mr. Bennet refuses to reveal any details about Mr. Bingley, and so it is that Mrs. Bennet learns that he is handsome as well as rich from her friend Lady Lucas. Mr. Bingley returns Mr. Bennet's visit but meets no one else in the family, and because of an engagement in London, he is unable to accept their dinner invitation. A ball (called an "assembly") in town gives the people a chance to meet Mr. Bingley, and he shows a keen interest in Jane, the eldest of the Bennet daughters. Mr. Darcy, Mr. Bingley's good friend, is also handsome and very wealthy, but he is overly proud at the ball, and many conclude that he is disagreeable. In addition, he insults Elizabeth by saying that he would not care to dance with her because she is not handsome enough. The theme of "pride and prejudice" is introduced in this chapter, as we will see that Darcy's pride stands in the way of his falling in love with Elizabeth. In the same way, his initial insult will prevent Elizabeth from making an objective assessment of his character. The fact that Elizabeth tells the story of his slight to all her friends shows her maturity and sense of humor.

Chapter 4. Jane and Elizabeth discuss Bingley, whom Jane greatly admires. Elizabeth says that his sisters, though, seem very haughty and proud. Although Darcy's reserve and superior attitude are greatly different from Bingley's open and agreeable nature, Bingley greatly admires his friend for his clever mind. In a contrasting scene, Bingley and Darcy discuss the ball, and decide that Jane is an agreeable girl, but Darcy claims to find all the people in the town dull. Among the upper classes in England in the early nineteenth century, business and commerce were looked down on as vulgar pursuits. The Bingley sisters are not the heirs to old, established fortunes, and they act very snobbishly to play down the origin of their wealth, commerce, and try to convey the impression that they are of the established gentry. One of the themes of this book is that snobbery is not an indication of good manners and occupations are not an indication of moral worth.

Chapter 5. The Lucases and the Bennets meet to discuss the ball, and Mrs. Bennet denounces Darcy's pride. Elizabeth says that she could forgive his pride if he had not offended hers. By now, we can see that Darcy and Elizabeth are the two main characters because of their superior intellects, and we also see that Elizabeth was more deeply hurt by Darcy's remark than she has admitted. We may also see a future to their relationship.

Chapter 6. The Bingley sisters and the Bennets exchange visits, and it becomes apparent that Jane is much attracted to Bingley. Elizabeth and her close friend, Charlotte Lucas, discuss marriage. Charlotte says that a woman must catch the man she wants before someone else does. Elizabeth says that one must first be sure of her feelings, but Charlotte believes that the most important thing is to get married, regardless of emotion. This conversation reinforces the theme: Elizabeth sees the necessity for affection as well as good economic status; Charlotte sees simply the importance of being married. Despite his criticism, Darcy is attracted to Elizabeth for her personality and spirit, and admits to one of Bingley's sisters that he finds Elizabeth most pleasing. Miss Bingley discourages his interest, saying no matter how pleasing Elizabeth may be, he would have to contend with the "common" Mrs. Bennet as a mother-in-law. Miss Bingley is single, and her interest in Darcy is not totally without self-serving notions.

Chapter 7. When Mr. Bennet dies, his daughters will receive no inheritance, due to the way in which the property was originally left to him. Mrs. Bennet has a small inheritance of her own as well as two relations who are engaged in trade. Kitty and Lydia are very excited that a military regiment is to pass the winter in the vicinity. Mr. Bennet is annoyed at the shallowness of his daughters, but Mrs. Bennet reminds him that she too was once much taken with soldiers. Jane receives an invitation to visit Bingley's sisters, and through Mrs. Bennet's clever machinations, she is invited to stay the night. Unfortunately, Jane becomes ill, and Elizabeth walks the three miles to see her, arriving splattered with mud. Despite her appearance, Darcy is struck with her beauty and she is invited to stay and help nurse Jane.

Chapter 8. After dinner that evening, Elizabeth returns to Jane's room while the Bingley sisters cynically discuss her appearance and family connections with trade. Darcy concludes that she will not stand a good chance of marrying someone of quality. The discussion turns to Darcy's fine estate, Pemberley, and we see the social differences between Darcy and Elizabeth.

Chapter 9. Elizabeth spends the night with her sister and sends for her mother, who arrives with her two youngest daughters. Mrs. Bennet exaggerates the severity of Jane's illness, insisting that Jane is not well enough to travel home. We see how vulgar and crude Mrs. Bennet can be.

Chapter 10. Darcy is now so taken with Elizabeth's character and appearance that if it were "not for the inferiority of her connections" he would seriously consider marriage. Caroline Bingley, desiring Darcy for herself, again attacks Elizabeth's family connections, and while Darcy does not reply, the barbs do have some sting.

Chapter 11. After dinner, Caroline Bingley tries to attract Darcy's attention by walking back and forth, showing off her figure, but it is only after Elizabeth joins her that Darcy looks up. It is plain that Darcy is taken with Elizabeth, but it is ironic that she is not even trying to attract him.

Chapter 12. Elizabeth writes to her mother that Jane is well, but her mother, contriving to extend their visit with Darcy and Bingley, refuses to send the carriage. Elizabeth borrows Bingley's carriage and returns home anyway.

Chapter 13. The next morning, Mr. Bennet reads a letter to his family that tells them that Mr. Collins, who is to inherit Bennet's estate, had been ordained in the Church of England and receives the patronage of a wealthy Lady, Catherine. He is to visit, the letter says, and he arrives that afternoon.

Chapter 14. Mr. Collins tells of his good fortune in receiving the patronage of Lady Catherine, and Mr. Bennet and Elizabeth are much amused at his pompous airs.

Chapter 15. Collins has decided to visit the Bennets partly to marry one of the daughters, which he feels will somewhat make up for his inheriting the estate. He focuses his attentions on Elizabeth. The next day they go for a walk and meet Mr. Wickham, an officer. They meet with Darcy, and Darcy and Wickham are visibly embarrassed at seeing each other. We see Collins as perhaps the most pompous, snobbish person in the book.

Chapter 16. The next evening, at a party, Wickham tells Elizabeth that Darcy's father had been his godfather and had informally bequeathed a very fine parish to Wickham, who was to enter the church. Darcy ignored his father's wishes, though, and so Wickham has had to enter the military to make a living. Elizabeth finds herself attracted to Wickham and feels that he has indeed been misused by Darcy. Wickham goes on to say that Collin's patron, Lady Catherine, is Darcy's aunt.

Chapter 17. The next day Elizabeth tells Jane what Wickham revealed. Jane, as usual, cannot believe ill of anyone. One of the themes here is appearance vs. reality. Elizabeth knows little of Wickham, yet she believes his tale based on his appearance, as well as Darcy's apparent pride. In the course of the action, Elizabeth learns that appearances can be deceiving. Another aspect of this theme involves the nature of trade, for it would appear that people engaged in commerce would or could be inferior. In reality, Elizabeth's aunt and uncle in London are morally superior to Caroline Bingley and Lady Catherine.

Chapter 18. At the ball, it is announced that Wickham is not attending because he wants to avoid Darcy. Elizabeth feels added resentment against Darcy, but when he asks her to dance, she is too surprised to refuse. He will not talk about Wickham, though, and he finds himself even more attracted to her. Later, Miss Bingley tells Elizabeth that Wickham is responsible for the bad feelings, but Elizabeth refuses to listen. Mrs. Bennet behaves badly, bragging that her daughter Jane will soon marry Bingley. We see Darcy struggle between the attraction of Elizabeth's wit and beauty and her vulgar and tasteless mother and family connections.

Chapter 19. The next day Mr. Collins proposes to Elizabeth and although she quickly declines, he takes this to be mere coyness. This scene is comic, as Collins, a true bore, refuses to believe that anyone could possibly refuse his offer of marriage.

Chapter 20. Mrs. Bennet tries to force Elizabeth to marry Collins, but her father backs her decision completely. Collins finally realizes that Elizabeth is serious and withdraws his offer. This scene, although comic, shows how wide the gulf is between Elizabeth and her mother.

Chapter 21. Elizabeth sees Wickham, and he admits that he missed the ball to avoid Darcy. Jane receives a letter from Caroline Bingley, who tells her that Bingley will marry Darcy's sister. Jane believes that Bingley has lost interest in her; Elizabeth does not agree.

Chapter 22. Collins proposes to Charlotte Lucas, Elizabeth's best friend, and to Elizabeth's astonishment, Charlotte accepts quite happily. This shows us one view of marriage—making a good business transaction. Both are satisfied.

Chapter 23. Lady Lucas arrives at the Bennets to brag of her daughter's engagement, but Mrs. Bennet is furious, since by the terms of the inheritance, Charlotte Lucas will one day be mistress of her home rather than one of her daughters, as she had schemed and planned.

Chapter 24. Jane receives another letter from Miss Bingley, who informs her that they are to stay in London all winter. She also claims that Bingley will marry Darcy's sister. Elizabeth does not believe this. She criticizes Charlotte's marriage, saying that for a marriage to be a success, both affection and material needs must be considered.

Chapter 25. Collins returns to the Bennet's neighborhood, and Mrs. Bennet's brother and his wife come for a Christmas visit. He and his wife are far superior in breeding to his sister, and Mrs. Gardiner, the sister-in-law, convinces Jane to return with them to London for a visit. Mrs. Gardiner had lived in the area and enjoys hearing news of it from Wickham. This will become very important later.

Chapter 26. Mrs. Gardiner discourages Elizabeth's interest in Wickham. Collins arrives for his marriage to Charlotte Lucas. Jane visits with Bingley's sister in London but is coolly received and becomes convinced that Bingley never really cared for her. Wickham has become very interested in a young woman who has inherited a considerable sum of money. It appears his idea of marriage is very much like Charlotte's.

Chapter 27. Elizabeth travels to London, where her aunt teases her about the loss of Wickham's attentions. Although she defends his action, it appears that she is upset by his turn to another for the sake of money.

Chapter 28. The next day Elizabeth and her friends pay a call on Mr. Collins, who speaks at great length about his patron, Lady Catherine. Elizabeth gets a look at the "sickly and cross" girl who is rumored to become the future Mrs. Darcy.

Chapter 29. While everyone is greatly impressed by Lady Catherine, the independent-minded Elizabeth finds her snobbish. Pride and good breeding, two of the themes of this book, are treated ironically in Lady Catherine, who despite her high birth, has neither. The theme is that good breeding does not belong only to the upper classes.

Chapter 30. Elizabeth stays on to visit with Charlotte, and it emerges that Lady Catherine is a general busybody. A week before Easter, Darcy and his cousin, Colonel Fitzwilliam, arrive for a visit.

Chapter 31. The next week, the Collinses and their guests visit Lady Catherine. Darcy is upset at his aunt's ill breeding. Elizabeth engages in banter with Darcy that only increases his attraction to her, but again she is not aware of it.

Chapter 32. Darcy and Elizabeth visit alone; he had expected others to be there and the visit is somewhat uncomfortable. Later, Charlotte suggests that Darcy's visit shows that he is attracted to Elizabeth, but Elizabeth quickly discounts this, despite his repeated visits during the next few days.

Chapter 33. Darcy and Elizabeth continue to meet during her solitary walks, but she is more interested in the attentions of his cousin, Fitzwilliam. He, however, tells her that as the younger son he does not stand to inherit any money and thus must consider money a factor when he marries. He also says that Bingley is much indebted to Darcy for saving him from a poor marriage. Elizabeth had believed that Miss Bingley was the leader in convincing her brother not to marry Jane and is very distressed by this news.

Chapter 34. Darcy calls on Elizabeth to propose marriage, explaining that his pride has stood in the way of his heart. To his astonishment, she refuses his offer, and tells him that she is angry that he prevented Jane and Bingley from marrying. Darcy's pride is so great that he feels compelled, even while he is proposing, to tell her what a great sacrifice he is making.

Chapter 35. The next morning Darcy hands Elizabeth a letter attempting to justify his actions. He also explains his side of the situation concerning Wickham. It emerges that Elizabeth has been mistaken about a number of things: Darcy's pride has not been all snobbishness and Wickham has not been honest and open.

Chapter 36. Elizabeth reads Darcy's letter with great excitement and realizes her great *prejudice* has stood in her way of understanding the situation fully. Now she sees that Wickham's behavior is not consistent and that she has been misled by appearances. She declares, "Till this moment I never knew myself," and begins to shed her prejudice and be honest with herself. Read this chapter very carefully; it shows the correct order of all that has been incorrectly perceived before.

Chapter 37. Elizabeth carefully thinks over what she has learned.

Chapter 38. Elizabeth leaves the Collinses residence and travels to London for a few days. She decides to wait until they return home to tell Jane what she has learned.

Chapter 39. The main function of this chapter is to tell the reader about Lydia's character. She is a great deal like her mother, coarse and vulgar.

Chapter 40. Elizabeth tells Jane what she has learned about Bingley from Darcy, as well as about her prejudice against him.

Chapter 41. Seeing her youngest sisters crying over the departure of the regiment, Elizabeth feels the truth of what Darcy has said about her family. Lydia is invited to join a young wife and follow the officers. Elizabeth tries to get her father to stop what is at best an imprudent and at worst a dangerous trip, but he does not want to upset the family peace. Wickham returns, and Elizabeth hints that she has learned a great deal about him. We see by his fear and refusal to talk with her that Darcy's side is correct. Lydia leaves on her trip.

Chapter 42. Elizabeth realizes that her father married her mother solely for her looks and quickly lost interest in her. This has been a poor example for the family, and he has tended to ignore all his daughters except Elizabeth. Elizabeth goes for a vacation with the Gardiners to the area around Darcy's estate, Mrs. Gardiner's childhood home.

Chapter 43. Elizabeth tours Darcy's home, secure that he is away. The housekeeper describes him in such glowing terms that she cannot believe this is the same man she knows. As they are leaving the house, Darcy appears. Elizabeth is overcome with shame that he will think she is pursuing him. Later, they meet him again, and he treats her and her family with great courtesy. Because she has shed her prejudice and he his pride, they can see each other more clearly and she sees his true interest in her.

Chapter 44. Darcy brings his sister to meet Elizabeth the same day, a great compliment, and because of his behavior, her aunt and uncle conclude that his intentions are sincere and his love true. Elizabeth explores her own feelings about him.

Chapter 45. Bingley's sister receives Elizabeth's visit, which is not warm and cordial, and after Elizabeth leaves, criticizes her. Darcy comes to Elizabeth's defense.

Chapter 46. Jane writes two letters to Elizabeth. The first says that Lydia has run off with Wickham; the second, that he does not intend to marry her. Elizabeth runs to catch her aunt and uncle and meets Darcy, who is very sympathetic toward her plight. She thinks that this disgrace will wipe away any affection he has for her. This is an important chapter, for we see that emotion (feeling) should always be governed by reason. The Gardiners leave to find Lydia.

Chapter 47. Elizabeth and the Gardiners discuss Lydia and Wickham. Elizabeth does not reveal the complete truth about his past, but enough so that the Gardiners realize that he is not honest. Meanwhile, Mrs. Bennet blames everyone but herself for Lydia's misfortune, not seeing that it is the result of a careless upbringing.

Chapter 48. Wickham owes money all over town. Collins writes a letter to the Bennets, in which he says that it would be better if Lydia were dead rather than to dishonor her family so. Again we see how shallow he is. Mr. Bennet tells Elizabeth that he is responsible for what has happened to Lydia, and we see that as with Darcy and Elizabeth, he too has a moment of realization, when he must acknowledge and confess his character faults.

Chapter 49. Gardiner has found Lydia and Wickham and has learned that Wickham has no intention of marrying her. Gardiner arranges a settlement: Wickham will marry Lydia for a sum of money. Elizabeth is worried about a marriage that starts so poorly; her mother, in contrast, is delighted that Lydia will marry. In Jane Austen's time, this was the only sensible solution to the problem, since a decent middle-class man would not marry a woman who had run off with another man. Therefore, Lydia would either have had to marry "beneath" her or remain unmarried.

Chapter 50. Mrs. Bennet looks for a house for Lydia and Wickham, but Mr. Bennet informs her that he will not give her any money and will never receive the couple in his home. Wickham and Lydia will move to another part of the country, and Elizabeth convinces her father to see Lydia off. Elizabeth now sees that she and Darcy would have had a model marriage, but she believes that the alliance between Lydia and Wickham, Darcy's enemy, is the final blow, for Darcy would never marry into such a family.

Chapter 51. Lydia and Wickham arrive and behave poorly. Lydia tells her sisters to go to Brighton, for that is where they will all find husbands. It does not bother her that she has nearly disgraced the family and that Wickham had to be bribed to marry her at all. Lydia reveals that Darcy was at their wedding, which astonishes Elizabeth.

Chapter 52. Mr. Gardiner writes to Elizabeth to tell her what Darcy has done. After Gardiner arrived in London, Darcy contacted him to tell him that he had heard about Wickham and Lydia and gone after them to try to change their minds. Darcy had arranged the financial settlement and had paid the full amount himself—but the Bennets were not to know. Finally, Darcy returned for the wedding and the final financial arrangements. Wickham comes to see Elizabeth, they discuss the truth of his past, and Elizabeth generously asks that they forget the past.

Chapter 53. Wickham and Lydia leave, and Mr. Bennet ironically says that Wickham is a fine fellow. We learn that Bingley is to return to his home in the country, and on the third day after their arrival, Bingley and Darcy come to pay a call on the Bennets.

Chapter 54. Some days later at dinner, Bingley and Jane are excited to be with one another again, but Darcy seems to treat Elizabeth coolly. She believes that this is because she has once refused his offer of marriage.

Chapter 55. Bingley proposes to Jane. Mrs. Bennet's moral and intellectual dullness are made clear by the way she reacts to her daughter's news: She treats it as she did Lydia's, apparently seeing no difference in the way Jane and Bingley regard each other from the way Wickham used Lydia.

Chapter 56. Lady Catherine appears at Elizabeth's door, rudely inquiring if it is true that Darcy is to marry her, since she wants Darcy to marry her daughter. Lady Catherine is insulting and vulgar. Her crude assault is an extreme form of the pride from which Darcy once suffered. All of Lady Catherine's wealth cannot make up for her poor breeding.

Chapter 57. Collins writes a letter revealing Darcy's plan to marry Elizabeth, but warning that it will be what Lady Catherine calls a "disgraceful match." Mr. Bennet is much amused, thinking that Elizabeth greatly dislikes Darcy. She is angry and confused. She would like to be engaged, and others think she is, but she is not.

Chapter 58. Darcy comes to visit and Elizabeth thanks him for what he has done for Lydia. He again proposes, and this time she accepts. They declare their mutual love. They review the details of their relationship, their pride and prejudice.

Chapter 59. Elizabeth tells her father of her match, and he cautions her to not marry unless she feels affection. She tells him that she does indeed love Darcy, despite her earlier condemnations of him. She informs her mother, who is thrilled that Elizabeth is to marry.

Chapter 60. Elizabeth and Darcy discuss how they fell in love. The Collinses come to visit, and Darcy patiently endures the dull Collins and vulgar Mrs. Bennet.

Chapter 61. Jane and Elizabeth each marry. A year later, Jane and Bingley buy an estate about thirty miles from Pemberely, where Darcy and Elizabeth live. Lydia writes to Elizabeth, asking for help. Elizabeth sends money, and Darcy helps Wickham with his army career. All the loose ends are tied up, and we see in Elizabeth and Darcy and Jane and Bingley the portrait of happy marriage, quite different from the business proposition pictured in Chapter 1.

Organization of Plot

The plot of *Pride and Prejudice* is organized *two* ways—by pairs of lovers and by places.

In the first scheme, we can divide the book into five parts:

Part I   The lovers meet, especially Darcy and Elizabeth, Jane and Bingley. The section ends with the marriage of Collins and Charlotte Lucas (Chapter 26).

Part II   Darcy proposes to Elizabeth; she refuses (chapters 27–41).

Part III Darcy and Elizabeth meet for the third time; Lydia and Wickham have run away (Chapter 42–47)

Part IV   Lydia and Wickham's story (chapter 43–52).

Part V   Double marriage of Elizabeth and Darcy, Jane and Bingley. Resolution of conflicts on all levels.

In the second method of organization, we also see five divisions, based on location:

Part I   Longbourn, Netherfield, Meryton

Part II   Hunsford and Rosings

Theme

The main idea of this book concerns the ways in which we ought to select spouses and conduct ourselves during the selection. Mrs. Bennet, for example, judges success in marriage strictly in economic terms, and we see that despite her conviction that her own marriage was a sound deal, her husband and she have little in common, and the marriage is actually very unsound. In the same way, Lydia's marriage is unsound, as we see in the end, when the author tells us they have little happiness. A "marriage of true affection" must combine emotional as well as practical considerations. Thus, personalities must match, and morality and social breeding must be considered. That is what we see in the models of Jane and Bingley and Elizabeth and Darcy.

Sample Questions to Consider

1. Explore the class structure of the novel: Explain what the hierarchy says about the author's theme.
2. How is the title important?
3. What does a close look at the vocabulary of this novel reveal about its moral underpinnings?

Answers

1. Marriage is the ultimate social act, because through its continuation society conserves and revivifies itself (or disintegrates). All society is hierarchical, there are ranks, orders, or classes. In the time of Elizabeth and Darcy, the late eighteenth century, these were acknowledged with greater formality than now and crossing class lines was a dramatic social event. These marriages afforded us a glimpse of the social facts of life of the eighteenth century: income ("fortune"); aristocratic ideals; snobbery; and breeding ("manners").
2. The novel deals with the effect of pride and prejudice on the characters. By "pride" the author means an unrealistic exaggeration of one's status, and by "prejudice," judging before all the evidence is at hand. While the main part of the story revolves around the relationship of pride and prejudice in Elizabeth and Darcy, it is also manifested in all the minor characters, most notably Lady Catherine, Mr. Collins, and Mrs. Bennet.
3. Certain words are frequently applied to certain people, which helps establish their characters in a subtle and highly effective manner. Thus, we have words dealing with business transactions—charge, worth, debt, business, etc.—applied to those who view marriage as a kind of business transaction, people like Charlotte, Mr. Collins, and Mrs. Bennet. On the other hand, we see abstract words dealing with moral standards—principle, sense, truth, folly, pride, prejudice, conduct, reason—applied to people who see marriage as the uniting of two like souls, people like Elizabeth and, to a lesser extent, Jane and Darcy. Naturally, the vocabulary a character uses ought to conform to the nature of his or her character. This is one of the standards by which we judge a quality work of literature.

EVALUATION OF *PORTRAIT OF THE ARTIST AS A YOUNG MAN*

Author: James Joyce
Date of Publication: 1916

Plot Summary

Chapter 1. The novel opens with some early childhood experiences of the main character, Stephen Dedalus. The scene then shifts to Clongowes, where Stephen is a student. Sensitive and standoffish, Stephen is unwilling to join his classmates in games. His mind wanders to the lavatory at school, the memory of which makes him feel hot and cold. Stephen is taken sick and admitted to the infirmary. He goes home for the Christmas holiday and we meet his family. Christmas dinner is the scene of a violent religious and political argument about Parnell, Ireland's dead hero, but Stephen does not understand what the fighting is all about. After the holidays, we shift back to the playground where Stephen listens to a conversation concerning certain boys leaving school. Again, he refrains from participation. In class Stephen is unjustly punished for neglecting his studies. The prefect of studies, Father Dolan, believes Stephen broke his eyeglasses on purpose to avoid having to do his lessons. Stephen tells the rector about the incident and is welcomed back to the playground as a hero by his classmates.

Chapter 2. His father has undergone a financial setback and Stephen has been withdrawn from school. He spends his free time reading romantic fiction. The family moves to Dublin and Stephen is sent to Belvedere school, where we see he is still proud and sensitive. He takes a trip with his father to Cork and is aware of his lack of communication with his father. In school, his pride and independence lead to trouble with the authorities. The final incident concerns an essay which has been judged to be heretical and which he is asked to recant. Stephen refuses to conform outside the classroom, defending Byron's verse and deriding Tennyson's, even though he is beaten for his opinions. With some prize money he has won, Stephen attempts to heal the rift between himself and his family. He lends them money, takes his family out, etc. but when all the money is gone, he realizes that his plan "to erect a breakwater of order and elegance" is doomed. At the same time, he feels that he is drifting into mortal sin and feelings of lust, feelings which impel him to wander Dublin's streets at night. He soon finds his way to the brothel section.

Chapter 3. Stephen's feelings of lust are sharply altered after Father Arnall's sermons on the horrors of hell and eternal damnation. Feeling that the sermons were directed at him personally, he is overcome with shame and guilt. Stephen is horrified by the graphic descriptions of hell. He is so overcome that back in his room he vomits. Later he prays for forgiveness and promises to reform his life.

Chapter 4. Partly because of his apparent devotion, Stephen is called in to speak with the director about the possibility of becoming a Jesuit priest. He realizes that this is impossible, however, for *non serviam,* I cannot serve, is his credo. He cannot leave the world by assuming a religious life; he must participate in it and accept the guilt and suffering. The symbol of his decision is the bridge over Tolka stream, as his eyes for a moment face the faded shrine of the Virgin and then turn toward his own house. The "disorder, the misrule and confusion of his father's house" is his choice. Later he goes to the shore, and the voice of the waves mingled with the voices of his friends gives shape to his name, Dedalus, the "fabulous artificer," and thus he is fated to become an artist. Seeing a lonely girl wading in the water, he feels he is reborn to the beauty of the world. As Stephen stretches out on the sand for a final vision of this new world, the novel reaches its climax, the point at which Stephen comes to understand not only literal reality but the greater reality that exists beyond.

Chapter 5. Back at the university, Stephen speaks of aesthetics (art) and we see sketches of his friends, Cranly, MacCann, and others. Remaining isolated, he refuses to sign the petition for universal peace, and we see that he is still alone, that his pride is still a motivating factor. A long discussion of aesthetic philosophy takes place between Stephen and his friend, Lynch, in which Stephen concludes that the artist must set his images between himself and "the market place," and that the forms of art must be considered as falling into three related categories: the *lyrical,* as the artist presents the image in relation to himself; the *epical,* as the image is presented in relation to himself and others; and the *dramatic,* as the image is presented in immediate relation to others. The last section of this chapter shows Stephen preparing to leave. An implied comparison is made between Stephen and Icarus, the son of Daedalus. The novel ends with Stephen recording in his diary his feelings about his upcoming escape to Europe, as he declares that his goal is "to forge in the smithy of my soul the uncreated conscience of my race."

Themes

1. Conformity to ritual (suggested by Stephen's dancing to the hornpipe).
2. Stephen's search for identity and, by extension, any artist's search for his own voice (suggested by Stephen's questions about his name).
3. Alienation and loneliness, probably the central theme (suggested by his behavior at school and with his family and friends; he is always alone, even in a crowd): The artist's search for identity and place in the hostile world.
4. Ireland, her history and politics (suggested at the very beginning by the "moocow," a symbol of Ireland, and later by the discussion of Parnell at Christmas dinner. Parnell is one of the most vivid symbols of the country.).
5. The gulf between generations, specifically the rift between father and son (suggested by the parents' behavior when Stephen gives them the prize money—how little difference it makes ultimately in their lives or his).
6. The conflict between the internal and external worlds, between imagination and reality (suggested by the contrast between heat and cold, red and green). The underlying theme in *Portrait* is the role of the artist as he seeks to discover or "forge" his place in an often hostile, or at best indifferent, world. The events take place during the artist's teen years, for this is when the conflict between the ideal (the artist) and the real (the world) is sharpest. Many who have felt themselves destined to create works of art, especially literature, have been very strongly drawn to this book, as *they* try to find a place in the world that often seems to reject them because they seem different from the norm.

Method of Development

Unlike the conventional novel, *Portrait of the Artist as a Young Man* does not depend on the *plot,* the chronological unfolding of events, to develop its themes. Rather, they are woven into the book by means of *expansion,* which takes several different forms. For example, the first, third, and fifth chapters build up ideas that are commented on in the second and fourth chapters. This rise and fall of interwoven ideas is one method of development. Another is the *recurrence of images or incidents,* as the opposites, hot and cold for example, reoccur throughout the novel. A third form of expansion is the movement from *the specific to the universal*—the specific shown, for example, in the scene where Stephen writes his name in the geography text, and moving through a series of wider definitions of himself, arriving finally at "the Universe." In these ways, Joyce was able to work around the straight line plot development of the traditional novel to use: *dialectic* (thesis-antithesis), *cyclic* (circles, returns, recurrences), and *inductive* (specific to general) means of development to suggest whole new meanings.

These expansions fit in with another of Joyce's means of development, the *architectonic,* a medieval concept that explains the integration of clearly defined parts into a unified whole. Therefore, we find a series of parts and motifs that occur again and again. Thus, for example, we see the playground at the beginning and at the end of the first chapter. Joyce's narrative structure has been termed *montage,* a term taken from the movies, a series of scenes that illustrate the daily progression of life. Some readers have felt that they could read *Portrait* in any order and it would still make sense. This would work only if the reader did not realize that one scene builds upon another to create a total effect, although on first reading the scenes may appear randomly selected.

Some Motifs in Detail

Names. Stephen's last name, Dedalus, has meaning on several levels: First, the Daedalus in Greek mythology was the man who tried to escape the ties of time and place by devising a pair of wings. Thus, he can be said to stand for the eternal conflict between man's quest for freedom and the limitations the world imposes. Daedalus also invented the labyrinth, and so, in this book, the name can also be symbolic of the mind's many twisting and turning paths that attempt to prevent the formulation of any absolute solutions.

Artistic consciousness. Very early on, Stephen is aware of his desire to create artistically. The verses that he intends to write, for example, are dedicated to E—— C——, copied from what he had seen in Byron's works. Byron was an exiled poet, as was the Count in *The Count of Monte Cristo,* one of Stephen's favorite works. Stephen will leave Ireland for Europe at the end of the work, becoming an exiled poet himself.

Role of the artist. The artist lives in isolation and solitude, Stephen/Joyce concludes. The role of the artist expressed here is taken from Flaubert's idea that the artist's role is similar to that of a priest (in the real world) and of God (in the ideal world). Yet we recall that Stephen also concludes that life is to be faced and lived, which is one reason he declined to accept the Jesuit's offer to become a priest. This apparent contradiction defines the role of the artist in the modern age: how to be a detached and preoccupied artist, yet go with the crowd at the same time. Stephen's friend MacCann accuses him of being "an antisocial being, wrapped up in [him]self" (Chapter 5), and Cranly suggests that Stephen is unable to communicate. Stephen wants to discover the way in which the artist can express himself freely, and to this end decides to use only "silence, exile, and cunning." It is for each of us to discover for ourselves the role of the artist and to evaluate Stephen's "sins"—pride and egoism. Are they necessary for the artist in the modern world? What *is* the artist's stance?

Sample Questions to Consider

1. What is Joyce's definition of "epiphany"? Give some examples from *Portrait*.
2. What is Stephen's philosphy of art? Is it the same as James Joyce's?
3. How do the sermons in Chapter 3 affect Stephen?

Answers

1. Joyce uses the term epiphany to mean a sudden realization, usually a recognition of the essence of something. Joyce himself said "its soul, its whatness leaps to us from the vestment of its appearance." In the end of *Portrait,* Stephen's epiphany comes when he realizes he must leave Ireland behind to, as he says, "forge in the smithy of my soul the uncreated conscience of my race."
2. Stephen's philosphy is based on the ideas of St. Thomas Aquinas and, and while his philosophy is simplistic it does contain important substance. Go back to lyric, epic, and dramatic (discussed previously) for the theory. Since most critics agree that Joyce is treating the young artist ironically here, most likely parodying himself at Stephen's age, it is likely that when he wrote *Portrait* he did not take these ideas very seriously himself. Much of what Stephen concludes *sounds* better than it is.
3. Impressed by the images in the sermons, Stephen attempts to use Christian faith to avoid reality. But this barrier, like his previous attempt to establish order in his life in Chapter 2, is doomed to fail, for the artist cannot escape the world, even through faith.

ESSAY QUESTIONS ON THE NOVEL

Following are some sample AP essay questions on the novel. Allow yourself 60 minutes to organize, write, and correct each essay. Be certain to cite specific examples from the work under discussion to prove your points. Follow the directions for generating and organizing your thoughts as described in **Part 2: Essay Writing Guide**. Be sure to leave time to revise and edit your essay at the end.

1. First chapters are often important in establishing the personality of a main character through language, symbolism, imagery, and so forth. Select any novel of recognized literary worth that you have read and show how this is true.
2. In the same manner, second and third chapters establish the personality of minor or secondary characters. Select any two novels of recognized literary worth that you have read and show how their second and third chapters establish the personality of secondary characters through the use of language, symbolism, imagery, and so forth.
3. The first chapter of a novel can also establish the *tone* of the entire work through word choice, imagery, symbolism, and language. Select any novel of recognized literary worth that you have read and show how this is true.
4. In some novels, the historical and/or social background is so important to the theme and plot that the work could not have been set in any other time or place. Show how this is true in any novel that you have read.
5. Occasionally the conclusion of a novel seems tacked on, not really an integral part of the narrative. It may seem that the author could not figure a way out of the action and so constructed an artificial ending, or that the beliefs of the time demanded that the book end in a particular way. Sometimes we may find two versions of a book: one with a conventionally expected ending, another with a very different outcome. Select any one novel and show how the ending does not seem to fit with the rest of the book.

6. On the other hand, there are novels whose endings seem perfect; there is no other way the action could have ended. Select any novel that you have read and show how the ending fits the rest of the book and is the best possible resolution of the theme and plot.

7. In some novels, setting is of very little importance. The novel could have taken place anywhere, anytime. Show how any one work you have read could have been set in another time and place with no loss to theme or plot, or perhaps even be improved by another setting.

8. Language is usually an important element in any work of literature. Sometimes it becomes the most significant element in a novel, a metaphor for the theme. Show how this is true in any one novel you have read.

9. Some first chapters set forth all the themes of the novel as well as establish character and setting. Show how this is true in any novel you have read. Trace the themes and show how they are introduced in the first chapter.

10. The final chapter of a novel is sometimes a letdown for the reader for a variety of reasons. Select a novel of recognized literary value and show how the ending does not live up to the promise of the beginning.

11. Oppositely, the ending of a novel may be better than you expected for a variety of reasons. Show how this is true in any novel you have read. Be sure to prove what makes the ending so much better than the text that preceded it.

12. Sometimes you may read and admire several works by the same author, then pick up another of his/her books to find that it is a great disappointment for a variety of reasons. Show how this is true in any one work you have read. First explain what made all the other books better, then show how this book was a disappointment.

13. The inverse may be true: You may not like any of the author's previous works but find one astoundingly good. Use one work you have read as an example. Explain what made the previous works disappointing and then show how this one is better. Refer to language, theme, setting, imagery, characterization, etc.

14. Select any one aspect of the novelist's craft—characterization, imagery, setting, theme, plot, etc.—and show how any one author has used that element to create a masterpiece. Select specific examples to prove your point.

SUGGESTED READING LIST

Austen, Jane	*Pride and Prejudice*
	Emma
Baldwin, James	*Go Tell It on the Mountain*
Balzac, Honoré de	*Père Goriot*
Bellamy, Edward	*Looking Backward*
Bellow, Saul	*Seize the Day*
Brontë, Charlotte	*Jane Eyre*
Brontë, Emily	*Wuthering Heights*
Buck, Pearl	*The Good Earth*
Camus, Albert	*The Stranger*
Cather, Willa	*My Antonia*
Chopin, Kate	*The Awakening*
Conrad, Joseph	*Lord Jim*
	Heart of Darkness
Crane, Stephen	*The Red Badge of Courage*
Defoe, Daniel	*Moll Flanders*
Dickens, Charles	*Great Expectations*
	David Copperfield
	Oliver Twist
	The Pickwick Papers
	A Tale of Two Cities
Dostoevski, Fyodor	*Crime and Punishment*
	The Brothers Karamazov
Dumas, Alexander	*The Count of Monte Cristo*
Eliot, George	*Silas Marner*
	The Mill on the Floss
Ellison, Ralph	*Invisible Man*
Faulkner, William	*The Sound and the Fury*
	As I Lay Dying
Fielding, Henry	*Joseph Andrews*
Fitzgerald, F. Scott	*The Great Gatsby*
Flaubert, Gustave	*Madame Bovary*
Forster, E. M.	*Passage to India*
Fowles, John	*The French Lieutenant's Woman*
Golding, William	*The Lord of the Flies*
Greene, Graham	*The Power and The Glory*
Hardy, Thomas	*The Return of the Native*
Hawthorne, Nathaniel	*The Scarlet Letter*
	The House of the Seven Gables
Hemingway, Ernest	*The Old Man and the Sea*
	For Whom the Bell Tolls
Howells, William D.	*The Rise of Silas Lapham*
Huxley, Aldous	*Brave New World*
James, Henry	*The Turn of the Screw*

Joyce, James	*A Portrait of the Artist as a Young Man*
Knowles, John	*A Separate Peace*
Lawrence, D. H.	*Sons and Lovers*
London, Jack	*Call of the Wild*
Lee, Harper	*To Kill a Mockingbird*
Mailer, Norman	*The Naked and the Dead*
Malamud, Bernard	*The Fixer*
Maugham, W. Somerset	*Of Human Bondage*
Melville, Herman	*Moby Dick*
	Billy Budd, Foretopman
Norris, Frank	*The Octopus*
Orwell, George	*1984*
	Animal Farm
Roth, Philip	*Goodbye, Columbus*
Shelley, Mary	*Frankenstein*
Steinbeck, John	*The Grapes of Wrath*
	Of Mice and Men
Stevenson, R. L.	*Kidnapped*
Swift, Jonathan	*Gulliver's Travels*
Thackeray, William M.	*Vanity Fair*
Turgenev, Ivan	*Fathers and Sons*
Twain, Mark	*The Adventures of Huckleberry Finn*
Updike, John	*Rabbit, Run*
Warren, Robert Penn	*All the King's Men*
West, Nathanael	*Miss Lonelyhearts*
Wharton, Edith	*Ethan Frome*
Woolf, Virgina	*To the Lighthouse*
	Mrs. Dalloway
Wright, Richard	*Black Boy*
	Native Son

Satire

The term "satire" is derived from the Latin "satura," which means "full," "a mixture of things." While it seems to have referred originally to food, it has come to be associated with a down-to-earth coarseness. While there are, of course, highly stylized, polite, and refined satires—Pope's *The Rape of the Lock* is a well-known example— these are not typical of satire as a whole. The function of satire was not defined by the Greeks, and so we have nothing comparable to Aristotle's analysis of tragedy. Two main conceptions of the purpose of satire have emerged, however.

TWO KINDS OF SATIRISTS

One type of satirist likes most people, but thinks they are foolish and blind to reality. He tells the truth pleasantly, so that he will not turn people away but rather cure them of that ignorance which is their worst problem. The other type of satirist hates people, and believes that wickedness and evil will triumph in the world. Swift is an example of the second type of satirist. He loves individuals, but hates mankind. He therefore desires not to cure, but to punish and destroy. The famous satirist Juvenal also falls into this category.

The two types have different views of evil. The misanthropic satirist feels that evil is rooted in man's nature and the structure of society. Nothing he can say will cure or eliminate it. Man, or the special group that he is discussing, deserves only hatred, and his laughter carries with it no identification. This type of satirist is close to the tragedian. Many readers find such satire difficult to read, for what is the purpose if man cannot be changed from the folly of his ways? The misanthropic satirist finds life not comic but contemptible.

The satirist who likes people is basically an optimist, believing that evil is not inherent in humanity, or if it is, it is like a disease which can be cured. Some people *are* incurable, and they are offered as examples in order to help the others who *can* mend the folly of their ways. Only those who understand what good really is can follow it and shed evil ways. Satirists such as Horace believed this, and they are kinder, more persuasive than denunciatory. At the worst, such satirists will say that the world's values are twisted, but offer this view as a comment on the ridiculous predicament of mankind. Usually they select a few of the worst offenders to hold up as examples. Even if the satire does cut a little too deeply, it doesn't matter, for they believe that the pain will result in a cure for the evils that they have pointed out.

WHY SATIRISTS WRITE

The different kinds of satirists naturally view their purpose differently. The optimist writes in order to correct man's problems; the pessimist writes in order to punish man for his transgressions. The optimistic satirist sees the world as essentially a healthy place, even though there are those among us who are ill and need to be cured; the pessimistic satirist sees a world full of incurable criminals, a world so mad that some have lost their wits just looking closely at it. So that he will not go insane like the rest of the sick world the pessimitic satirist uses all the hate and derision at his command. All satirists cannot be rigidly classified in this manner, however, for a writer may compose one work that is hopelessly pessimistic and follow it with another that is cheerfully optimistic. Various degrees of optimism/pessimism are even found within the same work, as the satirist's mood changes with his material.

Why does the satirist write? First, he is moved to action by a personal feeling about a specific subject, perhaps hatred or scorn, even though he may claim in his work that he has gotten rid of all personal feelings. He tries to justify his feelings and make his readers share in them. Some satirists have been moved by feelings of personal inferiority, of social injustice, of being excluded from a group to which they wished to belong. Pope and Dryden, for example, were both Roman Catholics in a Protestant country. Pope was unusually small and deformed. Juvenal and Cervantes were men of talent forced into careers they felt useless or beneath their talents.

Some satirists feel a pleasure in the material itself, and many feel the patterns of satire are especially interesting in their complexity. Any writer of satire needs a very large vocabulary, a good sense of humor and imagination, and especially good taste, allowing him to say shocking things without making the reader turn aside in disgust. This aesthetic appeals to some.

Still others like satire because it allows them to set up a model to copy and offer advice. Although some may be too bitter to give voice to positive beliefs and others may be too concerned with humor, we do find a great many satires that establish an ideal for emulation.

CHARACTERISTICS OF SATIRE

What is satire?

- It is topical, referring to its time and place.
- It claims to be realistic, although it is usually distorted or exaggerated.
- It is shocking.
- It is informal in tone and manner.
- It is funny, although it sometimes may be painful or grotesque.

It usually assumes one of three main forms:

1. *Monologue.* The satirist, usually speaking as himself or from behind an assumed mask or persona, addresses us directly. He states his view of the problem, provides examples, criticizes opponents, and tries to make his view ours.
2. *Parody.* The satirist takes an existing work of literature which was created with a serious purpose or a literary form in which some well-regarded books have been written and makes the work or the form look ridiculous, filling it with incongruous ideas or exaggerating its features. He may make the ideas look silly by placing them in an inappropriate setting or form.
3. *Narratives.* The satirist generally does not assume a narrative voice as he does in the monologue. The narratives may be stories, such as Voltaire's *Candide,* or dramatic fictions, such as *Troilus and Cressida.* This seems to be the most difficult type of satire to compose, and hardest for the reader to judge and understand.

If the forms are different, how can we tell what is a satire and what is not? What qualities make an entire work a satire, but another contain only satiric episodes?

HOW TO DETERMINE IF A WORK IS SATIRE

When a satirist writes a parody which follows the originally very closely, when his work is highly ironic, when his humor is subtle or mild, or when he pretends in such a manner as to convince the reader that he is really telling the truth, he may be mistaken for a dispassionate commentator, a skilled comedian, or a genuine admirer of the material he is ridiculing. There have been many readers who have missed the point of a satire entirely and have found themselves in agreement with the most ridiculous satiric suggestions. Fortunately, there are a number of ways to distinguish a satire:

First, the author may clue us in that he is writing a satire. Juvenal, for example, looked at the corruption rampant in Rome and wrote, "It is difficult *not* to write satire," and so we know that he is writing in the satiric mode.

Second, the author may cite previous satires to tell us what he is satirizing. When Erasmus, for example, says that his *Praise of Folly* is justified by such works as *The Battle of Frogs and Mice* and Apuleius' *Metamorphoses* (among others), he is telling us that his work follows the classical line of descent of other satirists.

Third is the choice of traditional satiric subject matter and its treatment. Often, the topic will derive directly from a previously published, well-known satiric work. This can also be accomplished by quoting another well-known satire, even without a direct statement or without mentioning the original author's name, trusting the reader to recognize it. The satirist favors *concrete, topical,* and *personal* subjects. Satires often deal with real cases and many even name real people or describe them unmistakably, and often unflatteringly. Satires often allude to the gossip of the moment in the city in which the writer resides, the here and now. Freshness is one of the most important characteristics of the satire. No one cares fifty or one hundred years later what the talk was about, and few can recall, if they are even concerned, the details of the crisis that had the whole city talking. Dryden's *Mac Flecknoe,* for example, is full of good jokes, but they pale when we have no knowledge of the participants, and we lose interest.

Fourth, while the subject matter varies, the *style* is easy to distinguish in most instances. Most satires contain cruel and even "dirty" words, and all contain comic words and terms. Many use colloquial and nonliterary terms to make their points. The satirist always tries to produce the unexpected, so in plot, tone, vocabulary, sentence structure, and phrasing, the satire will contain the unexpected, unlike the epic or the sonnet forms. We also find many typical satiric weapons—irony, paradox, antithesis, parody, anticlimax, obscenity, violence, vividness, and exaggeration. If these devices are used only in certain sections of work, then those sections can properly be considered satiric, but if they are present throughout the work, then the entire piece is considered a satire.

In almost all satires, two special attitudes, or methods, are usually present:

1. The first is the detailed description of an absurd or painful situation, or a foolish or wicked person or group of people. The satirist believes that most people are dulled by custom and must be made to see the truth as clearly as posible. A tone of scornful amusement may prevail.
2. The satirist may use blunt language to describe unpleasant people and facts in order to shock his readers into awareness. He wants to force them to look at something that they may have overlooked or may wish to overlook. Use of brutally direct language—nauseating images, crude slang, forbidden expressions—will make the people see the truth of what he is saying and be moved to feelings of protest.

There is one final test for satire. The author wishes the reader to feel a mixture of amusement and contempt. In some works the amusement far outweighs the contempt; in others, the amusement nearly vanishes in a grim. smile or a sneer of cold contempt.

A MODEST PROPOSAL

For Preventing the Children of Poor People From Being a Burthen to Their Parents or Country, and for Making Them Beneficial to the Public.

by Jonathan Swift

It is a melancholy object to those who walk through this great town, or travel in the country, when they see the streets, the roads, and cabin-doors crowded with beggars of the female sex, followed by three, four, or six children, *all in rags,* and importuning every passenger for an alms. These mothers, instead of being able to work for their honest livelihood, are forced to employ all their time in strolling, to beg sustenance for their helpless infants, who, as they grow up, either turn thieves for want of work, or leave their dear Native Country to fight for the Pretender in Spain, or sell themselves to the Barbadoes.

I think it is agreed by all parties that this prodigious number of children, in the arms, or on the backs, or at the heels of their mothers, and frequently of their fathers, is in the present deplorable state of the kingdom a very great additional grievance; and therefore whoever could find out a fair, cheap, and easy method of making these children sound useful members of the commonwealth would deserve so well of the public as to have his statue set up for a preserver of the nation.

But my intention is very far from being confined to provide only for the children of professed beggars; it is of much a greater extent, and shall take in the whole number of infants at a certain age who are born of parents in effect as little able to support them as those who demand our charity in the streets.

As to my own part, having turned my thoughts, for many years, upon this important subject, and maturely weighed the several schemes of other projectors, I have always found them grossly mistaken in their computation. It is true a child, just dropped from its dam, may be supported by her milk for a solar year with little other nourishment, at most not above the value of two shillings, which the mother may certainly get, or the value in scraps, by her lawful occupation of begging, and it is exactly at one year old that I propose to provide for them, in such a manner as, instead of being a charge upon their parents, or the parish, or wanting food and raiment for the rest of their lives, they shall, on the contrary, contribute to the feeding and partly to the clothing of many thousands.

There is likewise another great advantage in my scheme, that it will prevent those voluntary abortions, and that horrid practice of women murdering their bastard children, alas, too frequent among us, sacrificing the poor innocent babes, I doubt, more to avoid the expense than the shame, which would move tears and pity in the most savage and inhuman breast.

The number of souls in this kingdom being usually reckoned one million and a half, of these I calculate there may be about two hundred thousand couples whose wives are breeders, from which number I subtract thirty thousand couples who are able to maintain their own children, although I apprehend there cannot be so many under the present distresses of the kingdom, but this being granted, there will remain an hundred and seventy thousand breeders. I again subtract fifty thousand for those women who miscarry, or whose children die by accident or disease within the year. There only remain an hundred and twenty thousand children of poor parents annually born: The question therefore is, how this number shall be reared, and provided for, which, as I have already said, under the present situation of affairs, is utterly impossible by all the methods hitherto proposed, for we can neither employ them in handicraft, or agriculture; we neither build houses (I mean in the country), nor cultivate land: they can very seldom pick up a livelihood by stealing till they arrive at six years old, except where they are of towardly parts, although, I confess they learn the rudiments much earlier, during which time they can however be properly looked upon only as *probationers,* as I have been informed by a principal gentleman in the County of Cavan, who protested to me that he never knew above one or two instances under the age of six, even in a part of the kingdom so renowned for the quickest proficiency in that art.

I am assured by our merchants that a boy or a girl, before twelve years old, is no saleable commodity, and even when they come to this age, they will not yield above three pounds, or three pounds and half-a-crown at most on the Exchange, which cannot turn to account either to the parents or the kingdom, the charge of nutriment and rags having been at least four times that value.

I shall now therefore humbly propose my own thoughts, which I hope will not be liable to the least objection.

I have been assured by a very knowing American of my acquaintance in London, that a young healthy child well nursed is at a year old a most delicious, nourishing, and wholesome food, whether stewed, roasted, baked, or broiled, and I make no doubt that it will equally serve in a fricassee, or a ragout.

I do therefore humbly offer it to public consideration that of the hundred and twenty thousand children already computed, twenty thousand may be reserved for breed, whereof only one fourth part to be males, which is more than we allow to sheep, black-cattle, or swine, and my reason is that these children are seldom the fruits of marriage, a circumstance not much regarded by our savages, therefore one male will be sufficient to serve four females. That the remaining hundred thousand may at a year old be offered in sale to the persons of quality, and fortune, through the kingdom, always advising the mother to let them suck plentily in the last month, so as to render them plump, and fat for a good table. A child will make two dishes at an entertainment for friends, and when the family dines alone, the fore or hind quarter will make a reasonable dish, and seasoned with a little pepper or salt will be very good boiled on the fourth day, especially in winter.

I have reckoned upon a medium, that a child just born will weigh 12 pounds, and in a solar year if tolerably nursed increaseth to 28 pounds.

I grant this food will be somewhat dear, and therefore very proper for landlords, who, as they have already devoured most of the parents, seem to have the best title to the children.

Infants' flesh will be in season throughout the year, but more plentiful in March, and a little before and after, for we are told by a grave author, an eminent French physician, that fish being a prolific diet, there are more children born in Roman Catholic countries about nine months after Lent than at any other season; therefore reckoning a year after Lent, the markets will be more glutted than usual, because the number of Popish infants is at least three to one in this kingdom, and therefore it will have other collateral advantage by lessening the number of Papists among us.

I have already computed the charge of nursing a beggar's child (in which list I reckon all cottagers, labourers, and four-fifths of the farmers) to be about two shillings *per annum,* rags included, and I believe no gentleman would repine to give ten shillings for the carcass of a good fat child, which, as I have said, will make four dishes of excellent nutritive meat, when he hath only some particular friend or his own family to dine with him. Thus the Squire will learn to be a good landlord, and grow popular among his tenants, the mother will have eight shillings net profit, and be fit for work till she produces another child.

Those who are more thrifty (as I must confess the times require) may flay the carcass; the skin of which, artificially dressed, will make admirable gloves for ladies, and summer boots for fine gentlemen.

As to our City of Dublin, shambles may be appointed for this purpose, in the most convenient parts of it, and butchers we may be assured will not be wanting, although I rather recommend buying the children alive, and dressing them hot from the knife, as we do roasting pigs.

A very worthy person, a true lover of this country, and whose virtues I highly esteem, was lately pleased, in discoursing on this matter, to offer a refinement upon my scheme. He said that many gentlemen of this kingdom, having of late destroyed their deer, he conceived that the want of venison might be well supplied by the bodies of young lads and maidens, not exceeding fourteen years of age, nor under twelve, so great a number of both sexes in every country being now ready to starve for want of work and service: and these to be disposed of by their parents if alive, or otherwise by their nearest relations. But with due deference to so excellent a friend, and so deserving a patriot, I cannot be altogether in his sentiments; for as to the males, my American acquaintance assured me from frequent experience that their flesh was generally tough and lean, like that of our schoolboys, by continual exercise, and their taste disagreeable, and to fatten them would not answer the charge. Then as to the females, it would, I think with humble submission, be a loss to the public, because they soon would become breeders themselves: And besides, it is not improbable that some scrupulous people might be apt to censure such a practice (although indeed very unjustly) as a little bordering upon cruelty, which, I confess, hath always been with me the strongest objection against any project, however so well intended.

But in order to justify my friend, he confessed that this expedient was put into his head by the famous Psalmanazar, a native of the island Formosa, who came from thence to London, above twenty years ago, and in conversation told my friend that in his country when any young person happened to be put to death, the executioner sold the carcass to persons of quality, as a prime dainty, and that, in his time, the body of a plump girl of fifteen, who was crucified for an attempt to poison the emperor, was sold to his Imperial Majesty's Prime Minister of State, and other great Mandarins of the Court, in joints from the gibbet, at four hundred crowns. Neither indeed can I deny that if the same use were made of several plump young girls in this town, who, without one single groat to their fortunes, cannot stir abroad without a chair, and appear at the playhouse, and assemblies in foreign fineries, which they never will pay for, the kingdom would not be the worse.

Some persons of a desponding spirit are in great concern about that vast number of poor people, who are aged, diseased, or maimed, and I have been desired to employ my thoughts what course may be taken to ease the nation of so grievous an encumbrance. But I am not in the least pain upon that matter, because it is very well known that they are every day dying, and rotting, by cold, and famine, and filth, and vermin, as fast as can be reasonably expected. And as to the younger labourers they are now in almost as hopeful a condition. They cannot get work, and consequently pine away for want of nourishment, to a degree, that if at any time they are accidentally hired to common labour, they have not strength to perform it; and thus the country and themselves are happily delivered from the evils to come.

I have too long digressed, and therefore shall return to my subject. I think the advantages by the proposal which I have made are obvious and many, as well as of the highest importance.

For first, as I have already observed, it would greatly lessen the number of Papists, with whom we are yearly over-run, being the principal breeders of the nation, as well as our most dangerous enemies, and who stay at home on purpose with a design to deliver the kingdom to the Pretender, hoping to take their advantage by the absence of so many good Protestants, who have chosen rather to leave their country than stay at home, and pay tithes against their conscience to an Episcopal curate.

Secondly, The poorer tenants will have something valuable of their own, which by law be made liable to distress, and help to pay their landlord's rent, their corn and cattle being already seized, and *money a thing unknown.*

Thirdly, Whereas the maintenance of an hundred thousand children, from two years old, and upwards, cannot be computed at less than ten shillings a piece *per annum,* the nation's stock will be thereby increased fifty thousand pounds *per annum,* besides the profit of a new dish, introduced to the tables of all gentlemen of fortune in the kingdom, who have any refinement in taste, and the money will circulate among ourselves, the goods being entirely of our own growth and manufacture.

Fourthly, The constant breeders, besides the gain of eight shillings sterling *per annum,* by the sale of their children, will be rid of the charge of maintaining them after the first year.

Fifthly, This food would likewise bring great custom to taverns, where the vintners will certainly be so prudent as to procure the best receipts for dressing it to perfection, and consequently have their houses frequented by all the fine gentlemen, who justly value themselves upon their knowledge in good eating; and a skilful cook, who understands how to oblige his guests, will contrive to make it as expensive as they please.

Sixthly, This would be a great inducement to marriage, which all wise nations have either encouraged by rewards, or enforced by laws and penalties. It would increase the care and tenderness of mothers toward their children, when they were sure of a settlement for life, to the poor babes, provided in some sort by the public to their annual profit instead of expense. We should see an honest emulation among the married women, which of them could bring the fattest child to the market, men would become as fond of their wives, during the time of their pregnancy, as they are now of their mares in foal, their cows in calf, or sows when they are ready to farrow, nor offer to beat or kick them (as it is too frequent a practice) for fear of a miscarriage.

Many other advantages might be enumerated: For instance, the addition of some thousand carcasses in our exportation of barrelled beef; the propagation of swine's flesh, and improvement in the art of making good bacon, so much wanted among us by the great destruction of pigs, too frequent at our tables, which are no way comparable in taste or magnificence to a well-grown, fat yearling child, which roasted whole will make a considerable figure at a Lord Mayor's feast, or any other public entertainment. But this and many others I omit, being studious of brevity.

Supposing that one thousand families in this city would be constant customers for infant's flesh, besides others who might have it at merry-meetings, particularly weddings and christenings, I compute that Dublin would take off annually about twenty thousand carcasses, and the rest of the kingdom (where probably they will be sold somewhat cheaper) the remaining eighty thousand.

I can think of no objection that will possibly be raised against this proposal, unless it should be urged that the number of people will be thereby much lessened in the kingdom. This I freely own, and was indeed one principal design in offering it to the world. I desire the reader will observe, that I calculate my remedy for this one individual *Kingdom of Ireland, and for no other that ever was, is, or, I think, ever can be upon earth.* Therefore let no man talk to me of other expedients: *Of taxing our absentees at five shillings a pound: Of using neither clothes, nor household furniture, except what is of our own growth and manufacture: Of utterly rejecting the materials and instruments that promote foreign luxury: Of curing the expensiveness of pride, vanity, idleness, and gaming in our women: Of introducing a vein of parsimony, prudence, and temperance: Of learning to love our Country, wherein we differ even from* LAPLANDERS, AND THE INHABITANTS OF TOPINAMBOO: *Of quitting our animosities and factions, nor act any longer like the Jews, who were murdering one another at the very moment their city was taken: Of being a little cautious not to sell our country and consciences for nothing: Of teaching landlords to have at least one degree of mercy toward their tenants. Lastly, of putting a spirit of honesty, industry, and skill into our shopkeepers, who, if a resolution could now be taken to buy only our native goods, would immediately unite to cheat and exact upon us in the price, the measure, and the goodness, nor could ever yet be brought to make one fair proposal of just dealing, though often earnestly invited to it.*

Therefore I repeat, let no man talk to me of these and the like expedients, till he hath at least some glimpse of hope that there will ever be some hearty and sincere attempt to put them in practice.

But as to myself, having been wearied out for many years with offering vain, idle, visionary thoughts, and at length utterly despairing of success, I fortunately fell upon this proposal, which as it is wholly new, so it hath something solid and real, of no expense and little trouble, full in our own power, and whereby we can incur no danger in *disobliging* ENGLAND. For this kind of commodity will not bear exportation, the flesh being of too tender a consistence to admit a long continuance in salt, *although perhaps I could name a country which would be glad to eat up our whole nation without it.*

After all I am not so violently bent upon my own opinions as to reject any offer, proposed by wise men, which shall be found equally innocent, cheap, easy, and effectual. But before something of that kind shall be advanced in contradiction to my scheme, and offering a better, I desire the author, or authors, will be pleased maturely to consider two points. First, as things now stand, how they will be able to find food and raiment for an hundred thousand useless mouths and backs. And secondly, there being a round million of creatures in human figure, throughout this kingdom, whose whole subsistence put into a common stock would leave them in debt two millions of pounds sterling; adding those, who are beggers by profession, to the bulk of farmers, cottagers, and labourer with their wives and children, who are beggars in effect. I desire those politicians, who

dislike my overture, and may perhaps be so bold to attempt an answer, that they will first ask the parents of these mortals whether they would not at this day think it a great happiness to have been sold for food at a year old, in the manner I prescribe, and thereby have avoided such a perpetual scene of misfortunes as they have since gone through, by the oppression of landlords, the impossibility of paying rent without money or trade, the want of common sustenance, with neither house nor clothes to cover them from the inclemencies of the weather, and the most inevitable prospect of entailing the like, or greater miseries upon their breed for ever.

I profess in the sincerity of my heart that I have not the least personal interest in endeavouring to promote this necessary work, having no other motive than the *public good of my country, by advancing our trade, providing for infants, relieving the poor, and giving some pleasure to the rich.* I have no children by which I can propose to get a single penny; the youngest being nine years old, and my wife past child-bearing.

ANALYSIS OF "A MODEST PROPOSAL"

The best known of Jonathan Swift's shorter pieces, "A Modest Proposal" (1729), composed when he had long been Dean of St. Patrick's, the Protestant cathedral in Dublin, is consistently ironic and relentlessly harsh and satiric. Its aim, in the words of its long title, is to prevent "the children of poor people from being a burthen to their parents or country, and for making them beneficial to the public." Not a single sentence in the essay deviates from this bitter tone. Its persuasive power lies in its irrefutable indictment of Irish and English indifference and sheer folly in the face of unspeakable injustice and misery, but its first attraction is its wildly original and creative idea.

The pamphlet does not claim to be written by Swift himself; as with many monologues, as we mentioned earlier, the author assumes a mask. In this case, Swift claims the document has been penned by an anonymous Irish patriot, whose sole motive was to help the people of Ireland by solving their most pressing social and economic problems. The situation was that under English domination, the people of Ireland were starving to death. One radical solution, Irish independence, could not then be considered and so other measures of complete social, financial, and moral reorganization were obviously correct. Thus, they would never be considered or initiated, Swift felt with the pessimism of the satirist. So, behind the ironic mask of the anonymous philanthropist, he set forth a solution that was framed in blandly persuasive tones, but was so atrocious that no one could possibly take it seriously.

The solution that he proposes is that since so many Irish babies are being born every day, they should be treated as animals, not as humans, and be slaughtered and consumed. The best age at which to eat them, from the consumer's point of view, would be one year, for at that point they would be healthy and tender. Another suggestion is that the children be allowed to grow until the age of 12 or 13 and then served in place of venison, but he is not in favor of this, as the meat would be lean and tough. "And besides," he adds, with not a little touch of sarcasm and irony, "it is not improbable that some scrupulous people might be apt to censure such a practice (although indeed very unjustly) as a little bordering upon cruelty, which, I confess, hath always been with me the strongest objection against any project, however so well intended." In a serious manner, with all apparent concern for the welfare of the Irish people, who are miserably downtrodden and ill treated, the narrator describes the advantages of his modest little proposal. It will, he says, reduce the number of Catholics, increase the country's annual income, and even raise the general standard of living. Even in brief outline the ideas are revolting, but the arguments are so even tempered and well presented that the reader finds himself continuing to follow the argument, despite the horror that underlies the words. Swift, long tortured by the horrors he saw around him, put all his efforts into describing the practical details of actually cooking and serving a child. These details obviously add greatly to the effect he desires.

He claims that a child will provide two dishes at a party, but "the fore or hind quarters will make a reasonable dish" when the family dines alone. He notes that "seasoned with a little pepper or salt [it] will be very good boiled on the fourth day, especially in winter." These specific details—even to the extent of providing cooking directions—add to the satire, as he vents his spleen at the callousness of the authorities that allow people to continue to live in miserable hovels, starving to death.

What is the object of Swift's attack? It may, of course, be argued that his main purpose is to employ satire to reveal the full horror of the Irish economic situation. And we can see that this must be one of the aims, for the speaker implies that cannibalism is a reasonable alternative to the horrible status quo. But when we say that the main purpose of the essay is to underscore the dreadful conditions of the Irish peasants, we run into difficulties. It is true that as an introduction to the essay's proposal Swift gives an appalling view of the hopeless squalor and suffering which afflicted his countrymen. But the "proposal" itself does not serve to reinforce this distressing scene. The conclusion that one is tempted to draw is that the proposal is not itself more shocking than the existing state of affairs Swift had described for us in the beginning of the essay. Yet this implies that the proposal is real, that the ideas he sets forth are taken at face value, seriously—in short, that we are not dealing with satire, but rather with a straightforward proposal of the most brutal economic notion ever to be put to paper.

It is clear that thoughtful readers will not accept his argument at face value, but will look beyond his literal words for some essential object of attack, and thus regard the work as satiric. A number of theories concerning the real object of Swift's venom have been proposed. Some feel that it is the English—specifically the English legislators, landlords, and economic apologists. We can see his argument in this light as an exaggeration and distortion of English indifference to the most basic human needs of the Irish. The problem with this view is that the speaker never identifies himself with the English. Indeed, throughout, he is clearly addressing the Irish and regards the country as his own.

Some have seen "A Modest Proposal" as a parody of previous writings. Certainly in the glib and semi-scientific descriptions of cooking and addressing the children we see mocking echoes of what were, in Swift's time, all-too-familiar discussions of the Irish problem. But the bleakness with which the plight of the Irish peasant is presented, especially in the opening paragraphs, and the savage resentment which the narrator voices, cannot be explained by previous works on the same subject. Nowhere else has the same solution been offered in a published attempt to solve the Irish poverty problem.

We can also see that the Irish people themselves are a target of Swift's venom here, those people who determine the country's policies. Swift is acting the part of the angry preacher, determined to reveal the sloth and stupidity of his congregation. The famous passage which begins, "for this one individual *Kingdom of Ireland, and for no other that ever was, is, or, I think ever can be upon earth,*" shows that he is aiming at least part of his anger at the Irish people themselves. This passage contains a series of solutions that Swift had long advocated himself, and it is clear he bitterly resents that his common-sense ideas have been ignored. In a letter to Alexander Pope the year before "A Modest

Proposal" was written. Swift said that he was feeling ". . . perfect rage and resentment" at seeing daily the "mortifying sight of slavery, folly, and baseness about," which he was forced to endure.

The main satiric thrust, then, can be seen as a devastating assessment of the Irish people's own lethargy and foolishness in the face of horrible social and economic conditions. Their blindness appears all the more awful when we see, after Swift has pointed it out, that they have rejected all reasonable courses of action, and that the incredibly repellent proposal he sets forth is at least better than doing nothing. For a people who should, he thinks, truthfully "think it is a great happiness to have been sold for food at a year old," he offers, in rage and despair, a blueprint for the destruction of a nation which is no more shocking than the current state of affairs in that nation, resulting from their own folly.

Curiously, another plan to solve Ireland's problems, which actually outdid this one in its absurdity, was seriously suggested by an Irish patriot, Colonel Edward Despard. He told a friend that he could solve Ireland's problems through a separation of the sexes. Swift satrically proposed that the Irish institute a system of regulated cannibalism, while Despard very seriously proposed racial suicide, which, had it been instituted, would have eliminated the entire Irish population in a few short generations. In Colonel Despard's suggestion, what had been ironic in Swift became theoretical truth, for it was most seriously proposed.

SATIRE AND GEORGE ORWELL'S *1984*

George Orwell wrote *1984* with two main purposes in mind: To ensure, as far as it lay in his power, that the kind of society that he envisioned would not come about, and to satirize totalitarianism and linguistic abuses. *1984*, then, is a satire whose purpose is not to portray the future, but to warn the present, to alert those whom Orwell considered the decent and reasonable members of his generation to be on their guard against the rise of totalitarian societies.

1984 is a political satire of an activist nature, for Orwell hoped that his work might have some political effect by telling his readers of certain dangers he saw creeping into modern society. It is in the tradition of Utopian literature, which, taking its name from Sir Thomas More's *Utopia* (1515–16), extends back at least as far as Plato's *Republic*, and describes a mythical but ideal society which is intended to shed light on current-day society and change it to conform to the author's view of the ideal. A variation on this model is anti-Utopian society, in which the hypothetical land is presented not as an ideal to emulate, but a distortion of the real, often focusing on the worst and most frightening aspects of the real society. Its object is the same as that of the true Utopia, in that people are supposed to work to improve the society in which they live. Instead of holding up the model of a perfect land, the author of anti-Utopian literature presents a satirical criticism of mankind's pride and folly, combined with a warning that if tendencies shown in the anti-Utopian model are not corrected, man's condition will get worse instead of beter. The most famous anti-Utopian satirical fiction in English is Jonathan Swift's *Gulliver's Travels* (1726). Aldous Huxley's *Brave New World*, written in 1932, is also an example of this genre, but Orwell's *1984* stands as the most famous and influential anti-Utopian work of the twentieth century.

The real structure of the brutal society described in *1984* is explained in the political tract which Winston Smith, the main character, reads as he is about to be apprehended by the Thought Police. It is called "The Theory and Practice of Oligarchical Collectivism," and it was written by Emmanuel Goldstein, the enemy of Big Brother, the leader, and the Party which controls the society of 1984. Oligarchy means that a small group has control over the larger groups, and implies a certain corruption. Without doubt, the oligarchy here is corrupt, for the leaders tyrannize and brutalize the masses into submission.

In *1984* the world has been divided into three superstates: Oceania, Eurasia, and Eastasia. England has become a province of Oceania called Airstrip One. The three powers are constantly at war, although one will occasionally strike an alliance with another to gain an advantage. Partly through the enormous cost of the constant war, and partly through the waste of material and energy which the Party encourages to maintain its power, England has become poor and grim. Oceania has three classes: The Inner Party, the Outer Party, and the Proles. The Inner Party consists of only two percent of the total population and is the ruling class. It maintains its numbers not through hereditary succession, democratic election, or even brute force, but by the selection of people from time to time either from the Inner Party's children or from the most able members of the Outer Party. It is thus a selective aristocracy, including both talent and a fierce devotion to the aims of the Party. Big Brother, whose pictures are everywhere, is the symbol of the Inner Party. It is never clear if he is a real person or not; most likely he is simply the imaginary representative of the Inner Party and has been created by them out of the realization that people need a single all-powerful leader to look up to and even worship. The only member of the Inner Party we ever meet in the book in any detail is O'Brien, Winston Smith's torturer, and we never even learn his first name. As a matter of fact, only three characters in the depersonalized and dehumanized world of this novel are ever given their complete names.

Under the total control of the Inner Party is the Outer Party, made up of fifteen percent of the population and responsible for all the routine administrative duties. The Outer Party may be compared to a small and powerless, but nonetheless indispensable, middle class. Winston Smith, the 39-year-old hero of the book, is a member of the Outer Party. The action of the book revolves around his revolt against the oligarchy and the results of his decisions. His name is symbolic, for Smith is the most common name in the English language, thus suggesting that he is Everyman, representative of all of us. Winston is the first name of the great English war leader and Prime Minister, Winston Churchill, who is generally recognized as one of the greatest heroes of his age. The combination of these two names implies that while Winston Smith is Everyman, he is also unique. For example, in the beginning of the book, Winston Smith, as a minor employee of the Government's Ministry of Truth, sets himself up against Big Brother and the Party, even though he is fully aware that he cannot possibly succeed. All crimes in *1984* are understood to be simply different forms of the same crime—Thoughtcrime—which means having the wrong mental attitude toward the Party and Big Brother, and are punishable by death without a formal legal trial. Winston is a Thoughtcriminal, and this novel, in illustrating his decline and fall, takes us through the most representative parts of the complete society so we may understand the satire fully.

The government of *1984* is centralized in London, the capital city of Airstrip One (England), and is organized into four huge ministries: The Ministry of Truth, which is involved with news, entertainment, education, and the fine arts; the Ministry of Peace, concerned with war; the Ministry of Love, which rules law and order and controls the secret police; and the Ministry of Plenty, which governs economic affairs. In Newspeak, the official language of *1984,* these are referred to as Minitrue, Minipax, Miniluv, and Miniplenty. Winston Smith works for the Ministry of Truth.

His job, when we first meet him, is to rewrite—which means to falsify—history to make it conform to Party doctrine. This is done in accordance with the Party slogan: "Who controls the Past controls the Future." Winston has begun to keep a diary, which is technically not illegal, for since there are no written laws nothing can be considered illegal in the technical sense, but it is nevertheless dangerous, for it shows that one may have private thoughts and by putting them on paper may wish to communicate these private thoughts to others. This is forbidden or at least not at all encouraged, for the maintenance of the oligarchical totalitarianism in 1984 depends not on increasing communication between people by sharing thoughts, but rather on decreasing it to the minimum necessary to carry on a routine life. Therefore Winston's diary would make him suspect, a fact of which he is fully aware.

The three slogans of the Party upon which the government is constructed are:

WAR IS PEACE
FREEDOM IS SLAVERY
IGNORANCE IS STRENGTH

All three superstates are essentially the same: self-contained economies having little or no need for external support. Each has enough raw materials. War would provide them at most, a few million extra people for hard labor and a few more miles of land. Despite the fact that war is not at all an economic necessity, a constant state of war is maintained. War determines the population's condition, and overcrowding, chronic food shortages, and long hours of work for poor pay result. There are even added hours of "voluntary" work for the Outer Party, for which no additional pay is received.

In the past, the objective of war was largely economic, but in the society of *1984*, the purpose of war is not to win, but instead to maintain the status quo. War, therefore, is peace, for the state of war keeps society in balance. The slogan "War is Peace" holds true as long as the war does not build up, for the three states can keep their people too busy with the war effort to allow them any time to plan ways of changing the system. The three states hold each other up, despite their frequent differences, and provide ways of destroying the surpluses which would make life comfortable.

Members of the Party are expected to be hard-working and intelligent (within the narrow limits of Party allegiance, of course). At the same time, they are required to be ignorant fanatics whose prevailing moods are "fear, hatred, adulation (of Big Brother), and orgiastic triumph." The way that Party members can resolve this contradiction is through the practice of Doublethink, a process whereby a person may control his mind so that he will not even allow himself to think of things which are not approved by the Party. Thus the Party members convince themselves that Oceania is fighting a war which will end in victory, and in which Oceania will be the ruler of the world. To think in any other way is to be guilty of a Thoughtcrime.

When we first encounter Winston Smith he is in very dangerous shape, for Doublethink, Party conditioning, is breaking down and he is thinking for himself. He is aware of the mortal difficulty he is in, but he cannot help himself. One day, he hysterically writes in his diary:

DOWN WITH BIG BROTHER
DOWN WITH BIG BROTHER
DOWN WITH BIG BROTHER . . .

and with this forbidden thought and deed, his fate is sealed. Although his downfall will take some time, it is inevitable.

He becomes acquainted with two people from work who will have a great influence on his life: Julia, a 26-year-old woman, who will become his mistress, and O'Brien, a member of the Inner Party who will betray Winston and Julia.

Winston and Julia are expected to behave in a manner approved by the Party. The Party must approve all marriages, and is suspicious of romantic love, for it feels that any attachment of one human being for another will weaken the attachment to or affection for Big Brother. All good Party members are expected to love Big Brother above all else. The only affection tolerated by the Party is called Goodsex in Newspeak—the normal, marital relations between husband and wife only for the purpose of reproduction. Smith had previously been married to a fanatical Party member named Katherine, but they had separated after discovering they could not do their duty to the Party by having children. They have not been divorced, since the Party rarely allows divorces. The Proles, who are not considered important even though they make up 85 percent of the population, are not restricted in their sexual and marital behavior because Proles exist solely to provide soldiers and workers for the State. They are kept in ignorance, and if a Prole looks like he might cause a problem, he is destroyed by the Thought Police.

Julia works in a division of the Ministry of Truth which provides reading material for Proles to keep them out of trouble. The novels she works on have only six possible plots, shuffled around by machine. This pornographic material, along with cheap gin, is endlessly supplied to the Proles to keep them from any awareness of reality. Party members who indulge in such vices are punished.

Winston and Julia becomes lovers, and in so doing, set themselves up against the Party. They know too that no matter how careful they are, they will eventually be found out. "Thoughtcrime does not entail death; thoughtcrime is death," Winston writes in his diary, realizing that he is as good as dead as a result of his crime.

Big Brother is watching them in the form of O'Brien, an urbane and cultured member of the Inner Party who is several levels above Winston and Julia. He strikes up a relationship with them, and they visit his home. As a member of the Inner Party, he is allowed to turn off the two-way screen which constantly spies on all members of society. They tell O'Brien that they are Thoughtcriminals. Winston says that he has heard of a secret brotherhood, headed by Emmanuel Goldstein, that plots to overthrow Big Brother. But just as no one has ever seen Big Brother, no one has ever seen Goldstein either, and it is likely that both are Party creations.

Winston and Julia join the Brotherhood through O'Brien, whom they suppose is its representative. They are willing to do whatever is necessary to work toward the overthrow of Big Brother. O'Brien gives Winston a copy of Goldstein's book, and promises that they will meet again.

They next meet in the underground rooms of the Ministry of Love, where the Thought Police torture victims. At the same time, Winston and Julia have found a place free of telescreens, a cheap room above an antique shop run by a Mr. Charrington. There, one day while they are in bed, the Thought Police come to arrest them, and it is revealed that even Mr. Charrington is an agent of the Thought Police. Winston is taken to be tortured.

The Party does not wish to kill Winston. Rather, they wish to change his way of thinking, to make him a perfect follower of Big Brother. After this, he may be killed, but the party is far more concerned with the mental destruction than the physical destruction of its enemies.

Next we see Winston's torture, his betrayal of Julia, and his final spiritual destruction, so complete that by the end of the book he does indeed love Big Brother. Winston provides another way the Party can show its power. Since Power is what the Party worships above all, there must be limitless reasons to exercise Power or the Party will cease to exit. The end of Power is Power; and the goal of the Inner Party is to maintain its Power by whatever means are necessary. The last third of the book is a dialogue between Smith and O'Brien on the theme of the Party and Power, in which O'Brien leads Winston through the path that will show him that he must believe anything that the Party decides that he will believe.

The Party has won. No matter what happens to Winston now, the Party has him in its control, for he will think no thought that is not approved by the Party. Just as the Ministry of Peace is concerned with war, so the Ministry of Love is concerned with torture, all in the name of Big Brother. Winston's spirit has been thoroughly crushed by the end of the book, so much so that it matters little whether he lives or dies.

Satire on Totalitarianism

Orwell's satire on totalitarianism in *1984* revolves around the distorted notions of law and justice illustrated. Our ideas of justice have come from the idea that people have what the Declaration of Independence calls "certain inalienable rights," rights which cannot be given or taken away. These rights have no value in society unless they are guaranteed and backed up by law, since otherwise, there would be no way of enforcing them.

One of the rights which we assume to be ours is the right to be ruled by a code of government which does not allow a person to be convicted of a crime unless the person knows that the act (or the omission of an act) is in fact a crime. This means that no one can be punished for breaking the law unless the person knows that there *is* a law. A person does not have to read all the laws, but is expected to know the law; thus, ignorance of the law is not accepted as an excuse. For example, you are expected to know that a red light means stop. If you go through a red light and a police officer stops you and gives you a ticket, you will not be excused if you say that you did not realize that it was illegal to pass red lights.

In *1984* there are no written laws; thus, everything *can* be a crime, but no one knows what really *is*. All crimes are combined into what is called Thoughtcrime, which involves not forbidden acts but thoughts. Our laws take no account of thoughts, only acts. How can someone be held legally responsible for thinking forbidden thoughts? Further, how can this be if he doesn't even know what *is* forbidden? But this is exactly the position of the Party, and it leads to complete tyranny.

Certain rights we have come to expect have been abolished in this book. For example, we take as basic the right of a person held for a crime to be released if there is not enough proof to hold him, or released on bail or certain other ways if the judge rules so. This is called the right of *habeas corpus*. In *1984,* people can be held without trial for months or even years, without even being told what the charges against them are.

In *1984,* people simply vanish, as was the case with Smith's parents, since there are no safeguards imposed on the society to protect the individual. Another right we assume is the integrity of the individual, but this too is violated by the Party. This is what the Party does to Winston and Julia—degrade them to the point where they are no longer what we would consider human.

Common crimes—murder, theft, etc.—still exist in *1984* and while they are punished by the Party, they are not considered as serious as Thoughtcrimes. Ordinary criminals are even treated with some favoritism by the jailers in *1984.*

In short, the absence of a legal code leaves punishment up to the whim of the Party. In the totalitarian states of the 1930s and 1940s, Orwell saw such things as imprisonment without trial, secret murder, and political assassination employed as normal rules of state. He believed that unless people obtained a written guarantee of their rights and freedoms, they would have nothing except that granted by a not always benevolent government.

Linguistic Satire in *1984*

The linguistic satire here is similar to that found in the works of Jonathan Swift, a writer Orwell much admired. Swift's "Tale of a Tub" and Book III of *Gulliver's Travels* contain brilliant satire on the corruption of language for political or religious purposes. Swift's ideal in language involved precision of meaning, which he employs in the works just mentioned. In "Tale of a Tub," for example, a satire on religious controversy and true and false religions, Swift makes the point that if a work is clear and has meaning, the average reader will immediately be aware of it, for it does not take extraordinary intelligence to understand a clear and meaningful work of literature. On the other hand, if a writer decides to conceal his meaning, he will bombard the reader with a collection of ill-selected and imprecise words. Orwell also advocates precision and clarity of meaning.

Orwell felt that much political writing seeks not to reveal the truth but to conceal it. The corruption of language takes two forms: the first involves the limitation of meaning and thought, and the second, the deliberate lack of precision and meaning through the use of words selected to soothe and cover reality.

In the appendix to *1984,* Orwell explains what he means fully. "The purpose of Newspeak was not only to provide a medium of expression for the world-view and mental habits proper to the devotee of Ingsoc, but to make all other modes of thought impossible." This seems to be impossible, but it can be brought about by destroying the *connotations* of words, so that each word will have one and only one possible meaning. Of course, we find exaggeration here for the purposes of satire. Accompanying the destruction of connotative meaning is the decline of the precision of language for political and economic causes, whereby euphemisms (soothing expressions such as "passed on" for "died") are used to obscure the truth. Thus political opponents of a totalitarian regime are not murdered or shot; they are "eliminated" or "liquidated." These words do not carry the same connotations of brutality, and they obscure the truth. These words come to substitute for real thought. Both of these processes—the narrowing of meaning through the elimination of connotation and the use of euphemism—are satirized in *1984.*

Newspeak is used by the Party to help make certain thoughts impossible by removing the very ideas and ways in which these thoughts can be phrased in English. Thus, even a dictionary has political import, as it is used to narrow down the meaning of words. Thus "free" can not be used in any way as to suggest political freedom; it can only be used to suggest that an object is not held by another, as in "the yard was free of small animals." So Newspeak limits the range of thought and expression.

The Party wishes to abolish Oldspeak as soon as possible, but since much of it is still in use, the language in *1984* is a cross between Oldspeak and Newspeak. Newspeak contains three vocabularies, A, B, and C. The A words are used in everyday life; the B words have been invented for political reasons; and the C words are technical and scientific. In practice, then, anti-Party thoughts would be difficult if not impossible.

"Political language," Orwell wrote in his essay "Politics and the English Language," "is designed to make lies sound truthful and murder respectable, and to give the appearance of solidity to pure wind." The process he saw in motion in the totalitarian countries in the 1930s and 1940s were completed in his satiric *1984.* Yet he saw that the process could be reversed if people were aware of the debasement of language and took steps to use it properly, to clarify rather than obscure thought.

We can conclude that *1984* satirizes all absolutist systems of political control of populations, whether we call these systems Communism, Fascism, or Oligarchical Collectivism, which is the form of government in *1984.* What all these forms have in common is that none is democratic. Orwell believed that man was not fully capable of power on his own, and thus government had to be constructed on a system of checks and balances. This book was, therefore, a satiric projection of the trends that Orwell saw surrounding him in the 1930s and 1940s trends about which he hoped to warn people.

ESSAY QUESTIONS ON SATIRE

Allow yourself 45 minutes to organize, write, and correct an essay on any of the following topics. Follow the directions for generating and organizing your thoughts as described in **Part 2: Essay Writing Guide**. Be sure to leave time to revise and edit your essay at the end.

1. Explain the purpose of the satire in any one satiric work that you have read. What exactly is it that the author is attacking? Select specific words or phrases from the text to prove your point; be specific. If possible, explain the background of the subject.

2. Select any one satiric piece that you have read and define the *tone*. To make your point clearly, isolate specific words and phrases that prove your thesis.

3. What are the tools of the satirist? What devices does he/she have at his/her disposal to make a point? How do these literary devices differ from those of the novelist or the short story writer?

4. Define satire in the opening paragraph of your essay. Then, show how any one work of recognized literary value is satiric.

5. Select any one satire and explain its audience. Show the group at which the satire is aimed, and explain how you came to that conclusion. Use specific details from the work to make your point.

6. Select any one satire that you have read and isolate and define the following elements: characters, objects of satire, style, unifying elements. Show how they work together to make the satirist's point.

SUGGESTED READING LIST

Note: For those authors with no specific work listed, any of their works is acceptable for the AP exam.

Ancient Satire

Horace
Juvenal
Martial
Petronius Arbiter

Medieval Satire

| | *Roman de la Rose;* thirteenth-century dream allegory |
| Chaucer, Geoffrey | *The Canterbury Tales* (selected); see especially "The Miller's Tale" and "The Nun's Priest's Tale" |

Renaissance Satire

Brant, Sebastian
Rabelais, François — *Pantagruel* and *Gargantua*
Erasmus, Desiderius — *Praise of Folie*
Cervantes, Miguel de — *Don Quixote*
Barclay, Alexander
Butler, Samuel — *Hudibras*
Dryden, John — *Absalom and Achitophel*
Molière

Eighteenth-Century Satire

Gay, John — *Beggar's Opera*
Pope, Alexander — *Dunciad*
Addison, Joseph
Fielding, Henry
Austen, Jane
Smollett, Tobias George — *The Expedition of Humphry Clinker*
Voltaire — *Candide*

Nineteenth-Century Satire

Bierce, Ambrose — *Devil's Dictionary*
Thackeray, William
Twain, Mark
Dickens, Charles
Wilde, Oscar
Shaw, George Bernard

Twentieth-Century Satire

Lewis, Sinclair — *Babbitt*
Thurber, James
Waugh, Evelyn
Huxley, Aldous — *Brave New World*
West, Nathanael — *The Day of the Locust*
Nabokov, Vladimir
Grass, Günter
Hasek, Jaroslav — *The Good Soldier Schweik*
Heller, Joseph — *Catch-22*
Ellison, Ralph
O'Hara, John

The Essay

An essay is a literary composition which does not assume to treat a subject thoroughly. The word "essay," which comes from the French "essai," meaning an "attempt," was first used in the sixteenth century. Although usually written in prose, an essay may be written in verse, such as Pope's "Essay on Criticism." Because the main meaning of the term "essay" is a beginning study, an essay may be only a few pages long, or even less than a page, although there is no fixed length. There have been books of many essays and large books that contain only a single essay, but since the eighteenth century, most essays have appeared in magazines. Famous essayists include Addison, Steele, Lamb, Hazlitt, Macaulay, George Orwell, and Aldous Huxley. Around 1800, the Romantic writers employed a form of the essay called the *informal or familiar essay,* in which the author adopts a personal and chatty tone. He often reveals as much about himself as he does about the subject under discussion, as in Lamb's "Dissertation Upon a Roast Pig." *Formal essays,* in contrast, are impersonal analyses of various subjects, an example being John Locke's "Essay Concerning the Human Understanding." For more on the essay, consult Leslie Fiedler's *The Art of the Essay.*

DETERMINING TONE AND MOOD

An essayist often reveals a specific attitude in the course of developing his thesis. This is important because the speaker's tone or mood can often significantly affect the meaning of a passage; in some instances, the meaning depends on the speaker's attitude. Questions involving this aspect of a writer's craft often appear on Advanced Placement exams, and we find this especially important when considering an essay, which was usually written to convey a specific attitude in a very brief amount of space. A novelist has the room to expand his argument, a short story writer can rely on narration (telling a story) rather than persuasion (proving a point), but the essayist usually has a point to prove and tone/mood are among his most valuable tools.

The following passages illustrate this type of persuasive prose writing. Read them and answer the questions that follow each.

1. It takes no calendar to tell root and stem that the calm days of mid-summer are here. Last spring's sprouted seed comes to fruit. None of these things depends on a calendar of the days and months. They are their own calendar, marks on a span of time that reaches far back into the shadows of time. The mark is there for all to see, in every field and meadow and treetop, as it was last year and then years ago and when the centuries were young.

The time is here. This is the point in the great continuity when these things happen, and will continue to happen year after year. Any summer arrives at this point, only to lead on to the next and the next, and so to summer again. These things we can count on; these will happen again and again, so long as the earth turns.

The passage indicates that the author experiences a feeling of
(A) frustration
(B) fear of the forces of nature
(C) pessimism
(D) serene confidence
(E) regret at the rapid passage of time

The answer here is (D), serene confidence, as the phrases "calm days," "great continuity," and "we can count on" reveal. The author has no fear of nature nor any regret at the passage of time; rather, we sense, through the phrases cited above, a calm acceptance of the seasons.

> 2. Engineers say that the push-button factories may eventually permit a work schedule in which the weekend will be longer than the week. Educators see all this leisure promoting a scholastic renaissance in which cultural attainments will become the yardstick of social recognition for worker and boss alike. Gloomier observers fear the trend toward "inhuman production" will end by making men obsolete.

The passage is developed principally by means of
(A) cause and effect
(B) examples
(C) definition
(D) narration
(E) contrast

The answer is (A), cause and effect, for the causes, such as "push-button factories" result in the effects, such as "the weekend will be longer than the week." Leisure will result in an cultural renaissance; "inhuman production" will result in men becoming obsolete. There are no specific examples here (B), and the author does not define his terms. In the same manner, narration, telling a story, (D), is not an element of this passage, nor is contrast, (E), except between the final sentence and the first two, but the main means of development remains cause and effect.

The writer's *tone* is established through his choice of words and their placement in the passage. This, in turn, reveals his attitude toward the subject matter. The next passage illustrates how tone reveals attitude:

> Eventually the whole business of purveying to the hospitals was, in effect, carried out by Miss Nightingale. She, alone, it seemed, whatever the contingency, knew where to lay her hands on what was wanted; she alone possessed the art of circumventing the pernicious influences of official etiquette. On one occasion 27,000 shirts arrived, sent out at her insistence by the Home Government, and were only waiting to be unpacked. But the official "Purveyor" intervened; "He could only unpack them" he said, "with an official order from the Government." Miss Nightingale pleaded in vain; the sick and the wounded lay half-naked, shivering for want of clothing; and three weeks elapsed before the Government released the shirts. A little later, on a similar occasion, Miss Nightingale ordered a Government consignment to be forcibly opened, while the "Purveyor" stood by, wringing his hands in departmental agony.

1. The tone of the author reveals that his attitude toward Miss Nightingale is one of
   (A) amazement and chagrin
   (B) admiration and respect
   (C) prejudice and apathy
   (D) frustration and fright
   (E) dislike bordering on active hatred

2. The use of a phrase like "she alone" gives the reader an idea of Miss Nightingale's
   (A) loneliness
   (B) conceit
   (C) femininity
   (D) uniqueness
   (E) inefficiency

3. Describing the influence of official etiquette as "pernicious" reveals the author's awareness of the
   (A) dangers of red tape
   (B) efficiency of command procedure
   (C) lack of blood plasma
   (D) women's liberation movement
   (E) horrors of war

4. The description of the sick and wounded as "half-naked" and "shivering" serves as
   (A) an introduction of physical detail
   (B) weather information
   (C) historic documentation
   (D) contrast to bureaucratic lack of concern
   (E) a metaphor

5. The Purveyor seems concerned only with
   (A) humanity
   (B) the ill men
   (C) the men's needs
   (D) departmental procedure
   (E) Miss Nightingale's requests

6. In this selection, the author's tone is best communicated by his
   (A) metaphors
   (B) similes
   (C) onomatopeia
   (D) word choice
   (E) general figurative language

Answers

1. (B) admiration and respect. The final example, where she circumvented official policy to make sure that the suffering were taken care of, reveals his attitude toward her.
2. (D) uniqueness. The first sentence reveals that she alone is responsible for the welfare of the suffering
3. (A) dangers of red tape. The incident concerning the delay in unpacking shirts already in the hospital shows the author's feelings about "red tape," the official tendency to make things more difficult than they need be.
4. (D) contrast to bureaucratic lack of concern. The author underscores the same point with the example of the shirts unreleased.
5. (D) departmental procedure. That he could stand by and watch people suffer shows this. The final incident is the same type of example.
6. (D) word choice. As cited earlier, the use of phrases like "half-naked" reveal the importance of word choice.

SAMPLE AP QUESTIONS ON THE ESSAY

The Advanced Placement Committee suggests the following topics for consideration in the study of the essay: (1) organization and structure of the essay; (2) speaker; (3) tone and mood; (4) style and language; (5) ideas and theme; (6) elements of fiction; (7) audience.

Following are some typical AP questions on the essay. Suggestions for answers follow the last question.

1. As expressed in the essay that follows, what is the cost of man's reliance on and interest in amassing property? Examine the premise of "Reliance on Property" and write an essay in which you show that the author's thesis does or does not hold true today.

RELIANCE ON PROPERTY

And so the reliance on property, including the reliance on governments which protect it, is the want of self-reliance. Men have looked away from themselves and at things so long that they have come to esteem the religious, learned and civil institutions as guards of property, and they deprecate assaults on these, because they feel them to be assaults on property. They measure their esteem of each other by what each has, and not by what each is. But a cultivated man becomes ashamed of his property, out of new respect for his nature. Especially he hates what he has if he sees that it is accidental,—came to him by inheritance, or gift, or crime; then he feels that it is not having; it does not belong to him, has no root in him and merely lies there because no revolution or no robber takes it away. But that which a man is, does always by necessity acquire; and what the man acquires, is living property, which does not wait the beck of rulers, or mobs, or revolutions, or fire, or storm, or bankruptcies, but perpetually renews itself wherever the man breathes. "Thy lot or portion of life," said the Caliph Ali, "is seeking after thee; therefore be at rest from seeking after it." Our dependence on these foreign goods leads us to our slavish respect for numbers. The political parties meet in numerous conventions; the greater the concourse and with each new uproar of announcement, The delegation from Essex! The Democrats from New Hampshire! The Whigs of Maine! the young patriot feels himself stronger than before by a new thousand of eyes and arms. In like manner the reformers summon conventions and vote and resolve in multitude. Not so, O friends! will the God deign to enter and inhabit you, but by a method precisely the reverse. It is only as a man puts off all foreign support and stands alone that I see him to be strong and to prevail. He is weaker by every recruit to his banner. Is not a man better than a town? Ask nothing of men, and, in the endless mutation, thou only firm column must presently appear the upholder of all that surrounds thee. He who knows that power is inborn, that he is weak because he has looked for good out of him and elsewhere, and, so perceiving, throws himself unhesitatingly on his thought, instantly rights himself, stands in the erect position, commands his limbs, works miracles; just as a man who stands on his feet is stronger than a man who stands on his head.

—*Ralph Waldo Emerson*

2. Explain the literary devices the author uses in the essay that follows to show the difference between a "mere thinker" and "Man Thinking."

MAN THINKING

It is one of those fables which out of an unknown antiquity convey an unlooked-for wisdom, that the gods, in the beginning, divided Man into men, that he might be more helpful to himself; just as the hand was divided into fingers, the better to answer its end.

The old fable covers a doctrine ever new and sublime; that there is One Man,—present to all particular men only partially, or through one faculty; and that you must take the whole society to find the whole man. Man is not a farmer, or a professor, or an engineer, but he is all. Man is priest, and scholar, and statesman, and producer, and soldier. In the *divided* or social state these functions are parcelled out to individuals, each of whom aims to do his stint of the joint work, whilst each other performs his. The fable implies that the individual, to possess himself, must sometimes return from his own labor to embrace all the other laborers. But, unfortunately, this original unit, this fountain of power, has been so distributed to multitudes, has been so minutely subdivided and peddled out, that it is spilled into drops, and cannot be gathered. The state of society is one in which the members have suffered amputation from the trunk, and strut about so many walking monsters,—a good finger, a neck, a stomach, an elbow, but never a man.

Man is thus metamorphosed into a thing, into many things. The planter, who is Man sent out into the field to gather food, is seldom cheered by any idea of the true dignity of his ministry. He sees his bushel and his cart, and nothing beyond, and sinks into the farmer, instead of Man on the farm. The tradesman scarcely ever gives an ideal worth to his work, but is ridden by the routine of his craft, and the soul is subject to dollars. The priest becomes a form; the attorney a statute-book; the mechanic a machine; the sailor a rope of the ship.

In this distribution of functions the scholar is the delegated intellect. In the right state he is *Man Thinking*. In the degenerate state, when the victim of society, he tends to become a mere thinker, or still worse, the parrot of other men's thinking.

In this view of him, as Man Thinking, the theory of his office is contained. Him Nature solicits with all her placid, all her monitory pictures; him the past instructs; him the future invites. Is not indeed every man a student, and do not all things exist for the student's behoof? And, finally, is not the true scholar the only true master?

—*Ralph Waldo Emerson*

3. In the essay that follows the author objects to man traveling in hopes of "get[ting] somewhat which he does not carry." Explain what this means by specific references to the essay.

TRAVELING

It is for want of self-culture that the superstition of Traveling, whose idols are Italy, England, Egypt, retains its fascination for all educated Americans. They who made England, Italy, or Greece venerable in the imagination, did so by sticking fast where they were, like an axis of the earth. In manly hours we feel that duty is our place. The soul is no traveler; the wise man stays at home, and when his necessities, his duties, on any occasion call him from his house, or into foreign lands, he is at home still and shall make men sensible by the expression of his countenance that he goes, the missionary of wisdom and virtue, and visits cities and men like a sovereign and not like an interloper or a valet.

I have no churlish objection to the circumnavigation of the globe for the purposes of art, of study, and benevolence, so that the man is first domesticated, or does not go abroad with the hope of finding somewhat greater than he knows. He who travels to be amused, or to get somewhat which he does not carry, travels away from himself, and grows old even in youth among old things. In Thebes, in Palmyra, his will and mind have become old and dilapidated as they. He carries ruins to ruins.

Traveling is a fool's paradise. Our first journeys discover to us the indifference of places. At home I dream that at Naples, at Rome, I can be intoxicated with beauty and lose my sadness. I pack my trunk, embrace my friends, embark on the sea and at last wake up in Naples, and there beside me is the stern fact, the sad self, unrelenting, identical, that I fled from. I seek the Vatican and the palaces. I affect to be intoxicated with sights and suggestions, but I am not intoxicated. My giant goes with me wherever I go.

—*Ralph Waldo Emerson*

4. Read the address that follows and then answer the questions about it.

SECOND INAUGURAL ADDRESS, MARCH 4, 1865

Fellow Countrymen: At this second appearing to take the oath of the presidential office, there is less occasion for an extended address than there was at the first. Then a statement, somewhat in detail, of a course to be pursued, seemed fitting and proper. Now, at the expiration of four years, during which public declarations have been constantly called forth on every point and phase of the great contest which still absorbs the attention and engrosses the energies of the nation, little that is new could be presented. The progress of our arms, upon which all else chiefly depends, is as well known to the public as to myself; and it is, I trust, reasonably satisfactory and encouraging to all. With high hope for the future, no prediction in regard to it is ventured.

On the occasion corresponding to this four years ago, all thoughts were anxiously directed to an impending civil war. All dreaded it—all sought to avert it. While the inaugural address was being delivered from this place, devoted altogether to saving the Union without war, insurgent agents were in the city seeking to destroy it without war—seeking to dissolve the Union, and divide effects, by negotiation. Both parties deprecated war; but one of them would make war rather than let the nation survive; and the other would accept war rather than let it perish. And the war came.

One eighth of the whole population were colored slaves, not distributed generally over the Union, but localized in the southern part of it. These slaves constituted a peculiar and powerful interest. All knew that this interest was, somehow, the cause of the war. To strengthen, perpetuate, and extend this interest was the object for which the insurgents would rend the Union, even by war; while the government claimed no right to do more than to restrict the territorial enlargement of it.

Neither party expected for the war the magnitude or the duration which it has already attained. Neither anticipated that the cause of the conflict might cease with, or even before, the conflict itself should cease. Each looked for an easier triumph and a result less fundamental and astounding. Both read the same Bible, and pray to the same God; and each invokes His aid against the other. It may seem strange that any man should dare to ask a just God's assistance in wringing their bread from the sweat of other men's faces; but let us judge not, that we be not judged. The prayers of both could not be answered—that of neither has been answered fully.

The Almighty has His own purposes. "Woe unto the world because of offenses! for it must needs be that offenses come; but woe to that man by whom the offense cometh." If we shall suppose that American slavery is one of those offenses which in the providence of God, must needs come, but which, having continued through His appointed time, He now wills to remove, and that He gives to both North and South this terrible war, as the woe due to those by whom the offense came, shall we discern therein any departure from those divine attributes which the believers in a living God always ascribe to Him? Fondly do we hope—fervently do we pray—that this mightly scourge of war may speedily pass away. Yet, if God wills that it continue until all the wealth piled by the bondman's two hundred and fifty years of unrequited toil shall be sunk, and until every drop of blood drawn with the lash shall be paid by another drawn with the sword, as was said three thousand years ago, so still must be said, "The judgments of the Lord are true and righteous altogether."

With malice toward none; with charity for all; with firmness in the right, as God gives us to see the right, let us strive on to finish the work we are in; to bind up the nation's wounds; to care for him who shall have borne the battle, and for his widow and his orphan—to do all which may achieve and cherish a just and lasting peace among ourselves, and with all nations.

—*Abraham Lincoln*

Questions on Lincoln's "Second Inaugural Address"

1. According to the passage, what was the North's purpose in entering the war?
2. According to the passage, what was the author's own feeling toward slavery?
3. Did the author believe that the preservation of the Union was important?
4. Why are there quotations from the Bible in this address? What purpose do they serve?
5. Would this address be considered an example of good—even superior—writing? Consider writing elements such as word choice, sentence variety, use of figurative language, tone, etc. in answering this question.

Suggested Answers to Sample Questions on the Essay

1. In "Reliance on Property," Emerson asserts that man's interest in amassing property is achieved at the expense of his self, his independence and self-reliance. "Men have looked away from themselves . . ." would be a line to support this, as would, "They measure their esteem of each other by what each has, and not by what each is." Whether or not this is true today is, of course, a matter of opinion, but most would agree that it is and could cite people's adherence to cults as proof that we seek some sense of self.
2. As stated in "Man Thinking," a "mere thinker" is a person following an intellectual exercise that he is unable to relate to what is happening about him, while a "Man Thinking" is a person who is able, using all his abilities, to experience

feelings of total awareness. The fable is the main literary device employed here; trace its development and parallels to the thesis.

3. In "Traveling," Emerson is referring to knowledge and wisdom, cultural and spiritual growth, and self-awareness, all of which escape those who travel to run away from themselves and their inner lives. The "giant" of the last line is the self that is unable to find beauty at home and cannot be affected by the simple experiences of daily life. No matter where we travel, we can never escape from ourselves.

4. Lincoln's "Second Inaugural Address"

a) The purpose of the North's involvement was to preserve the Union as well as restrict "territorial enlargement" of slavery.

b) Lincoln regarded slavery as a moral offense for which God had punished the nation by inflicting war.

c) The preservation of the Union was Lincoln's main concern. Slavery was regarded as a secondary concern, although he realized it was the underlying cause of the conflict.

d) The quotation from Matthew 7:1 foreshadows the lack of vindictiveness in the final paragraph: "With malice toward none; with charity for all. . . ." Those quotes from Matthew 18:7 and Psalms 19:9 are used to indicate a share in the responsibility.

e) The speech is extraordinarily effective in what it seeks to accomplish. It is especially well written for the glimpse that it gives us of the speaker, who reveals himself here to be a wise and compassionate man. It is also almost free from recrimination, the assignment of blame. Slavery is attacked on moral grounds, but the ethics of men "wringing their bread from the sweat of other men's faces" is set forth with little heat, while the "two hundred and fifty years of unrequited toil" and the "blood drawn with the lash"—which are the most emotional lines in the speech—are presented in almost biblical language and thus seem to be missing a lot of their vengeful quality. The diction is simple for the most part, but there are times when the choice of words is amazingly precise and apt. The second sentence of the third paragraph, for example; "These slaves constituted a peculiar and powerful interest." There is nothing that could be substituted for "interest" and "peculiar" without seriously changing the exact meaning that the author desired. It is also a sign of good writing that so much of American history is contained in the words "strengthen, perpetuate, and extend this interest," which follows in the next sentence. Lincoln is also adept at varying his sentences to achieve specific effects. For example, he uses inversion, the switching of the normal, expected order of words within the sentence, to attract attention to specific sentences. Thus, "Fondly do we hope" and the opening sentences of the last paragraph attract our attention by their difference. While his sentences tend to be long and complex in style, he is careful to mix in some short statements for balance. This can be seen in the second and third paragraphs especially. At some points his prose borders on the poetic, as "Fondly do we hope—/ fervently do we pray—/ that this mighty scourge of war/ may speedily pass away." There are also numerous instances of specific poetic techniques such as assonance and alliteration, metaphor, and personification. "Bind up the nation's wounds" in the final paragraph would be an example of personification. But in the final analysis it is not the poetic devices that achieve the success here, but the restrained tone. The holding back of tone, the avoidance of excessive zeal, helps to convey the message of utter sincerity, especially in the final paragraph. The language of this address evokes the ugly realities of the war as well as the hope of people everywhere for a just and lasting peace. It is an especially effective example of clear, persuasive prose.

SUGGESTED READING LIST

The following authors have all written important essays:

Adamic, Louis
Bacon, Francis
Beauvoir, Simone de
Benedict, Ruth
Carson, Rachel
Donne, John
Emerson, R. W.
Forster, E. M.
Hemingway, Ernest
Hersey, John
Irving, Washington
Keller, Helen
King, Martin Luther, Jr.
Lamb, Charles
Mead, Margaret
Sandburg, Carl
Steffens, Lincoln
Stevenson, R. L.
Thoreau, H. D.
Trilling, Lionel
White, W. A.
Woolf, Virginia

Addison, Joseph
Baldwin, James
Benchley, Robert
Broun, Heywood
Cousins, Norman
DuBois, W. E. B.
Faulkner, William
Galsworthy, John
Henry, Patrick
Huxley, Thomas
Jefferson, Thomas
Kennedy, John F.
Krutch, Joseph Wood
McCarthy, Mary
Packard, Vance
Sontag, Susan
Steinbeck, John
Swift, Jonathan
Thurber, James
Twain, Mark
Wilson, Edmund

Part 4

Understanding Poetry

How to Read and Interpret Poetry

While there are different methods of approaching poetry, the following steps have proved helpful: Read the poem through once and see how much of the author's meaning you can immediately grasp. Then, go back through the poem a second time, line by line, and define all the unfamiliar words, concepts, ideas, and references. Figure out all the images and symbols, referring, if necessary, to outside works or other poems by the same author. Sometimes, it is helpful to "translate" each line into prose, or simply to substitute simpler words for the more difficult ones. When you understand all the basic words and ideas, reread the poem a few more times and pull it all back together.

Poetry will make a great deal more sense to you if you read it in a normal speaking tone, letting the accents fall where they seem natural. Pay attention to the punctuation the author uses, ending a line only when the punctuation indicates it is correct to do so. The punctuation marks in poetry tell us how the author wishes the work to be read. A period or an exclamation mark can be thought of as a complete stop, while a comma, in contrast, would be a half-stop. So there is no need to stop at the end of a line unless there is some punctuation mark to indicate that we must.

> Farewell, too little, and too lately known,
> Whom I begin to think and call my own;
> For sure our souls were near allied, and thine
> Cast in the same poetic mold with mine.

These first four lines of John Dryden's "To the Memory of Mr. Oldham" show several uses of the pause. When a line of verse has a pause at its end, as in "known," "own," and "mine," the line is called *end-stopped*. But when there are pauses indicated within the line, as after "little" and "allied," the term employed is *caesura*. This simply means a "little pause." When there is no pause at the end of the line, as in line 3 of this example, one line flows into the next and the line is called a *run-on line* or an *enjambement*. These effects are common in modern verse especially.

When reading poetry, follow the author's directions. Do not insert punctuation where none is indicated, and do not force a word to be stressed that would not normally be so. Some poets, Gerard Manley Hopkins, for one, frequently indicate to the reader that a certain word is to be stressed by the addition of a stress mark. Readers, of course, should follow such leads. Some lines may be read in more than one way, depending, for example, on the reader's background. A poem read by a Southerner sounds very different from one read by a New Englander, for example. Use your common sense and pronounce each line as you would normally speak, and the poem will make a great deal more sense.

Let's apply the suggestions outlined above to the reading and interpretation of the poems that follow.

SAILING TO BYZANTIUM

1

That is no country for old men. The young
In one another's arms, birds in the trees
—Those dying generations—at their song,
The salmon-falls, the mackerel-crowded seas,
5 Fish, flesh, or fowl, commend all summer long
Whatever is begotten, born, and dies.
Caught in that sensual music all neglect
Monuments of unaging intellect.

2

An aged man is but a paltry thing,
10 A tattered coat upon a stick, unless
Soul clap its hands and sing, and louder sing
For every tatter in its mortal dress,
Nor is there singing school but studying
Monuments of its own magnificence;
15 And therefore I have sailed the seas and come
To the holy city of Byzantium.

3

O sages standing in God's holy fire
As in the gold mosaic of a wall,
Come from the holy fire, perne in a gyre.
20 And be the singing-masters of my soul.
Consume my heart away; sick with desire

And fastened to a dying animal
It knows not what it is; and gather me
Into the artifice of eternity.

4

25 Once out of nature I shall never take
My bodily form from any natural thing.
But such a form as Grecian goldsmiths make
Of hammered gold and gold enameling
To keep a drowsy Emperor awake;
30 Or set upon a golden bough to sing
To lords and ladies of Byzantium
Of what is past, or passing, or to come.

—*Willam Butler Yeats*

INTERPRETATION OF "SAILING TO BYZANTIUM"

The first thing to discover here is the meaning of the title. According to the dictionary, Byzantium was an ancient Greek city on the Bosporus and the Sea of Marmara. Its buildings were characterized by highly formal structure and the use of rich color. This, however, doesn't tell us why Yeats selected this particular empire; there were, after all, many other ancient cities noted for the same qualities. Looking through other poems by the same author as well as critical studies of his work, we find that Byzantium had become for Yeats the symbol for art or artifice as contrasted with the natural world of biological activity. As he matured, he turned away from the sensual world of growth and constant change to the world of art. Later, though, he returned to the sensual world. As he wrote in his work, *A Vision,* "I think that if I could be given a month of antiquity and leave to spend it anywhere I chose, I would spend it in Byzantium [what we today call Istanbul] a little before Justinian opened St. Sophia and closed the Academy of Plato [around 535 A.D.] . . . I think that in early Byzantium . . . religious, aesthetic, and practical life were one, that architects and artificers . . . spoke to the multitude in gold and silver." In his old age, the poet rejected the world of growth and death—biological change—to turn instead to structures of what he called "unaging intellect."

This discussion fits in with the opening line reference to "old men," which we also could have discovered by looking up Yeats' age when he wrote this poem and the date of the poem itself. Yeats lived from 1865 to 1939, and this poem was published in 1927 when he was obviously in his later years. Thus, we can also infer that the poem has some autobiographical learnings.

The entire first stanza discusses the natural world of biological activity: the endless process of creatures being "begotten, born," and dying. He is the old man, as he states, turning away from all this.

The second stanza continues with the theme of the aging man, here made into the brilliant and oft-quoted symbol of the "tattered coat upon a stick." And so, seeking the unchanging world of art, the speaker comes, symbolically, to all that Byzantium has come to represent.

The "gold mosaic" in the third stanza refers to the mosaic figures on the walls of the Church of the Hagia Sophia ("Holy Wisdom") in Byzantium. There are two words that must be explained in the third stanza. The first is "perne," which means a bobbin, reel, or spool, and can also be spelled "pirn." The second is "gyre," which means to whirl around in a spiral motion. This became a favorite word of Yeats', and he used it as a verb, meaning "to spin around." He associated this spinning with the spinning of fate. Here he is asking the saints on the wall to descend and enter into this symbolic spinning motion, and thus help *him* enter into their state of being. We see this in the final line of this stanza, ". . . and gather me/Into the artifice of eternity."

Once he is able to leave the natural flux, he says in the final stanza, he shall not again assume a natural shape. Rather, he will assume a form that Grecian workers in gold might fashion. The form is specifically that of a bird. His notes say that he had read somewhere "that in the Emperor's palace in Byzantium was a tree made of gold and silver, and artificial birds that sang."

Therefore, we can conclude that "gyre" and "Byzantium" were key words in the poems of W. B. Yeats, whose special meanings are very important to how he felt about life, art, and approaching old age. Here he is turning away from the natural world to embrace the timeless world of art, represented for him in the symbol of Byzantium.

AMONG SCHOOL CHILDREN

1

I walk through the long schoolroom questioning;
A kind old nun in a white hood replies;
The children learn to cipher and to sing,
To study reading-books and history,
5 To cut and sew, be neat in everything
In the best modern way—the children's eyes
In momentary wonder stare upon
A sixty-year-old smiling public man.

2

I dream of a Ledaean body, bent
10 Above a sinking fire, a tale that she
Told of a harsh reproof, or trivial event
That changed some childish day to tragedy—
Told, and it seemed that our two natures blent
Into a sphere from youthful sympathy,
15 Or else, to alter Plato's parable,
Into the yolk and white of the one shell.

3

And thinking of that fit of grief or rage
I look upon one child or t'other there
And wonder if she stood so at that age—
20 For even daughters of the swan can share
Something of every paddler's heritage—
And had that color upon cheek or hair,
And thereupon my heart is driven wild:
She stands before me as a living child.

4

25 Her present image floats into the mind—
Did Quattrocento finger fashion it
Hollow of cheek as though it drank the wind
And took a mess of shadows for its meat?
And I though never of Ledaean kind
30 Had pretty plumage once—enough of that,
Better to smile on all that smile, and show
There is a comfortable kind of old scarecrow.

5

What youthful mother, a shape upon her lap
Honey of generation had betrayed,
35 And that must sleep, shriek, struggle to escape
As recollection or the drug decide,
Would think her son, did she but see that shape
With sixty or more winters on its head,
A compensation for the pang of his birth,
40 Or the uncertainty of his setting forth?

6

Plato thought nature but a spume that plays
Upon a hostly paradigm of things;
Soldier Aristotle played the taws
Upon the bottom of a king of kings;
45 World-famous golden-thighed Pythagoras
Fingered upon a fiddle-stick or strings
What a star sang and careless Muses heard:
Old clothes upon old sticks to scare a bird.

7

Both nuns and mothers worship images,
50 But those the candles light are not as those
That animate a mother's reveries,
But keep a marble or a bronze repose.
And yet they too break hearts—O Presences
That passion, piety, or affection knows.
55 And that all heavenly glory symbolize—
O self-born mockers of man's enterprise;

8

Labor is blossoming or dancing where
The body is not bruised to pleasure soul,
Nor beauty born out of its own despair,
60 Nor blear-eyed wisdom out of midnight oil.
O chestnut tree, great-rooted blossomer,
Are you the leaf, the blossom, or the bole?
O body swayed to music, O brightening glance,
How can we know the dancer from the dance?

—William Butler Yeats

INTERPRETATION OF "AMONG SCHOOL CHILDREN"

This poem can be read in the same manner as "Sailing to Byzantium." Also by Yeats, it is used here as an example to show how an author's body of work functions as a unified whole. The more examples of a poet's art you read, the more you will understand the symbols and allusions that artist employs.

The first stanza tells us that the speaker, a "sixty-year-old smiling public man," is touring a parochial school (note the reference to a nun), asking what the children are learning. Again, we can infer that the speaker bears some relation to Yeats, as we check the dates and discover that he was indeed in his early sixties when he wrote this poem. A quick look at a biography reveals that he was very well known and well respected at this time.

The second stanza contains many difficult allusions. Zeus visited Leda in the form of a swan. As a result of the union Leda gave birth to Helen of Troy. Yeats saw Zeus' visit as an "annunciation marking the beginning of Greek civilization." In Yeats's private mythology, this is used as a reference to Maud Gonne, a woman he very much admired, who functions in his verse as a kind of Helen, a shining ideal of womanhood—and betrayal. The first two lines of this stanza refer to Aristophanes' explanation of Love in Plato's *Symposium*. He suggested that the primeval man was round with four hands and four feet, back and sides forming a circle, one head having two faces. After the division, the two parts of man, desiring the other half, throw their arms around each other in embrace, not wanting to be alone. As the daughter of Leda and the swan, Helen would have been born from an egg, and this suggests Yeats's image for the coming together. This stanza, then, describes the child telling the speaker some tale that changed their normally happy and carefree childhood day to tragedy (as it would seem to a child). After they shared the sadness of the event, they were in such sympathy and agreement that their very natures bent into the form of a single being. Thus, it suggests how two persons can share the grief and blend into one when their natures are in accord.

Suddenly back in the present again, the speaker wonders if any of the little girls before him look as Maud did all those years ago when they were children. In this third stanza, he suddenly sees a little girl who looks just as Maud did many, many years ago, and his "heart is driven wild."

In the fourth stanza, he thinks of how she looks today, in the present, a mature woman. Quattrocento is a reference to the fifteenth century, and here he is calling to mind the painters of that period, especially Botticelli, noted for his lovely portraits of women. The speaker notes that although he was never as handsome as she was beautiful, he did have "pretty plumage once." He stops his remembrances there, for that is all passed now, and it is better to smile about the past for the sake of all the schoolchildren looking at the famous figure. He now sees himself as a "comfortable kind of old scarecrow," smiling nicely for the children.

In the fifth stanza he thinks of his mother, looking at her infant son now sixty years old. The references here are complex. The phrase "honey of generation" was taken from Porphyry's essay, Yeats tells us, but Porphyry did not consider it a "drug" that destroys the memory of pre-birth freedom. Porphyry was a philosopher who wrote during the third century A.D. "Honey of generation," by erasing the memory of happiness before birth, "betray[s]" an infant into being born into the world. The infant will either "sleep" or "struggle" to escape from the world, depending on whether the drug works or the memory of the bliss of life before birth takes over. Would his mother, looking at her 60-year-old son, think that his present "shape" (ie, condition, status, fame) was compensation for the pain of his birth or her fear of what fate would allot to him?

In the sixth stanza, we see that Plato believed that nature was but an appearance ("spume") covering the final spiritual and mathematical reality ("ghostly paradigm"). Aristotle believed that form was really in the matter of nature and thus nature itself had reality; thus Yeats calls him "soldier." Aristotle was Alexander the Great's tutor and punished him by using "taws," or straps, to beat him. So the first two lines here explain what Plato thought about nature, and the second two tell us that Aristotle disciplined Alexander (the king of kings) with a strap. Pythagoras was a Greek philospher who lived during the early sixth century B.C. and was interested in mathematics and music. His followers, called the Pythagoreans, developed a mythical philosophy of numerical relationships and tied together the fields of mathematics and astronomy in a theory of the music of the spheres. These followers regarded their master as a god with a golden thigh. Thus, these three lines refer to Pythagoras and his followers. The final line of this stanza is a contemptuous description of all three philosophers.

The beginning of the seventh stanza says that both nuns and mothers worship images: Nuns worship images of Christ or the Virgin; mothers worship their own inward images of their children. Mothers do not worship the same images as nuns do, the next line states.

The final stanza expresses Yeats' theme: Life is a cosmic dance, in which every human ability and part joins in smoothly. The individual becomes part of the whole, as the dancer becomes part of the dance. He sees this cosmic dance as a means of bringing together the conflicting parts of everyday life.

A Brief History of Meter

From the very first poems, oral accounts of adventures we date from the eighth century, an individual line of poetry has been the basic unit we recognize as "poetic." Up until the time of Walt Whitman's revolutionary poetic experiments, we were even able to say that a poem "looked like a poem," by which we meant that the lines stood apart in a certain recognizable manner and did not run together like a prose paragraph. The act of breaking down poetic lines into their basic units to discover their rhythm and rhyme is called *scansion*. *Scanning* a poem is not an attempt to discover its meaning; it is breaking down the verse into its textual parts. When we scan, we will discover that there are four basic types of verse: *accentual, syllabic, accentual-syllabic,* and *free verse*.

ACCENTUAL VERSE

The earliest recorded poetry, the eighth-century Anglo-Saxon verse mentioned above, was measured neither by rhyme nor by meter. From its inception in other languages, English has been an *accented* language. This means that certain words receive more spoken emphasis than others, that we stress certain parts or sounds within the word. The Anglo-Saxon poets used this system of accents as the basis of their poetry. The accents determined the length of the line of poetry. We use this system to indicate accents: An ictus (´) over a syllable means that it is to be accented. A breve (˘) over a syllable means that it is *not* accented.

If we look at a few sample lines from the poem <u>Beowulf</u>, from the eighth century, we see how the accentual system works to determine meaning:

Hwæt! Wē Gār-Dena   in geār-dagum,

þēod-cyninga,   þrym gefrūnon,

hū ðā æþelingas   ellen fremedon!

The first line has nine syllables; the second, ten; the third, ten or eleven. But the number of syllables per line doesn't matter in verse that is scanned by accent. What is important is that each line have the same number of accents. Going through the poem, it becomes apparent that *four* accents predominate per line. No matter how you read the lines, though, no one would stress words such as "the" and "to."

Accentual verse comes up again in the works of Gerard Manley Hopkins, mentioned previously. Hopkins, who lived from 1844 to 1889, reintroduced accented verse to the modern ear with a variation called *sprung rhythm,* in which strongly accented syllables are pushed up against unaccented ones to produce a new way of scanning verse. Hopkins hoped to shake up the reader to his meaning by forcing us to look at his words in a new light.

SYLLABIC VERSE

Syllabic verse, has a different basis from *accented verse*. The French language, unlike English, makes little use of strongly accented words. One rarely counts out the number of accents in a line of French verse. Instead, the French developed a way of counting the number of syllables to establish the length of their lines of verse. When William the Conqueror invaded England in 1066, he introduced French poets experienced in syllabic rhythms and rhyme. The next few centuries, until the 1400's, saw the change from Old English (*Beowulf,* as we saw before, for example) to Middle English. Old English and French melded together; the language of the lower classes and the language of the court meshed to form Middle English, a midpoint between Old English and modern English. For a short period, the English court spoke French and listened to French poets composing verse within the strict confines of a syllabic line. Although this was a brief period and syllabic verse was altered quickly into accentual-syllabic poetry, later poets occasionally utilized lines determined solely by the number of syllables. In these verses, the number of accents could vary as long as the number of syllables remained constant. Modern poets continue to experiment with the syllabic idea, for it enables the author to escape the boundaries of a more regulated and often jingling or monotonous rhythmic cadence. Dylan Thomas, the Welsh poet who lived from 1914 to 1953, constructed such a syllabic verse:

> In my craft or sullen art
> Exercised in the still night
> When only the moon rages
> And the lovers lie abed . . .

Each line has seven syllables, even though the accents change in each line, both in their number and position.

ACCENTUAL-SYLLABIC VERSE

Accentual-syllabic verse is the kind of poetry that most people would identify immediately as "poetry." It often rhymes, has a definite beat—called *meter*—and usually moves with a predictable regularity. From the fourteenth century to the present, accentual-syllabic verse has been the norm, following rules strictly enforced. In some instances, the skill of the poet has been equated with ability to follow these rules and manipulate words within their confines.

Accentual-syllabic verse came into being when the counting of accents and the counting of syllables in a line occurred at the same time. Although many modern poets feel that this type of verse sounds forced and artificial, for centuries few were bothered by this at all. Rather, they felt it lovely and truly "poetic"—the measure of the craftsman's skill in forging words and ideas into a preconceived pattern. Poetry was closely linked to music and understood to be little more than the construction of a series of sounds, a work of skill and art. Conventional verse gains much of its success and beauty from the fact that English is a language in which word order is highly significant. When the poet is able to fashion language into a verse that moves with ease, a tension and power are created. It is like a formal garden, trained under the craftsman's eye for symmetry and order. Nature has been subdued, brought under man's control, and the work that results has a structure that many find enormously pleasing.

The *foot* of English poetry was created by counting out the number of accents and syllables together. Because English has an accented base, dividing a line into stressed and unstressed syllables creates certain recurring patterns. These measures also fit the patterns of classical Greek and Latin. In counting stresses, the two classical languages were also counting duration—the length of time it took to express an idea. In Greek and Latin, syllables were separated according to length, not stress. Long and short syllables were equated to what English terms stressed or unstressed, the *quality* of a syllable. Therefore, counting in accentual-syllabic verse came to be measured in *feet*.

There are four basic types of metrical feet in English verse:

IAMB	˘ ´	ANAPEST	˘ ˘ ´
TROCHEE	´ ˘	DACTYL	´ ˘ ˘

A foot is composed of either two or three syllables, such that the nature of the foot is determined by the placement of the accent. Every English sentence, no matter whether classified poetry or prose, is made up of these units. Their placement determines the *rhythm* of a line. Even more significantly, they establish the *meter* of a line, the regularity of a verse in an accentual-syllabic piece. One particular foot determines the poem's rhythm.

The following examples illustrate the four basic English feet:

Iamb	Ĭ táste/ ă líq/ uŏr név/ĕr bréwed
Trochee	Eárth, rĕ/ céive aň/ hońorĕd/ guést
Anapest	Tˇe Ašsyŕ iaň caḿe dowń/ likĕ tˇe wólf/ oň tˇe fóld
Dactyl	Oút ŏf tˇe/ crádlĕ/ eńdlešslў/ roćkiňg

A slash / is used as a divider to separate feet in a line.

Poetic lines are usually not composed of only one type of metrical foot, for this would sound dull. Variations are constructed to give the line more exciting movement. There are two rare feet,

SPONDEE	´ ´
PYRRHIC	˘ ˘

that are occasionally mixed in with the more usual ones. An iambic line, thus, may contain other feet, such as trochees, just as a trochaic line could contain iambs for variety. In lines with mixed feet, whichever foot is most prevalent determines the type and name of the line. Thus, a line with six iambs and four trochees would be called an iambic line.

After we figure out the predominant foot in the line, we mark the accents and count the number of feet in order to determine the total length of the line. For example:

Ĭ taśte/ ă liq́/ uŏr név/ eř bréwed

has a total of four iambic feet. This is called iambic tetrameter. The following chart explains the number of feet and the length of the line:

Number of Feet	**Line Length**
one	monometer
two	dimeter
three	trimeter
four	tetrameter
five	pentameter
six	hexameter
seven	heptameter

While it is possible to have a line containing more than seven feet, in actual practice, the heptameter line—a line from 14 to 21 syllables long—approaches the outer limits of most poems.

The most common foot in English is the iamb, perhaps because the use of articles—the, a, an—establishes that an unstressed syllable will occur before a stressed one. Children's verse, such as nursery rhymes, often has trochees dominating. This is also because children don't use as many articles as adults do in speech. The most common line in English poetry is the iambic pentameter line, in part because a line greater than ten syllables in length requires an intake of breath, which translates as requiring another line.

Even though the measurement of an accentual-syllabic line can be very precise, as illustrated earlier, there is a way for the poet to shorten or lengthen the line, even within strict metrical lines. This is called *elision*. For example, two vowels placed side by side may become a single syllable. We consider the letters h, w, and v as vowels, as well as the more easily recognized a, e, i, o, and u. These four lines by Raleigh illustrate the process:

> The flowers do fade, and wanton fields
> To wayward winter reckoning yields;
> A honey tongue, a heart of gall,
> In fancy's spring, but sorrow's fall.

This poem, "The Nymph's Reply to the Shepherd," is written in iambic tetrameter, which means that it should have eight syllables per line. The first two lines though, count out to nine syllables apiece, while the second two come out to the expected eight. We deal with the extra syllable in the first line by taking the word "flowers" and treating it differently. The vowels o, w, and e come together to create what we call a *diphthong,* meaning two syllables which may be counted or pronounced as one if the poet should so desire. The same is done with the word "reckoning" in the second line, compressing into two syllables what might have been considered three with more formal pronunciation. The same process can be seen in Milton's sonnet "On the Late Massacre," which has an iambic pentameter line with eleven syllables instead of the usual ten:

> . . . and they
> To Heaven. Their martyred blood and ashes sow
> O'er all th'Italian fields where still doth sway
> The triple tryant;

Elision occurs here with the words "To Heaven" where the two-syllable word "Heaven" is treated as though it had only one syllable. In the next line, "Over" is written "O'er," indicating elision by spelling. In the same manner, "the Italian fields" is shortened to "th'Italian fields." It is rare today to find words contracted as Milton did to show the elision, for it is felt to be old-fashioned, but it is nonetheless present in modern accentual-syllabic verse. You will be able to find it when you read the lines for their meter.

Accents may also be used to give the poet greater leeway at the end of a line of verse. A line is said to have a *feminine ending* when it ends on an unaccented syllable, a *masculine ending* when it ends on an accented one: These lines from Milton's epic *Paradise Lost* have a feminine ending:

> Thus they in mutual accusation spent
> The fruitless hours, but neither self condemning

The second line has an extra syllable because of its feminine ending, but as an unaccented additional syllable at the close of a line, the "ing" may be discounted. Thus a line that counts out to 11 syllables may, at the poet's decision, become technically a 10-syllable line thanks to the feminine ending.

FREE VERSE

Free verse has no fixed metrical pattern: It is free from counting, measuring, meter. Free verse replaces the expected pattern of a particular foot with a looser movement called *rhythm.* Free verse shares a common basis with accentual and syllabic verse, but it must be devoid of all predominant measurements to be considered truly "free." The placement of accents must follow no pattern; the syllables must not be able to be measured with any regularity. In the same manner, *rhyme,* if used at all, is irregular. A poem may be considered free verse if you can find no accentual or syllabic pattern. It may, of course, have other regularities. This type of verse can be found in the work of e.e. cummings and Walt Whitman, among others.

There are some modern poets who consider free verse to be anything in which no attempt has been made to make the lines of verse fit a definite pattern, even though they do, in fact, have patterns at intervals. Often a page of poetry will look like free verse, but upon closer examination, will reveal itself to be syllabic or accentual. The poems of T. S. Eliot and Dylan Thomas are of this type. There are many other modern poems that have no metric regularity and are thus considered free verse, although they have a great deal of rhythm, such as the work of Lawrence Ferlinghetti.

Some poets have carried matters to such a length that they have created poems where the shape, not the words, is what matters. These are called *concrete poems.* Sometimes just repeating one letter of the alphabet, they leave it to the reader's eye to create a pleasing or important shape and meaning.

We have looked thus far at rhythm and accents, syllables and lines, but it's obvious that these can be grouped in several ways. Often these lines arrange themselves into blocks of specific numbers—two lines, four lines, six lines, etc. Usually there is a space, followed by an equal grouping of lines. A grouping of lines is called a stanza, roughly the same as a paragraph in a prose work. Stanzas may be classified as follows:

Couplets	2-line stanzas
Quatrains	4-line stanzas
Sextets	6-line stanzas
Octets	8-line stanzas

A Quick Review of Meter

Scansion	The act of breaking down lines into their basic units to discover rhythm and rhyme.
Accent	Emphasis or stress on certain words or parts of words.
Ictus	´ mark over the syllable to indicate that it is accented.
Breve	˘ mark over the syllable to indicate that it is not accented.
Sprung Rhythm	A reintroduction of accentual verse in the works of Gerard Manley Hopkins (1844–1889), in which strongly accented syllables are pushed up against unaccented ones to produce greater tension and emphasis within the verse.
Accentual Verse	A system of verse in which accents are used to determine the length of lines of poetry. The number of syllables per

line is unimportant. This is found mainly in the works of the earliest poets, dating from the eighth century.

Syllabic Verse
A system of verse in which syllables are used to determine the length of a line of poetry. This type of verse flourished mainly in the period between 1066–1400, although modern poets have experimented with it.

Accentual-Syllabic Verse
A type of verse in which the counting of accents and syllables occurs within the same line. It is the type of poetry most people instantly recognize as "poetic," for it has a definite beat and often rhymes.

Meter
The "beat" of a line of verse determined by the kind and number of poetic feet.

Foot/Feet
A group of stressed and unstressed syllables combining to form a unit of verse.

iamb ˘ ´ — An unstressed syllable followed by a stressed one
trochee ´ ˘ — Stressed, unstressed syllables
anapest ˘ ˘ ´ — Two unstressed followed by a stressed
dactyl ´ ˘ ˘ — Stressed followed by two unstressed
spondee ´ ´ — Two stressed syllables
phyrrhic ˘ ˘ — Two unstressed syllables
/ — Used as a divider to separate feet in a line

Number of Feet	line length
one	monometer
two	dimeter
three	trimeter
four	tetrameter
five	pentameter
six	hexameter
seven	heptameter

Elision
The elimination of a vowel, consonant, or syllable in pronunciation. It usually occurs in verse at the end of a word when the next word begins with a vowel, and is used to shorten or lengthen a line to make it fit metrical requirements.

Diphthong
Two syllables that are counted and pronounced as one, used in poetry to make the words fit the metrical requirements.

Feminine Ending
A line that ends on an unaccented syllable.

Masculine Ending
A line that ends on an accented syllable.

Free Verse
Poetry without a fixed metrical pattern. The rhythmical lines vary in length and are usually unrhymed. Although the form may appear unrestrained, there is a firm pattern to the words.

Concrete Verse
Poems shaped like a specific object.

Stanza
An arrangement of a certain number of lines forming the divisions of a poem.

Types of Stanzas
couplets — 2-line stanzas
quatrains — 4-line stanzas
sextets — 6-line stanzas
octets — 8-line stanzas

Rhyme and Figurative Language

Rhyme is the repetition of the same or similar sounds often occuring at set intervals in a poem. Many find it pleasant in itself, and it also serves to suggest order and pattern. In addition, it often relates to the meaning of the verse, for it brings words together and suggests relationships.

The most obvious type of rhyme is called end rhyme, since it appears at the end of a line. For example, the word "light" rhymes with "fight," "sight," etc. The rhyming constant is the sound "ight," on which the poet forms other rhymes by changing the first letter or letters. To some extent, the use of rhyme is similar to the musical pattern of returning to a recognized theme or note. In ancient poetry, before the advent of writing, rhyme was invaluable, for it was far easier to commit to memory poetry that had a strong pattern of rhyme.

KINDS OF RHYME

True or *perfect rhyme* occurs when the first consonants change, but following consonants or vowels stay the same. This can also be referred to as *exact rhyme*. These involve identity of sound, not spelling. "Fix" and "sticks," like "buffer" and "rougher," though spelled diffeently, are perfect rhymes. Anne Bradstreet's "Before the Birth of One of Her Children" (1678) illustrates true rhyme:

> All things within this fading world hath end,
> Adversity doth still our joys attend;
> No ties so strong, no friends so dear and sweet,
> But with death's parting blow is sure to meet.

In the lines quoted, "end," which we shall call *a,* rhymes with "attend," also called *a,* while "sweet," called *b,* rhymes with "meet." The *rhyme scheme,* then, is *aabb,* etc.

Half-rhyme (also called *slant rhyme, approximate rhyme, near rhyme,* or *off-rhyme*) occurs when there are changes within the vowel sounds of words intended to rhyme and only the final consonant sounds of the words are identical. The stressed vowel sounds as well as the initial consonant sounds (if any) differ. Examples include: soul:oil; firth:forth; trolley:bully. The following lines from William Whitehead's "Je Ne Sais Quoi" exemplify half-rhyme:

> Tis not her face that love creates,
>   For there no grace revel;
> Tis not her shape, for there the Fates
>   Had rather been uncivil.

"Revel" and "uncivil in lines 2 and 4 above illustrate half-rhyme because the vowel sound changes, but the "vl" sound has remained the same.

Assonance occurs when the vowels in the words are the same, but the consonants are not, for example, in the words "seat" and "weak." *Consonance* occurs when the consonants agree but the vowels do not, as in the words "luck" and "lick." "Tide" and "mine" are assonantal. Assonance and consonance are both variations of half-rhyme.

Internal rhyme occurs within the line instead of at the end. Oscar Wilde's "Each narrow cell within which we dwell" would be an example of internal rhyme because the words "cell" and "dwell" rhyme.

Masculine and *feminine rhymes* are the equivalents of masculine and feminine line endings. Rhymes that end on a stress, such as "van" and "span," are masculine, while those ending on an unstressed syllable, such as "falling" and "calling," are called feminine. Thus, "stark/mark" and "support/retort" would be masculine while "revival/arrival" and "flatter/batter" are feminine. Feminine rhyme is also referred to as *double rhyme*. Also a feminine rhyme, *triple rhyme* as defined in *A Handbook to Literature** is a rhyme in which the correspondence of sound lies in three consecutive syllables. "Machinery/scenery" and "tenderly/slenderly" are two examples.

Alliteration is the repetition of an initial sound in two or more words. Although not technically considered a type of rhyme, it will be treated here because its use adds to the musical quality of a poem.

About the lilting house and happy as the grass was green

shows alliteration in the repetition of *h* in "house" and "happy" and the *gr* in "grass" and "green." Alliteration is also called *initial rhyme*. In Macbeth's line, "after life's fitful fever," true alliteration is found in the repeated *f*s of "fitful fever" and *hidden alliteration* is found in the *f*s of "after," "life," and "fitful." Accentual Anglo-Saxon poetry, used alliteration a great deal to create the balance and music of its verses.

Eye-rhyme occurs when words are spelled the same and look alike but have a different sound, see the following lines 3 and 4 of Sir Walter Raleigh's poem "The Nymph's Reply to the Shepherd."

"These pretty pleasures might me move
To live with thee and be thy love"

The words "move" and "love" are an example of eye rhyme. These rhymes are also called *historical rhymes* as, in the above example by Sir Walter Raleigh, the pronunciation has changed over the years. The word "tea," for example, once rhymed with "day," but today these two words are, at best, *half-rhymes*.

Onomatopoeia occurs when the sound of word echoes or suggests the meaning of the word. "Hiss" and "buzz" are examples. There is a tendency for readers to see onomatopoeia in far too many instances, in words such as "thunder" and "horror." Many words that are thought to echo the sound they suggest merely contain some sound which seems to have a resemblance to the thing it suggests. Tennyson's lines from "Come Down, O Maid" are often cited to explain true onomatopoeia:

"The moan of doves in immemorial elms
And murmuring of innumerable bees."

Euphony is the use of a pleasant-sounding or harmonious combination of words, while *cacaphony* is harsh or discordant sound used to produce an unharmonious effect.

FIGURATIVE LANGUAGE

Robert Frost, the twentieth-century American poet, once said, "Poetry provides the one permissible way of saying one thing and meaning another." Of course, this is an exaggera-

*William Flint Thrall and Addison Hibbard, *A Handbook to Literature,* ed. C. Hugh Holman (New York: The Odyssey Press, 1960) p. 495.

tion, but it does underline the importance of *figurative language*—saying one thing in terms of another. Words have a literal meaning that can be looked up in any dictionary, but they can also be employed so that something other than that literal dictionary meaning is intended. What is impossible or difficult to convey to a reader through the literal use of language may be highly possible through the use of *figures of speech,* also called *tropes.* *Figures of speech* make language significant, moving, and fascinating. "My love is a rose" is, when taken at face value, ridiculous, for few love a plant with a prickly, thorny stem. But "rose" suggests many other possible interpretations—delicate beauty, soft, rare, costly, etc.—and so it can be implied in a figurative sense to mean "love" or "loved one."

If a reader comes across the phrase "Brutus growled," he/she is forced, if the poem has indicated that Brutus is a human, to accept "growled" in a nonliteral manner. We understand that it is likely that the poet is suggesting that Brutus spoke like an animal, perhaps a lion or a bear, and indicates Brutus' irritation or unrest. The author calls forth the suggestion of wild animals to describe Brutus most vividly and accurately. It is far more effective than saying "Brutus spoke like an animal," or "Brutus acted like an animal." By using a figure of speech, the author calls the reader's imagination into play.

THE FIGURES OF SPEECH

Simile. A simile is a comparison between unlike objects introduced by a connective word such as "like," "as," or "than," or a verb such as "seems." The following are some examples:

> My heart is like a singing bird (C. Rossetti)
> I am weaker than a woman's tear (Shakespeare)
> Seems he a dove? His feathers are but borrowed (Shakespeare)

Metaphor. A metaphor is a comparison without the "like" or "as." Once established, this relationship between unlike objects alters our perception of both. In the most basic metaphor, such as "My love is a rose," "rose" and "love" are equated. They are not alike, but they interact with one another, so the abstract word, "love," becomes concrete. Now it is not a vague internal emotion but an object that could be picked and caressed. We can make the comparison even more specific by describing the rose in more detail—color, variety, and so forth. The subject of the comparison—in this case, love— is called the *tenor,* and the figure that completes the metaphor—the rose—the *vehicle.* These terms were coined by critic I.A. Richards. In the following metaphor by John Donne, the poet's doctors become the map-makers of the heavens, while the poet's body becomes the map in which the ultimate destiny of his soul can be divined:

> Whilst my physicians by their love are grown
>   Cosmographers, and I their map, who lie
> Flat on this bed . . .

Implicit or Submerged Metaphor. If we do not have both terms of the metaphor present ("My winged heart" instead of "My heart is a bird"), we have what is called a submerged metaphor.

Mixed Metaphor. A mixed metaphor combines two metaphors, often with absurd results. For example, "Let's iron out the bottlenecks," would be silly, for it is obvious that it is an impossibility.

Dead Metaphor. A metaphor that has lost its figurative value through overuse is called a dead metaphor. "Foot of a hill" or "eye of a needle" are examples.

Extended Metaphor. An extended metaphor results when a metaphor becomes elaborate or complex. It has length and the ideas are more fully illustrated.

Conceit. A metaphor that goes beyond the original tenor and vehicle to other tenors and vehicles is called a conceit. In "A Valediction Forbidding Mourning" by Donne, the souls of two lovers become the same as the two legs of a draftsman's compass:

> If they be two, they are two so
>   As stiff twin compasses are two;
> Thy soul, the fixed foot, makes no show
>   To move, but doth, if th'other do.
>
> And through it in the center sit,
>   Yet when the other far doth roam,
> It leans and harkens after it,
>   And grows erect, as that comes home.

Metonymy. Metonymy is the substitution of one item for another item that it suggests or to which it is closely related. For example, if a letter is said to be in Milton's own *hand*, it means that the letter is in Milton's own handwriting. As another example, Sidney wrote in his sonnet "With How Sad Steps, O Moon," "What, may be that even in heav'nly place/That busy archer his sharp arrows tries?" "That busy archer" is a reference to Cupid, the god of love frequently depicted as a cherubic little boy with a quiver full of arrows. Here he is at his usual occupation—shooting arrows into the hearts of unsuspecting men and women. Thus an archer, by relating to the god of love, describes love without specifically using the word.

Synecdoche. Synecdoche substitutes a part of something for the whole, or the whole is used in place of one of the parts. "Ten sails" would thus stand for ten ships. In the stanza below by American poet Emily Dickinson, "morning" and "noon," parts of the day, are used to refer to the whole day. In the same manner, "Rafter of Satin" refers to a coffin, by describing its inner lining rather than the entire object:

> Safe in their Alabaster Chambers—
> Untouched by Morning—
> And untouched by Noon—
> Lie the meek members of the Resurrection—
> Rafter of Satin—and Roof of Stone!

Transferred Epithet. Transferred epithet is a word or phrase shifted from the noun it would usually describe to one which has no logical connection with it, as in Gray's "drowsy tinklings," where "drowsy" literally describes the sheep who wear the bells, but here is figuratively applied to the bells. In current usage, the distinction between metonymy, synecdoche, and transferred epithet is so slight that the term metonymy is often used to cover them all.

Personification. Personification is the attribution of human characteristics and/or feelings to nonhuman organisms, inanimate objects, or abstract ideas. "Death, Be Not Proud" by John Donne addressed Death as if it were a person capable of hearing as well as possessing human emotions, such as pride. Tennyson's "Now sleeps the crimson petal, now the white" and Shakespeare's reference to "Time's cruel hand" are both examples of this process at work.

Pathetic fallacy. This is a specific kind of personification in which inanimate objects are given human emotions. John Ruskin originated the term in *Modern Painters* (1856). Ruskin uses the example of "the cruel crawling foam" of the ocean to discuss the pathetic fallacy: The ocean is not cruel, happy to inflict pain on others, as a person may be, although it may well seem cruel to those who have suffered because of it. Ruskin obviously disapproved of such misstatement, and allowed it only in verse where the poet was so moved by passion that he could not be expected to speak with greater accuracy. But in all truly great poetry, Ruskin held, the speaker is able to contain his excess emotion to express himself accurately. The term is used today, however, without this negative implication.

Apostrophe. Apostrophe is also closely related to personification. Here, a thing is addressed directly, as though it were a person listening to the conversation. For example we have Wordsworth's "Milton! thou should'st be living at this hour," although Milton has obviously passed on. Apostrophe and personification go hand-in-hand in Donne's "Busy old fool, unruly Sun," and Wyatt's "My lute, awake." Milton's apostrophe has only a hint of the laurels as listening things in "Yet once more, O ye laurels."

Invocation. Invocation is an address to a god or muse whose aid is sought. This is commonly found at the beginning of an epic. For example, Milton's "Sing, Heavenly Muse" at the opening of his *Paradise Lost*.

Hyperbole or Overstatement. This is exaggeration for a specific literary effect. Shakespeare's Sonnet 97 contains this example:

> How like a winter hath my absence been
> From thee, the pleasure of the fleeting year!
> What freezings have I felt, what dark days seen!
> What old December's bareness everywhere!

We realize obviously that Shakespeare did not literally freeze with real cold when he was apart from his loved one. We also realize that the days did not turn dark, or June turn to December, but he is saying this to illustrate the depth of his despair at their separation. The same process is at work in Lovelace's "When I lie tangled in her hair/And fetter'd to her eye . . .". Obviously, he is not captured in her hair nor chained to her eye; what he is suggesting, however, is that he is a prisoner to her beauty and finds himself unable to escape its spell.

Understatement. Understatement is the opposite of exaggeration, a statement that states less than it indirectly suggests, as in Jonathan Swift's "Last week I saw a woman flayed, and you will hardly believe how much it altered her person for the worst." In the same way, Auden's ironic poem "The Unknown Citizen" has a great many examples of understatement that combine to show how numbers cannot evaluate the ultimate happiness of a person's life.

Litote. Litote is a special form of understatement. It affirms something by negating its opposite. For example, "He's no fool" means that he is very shrewd.

Synesthesia. This takes one of the five senses and creates a picture or image of sensation as perceived by another. For example, "the golden cry of the trumpet" combines "golden", a visual perception of color, with "cry," hearing. In the same manner, Emily Dickinson speaks of a fly's "blue, uncertain stumbling buzz."

Oxymoron. Oxymoron is the combination of contradictory or incongruous terms. "Living death," "mute cry," and Milton's description of hell as "no light, but rather darkness visible" are all examples of this process. The two words that are brought together to form a description of this nature ought to cancel each other out by the nature of their contradictions; instead, they increase the sense of each word. Thus "sweet pain" aptly describes certain experiences of love.

Onomatopoeia. As mentioned earlier, onomatopoeia refers to the repetition of a sound intended to echo what it is describing. The famous last lines of Tennyson's "Come Down, O Maid," contain an example. "The moan of doves in immemorial elms,/And murmuring of inumerable bees" suggests the sounds of birds and bees among old trees.

Symbolism. Symbolism occurs when an image stands for something other than what was expected. The ocean, for example, may be said to symbolize "eternity," and the phrase "river to the sea" could stand for "life flowing into afterlife." In most instances the symbol does not directly reveal what it stands for; the meaning must be discovered through a close reading of the poem and an understanding of conventional literary and cultural symbols. For example, we realize that the "stars and stripes" stands for the American flag. We know this because we are told it is so, for the flag itself in no way looks like the United States. Without cultural agreement, many of the symbols we commonly accept would be meaningless.

Irony. Irony states things in one tone of voice when in fact the opposite meaning is intended. Auden's "Unknown Citizen," for example, ends ironically by making a statement that the reader knows to be false. As a matter of fact, the entire poem is ironic in that it condemns the State by using the State's own terms of praise: "Was he free? Was he happy? The question is absurd;/Had anything been wrong, we should certainly have heard."

Socratic Irony. This form of irony is named for Socrates, who usually pretended to be ignorant when he was in fact cautious or tentative. The person who states "I do not understand; please explain this to me . . ." is a Socratic ironist, and his words are ironic, for he clearly does understand.

Verbal Irony. This form of irony involves a contrast between what is stated and what is more or less wryly suggested. The statement is somehow negated by its suggestions. Thus, Pope attacks the proud man by ironically encouraging his pride:

> Go, wiser thou! and, in thy scale of sense,
> Weigh thy opinion against Providence . . .
> Snatch from His hand the balance of the rod,
> Re-judge his justice, be the God of God.

What is stated ironically need not always be the direct reverse of what is suggested; irony may, for instance, state less than what is suggested, as in the following understatement: "Men have died from time to time."

Sarcasm. Sarcasm is crude and heavy-handed verbal irony.

Dramatic Irony, Sophoclean Irony, Tragic Irony. Here the irony refers to conditions or affairs which are the tragic reverse of what the participants have expected. Thus, it is ironic that when Eve eats the forbidden fruit she is faced with great sorrow, for she had expected great joy and happiness. Macbeth expected great happiness to follow his killing of King Duncan; instead, he finds that he forfeits all that makes life worth living by his deed. Sophocles' King Oedipus accuses the blind prophet of corruption, but by the end of the play he learns, as we had realized all along, that he is himself corrupt, that he has been blind to what is real, and that the prophet's visions were indeed correct. As in verbal irony, dramatic irony is marked by contrast, but here it is not between what the speaker says and means, but between what he says and means and the real state of affairs.

Irony of Fate or Cosmic Irony. This term describes the view that God, Fate, or some supernatural being is amused to manipulate human beings as a puppeteer would manipulate puppets. It is an irony of fate that the prisoner receives his pardon a moment too late.

Romantic Irony. Romantic irony is most commonly found in German literature and shows the creator detaching himself from his creation to treat it playfully or objectively.

Contrast. Contrast shows the difference between two objects. In this sense it is the opposite of comparison, which shows similarities. In the following example by William Shakespeare, we see his mistress contrasted to various accepted symbols of adoration:

> My mistress' eyes are nothing like the sun;
> Coral is far more red than her lips' red;
> If snow be white, why then her breasts are dun;
> If hairs be wires, black wires grow on her head.

Connotation and Denotation. Connotation is the generally accepted meaning(s) of a word, in contrast to the denotation, which is the dictionary meaning. Connotation adds additional richness to a word's, and by extension a poem's, meaning. In the line, "She was the sickle; I, poor I, the rake," the word "rake" has a clear denotation—a gardening tool designed to pick up clippings from a lawn or a garden that a sickle might have cut down. In the context of the entire poem, though, the word "rake" has the connotative meaning of a debauched man. The two meanings work together to give the poem greater depth and further the author's theme.

Ambiguity. Ambiguity allows multiple meanings to coexist in a word or a metaphor. It does not mean that the word or term is unclear; rather, it means that the perceptive reader can see more than one possible interpretation at the same time. Puns, for example, offer ambiguity, as these lines from Wyatt's "They Flee From Me" show: "But since that I so kindely [*sic*] am served/I fain would know what she hath deserved." The word "kindely" means both "served by a group" and "courteously."

Allegory. Allegory occurs when one idea or object is represented in the shape of another. In medieval morality plays and in some poems, abstract ideas such as virtues and vices appear as people. In this way the reader can understand a moral or a lesson more easily. In Emily Dickinson's poem "Because I Could Not Stop For Death," death appears as the allegorical figure of a coachman, kindly stopping to pick her up on the road to eternity.

Types of Poems and Poetic Movements

POETIC FORMS

Ballads. The *traditional* or *popular ballad* is a story told in song form which has been passed by word of mouth from singer to singer, generation to generation. Unlike formal written verse, ballads underwent change. They were common in the fifteenth century, and one, "Judas," is known to have passed down from the thirteenth century. The oral nature is shown in the effective transitions in the narrative, for weak verses tended to get taken out and forgotten, resulting in a highly effective series of pictures in words.

The tradition of the ballad runs through English and American verse. The anonymous ballads of the fifteenth century have their counterpart in the ballads of the twentieth century, in songs of social protest and stories of ordinary people. Traditional ballads were produced throughout the nineteenth century also, in America, commonly by sailors, loggers, and plantation workers—relatively isolated and illiterate people. In rural areas, such ballads are still flourishing today.

When professional poets write stanzas of this type, such as Auden's "I Walked Out One Evening," they are called *literary ballads*. English and Scottish ballads have been imitated by serious poets. Probably the most famous ballads are Coleridge's "Rime of the Ancient Mariner" and Keats's "La Belle Dame sans Merci."

The ballad stanza rhymes *abcb*. ballads often contain *refrains,* musical reptitions of words or phrases. Some critics believe that ballads were originally two-line rhyming songs, thus explaining why there are only two rhymes in a four line stanza. Because early ballads were nonliterary, half-rhymes and slant rhymes are often used. The common stanza is a quatrain of alternating lines of iambic tetrameter and iambic trimeter. Ballads sometimes employ *incremental repetition*, the repetition of some previous line or lines, but with a slight variation to advance the narrative, as in these lines from "The Cruel Brother":

> O what will you leave to your father dear?
> The silver-shode steed that brought me here.
> And what will you leave to your mother dear?
> My velvet pall and my silken gear.

Interestingly, there are frequent nonsense lines in the refrains—"Every rose is merry in time" is a misunderstanding of "Savory, rosemary, and thyme"—perhaps because of oral transmission.

Though the singers of ballads were usually common folk, the subjects were often noble, and the usual theme was tragic love.

A *broadside ballad* was a poem of any sort printed on a large sheet—thus the "broadside"—and sold by street singers in the sixteenth century. Not until the eighteenth century was the word "ballad" limited to traditional narrative song.

Blank Verse. Blank verse is unrhymed iambic pentameter. It was introduced into English poetry in the middle of the sixteenth century. By the end of the century it had become the standard medium of English drama. An example, by William Shakespeare, is: "Time hath, my Lord, a wallet at his back,/Wherein he puts alms for oblivion."

Burlesque. Burlesque is not a type of verse, but any imitation of people or literary type which, by distortion, aims to amuse. Its tone is neither savage nor shrill, and it tends to ridicule faults, not serious vices. Thus it is not to be confused with Satire, for burlesque makes fun of a minor fault with the aim of arousing amusement rather than contempt or indignation. Also, it need not make us devalue the original. For example, T. S. Eliot's "The Hollow Men" is parodied in Myra Buttle's "Sweeniad." The original reads:

> Between the conception
> And the creation
> Between the emotion
> And the response
> Falls the shadow

while the burlesque is:

> Between the mustification
> And the deception
> Between the multiplication
> And the division
> Falls the Tower of London.

Travesty. Also known as *low burlesque,* travesty takes a high theme and treats it in trivial terms, as in the Greek "Battle of the Frogs and Mice," which travesties Homer.

Mock Epic or Mock Heroic. This is also known as *high burlesque,* the reverse of travesty, for it treats a minor theme in a high, lofty, style. Despite its name, it does not mock the epic, but rather mocks low activities by treating them in the elevated style of the epic. The humor results from the difference between the low subject and the lofty treatment it is accorded. In the theatre, a burlesque may be a play that humorously criticizes another play by imitating aspects of it in a grotesque manner, as in John Gay's "Beggar's Opera," which make fun of serious operas. The term is also used, especially in America, for a sort of variety show stressing crude humor and sex.

Didactic Literature. Didactic literature intends to instruct or teach. It is sometimes used in contrast to *pure poetry,* which is said to be free from instruction and moral content and intends merely to delight and entertain. The term need not be pejorative, though many use it in this manner. A good case can be made that almost all of the world's finest poetry is didactic in some way. Satire makes fun of certain modes of behavior; Milton wrote *Paradise Lost* to "justify the ways of God to men." The problem, then, is one of degree, as true didactic literature deals mainly with instruction. This does not make it any less "poetic." These lines by John Gay, explaining how to clean worms, are an illustration of didactic literature:

> Cleanse them from filth, to give a tempting gloss,
> Cherish the sully'd reptile race with moss;
> Amid the verdant bed they twine, they toil,
> And from their bodies wipe the native soil.

Doggerel. Doggerel is verse made comic because irregular metrics are made regular by stressing normally unstressed syllables. In Butler's lines:

> More peevish, cross, and splenetic
> Than dog distract or monkey sick.

If the subject matter is mock heroic (see previous definition) and the lines are iambic tetrameter couplets (as in the example quoted above), the poem is also referred to as *hudibrastic,* after Samuel Butler's "Hudibras."

Dramatic Monologue. The speaker in a dramatic monologue is usually a fictional character or an historical figure caught at a critical moment. His words are established by the situation, and are usually directed at a silent audience. The speaker usually reveals aspects of his personality of which he is unaware. To some extent, every poem is a dramatic monologue, as an individual speaker is saying something to someone, even if only to himself, but in a true dramatic monologue, the above conventions are observed. Fine examples of this mode include Robert Browning's "My Last Duchess," in which a duke who has eliminated his last duchess reveals his cruelty to an emissary, who wants to arrange for the marriage to the latest duchess. T. S. Eliot's "The Love Song of J. Alfred Prufrock," in which the speaker's timid self addresses his agressively amorous self, would serve as another example.

Elegy. An elegy is a poem that deals solemnly with death. In Greek and Latin verse, they are poems that alternate lines of dactylic hexameter and dactylic pentameter. Gray's "Elegy Written in a Country Churchyard" is an example in point. If an elegy is a short funeral lament, it may be called a *dirge,* which in ancient times was a funeral song. *Threnody* and *monody* are terms used for funeral poems also, although the monody is often more complex and recited by an individual mourner. The elegy is frequently a *pastoral,* in which shepherds mourn the death of a fellow shepherd. They use the conventions of this type of verse, including invocation to the muses, processions of mourners, and lists of flowers. Many poets have used this form to advantage, including Walt Whitman's elegy on Abraham Lincoln, "When Lilacs Last in the Dooryard Bloomed" and Milton's "Lycidas."

Eulogy. Frequently confused with elegy, a eulogy is a poem praising the memory of the living or the dead.

Emblematic Poems. Emblematic poems take the shape of the subject of the poem. An emblematic poem on a swan, for example, would be in the shape of a swan. George Herbert's "Easter Wings" is an example of an emblematic poem.

Epic. An epic is a long and serious narrative poem (a poem that tells a story) about a hero and his heroic companions, often set in a past that is pictured as greater than the present. The hero often possesses superhuman and/or divine traits. In Homer's *Iliad,* for example, the hero, Achilles, is the son of a goddess; in Milton's *Paradise Lost,* the characters are God the Father, Christ, angels, and Adam and Eve. The action is usually rather simple, Achilles' anger in the *Iliad* and the fall of man in *Paradise Lost,* but it is increased by figurative language and allusions that often give it cosmic importance. The style is elevated to reflect the greatness of the events, and certain traditional procedures are employed. For example, the poet usually calls to the muses for help, asks them what initiated the action (the *epic question*), and often begins his tale in the middle of the action (*in medias res*). At this point, the hero is at his lowest fortunes, and later recounts the earlier part of the tale. Gods often participate in the tale, helping the heroes. There may be a trip into Hades. The *epic simile,* also called the *Homeric simile,* is an extended comparison, as a subject is compared to something that is presented at such length or detail that the subject is momentarily lost in the description. For example, in *Paradise Lost,* Satan walking in Eden is compared to a vulture:

> Here walk'd the Fiend at large in spacious field,
> As when a Vultur on Imaus bred,
> Whose snowy ridge the roving Tartar bounds,
> Dislodging from a Region scarce of prey
> To gorge the flesh of Lambs or yearling Kids
> On Hills where Flocks are fed, flies toward the Springs
> Of Ganges or Hydaspes, Indian streams;
> But in his way lights on the barren Plains
> Of Sericana, where Chineses drive
> With Sails and Wind their cany Waggons light:
> So on this windy Sea of Land, the Fiend
> Walk'd up and down alone bent on his prey.

There are two types of epics: the *primary epic* (sometimes called the *primitive epic* or a *folk epic*), which is a stately narrative about the noble class recited to the noble class; and the *secondary epic* (also called *literary epic* or *artificial epic*), a stately narrative about great events designed for a literary person to read from a book. Primary epics include Homer's *Iliad* and *Odyssey* and the anonymous Old English *Beowulf,* while secondary epics include Vergil's *Aeneid* and Milton's *Paradise Lost.* The poet of the primary epic speaks as the voice of the community, whereas the poet of the secondary epic may show more individuality. For example, Homer is not introspective; Milton sometimes is. Homer's poems and *Beowulf* share discussion of aspects of an "heroic age" (virtue is identified with strength, celebrated by the poets). Because the poets in these heroic societies sang memorized poems, their chants contain a great many *stock epithets* and repeated lines. When such repetitions occur at particular positions in lines they are called *formulas,* and they served to help the poet compose his material and remember it. An example of *formulaic poetry* is Longfellow's "The Song of Hiawatha." Modern epics include Hart Crane's "The Bridge," William Carlos Williams's "Paterson," and Ezra Pound's "Cantos." The first two are examples of American epics; the last a case for Western civilization. Epics vary in structure. *Beowulf,* for example, uses alliteration and accentual stress, not rhyme or stanza length, to structure the poem.

Epigram. Originally meaning an "inscription," the epigram became for the Greeks a short poem, usually solemn. But the Romans used the term to mean a short witty poem, with the sting at the end. An example by John Wilmot:

> We have a pretty witty King,
> Whose word no man relies on,
> Who never said a foolish thing,
> Nor ever did a wise one.

The term has come to mean any cleverly expressed thought in verse or prose.

Epitaph. An epitaph is a burial inscription, usually serious but sometimes humorous. John Gay's own serves as an example: "Life is a jest and all things show it:/I thought so once, but now I know it."

Epithalamion. (also spelled **epithalamium**). This is a lyric poem in honor of a bride or bridegroom or both. It is usually ceremonial and happy, and is not simply in praise of marriage, but of a particular marriage. Spenser's "Epithalamion" is the greatest in English. It begins, like its models in Greek and Roman literature, with an invocation, and follows Catullus in calling on young people to attend the bride, in praising the bride, and in welcoming the night. Spenser added deep Christian feeling and realistic description of landscape.

Free Verse. (also called **vers libre**). Free verse is composed of rhythmical lines varying in length, following no fixed metrical pattern, usually unrhymed. Often, the pattern is based on repetition and parallel grammatical structure. Although it may appear unrestrained, it does follow the rules outlined above. An example from Walt Whitman's "Song of Myself":

> I celebrate myself, and sing myself,
> And what I assume you shall assume,
> For every atom belonging to me as good belongs to you.

Haiku. Haiku is an Oriental verse form composed of seventeen syllables in three lines. Such forms were greatly admired models for the Imagist school, an early twentieth century movement that attempted to shed excess words to create poems of clear, concise details.

Idyll. An idyll is a short picturesque piece, usually about shepherds but sometimes a little epic, also called an *epyllion*. It presents an episode from the heroic past, but stresses the pictorial rather than the heroic. The most famous English example is Tennyson's "Idylls of the King," with its detailed descriptions of several aspects of the Arthurian legends.

Light Verse. Light verse is considered playful poetry, since it often combines lightheartedness or whimsy with mild satire as in Suckling's "Why So Pale and Wan, Fond Lover?" which concludes, "If of herself she will not love,/Nothing can make her;/The devil take her." The definition of light verse changed in the late nineteenth century, however, to include less polished pieces such as nursery songs with funny rhymes and distorted pronunciations.

Limerick. A form of light verse, a limerick is a jingling poem composed of three long and two short lines, the long lines (first, second, and fifth) rhyming with each other, and the short lines (third and fourth) rhyming with each other. The rhyming words in the first line can sometimes be misspelled to produce a humorous effect. The following limerick from an early sixteenth century songbook is an example:

> Once a Frenchman who'd promptly said "oui"
> To some ladies who'd asked him if houi
>   Cared to drink, threw a fit
>   Upon finding that it
> Was a tipple no stronger than toui

Lyric. Lyrics have regular rhyme schemes and are of a limited length, as in the fourteen-line sonnet. Burns' famous drinking song "Auld Lang Syne," Robert Frost's short poems, and George Herbert's religious meditations are examples of this form. If the emotion is hate or contempt, and its expression is witty, the poem is usually called a satire, or if very brief, an epigram. A *complaint* is a lyric expressing dissatisfaction, usually to an unresponsive love. Chaucer's humorous "Complaint to His Purse," for example, begins: "To you, my purse, and to noon other wight,/Complayne I, for ye be my lady dere!" For a brief period in the 1800s, nature as well as love became a major subject for lyrics, and poets such as William Wordsworth expressed their thoughts on clouds and daffodils more frequently than those on love.

Macaronic Verse. Macaronic verse is verse containing words resembling a foreign language or a mixture of languages. For example:

> "Mademoiselle got the croix de guerre,
> For washing soldiers' underwear,
> Hinky-dinky, parley-vous."

Narrative Verse. See epic.

Nonsense Verse. See light verse.

Occasional Poems. Poems that commemorate battles, anniversaries, coronations, or any other occasions worthy of poetic treatment.

Ode. This form was usually a song in honor of gods or heroes, but is now usually a very long lyric poem characterized by elevated feelings. The *Pindaric ode,* named for the Greek poet Pindar (c. 522–443 B.C.), has two structurally identical stanzas, the *strophe* and *antistrophe* (Greek for "turn" and "counterturn"). These are followed by a stanza with a different structure, the *epode* (Greek for "stand"). The line length and rhyming patterns are determined by the individual poet. In the original Pindaric ode, the chorus danced a pattern while singing during the strophe, retraced the same pattern while singing during the antistrophe, and sang without dancing during the epode. The odes were characterized by great passion. Notable English Pindaric odes are Gray's "The Progress of Poesy" and Wordsworth's "Ode: Intimations of Immortality." *Horatian odes,* named after the Latin poet Horace (65–8 B.C.), are composed of matched regular stanzas of four lines which usually celebrate love, patriotism, or simple Roman morality. Notable English Horatian odes include Marvell's "Horatian Ode Upon Cromwell's Return to Ireland," and Collins' "Ode to Evening." Keats' "Ode to a Grecian Urn" is probably the best known Horatian Ode. Although the ode is a serious poem expressing the speaker's passion, it may be passion about almost anything. Especially during the 1800s, the ode tended to become less public and more personal and introspective. Shelley's "Ode to the West Wind" or Keats' "Ode to a Nightingale" are examples of this introspection. The *irregular ode,* such as Wordworth's "Intimations on Immortality," has stanzas of various shapes, irregular rhyme schemes, and elaborate rhythms.

Sonnet. For the Elizabethans, sonnet and lyric were often considered one and the same, but to the modern sensibility, sonnet has come to mean a poem of fourteen lines (sometimes twelve or sixteen, but this is rare), written in iambic pentameter. There are two main kinds of sonnet: the *Italian sonnet* (or *Petrarchan*) and the *English sonnet* (*Elizabethan* or *Shakespearean*). The Italian sonnet has two divisions: The first eight lines are called the *octave,* rhyming *abba abba cde cde.* The section sets forth the theme of the poem, traditionally love and romance, and elaborates on it. The second section, the *sestet,* which rhymes *cd cd cd,* or a variant, reflects upon the theme and comes to a conclusion that ties everything together. Sidney's sonnets in English are Petrarchan, while Spencer's are linked rhymes with a variation. Milton, Wordsworth, and Keats have also written notable sonnets in the Italian form. The English sonnet, in contrast, is arranged in three quatrains and a couplet, rhyming *abab cdcd efef gg.* In the Shakespearean sonnet, themes and recapitulations are developed the same way as in the Italian, but seven different rhymes are used instead of four or five. In many sonnets, there is a marked correspondence between the rhyme scheme and the development of thought. Thus the Italian sonnet gives the generalization in the octave and specific examples in the sestet. The English sonnet may give three examples, one in each quatrain, and draw a conclusion in the couplet.

A *sonnet sequence* is a group of sonnets linked by a common theme, such as love betrayed, love renewed, love itself, etc. Some notable sonnet sequences include those of Elizabeth Barrett Browning ("Sonnets from the Portuguese"), George Meredith ("Modern Love"), W. H. Auden ("The Quest"), and Dylan Thomas ("Altarwise by Owl-light").

The *Miltonic sonnet* kept the Italian rhyme scheme, but changed the way the octet and sestet are constructed. Here, the sonnet no longer breaks at the octet but flows over or *enjambs* from line to line into the sestet. This type of sonnet appears to be more unified, beginning at one point and moving toward its inevitable conclusion. Milton also changed the theme of the typical sonnet. He moved into larger intellectual and religious concerns, a development begun by Donne.

Villanelle. A villanelle is a poetic form that not only rhymes but also repeats lines in a predetermined manner, both as a refrain and as an important part of the poem itself. Five stanzas of three lines each are followed by a quatrain. The first and third lines of the first stanza are repeated in a prescribed alternating order as the last lines of the remaining tercets, becoming the last two lines of the final quatrain. Dylan Thomas's "Do Not Go Gentle Into That Good Night" is an example of a modern villanelle.

POETIC MOVEMENTS AND TRENDS

Aesthetic Movement

In the early nineteenth century, a devotion to beauty developed in France. Beauty was thought good and desirable not because it reflected the mind of God, but because in a materialistic and chaotic world, it remained good in and of itself. This movement rejected the notion that the value of literature was related to morality—a sense of right and wrong—or some sort of usefulness. Instead, it put forth the idea that art was independent of any moral or didactic (instructive) end. This was in defiance of much of the traditional thought on the subject of art's place and purpose. The slogan was "art for art's sake" ("*l'art pour l'art*"), and many of the writers involved actively attacked the idea that art should serve any "purpose," in the traditional sense. In the late 1900's in England, the movement was represented by Oscar Wilde and Walter Pater. The term "*fin de siècle*" ("end of the century"), which earlier stood for progress, came to imply decadence—great refinement of style but a marked tendency toward the abnormal or freakish in content. When used as a proper noun, Decadence refers to the aesthetic movement.

Imagists/Imagism

At their peak between 1912 and 1914, these poets sought to use common language, to regard all the world as possible subject matter, and to present in vivid and sharp detail a concentrated visual image. "There should be no ideas but things," said poet William Carlos Williams. Imagists usually wrote in free verse. The most frequently cited example of their aims is summed up in this verse by Ezra Pound, the leader of the Imagist movement:

The apparition of these faces in the crowd;
Petals on a wet, black bough.

The title, "In a Station of the Metro," informs the reader that the poem is about a metro, a European subway, but the poem presents its statement without directly telling the reader what conclusions to draw. The poem means that the colorful faces of people in the subway are like flower petals against dark branches. The poet selects his images and arranges them; the reader must sense the relationships to experience the picture the poem presents.

Imagist poets avoided the old accentual-syllabic rhythms and depended on the poem's image or picture in the reader's mind to create the effect. Poems with obviously spelled-out messages were avoided at all costs. Oriental models, most especially the seventeen-syllable three-line haiku, were much admired. Poems of all kinds contain imagery, carefully described objects of the world, but this movement went further than describing what was seen to create a theory of verse around the idea of the picture.

Metaphysical Poets

The most important Metaphysical poets include John Donne (1572–1631) and his seventeenth-century followers, Andrew Marvell, George Herbert, Abraham Cowley, Richard Crashaw, and Henry Vaughan. These poets reacted against the traditions and rules of Elizabethan love poetry to create a more witty and ironic poetry. Modern critics have also concluded that the verse was more passionately intense and psychologically probing than the Elizabethan poems. Instead of penning smooth lines comparing a woman's beauty to something traditional like a rose, these poets wrote colloquial and often metrically irregular lines, filled with difficult and more searching comparisons. A comparison of this nature is called a *conceit,* which came to refer to a striking parallel of two highly unlike objects, such as the sun partly hidden by a cloud to a lover's head reclining on a pillow. Certain *Petrarchan conceits* were often used in English poetry during this time. They included a lover as a ship tossed by a storm, shaken by his tears, frozen by the coldness of his love. The *Metaphysical conceit* is closely allied, although it may be more original then the Petrarchan conceit. New, rather than traditional, and drawn from areas not usually considered "poetic" (commerce and science, for example), metaphysical conceits usually strike the reader with an effect quite different from the Petrarchan conceit.

Pastoral

Any writing concerning itself with shepherds may be called pastoral. Often set in *Arcadia,* a mountainous area in Greece, known for its simple shepherds who live an uncomplicated and contented life, a pastoral can also be called a *bucolic, idyll,* or an *eclogue.* An idyll sometimes refers to a minature epic, while an eclogue is usually a dialogue between two shepherds.

Rural life is usually shown as superior to tainted city life. Christian poets sometimes added their traditions to the Greek-Roman conventions and painted the shepherd as a holy man, as Christ the Shepherd. The *Georgic* is a poem dealing with rural life, and unlike the pastoral, shows a life of labor rather than a happy existence of singing and dancing through the day.

How Poets Create a Vision

There are three basic parts of any poem: its vision, the speaker who expresses that vision, and the language the poet uses to create voice and vision. This section will examine the ways in which language creates that vision.

When we use the term "vision" in relationship to verse, we are saying that the poet's vision is shared by the audience. By the end of a successful poem, then, we should have something that we recognize, perhaps even a reflection of our inner selves, as we have not before experienced it.

There are two ways in which a poet can create this successful vision. The first is to express his view so clearly that we feel that we are seeing what the poet wishes us to see with a new closeness and clarity. The second way involves using figures of speech or unexpected comparisons or juxtapositions of words that force us to make comparisons we have never before imagined. A look at two poems that use these different methods will show how language operates in each:

THE DALLIANCE OF THE EAGLES

Skirting the river road, (my forenoon walk, my rest,)
Skyward in air a sudden muffled sound, the dalliance of the eagles,
The rushing amorous contact high in space together,
The clinching interlocking claws, a living, fierce, gyrating wheel,
5 Four beating wings, two beaks, a swirling mass tight grappling,
In tumbling turning clustering loops, straight downward falling,
Till o'er the river pois'd, the twain yet one, a moment's lull,
A motionless still balance in the air, then parting, talons loosing,
Upward again on slow-firm pinions slanting, their separate diverse
flight,
10 She hers, he his, pursuing.

—*Walt Whitman*

THE EAGLE

He clasps the crag with crooked hands;
Close to the sun in lonely lands,
Ringed with the azure world, he stands

The wrinkled sea beneath him crawls;
5 He watches from his mountain walls,
And like a thunderbolt he falls.

—*Alfred, Lord Tennyson*

It is easy to see that these poems are very different. Tennyson's work, depicting a lone eagle who remains still throughout most of the poem, creates a feeling of space and solitude; Whitman's, dealing with two eagles, seems to have captured a constant rush of movement. This difference in feeling is created in part by the sounds of the words the poets have selected. Tennyson's words, lines, and sentences are all short, and the stop at the end of each line is very sharply marked. Whitman, in contrast, uses longer lines, with less sharp breaks between them, and his sentences are complex and involved. This technique keeps the reader's mind in almost constant motion—like that of the eagles' flight. Yet the basic difference in the presentation of these two poems lies not in the motion or motionlessness of the eagles, but rather in the imagery used to describe them.

A close examination of the poems reveals this difference in imagery. Whitman uses a great many adjectives, especially participles (adjectives formed from verbs), such as, "clinching," "interlocking," "living," "beating," and "grappling" to convey a sense of motion and action, and contribute much of the force of the poet's description. The poet is an observer here. Taking a walk, he has been startled first by the "sudden muffled sound" and then by the sight of the eagles. He describes these two sensations as carefully and fully as he can: "The clinching interlocking claws, a living, fierce, gyrating wheel,/ Four beating wings, two beaks, a swirling mass tight grappling".

Tennyson's verse is also descriptive, but it varies greatly from Whitman's in the types of words chosen to describe the eagle. Where Whitman uses words that could easily be applied to eagles, Tennyson uses words that are not usually associated with birds. His eagle is described in terms which compare it to other things: an old man, grown crooked with age; an explorer in "lonely lands"; a thunderbolt. By calling our attention to the comparison between the eagle and other objects, he draws upon our feelings for these other objects (respect or awe, for example) and uses those emotions to influence our feelings about the eagle itself. Thus, instead of saying, as Whitman does, that the eagle has "clinching . . . claws," Tennyson gives his eagle "crooked hands." He "stands"—a human rather than a birdlike act—and "watches," as both men and birds do. The landscape is also humanized. The lands are described as "lonely," the sea is pictured as "wrinkled," and it "crawls." There are examples of hyperbole (exaggeration) as well. The eagle is said to have a perch "close to the sun," which of course is impossible. In the same way, the sky against which he is pictured is an entire "azure world," and the eagle falls like "a thunderbolt." High and remote, yet in these very qualities very human, Tennyson's eagle presents a stunning image of a being in isolation.

By linking things that we would not ourselves associate, the poet creates new images and calls forth new emotions which make the reader look at things in a different light. Abstract ideas become specific through the use of precise visual images and specific words. The reader derives very different feelings from Whitman's waterfall of precisely denotative adjectives and Tennyson's careful balance of connotations of space, people, and isolation. A closer look at other forms of comparison can show us how imagery works in different settings. Comparative figures of speech include explicit comparisons, similes and metaphors, and implicit comparisons, implied metaphors, and personification.

SIMILES, METAPHORS, AND PERSONIFICATION

Similes are comparisons using the words "like," "as," or a similar word of comparison. Usually the objects under comparison resemble each other in only one or two ways, differing in all other aspects. For example, an eagle and a thunderbolt are really not very much alike, but the fact that they both can travel from the sky to the ground allows Tennyson to use this comparison to say that the eagle falls "like a thunderbolt." The strength of the simile lies in the difference between the eagle and the thunderbolt. The fact that the thunderbolt is much more powerful and dangerous than the eagle gives a sense of speed, power, and danger to the bird's fall. Langston Hughes constructed an entire poem, "Harlem," on the basis of similes. He compares a dream that has been put off to various physical items that have in some manner changed their appearance. He calls forth the image of a raisin, a dried grape, and a cut that has become infected. All the similes he uses in some way appeal to our senses and tell us that deferring our dreams will cause horrible things to happen. No matter how the change occurs in any event, lives will not remain untouched by the disappointment of deferred dreams. While the structure and language used are simple, at least on the surface, the similes lend extraordinary power to the poet's theme.

Like similes, *metaphors* are comparisons of two unlike objects. In this instance, though, the joining of the two objects is more complete, for there is no intervening word such as "like" or "as." Instead, the metaphor simply states that A *is* B; one element of the comparison becomes the other. Some metaphors go one step further and omit the "is." They talk about A as though it were B, and in some cases may not even use the name for B at all, forcing the reader to guess what B is by the language used. In this instance, the metaphor is called an *implied metaphor*.

The following poem by John Keats makes use of metaphors:

ON FIRST LOOKING INTO CHAPMAN'S HOMER

Much have I travelled in the realms of gold,
   And many goodly states and kingdoms seen;
   Round many western islands have I been
Which bards in fealty to Apollo hold.

5 Oft of one wide expanse had I been told
   That deep-browed Homer ruled as his demesne;
   Yet did I never breathe its pure serene
Till I heard Chapman speak out loud and bold:
Then felt I like some watcher into his ken;
10   When a new planet swims of the skies
Or like stout Cortez when with eagle eyes
   He stared at the Pacific—and all his men
Looked at each other with a wild surmise—
   Silent, upon a peak in Darien.

—John Keats

The vocabulary in the first eight lines of this poem is drawn mainly from the Middle Ages and its system of feudalism. The word "realms" is used for kingdoms, "bards" for poets, and "fealty" for the system under which a nobleman owed his allegiance to a king or other nobleman with more extensive power. "Demesne" is the word for the nobleman's domain, and "ken" means knowledge. In the same way, we no longer use "serene" for air or "oft" for often. Apollo, in contrast, is drawn from classical mythology, and stands for the god of poets. Homer is an ancient Greek poet and Chapman a sixteenth-century English poet who was noted for his translation of Homer's *Iliad* into English. What we must ask ourselves, then, is why the poet would use the language of the Middle Ages and the metaphor of traveling to talk about his joy in reading poetry and the delight he experienced when his discovery of Chapman's translations made him feel that he was really reading Homer for the first time. (Perhaps he selected the Middle Ages metaphor to show the timelessness of true verse, how it transcends the boundaries of time to speak for all people at all times.)

Here are some further questions to consider:

1. When Keats finds Chapman's translation, two new similes come to him that support the metaphor of the traveler. What is the first, found in lines 9–10? How does the new identity of the poet resemble his earlier pose as a traveler? How is it different? What sorts of feelings go with each identity?
2. The second simile is set forth in lines 11–14. Who does the poet feel like now? How do his new feelings form a climax to the poem?

Answers

1. In lines 9–10, the poet compares his feelings to those of an astronomer discovering a new planet.
2. In lines 11–14, he compares his feelings to those of an explorer (Cortez) discovering a new ocean (the Pacific). It will make no difference in your enjoyment of the poem, but it was Balboa, not Cortez, who was the first European to see the Pacific Ocean. From these two similes we can sense the poet's great excitement and wonder.

Personification. Personification is a type of implied metaphor, in this instance, speaking about something nonliving as though it were living. Or, as in the case of Tennyson's eagle, the attribution of human characteristics ("crooked hands") to something nonhuman (the bird).

One way to read a poem is to scan it once, and then go back and note all the figures of speech. Identify each one and decide what elements make up the comparison—what is being compared to what? Make some notes about why the poet would want his readers to think about these specific comparisons. Then, read the poem through once again. Look again at the figures of speech that you have noted and see how each relates to the meaning of the poem. Decide what the speaker's feelings are toward the subject and how many subjects of comparison there are. Is each subject compared to one thing, or is one subject compared to several? Is the comparison developed at length? If it is, to what purpose? What is the point that the poet is making through an extended metaphor? If the subject is compared to several things, how do the different images fit together? Are they unrelated so that the job of fixing them into a pattern is left to the reader? Or does the poet suggest some sort of relationship or contrast between/among them? How does the pattern thus created form your sense of the poet's vision, meaning, progression? Finally, read the poem through once again to see if the conclusions you have reached hold up. This may sound like a very complex and time-consuming practice, but it is only one way of looking at verse. It is handy for exams when you are expected to be fully aware of the poet's techniques and must be able to discuss how and why he did what he did. Of course, verse may be read in many other ways for many different reasons, but here we are dealing with gaining a clear understanding of poetic conventions and meanings.

Take a look at the two poems that follow. Using the method outlined, see what poetic techniques and meanings you can extract.

From A PINDARIC ODE

It is not growing like a tree
 In bulk, doth make man better be;
Or, standing long an oak, three hundred year,
To fall a log at last, dry, bald, and sear:
5 A lily of a day
   Is fairer far, in May,
 Although it fall and die that night;
 It was the plant and flower of light.
In small proportions we just beauties see,
10 And in short measures life may perfect be.
       —*Ben Jonson*

COMPOSED UPON WESTMINSTER BRIDGE, SEPTEMBER 3, 1802

Earth has not anything to show more fair:
Dull would he be of soul who could pass by
A sight so touching in its majesty;
This City now doth, like a garment, wear
5 The beauty of the morning; silent, bare,
Ships, towers, domes, theaters, and temples lie
Open unto the fields, and to the sky;
All bright and glittering in the smokeless air.
Never did sun more beautifully steep
10 In his first splendor, valley, rock, or hill;
Ne'er saw I, never felt, a calm so deep!
The river glideth at his own sweet will:
Dear God! the very houses seem asleep;
And all that mighty heart is lying still!
　　　　　　　　　—*William Wordsworth*

Most metaphors have a certain timelessness to them, a quality that endures through the ages. Thus, Wordsworth's picture of London asleep is a vision of something real that holds for all time. We can feel it today, more than a century later, as he must have felt it then. There are poems, usually very modern, that contain metaphors that are transitory and illusory. This is true of the work of Richard Wilbur, particularly the poem entitled "Love Calls Us to the Things of This World." In all poems, metaphors serve to illuminate the poet's view of the world.

SYMBOL AND ALLEGORY

Similes and metaphors tend to make points quickly, for they usually occupy little more than a line or two. They can be linked to others of their kind to make further points, or they may stand alone, secure in their power. Symbol and allegory, though, tend to dominate the poems in which they are used. Further, they tend to stand alone, they are not piled one upon the other as metaphors and similes may be. One symbol or allegorical device is usually all a poem can maintain.

Similes and metaphors are used to make us take a closer look at a subject, or to look at a subject in a new light. Symbols and allegory, in contrast, force us to look beyond the literal meaning of the poem's statement or action. The following poem provides an example:

THE TYGER

Tyger! Tyger! burning bright
In the forests of the night,
What immortal hand or eye
Could frame thy fearful symmetry?

5 In what distant deeps or skies
Burnt the fire of thine eyes?
On what wings dare he aspire?
What the hand, dare seize the fire?

And what shoulder, & what art,
10 Could twist the sinews of thy heart?
And when thy heart began to beat,
What dread hand? & what dread feet?

What the hammer? what the chain?
In what furnace was thy brain?
15 What the anvil? what dread grasp
Dare its deadly terrors clasp?

When the stars threw down their spears,
And water'd heaven with their tears,
Did he smile his work to see?
15 Did he who made the Lamb make thee?

Tyger! Tyger! burning bright
In the forests of the night,
What immortal hand or eye
Dare frame thy fearful symmetry?
　　　　　　　　　—*William Blake*

In this poem, Blake wishes to focus our attention not on the topic of tigers but on the awesome qualities suggested by the tiger's beauty and the godlike powers involved in its creation. This poem may lead the reader to the question of the existence of evil as symbolized by the tiger's murderous nature. How far the symbol or allegory is carried is frequently left in the reader's hands.

Allegory always tells of an action. The events of that action should make literal sense, but they carry much more meaning in a second interpretation. Usually that second interpretation will have a spiritual or psychological level of meaning, for allegories tend to use physical actions to describe the workings of the mind. Thus, allegory presents a correspondence between some physical action (usually some sort of encounter) and a second action (usually psychological or physical), with each step of the literal tale matching the allegorical one. Symbolism, too, may involve the use of a tale, but it may also set forth a description of some unchanging being or object. And it's far more likely to suggest several different interpretations than to insist on a single one. The following poem, for instance, presents a symbolic tale of a king's fall from power:

OZYMANDIAS

I met a traveler from an antique land
Who said: Two vast and trunkless legs of stone
Stand in the desert . . . Near them, on the sand,
Half sunk, a shattered visage lies, whose frown,
5 And wrinkled lip, and sneer of cold command,
Tell that its sculptor well those passions read
Which yet survive, stamped on these lifeless things,
The hand that mocked them, and the heart that fed:
And on the pedestal these words appear:
10 "My name is Ozymandias, king of kings:
Look on my works, ye Mighty, and despair!"
Nothing beside remains. Round the decay
Of that colossal wreck, boundless and bare
The lone and level sands stretch far away.

—*Percy Bysshe Shelley*

The whole tale of the king's loss of power is symbolic, but within the tale, the most striking symbol is the broken statue with its boastful inscription. For many readers, the vision of the statue comes to mind when anyone says "Ozymandias." The full story of the king tends to come as an afterthought.

And what of the symbolism here? Does the king's loss of power symbolize the fall of the proud, which would lend a moral interpretation to the poem? Or is it rather the fall of tyranny, which would throw a political cast on the poem's theme. Or is it simply the inescapable destruction of human lives and civilization by the unceasing motion of time? All three levels of meaning can be read into the poem's symbol, and this contributes to the lasting power of the work. Without doubt, the tyrant with his "sneer of cold command" seems unsavory enough for the reader to welcome his overthrow. But the sculptor, with "the hand that mocked," is dead too, and even the work that was to endure is half destroyed. The picture this sonnet paints is simple enough on the surface; the interpretation of the symbol gives it additional strength.

The following poem is an example of conventional symbolism in verse:

THE LAMB

Little Lamb, who made thee?
  Dost thou know who made thee?
Gave thee life & bid thee feed,
By the stream & o'er the mead;
5 Gave thee clothing of delight,
  Softest clothing wooly bright;

Gave thee such a tender voice,
Making all the vales rejoice!
  Little Lamb who made thee?
10 Dost thou know who made thee?

Little Lamb I'll tell thee,
Little Lamb I'll tell thee!
He is callèd by thy name,
For he calls himself a Lamb:
15 He is meek & he is mild,
He became a little child:
I a child & thou a lamb,
We are callèd by his name.
  Little Lamb God bless thee.
20 Little Lamb God bless thee.
                    —*William Blake*

Here Blake is relying on the traditional association of Christ with the lamb, and thus the meaning is less difficult to discern than in other poems where the author may invent a private symbol and an interpretation as well.

CONCEITS AND ALLUSIONS

Metaphors and similes, because they are so easy to recognize and usually easy to understand, are the first kind of figurative language we notice when reading verse. Symbols and allegories need a much closer reading, but are rewarding because they offer richness and deeper significance. Conceits and allusions may be brief or run the entire length of the poem, but in any case, they tend to be the most difficult to discern, often requiring some outside knowledge to make their meaning clear.

A *conceit* is a comparison between two very unlike objects; some have even called it an "outrageous metaphor." Conceits are usually developed at length, comparing and contrasting many different aspects of two objects to make their meaning clear. In love verse, conceits often derive from the Renaissance tradition that paints the woman as the walled village and the man as the conquering warrior; he attacks and she defends or surrenders. Or she might be the warrior, harming him with sharp looks and sharp words. She could be depicted as a goddess of love, and the list goes on and on. Some poets take these poetic conventions very seriously; others use them in fun, making use of the shock that comes from turning an expected comparison upside down.

The unexpected was a crucial part of the poetic conceit for the Metaphysical poets of the seventeenth century. They used conceits in religious verse as well as love verse, and succeeded in forging poetry of unequalled complexity. Any of the sciences—physics, astronomy, navigation—could yield a conceit which charted the soul's progress in relation to the physical universe. Such metaphysical conceits can be very difficult to understand, but they can be very rewarding for the depth of vision they offer.

The following poem provides examples of the use of metaphysical conceits. Note that there are two main groups of imagery in the poem. The first concerns maps and voyages; the second the image of Christ as the second Adam. Also note that the two images are interwoven by the idea of the soul's journey to salvation as an annihilation of time and space and by the physical image of the sick man, flat on his back in bed and suffering with fever.

HYMN TO GOD MY GOD, IN MY SICKNESS

Since I am coming to that holy room,
    Where, with thy choir of Saints for evermore,
I shall be made thy music; as I come
    I tune the instrument here at the door,
5   And what I must do then, think now before.

Whilst my physicians by their love are grown
    Cosmographers, and I their map, who lie
Flat on this bed, that by them may be shown
    That this is my Southwest discovery
10   *Per fretum febris,* by these straights to die,

I joy, that in these straits, I see my west;
    For, though their currents yield return to none,
What shall my west hurt me? As west and east
    In all flat maps (and I am one) are one,
15   So death doth touch the Resurrection.

Is the Pacific Sea my home? Or are
    The eastern riches? Is Jerusalem?
Anyan, and Magellan, and Gibraltàr,
    All straits, and none but straits, are ways to them,
20   Whether where Japhet dwelt, or Cham, or Shem.

We think that Paradise and Calvary,
    Christ's Cross, and Adam's tree, stood in one place;
Look Lord, and find both Adams met in me;
    As the first Adam's sweat surrounds my face,
25   May the last Adam's blood my soul embrace.

So, in his purple wrapped receive me, Lord,
    By these thorns give me his other crown;
And as to others' souls I preached thy word,
    Be this my text, my sermon to mine own,
30   Therefore that he may raise, the Lord throws down.
—*John Donne*

Conceits demand that we bring some outside knowledge to our understanding of the poem under study. For example, we must be able to grasp the distortions of space involved in making a flat map represent a round world if we are to fully grasp Donne's hymn. In the same way, an *allusion* demands that we bring knowledge to our reading. An allusion is a reference to a previous work of literature, or to some well-known person or event. If we do not understand the reference, we may misunderstand the poem. Notice how the speakers in the three poems that follow use conceits or allusions to praise the women they love and expound on the benefits of love. Begin by looking carefully at each poem's imagery, but note also the use of apostrophe, or direct address, and the different tones used in each example.

FROM AMORETTI—SONNET 15

Ye tradefull Merchants, that with weary toyle,
Do seeke most pretious things to make your gain,
And both the Indias of their treasure spoile,
What needeth you to seeke so farre in vaine?
For loe, my love doth in her selfe containe,
All this worlds riches that may farre be found:
If saphyres, loe her eies be saphyres plaine;
If rubies, loe hir lips be rubies sound;
If pearles hir teeth be pearles both pure and round;
If yvorie, her forehead yvory weene;
If gold, her locks are finest gold on ground;
If silver, her faire hands are silver sheene:
    But that which fairest is but few behold:—
    Her mind, adornd with vertues manifold.
—*Edmund Spenser*

Some Questions for Your Consideration

1. Toward whom is the poet addressing his remarks? Focus on the first four lines.
2. Why should he select this particular audience?
3. What do the words "weary toyle" and "in vaine" suggest about this audience or their activities?
4. How are the metaphors in lines 7–12 connected?
5. How does the conclusion continue the theme of treasure? How does it change the theme?
6. What new questions does the conclusion raise about the merchants' quest for precious things?

Answers

1. The poet is addressing merchants.
2. He might have selected the merchants because they traveled far and wide to seek riches, in contrast to the poet's feeling that all the riches of the world are right at home, in the person of his loved one.
3. The words suggest that all the travels are useless, for real riches rest in love, not commodities.
4. The poet describes the beauty of his love in terms of the most precious substances on earth: gems, gold, silver, and ivory.
5. The conclusion fits in with the theme of treasure in that the mind of the poet's loved one is also "adornd" with riches. It changes the theme since the mind cannot really be seen, and her virtues, the most valuable of her treasures, cannot be gathered like so many jewels.
6. According to the poet, the merchants' quest is absurd, for all we should seek are the virtues hidden in a fine mind, not the outward show of precious metals and stones.

SONNET 18

Shall I compare thee to a summer's day?
Thou are more lovely and more temperate:
Rough winds do shake the darling buds of May,
And summer's lease hath all too short a date:
5 Sometime too hot the eye of heaven shines,
And often in his gold complexion dimmed;
And every fair from fair sometime declines,
By chance or nature's changing course untrimmed:
But thy eternal summer shall not fade
10 Nor lose possession of that fair thou ow'st,
Nor shall Death brag thou wand'rest in his shade,
When in eternal lines to time thou grow'st.
　　So long as men can breathe or eyes can see,
　　So long lives this, and this gives life to thee.
　　　　　　　　　　　　—William Shakespeare

This sonnet also starts with questions relating to physical qualities and concludes with intangible ones.

Questions

1. By means of what comparisons does Shakespeare achieve this movement from tangible to intangible?
2. Trace his logic to show how he arrived at the movement in question 1.
3. Compare and contrast this poem to Sonnet 15 by Spenser. How are they the same? How are they different?

Answers

1. Shakespeare compares a woman's beauty to the beauty of a summer's day to conclude that art—in the form of this sonnet—insures her immortality. The final line, "So long lives this [the sonnet], and this gives life to thee" sums up the movement from tangible to intangible.
2. See lines 1–12 for the development of the theme. The final couplet presents the conclusion and makes the poet's point. Note especially the phrase "summer's day" (line 1), "the eye of heaven" (line 5), and "eternal summer" (line 9). These phrases signal the beginning of the three stages of the author's argument, with the final two lines marking the conclusion. Also, be aware that "fair" has three meanings: a noun meaning "a lovely thing," an adjective meaning "lovely," and a noun meaning "beauty."
3. Both poems are the same in that they praise a loved one for her appearance. They are different in that Shakespeare's sonnet makes the specific point that this particular poem will immortalize the person spoken of in the poem.

Here's another poem to analyze in the same manner:

THE SUN RISING

Busy old fool, unruly sun,
    Why dost thou thus
Through windows and through curtains call on us?
Must to thy motions lovers' seasons run?
5   Saucy, pedantic wretch, go chide
    Late schoolboys and sour 'prentices,
  Go tell court huntsmen that the king will ride,
  Call country ants to harvest offices.
Love, all alike, no season knows nor clime,
10 Nor hours, days, months, which are the rags of time.

Thy beams, so reverend and strong
    Why shouldst thou think?
I could eclipse and cloud them with a wink,
But that I would not lose her sight so long.
15   If her eyes have not blinded thine,
    Look, and tomorrow late tell me
  Whether both th' Indias of spice and mine
  Be where thou left'st them, or lie here with me;
Ask for those kings whom thou saw'st yesterday,
20 And thou shalt hear: All here in one bed lay.

She's all states, and all princess I;
    Nothing else is.
Princes do but play us; compared to this,
All honor's mimic, all wealth alchemy.
25   Thou, sun, art half as happy as we,
    In that the world's contracted thus;
Thine age asks ease, and since thy duties be
To warm the world, that's done in warming us.
Shine here to us, and thou art everywhere;
30 This bed thy center is, these walls thy sphere.
                    —John Donne

Question

Here again earthly riches are equated with the beauty of a woman and then are devalued by it, as time gives way to timelessness. How does Donne's treatment of these conceits differ from those of Shakespeare and Spenser? How is it the same?

Answer

Donne's treatment is different from Shakespeare's since he is *not* saying that this poem will afford the woman immortality. Also, Shakespeare does not place the woman in the center of the universe ("This bed thy center is, these walls thy sphere.") as Donne argues. Of the three, you could make a case for Spenser's poem being the least sophisticated, because he simply praises the woman for her beauty and virtues, while the other two poets make further arguments. Donne's poem is far more earthly than either Shakespeare's or Spenser's, making specific reference to their love.

IMAGERY

We have isolated the various figures of speech to discuss each one individually with examples, but in actual practice, the various poetic devices are almost always found in combination with one another. Just as form and meaning serve to reinforce each other, so the poem's figures of speech work together to echo the poem's pattern of meaning and imagery. When you first begin to read a poem, you may focus on one striking aspect, but once you have studied it well, the entire pattern should come together and the various figures of speech will enter into your understanding of the poem's meaning.

An *image* is a word or a phrase that appeals to the sense—sight, smell, taste, touch, or sound—in such a way as to suggest objects or their characteristics. Images serve to create pictures in the reader's mind and aid in conveying the poem's theme.

Renaissance poems tended to begin with a position and then build on it, showing little movement within the verse. Metaphysical poems showed more movement, as they often followed a speaker's mind through the ramifications of an idea or situation. Modern poets may create scenes, moods, and speakers with even greater movement and further use of sound and imagery. The nineteenth-century American poet Walt Whitman, for example, relied on a pattern of imagery to give structure to his verse rather than on the more conventional rhymes and meters. "There Was A Child Went Forth' is one example. Read the poem and answer the questions that follow.

THERE WAS A CHILD WENT FORTH

There was a child went forth every day,
And the first object he look'd upon, that object he became,
And that object became part of him for the day or a certain part of the day,
Or for many years or stretching cycles of years.

5 The early lilacs became part of this child,
And grass and white and red morning-glories, and white and red clover, and the song of the phoebe-bird,
And the Third-month lambs and the sow's pink-faint litter, and the mare's foal and the cow's calf,
And the noisy brood of the barnyard or by the mire of the pond-side,
And the fish suspending themselves so curiously below there, and the beautiful curious liquid,
10 And the water-plants with their graceful flat heads, all became part of him.

The field-sprouts of Fourth-month and Fifth-month became part of him,
Winter-grain sprouts and those of the light-yellow corn, and the esculent roots of the garden,
And the apple-trees cover'd with blossoms and the fruit afterward, and woodberries, and the commonest
    weeds by the road,
And the old drunkard staggering home from the outhouse of the tavern whence he had lately risen,
15 And the schoolmistress that pass'd on her way to the school,
And the friendly boys that pass'd, and the quarrelsome boys,
And the tidy and fresh-cheek'd girls, and the barefoot Negro boy and girl,
And all the changes of city and country wherever he went.

His own parents, he that had father'd him and she that had conceiv'd him in her womb and birth'd him,
20 They gave this child more of themselves than that,
They gave him afterward every day, they became part of him.

The mother at home quietly placing the dishes on the supper-table,
The mother with mild words, clean her cap and gown, a wholesome odor falling off her person and clothes
    as she walks by,
The father, strong, self-sufficient, manly, mean, anger'd, unjust,
25 The blow, the quick loud word, the tight bargain, the crafty lure,
The family usages, the language, the company, the furniture, the yearning and swelling heart,
Affection that will not be gainsay'd, the sense of what is real, the thought if after all it should prove unreal,
The doubts of day-time and the doubts of night-time, the curious whether and how,
Whether that which appears so is so, or is it all flashes and specks
30 Men and women crowding fast in the streets, if they are not flashes and specks what are they?
The streets themselves and the facades of houses, and goods in the windows,
Vehicles, teams, the heavy-plank'd wharves, the huge crossing at the ferries,
The village on the highland seen from afar at sunset, the river between,
Shadows, aureola and mist, the light falling on roofs and gables of white or brown two miles off,
35 The schooner near by sleepily dropping down the tide, the little boat slack-tow'd astern,
The hurrying tumbling waves, quick-broken crests, slapping,
The strata of color'd clouds, the long bar of maroon-tint away solitary by itself, the spread of purity it lies
    motionless in,
The horizon's edge, the flying sea-crow, the fragrance of salt marsh and shore mud.
These became part of that child who went forth every day, and who now goes, and will always go forth
    every day.

                —*Walt Whitman*

Questions on "There Was a Child Went Forth"

1. Describe the image in each of the following group of lines: 1–13; 14–17; 19–26; 30–34; 35–38.
2. Do these images form a pattern? If so, what is it?

3. How does the imagery serve to unify and connect the poem?
4. Discuss the meaning of lines 19–21. How did the child's parents become "part of him"?
5. What is the poet describing through the use of the images in line 37?
6. How long is the time span in the poem?

Answers

1. 1–13: Spring morning in the country, the beginning of both plant and animal life; 14–17: Fall and re-entry into the town and the world of people; 19–26: Home and the child's parents; 30–34: The movement of the city; 35–38: The shore and nightfall
2. There are several patterns evident here: There is a movement from childhood to adulthood, from home to shore, from morning to evening, from country to city, from self outward to others, through the progression of the seasons (spring-summer-fall), from acceptance to doubt, and finally back to a reaffirmation of life and the goodness of the universe.
3. All the images are connected by the child. He embraces the country and the city, land and water, spring and fall, etc. He is the link that connects all the various pictures the poet creates.
4. The child is more than the result of love between his parents. He is a creation whose development depends on the continued care of his parents. They present him with lessons on how to live, lessons that the child blends into his own self-image.
5. Sunset over the water is the image described here.
6. The poem takes place in one day, from sunrise to sunset.

MEETING AT NIGHT

The gray sea and the long black land;
And the yellow half-moon large and low;
And the startled little waves that leap
In fiery ringlets from their sleep,
5 As I gain the cove with pushing prow,
And quench its speed i' the slushy sand.

Then a mile of warm sea-scented beach;
Three fields to cross till a farm appears;
A tap at the pane, the quick sharp scratch
10 And blue spurt of a lighted match,
And a voice less loud, through its joys and fears,
Than the two hearts beating each to each!
—Robert Browning

This is a poem about love, but despite the number of things that we can infer about love—it is a sweet and exciting time when everything seems beautiful and the most minor things become significant—nothing is told to us directly. As a matter of fact, the author does not even use the word "love" in the poem. He is conveying a feeling and an experience, to the readers. This is accomplished by presenting a situation—a man going to meet his love—and describing that situation so clearly in terms of sensory impressions that the reader is able to share in the poet's experience.

Every line in the poem centers about an image: the gray sea, the long black land, the yellow half-moon, the blue spurt of the lighted match. These images allow the reader to experience with the poet, to enter into his world and become part of it. The warm sea smell of the beach appeals to both our sense of smell and touch while the quiet speech of the lovers engages our sense of hearing. By engaging the reader's senses, the poet is able to attract the reader's attention and convey his feelings on the subject under discussion. Read the two Edgar Allan Poe poems that follow. Then, answer the questions about each selection.

ANNABEL LEE

It was many and many a year ago,
  In a kingdom by the sea,
That a maiden there lived whom you may know
  By the name of Annabel Lee;
5 And this maiden she lived with no other thought
  Than to love and be loved by me.

I was a child and *she* was a child,
  In this kingdom by the sea,
But we loved with a love that was more than
    love—
10   I and my Annabel Lee;
With a love that the wingèd seraphs of heaven
  Coveted her and me.

And this was the reason that, long ago,
  In this kingdom by the sea,
15 A wind blew out of a cloud, chilling
  My beautiful Annabel Lee;
So that her highborn kinsmen came
  And bore her away from me,
To shut her up in a sepulcher
20   In this kingdom by the sea.

The angels, not half so happy in heaven,
  Went envying her and me—
Yes! that was the reason (as all men know,
  In this kingdom by the sea)
25 That the wind came out of the cloud by night,
  Chilling and killing my Annabel Lee.

But our love it was stronger by far than the love
  Of those who were older than we,
  Of many far wiser than we;
30 And neither the angels in heaven above,
  Nor the demons down under the sea,
Can ever dissever my soul from the soul
  Of the beautiful Annabel Lee;

For the moon never beams, without bringing me
    dreams
35   Of the beautiful Annabel Lee;
And the stars never rise, but I feel the bright eyes
  Of the beautiful Annabel Lee;
And so, all the night-tide, I lie down by the side
Of my darling—my darling—my life and my bride,
40   In the sepulcher there by the sea.
  In her tomb by the sounding sea.

TO HELEN

Helen, thy beauty is to me
Like those Nicean barks of yore,
That gently, o'er a perfumed sea,
The weary, wayworn wanderer bore
5 To his own native shore.

On desperate seas long wont to roam,
Thy hyacinth hair, thy classic face,
Thy Naiad airs, have brought me home
  To the Glory that was Greece
10 And the grandeur that was Rome.

Lo! in yon brilliant window niche
How statuelike I see thee stand,
The agate lamp within thy hand!
Ah, Psyche, from the regions which
15 Are Holy Land!

Questions on Poe's Poems

1. Characterize the descriptions of women in these poems. What are they like?
2. The meaning of "To Helen" depends on the classical imagery in which it is expressed. What parallel does Poe draw between Helen and the "Nicean barks" in the first stanza?
3. How does the simile of the above question serve to describe the poet?
4. Find the metaphors in the second and third stanzas of "To Helen." Then, show how they reinforce Poe's theme. What *is* the theme of this poem?
5. Find examples of the following types of figurative language:
   Alliteration
   Assonance
   Repetition
6. Find examples of rhyme, especially end rhyme.

Answers

1. While it appears that women are at the center of both poems, these women seem less than real. What we have here are idealized portraits, removed and abstract. Those women are both untouchable—Annabel Lee because she is firmly in the grave, Helen because she is set so high on a pedestal of classical perfection that it seems impossible to see in her any human quality, "To Helen" has a line that sums this up: "How statuelike I see thee stand."
2. Poe compares Helen's beauty to a ship for it can carry him to the heights of happiness experienced by a weary traveler brought home at last. The meaning of this poem has been much discussed and disagreed upon. It may be that the author was drawing from the people of what is now Nice, France, who were a great seapower in the later part of the Middle Ages. The phrase "perfumed sea" calls forth Nicea (now called Iznik), located just southeast of the Bosporos. This city was important because it was located on the early trade routes to the Orient, but it was not on the sea. The Phaeacians—"lovers of the sea"—are another reference to classical imagery. They were the ones to whom Odysseus recounted his adventures and who sent him home in their enchanted bark (ship).
3. This simile shows the poet, exhausted by his travels on the sea of life, finding succor in thoughts of Helen's ideal beauty, which he seems to link to the happy days of his youth.
4. "Hyacinth hair" serves to call forth the image of beauty and makes a classical reference to Hyacinthus. "Naiad airs" may refer to the Ulysses story, and also reinforces the impression of beauty. "Psyche" in the third stanza is also a classical reference. Psyche was separated from her lover, Cupid, when she ignored his instructions and took a lamp to look at him. She searched for Cupid for years, and finally she was reunited with him. The theme of this poem revolves around the contemplation of Helen's beauty. By thinking of Helen, the ideally remembered figure from his childhood, the poet is able to recapture the classic beauty of the state of mind he enjoyed during his youth. He implies that this state of mind must have been common when the world itself was "young"—in the classical age.
5. Alliteration, the repetition of the initial sound of two or more closely related words, is found, for example, in the last stanza of "Annabel Lee." Line 40 has "sepulcher" and "sea"; "sounding" and "sea" appear in line 41.

   Assonance, the sound of the vowel repeated in two or more accented syllables, can also be found in the last stanza of "Annabel Lee." The long *e* sounds of the internally rhymed words "beams" and "dreams" (line 34) also appears in the "me" of the same line and in "feel" (line 36) and "sea" (lines 40 and 41). Also, the long *i* sound of "rise" and "eyes" (line 36), "night-tide" and "side" (line 38), and "bride" (line 39), is repeated in "bright" (line 36), "lie" (line 38), "my" and "life" (line 39), and "by" (lines 38, 40, and 41). The *o* in "moon" (line 34) is repeated in "tomb" (line 41), and is closely related to the sound in "beautiful" (lines 35 and 37).

Repetition may be seen in "Annabel Lee" in the phrase "kingdom by the sea" (lines 2, 8, 14, 20, and 24). The word "love" is repeated in lines 6, 9, 11, and 27.

6. End rhyme is obvious in both works, but Poe also uses the far more elaborate internal rhyme. This can be seen in the last stanza of "Annabel Lee": "beams" in line 34 rhymes with "dreams"; "rise" in line 36 rhymes with "eyes". "Night-tide" and "slide" in line 38 rhyme with each other and with "bride" at the end of line 39.

TONE

Tone is the writer's or speaker's attitude toward his subject, audience, or himself. It brings emotional power to the poem and is a vital part of its meaning. In spoken language, tone is conveyed through the speaker's inflections, and it may vary from ecstatic to incredulous to despairing to bleak and resigned. A correct interpretation of tone is vital to a correct interpretation of meaning. It is more difficult to discern tone in writing than in speech since inflection cannot be determined in text. To understand tone, we must analyze all the poetic elements that we have previously discussed: imagery, simile, metaphor, irony, understatement, rhythm, sentence structure, denotation, connotation, and so forth. Tone is a combination of all these elements. Let's try to determine the tone of the two poems that follow.

CROSSING THE BAR

Sunset and evening star,
   And one clear call for me!
And may there be no moaning of the bar
   When I put out to sea,

5 But such a tide as moving seems asleep,
   Too full for sound and foam,
When that which drew from out the boundless deep
   Turns again home.

Twilight and evening bell,
10   And after that the dark!
And may there be no sadness of farewell
   When I embark;

For though from out our bourne of Time and Place
   The flood may bear me far,
15 I hope to see my Pilot face to face
   When I have crossed the bar.

              —*Alfred, Lord Tennyson*

Questions

1. What are the two different figures that the poet uses to stand for death?
2. What is the exact moment of death in each instance?
3. What kind of death is the poet wishing for here? Why does he say he wants "no sadness of farewell"?
4. What is the "boundless deep"?
5. What is the tone of this poem?

Answers

1. Each figure begins a section of the poem. The first occurs in line 1, "Sunset and the evening star," while the second is found in line 9, "Twilight and evening bell."
2. In the first instance, death occurs "When that which drew from out the boundless deep/Turns again home" (lines 7–8). In the second, death occurs when the speaker has "crossed the bar" (line 16).
3. The poet is wishing for a death that causes "no sadness of farewell," a death that is neither painful nor protracted. He does not want extended leave-takings, nor people gathering around the bedside of a dying man.
4. The "boundless deep" is that which awaits us after death.
5. The tone is one of calm resignation since the speaker is peaceful and relaxed as he faces death.

ONE DIGNITY DELAYS FOR ALL

> One dignity delays for all,
> One mitred afternoon.
> None can avoid this purple,
> None avoid this crown.
>
> 5 Coach it insures, and footmen,
> Chamber and state and throng;
> Bells, also, in the village,
> As we ride grand along.
>
> What dignified attendants,
> 10 What service when we pause!
> How loyally at parting
> Their hundred hats they raise!
>
> How pomp surpassing ermine
> When simple you and I
> 15 Present our meek escutcheon
> And claim the rank to die!
> —*Emily Dickinson*

Questions

1. What is the "dignity" that "delays for all"?
2. What is being discussed in the second and third stanzas?
3. Look up the following words if you're not sure of their meaning: mitred, escutcheon.
4. What is the tone of this poem and how does it differ from that of Tennyson's "Crossing The Bar?"

Answers

1. This "dignity" is death.
2. The second and third stanzas discuss the actual process of dying.
3. "Mitred" means "raised to a high rank." The poet is using it to describe a very special afternoon, the afternoon of her death. "Escutcheon" is a shield with a coat of arms.
4. The tone of this poem is decidedly more playful than that of "Crossing The Bar."

METER

Sound in verse is created by two elements: the rhythm of a poem's lines and the sound of its words. We have already discussed *meter,* the rhythm of a poem determined by the number of stressed and unstressed syllables, and the common varieties of meter, such as *iambic pentameter. Scanning* a poem is determining its rhythm or meter. As a brief review:

Dimeter	2 stresses per line	Díe soón
Trimeter	3 stresses per line	Dóst thou knów who máde thee?
Tetrameter	4 stresses per line	Tell áll the trúth but tell it slánt
Pentameter	5 stresses per line	Leáve me, O Lóve, which reáches bút to dust
Hexameter	6 stresses per line	Whích, like a wóunded snaké, drágs its slow length alóng.

As we have said before, seldom does the pattern of a poem remain perfectly regular, for to hold too closely to one meter can cause monotony. Poets seek to avoid such monotony by shifting stresses, so that a poem written in iambic meter may have some feet that are spondaic and others that are trochaic. More important, the poet varies meter by making the poem's meaning and the speaker's voice move with the rhythm. These few lines from Matthew Arnold's "Dover Beach" (printed in its entirety on page 64), show this process at work:

> The sea is calm tonight.
> The tide is full, the moon lies fair
> Upon the straits;—on the French coast the light
> Gleams and is gone; the cliffs of England stand,
> Glimmering and vast, out in the tranquil bay.

The first statement meshes beautifully with the meaning of the first line. But the next overlaps the second line, so that you cannot stop reading on "fair," but must continue with "Upon the straits" to make sense of the line. After a pause, the thought continues through that line and half of the next, then pauses more briefly, finishes the line with a slight pause, and comes to an end at the fifth line. The first and fifth lines are called *end-stopped,* because a longer pause is called for at the end of these lines. In the same manner, the second, third, and fourth lines which force your voice to continue are called *run-on* lines. Both end-stopped and run-on lines may contain internal pauses. there is one such pause after the word "full" in the second line. These pauses are called *caesuras,* and their placement gives to poetry the sound of the speaking voice.

Blake's "The Lamb" and "The Tyger" (see pages 187 and 185) offer a marked contrast to Arnold's "Dover Beach." Because of the many end-stopped lines and the regularity of their rhythm, the two Blake poems sound almost like incantations, very different from the musing, gentle tone of Arnold's poem. But even in these two poems Blake varies the length of the lines and includes some caesuras and run-on lines.

> What the hammer? what the chain?
> In what furnace was thy brain?
> What the anvil? what dread grasp
> Dare its deadly terrors clasp?

Blake holds himself to seven-syllables lines in "The Tyger" and a patterned alternation between trimeter and tetrameter lines in "The Lamb," while Arnold varies the length of the lines in "Dover Beach," the lines getting longer as the speaker's argument continues. It is also clear that all the lines quoted from both Blake and Arnold end with stressed syllables. The rising voice at the end of a line creates what is called *rising rhythm*. In contrast, lines that end in unstressed syllables create a *falling rhythm*. "O wild West Wind, thou breath of Autumn's being" is an example of falling rhythm.

Let's look at the following poem to determine both its meaning and its rhythm:

PIED BEAUTY

> Glory be to God for dappled things—
>   For skies of couple-colour as a brindled cow;
>   For rose-moles all in stipple upon trout that swim;
> Fresh-firecoal chestnut-falls; finches wings;
> 5 Landscape plotted and pieced—fold, fallow, and plough;
>   And áll trádes, their gear and tackle and trim.
>
> All things, counter, original, spare, strange;
>   Whatever is fickle, freckled (who knows how?)
>   With swift, slow; sweet, sour; adazzle, dim;
> 10 He fathers-forth whose beauty is past change:
>   Praise him.
>   —*Gerard Manley Hopkins*

Questions

1. How do the examples of "dappled things" given in lines 2–4 differ from those in lines 5–6? How do the examples in the first stanza (lines 2–6) differ from those in the second stanza (lines 7–9)?
2. What has Hopkins done to his first definition of "dappled things"?
3. In what way are all these images and examples unified?
4. How important is the speaker's vision of "pied beauty"?
5. What is the rhythm here?

Answers

1. Lines 2–4 present *specific* items (line 2, skies; line 3, trout; line 4, chestnuts, birds' wings), while lines 5–6 present *general* descriptions (line 5, landscape; line 6, trades).
2. Hopkins has gone from the specific to the general to include all of creation as he sees it.
3. The images and examples are connected by theme and language. In the first in-

stance, the theme is that all of the universe is God's glory and reflection. In the second, we see an echo of language techniques:

line 5 fold, fallow, plough

line 9 swift, slow, sweet, etc.

Both these lists show a common technique and serve to unify the poem.

4. The speaker's vision is, of course, the most important thing in the world to him, for he was a priest and saw God's hand in all.

5. This is an example of Hopkins' sprung rhythm, explained earlier.

Rhymed and Unrhymed Verse

Unrhymed verse is rather easy to classify, and can be divided into three main types. First is *accentual verse,* which originated in the eighth century, the earliest known kind of verse. *Beowulf* is an example of early accentual verse and Gerard Manley Hopkins' "Pied Beauty" is an example of nineteenth century accentual verse. Second is blank verse, unrhymed iambic pentameter, a sixteenth-century invention made famous by Shakespeare. Third is modern *free verse,* found in the work of such poets as Walt Whitman, e. e. cummings, Ezra Pound, and Denise Levertov.

Rhymed verse cannot be divided into three simple categories. There are those forms with a fixed length: the limerick with five lines, the sonnet with fourteen lines, and the villanelle with nineteen lines. There are other forms that do not have a fixed number of lines, although almost all are composed of stanzas. While each stanza usually has a fixed length, the number of stanzas may vary, so that a poem can be any length at all. There are a series of patterns, though, that we can isolate and discuss in depth.

The *couplet* is a stanza that has two lines that rhyme. A couplet is found at the end of an English sonnet to make the point and conclude the discussion. An example from Shakespeare:

> So long as men can breathe or eyes can see,
> So long lives this, and this gives life to thee.

The *triplet* or *tercet* is composed of three rhyming lines, as we see here:

> He clasps the crag with crooked hands,
> Close to the sun in lonely lands,
> Ringed with the azure world, he stands.

Another three-line stanza in which only the first and last lines rhyme is called *terza rima.* When several stanzas of *terza rima* are grouped together, the middle line of one stanza will rhyme with the first and third lines of the following stanza. For example:

> O wild West Wind, thou breath of Autumn's being,
> Thou, from whose unseen presence the leaves dead
> Are driven, like ghosts from an enchanter fleeing,
>
> Yellow, and black, and pale, and hectic red,
> Pestilence-stricken multitudes: O thou
> Who chariotest to their dark wintry bed

The *quatrain* is a stanza composed of four lines which may have several different rhyme schemes: the second and fourth lines (*abcb*); the first and third, and the second and fourth (*abab*); the first and fourth and the second and third (*abba*); and the first and second, and third and fourth (*aabb*). Any one of these patterns may be used, or they may be combined in any variation. Thus, you cannot assume that if the first few stanzas follow a certain pattern, the rest of the poem will continue that pattern. It is always best to check the rhyme in each and every line to make sure the pattern follows what you assume. Here are some examples to study:

(*abcb*)   When I was one-and-twenty
          I heard a wise man say,
          "Give crowns and pounds and guineas
          But not your heart away;"

(*abab*) She even thinks that up in heaven
          Her class lies late and snores,
          While poor black cherubs rise at seven
          To do celestial chores.

(*abba*) Earth hath not anything to show more fair!
          Dull would he be of soul who could pass by
          A sight so touching in its majesty
          The city doth now, like a garment, wear.

(*aabb*) "O, Melia, my dear, this does everything crown!
          Who could have supposed I should meet you in Town?
          And whence such fair garments, such prosperi-ty?"—
          "O didn't you know I'd been ruined?" said she.

THE NARRATIVE POEM

A narrative poem tells a story, recounting actions and events. The sequence of events in a narrative poem is called the *plot,* and it must be controlled and directed by the *narrator,* the person telling us the tale. The *point of view,* the position from which the narrative is recounted, must also be controlled, which is accomplished in part by the grammatic *person* in which the author chooses to write. Narrative verse is less popular today, as more stories are told in prose forms.

The following is an example of a *narrative poem:*

MY LAST DUCHESS

1   That's my last Duchess painted on the wall,
    Looking as if she were alive. I call
    That piece a wonder, now: Frà Pandolf's hands
    Worked busily a day, and there she stands.
5   Will't please you sit and look at her? I said
    "Frà Pandolf" by design, for never read
    Strangers like you that pictured countenance,
    The depth and passion of its earnest glance,
    But to myself they turned (since none puts by
10 The curtain I have drawn for you, but I)
    And seemed they would ask me, if they durst,
    How such a glance came there; so, not the first
    Are you to turn and ask thus. Sir, 'twas not
    Her husband's presence only, called that spot
15 Of joy into the Duchess' cheek: perhaps
    Frà Pandolf chanced to say, "Her mantle laps
    Over my lady's wrist too much," or "Paint
    Must never hope to reproduce the faint
    Half-flush that dies along her throat:" such stuff
20 Was courtesy, she thought, and cause enough

    For calling up that spot of joy. She had
    A heart—how shall I say?—too soon made glad,
    Too easily impressed; she liked whate'er
    She looked on, and her looks went everywhere.
25 Sir, 'twas all one! My favour at her breast,
    The dropping of the daylight in the West,
    The bough of cherries some officious fool
    Broke in the orchard for her, the white mule
    She rode with round the terrace—all and each
30 Would draw her alike the approving speech,
    Or blush, at least. She thanked men,—good! But thanked
    Somehow—I know not how—as if she ranked
    My gift of a nine-hundred-years-old name
    With anybody's gift. Who'd stoop to blame
35 This sort of trifling? Even had you skill
    In speech—(which I have not)—to make your will
    Quite clear to such a one, and say, "Just this
    Or that in you disgusts me; here you miss,
    Or there exceed the mark"—and if she let
40 Herself be lessoned so, nor plainly set

Her wits to yours, forsooth, and made excuse,
—E'en then would be some stooping; and I choose
Never to stoop. Oh sir, she smiled, no doubt,
Whene'er I passed her; but who passed without
45 Much the same smile? This grew; I gave commands;
Then all smiles stopped together. There she stands
As if alive. Will't please you rise? We'll meet
The company below, then. I repeat,

The Count your master's known munificence
50 Is ample warrant that no just pretence
Of mine for dowry will be disallowed;
Though his fair daughter's self, as I avowed
At starting, is my object. Nay, we'll go
Together down, sir. Notice Neptune, though,
55 Taming a sea-horse, thought a rarity,
Which Claus of Innsbruck cast in bronze for me!
—*Robert Browning*

Discussion

This is a narrative poem, in which we listen to the Duke speak of his dead wife. He tells the story of their marriage and her death. Browning uses a technique called the *dramatic monologue,* and the reader feels almost as though he is overhearing the Duke as he speaks. From his conversation, we are able to piece together the situation, both past and present, and we are able to see what sort of person the Duke is as well as what sort of person his wife was. By the end of the poem, we are even able to see what the poet thought of them both.

Line-by-line Analysis of "My Last Duchess"

Lines 1–2. Addressing an unidentified audience, the Duke discusses a portrait of his "last Duchess." The word "last" hints that the Duke may have had more than one previous wife, and also suggests that he is once again "shopping" for another. The word also intimates that a wife is a commodity, something to acquire as one would any other possession. We know immediately she is dead from the phrase "Looking as if she were alive" (line 2).

Lines 3–4. The Duke is very impressed with the painting, and makes sure to mention the painter. This tells us that he admires works of art and that he is very conscious of status. Already we can tell that he treasures *objects* above *people*.

Lines 5–10. The Duke is eager to talk about the look on his former wife's face. It is also important that he tells us that he is the only one to uncover her face. Even in death, he is in control, the one to allow her to be seen.

Lines 11–24. In line 14, the Duke says that it was not only his presence that called "that spot/ Of joy" to her cheek. She had what he calls "A heart . . . too soon made glad" (line 22), and she liked "whate'er/She looked on" (lines 23–24). This causes him great distress, for he is used to being the one in control, the one—and only one—able to call forth her joy.

Lines 25–30. These lines reinforce the Duke's distress, as he tells us that his admiration was, to the Duchess, the same as the sunset or a gift of a bough of cherries. He feels that he should be the only one able to please her and resents all other things that cause her happiness. We also see that the Duchess was gracious and kind, easy to please, and happy with the simple pleasures of life.

Lines 31–43. Lines 31–32 tell us that the Duke bitterly resented the way his Duchess seemed to rank all gifts the same. What right had she to rank the gift of his name (in marriage) with anyone else's gift, he asserts. He was unwilling to speak with her about her graciousness to all, for he felt that even if he had the skill with language, he would not stoop to correct her (lines 42–43).

Lines 44–46. The Duchess, happy with her life, smiles at each and all. The Duke, furious with what he perceives as a slight, gives commands, "Then all smiles stopped together" (line 46). This line is brilliantly juxtaposed with the next, "There she stands/As if alive," so we know that his command destroyed her, directly or indirectly. Perhaps he deprived her of the daily pleasures that give life its savor—the beauty of nature, human company— or perhaps he did something even more heinous.

Lines 47–53. Here we learn that the Duke has been addressing someone sent by a Count to arrange a marriage between the Count's daughter and the Duke. The Duke smoothly asserts that his main goal is the Count's "fair daughter," but that he fully intends to obtain a fitting dowry in the deal.

Lines 53–56. As they walk down, the Duke points out another of his possessions, a bronze statute of Neptune "Taming a sea-horse." Neptune has tamed the sea-horse much as the Duke tamed his "last Duchess," destroying her spirit—through his unbending pride.

   The Duke emerges as arrogant and ruthless, determined to have his will prevail regardless of the cost. That his child-like wife would find innocent pleasure in commonplace events is insufferable to such an egotist, and so he "gives commands" that reassert his will—and destroys his wife's.

LYRIC VERSE

   As stated earlier, lyric verse was originally a term used to describe short poems meant to be sung to the music of a lyre, but the term has evolved to mean any short poem, regardless of meter or rhyme scheme, that expresses an emotion or records a thought rather than tells a tale. Probably the most common emotion in lyrics is love, or the despair brought on by unreturned love, though grief and pain are also frequent subjects. The following is a lyric from a sixteenth-century songbook:

Western wind, when wilt thou blow,
    The small rain down can rain?
Christ, if my love were in my arms,
    And I in my bed again!

There are many different kinds of lyrics:

epigram	a brief witty expression, usually of contempt
satire	a longer expression of hate or contempt
complaint	an expression of dissatisfaction, usually to a loved one
elegy	a melancholy or mournful contemplative poem
ode	a long poem characterized by heroic or elevated emotions
dirge	a short funeral lament
pastoral	a poem of mourning set in a country setting, usually a shepherd mourning the death of a fellow shepherd
threnody	a funeral poem
monody	a longer and more complex funeral poem
sonnet	a fourteen-line poem expressing emotion
ballad	a simply structured poem, usually dealing with an emotional event

The following is an excerpt from a lyric poem, Walt Whitman's "Crossing Brooklyn Ferry." Here Whitman begins with a seemingly simple topic, the daily trip by ferry from Manhattan to Brooklyn, and uses it to create a lyrical meditation on the diversity, unity, and continuity of all objects, people, places, and time. This poem demonstrates that a lyric is more personal and subjective than other poetic forms, falling back on the imaginative to express personal emotions, thoughts, and attitudes.

CROSSING BROOKLYN FERRY

1

Flood-tide below me! I see you face to face!
Clouds of the west—sun there half an hour high—I see you also face to face.

Crowds of men and women attired in the usual costumes, how curious you are to me!
On the ferry-boats the hundreds and hundreds that cross, returning home, are more curious to me than you suppose,
And you that shall cross from shore to shore years hence are more to me, and more in my meditations, than you might suppose.

2

The impalpable sustenance of me from all things at all hours of the day,
The simple, compact, well-join'd scheme, myself disintegrated, every one disintegrated yet part of the scheme,
The similitudes of the past and those of the future,
The glories strung like beads on my smallest sights and hearings, on the wall in the street and the passage over the river,
10 The current rushing so swiftly and swimming with me far away,
The others that are to follow me, the ties between me and them,
The certainty of others, the life, love, sight, hearing of others.

Others will enter the gates of the ferry and cross from shore to shore,
Others will watch the run of the flood-tide,
Others will see the shipping of Manhattan north and west, and the heights of Brooklyn to the south and east,

Others will see the islands large and small;
Fifty years hence, others will see them as they cross, the sun half an hour high,
A hundred years hence, or ever so many hundred years hence, others will see them,
Will enjoy the sunset, the pouring-in of the flood-tide, the falling-back to the sea of the
    ebb-tide.

3

20 It avails not, time nor place—distance avails not,
I am with you, you men and women of a generation, or ever so many generations hence,
Just as you feel when you look on the river and sky, so I felt,
Just as any of you is one of a living crowd, I was one of a crowd,
Just as you are refresh'd by the gladness of the river and the bright flow, I was refresh'd,
Just as you stand and lean on the rail, yet hurry with the swift current, I stood yet was
    hurried.
Just as you look on the numberless masts of ships and the thick-stemm'd pipes of steamboats,
    I look'd.

I too many and many a time cross'd the river of old,
Watched the Twelfth-month sea-gulls, saw them high in the air floating with motionless
    wings, oscillating their bodies,
Saw how the glistening yellow lit up parts of their bodies and left the rest in strong shadow,
30 Saw the slow-wheeling circles and the gradual edging toward the south,
Saw the reflection of the summer sky in the water,
Had my eyes dazzled by the shimmering track of beams.
Look'd at the fine centrifugal spokes of light round the shape of my head in the sunlit water,
Look'd on the haze on the hills southward and south—westward.

Look'd on the vapor as it flew in fleeces tinged with violet,
Look'd toward the lower bay to notice the vessels arriving,
Saw their approach, saw aboard those that were near me,
Saw the white sails of schooners and sloops, saw the ships at anchor,
The sailors at work in the rigging or out astride the spars,
40 The round masts, the swinging motion of the hulls, the slender serpentine pennants.

THE ODE

The *ode* has a regular rhythmic pattern, although meter and verse lengths may vary from time to time. Originally a song in honor of the gods characterized by elevated feelings, there are now three main types of ode:

1. Pindaric or regular ode has three parts: a strophe (where the chorus danced while singing), an antistrophe (where the chorus sang without dancing), and the epode (where the chorus sang without dancing). Within these fixed divisions there are lines of uneven length. More modern models include Gray's "The Progress of Poesy" and Wordsworth's "Ode: Intimations of Immortality."
2. Horation or homostrophic ode has one repeated stanza type, but may vary within its form. Examples include Marvell's 'Horatian Ode upon Cromwell's Return from Ireland," Collins' "Ode to Evening," and Keats' "Ode to Autumn."
3. Irregular odes disregard the strophe and stanza rules of their model, the Pindaric ode. They tend to show great flexibility with regard to length, meter and rhyme, and are thus the most popular form.

The ode that follows, by William Wordsworth, one of the leaders of the Romantic movement in England, uses both rhyme and rhythm to great advantage, but also manages to keep a freshness of style and tone that combine to make it pleasant reading long after its composition. It is an irregular ode, for the stanzas vary among themselves, following the poet's argument. The meter is iambic throughout, although the length of the lines and the rhymes shift. The poem discusses relationships among the human soul, nature, and immortality. It suggests that we know what immortality is after death, but even more interesting, it says that we could also know immortality before birth: "trailing clouds of glory do we come/From God, who is our home" (lines 64–65). It revels in the joy that a child sees in the world of nature as well as laments the fact that the child turns his attention to earthly things, quickly dulling that initial joy. But even so, the conclusion is not sorrowful, as the poet passes beyond mourning this loss to celebrating joys that the mature human soul is capable of appreciating. Trace the way the poet develops his arguments, and notice how the poem has been shaped to echo this train of thought. See how the different stanzas reflect the speaker's change in emotion.

INTIMATIONS OF IMMORTALITY FROM RECOLLECTIONS OF EARLY CHILDHOOD

The Child is father of the Man;
And I could wish my days to be
Bound each to each by natural piety.

1

There was a time when meadow, grove, and stream,
The earth, and every common sight,
    To me did seem
    Apparelled in celestial light,
5 The glory and the freshness of a dream.
It is not now as it hath been of yore;—
    Turn wheresoe'er I may,
    By night or day,
The things which I have seen I now can see no more.

2

10   The Rainbow comes and goes,
    And lovely is the Rose,
    The Moon doth with delight
Look round her when the heavens are bare;
    Waters on a starry night
15   Are beautiful and fair;
    The sunshine is a glorious birth;
    But yet I know, where'er I go,
That there hath past away a glory from the earth.

3

Now, while the birds thus sing a joyous song,
20   And while the young lambs bound
    As to the tabor's sound,
To me alone there came a thought of grief:
A timely utterance gave that thought relief,
    And I again am strong:
25 The cataracts blow their trumpets from the steep;
No more shall grief of mine the season wrong;

I hear the Echoes through the mountains throng,
The Winds come to me from the fields of sleep,
    And all the earth is gay;
30   Land and sea
    Give themselves up to jollity,
    And with the heart of May
    Doth every Beast keep holiday;—
    Thou Child of Joy,
35 Shout round me, let me hear thy shouts,
thou happy Shepherd-boy!

4

Ye blessèd Creatures, I have heard the call
    Ye to each other make; I see
The heavens laugh with you in your jubilee;
    My heart is at your festival,
40   My head hath its coronal,
The fulness of your bliss, I feel—I feel it all.
    Oh evil day! if I were sullen
    While Earth herself is adorning,
    This sweet May-morning,
45   And the Children are culling
    On every side,
    In a thousand valleys far and wide,
    Fresh flowers; while the sun shines warm,
And the Babe leaps up on his Mother's arm:—
50   I hear, I hear, with joy I hear!
    —But there's a Tree, of many, one,
A single Field which I have looked upon,
Both of them speak of something that is gone:
    The Pansy at my feet
55   Doth the same tale repeat:
Whither is fled the visionary gleam?
Where is it now, the glory and the dream?

5

Our birth is but a sleep and a forgetting:
The Soul that rises with us, our life's Star,
60   Hath had elsewhere its setting,
      And cometh from afar:
    Not in entire forgetfulness,
    And not in utter nakedness,
But trailing clouds of glory do we come
65   From God, who is our home:
Heaven lies about us in our infancy!
Shades of the prison-house begin to close
    Upon the growing Boy,
      But He
70 Beholds the light, and whence it flows,
    He sees it in his joy;
The Youth, who daily farther from the east
    Must travel, still in Nature's Priest,
    And by the vision splendid
75   Is on his way attended;
At length the Man perceives it die away,
And fade into the light of common day.

6

Earth fills her lap with pleasures of her own;
Yearnings she hath in her own natural kind,
80 And, even with something of a Mother's mind,
    And no unworthy aim,
    The homely Nurse doth all she can
To make her Foster-child, her Inmate Man,
    Forget the glories he hath known,
85 And that imperial palace whence he came.

7

Behold the Child among his new-born blisses,
A six year's Darling of a pigmy size!
See, where 'mid work of his own hand he lies,
Fretted by sallies of his mother's kisses,
90 With light upon him from his father's eyes!
See, at his feet, some little plan or chart,
Some fragment from his dream of human life,
Shaped by himself with newly-learnèd art;
    A wedding or a festival,
95   A mourning or a funeral;
    And this hath now his heart,
    And unto this he frames his song:
    Then will he fit his tongue
To dialogues of business, love, or strife;
100   But it will not be long
    Ere this be thrown aside,
    And with new joy and pride
The little Actor cons another part;
Filling from time to time his "humorous stage"
105 With all the Persons, down to palsied Age,
That Life brings with her in her equipage;
    As if his whole vocation
    Were endless imitation.

8

Thou, whose exterior semblance doth belie
110   Thy Soul's immensity;
Thou best Philosopher, who yet dost keep
Thy heritage, thou Eye among the blind,
That, deaf and silent, read'st the eternal deep,
Haunted for ever by the eternal mind,—
115   Mighty Prophet! Seer blest!
    On whom those truths do rest,
Which we are toiling all our lives to find,
In darkness lost, the darkness of the grave;
Thou, over whom thy Immortality
120 Broods like the Day, a Master o'er a Slave,
A Presence which is not to be put by;
Thou little Child, yet glorious in the might
Of heaven-born freedom on thy being's height,
Why with such earnest pains dost thou provoke
125 The years to bring the inevitable yoke,

Thus blindly with thy blessedness at strife?
Full soon thy Soul shall have her earthly freight,
And custom lie upon thee with a weight,
Heavy as frost, and deep almost as life!

9

130   O joy! that in our embers
    Is something that doth live,
    That nature yet remembers
    What was so fugitive!
The thought of our past years in me doth breed
135 Perpetual benediction: not indeed
For that which is most worthy to be blest;
Delight and liberty, the simple creed
Of Childhood, whether busy or at rest,
With new-fledged hope still fluttering in his breast:—
140   Not for these I raise
    The song of thanks and praise;
    But for those obstinate questionings
    Of sense and outward things,
    Falling from us, vanishings;
145   Blank misgivings of a Creature
Moving about in worlds not realised,
High instincts before which our mortal Nature
Did tremble like a guilty Thing surprised:
    But for those first affections,
150   Those shadowy recollections,
    Which, be they what they may,
Are yet the fountain-light of all our day,
Are yet a master-light of all our seeing;
Uphold us, cherish, and have power to make
155 Our noisy years seem moments in the being
Of the eternal Silence: truths that wake,
    To perish never:
Which neither listlessness, nor mad endeavor,
    Nor Man nor Boy,
160 Nor all that is at enmity with joy,

Can utterly abolish or destroy!
    Hence in a season of calm weather
      Though inland far we be,
Our Souls have sight of that immortal sea
165   Which brought us hither,
      Can in a moment travel thither,
And see the Children sport upon the shore,
And hear the mighty waters rolling evermore.

10

Then sing, ye Birds, sing, sing, a joyous song!
170   And let the young Lambs bound
      As to the tabor's sound!
We in thought will join your throng,
      Ye that pipe and ye that play,
      Ye that through your hearts to-day
175   Feel the gladness of the May!
What though the radiance which was once so bright
Be now for ever taken from my sight,
    Though nothing can bring back the hour
Of splendor in the grass, of glory in the flower;
180   We will grieve not, rather find
      Strength in what remains behind;
      In the primal sympathy

      Which having been must ever be;
      In the soothing thoughts that spring
185   Out of human suffering;
      In the faith that looks through death,
In years that bring the philosophic mind.

11

And O, ye Fountains, Meadows, Hills, and Groves,
Forebode not any severing of our loves!
190 Yet in my heart of hearts I feel your might;
I only have relinquished one delight
To live beneath your more habitual sway.
I love the Brooks which down their channels fret,
Even more than when I tripped lightly as they;
195 The innocent brightness of a new-born Day
      Is lovely yet;
The Clouds that gather round the setting sun
Do take a sober coloring from an eye
That hath kept watch o'er man's mortality;
200 Another race hath been, and other palms are won.
Thanks to the human heart by which we live,
Thanks to its tenderness, its joys, and fears,
To me the meanest flower that blows can give
Thoughts that do often lie too deep for tears.
              —*William Wordsworth*

THE SONNET

    The most popular of the defined poetic forms is the sonnet. It is a lyric poem of fourteen lines, written in iambic pentameter (five accents per line). There are two main sonnet forms. The first was originated by the Italian poets in the thirteenth century and reached its final form a century later in the work of Petrarch, thus, it came to be called the *Petrarchan or Italian* sonnet. The first eight lines, called the *octave,* rhyme *abbaabba* and present the subject of the poem; the final six lines, called the *sestet,* rhyme *cdecde* and resolve the problem or situation set forth in the first eight lines. The English poets of the sixteenth century altered the rhyme scheme of the Italian sonnet, creating an *abab/cdcd/efef/gg* pattern, which has come to be called the *Shakespearean or English* sonnet. Some claim the Shakespearean sonnet is easier to write, for no sound needs to be written more than twice. It is also said that the Italian sonnet has a smother flow and is more graceful. Originally both forms came into the language as love verse, but sonnets have been used for many different themes and subjects. A close look at the models that follow will show this variety. Examine each sonnet and decide (1) Is it an Italian or an English sonnet? (2) What is the rhyme scheme? (3) What is the poet's theme or main idea? (4) How does figurative language and other poetic devices enhance the theme?
    From Shakespeare:

SONNET 116

Let me not to the marriage of true minds
Admit impediments. Love is not love
Which alters when it alteration finds,
Or bends with the remover to remove.

5 O no! it is an ever-fixèd mark
That looks on tempests and is never shaken;
It is the star to every wand'ring bark,
Whose worth's unknown, although his height be taken.
Love's not Time's fool, though rosy lips and cheeks
Within his bending sickle's compass come.
Love alters not with his brief hours and weeks,
But bears it out even to the edge of doom.
    If this be error, and upon me proved,
    I never writ, nor no man ever loved.

SONNET 73

That time of year thou mayst in me behold
When yellow leaves, or none, or few, do hang
Upon those boughs which shake against the cold,
Bare ruined choirs where late the sweet birds sang.

5 In me thou see'st the twilight of such day
As after sunset fadeth in the west,
Which by and by black night doth take away,
Death's second self that seals up all in rest.
In me thou see'st the glowing of such fire
10 That on the ashes of his young doth lie,
As the deathbed whereon it must expire,
Consumed with that which it was nourished by.
    This thou perceiv'st, which makes thy love more strong
    To love that well which thou must leave ere long.

Henry Wadsworth Longfellow wrote a series of sonnets with especially deep feeling. In July of 1861, his wife was tragically burned to death, despite Longfellow's frantic efforts to save her. Overcome with grief, he sought relief in his work, and set forth an especially difficult task for himself—translating into English Dante's *Divine Comedy*. The poem has three parts, which describe Dante's fictional journey into Hell, Purgatory, and Paradise. In his version, Longfellow opened each section with two sonnets. While Longfellow's writings said that his purpose here was to describe Dante's verse as a cathedral, he is seemingly using Dante's poem to comfort himself in his grief. The two sonnets which follow preface the first part of Longfellow's translation.

Oft have I seen at some cathedral door
    A laborer, pausing in the dust and heat,
    Lay down his burden, and with reverent feet
    Enter, and cross himself, and on the floor
5 Kneel to repeat his paternoster o er;
    Far off the noises of the world retreat;
    The loud vociferations of the street
    Become an undistinguishable roar.
So, as I enter here from day to day,
10   And leave my burden at this minster gate,
    Kneeling in prayer, and not ashamed to pray,
The tumult of the time disconsolate
    To inarticulate murmurs dies away,
    While the eternal ages watch and wait.

How strange the sculptures that adorn these towers!
  This crowd of statues, in whose folded sleeves
  Birds build their nests; while canopied with leaves
  Parvis[1] and portal bloom like trellised bowers,
5 And the vast minister seems a cross of flowers.
  But fiends and dragons on the gargoyled eaves
  Watch the dead Christ between the living thieves,
  And, underneath, the traitor Judas lowers!
Ah! from what agonies of heart and brain,
10   What exultations trampling on despair,
  What tenderness, what tears, what hate of wrong,
What passionate outcry of a soul in pain,
  Uprose this poem of the earth and air,
  This medieval miracle of song!

SAMPLE AP QUESTIONS ON POETRY

1. Considering the sonnet printed below, explain what the author wishes to be loved for and why she feels this way. Time—20 minutes.

SONNET 14

If thou must love me, let it be for nought
Except for love's sake only. Do not say,
"I love her for her smile—her look—her way
Of speaking gently,—for a trick of thought
5 That falls in well with mine, and certes brought
A sense of pleasant ease on such a day"—
For these things in themselves, Belovèd, may
Be changed, or change for thee,—and love, so wrought,
May be unwrought so. Neither love me for
10 Thine own dear pity's wiping my cheeks dry,—
A creature might forget to weep, who bore
Thy comfort long, and lose thy love thereby!
But love me for love's sake, that evermore
Thou may'st love on, through love's eternity.
          —*Elizabeth Barrett Browning*

Answer

  The first two lines state what the author wishes to be loved for "nought [nothing]/ Except for love's sake only." This is picked up again in the final two lines, "But love me for love's sake . . . ." She wishes to be loved for "love's sake" because if love is not based on mere physical attractions ("her smile," "her look," "her way/Of speaking gently"), it will be able to endure for eternity (see last line).

2. Contrast the sonnet below, number 43, with the one above and show how the similarities and differences in the description of love. What is the difference in speaker? Theme? Use specific references to make your point. Time—30 minutes.

SONNET 43

How do I love thee? Let me count the ways.
I love thee to the depth and breadth and height
My soul can reach, when feeling out of sight
For the ends of Being and ideal Grace.
5 I love thee to the level of everyday's
Most quiet need, by sun and candle-light.
I love thee freely, as men strive for Right;
I love thee purely, as they turn from Praise.
I love thee with the passion put to use
10 In my old griefs, and with my childhood's faith.
I love thee with a love I seemed to lose
With my lost saints,—I love thee with the breath,
Smiles, tears, of all my life!—and, if God choose,
I shall but love thee better after death.
　　　　　　　　　　　　—*Elizabeth Barrett Browning*

Answer

While each sonnet discusses love, there are differences in speaker and theme. In Sonnet 14, the author is explaining the love someone else feels for her; in Sonnet 43, she is discussing the love *she feels* for someone else. The first sonnet stresses the mutability and impermanence of the outward show of love, rejecting love based on physical attraction for a love that will endure for eternity. The second sonnet stresses the love she feels here and now for the man, but adds that if God chooses, she will love him even better after death.

3. Show how the two parts of "How Soon Hath Time" are united by the theme. You will have to:
   - find and explain the two parts of the poem
   - describe the theme
   - show how the theme unites the poem. Time—30 minutes.

HOW SOON HATH TIME

How soon hath Time, the subtle thief of youth,
Stolen on his wing my three-and-twentieth year!
My hasting days fly on with full career,
But my late spring no bud or blossom shew'th.
5 Perhaps my semblance might deceive the truth
That I to manhood am arrived so near;

And inward ripeness doth much less appear,
That some more timely-happy spirits endu'th.[1]
Yet be it less or more, or soon or slow,
10 It shall be still in strictest measure even
To that same lot, however mean or high,
Toward which Time leads me, and the will of Heaven;
All is, if I have grace to use it so,
As ever in my great Taskmaster's eye.
　　　　　　　　　　　　—*John Milton*

Answer

The first part of the poem, lines 1–6, discusses the outward changes the speaker has undergone. Such changes are reflected in the statement "Perhaps my semblance might deceive the truth/That I to manhood am arrived so near" (line 5–6), which shows, in the word "semblance", the *outward* changes time has wrought.

The second part of the poem concerns *inward* changes, as found in the phrase "inward ripeness" (line 7).

The theme, stated in the final four lines, is that the changes the speaker has experienced are the will of heaven.

4. Using "How Soon Hath Time," show how the author's theme is reflected in the poem's form. Explain why the particular form selected is best suited to this theme. Discuss the sonnet. Why was this form of the sonnet used here? Time—30 minutes.

Answer

The sonnet takes two forms, the Italian (Petrarchan) and English (Elizabethan). This is an Italian sonnet, which has eight lines (the octave), rhyming *abbaabba,* which present the poet's subject, followed by six lines (the sestet), rhyming *cdecde,* which indicate the importance of the facts set forth in the octave and resolve the problem established there. Milton used the Italian sonnet form rather than the Elizabethan (*abab/cdcd/efef/gg* rhyme) because the Elizabethan form resolves the conflict in the final couplet (*gg*) and usually has a witty turn of phrase. The Italian form allows him six lines to make his point—the changes God wills in man—without any wit or humor at the end.

Milton selected the sonnet form because it allows for a brief and clear presentation of theme. He did not need a narrative—a long story—nor an ode—in elevated language—to make his point about the changes he has undergone and their reason.

5. What appalls Captain Ahab so is the "whiteness" of Moby-Dick, the great whale. Robert Frost is working with that symbolism in the poem below. Discuss the *symbolism* of "Design" and explain how the "whiteness" represents the *theme*. Time—30 minutes.

DESIGN

I found a dimpled spider, fat and white,
On a white heal-all, holding up a moth
Like a white piece of rigid satin cloth—
Assorted characters of death and blight
Mixed ready to begin with morning right,
Like the ingredients of a witches' broth—
A snow-drop spider, a flower like a froth,
And dead wings carried like a paper kite.

What had that flower to do with being white,
The wayside blue and innocent heal-all?
What brought the kindred spider to that height,
Then steered the white moth thither in the night?
What but design of darkness to appall?—
If design govern in a thing so small.

—*Robert Frost*

Answer

Follow the white items listed in the first four lines: spider, fat and white; white heal-all; moth, looking like a white piece of cloth. All are linked by the remark in line 4: "Assorted characters of death and blight." These pictures of death and decay continue: witches' broth, dead wings.

The items listed above are pulled together in the final two lines as the speaker expresses surprise that there is some power governing even the formation and design of items as small and seemingly insignificant as the ones he lists. If there is a hand behind even these petty items, what then rules our lives which we hold so very significant?

6. Show how the form of "Design" is suited to the theme. Time—30 minutes.

Answer

This poem is a sonnet, having fourteen lines with the rhyme scheme:

white	a
moth	b
cloth	b
blight	a
right	a
broth	b
froth	b
kite	a
white	a
heal-all	c
height	a
night	a
appall	c
small	c

This is a variation on the Italian sonnet, whose form is *abbaabba cdecde*. This pattern is followed through the octave (*abbaabba*), but breaks form in the sestet, to *acaacc*, with a final rhyming couplet, the *cc*.

An excellent case could be made that the form is followed in the first eight lines because Frost is talking about *design* and so follows a rigid form. In the conclusion, though, he breaks out of the design to create a new pattern. This is reflected in the theme of design ruling even the smallest item in nature, but not in *his* creation, the poem.

7. Read the poem below and answer the following questions: What is "fire" and what is "ice"? Why does the poet conclude that ice will also suffice for destruction? Time—20 minutes.

FIRE AND ICE

Some say the world will end in fire,
Some say in ice.
From what I've tasted of desire
I hold with those who favor fire.
But if it had to perish twice,
I think I know enough of hate
To say that for destruction ice
Is also great
And would suffice.
—*Robert Frost*

Answer

Fire is passion and desire, that which heats up our lives. Ice is cold, hard hate, devoid of the heat of passion. The poet feels that hatred is strong enough to cause the destruction of the world, even though most might feel that desire, fire, is most apt to set things aflame.

SUGGESTED READING LIST

The following books are helpful for understanding poetry and poetic theory:

Brooks, Cleanth and Robert Penn Warren. *Understanding Poetry*. New York: Holt, Rinehart and Winston, 1960.

Ciardi, John. *How Does a Poem Mean?* Boston: Houghton, Mifflin Company, 1960.

Perrine, Lawrence. *Sound and Sense: An Introduction to Poetry*. New York: Harcourt Brace Jovanovich, 1973.

And for brief essays on poets' lives as well as extended discussions of poetic movements and social settings, consult the appropriate volume of *The Norton Anthology of Literature* (New York: W.W. Norton, 1986). There are two volumes on English Literature (I, II) and two on American Literature (I, II).

NOTE: In some instances specific works will be listed; in others, author's names. When an author is listed with no specific work following his name, any of his poems are suitable for analysis on the Advanced Placement exam. Where all of a poet's work is suitable but specific works are recommended for study these works are listed followed by the word "poems."

	Eighth Century
anonymous	*Beowulf*
	Thirteenth/Fourteenth Century
anonymous	ballads
Chaucer	
	Sixteenth Century
Christopher Marlowe	*Doctor Faustus*
William Shakespeare	sonnets
	songs from plays
Sir Philip Sidney	sonnets
Edmund Spenser	sonnets
Sir Thomas Wyatt the Elder	poems
	Seventeenth Century
Anne Bradstreet	poems
John Donne	sonnets
John Dryden	poems
John Gay	poems
Robert Herrick	poems
George Herbert	poems
Samuel Johnson	poems
Ben Jonson	poems
Andrew Marvell	poems
John Milton	"On His Blindness"
	Paradise Lost
Alexander Pope	"Ode on Solitude"
	"An Essay on Man"

Eighteenth Century

Robert Burns	poems
Thomas Gray	"Elegy Written on a Country Churchyard"

Eighteenth/Nineteenth Century

William Blake	*Songs of Innocence*
	Songs of Experience
William Cullen Bryant	"Thanatopsis"
Lord Byron	"She Walks in Beauty"
Samuel Taylor Coleridge	"Kubla Khan"
John Keats	"Ode to a Grecian Urn"
	"Ode to a Nightingale"
Percy Bysshe Shelley	"Ozymandias"
	"Ode to the West Wind"
William Wordsworth	poems

Ninetheenth Century

Matthew Arnold	"Dover Beach"
Elizabeth Barrett Browning	*Sonnets from the Portuguese*
Robert Browning	poems
Lewis Carroll	"Jabberwocky"
Emily Dickinson	poems
Ralph Waldo Emerson	poems
Edward Fitzgerald	"The Rubáiyát of Omar Khayyám of Naishápúr"
Thomas Hardy	poems
Gerard Manley Hopkins	"Pied Beauty"
	"Spring and Fall"
Henry Wadsworth Longfellow	poems
Herman Melville	"Clarissa"
Edgar Allan Poe	"To Helen"
	"Annabel Lee"
Alfred, Lord Tennyson	"Ulysses"
	"Crossing the Bar"
Henry David Thoreau	poems
Walt Whitman	"Out of the Cradle Endlessly Rocking"
	"A Noiseless Patient Spider"
	poems

Twentieth Century

Rupert Brooke	poems
T.S. Eliot	"The Love Song of Alfred J. Prufrock"
	"The Hollow Men"
	"Journey of the Magi"
	Four Quartets
Robert Frost	"Stopping by Woods on a Snowy Evening"
	"The Road Not Taken"
	"Design"
	poems
A.E. Housman	*A Shropshire Lad*
Randall Jarrell	poems
Philip Larkin	poems

D.H. Lawrence	poems
Robert Lowell	poems
Archibald MacLeish	"Ars Poetica"
	"You, Andrew Marvell"
W.S. Merwin	poems
Marianne Moore	poems
Ezra Pound	"In a Station of the Metro"
	poems
John Crowe Ransom	poems
E.A. Robinson	"Miniver Cheevy"
Carl Sandburg	"Fog"
Anne Sexton	poems
Wallace Stevens	"The Snow Man"
	all poems
William Carlos Williams	"The Dance"
	"The Red Wheelbarrow"
	"The Yachts"
William Butler Yeats	"Leda and the Swan"
	"When You are Old"
	"Sailing to Byzantium"
	"The Second Coming"
	poems

Part 5

Analyzing Drama

A Brief Overview of Drama

Drama is a presentation in which actors and actresses imitate for an audience an event (the term "drama" comes from the Greek *dran,* which means "to do") through words and/or gestures. The *mis en scène* is the term used for the actual staging of the performance, including any scenery and *properties* (movable furniture) as well as the actors and actresses themselves. If no words are used and the events are told entirely through the use of gestures, the performance is called a *pantomime* or *dumb show.* The last term is often applied to a silent performance within a performance, as in the second scene of the third act of *Hamlet,* where the players, under Hamlet's direction, wordlessly enact the murder of a king.

Chronological List of Periods and Types of Drama

I. **Ancient Drama**
  A. *Classical tragedy:* A dramatic representation of "an action of high importance," according to Aristotle. In the twentieth century, we generally define tragedy as any play of serious intention ending with the hero either dead or spiritually crushed.
  B. *Classical comedy:* A kind of drama that amuses the audience, showing a movement from unhappiness to happiness that entertains rather than distresses the audience and ridicules rather than upsets.

II. **Middle Ages**
  A. *Mystery play:* Dramatization of a biblical story concerning a saint's life that included much secular material, especially in the late Middle Ages. *The Second Shepherds' Play,* for example, takes 6/7 of its space to tell the humorous story of a sheep-stealer, leaving only 1/7 to the events of Christ's birth.
  B. *Miracle play:* Also dramatization of a biblical story, such as the story of Cain and Abel. Popular from the twelfth through the fifteenth centuries.
  C. *Morality play:* Allegorical dramatization of the conflict between good and evil, including stock characters such as Everyman, Good Deeds, and Avarice. A late medieval development which remained popular far into the sixteenth century.

III. **The Renaissance**
  A. *Masque* (also spelled *Mask*): An entertainment given in the Renaissance court, as noblemen and women performed a dignified little play, usually allegorical and mythological in nature. It was frequently lavish in production but the structure was simple, as the so-called masquers, costumed and masked noblemen, entered, supposedly having traveled from afar. They invited the ladies of the court to dance, they dance, and the masquers leave. Shakespeare's *Henry VIII,* I, iv reenacts the masque at which the king first encountered his second wife, Anne Boleyn. Renaissance England's greatest writer of masques was Ben Jonson, who created them with the famous architect Inigo Jones.
  B. *Antimasque* (popularized by Ben Jonson): A grotesque dance of monsters or clowns. The performance was enacted by professionals representing chaos, who are broken up by the courtly performers. "Anti" is derived from the term "antic," meaning a "grotesque caper" or "fool" and does not mean "against" as we might assume today.
  C. *Pastoral:* Any writing having to do with shepherds. These plays described rural life as unspoiled and superior to urban existence. They are frequently set in Arcadia, a mountainous district in Greece, well known for its peaceful shepherds.

D. *Chronicle play:* A dramatization of historical material (or material assumed to be historical) for a public ready to view its past. These plays are registers of facts, a history in chronological order. There is some confusion between a tragedy with historical figures, such as Shakespeare's *Richard II,* and a chronicle play with tragic events.

E. *Tragedies and Comedies:* To be discussed later in detail.

IV. Restoration (1660–1700) and the Eighteenth Century

A. *Comedy of manners* (also called comedy of wit): A form of comedy, often cynical in tone, that involved much witty *repartee* (quick and unexpected come-back answers). The best-known authors of such comedies were Etherege, Wycherly, and Congreve. The most common theme was that love, marriage, and commonly held notions of romance are silly. People emerge as selfish, pleasure-loving, and skeptical of traditions that cannot stand up to close study. About 1700, Restoration comedy ended when the satire came to be directed against heartless cleverness rather than deviations in manners. At the same time *sentimental comedy* developed.

B. *Commedia dell'arte:* A dramatic comedy that used so-called stock characters including such figures as the Merchant, the Doctor, Young Lovers, Clever Servants, etc. It was performed especially by Italian troops of actors who improvised as they went along.

C. *Sentimental comedy and drama:* Developed at the end of this period, portray man as basically good. The few who are evil quickly repent, often in a sea of soggy sentiment. There is little wit; the characters are usually drawn from the middle class; and they indicate their virtue by weeping at the sight of any kind of distress.

V. Nineteenth Century

A. *Melodrama:* Originally drama with music expressing the character's thoughts (as is done in the movies today), but by the nineteenth century, it had come to stand for a drama wherein characters who are clearly good or evil are posed against each other in sensational situations filled with suspense. In the nineteenth century, there was an element of exotic horror represented by castles and dungeons, but it was later replaced by local evil, including the wicked landlord. The plot is unbelievable or unlikely, and virtue triumphs over adversity.

B. *Social plays:* Depict social setting and people in their environment.

VI. Twentieth Century

A. *Problem plays:* Ask the audience to address itself to a sociological problem of some sort. Ibsen's *A Doll's House* invites debate on the relationship between a husband and a wife, and Shaw's *Major Barbara* (discussed in the following chapter in depth) involves the audience in a discussion of the merits of the Salvation Army, the ethics of businesses and the people that run them, and the responsibility for war. It may not be either tragic or comedic, but the emphasis is on the social aspects of the problem rather than the fate of individual characters.

B. *Theatre of the absurd:* To be discussed in the following chapter in detail.

The Elements of Drama

TIME

Drama, theater, and the play are all closely related, but for our purposes here, the term *drama* shall be restricted to the written form, the creation of the *dramatist*. Going back 2300 years to Aristotle's *Poetics,* drama is defined as consisting of a *story* (or *fable*) with a beginning, a middle, and an end, which must be told within a specific *time* period. Following the conventions of the ancient Greeks, the modern dramatist, too, must complete his story within the few hours allowed to him, for the audience cannot put his story down and come back tomorrow, nor sit for more than a few hours at a time. Within the strict limits of the time he has, the dramatist must tell his tale in such a way as to get his meaning across and hold the audience's attention. Some of this has changed—rather drastically, too—in contemporary drama, as you will see later, but the theater experience is basically still limited to a few short hours at a time.

Even within the strict limits of the time allowed to him, the dramatist has some freedom. This can be seen even in plays by such traditional playwrights as Shakespeare. There are two distinct "times" in *Othello,* for example. The first, from the beginning of Act II until the end of the play, takes only 33 hours of "play" time (just a few hours—or less, depending on interpretation—of "theater" time). But this is not enough time to account for the repeated adultery with which Iago accuses Desdemona. There would not have been time for the alleged affair between Cassio and Desdemona either in Cyprus or in the brief time in Venice. This is accounted for by a period of time in Cyprus lasting over a week: Bianca scolds Cassio for having been away from her for so long; Lodovocio has time to sail from Venice and reach Cyprus after the news of the Turkish defeat has reached Venice.

SPEAKERS/CHARACTERS

Having decided upon the story, the dramatist must next consider who will tell his tale and perform the action. There must not be too many people on the stage at any one time, for if the stage becomes too crowded, the audience may not be able to follow the action. In Greek drama, for example, each playwright was limited to three speaking actors: one involved in the actor's contest (for best actor) and two others, who divided the remaining roles between them. In tragedy, the number of actors never exceeded three, although in comedy there were sometimes extras who were assigned a few lines. In both tragedy and comedy, there were an unlimited number of nonspeaking walk-on parts. The audience must be able to identify with the characters to establish the dramatist's desired relationship. Because the characters are visible and live, the dramatist must constantly be aware of physical appearance and capabilities of his characters. Will they require costumes? Will they have to appear older? Younger?

The *major characters* are those at the center of the drama. They are either the cause of the crisis or caught up in it through no fault of their own. We see this in Aeschylus' *The Choephori* and Euripides' *Electra.* Orestes and Electra are major characters in both works, and their crisis is the decision to kill Clytemnestra. In a tragedy, the audience must feel sympathy for the major characters, for we must be emotionally affected by the fate of these characters if the play is to be successful. This is not necessarily true for comedy. There we do not forge a bond with the main characters, who are not usually drawn as fully as are the characters in a tragedy.

Minor characters may or may not help to advance the plot, and the audience is not usually as caught up in their fate. They may serve to advance the plot through their roles as messengers or servants. In Greek drama, violence was not allowed to be performed on stage, so the minor characters often gave long speeches describing violent acts that took place out of sight of the audience.

Stock characters are characters whom we instantly recognize as "types." Pylades in *The Choephori* and *Electra* is "the faithful friend." Cadmus appears to be "the foolish old man" in the beginning of *The Bacchae,* but by the play's end, he has discarded his stereotype and grown in stature. Other stereotypical roles include "the sweet young maiden," "the brave soldier," "the dirty old man," etc.

Motivation is essential to a successful play. The audience must be made to feel that the characters have reasons for doing what they do. In Greek tragedy, one of the key motivations is revenge (getting back at a person for what he has done to the main character). Family ties are sacred, and one of the chief responsibilities of family is to revenge wrongs done to relatives. Romantic love as we define it today was not a key motivation in early plays. Since most marriages of the time were arranged for personal or political reasons, little attention was paid to romantic love as a motivating force. This, of course, is very different today, and so we find romantic love as an important motivation in modern drama.

Character development is another major element of drama. How does the character change as the play progresses? Does the character mature in stature or is this not a necessary function of that character in that play? Hippolytus in Euripides' play is an unbearable egotist through most of the drama. When he is close to death, though, he realizes his error of pride and becomes more likable, allowing the audience to feel for him. Comedy, in contrast, usually does not feature character change. Strepsiades is as silly and unthinking at the conclusion of *The Clouds* as he was in the beginning.

There are several ways in which an author can indicate characterization. The first is through *dialogue.* The way in which a character speaks, the words he selects, his specific accent, and his use of grammar and syntax tell us something about him.

A character's *actions* also reveal his personality. How he acts and reacts to events tell us a great deal about him.

The most difficult aspect of characterization for the dramatist is the indication of a *character's thoughts.* Playwrights have adopted several means for stepping inside a character's mind to show what he is thinking. One of these methods is the *soliloquy,* in which a character stands alone on the stage and addresses the audience. Another is the *prologue,* a feature of Greek tragedy in which a character appears before the start of the action to share his thoughts with the audience. Another method used to reveal thoughts in Greek drama involves using the *chorus* as a kind of sounding board. Frequently the chorus is sworn to silence by a character who feels that he has revealed too much.

Other characters also help to define a major character, for what others say about a person can be very revealing. Sometimes, one character has a personal grudge against another character, and so we must carefully sift what is said, recognizing the possibility of bias.

Often the characters in drama function to give *unity* to the plot. The events of a play can be held together because they happen to the same character or are enacted by the same character. Euripides, for example, has been criticized because often the only thing that holds the two halves of his plays together is the fact that they concern the same character. *Hecuba* is a good example of this type of relationship. When plots are held together through time or character, they are said to be *loose* or *episodic.* This is not to say that any one type of structure is superior to another, but naturally some critics and viewers favor one over the other.

DIALOGUE

Dialogue is of vital importance to successful drama. Aristotle wrote that what is said (*thought*) and how it is said (*diction*) are next in importance to character, and if the dialogue is not accurate, the audience will be unable to follow the dramatist's ideas. Even the finest writers of fiction are often unable to pen good dramatic dialogue. Such was the case with Henry James, whose stories have held readers spellbound, but whose plays were all failures. Ironically, many of his stories, when adapted for the stage by good dramatists, were successes. Thus, dialogue is crucial, for it is the only way we can learn what is going through a character's mind. Dialogue is a curious thing, though. Because it keeps going without a pause in traditional plays, it becomes essentially unreal. Yet it must *appear* real. The characters must seem to speak in that manner, whether or not anyone really does. The quality of the dialogue, then, makes the difference between merely *literate* drama and real *dramatic literature*. While all drama is literate, it is the exceptional drama that is passed down through the ages as great, enduring literature. Whether it is written in poetry or prose, enduring dialogue must have a sense of the patterns of speech that are fitting to each speaker and the special situation in which he is placed. The speakers must hold the audience by their words and, simultaneously, reveal the theme.

Shakespeare had four basic tools for dialogue:

1. blank verse
2. prose of different kinds, such as comic prose of clowns, familiar speech of gallants
3. variations on ten-syllable lines, such as couplets, quatrains, stanzas, etc.
4. shorter rhymed lines, usually six or eight syllables each, in couplets or quatrains

The following examples show that we can clearly distinguish the difference between various forms:

> Now, fair Hippolyta, our nuptial hour
> Draws on apace: four happy days bring in
> Another moon: but, O, methinks how slow
> This old moon wanes! She lingers my desires,

and

> Over hill, over dale,
>   Through bush, through briar,
> Over park, over pale,
>   Through flood, through fire,
> I do wander everywhere.

It cannot be overstressed that Elizabethan audiences would be much more readily attuned to differences in sound; indeed, we know from the following example that their ears were acute enough to be able to recognize blank verse from a single line. In *As You Like It,* Orlando says, "Good day, and happiness, dear Rosalind." One of the other characters responds, "Nay then, God buy you, as you talk in blank verse." The point of the joke rests in Shakespeare's assurance that the audience will pick up the blank verse as quickly as Jacques did. The difference in dialogue also alerted the audience to characterization.

In the opening of *Macbeth,* for example, the witches utter the following lines:

> When shall we three meet again,
> In thunder, lightning or in rain?

Immediately, the octosyllabic lines, in place of the expected blank verse, suggest the supernatural, while the falling (trochaic) movement suggests that things are turned upside down, inverted from the normal order. "Fair is foul and foul is fair" illustrates this also.

Similarly, the language used in the opening of *Hamlet* alerts the audience to what is happening. In the first seven short utterances of the play there are three regular blank verse lines.

> Nay, answer me: stand and unfold youself . . .
> You come most carefully upon your hour . . .
> 'Tis now struck twelve; get thee to bed, Francisco.

This is what the play-goers would have expected. However, the rest of the lines in this section are broken, lines such as "Who's there?" and "He." This suggests to the audience that the atmosphere is broken with tension and anxiety, as the blank verse is disrupted with short, disturbing messages.

These passages from *Macbeth* and *Hamlet* show the link between verse form and scene content. Different verse forms are also used for contrast. The balcony scene in *Romeo and Juliet,* for example, is rich in lyrical blank verse, as the following excerpt shows:

> But, soft! what light through yonder window breaks?
> It is the east, and Juliet is the sun.
> Arise, fair sun, and kill the envious moon,
> Who is already sick and pale with grief,
> That thou her maid art far more fair than she: . . .
> O Romeo, Romeo! wherefore art thou Romeo?
> Deny thy father and refuse thy name;
> Or, if thou wilt not, be but sworn my love,
> And I'll no longer be a Capulet. (II, ii, 1–37)

But the following scene, with Friar Lawrence, uses rhymed couplets and heavy spondaic measures to achieve a poetic, serious, and dignified atmosphere:

> Benedicite!
> What early tongue so sweet saluteth me?
> Young son, it argues a distemper'd head
> So soon to bid good morrow to thy bed:
> Care keep his watch in every man's old eye,
> And where care lodges, sleep will never lie;
> But where unbruised youth with unstuff'd brain
> Doth couch his limbs, there golden sleep doth reign (II, iii, 31–38)

LANGUAGE

The *language* of a work of literature refers to the diction, sentence structure, syntax, and so forth. Since some of the words used during the Renaissance, for example, will obviously be unfamiliar to modern readers, we will initially have to put more effort into grasping their meaning and then turn our attention to an appreciation of style. The problem is even more obvious in older works, such as those from the Greek, or in foreign works, such as Molière's plays. Since you will be reading all such plays in translation, you will have to select a well-known edition, preferably one recommended or clearly the work of a well-known, accomplished translator. A poor translation, or one that was done before the discovery of additional material, will hamper your understanding of the play as well as your appreciation of the style.

Aristotle spoke of diction as crucial to an effective style. Diction, as explained in the Writing section, is word choice. *Diction in tragedy,* according to Aristotle, must be elevated in keeping with the lofty themes and concerns. If this rule is not followed strictly, the work is usually classed as a *tragi-comedy.* In the same way, the characters and images must be elevated, focusing on kings or nobles and such significant events as battles or great storms.

Diction in comedy is usually much less elevated and lofty, and here we find scatological words and images. The wit is also coarser, and generally the entire play relies less on descriptions of the upper strata of society. This is not to say that there are not passages of great beauty, but this is not the main goal of comedy.

Song is an important part of Greek comedy and tragedy. There are choral odes that divide the scenes in tragedy, commenting on the action or the theme. They follow a rigid verse form and refer to mythology and history. These odes are not as important to comedy and are usually used to comment on current events or people.

At the heart of all discussions of style is *language,* for the words a playwright selects are obviously crucial to the meaning of his work. Nowhere is this more evident than in Shakespeare's works. In *Othello,* for example, several language motifs are used to make very specific thematic points:

1. **Military Words.** The major characters are army officers, and four of the five acts take place in a town of war. Thus Othello is called "General" (also referred to as "Captain," an Elizabethan word meaning the same). He is a mercenary, as it was the practice of some Italian city-states to employ a foreigner as the head of the army. Cassio is called "Lieutenant"; Iago is called "Ancient," which is the same as "Ensign." Othello as captain selects his two officers, lieutenant, and ensign, and fires one of them.

2. **"Honest."** When applied to Desdemona, it has a double meaning: "chaste" as well as "upright." When applied to Cassio, it usually means "honorable." When used with Iago, the term is an ironic reference to Iago as a virtuous and trustworthy man. Thus, Iago would be able to distinguish vice in others and enjoy the freedom of cynical and truthful speech. Obviously, this is ironic.

3. **"Think."** This word has not changed meaning over the years, and applies mostly to Iago, whereas Othello has been used to *knowing* and then acting. Iago uses it when he is trying to rouse Othello's suspicions, and we see its climax in Othello's description of his torment:

> By the world,
> I *think* my wife be honest, and *think* she is not;
> I *think* that thou are just, and *think* thou are not.
> I'll have some proof. (III, iii, 383–386)

Imagery, another aspect of style, is extremely effective in a play. In *Othello,* continuing with the previous example, the images, pictures suggested by words and phrases, fall into three groups:

1. **Light and Dark.** This is most obvious in the marriage of black and white, Othello and Desdemona, which would have startled an Elizabethan audience to whom a Moor would have been a rare sight. The following are a sampling of quotes that show this kind of imagery. You will be able to find many more.

(I, i, 76–77)   "As when, by night and negligence, the fire/Is spied in populous cities."
Fire in the night, a recurrent light/dark image in the play, reaches its climax when Desdemona sees Othello holding a burning candle, standing by her bed.

(I, iii, 409–10)   "Hell and night/must bring this monstrous birth to the world's light."
This image is used to describe Iago's hellish plan, as darkness and hell bring forth evil thoughts into the light of consciousness.

(III, iii, 386–88)   "Her name, that was as fresh/As Dian's visage, is now begrim'd and black/As mine own face."
Through Iago's suggestions, Othello sees Desdemona so marred by blackening evil that she seems to be as black as he is physically.

2. **Animal Images.** Several critics have noticed that the more Othello listens to Iago's evil suggestions, the more "lower" animals are used to describe him. The most well-known of these are the "goats and monkeys" (IV, i, 274) Othello mentions when speaking to Lodovico, echoing the suggestion Iago had made of these lecherous creatures in III, iii, 403. These images are frequently lewd and obscene. For example:

(I, i, 88–89)   ". . .an old black ram/Is tupping your white ewe." Iago sees Othello as an "old black ram," Desdemona is the innocent lamb, and suggests Othello is defiling the innocent woman.

3. **Ocean Storms.** The Renaissance used images of the larger world, called the "macrocosm" to reflect the actions of man in the little world, called the "microcosm." The storms of the ocean represent what is happening to the characters, emotionally and spiritually. In I, i, 30, Iago describes himself as "belee'd and calm'd," and describes the success of his plan in terms of a ship being helped on its way by winds and currents: "If consequence do but approve my dream,/My boat sails freely, both with wind and stream" (II, iii, 64–65). There is nothing romantic about his view of the sea, and it has no storms, no danger, and ultimately, no beauty. Each character is compared to the sea, and the way the character reacts to the ocean imagery tells us about him. In V, ii, 267–68, for example, Othello compares the end of an ocean journey to the approach of death. Both the tempest and the icy currents, the swell of life, with their beauty and their motion, are now gone: "Here is my journey's end, here is my butt,/ And very seamark of my utmost sail."

For further study of imagery, see Robert B. Heilman's discussion of various images in *Othello,* including birth, burning, pain, clothing, etc. Wolfgang Clemen has also studied this aspect of the play, especially the contrasting imagery of Iago and Othello.

THEATER STYLE AND PRODUCTION

The manner in which a play is presented has only become important in the last hundred years. The style of drama has varied through the years, designed as it was for specific theaters, the space determining the *manner* and *method* of production. Until about a hundred years ago, the style of drama and the style of the physical space within which it was presented had not changed for a period of a hundred years or more. Regardless of subject, theme, or character, for instance, Shakespearean style remained the same with regard to costuming, staging, theater structure, and so forth from about 1576 (the opening of the first commercial theater) until the theaters were closed by the Puritans in 1642. In the same way, the style of the theater remained the same from the time the theaters were reopened by Charles II after the Restoration in 1660 for quite a long time. Today this has changed, as theater style has adapted to many different forms. There are several different styles to be considered.

The *classic* style is structured in the manner of Greek drama, with the subject matter devoted to a single plot line, dealing mainly with heroic legends or historical myths and tales. There is little physical violence—what there is takes place off-stage—although the physical and mental agonies of many of the characters, such as those of Oedipus, are in full view. Action takes place during a single time span and in a single place. Dialogue is elevated in tone, almost poetic, carefully planned and arranged in long set pieces that alternate with quick exchanges between the main characters. Staging is simple, suggesting the clean lines of classical buildings. These plays are concerned with the relationship of the larger-than-life characters to the gods, or God, Nature, or the Universe as well as to each other, and frequently raise deep questions about the forces that control human behavior. Usually the classic and tragic views are found together.

The *romantic* style is quite different from the classic. Because the romantic writer sees man as essentially good, unaffected by the gods and untainted by original sin, he is uncomfortable with the rigid uniformity of subject matter, theme, and set design of the classic theater. He favors originality, freedom to move about in time and space, and to weave multiple plot lines. This, in turn, results in a great deal of colorful spectacle and exciting adventure. Romantic plays tend to appeal to the emotions. Central to these plays is the notion that man's various difficulties are the result of the façade forced upon him by "civilization," hiding and stifling his true nature. When this artificial cover is stripped away, man will shine forth in all his goodness. "Natural man" is pure and uncontaminated, and thus the romanticist looks to nature, to the woods and streams, sunshine and rain, for an understanding of mankind. Also, since the past is invariably seen as better than the corrupted present, the romanticist is historically oriented. These plays emphasize nostalgia, undying devotion, and love; they are eternally optimistic. Oppositely, the romanticist is also obsessed with evil and the mysteries of death, and is far more drawn to the hellish than the heavenly. What is on the other side of the grave? Can we ever know it? The romanticist probes the supernatural, the magical, the fantastic, and the exotic, setting his tales in mysterious valleys and deeply hidden mountains. He is also not above changing history to suit his own needs, preferring as he does the ideal to the real. This trait can be found in the works of Frederich Schiller, the German romanticist.

The *realistic* and *naturalistic* styles are very different from the classic and romantic styles. A realistic play accepts man pretty much as he is, and presents him as a product of his society. The subject matter mirrors reality, as the characters on stage move through actions that would be found in real life. The characters are closely identified with the audience, for they are presented as products of their society, unromanticized and unsentimentalized. The characters are neither totally good nor totally evil, but rather totally human, appearing strong or weak, heroic or fearful, as the situation demands. The dialogue also fits in with this characterization, and the characters speak as real people, in the rhythms of normal speech.

The naturalistic style makes use of the same subject matter as the realistic style, but the characters are regarded more objectively, even scientifically. To the naturalistic writer, the characters are used as subjects for close analysis, as the naturalist is interested in what makes man function as a creature in the natural world. According to his theory, society has placed upon the individual a certain pattern of behavior made up of the customs of civilized behavior. If that covering is ripped away, man stands revealed in all his animalistic primitiveness. Because naturalists tend to dwell on these things and are not especially selective in the details they highlight, they have been accused of being sensationalists. Naturalists defend themselves on the grounds that it is necessary to strip away society's veneer in order to be able to probe the forces of nature that have combined to make man what he really is. As a result, the naturalist sees life as a jungle. He avoids concerning himself with the past, seeing little to be gained there. He looks at the future darkly, as contrasted to the realist, who is neither a pessimist nor an optimist. The naturalist sees little possibility of things changing for the better. He offers no particular solution to the effect the forces of nature have worked on man, uncertain as to whether or not there are any solutions for the problem. The realist often takes a sharp stand on the social issues of his day, backing a cause, and even offering a solution. Henrik Ibsen, considered the first great dramatic realist, once explained what he saw as the difference between himself and Émile Zola, one of the greatest naturalists of the nineteenth century. Ibsen is supposed to have said, "When I go down to the sewer, I go to clean it out. When Zola goes down, he takes a bath."

Realism has come to be equated with "modern" drama, which is generally dated from about 1880 to the present. Any departure from this style is called *stylization,* which can be the staging of a modern play in a different manner or the revival of an older play in a different fashion. *Expressionism,* first commented upon in 1902 by the Swedish realist August Strindberg, presented a very subjective view of life. In his play *The Dream Play,* Strindberg blended a nightmare in which time, place, and characters chaotically mingled in the manner of a dream. The expressionist fashions reality as he sees it, not as daily life, but as it appears to him. If a person seems to be the same as the machines he operates, that person will act like a machine, speaking in the manner of a mechanical object. If a person's actions seem to make no sense, then that person will speak in gibberish or singsong. Thus, the expressionist expresses his views and displays them with the greatest possible dramatic and theatrical distortion. His work is socially oriented and concerned with the present that man has forged for himself. The expressionist, like the naturalist, has little faith in the lessons of the past, and the present doesn't seem to offer much hope for the future. This style was popular for only two or three decades in the early twentieth century, but it has had a lasting effect on the theater. The expressionist opened up the use of the stage, including even the audience as an acting area, and imposed no limits on what could or could not be done within the theatrical experience.

Impressionism seeks not to create a distorted "expression" but a highly personal "impression" of what the author sees. Thus we find life viewed from a very particular vantage point, through the clouds of personal or physical distance, making use of a variety of sights and sounds neither totally real, nor totally unreal.

The *absurdist* sees life as a ridiculous joke, a pointless experience, a confusing contest with unknown, uninterested forces. He often sends his characters through a totally stylized world to make his point.

The outward, literal, objective presentation of what the dramatist sees is called realism; the inward, imaginative subjective presentation is expressionism. The push and pull of these two styles combined to bring to the modern theater a great many exciting and innovative changes.

ACTION

Aristotle believed the *fable,* or the story, is the soul of drama and the *agon,* or argument, is the heart. He defined tragedy as "the imitation of an action," and the drama must have action in it. Narration, or the mere telling of a story, he left for the epic poem. The elements of drama we shall consider here are action, plot, and conflict.

Action means the things that happen in a play. It consists of several elements that have a unity unto themselves, yet are so interrelated that they become fully understood only when considered as a whole. These elements can be divided up into two distinct types:

1. Outward action, which includes the events we can see each as Orestes' murder of his mother in Aeschyulus' *The Choephori* and Euripides' *Electra.*
2. Inward action, which includes the events that take place in the minds of the characters, such as major decisions, acceptances, plottings not spoken of to the audience, dislikes, etc. An example of inward action would be how Medea decided to kill her children in Euripides' play, as the audience was not privy to her thoughts.

Plot is the arrangement of the action to produce a unified and coherent whole. According to Aristotle, all the events in a drama must be so closely connected that the removal of any one of them would "disjoint and dislocate the whole."

The *conflict* surrounding the argument centers on the opposition of two forces:

1. The protagonistic force, which may be one person or many.
2. The antagonistic force, which may be a person, group, thing, or force that is supernatural, natural, or divine.

The way in which the argument unfolds is the *form* of the play, involving the beginning, middle, and end. First, there must be a starting point, known as the *point of attact,* from which the dramatist leads his audience into the action. If he starts at the beginning and reveals events as they occur, he is using an *accretive plot.* If he starts in the middle of the action and lets the story reveal what has already transpired, he is using a *climactic plot.* Shakespeare's *Hamlet* is an example of an accretive plot; Sophocles' *Oedipus* is climactic.

In *Hamlet,* we have the following order of events:

I.i.	The ghost of Old Hamlet appears to the guards on the platform of Elsinore Castle.
I.ii.	King Claudius speaks about his brother's death and his assumption of power; Voltemand and Cornelius are dispatched with letters to rulers of Norway; Hamlet agrees to remain in Denmark; Horatio tells Hamlet of the ghost.
I.iii.	Laertes and Polonius advise Ophelia to shun Hamlet's advances.
I.iv.	The ghost appears to Hamlet and the guards.
I.v.	The ghost tells Hamlet about his murder at his brother's hand and commands Hamlet to avenge his death.

II.i	Polonius sends his servant Reynaldo to France to spy on Laertes; Ophelia tells her father of her upsetting meeting with Hamlet; Polonius decides to report Hamlet's mad behavior to Claudius.
II.ii	Claudius asks Rosencrantz and Guildenstern to spy on Hamlet. Hamlet greets the players.
III.i.	After contemplating suicide ("To be or not to be . . ."), Hamlet berates Ophelia for her falseness; Claudius plans to send Hamlet to England.
III.ii.	Claudius' shocked reaction to the play-within-a-play reveals his guilt.
III.iii.	Hamlet spares Claudius as the king tries to pray.
III.iv.	While berating his mother. Hamlet kills Polonius. The ghost appears.
IV.i.	Gertrude tells Claudius that Hamlet is mad.
IV.ii.	Hamlet refuses to reveal where he has hidden Polonius' body.
IV.iii.	Claudius sends Hamlet to England to be killed.
IV.iv.	The sight of Fortinbras' army moves Hamlet to soliloquize on his delayed revenge.
IV.v.	Ophelia goes mad and Laertes returns, bent on avenging Polonius' death.
IV.vi.	Hamlet announces his return to Denmark in a letter to Horatio.
IV.vii.	Claudius and Laertes plot Hamlet's death; Gertrude reports Ophelia has drowned.
V.i.	While walking through the churchyard with Horatio, Hamlet ponders human mortality; encounters gravediggers. Ophelia's funeral.
V.ii.	Treachery in the fencing match leads to the deaths of Gertrude, Laertes, Claudius, and Hamlet. Fortinbras assumes the throne.

As you can see, the plot unfolds in an orderly fashion, from the beginning to the end. With the exception of King Hamlet's murder, which occurred before the beginning of the play, the events unfold as we watch in this type of plot.

No matter which way the dramatist decides to structure the action, he must first establish for the audience what is going on and who is involved, which he does with a technique called *exposition,* showing and telling the facts. This can be accomplished by having two characters tell each other—and thus the audience—what is going on, or simply by plunging us into the action, as Shakespeare does in the opening scenes of *Hamlet.* In *Macbeth,* too, the first scene is structured to attract our attention, as the witches speak:

First witch:	When shall we three meet again In thunder, lightning, or in rain?
Second witch:	When the hurlyburly's done, When the battle's lost and won.
Third witch:	That will be ere the set of sun.
First witch:	Where the place?
Second witch:	Upon the heath.
Third witch:	There to meet with Macbeth.

From this brief exchange, we know immediately that there is to be a battle, and it will end before sunset. Somehow Macbeth will be involved with the battle, but what could he have to do with three witches? This first scene has only twelve lines, and the last two, very well known, express one of the themes of the play:

All:	Fair is foul and foul is fair. Hover through the fog and filthy air.

The play will be concerned with the differences between appearances and reality. Things will be reversed and we shall not know who to trust, as the loyal and wise Duncan is overthrown by Macbeth, his host for the evening. It is a double treachery, as Macbeth was a trusted soldier, well rewarded by Duncan for his brave deeds and loyalty. Act I, scene ii tells us a great deal more, as we learn details of the battle and Macbeth's bravery and rich rewards:

> *Sergeant:*   ... The merciless Macdonwald
> (Worthy to be a rebel, for to that
> The multiplying villainies of nature
> Do swarm upon him) from the Western Isles
> Of kerns and gallowglasses is supplied;
> And Fortune, on his damnèd quarrel smiling,
> Showed like a rebel's whore. But all's too weak:
> For brave Macbeth—(well he deserves that name)—
> Disdaining Fortune, with his brandish'd steel
>
> . . . .
>
> Like valour's minion carved out his passage
> Till he faced the slave;
>
> . . . .
>
> Till he unseam'd him from the nave to the chops

Macbeth has performed valiantly during battle, disdaining personal safety to kill the traitor Macdonwald. For this he is rewarded with the traitor's land and his title, Thane of Cawdor. This opening scene also foreshadows Macbeth's treachery, for he becomes a far greater enemy than Macdonwald in that he does succeed in killing his king. So these opening passages tell us the themes—loyalty and disloyalty, appearance and reality—and explain what is going on, as King Duncan and his troops are completing a battle and prizes are awarded. Once the events are established, the dramatist can continue to the climax and eventual resolution of events. To return to further exposition after this point would most likely confuse the audience.

In Greek drama, *exposition* is usually accomplished in the prologue. A character comes out on the stage and tells the audience what it must know of past events and character relationships before the play can begin. Modern drama has built upon the Greek tradition: We see in Thornton Wilder's *Our Town,* for example, the role of the Stage Manager, built directly on the prologue tradition.

Having established the situation, the dramatist sets forth *complications* that add depth to the action. These complications form the *rising action:* the building of suspense, emotional response, and audience involvement. All these events carry the plot to its *climax,* where all that has happened is pulled together. The protagonistic and antagonistic forces have established their sides of the agon, and have met, face to face, in one way or another. The climactic showdown, or *obligatory scene,* the one that everyone has come to expect, is the turning point after which nothing new is added. Any other high point that follows is called the *anticlimax,* and may lose dramatic emphasis for being placed after the climax. The climax may be one single event, as when Oedipus finally learns who and what he is, or it may be a series of events, as in *Hamlet,* proceeding from the middle of the play on.

The climax is followed by the *falling action,* a winding down of the action. Things fall into place, and the play heads for its conclusion, its *denouement,* or as the Greeks called it in referring to tragedy, its *catastrophe.* The denouement is the resolution of the plot. It is vital that the conclusion be believable, as the audience must feel that the action has been resolved in an acceptable manner.

The denouement may not always leave the audience satisfied. In Euripides' plays particularly, the plots are so confused with subplots that there is often no clear way out. In such cases, Euripides resorted to the *deus ex machina*. Literally a god lowered by a machine from the roof of the playhouse, the term more commonly refers to the employment of an outside agency to resolve the crisis. Artemis appears in Euripides' *Hippolytus* for this purpose. The modern reader tends to judge this type of conflict resolution as unsatisfactory. However, the device has proved successful in comedies, as when Aristophanes had Socrates appear in a basket lowered from the roof in *The Clouds* and Trygaeus ascends to heaven on the back of a giant beetle in *Peace*.

Plays that follow the pattern just outlined are called *well-made,* because the structure rather than the theme or plot becomes the crucial element. Because these plays tend to emphasize popular entertainment, the term "well-made" has long been held in critical disfavor. But many of the most stunning examples of lasting dramatic art are essentially well-made, such as *Hamlet* and *Oedipus*. It is what the dramatist does with the development of character, the conflict of the fable, the clash between the protagonist and antagonist, that makes the real difference in quality.

MEANING

The central question concerning any work of art, no matter what its form, is what does it all mean? Sometimes the meaning is very clear, as in Aristophanes' *Peace*—war is useless and must be stopped. Sometimes in Greek drama the meaning concerns the origin of a religious rite, such as Euripides' *Iphigenia in Aulis,* which explains the substitution of animal for human sacrifice. There are, however, instances where the modern reader will be unable to fathom the meaning of Greek drama because the historical allusions have been lost or because part of the play itself has been lost.

There are several ways to discern meaning.

Plot. Sometimes a brief summary of the plot will help make the meaning clear, hence all the plot summaries given in this guide. When all the events are set down on paper, often the meaning becomes clear. You can, of course, chart the events of the play for yourself.

Conventions. Sometimes the playwright uses a well-known device to make his meaning clear. In Greek drama, this device is usually the chorus, which explains the main ideas of the play as no character is able to do, standing both within and outside of the action. *Deus ex machina* is another device that may be used to make sure the audience and the characters understand what has happened.

Symbols. In some instances, especially in modern drama, symbols can illuminate meaning. Ibsen's *A Doll's House* is a case in point.

Images. Like symbols, images are often used to reinforce meaning. See the section on *Othello* for a discussion of various images and their meaning.

No matter what the meaning or how you have discerned it, when you are writing your essay, you must back up your assertions with clear, specific examples drawn directly from the text. This means that you will use specific passages and incidents to describe symbols, images, and so forth.

SPECTACLE AND AUDIENCE

The dramatist must ultimately be aware that his play will be performed before a live audience, and he must be versed in theatrical considerations, or *spectacle* in Aristotle's terms. Actually, Aristotle placed *spectacle* very far down his list of important dramatic considerations, for he believed that the dramatist who was concerned mainly with the showy parts of theater would write inferior drama. Furthermore, this entire aspect of theater—costumes, scenery, lighting, etc.—is intended to serve the drama, not to dominate it. The *director* alone has the final say on what will appear on the stage. He approves the setting, lighting, costumes, sound and special effects, and so forth. More important, he is the one who selects the actors, with or without the advice of the dramatist, and in his hands rests the final responsibility for the production.

The *audience* also figures in the final production, for the dramatist and director must be concerned with the living group of people who will willingly suspend their disbelief (to paraphrase Samuel Taylor Coleridge) and accept as truth what is being presented on the stage. Both the actors and the audience participate in this suspended belief: the actors in pretending that they are who they are playing, and the audience in believing that, for the moment, Mary Smith is indeed Shakespeare's Ophelia. For this process to work, there must be a balance between the actor and the spectator. On one side there is *empathy,* an emotional identification with the character and his difficulties. The audience must be interested in and identify with the character. On the other side is *aesthetic distance,* which means that even as it is moving toward emotional identification with the characters, the audience must constantly pull back with the knowledge that what it is seeing is art, not life.

Tragedy

ARISTOTLE'S DEFINITION OF TRAGEDY

All discussion of serious drama begins with an examination of Aristotle's *Poetics*. Tragedy is "an imitation of an action that is serious, complete, and of a certain magnitude; in language embellished with each kind of artful ornament, the several kinds being found in separate parts of the play, in the form of action, not of narration; through pity and fear effecting the proper purgation of these and similar emotions." To fully understand Aristotle's definition, you must comprehend the meaning of his terms:

Imitation means getting at the heart of the situation; finding the universal in the particular.

Action means more than just the moving about of characters; it refers to the great decisions that the central character makes, and the ramifications that these decisions cause.

Magnitude means that the action and characters must rise above the ordinary. Arthur Miller challenged this assumption in *Death of a Salesman* with the creation of Willy Loman, the "low man" common to all of us. For Aristotle, the plays had to revolve around kings, gods, or great military leaders.

Ornament includes *diction* and *song*. The diction must be elevated; people must talk in a refined manner. The songs, choral odes, are sung in ritualistic and often complicated manners. Different ornaments are suited for different parts of the play. Arthur Miller challenged this notion too, with the diction he used in *Salesman,* the everyday talk of a common man.

Purgation, or in Aristotelian terms, *catharsis,* refers to the cleansing that the audience experiences at the end of the play. We feel fear for the fate of the main character, and we pity this character, basically noble and good, who has been put through such travail.

The term tragedy does not refer to a sad play with an unhappy ending. The root of the word has nothing to do with sadness and death. Rather, it comes from the Greek *tragos,* or goat, plus *aedein,* to sing, which means the "singing of the goat." The goat was a sacred animal to Dionysus, god of wine and fertility, in whose honor the early festivals of song and dance were held out of which drama evolved. The entire notion of tragedy as we now accept it is a product of Greek civilization, founded on the special view Greeks held with regard to man and his relationship to the gods. The Greeks created their gods in their own image, endowing them with beauty, power, and immortality, yet subjecting them to the same passions endured by mortal men and women. Thus, Zeus, the king of the gods, could fall in love with an earthly being, and his queen, Hera, could be jealous. The gods did not always possess common sense, no more than did their human models. When they did act, it was following human lines which could be understood by mortals if not always entirely appreciated. The Greek gods were not independent, for they were under the rule of the Fates, the three sisters who controlled the thread of life. From this we can see how tragedy developed. As an assertion of the basic greatness of man, it demonstrates the individual's ability to ascend to the heights of human possibility in the face of an antagonistic force he knows will eventually destroy him. The protagonist of a tragedy, do what he will, may suffer from the curses of the gods for generations, for the gods, like their mortal counterparts, are capable of carrying grudges and taking offense. The point of all tragedy is that the protagonist, even when faced with the knowledge that the forces laid out against him are to cause his literal or symbolic death, can rise and assert his splendor, defy the forces, and even bring the forces down with him on occasion. There is no possibility of escape, and we watch as the hero proceeds in full recognition of his fate. Since the forces move with an absolute finality, it is what the protagonist does in the struggle that counts. The hero rises in the ultimate human courage and defiance to display the godlike qualities that lie within each of us.

Thus, tragedy is not a sad or depressing genre. It is positive and optimistic in its view of the possibilities of human beings. The tragic protagonist is not a martyr, for the martyr suffers for a certain cause and his death implies that something will follow, making the suffering and sacrifice worth the effort. The martyr, having a cause, may actually seek his own end. The tragic protagonist, in sharp contrast, has every reason to survive, and makes a heroic struggle to that end. At the moment of his death, he has shown the very best qualities of mankind, and his death is a very real loss. In displaying his greatness, the protagonist actually becomes godlike, and the giving of his life is a kind of reverse act, a sacrifice for mankind, not for the gods.

At the end of a tragedy there is usually a deep emotional involvement on the part of the audience. Aristotle discussed this when he spoke of *catharsis,* the arousal in the audience of pity, terror, and fear. When we view a tragedy, we are moved by a compassionate pity for the protagonist. In the same manner, we feel terror when we realize the size and the power of the forces that have caused the protagonist's downfall. At the tragedy's end, a calmness descends, and the audience undergoes a spiritual cleansing when it realizes how great the human being can be when called to the proper occasion.

Aristotle described the "ideal" tragic hero as human, not a god, and of noble stature. By this he intended royalty, for those were the deaths that could make empires crumble. Today we have redefined the term to mean that the individual must contain within himself a greatness and a stature beyond the ordinary. Thus, in modern tragedies, the protagonist may be a "little man," but not in any sense a "little person." The tragic hero cannot be predominantly evil, for then the audience would welcome his demise. Neither can he be all good, for then his death would be truly shocking, and displeasing to the audience.

Aristotle attributes *hamartia* to the tragic hero, which we translate as a "tragic flaw" or "shortcoming." In many plays, it is a character flaw or a vice, such as *hubris,* a Greek word meaning overwhelming arrogance or pride, that leads to his demise. But in other plays, a hero's flaw may be merely a poor choice, or a choice that turns out badly. There have been instances in which the tragic hero is undone because of his virtue, as he may be courageous when others are not. Therefore, the tragic hero need not always have a flaw. For instance, in the case of Romeo and Juliet, neither rashness nor lust fits their case, and they are undone more by circumstance than by anything they themselves lack or have caused. Regardless of the reason, the hero suffers and then comes to some sort of an awareness, either of his vice—if he has one—or his virtue—which he now sees cannot exist in the world of ordinary people.

In the end, the hero must be fully aware of what has happened to him and must face that realization. He proclaims his defiance, as Macbeth did in the end of the play, and welcomes his adversary.

Tragedy is ironic, as the audience, aware of what is going to happen, waits for the protagonist to reach awareness. Tragedy may involve the twists of fate: the harder the protagonist may seek to avoid his fate, the faster it approaches. This is true in *Hamlet,* for example.

There are two more terms to consider when discussing Aristotle's definition of tragedy.

Peripeteia (also spelled peripety) occurs when an action produces the opposite of what was intended or expected. It is a *reversal.* Thus, Macbeth kills his king, Duncan, to gain happiness through power, but reaps misery instead.

Anagnorisis means disclosure, discovery, or recognition. For Aristotle, the disclosure was usually a simple recognition of who was who through a clear external sign such as a birthmark or even clothing, but the term has been extended to include the tragic hero's recognition of himself or his place in the universe. So we see that Othello, who killed his faithful wife, learned that he was tricked into thinking her dishonest, and finally sees himself as "one not easily jealous, but being wrought/Perplexed in the extreme" and enacts justice by killing himself.

Melodrama, like tragedy, has come to mean something quite different from what its word roots would seem to portray. *Melo* (music) and *drama* (play) originally meant "a play with music." The term was coined during the eighteenth century, when the popular theaters of the day, offering diversion outside the "classical" theatres, made extensive use of background music. These plays were full of broad action, blood, and excitement. By the end of the eighteenth century, the innocent maiden persecuted by villains and saved by dashing heroes had been added to the format. The difference between tragedy and melodrama lies in the degree of emphasis, for while action is an integral part of a tragedy, melodrama creates action for its own sake, to divert the audience and keep it amused. Characters in tragedy are well-rounded and fully developed; those in melodrama tend to be "types" easily recognized so the plot can move quickly without the dramatist's having to establish motives. The tragic end is unrelated to justice; melodrama punishes the bad and rewards the good. Melodrama sets up the action so that things will work out well for all but the villain in the end.

The nontragic, nonmelodramatic, noncomedic play known as the *middle genre,* the *"straight" drama* or the *drame* comes from the traditions of literary realism. It achieves its success in describing people in terms of their humanity, in everyday situations, not in terms of the contrived plots and settings of the melodrama nor the outrageous fortunes of someone like Hamlet. In this genre, people face the challenges of everyday life in a recognizable setting. These very human figures may sway an audience far more easily than do those of tragedy and melodrama.

Summary of Tragedy

1. The term "tragedy" is applied to literary and especially dramatic representations of serious actions which turn out disastrously for the chief character.
2. "Comedy" is applied to dramatic works in which the characters undergo embarrassments which, on the whole, are so managed that they interest and amuse us without engaging our profoundest sympathy. In comedy, the action turns out well for the chief characters.
3. Discussion of tragedy begins with Aristotle's *Poetics,* where he defined tragedy as "the imitation of an action that is serious and also, as having magnitude, complete in itself." Tragedy must be presented dramatically in poetic language rather than as narrative, with "incidents arousing pity and fear, wherewith to accomplish its catharsis of emotion."
4. "Catharsis" is the feeling of relief on the part of the audience that leads to a cleansing of the mind.
5. Since tragedy must elicit pity and fear from the audience, the tragic hero will do this most effectively if he is neither thoroughly good nor thoroughly evil, but human with flaws like the rest of us. The tragic hero suffers a change in fortune from happiness to misery because of a mistaken act due to his "tragic flaw" or to a tragic error in judgment. One tragic flaw is "hubris," pride that leads man to overlook a divine warning or to break a moral law.
6. The tragic hero whose character is marked by some tragic flaw, which is ultimately responsible for his downfall, moves us to pity, because his misfortune is greater than he deserves, and to fear, because we recognize similar possibilities and consequences in our own fallible selves.

GREEK TRAGEDY

Greek theater grew out of the worship of the god Dionysus, known to the Romans as Bacchus, who was especially significant to the Greeks as a fertility figure. Once every spring he died, was buried, and rose again, standing for the rebirth of the crops which sustained life.

Most likely the first literary form developed to help in the religious ritual was the *dithyramb,* a poem chanted and danced by a chorus of priests. Critics have theorized that as the service became more complex the dithyramb became a *dialogue,* with verses sung or chanted alternately by the religious leader and the chorus, much as is practiced today in religious services. From this it is thought that the leader would assume the role of another, usually a god. From this point on, the Dionysian religious service can be considered drama.

In Athens in the fifth century B.C., drama was organized and run by the state as the main feature of an important religious event, the worship of the god Dionysus, as outlined above. In addition, it was part of a contest. The plays were judged and prizes awarded to the best comedy and best tragedy. There were two main festivals, the more important of the two being the Greater Dionysia, which took place at the end of March or the beginning of April and lasted three days. During the last quarter of the fifth century B.C., three playwrights competed in the tragedy division, three in comedy. Each tragedian entered three plays in the morning contest, and each comedic writer contributed one play to the afternoon festivities.

The second festival was called the Lenaea, and took place at the end of January or the beginning of February. It emphasized comedy and three comedic writers entered, each with one play. Three tragedians also took part, but with two plays each instead of the three allowed in the Greater Dionysia.

The actual production of the plays in both festivals lay entirely in the state's hands. Athens annually elected two officials called "archons," who were in charge of the festivals. Any interested playwright could submit a script to these officials, and the archons decided which ones were to be produced. All entries were in verse, for no prose was allowed, and most scenes were written in iambic hexameter lines, which the actors delivered in ordinary speech. There were also more complex rhymes and lyric passages, which were sung with the accompaniment of a flute or lyre.

The state took care of all expenses, the most significant of these being the chorus. There were 24 people in the chorus of a comedy who had to be paid, costumed, and trained by a dancing coach and a flute player. Since the cost of all this was too great for the state to assume directly, the archon assigned a "choregus," or "chorus handler" to each playwright. These more wealthy Athenians paid all expenses.

The next most significant expense was the actors. In the very early days of the Greek drama, the playwright himself played the leading role, but soon professional actors came to be used. The archon selected the leading men and assigned them to each playwright. The leading men competed against each other for the prize awarded to the best comic actor and the best tragic actor. The state also paid for all the other actors required, and for reasons not clear to us today—perhaps cost—each playwright was limited to only three speaking actors. No female actors were allowed on the stage. The playing of multiple roles was made easier by the use of masks. Made of linen and stiffened with clay, these masks covered the whole head and rested on the shoulders. Actors in comedies also wore silly padded costumes. Because the audience sat far away from the stage in most instances, the masks stood for different facial expressions. We are most familiar with the masks representing tragedy and comedy, but there were masks which stood for a wide variety of emotions. In tragedy, regardless of the emotion represented, the masks often served to maintain nobility and a high tone, while in comedy they were often ugly and ridiculous. Some critics and historians feel that the masks also served to amplify the sound, as the mouthpiece could function as an amplifier. The masks also distanced the audience and the actors, removing the actor from everyday life and rendering him unrecognizable. This would tend to give his actions a significance they would not otherwise carry. The tragic actor also wore high-heeled boots, called *cothurnus,* which added to his distance and impressiveness.

On the morning of the contest, people arrived early, bringing food and cushions, for the seats were hard and the day long. Although the state charged admission to cover the cost of maintaining the theater, there were funds set aside to pay for admission for all those who could not afford it. The first row was set aside for dignitaries.

When the last play was concluded, the panel of ten judges announced the ratings, and the first-place winners were crowned with ivy leaves. The names of the winners, and the order of placement of the losers, was inscribed in stone.

All plays during the fifth century B.C. were performed in the Theatre of Dionysus on the south side of the Acropolis. It looked very different then than it does today, for there was no stage and the construction was, for the most part, of wood. There were enough seats for 14,000 people set into the steep hillside. The first row was a great circle, about 85 feet in diameter. Within it was a smaller circle, about 65 feet around, where the chorus performed. In back of this circle was a building called the *skene*—the "scene building"—that served as a backdrop and the actors' dressing rooms. It was a long, two-story building flanked by two wings opening toward the circle, the whole in the shape of a U with a wider opening. The backdrop had three doors that could be used for entrances and exits and spaces that separated the scene building from the seating area. The entire theater was called the *theatron* or *koilon* and was most like the half-circle end of a football stadium. The *orchestra* is the end zone; the *skene* is on the goal line. The entrance ramps were called *parodos* and were used by the actors and the audience. There was a machine on the roof, called a *logeion,* that was used to raise or lower a symbolic god onto the stage.

This setting limited possible action in Greek plays. Most of the scenes had to take place outside, in front of the same place or setting, if possible. If an indoor scene was necessary, the skene could be opened or set on wheels, called an *eccyclema,* which would be rolled out from inside the skene. Every now and again, painted flats showing mountains or forests were placed against the skene walls. The Greek audience did not expect a great deal of scenery, relying upon imagination to create the atmosphere. There was, of course, no curtain, nor were there any acts or scene divisions. The plays were very short, running about an hour, and when breaks in the action were necessary, the chorus took over for a brief song and dance.

MEDEA BY EURIPIDES

Background

Jason was the heir to the throne of the Greek city Iolcos, but his place was usurped by his uncle, Pelias. Trying to kill his nephew, Pelias sent him to obtain the magic Golden Fleece, which the barbarian Aeetes, King of Colchis, had in his possession. Medea, Aeetes's daughter and a magician in her own right, fell in love with Jason. By deceiving her father and killing her brother, she helped Jason get the Fleece. Back in Iolcos, Medea brought about the death of Pelias, but Jason still could not ascend to the throne. Jason,

Medea, and their two sons fled to Corinth, where Jason, still trying to advance his position, deserted Medea and married Glauce, daughter of the Corinthian King Creon.

Summary of the Play

Standing in front of Medea's house in Corinth, the old Nurse describes Medea's grief over Jason's desertion. An attendant says that he has heard that Creon is to banish Medea and her sons from Corinth. The chorus, hearing Medea's lamentation, tries to soothe her by discussing the unfairness of women's position. Creon enters and tells Medea that she is indeed to be banished, but he allows her 24 hours to find refuge. After Creon leaves, Medea tells the chorus that she plans to murder Jason, Glauce, and Creon, although she does not have a plan yet. Jason, showing little sympathy or tact, arrives to tell Medea that he has married Glauce to provide a better life for Medea and her children. She tells him all the things that she has done to help him, including the murders, but he responds that she should be glad that he has brought her to a place as civilized as Greece. He offers her money, but she refuses. The chorus sings. The King of Athens, Aegeus, enters, and Medea promises that she will help him overcome his childlessness if he will grant her and her children refuge. He agrees, but only if she can get to Athens on her own, for he is worried about angering the Corinthians. She tells the chorus of her plan for the murders: She will send her children to Jason with a present for his bride—a headdress and robe that will burn to death anyone touching them—then murder her children and flee to Athens. Jason returns, and Medea sends the gift and her sons with him. The children return, and she takes them inside, determined to kill them so that Jason will be left with nothing. A messenger arrives to tell Medea that Glauce was engulfed in flames; Creon, coming to her aid, was also burned to death. She rushes inside to kill her children. Jason rushes in search of his children, and the chorus tells him they are dead. Suddenly Medea appears above the house in a chariot drawn by dragons; she tells Jason that she is now beyond his reach. He calls her a monster; she tells him he is not able to love fully. She refuses to allow him even the consolation of burying his children's bodies.

Like Othello, Medea has "loved not wisely, but too well." The extent to which she goes to punish Jason indicates this. She has committed murder to further Jason's career and to be cast aside for another is more than she can bear. Her violent nature erupts, destroying everything that Jason values. Jason, in contrast, is a reversal of the traditional portrayal of a hero. He is usually regarded as a sympathetic person, an adventurer searching for the Golden Fleece. Here, however, he is an opportunist who uses women to obtain what he desires. This play advocates that the dramatic contrasts between cultures—the Greek and the barbarian, for example—would make marriage outside one's caste unwise. Jason makes this point at the end of the play.

Discussion and Essay Questions on Medea

1. *Medea* is set in the city of Corinth, but for the resolution of its problem, the cleansing of guilt, the play looks to Athens. Why?
2. In *Electra,* Orestes' guilt was incurred wittingly, by command of a god; in *Heracles,* the crime was committed innocently. By sharp contrast, Medea's only excuse was her natural passion for revenge and her barbarian heritage. Why, then, is she granted sanctuary?
3. Was Jason a man of entirely respectable ambitions? Can we say that Medea brought her fate upon herself by standing in the way of Jason's ambitions? After

all, she had involved him in a murder before he ever came to Corinth, and as a non-Greek, she could never be recognized by Greeks as his legal wife.

4. Does Jason stand for a civilized life: a life without excess, a life of control and order? If this is the case, can we say that he is opposed to barbarism and all of its ways?
5. Can we conclude that Jason's concern for civilized values is joined with a calculating coldness and an unscrupulous want of feeling?
6. Is the theme of this play that civilized people ignore—at their dire peril—the world of instinct, emotion, and irrational experience; that their carefully worked out notions of right and wrong are mortally dangerous unless these ideas are flexible and allow for constant adjustment?
7. Is it true, that in his revenge plays Euripides first enlists the spectators' sympathy for the avenger and then extends that sympathy to the avenger's victim?
8. Is Medea selecting the most effective way of punishing Jason when she decides to enact her revenge on their children? Support your answer with specific references from the play and your own experiences.
9. Which gods, if any, determine Medea's passion? How does this fit in with other works by Greek playwrights that you have read from this period?
10. Which of her adversaries, if any, have sufficient stature to modify the plot?
11. Is Medea simply the victim of circumstance? Is what happens to Medea more the result of her own nature than anything else?
12. It has been said that Medea is not really different in the end of the play than in the beginning, and it is a mistake to see her as a good but a passionate woman who descends into the ultimate horror only when forced to by circumstances. Agree or disagree with this statement.
13. Some critics claim that Medea is not tragic. Rather, they say, she is a purely passive figure, a helpless victim of her own passions, doomed by her nature to suffer and cause disaster.
14. Others regard Medea as a real tragic heroine, engaged in a real agon and a real choice. Decide whether you see Medea as a helpless victim or a tragic heroine, and support your argument with specific references from the drama.

RENAISSANCE TRAGEDY

During the first half of the sixteenth century, teachers in England began to produce Roman plays in the schools. The effect of this became clear when Nicholas Udall wrote *Ralph Roister Doister* (1538–1553), the first "true" English comedy, based on these Latin models. Strolling bands of players obtained these new plays as soon as they were available, and dozens of new plays, of dubious literary value, flooded the stages.

In 1572, laws were passed that categorized strolling players as vagabonds, and forbade their presence on the streets of London. The effect of these laws was to bring the players under the patronage of the nobility and eventually under the crown itself. Best known of all such troops was the King's Servants, so named after James I ascended to the throne.

Because of local opposition, when the first public theater was built in 1576 by James Burbage, it was located outside the city proper. James Burbage's sons rebuilt their theater in 1599 and named it the Globe. It was known as London's finest theater until it burned down in 1613, during a performance of Shakespeare's *Henry VIII*. It was rebuilt shortly thereafter.

Although there were individual differences, the theaters were basically very much alike. The playhouse itself was round or octagonal, with an open space or courtyard in the center. Spectators' seating surrounded the yard on three levels: At the front and projecting into the yard was the stage itself. Behind the stage were dressing rooms, script rooms, and a space for properties and costumes.

Most scholars believe that the stage had two parts: the inner stage, which was under the roof and fitted with a curtain, and the outer stage, which extended into the yard. In the later theaters, performances could take place on three levels of the inner stage. There was a trapdoor near the center of the apron (outer) stage.

Performances took place during the day. Evening was represented by characters carrying candles or torches, or saying appropriate lines of dialogue. There was copious use of music and elaborate, costly costumes.

OTHELLO BY WILLIAM SHAKESPEARE

Plot Summary

Act I. Iago and Roderigo are discussing Othello's marriage to Desdemona. Roderigo had been one of Desdemona's suitors, and he is furious that he did not know about the affair. Iago declares that since he was passed over for Othello's lieutenant, he too has reason to hate the Moor. They arrive at Brabantio's home to tell him that his daughter has eloped with Othello. Cassio tells Othello that he has been called before a military council. Brabantio and Roderigo enter and the scene becomes violent, as Brabantio, accusing Othello of having bewitched his daughter, demands that he be thrown into jail. Othello convinces him to take his complaint before the Duke. Later that night, Brabantio presents his case before the Duke. Othello tells how he courted his wife. Desdemona arrives, and while making it clear that she still loves her father, she asserts that she now belongs to Othello. Brabantio rejects his daughter. The Duke returns his attention to the war effort, directing Othello to defend Cyprus and become its new governor. Desdemona will rejoin him later. All the others leave, and Iago convinces Roderigo that he still may have a chance to win Desdemona. When Roderigo leaves, Iago asserts that money and fun are his real reasons for befriending Roderigo. Then he begins to plan his deception of Othello.

Act II. A storm at sea has crippled the Turkish fleet and delayed Othello's arrival at Cyprus. Iago's ship, with Desdemona on board, arrives before Othello's does, and Iago jokes to reassure her that her husband will arrive safely. Iago privately notes that Cassio is also distracting her with polite conversation, and makes plans to use this against him later. Finally Othello arrives and he and Desdemona joyously reunite. After they leave the stage, Iago convinces the foolish Roderigo that Desdemona actually loves Cassio and urges him to pick a fight with the lieutenant that night. Alone, Iago tells his wife, Emilia, about his suspicions concerning Othello's and Cassio's affairs. That night they feast in celebration of safe arrival and Othello's wedding, and Iago succeeds in making Cassio drunk and quarrelsome. Urged on by Iago, Cassio and Roderigo fight. Montano breaks in, accusing Cassio of being drunk. Enraged, Cassio wounds him, and Roderigo sounds the alarm. Othello hurries in, and based on what Iago implies, Othello finds Cassio at fault and fires him. Cassio realizes what has happened, and Iago convinces him to try to regain Othello's favor through Desdemona. Iago gloats over the trouble he has caused.

Act III. Some musicians serenade Othello and Desdemona as Iago helps Cassio arrange a private meeting with Desdemona. After Iago leaves, his wife takes Cassio to Desdemona.

Othello requests that Iago meet him to inspect the castle fortifications. Desdemona promises Cassio that she will do all that she can to help his cause. Othello and Iago enter, and Cassio, feeling ill at ease, leaves quickly. Othello notices this, and Iago points out how "guilty" Cassio seemed. Desdemona immediately presents Cassio's case, and Othello bends to her wishes. Iago begins to undermine Othello's faith in Desdemona, going so far as to suggest that she and Cassio are having an affair. Iago leaves, and Desdemona enters. She tries to soothe Othello's headache with a handkerchief, and they depart, the handkerchief left behind. Emilia picks it up and gives it to Iago, not realizing its importance: It was the first gift Othello gave to Desdemona. Othello re-enters, and demands that Iago give him proof of Desdemona's unfaithfulness. Iago responds that he heard Cassio talking in a dream of making love to Desdemona and says that he has seen Cassio wipe his beard with Desdemona's handkerchief. Enraged, Othello plots revenge and promotes Iago. Later, Desdemona again brings up Cassio's case, but Othello is only concerned about the handkerchief. Desdemona lies and says that she has not lost it, for Othello had told her that the token had magical powers and its loss would be a misfortune. Othello leaves. Iago and Cassio enter and discuss Othello's bad temper. Later, Cassio meets Bianca and asks her to copy the embroidery of the handkerchief, which he had found in his room.

Act IV. Othello rages when Iago tells him that Cassio admits that he is having an affair with Desdemona. Cassio enters, but Iago tells him to leave, for Othello has suffered an epileptic fit. Othello, recovered, agrees to hide while Iago questions Cassio about his behavior. Iago speaks to Cassio about his girlfriend, Bianca, but Othello, who cannot hear well where he is hiding, misinterprets the discussion, and assumes they are speaking about Desdemona. Bianca enters and refuses to copy the embroidery on the handkerchief; she and Cassio leave. Again Othello is enraged at what he sees as proof of his wife's infidelity. At Iago's suggestion, he agrees to strangle Desdemona in her bed while Iago murders Cassio. Lodovico arrives with a letter that orders his return to Venice and appoints Cassio Governor of Cyprus. Desdemona tells Lodovico of the breach between Othello and Cassio. Her sympathy for Cassio angers Othello and he strikes and torments her. Othello, who has lost all control, leaves. Othello questions Emilia, who swears that Desdemona is true to him. He sends for Desdemona and she too swears that she has been chaste, but he will not believe her. She sends for Iago and asks how she can make Othello believe her. He tells her to remain calm. Later, Iago convinces Roderigo that they must murder Cassio. Emilia helps Desdemona prepare for bed and Desdemona swears that she loves her husband and would never deceive him.

Act V. Iago and Roderigo wait to murder Cassio. Cassio wounds Roderigo, and Iago wounds Cassio without being seen. Othello, passing by, hears Cassio calling out and believes that Iago's plan has succeeded and Cassio is dying. Lodovico and Gratiano enter, and we see that Cassio is still alive. Iago stabs Roderigo fatally while no one is watching. Bianca enters and Iago tries to fix the blame on her. Emilia enters and Iago sends her to Othello to tell him what has happened. Othello enters Desdemona's bedroom and smothers her, despite her pleas for mercy. Emilia pounds at the door with the news of Roderigo's murder, but Othello does not let her in until Desdemona seems to be dead. With her dying breath, Desdemona tries to hide Othello's guilt. Othello confesses the truth, explaining that Iago convinced him Desdemona was unfaithful. Emilia, horrified, tells him that Iago was lying and rushes out to publicize the crime. Othello explains what has happened to the others as they rush in. Emilia, realizing his error, explains that she took the handkerchief herself for Iago. Furious, Iago kills his wife. Othello wounds Iago for his lies, as the full truth is exposed. In complete despair over Desdemona's death, Othello stabs himself and dies kissing his wife.

Theme of Othello

The theme of this play is *jealousy,* affecting all the characters, but most evident in Othello when interwoven with his *pride.* For example, in III, iii, Othello says concerning his wife:

> I had rather be a toad
> And live upon the vapour of a dungeon
> Than keep a corner in the thing I love
> for others' uses. (III, iii, 270–73)

At first Othello thinks that the solution to jealousy is easy: he need only convert his love to hate. But he finds that this is impossible, for the love and hate are interwoven, and in his conflict, he convinces himself that killing Desdemona will bring about justice (V, ii, 1–17). But after he is convinced of his horrible error, he berates himself before rising to the proud resolution of his final speech. Although jealousy is shown most heartrendingly in Othello, the motivating spirit of envy is Iago.

If we believe what Othello himself says, he is not easily made jealous (V, ii, 345), while Iago, in contrast, is the very embodiment of the emotion. We see in him pride and hate, love transformed into self-admiration. Iago has been considered by several critics, Samuel Taylor Coleridge the most well known, to be an incarnation of "motiveless malignity"; others have seen him as a morality Vice figure. If we consider him a true portrait of a human being, his jealousy—as well as any motivation for it—is difficult to account for. He may, as critic Marvin Rosenberg has suggested, be a proud man resentful of the necessity of bowing before his superiors. It may also be that his hatred is abnormal and irrational, especially as directed toward women. What we can be sure of is the strength of his anguish; it gnaws at his innards (II, i, 306).

Other characters who exhibit signs of jealousy are Roderigo, Bianca, and as some have suggested Brabantio. The most obviously jealous of these characters is Roderigo, whose unrequited love for Desdemona leads him, with Iago's backing, to attempt murder.

Setting of Othello

The setting here of *Othello* is not as crucial as it is in *Macbeth* or *King Lear,* and there is no symbolic enlargement of the scene from the realm of the physical to that of the supernatural. There are two clear settings: The play begins in Venice, and at the beginning of Act II, moves to Cyprus for the rest of the action. Venice is the base of the action, and all the major characters except Othello and Cassio are Venetians. They bring with them to Cyprus what they had been in Venice. Venice represents a peaceful, sophisticated, law-abiding city, as the scene with the Duke (I, iii) shows. We see that despite Brabantio's hysteria over his daughter's elopement, Venice metes out fair judgment and all of its citizens, except Iago, are fair people. We see the sophistication in Brabantio's description of the kind of possible husbands his daughter had rejected (I, ii). Cyprus, in sharp contrast to Venice, is "a town at war,/Yet wild, the people's hearts brimful of fear" (II, iii, 213–14). When she elects to follow her husband to Cyprus, Desdemona leaves behind all friends and family, creating an island of fatal isolation. As with other islands in Shakespeare, Cyprus is the site of strange happenings. But unlike many of his other plays, the events taking place on the island are not supernatural, for without Iago, Cyprus would be peaceful and pleasant.

Discussion/Writing Questions on *Othello*

1. Evaluate the "completeness" of Othello's love for Desdemona. Othello is convinced of her faithlessness by Iago, and some critics have said that he is too ready to believe her treacherous. Is this a flaw in Othello's character or is it evidence of a less than total love? Consider, for example, the following quote from I, iii, 167–68: "She lov'd me for the dangers I had passed,/And I lov'd her that she did pity them."

2. Some critics have said that Othello's tragic flaw is excessive pride; others have claimed that he is but the pawn of circumstances with a nature too open and easily convinced. Consider the following quote in your evaluation: "Come, Desdemona, I have but an hour/Of love, or worldly matters and direction,/To spend with thee. We must obey the time." (I, iii, 299–301)

3. Is Othello able to feel the sorrow of his ideal being corrupted, even in the midst of his passion? If so, how does this affect our opinion of him, and indeed, his stature as a tragic hero? Consider the following quotation: "So delicate with her needle! . . . Of so high and plenteous wit and invention! . . . But yet the pity of it, Iago! O Iago, the pity of it, Iago!" (IV, i, 198–207)

4. The idealism which colors Othello's love and creates his jealous rage is the cause of some of his self-deception, and turns the murder from passion into a ritual purge. Does Othello at last realize that it is not simple to cast off love? Does he ever fully understand his own motivation for the murder? Consider: "It is the cause, it is the cause, my soul. . . . Yet I'll not shed her blood, . . . Yet she must die, else she'll betray more men. . . . and I will kill thee,/And love thee after. . . . This sorrow's heavenly;/It strikes where it doth love." (V, ii, 1–22)

5. Describe Othello's character in the beginning of the play, especially as shown through the actions and descriptions of others. Consider I, iii, 284–286 and I, iii, 405–06. How do these early descriptions affect his later downfall?

6. Some critics have seen Othello's confidence in himself as a kind of naive complacency. Consider I, iii, 81–87: "Rude am I in my speech,/And little blessed with the soft phrase of peace; . . . And little of this great world can I speak/More than pertains to feats of broil and battle."

7. Samuel Johnson believed that the first act of the play could be omitted without harming the play in any way. What would change in not initially presenting the character of Brabantio, the setting, and the scene where the two lovers defend their marriage?

8. Do most of the vital scenes of the play take place in the evening or the daytime? What effect does this have on the atmosphere and theme of the play?

9. Iago calls the pair "an erring barbarian and a supersubtle Venetian," and some critics have seen this to refer to Othello and Desdemona as opposites. Explain what he means. Is this the reason for what follows in the play or is the tragedy caused by other factors? Explain.

10. Samuel Taylor Coleridge and Harley Granville Barker call Iago "motiveless," believing that he has no reasons for his actions. What reasons does Iago himself give? Other critics, such as Marvin Rosenberg credit him with definite reasons for his actions. Explain who is correct by citing specific reasons for your belief.

11. Of the main characters, Desdemona has the fewest lines, yet her character—courage, devotion, chastity among the most evident qualities—is very clear. How is this accomplished? Trace specific examples.

12. Can nontraditional interpretations of the play be justified? For example, Sir Laurence Olivier portrayed Iago as a homosexual. Use specific examples to support your point of view.

13. Roderigo is the only character to whom Iago reveals his evil nature. What does this tell you about Roderigo's character?

14. Does the "universal appeal" of Othello suffer because Othello is less intellectually gifted than Hamlet or less socially important than Lear? Support your answer.

15. What "moral" can we draw from this play? What lessons does it have to teach us?

16. Iago believes that he is exacting revenge. If so, for what slights(s)?

17. Reconcile Emilia's lie to Desdemona about the stolen handkerchief with her impassioned defense of Desdemona in the final scene.

18. How does Othello's view of love change throughout the play? Is it ever a view held by another character?

19. Write an essay in which you describe one character as he/she appears through the eyes of another, such as Iago as seen by Othello.

MODERN TRAGEDY

Departing from conventional notions of realism, Arthur Miller redefined tragedy in his best-received play, *Death of a Salesman* (1949). His essay written the same year, "Tragedy and the Common Man," explains his aims in this play.

Miller begins by noting that there have been very few tragedies written in the modern age, most likely because man is "often held to be below tragedy—or tragedy above us." But he believes that "the common man is as apt a subject for tragedy in its highest sense as kings were." When tragedy is not the issue, he says, we never hesitate to attribute the same emotional and mental processes to the lowly as to the well-born, and if the tragic ability were truly only for the kingly, it would not happen that the mass of people would cherish tragedy above all other forms, let alone understand it.

He feels that "the tragic feeling is evoked in us when we are in the presence of a character who is ready to lay down his life . . . to secure personal dignity." Tragedy, then, is the result of a person's desire to evaluate himself justly.

A tragedy reveals in the hero what has been called the "tragic flaw," a characteristic not unique to the high-born. Miller feels that this flaw is not necessarily a weakness, but rather "an inherent unwillingness to remain passive in the face of what he [the hero] perceives to be a challenge to his dignity, his image of his rightful status." Those who accept their fate without active struggle are the flawless, he says, and most people fall into that category.

The terror and fear that are associated with tragedy result when this person acts against the scheme of things and, in the process, everything that has previously been blindly accepted is taken out and examined. In this attack on the seemingly stable universe, the individual and the audience feel the tragic emotions of terror and fear.

Most important, he concludes, we learn from this process, and we fear being displaced from our niche in the world, of losing our images of ourselves. It is the common man who experiences this fear most profoundly.

If we accept that tragedy is the result of man's desire to evaluate himself fairly, his destruction in the attempt points to an evil in the environment, not in himself, Miller asserts. This is the discovery of moral law.

Tragedy celebrates, then, the desire for freedom, and the struggle to assert this freedom demonstrates the "indestructible will of man to achieve his humanity." As opposed to the Greek definition, Miller feels that in tragedy the possibility of victory must be present; otherwise it descends to the level of pathos.

It is time, he concludes, that the modern civilization, bereft of kings, takes up the mantle of tragedy and locates it in its logical place—"the heart and spirit of the average man."

DEATH OF A SALESMAN BY ARTHUR MILLER

Plot Summary

As the play opens, Willy Loman, a traveling salesman for 34 years, has returned from a trip to New England. Exhausted, he tells his wife, Linda, that he is having difficulty keeping his mind on driving. He asks about his 34-year-old son, Biff, who has come home after being away a long time. Willy thinks back on the climactic football game of Biff's high school career, some 14 years ago, when universities around the country offered Biff football scholarships. But something thus far unexplained happened that year, and Biff flunked math, never graduated from high school, and never fulfilled his early promise. Later in the play, we find out that Biff had gone to Boston to tell his father that he had flunked math, confident that Willy, whom he greatly admired, would be able to reason with the math teacher. Biff discovered his father having an affair, and crushed that his idol could dishonor his family, lost all faith in Willy and to this day has held a grudge against his father.

Now Biff has returned home. He and his brother, Happy, discuss various jobs for which Biff might be suited. They decide that Biff should ask a former employer, Bill Oliver, for a $10,000 loan to start a business. They tell Willy of their plans, and Willy responds that together the "Loman Brothers" could conquer the world. Willy explains that the important thing is to be "well-liked" and personally attractive. They make plans to meet in a fancy restaurant the next day to celebrate.

Willy is so pleased with his boys' plans that he decides to ask his present boss, Howard Wagner, for a transfer from the New England territory to New York. Howard refuses his request and fires Willy, explaining that Willy's erratic behavior has been harming the firm. Willy, crushed and disoriented, goes to an old friend, his next-door neighbor Charley, to borrow enough money to pay his insurance premium. We find out that Willy has been borrowing $50 a week from Charley for quite some time, and pretending to Linda that he is still being paid salary and commission, when in fact he has received no salary for months. Even though Charley offers Willy a good job in New York, Willy refuses, saying he could never work for Charley. He goes to the restaurant.

Biff and Happy meet, and Biff tells Happy that his whole life has been an illusion. He explains to Happy that he has stolen himself out of every job that he has had, and wants to make everyone, especially Willy, understand that he no longer is bringing home any prizes. But when Willy arrives, he tells his sons that he has been fired, and he refuses to listen to Biff's realizations. Willy pretends that Biff has another appointment with Bill Oliver the next day, despite Biff's confession that he was fired from Oliver's employ for stealing a carton of basketballs. Willy is furious and about to make a scene. When Willy gets up to go to the bathroom, Biff leaves the restaurant. Happy, who has picked up two women—his usual behavior—follows suit, leaving Willy all alone when he returns to the table.

Later that night, Biff returns home to find Willy planting seeds in the backyard and talking to his long-dead brother, Ben. Biff explains to Willy that he thinks it would be better for the whole family if they break off and never see each other again. He again explains that he is a "lo-man," a "dime a dozen," and not a leader of men. But Willy once again refuses to see the truth in what Biff is saying, and Biff breaks down and cries to Willy to see what they really are. Willy thinks Biff is still a child who once again needs him and resolves to commit suicide to leave Biff the $20,000 insurance money and enable him to once again be magnificent. Willy goes through with his plan, but at his funeral we see that he has died a forgotten man, mourned by a handful of family and friends.

Structure

The structure of the play is unusual, told partly through the mind and memory of Willy Loman. Thus, the time fluctuates between 1942 and 1928, and the audience must be aware of the differences in time. To accomplish this, the *setting* must be employed in a suggestive way. When the action is in the present (1942), the characters observe all the doors and walls, but when the time shifts, they ignore the physical barriers and walk right through them. Another tool to show the shift in time is music. When the time shifts into the past, we have the flute, evocative of Willy's father and his lost youth; the blaring music of Willy's affair; the joyous music of the boys' past accomplishments. The characters' posture also changes to show the change in time. In the present, Willy is stooped with the weariness of an old man, but in the flashbacks, he carries himself forcefully. In the same way, Biff and Happy change, appearing in the past dressed as youngsters. The structure of the set underscores one of the main themes of the play, *illusion versus reality,* and shows how Willy has carried the illusions of the past into the present, especially when he calls on his dead brother Ben to guide him.

Recurrent Motifs

Debts. Willy and Linda, unable to afford all they wish, have bought many items on installment and discover that the items break before the payments are finished. They are constantly in debt, as they fall victim to the advertisements for the "best" of everything. The motif rises to the tragic as Willy makes the last payment on his house and then commits suicide so that as the house is all paid up, he is all used up. This is summarized in the "Requiem."

Personal attractiveness/Being well-liked. Willy believes that a person must not just be liked, but must be *well*-liked in order to be a success. Willy decided this after an encounter with a salesman named Dave Singleman (Single-man vs. Lo-man), who was so loved and respected that he could enter any town, pick up a phone, and get an order. When he died, people came from all over to his funeral. Willy decided that this is what he wants for himself, and for his favorite son, Biff. He cannot understand why a boy with such personal attractiveness could be so lost. We discover that Willy has rationalized many of the boy's mistakes and outright crimes with the notion of personal attractiveness: Willy tells Biff early on that the coach won't mind that Biff has stolen a ball because Biff is "well-liked." We see at the funeral that despite his belief, being well-liked does not guarantee success or happiness and that Willy's life has been based on false dreams.

Stealing. We see that Biff has stolen himself out of every job that he has ever had, and that Willy excuses the thefts if performed by someone who is well-liked. This motif brings the drama to its climax, for when Biff steals the pen from Bill Oliver's office during the interview, he is forced to face the fact that he is a thief. This, in turn, makes him see himself and try to explain his character to his father.

Vital to New England. Willy refuses to ask for a transfer to New York initially because he says that "he is vital to New England." We see clearly that he is a hindrance to the company, but for his own self-respect, Willy must continue to believe that he is the cornerstone of New England sales. In a flashback, we see Willy promising to take his sons to New England, but the plan never materializes, for it would force Willy to see that he is not important there or anywhere else. He cannot face the fact that he is not popular or well-liked, and has no friends. He falls easily for the affair, as it serves to build his ego. Here he feels the importance that is denied him as he waits outside closed doors hoping for orders. When Howard fires him, he must construct new illusions, but the world that he has created is so strong that he retreats further and further into his illusions. As he is preparing for suicide, he visualizes all the hundreds of salesmen and buyers who will come to his funeral—but none did come. This motif comments on Willy's life of illusion and how he has transformed illusion to reality to enable him to continue his drudgery of daily life. When maintaining the illusion becomes impossible, there is no reason for him to continue living.

Boxed in. The physical image that best describes Willy's inner state is one of enclosure. The more Willy feels boxed in, the more he feels the need to do something with his hands, to leave something physical for his family. This is introduced in the first scene, as Willy comments that their house has become so boxed in by the larger apartments around them that they no longer have any sunlight and cannot grow anything in the garden. Later we see that Biff feels the same way that Willy does, but when Biff suggests that the Lomans should be "mixing cement on some open plain," Willy refuses to acknowledge even this truth, and responds that even "your grandfather was better than a carpenter." We see throughout the play that Willy is boxed in by the city and that the only way out is through his death. After his death, with his sons unworthy of the sacrifice, Willy is permanently boxed in his little plot of ground.

Time: "The woods are burning". When Willy says that "the woods are burning," he means that life is closing in on him, and he no longer has the time to accomplish what he once thought he could. This is contrasted to Willy's image of his brother, Ben, who escaped to conquer the jungle of life. Ben walked into the jungle at 17 and walked out four years later a rich man. This is what Willy so desired for himself—to conquer life, not to be conquered by it. Therefore, to Willy, life is a jungle that he is unable to penetrate, and it becomes a burning woods constantly closing in on him. By the end, when time has completely closed in on him, the jungle becomes the darkness of death which Willy thought he could conquer by suicide.

Ben. Willy's brother, Ben, stands for all that Willy wants to be. Ben is a financial success, the opposite of Willy. Ben is also shown as cruel and cold, ruthlessly manipulative. He represents another side of Willy's illusions, as Willy refuses to see Ben for what he really is and admires him unquestioningly for his financial success.

Flute. Flute music opens and closes the play. We discover halfway through the play that Willy's father made and sold flutes. His father was also a salesman, but with one important difference: Willy sells things that others have made; his father sold items he made himself. Unlike Willy, his father was a great adventurer. Thus, the flute at the end mocks Willy, capturing his inability to be bold and brave, and suggesting the failure of the illusions that have controlled his world.

Stockings. Linda mends stockings and seems to be continually doing laundry, suggesting she is the eternal wife and mother figure, unable to help Willy strike out on his own.

There has been much written on Linda: Some say she is as guilty as Willy for tying him down to his meaningless illusions; others say she was the mainstay that gave him the strength to continue as long as he did. The mended stockings also evoke the image of the stockings that Willy gave to his mistress, showing, to Biff at least, that Willy denied things to Linda to support his wanderings with at least one other. Therefore, the stockings symbolize both Linda's personality and Willy's guilt.

Losing Weight. Happy is the neglected son, all the attention having been focused for so long on Biff. Thus it comes as no surprise when Happy deserts Willy at the restaurant, for he is acting toward Willy as he perceives Willy acted toward him. He speaks of losing weight in an attempt to gain attention, as he lies down and backpedals to illustrate the sincerity of his efforts, but no one pays him any attention. In the same way, he announces that he is going to get married when the scene gets too tense or he wishes attention. It should come as no surprise that he is shallow and a dedicated chaser of women.

Miller's style

Miller tries to recast tragedy into an American mold, using a "lo-man" as the hero rather than the traditional high-born, heroic model. Additionally, he captures the essential patterns of American speech and recasts them into phrases that remain in our minds, like the refrains of ballads. "Isn't it remarkable" and "He is not just liked but well-liked" are examples. The scenes of the present have a heavy and serious quality to the speech while the past carries a lighter, happier note.

Sample Questions to Consider

1. In what ways is this play a reworking of the traditional notions of tragedy?
2. Does Willy qualify as a tragic hero? Support your answer with specific examples and compare Willy's situation and behavior with the traditional mold.
3. Who is the central character of this play and why?
4. Is Linda Loman the helping, caring wife she appears to be on the surface or is she another force that drags Willy down, tying him to his pathetic illusions?
5. How much of Willy's tragedy is caused by his own personality and how much is caused by the reality of American life? What comments on American society is Miller making in this play?
6. How do illusion and reality function in this play?

Modern Drama

PSYCHOLOGICAL DRAMA—EUGENE O'NEILL

Eugene O'Neill (1888–1953) is considered by many modern critics to be the only American dramatist who can be ranked among the great figures of the European theatre. His brooding presence looms over the landscape of modern drama to affect all subsequent dramatists. His seriousness and devotion to artistic integrity remain landmarks in the American theater tradition. Most see August Strindberg as the main literary influence upon O'Neill, as both mercilessly exposed the corrosive and destructive cruelty family members can practice against one another when bound together in an ultimately fatal love-hate relationship. What some see as the best of his long plays appeared between 1928 and 1933: *Strange Interlude, Mourning Becomes Electra,* and *Ah, Wilderness* (his only successful comedy).

O'Neill's Philosophy

The Atmosphere of the Times. Many had begun to question the traditional values of Western civilization, feeling that God was dead and that it was up to man to create an ideal world using science in place of religion. This new world would benefit the common man, so long repressed by the wealthy. We can see this change acted out in the schools of Naturalism and Realism, which flourished in the modern period. As mentioned previously, the Naturalists felt that man was prey to the twin influences of environment and heredity. Stephen Crane, Frank Norris, and Theodore Dreiser, the chief Naturalists, often exposed conditions in the lower classes of society. This intellectual change was paralleled in social swings, as the rise of mass media (movies, chiefly), affordable automobiles for the masses, and a shift to the cities from the country, brought about the decline of the close-knit family.

Schopenhauer and Nietzsche. Arthur Schopenhauer (1788–1860) and Friedrich Nietzsche (1844–1900) were two German philosophers who had a great influence upon O'Neill. From Schopenhauer, O'Neill concluded that man is at the mercy of his emotions and that individuality and originality are thus illusions. From Nietzsche, he found encouragement to rebel against Christianity and the middle-class values of the day and to embrace the credo of an atheistic freethinker who had rejected middle-class mores. This, of course, fit right in with the change in temper of the beginning of the twentieth century.

Freud. Sigmund Freud (1856–1939), an Austrian physician and psychiatrist, had a profound influence on the literature of the early twentieth century with his writings on the unconscious, the underside of man's personality. He felt that the unconscious, which holds the keys to man's sexuality, was the determining factor in all of man's actions. This was corrupted into the notion that it is not good to repress basic desires, particularly sexual desires. Freud felt that religion would fade away as science came to dominate all of life. These notions were also shown in the temper of the time.

In the works of these three men, O'Neill found backing for his belief that man is controlled by forces he can neither understand nor control. Man's goal is to be able to express himself freely and to set himself against these forces. Despite the ensuing battle, which may be wonderful in its power, life is, in the end, meaningless and sad, especially when man is no longer in his prime.

O'Neill's Changes in the Theater

O'Neill is considered an important playwright because his plays almost singlehandedly created a *serious* American theater; before O'Neill, little had been performed but romantic melodrama. With the coming of O'Neill, the theater became a place where audiences could question man's place in the scheme of things and probe the darker sides of their own natures.

In O'Neill's plays, man is pitted against human and physical nature, as man is indifferent to his fellow man, competing for sexual and individual fulfillment. Above all, man is in conflict with a force that drives him to his doom. He is compelled to fight against this power, even though his efforts are always doomed to fail.

The main structural change O'Neill effected in the theater is the *long monologue*. This is paralleled in the experimental novel, as practitioners of both forms were seeking means to express internal workings to their audience. In *Strange Interlude*, the characters wear masks in an attempt to externalize the internal; in *The Hairy Ape* O'Neill uses backdrops to express the play's meaning symbolically.

MOURNING BECOMES ELECTRA

Source

O'Neill's play is taken from the Greek trilogy, the *Oresteia*, by Aeschylus (525–456 B.C.). The source describes the Trojan War and the events that follow. The Atreus family has been cursed by a terrible deed: When Thyestes seduced his wife, Atreus chopped up Thyestes' children and served them to him to eat. Only Aegisthus escaped. Many years later when Atreus' two sons, Menelaus and Agamemnon, had grown up, Paris, a visitor from Troy, kidnapped Menelaus's wife, Helen, setting off the Trojan War. Agamemnon, commanding the Greek army, met with ill fortune and sacrificed his daughter, Iphigenia, to ensure calm winds and a good voyage. His wife, Clytemnestra, pledged revenge. She gave her son, Orestes, to the King of Phocis (for him to raise) and waited for the day she could get her revenge. Aegisthus and Clytemnestra became lovers, and plotting together, were able to bring about Agamemnon's death. Orestes returned and vowed to avenge his father's murder, urged on by the promptings of his sister, Electra. Orestes killed both his mother and her lover, Aegisthus. He was punished by the Furies, spirits of vengeance, who drove him from place to place. After a trial held by the gods, Orestes was freed from the Furies.

O'Neill's Changes in the Source

Classical Greek drama has at its root the belief that man is controlled by the gods. O'Neill used the twin forces of heredity and environment instead of the Furies, thereby making Fate an internal force. Thus a person's behavior is determined by his past and his psychological background.

Instead of basing the play around the male figure, Orestes, O'Neill decided to use the female, Electra, as his protagonist.

Also there is no matricide. Instead, the mother, here called Christine Mannon, kills herself after murdering her husband.

There is no idea of justice—only the haunting of the living by the sins of the dead. Here we follow the aftermath of a crime of passion, not its expiation.

Comparison chart

Clytemnestra = Christine Mannon
Electra   = Lavinia Mannon
Agamemnon = Ezra Mannon
Orestes   = Orin Mannon
Aegisthus = Adam Brant

Setting

There are three plays here, which take place either in the spring or summer of 1865–66, as he tells us in the beginning. The plays are set "on the outskirts of one of the small New England seaport towns." Some critics have said that O'Neill often selected New England settings because the tradition of that part of the United States is characterized by introspection, religious and philosophic questioning, and deep relationships between people. (This is found in the writings of Ralph Waldo Emerson, Henry David Thoreau, and Emily Dickinson, to name a few of the New England writers of the middle to late nineteenth century). Most of the action takes place in the Mannon house itself, built as a Greek temple, with six tall columns. In *Homecoming*, the first play of the trilogy, the first act begins at sunset outside the home. The second takes place in Ezra's study, at the same time of day. The third act is outside the house during the night. The fourth act is in Ezra's bedroom at night. The background music is "Shenandoah," which O'Neill felt "more than any other [song] holds in it the brooding rhythm of the sea." In *The Hunted*, the second play, the first act takes place outside the house during the night. The second act is in the sitting room; the third act in the study. The fourth act is set in the clipper ship; the fifth act again in front of the house. The music is the same. In *The Haunted*, the final play, we begin in Act I outside the house, but this time the house is all boarded up. In Act I scene 2, we move inside and remain there for the next two acts; we go back outside for Act 4.

Theme

The characters in the play destroy themselves because they cannot get along with one another—or with anyone else, for that matter. They will not reach out to form relationships, and so they cannot love. We see here the *isolated self*, in an *amoral universe*, as the characters act out what seems right to them without regard for those around them. What they see as vital is self and self-gratification. Only in the sexual act do we see the possibility of the desire to live a full life, as we see in the relationship of Christine and Adam, and in the world of Adam's mother. They are warm and unrestrained, and represent life, as the Mannons—especially Ezra and Lavinia—represent death.

Structure

Mourning Becomes Electra is divided into three parts, as mentioned earlier. The first and third plays have four acts each; the middle play has five. Obviously, O'Neill was balancing the plays this way.

The play is also organized in a *circular* manner. We see this in the character of Lavinia. In *Homecoming*, she is an unattractive and sexless woman, but by the beginning of the final play, she is a mature and attractive woman. At the conclusion of the trilogy, she is once again wooden and lifeless, cloistered within the Mannon house. Her character development, to trace just one of the players, demonstrates O'Neill's use of a circular organization.

The play is also organized *thematically*. In *Homecoming,* for example, the themes of return, retribution, and curse form a thematic unity. The play marks a return to center as the Mannons move back into their house to work out the old hatreds. Here, though, we have an inversion of the usual meaning of "center" from a place of love and comfort to a place of hatred and evil. The characters must work through the hatred until death can expiate all sins.

Sample Questions to Consider

1. Why is Eugene O'Neill considered the most important dramatist of the twentieth-century American stage?
2. What is O'Neill's philosophy and how did it evolve from the contemporary intellectual movements of his day?
3. How did O'Neill change the theater and its conventions?
4. What was the source of *Mourning Becomes Electra* and how did O'Neill change it to suit his thematic needs?
5. How is the setting of this play important to its theme?
6. Does O'Neill's notion of structure differ from or concur with the classic Aristotelian theory?
7. Does O'Neill follow the traditions of tragedy with regard to theme here?
8. What symbols are present here and how do they function?

A VARIATION ON FORM—THORNTON WILDER

Thornton Wilder (1897–1975), unlike such contemporary dramatists as Samuel Beckett, Harold Pinter, and Eugène Ionesco, felt that man is welcome in the universe and that his attitude must be one of affirmation, not despair. This is shown in his theory of drama. In "Some Thoughts on Playwriting" (1941), Wilder sets forth his guidelines:

- Drama depends on collaborators, and a dramatist should write so as to take advantage of the skills of an actor.
- Drama must appeal to the majority of people. To hold the audience, the main techniques must be action and movement.
- Drama depends on pretense, so little spectacle is necessary.
- Time is always in the present (He violates this in "The Skin of Our Teeth").

These precepts are evident in his best-known play, *Our Town.* It has universal appeal, as shown first in the *setting,* a typical and fictional small town in America called Grover's Corners. The stage set is also in keeping with his precepts, for there is a very minimal set here—a table and a few chairs, two ladders, and two stools. The ladders are used at one point to stand for the second-floor rooms of the Gibbs and Webb homes; at another, they represent the drug store counter. The *time* is the present, as the stage manager tells us. The *characters* also evince this universality, for Wilder provides all we would expect in Small Town, U.S.A.: a paperboy, a milkman, a soda jerk, a high school sports hero, a church organist, a country doctor, the next-door neighbors who fall in love, etc. We also see this in the names, common to any American town. The action takes place from 1901 to 1913, covering the cycles of love, marriage, and death. The events of this small town achieve mythic proportion as the Stage Manager links them to the same cycle of an ancient Babylonian George and Emily, and we realize that love, marriage, and death are events common to all people at all times.

ANALYSIS OF *OUR TOWN*

Structure and Time

As the play opens, we see that there is no curtain and little scenery. The most unusual aspect of this play is the Stage Manager, a figure who can most probably be traced back to Greek drama and the chorus. The chorus commented on the play, interspersing its observations with the characters' dialogue. As the number of characters in the Greek plays increased, the chorus's role diminished. This same technique is also used in some of the plays by Eugene O'Neill, T. S. Eliot, and Tennessee Williams. In *Our Town,* the Stage Manager assumes the roles of a woman in the street, the druggist, and the minister. The play is divided into the usual three acts, and the Stage Manager opens each. He is also the last character to speak in each, and so functions as a framing device. His final remarks in acts I and II are brief, but at the end of act III he talks at greater length, in order to recapture the informal mood of the beginning of the play.

Act I, called "Daily Life," takes place on May 7, 1901, and is a typical day in the life of a small New England town. Act II is called "Love and Marriage," and the majority of the action takes place on July 7, 1904, the day George and Emily are married. There is a flashback in this act which takes us back to the day George and Emily first realized their love for each other. Act III takes place on a summer day in 1913. The act is not directly named, but the reader can surmise that it concerns death since most of the action concerns Emily's funeral and conversations among the dead in the graveyard. There is a flashback in this act also, to February 11, 1899, the date of Emily's twelfth birthday. The development of the action in acts I and II is parallel, as the dialogue switches from the Gibbs to the Webb home. The two scenes played in this way are the breakfast scene and the wedding morning scene.

Scenery

As mentioned earlier, there is no curtain and little scenery. The stage is half lit, and as the audience enters, the Stage Manager is placing a table and three chairs on the left of the stage and another table and three chairs on the right. He also sets out a bench which represents the corner of the Webb home and two flower-covered trellises which show the backyards of the adjacent Gibbs and Webb homes.

Through his gestures and descriptions, the Stage Manager creates an impression of the town, bordered by mountains and hills, and containing the railroad station, the churches, and the various ethnic neighborhoods. The town hall, post office, and jail are contained in the same building. He then describes the cemetery and the train whistle announces the arrival of the 5:45 train for Boston.

Many of the conventional props in the kitchen are imaginary, and the actors pretend they are using them. Thus Mrs. Gibbs raises an imaginary kitchen shade; Dr. Gibbs sets down an imaginary black doctor's bag; Mrs. Webb goes through the motions of putting wood on the stove, lighting it, and then preparing breakfast; Dr. Gibbs reads an imaginary newspaper. The actual props are few: an apron for Mrs. Webb, and hat and handkerchief for Dr. Gibbs, and books encircled by a strap for the children hurrying off to school. We hear the sound of milk bottles rattling, but Howie Newsome carries imaginary bottles, and strokes Bessie, the imaginary horse. This continues through the play, as Mr. Webb mows an imaginary lawn, and the children mount ladders to the imaginary second floor. In the flashback in the final act, on the day of Emily's twelfth birthday, the audience is given a summary of all the imaginary props and scenes of the beginning of the play, including the newspaper, milk bottles, and breakfast scene.

Some of this technique is taken from the Japanese Noh drama, where a player walks around the stage to indicate a long journey or rides a stick to simulate a horse.

Music

Music is used symbolically to underscore the theme of the typical small town and the universality of its appeal. The works are well known to the audience. At Emily's wedding, for example, Simon plays the traditional entrance hymn from Lohengrin and the familiar exit hymn from Mendelssohn's "Wedding March." As weddings are the most staid and traditional of the archetypal ceremonies common to most people, the music is exactly what we would expect to hear. In the same manner, the choir sings "Blessed Be The Tie That Binds" and "Love Divine, All Loves Excelling" at the wedding. Another traditional hymn is practiced by the choir in act I: "Art Thou Weary, Art Thou Languid." These selections fit perfectly with Wilder's description of Grover's Corners as a symbolic farm town.

Sound Effects

Sound effects function here in the same manner as the music, to underscore the nature of Grover's Corners and the appeal the small town holds for all of us. Only those sounds common to a small town in the early 1900s are used, and these are kept to a minimum. Since the story begins at dawn, we hear the cock crow and the whistle from the train headed toward Boston. This is followed by the sounds of Howie Newsome's imaginary horses and the clinking of imaginary milk bottles. Later in the morning, we hear the factory whistle from the Cartwright factory, the sounds of children headed for school, and the sounds of Mrs. Gibbs feeding the chickens.

Theme

Juxtaposed against the backdrop of the small town, Wilder is telling us that we do not appreciate life and all the wonderful little moments it has to offer until it is too late. Wilder celebrates all these little moments: rising, eating breakfast, going off to school, homework, etc., and he succeeds in raising these little pieces of time, the common events of daily life, to the level of ritual, a sequential celebration of the rites of life. This is important in the mainstream of twentieth-century literature, for most of Wilder's contemporaries were satirizing small-town America at the very time Wilder was celebrating it. Sinclair Lewis' *Main Street,* Sherwood Anderson's *Winesburg, Ohio,* Hamlin Garland's *Main Travelled Roads,* and Edgar Lee Master's *Spoon River Anthology* all decry the stultifying effects of the small town on the inhabitants, particularly on the sensitive artistic soul, who must escape to survive. Many of the writers of this period came from such small towns themselves—F. Scott Fitzgerald, Ernest Hemingway, Ezra Pound, T. S. Eliot, Sherwood Anderson, Sinclair Lewis—and initially did not look upon their hometowns with pleasure. Even people like Edith Wharton, who came from a very wealthy

New York area, created a mean and nasty vision of small town life in her "Starkfield" (the very name is symbolic) in *Ethan Frome*. The bitter cold of the town is reflected in the cold of the inhabitants' hearts, and the town, as much as the character's personality and circumstances, traps the individual and destroys him. Wilder, in sharp contrast to his contemporaries, points out these little details of small town life as vital and strengthening. Emily regrets that she never lived her life more fully, appreciating every tiny detail of everything about Grover's Corners. While some critics have said that the real theme and tragedy of *Our Town* is that the characters are not interested in anything beyond Grover's Corners and their everyday mundane life, the fact remains that the people here do not view life any differently and less intensely than any other person in any other setting, despite what other writers were saying at this time about the soul-destroying effects of small-town life.

Symbols

In order to underscore the universality of his message, Wilder uses the symbol of numbers. For example, the Stage Manager does not say that three years have passed but that the sun has risen over a thousand times. When he tells us how hardworking Mrs. Gibbs and Mrs. Webb are, he mentions the thousands of meals they have cooked in their lives, and adds that all 2,642 of the town's inhabitants have eaten dinner and that all those dishes have been washed. His purpose here is to give the play the necessary size to make its theme meaningful to every person, not just the handful that actually live in small towns in America.

THEATER OF THE ABSURD

"Absurd" originally meant "out of harmony" in a musical sense, and in common language, "ridiculous," but when applied to the Theater of the Absurd, the term takes on a different meaning. According to Eugène Ionesco, "Absurd is that which is devoid of purpose." When man is cut off from his roots, all his actions become senseless, useless, and absurd. This sense of anguish and uselessness in man's contemporary condition is found in the works of Samuel Beckett, Arthur Adamov, Eugène Ionesco, Jean Genet, and even Jean-Paul Sartre and Albert Camus, slightly earlier writers. The main difference between Sartre and Camus and the others in the list is that these two present their themes—the senselessness of life and devaluation of ideals—in a lucid and highly structured manner, while the other dramatists do not. The Theater of the Absurd expresses its themes through the disregard of rational devices and anticipated forms of structure. The Theater of the Absurd strives to blend form and content: If the world lacks form and focus, if all is useless, then the *form* of the play must be equally amorphous. The Theater of the Absurd does not *argue* about the absurdity of man's condition; it simply *presents* it, in terms of concrete stage images of the uselessness of life in the modern world. It is this attempt at integration of matter and form which distinguishes the Theater of the Absurd from the Existentialist theater (Camus and Sartre).

Luigi Pirandello. Pirandello has sometimes been considered the first of the Absurdists. Certainly he was one of the first to question who we are and how we appear to ourselves and others. Much of what he writes is hilariously funny, but it is also terrifying in what it says about man and the contemporary world. In *Six Characters in Search of an Author,* we are set in the middle of a play-within-a-play, and we must set aside our ability to rationalize, for in this play "real" people play at being what they are not. Suppose, questions the author, that there is a further "reality" that transcends "real" actors and "real" theater. Suppose there is an absolute reality that is art, the reality experienced by the characters the artist has created, who have undergone such an immediate reality that they must be set aside. And further suppose that they turn up in the world of make-believe that people create in the theater, and feel that their own version of "reality" is not able to be imitated and interpreted, existing as it does in an absolute that is known only to themselves and is not accesible to "real" people. Thus Pirandello is questioning what makes up reality and illusion. The audience realizes that the characters exist in a loop of time that circles back onto itself, as the characters are doomed to be what they are, nothing more and nothing less, for all eternity of written expression. They are, in the final analysis, far more "real" than the audience, who lives, after all, in a world of its own illusions. What we are left with is the question of what is real and who is really alive? What is imagination and who is trapped within it?

Harold Pinter. Harold Pinter generally rejects all labels, but his work is usually classified with the Theater of the Absurd, because of the elements of his plays. Thus the settings are often claustrophobic rooms and the atmosphere or mood is so frightening as to lead one critic to call his plays the "Comedy of Menace." Like Kafka and Beckett, Pinter finds menace in the ambiguity of the contemporary world. The characters express themselves in language that is often inarticulate and sometimes incoherent. As with the language of many other Absurdist plays, the rhythm of the idiom delves more deeply into reality than does the commonplace speech it seems to echo. The language expresses one of Pinter's themes: There can be no verbal certainty in this modern universe. We also find enormous violence in his plays, a reflection of the violence in twentieth-century life. In his later works, sex becomes a metaphor for the destruction of the individual. *The Dumb Waiter* is a case in point.

Edward Albee. Edward Albee's *themes* are similar to Pinter's: the substitution of false for real values in contemporary society, a criticism of smugness, and an exploration of violence and its effects. *The Zoo Story,* for example, looks into the animalistic violence that is barely covered by a thin veneer of civilization; this violence is revealed by the end of the play. It also details the loneliness and frustration of contemporary man, isolated from human contact by society and self. Albee's *symbols* and *allusions* underscore the emptiness of man's life today. Classical mythology, recalling the greatness of myths no longer applicable to modern life, is summoned up in Jerry's reference to his landlady and her dog as "the gatekeepers of my dwelling" and to the dog as "a descendant of the puppy that guarded the gates of hell or some such resort." Biblical parallels, suggesting how empty man's life is without faith, are present in such lines as Jerry's "So be it!" and "I came unto you . . . and you have comforted me. Dear Peter." Peter's response, "Oh my God!" is ironic in this context. Several critics have noticed parallels between Peter and the rock on which institutions are erected and Jerry as a Christ-figure or a Christ-parody. In any event, Albee's plays echo the themes and techniques of the Theater of the Absurd.

COMEDY

Comedy is a type of drama wherein the audience is amused. Generally it shows a movement from unhappiness to happiness, entertaining rather than distressing the audience.

Comedy is generally divided into two categories: *high* and *low*. High comedy is also called *social comedy, comedy of manners,* or *drawing room comedy.* It is intellectual and sophisticated. There may not be much action as it is given more to words than to frantic rushing around. The character development tends to be rather extensive, and the humor arises through a reversal of normal values. At the other end of the scale is *farce,* which shares many of the qualities of melodrama, but is intended to amuse and provoke laughter. Farce is defined as *low comedy,* but that does not imply it is of lesser quality than high comedy. High comedy tends to have a rather narrow intellectual appeal, while low comedy, such as farce, has a much broader, anti-intellectual appeal. There are a great many jokes and sight gags in low comedy, operating on the premise that this is a wacky world, populated by a lot of wild people, where logic and reason have flown out the window. The more a character attempts to find sanity in this insane world, the more likely things are to go awry.

Etherege, Wycherley, Congreve, and other playwrights immediately following the Restoration of Charles I to the throne of England in 1660 wrote what is called *Restoration comedy* of a special sort often referred to as *comedy of manners* or *comedy of wit,* full of cynical and quick repartee.

Comedy of humors is a term applied to plays whose characters represent types of moods, such as the jealous husband, the silly wife, and so forth. A "humor" was the term applied to body fluids that were thought to control man's behavior. There were four "humors"—blood, phlegm, yellow bile, and black bile—and a proper mixture of these elements was thought to produce a well-adjusted person while too much of any one element would distort personality. The word "humor" survives in such phrases as "He's in a bad humor today." Words like "phlegmatic" and "choleric" are still applied to personality. Ben Jonson's plays exemplify this type of comedy.

"Humor" characters are common in *situational comedy,* where the characters are placed by a clever plot into a situation that displays their absurdity; for example, a man who wishes for nothing but silence is forced into the company of a woman who talks constantly.

Farce is a variety of comedy that is based not on clever language or character subtleties, but on broadly humorous situations, such as a man entering the ladies' room by mistake. There is usually a great deal of meaningless movement and very broad facial expressions.

Slapstick is farce that relies on physical assault for humor. There is a lot of falling down and hitting in these works.

There is an in-between area of comedy, neither low nor high, which we call *straight comedy,* or *comedy of sensibility.* Like their counterparts in the drama, the characters here tend to be unsophisticated people who can experience suffering as well as fun. The plot is developed mainly through characterization, shunning what it sees as the vulgarities of farce as well as the narrow intellectualization of high comedy. This genre shows the charm of the ordinary man, not allowing the audience to become sentimental, even if the pain and suffering strike a little too close to home.

Comedy can also be classified according to specific subject matter:

Romantic comedies   show the stage-universe as a delightful pretend land where the main figures are lovers and all works out for the best. This is seen in Shakespeare's comedies.

Critical comedies	have main characters who are often ridiculed, seen especially in Molière's works.
Rogue comedies	such as Jonson's *Alchemist,* have as main characters pleasant scoundrels whose adventures entertain us, perhaps because they represent what we would like to experience in our more rebellious moments.

WHAT IS COMIC?

What is comic has been the topic of studies too numerous to count. Most begin with the distinction between *wit* and *humor. Wit,* from the Old English "witan," to know, has various meanings, but most agree with John Locke's definition: "The assemblage of ideas, and putting those ideas together with quickness and variety." In the court of Charles II, a wit was an intellectual, as defined by the above. But "wit" has had various definitions, even within the work of a single author. In the eighteenth century, Alexander Pope, in his "Essay on Criticism," speaks of works that are "one glaring chaos and wild heap of wit," where "wit" is defined as something like fanciful imagination instead of judgment. But Pope also says that "True wit is nature to advantage dressed,/What oft was thought, but ne'er so well express'd." Here "wit" means something like a well-phrased and true common expression, or good sense. Later in the eighteenth century, Dr. Johnson commented on Pope's second definition, and called "wit": "That which is not obvious is, upon its first production, acknowledged to be just." In our day, wit has come to be associated with a particular kind of cleverness that is compressed and mocking, a striking observation so phrased as to evoke laughter and amusement. *Humor,* in contrast, is genial and pokes fun at eccentricities, including the speaker's. As George Meredith says in *On the Comic Spirit,* "If you laugh all round him [a ridiculous character], tumble him, roll him about, deal him a smack, and drop a tear on him, own his likeness to you, and yours to your neighbor, spare him as little as you shun, pity him as much as you expose, it is a spirit of Humor that is moving you." Sometimes wit is said to be a recognition of resemblances while humor is the recognition of incongruities.

Theories about what is funny generally fall into two categories: (1) laughter is evoked by "a kind of sudden glory" (in Hobbes' famous phrase), as the spectator suddenly realizes his superiority to others, for example, when he sees how ridiculous someone looks who has slipped on a banana peel; (2) laughter is called forth by a "transformation of a strained expectation into nothing" (in Kant's famous phrase), as when we find funny a comedian who says, "I have enough money to last me the rest of my life—provided I die a week from Friday." In this instance the humor arises when we suddenly release the tension we have held in because we think we are with a very wealthy person. A great deal has been written on the division between wit and humor, as well as what actually constitutes "funny."

Aristotle did not write about comedy as extensively as he did tragedy (or his writings have been lost), but he did say that tragedy shows men greater than they are, while comedy shows them lesser. Comedy reminds us how unlike the gods we are, no matter how we may wish to emulate them. A comedy is usually thought of as "funny," and as having a happy ending. While this may be true, there may also be a great deal of suffering and even death along the way.

The main difference between comedy and tragedy is that comedy has a *detached point of view.* Comedy forces us to keep our distance, as we see the pain is not permanent nor the disaster real. We do not become emotionally involved with the characters, for if we do, the comedy has ended. Comedy emphasizes the foolishness of many of our poses, tripping us by a sudden reversal, a silly comparison, a gross exaggeration. Even as we fall flat on the ground, those watching us do not take the pain seriously, and so do not become involved with our pratfalls. While things that make people laugh have not changed drastically through the ages, artistic taste has altered. Physical defects, race, or mental problems are no longer acceptable comic devices, but still with us are the sexual jokes, the pratfall, the pie-in-the-face routine, the wit, and wisecrack.

GREEK COMEDY

Comic drama appears to have been drawn from ancient fertility rites, as it usually celebrates renewal, variety, and man's triumph over life's harshness. Even enraged parents and horrible natural events—earthquakes and shipwrecks—cannot prevent happy endings. *Greek comedy,* the earliest form of comedy, is usually divided into three categories: (1) old comedy; (2) middle comedy; and (3) new comedy.

Old comedy is best represented by Aristophanes (445?–380? B.C.) and combines fantastic elements, such as a utopia founded by birds, with wild political satire. Aristophanes was only one of a number of talented writers of comedy during this time, but after his death, his reputation far exceeded all others. The only examples of old comedy that survive are his, about 11 of the 40 plays he wrote.

Since Greek comedy was part of a religious festival, its purpose was to educate as well as entertain. This is true of Aristophanes' comedies. He used humor and satire to urge his audience to become good citizens, to drive away hypocrisy from the Athenian culture. Nevertheless, he had his own set of preconceived ideas, coming as he did from a wealthy family, whose aristocratic and conservative upbringing brought him into conflict with the popular political parties of the day. He tended to see hypocrisy there more easily than in the party he supported.

All of his plays concern three main themes: politics and the war with Sparta; literature, especially the writings of Euripides; and education, especially the teachings of the Sophists, whose beliefs he did not support. This can make much of what he wrote very difficult for the modern audience to understand. Since almost all of his humor was topical, it is necessary for us to refer to notes by critics and scholars.

When Aristophanes presented his first play in 427 B.C. (the earliest surviving comedy in Western literature), Athens was locked in a life-and-death struggle with the other leading power of Greece, Sparta. Athens was no longer the greatest nation on earth; Pericles was dead and his power dissipated.

In 404 B.C., after 27 years of fighting, the war finally ended in complete victory for Sparta. Athens was stripped, her treasure gone. We see this in Aristophanes' final plays.

Although Athens regained her former glory, old comedy never returned. In 338 B.C., Athens fell under the rule of the kings of Macedonia, and freedom of speech became a thing of the past. Life was dictated from above and was terribly unsure. The purpose of new comedy was to entertain, its subject was people, and its main source of humor derived from the gentle mockery of all. It soon became even more popular than tragedy.

Middle comedy does not survive. Many critics have seen it as a bridge to new comedy.

New Comedy is best represented by Menander (342?–291?B.C.) and has the plot we've come to expect in a comedy: Boy meets girl, boy and girl encounter problems, boy and girl overcome problems. There are adventures interwoven with tales of ordinary life. Even though he was not very popular during his lifetime (his rivals' humor had far greater appeal), Menander's reputation caught fire after his death. Some of his work was discovered in 1905 in an Egyptian tomb, greatly adding to his fame. His "formula" was continued in Rome by Plautus (254?–184? B.C.) and Terence (190–159? B.C.).

A century after Aristophanes, Greek comedy had spread to the world. It played in theaters from Italy to Asia Minor, although a performance in Athens remained the goal of every playwright.

Greek comedy generally followed a set formula, having three elements:

Idea: A character thinks of a "happy idea," and calls together a group to discuss it.

Application: After the discussion, the idea is put into practice, usually with very silly results.

Conclusion: There is some sort of union of the sexes at the end of a comedy. Some critics have again seen this as allied to the fertility rites of the ancient Greeks.

Some further qualities of Greek Comedy:

Characters: All are treated in a light manner, no matter what their status.

Purpose: To reform man through laughter. Ideas that people foolishly hold to be true are shown to be ridiculous, so that people will reform their ways.

Diction: Spans all levels, from crude and coarse jokes to lovely poetical passages. Often these shifts are used to illuminate character or theme, showing someone's personality through language.

Plot: Often came from political situations and philosophical questions. Wars, subsequent peace treaties, abuses in power, and prevailing philosophical ideas were often bantered around. While playwrights invented characters, it was not uncommon for well-known citizens to figure in the action.

ANALYSIS OF *THE FROGS* BY ARISTOPHANES

The Frogs was presented at the Lenaea in 405 B.C. and won first prize. The Athenians had been at war almost continually since 431 B.C., and their position was desperate; one defeat would lose the war. Six months after *The Frogs* was performed, Athens did indeed lose to Sparta. But when Aristophanes was writing this play, one great victory could still enable the Athenians to be victorious, provided that they used such a victory wisely, as a bargaining point for a lasting peace.

This was Aristophanes' view, and he felt that if all people banded together their talents and resources, a lasting peace could be achieved. The last lines of the play can be read in this manner.

The first part of *The Frogs* takes the form of a comic journey beyond the limits of the world, similar to *The Birds*. During the course of the journey, the Dead are encountered, who are used to voice the poet's own views and speak on behalf of peace. At the end of the journey, a conversation between two slaves, Xanthias and Aiakos, introduces the final *agon* between Euripides and Aeschylus.

The agon, after introductory preparation, is argued on five issues or rounds, as follows:

1. General style, subject matter, and effect upon audiences
   Choral interlude
2. Prologues, including skill at exposition and the use of iambic meter
   Choral interlude
3. Lyrics and lyric prose
   Choral interlude

4. The weighing of lines
   Interlude by Dionysos and Pluto
5. Advice to the Athenians

In each round, Euripides attacks first. In the first three rounds he achieves some victories. But Aeschylus, the ultimate winner, has the better position for an agon, since the last word belongs to him.

The arguments are as follows:

Round 1. Euripides says that Aeschylus' work is turgid, undramatic, obscure, and too militaristic. His own plays, in contrast, are lucid, plausible, and meaningful for all. Aeschylus responds that he has always maintained a high heroic standard and urged the citizens to greater virtue, while Euripides, in lowering tragedy by bringing it down to earth, has dragged it in the dust. Especially with his morbid interest in sex, he had succeeded in unmanning the Athenians.

Round 2. Euripides charges Aeschylus with an obscure and repetitious style. Aeschylus retorts with a charge of metrical monotony. In prologue after prologue of Euripides, the main verb is delayed and a subordinate clause completed in such a way as to conclude both the metrical line and the sentence.

Round 3. Aeschylus, having raised the question of metrical dullness, spurs Euripides to respond in kind. Aeschylus' lyrics are monotonous, he charges, for however he may begin, he always ends with a dactyl phrase. This can be seen in a line such as "O ho what a stroke come you not to the rescue?" These metrical criticisms repeat the general criticism of style: When Euripides makes sense, he is dull; when Aeschylus sounds wonderful, he means little. Aeschylus responds by saying that Euripides writes free verse and the lyric meters lose their form and lines cease to make any sense. This results in a shoddy, sentimental flow of words, especially marked by one special flaw which Aristophanes always finds in Euripides: the combination of magnificence and homeliness.

Round 4. The weighing of lines has often been regarded as the least important section of the play, but nevertheless it advances the opinion that the verse of Aeschylus has more mass and substance than that of Euripides.

Round 5. What shall Athens do? The speakers may be taken to represent the poet's own struggle. Euripides expresses Aristophanes' doubts about the good purpose of the heirs of Pericles, those who follow the support of naval warfare, while Aeschylus speaks for Aristophanes' unwilling conclusion, that these people alone have a chance to save what remains of the city.

We can conclude from all this that Euripides' Aeschylus, even in parody, is not as simple a figure as we might conclude from his plays. *Seven Against Thebes* is more than a simple-minded glorification of patriotism. *Agamemnon* condemns war-makers and sackers of cities. Aristophanes picked out and exaggerated certain aspects of Aeschylus, not from ignorance, but because he was concerned with the success of his agon rather than the validity of his presentation of historical people. The attack is on the moderns, and Euripides is their spokesman. Whatever Euripides is, Aeschylus must, for argument's sake, be the opposite. So, if Euripides is against war, Aeschylus must be pro-war. If Euripides takes the women's side in discussions, Aeschylus must be against women. And since Euripides was popular with the audience (although he did not win with the judges), Aeschylus must be unpopular, haughty, and aristocratic.

FRENCH COMEDY

During the seventeenth century, tragedy dominated the French theater. It was generally felt that all art must follow the Greek and Roman models and adhere to Aristotle's theories. Although Greek and Roman comedies were known, there were no established rules for comic drama. Molière (Jean-Baptiste Poquelin) stepped in to fill the void in the theater and create an original form.

While Molière is not considered solely a writer of comedies, many of his plays are very witty and humorous. He excelled at using humor to make a serious point. One of the main influences on Molière's work was the tradition of *farce*: a short skit, broadly humorous and satirical of society and its followers. Molière first won acclaim for his farces and returned to this form frequently. His last play, *The Imaginary Invalid,* is largely farcical.

TARTUFFE BY MOLIÈRE

Tartuffe, originally written in verse rather than prose, is Molière's most controversial play. It is based on a particular incident as well as a general problem of his day: There was a real priest who, while serving as the spiritual guide for a family, stole their money and committed adultery with the wife. Molière was also attacking a secret society of religious fanatics who tried to gain entrance to homes and control the personal lives of the families. It is not surprising that these people, seeing themselves so accurately portrayed on the stage, sought to destroy Molière. Many moderate churchmen as well as laypeople attacked the play because they viewed it as the work of an atheist and a freethinker. To them, *Tartuffe* denounced the church, religion, and religious practices.

The present version of *Tartuffe* is not the original script, which was banned by the king in 1664. That play is thought to have concluded in Tartuffe's victory over his enemies, Orgon's declaration of trust in his spiritual advisor, and his assent to Tartuffe's watch over his wife, Elmire. Louis XIV lifted the ban with the revised edition, submitted five years later. We can conclude that one of the reasons for the very weak conclusion, the use of the *deus ex machina* (an incredible and unbelievable device to solve the plot), was to flatter the king. How could Louis XIV not permit a play which praised him as the defender of the mistreated, the wise judge of all wrongs? When the revised edition was performed, it was hailed as a great success. Today it is one of Molière's best-known and most highly admired plays.

The theme is religious hypocrisy, obviously, but the play is also concerned with character and manners. The play focuses on the three points of view of Tartuffe, Orgon, and Cleante. It is difficult to support the thesis that Tartuffe is the main character, for he does not appear directly in the action until act III. The manners of the day, both religious and social, are noted in great detail here, along with the role of religion in family and household, the relations between family members, and the role and nature of friendship.

Summary of Tartuffe

Act I. The play opens in the midst of a family quarrel. Mme. Pernelle is very unhappy with the way her son's household is being managed. She complains about the children's manners and especially criticizes her daughter-in-law Elmire's extravagance. Mme. Pernelle rebukes the entire family for their disregard of Tartuffe, whose presence everyone except Mme. Pernelle resents. Damis, Orgon's son and Elmire's stepson, is the most outspoken, calling Tartuffe a pious fraud. They all describe him as a hypocrite enriching himself at the family's expense. They equally mistrust his servant, Laurent. Mme. Pernelle replies that Tartuffe hates sin and is trying to rescue their souls from eternal damnation. Dorine cannot accept his dictate that the family not be allowed visitors and claims that Tartuffe is emotionally interested in Elmire. Mme. Pernelle claims that visitors cause scandal, and Cleante, Elmire's brother, supports the majority of the family by asserting that they live innocently and have nothing to fear from visitors. Once gossipers start, he says, there is no stopping them. They cite the example of Orante, a neighbor whose current virtuous life-style conceals a wild past. Mme. Pernelle, realizing that she cannot sway the family, delivers one long final speech before her departure, saying that her son's actions in admitting Tartuffe to the house were correct, for he will rid it of evil. She warns them that unless they give up parties and evil ways, she will not visit them again. Cleante and Dorine discuss the reason for Tartuffe's overwhelming influence over Orgon. Prior to Tartuffe's arrival, he was a man of good sense and reason. The others return, and Damis asks Cleante to intercede with Orgon about Mariane's marriage to Valere, which Tartuffe opposes. Orgon enters and shows no interest in his wife's illness of the previous night; rather, he is concerned about Tartuffe's welfare. Cleante tries to make Orgon see how foolishly he is behaving, but Orgon says that Tartuffe has caused all worldly cares to vanish. He even goes so far as to say that he would not be upset if any of his family died. Orgon then explains how he met Tartuffe: his pious behavior in church, his entrance into the family, the upward turn in family fortunes. Cleante thinks that Orgon has lost all reason, and states with vigor that true religion does not concern itself with the blind acceptance of appearances. Why will man not stay within the boundaries of reason and seek the middle path of moderation? Why does man have so much difficulty distinguishing between appearance and reality? The main thrust of his attack is against religious hypocrisy, and he denounces those who use religious practices for their own ends. He praises those who practice what they preach. Insulted, Orgon wants to leave, but Cleante asks him about Valere and Mariane's marriage plans. Orgon says that he will follow the will of heaven—Tartuffe—and Cleante knows that the path will be rocky.

Act II. Orgon and Mariane discuss her wedding. He stresses obedience; she agrees, until he announces that Tartuffe is to be her husband. She refuses, and they quarrel. Dorine enters unnoticed, and Orgon scolds her for being an eavesdropper. She defends herself with an attack on Tartuffe. For example, she does not understand why he could want Tartuffe for a son-in-law, since Tartuffe is penniless. Orgon defends Tartuffe by saying that he has renounced all earthly possessions, including land that would make him rich. Dorine claims that these boasts are not signs of humility. They discuss the wedding, and Dorine says that Mariane will be wretched with Tartuffe as a husband. Orgon objects to Valere because he has heard that Valere does not attend church and plays cards. He believes that piety will bind together Tartuffe and Mariane as love cannot. He finally threatens to strike Dorine unless she keeps quiet, although she continues to make snide comments. Every time he tries to hit her she ceases, but she is at last forced to flee from his rage. Orgon is so angry that he has to leave the room, and Dorine returns to encourage Mariane in her rebellion. Mariane is torn between love and duty. Valere enters and demands to know if the rumor he has heard concerning Tartuffe as his love's intended is true. Mariane seems to be passively accepting her fate and he, too, mocks her. Dorine intervenes and effects a truce between the lovers. She tells Mariane to pretend to accept Tartuffe but to keep postponing the marriage as long as possible.

Act III. Damis and Dorine make plans to trap Tartuffe. Tartuffe enters and begins to assume pompous and false airs, warning against the temptation of the flesh and giving various orders. Elmire begins to discuss the wedding plans with Tartuffe, but he begins to flirt with her, declaring his love and saying he wishes to seduce her. She sets this condition: Tartuffe must give his support to Valere and Mariane's wedding or she will tell Orgon of Taruffe's bold seduction attempt. Damis rushes from the closet where he has been hiding, determined to tell his father what Tartuffe really is like. Orgon enters, and Elmire confirms Damis' tale. Tartuffe refuses to defend himself, kneeling before Damis to hypocritically accept all accusations. Orgon rises to Tartuffe's defense, and Tartuffe has to convince Orgon not to punish his son. Orgon claims the family is jealous of the man—Tartuffe—who is trying to help them. He vows to arrange the marriage sooner as a lesson to the family. Damis objects and Orgon drives him from the house. Tartuffe offers to leave, but Orgon wants him to stay, remain near his wife, be the sole heir to his fortunes, and marry Mariane. Tartuffe pretends to demur, but agrees only to be in accord with the will of heaven.

Act IV. Cleante tells Tartuffe that the townspeople are gossiping about his role in Damis' exile from his own home, and that Tartuffe should mend the fight between father and son for the sake of his, Tartuffe's, reputation. Tartuffe declines to get involved, invoking God's will. In order to escape Cleante's valid criticisms, Tartuffe leaves the room. Elmire, Mariane, and Dorine run in, asking Cleante to protect them against Orgon. When Orgon enters, Mariane begs him not to make her marry Tartuffe; she would rather enter a convent. Elmire is deeply upset by Orgon's acceptance of Tartuffe's version of affairs, and in desperation, asks Orgon if he would believe her if he could see Tartuffe trying to seduce her. He accepts the challenge, and Elmire hides him under the table as the others leave the room. Elmire and Tartuffe flirt, and although initially suspicious about her change in heart toward him, he soon accepts her words completely. She asks Tartuffe how he can justify his sin with his religious beliefs. He hypocritically says that sinning in silence is no sin at all and that he can warp conscience to justify behavior. When she mentions her husband to Tartuffe, he laughs and says that he can lead the foolish Orgon around by the nose. While Tartuffe checks to make sure the coast is clear, Orgon comes out from hiding too soon, and Elmire hides him quickly behind herself. As Tartuffe returns and continues his advances, Orgon comes out from hiding and demands that he leave the house immediately, but Tartuffe brazenly refuses to go, saying that the house is his. Orgon recalls the deed in inheritance he has signed and wants to get to his safe at once.

Act V. Orgon's safe is missing, and in despair, he asks for Cleante's advice. Damis and his father reunite to defeat Tartuffe, and although Mme. Pernelle still refuses to admit any wrongdoing on Tartuffe's part, the rest of the family is solidly against the faker. When Tartuffe sends a notice of eviction to the family, they believe all is lost. Even Mme. Pernelle now accepts Tartuffe for what he is. Valere hurries in to advise Orgon to leave the country; Tartuffe has turned the missing safe over to the king and some papers inside have made it appear that Orgon is a traitor for aiding an outlaw. Before Orgon can escape, Tartuffe comes with a policeman to arrest him. In a surprising ending, the police arrest Tartuffe, not Orgon. The policeman offers a very flattering speech that Louis XIV had immediately recognized Tartuffe for what he is. The king declared the contract between Orgon and Tartuffe null and void, and straightened out the matter of Orgon's friend the outlaw. Cleante does not allow the family to attack Tartuffe physically, but turns him over to the police.

SUGGESTED READING LIST

The following critical studies contain material useful for studying drama.

Boynton, Robert and Maynard Mack. *Introduction to the Play*. Rochelle Park, New Jersey: Hayden, 1969.

Brooks, Cleanth and William Heilman. *Understanding Drama*. New York: Holt, Rinehart and Winston, 1948.

Cubeta, Paul. *Modern Drama for Analysis*. 3rd ed. New York: Holt, Rinehart and Winston, 1962.

Felheim, Marvin, ed. *Comedy: Plays, Theories, and Criticism*. New York: Harcourt Brace Jovanovich, 1969.

Kernan, Alvin. *Character and Conflict: An Introduction to Drama*. New York: Harcourt Brace Jovanovich, 1969.

Levin, Richard, ed. *Tragedy: Plays, Theory, and Criticism*. New York: Harcourt Brace Jovanovich, 1960.

Aeschylus	*Agamemnon*
Albee, Edward	*Who's Afraid of Virginia Woolf*
	Zoo Story
Anonymous	*Everyman*
	The Second Shepherd's Play
Aristophanes	*The Frogs*
Beckett, Samuel	*Endgame*
	Waiting for Godot
Bolt, Robert	*A Man for all Seasons*
Brecht, Bertold	*The Caucasian Chalk Circle*
Capek, Karel	*R.U.R.*
Chekhov, Anton	*The Cherry Orchard*
	The Sea Gull
Congreve, William	*The Way of the World*
Eliot, T. S.	*Murder in the Cathedral*
	The Cocktail Party
Euripides	*Medea*
Gibson, William	*The Miracle Worker*
Gilbert, W. S.	*The Mikado*
Goldsmith, Oliver	*She Stoops to Conquer*
Hansberry, Lorraine	*A Raisin in the Sun*
Ibsen, Henrik	*A Doll's House*
	Ghosts
	The Enemy of the People
	The Wild Duck
Ionesco, Eugene	*The Lesson*
Lerner and Loewe	*My Fair Lady*
MacLeish, Archibald	*J. B.*
Marlowe, Christopher	*Dr. Faustus*
Miller, Arthur	*The Crucible*
	Death of a Salesman
Molière	*Tartuffe*
	The Physician in Spite of Himself

O'Casey, Sean	*Juno and the Paycock*
	The Plough and Stars
O'Neill, Eugene	*The Emperor Jones*
	The Hairy Ape
	Mourning Becomes Electra
Pinter, Harold	*The Birthday Party*
Pirandello, Luigi	*Six Characters in Search of an Author*
Rostand, Edmond	*Cyrano de Bergerac*
Sartre, Jean-Paul	*No Exit*
	The Flies
Shakespeare, William	*Hamlet*
	King Lear
	Othello
	Julius Caesar
	As You Like It
	Macbeth
	Romeo and Juliet
	The Tempest
Shaw, George Bernard	*Arms and the Man*
	Man and Superman
	Major Barbara
	St. Joan
	Pygmalion
Sheridan, Richard	*The Rivals*
	The School for Scandal
Sophocles	*Antigone*
	Oedipus Rex
Stoppard, Tom	*Rosencrantz and Guildenstern Are Dead*
Synge, John Millington	*Playboy of the Western World*
Vidal, Gore	*Visit to a Small Planet*
Wilde, Oscar	*The Importance of Being Earnest*
Wilder, Thornton	*Our Town*
Williams, Tennessee	*The Glass Menagerie*
	Cat on a Hot Tin Roof

Part 6

Three Sample Advanced Placement Exams in Composition and Literature

Sample Examination A

SECTION 1

Part A: Time—25 minutes

Directions: Read the poem and answer the questions that follow it.

NATURE

1 As a fond mother, when the day is o'er,
Leads by the hand her little child to bed,
Half willing, half reluctant to be led,
And leave his broken playthings on the floor,
5 Still gazing at them through the open door,
Nor wholly reassured and comforted
By promises of others in their stead,
Which, though more splendid, may not please him more;
So Nature deals with us, and takes away
10 Our playthings one by one, and by the hand
Leads us to rest so gently, that we go
Scarce knowing if we wish to go or stay,
Being too full of sleep to understand
How far the unknown transcends the what we know.
—*Henry Wadsworth Longfellow*

1. What two situations are being compared here?
   (A) A mother reassuring her child that his broken toys will be replaced to Nature's destruction of the world's "toys."
   (B) Life to sleep
   (C) Death to sleep
   (D) Parenthood to childhood
   (E) A "fond mother" and her sleepy child to "Mother Nature" and natural disasters

2. What is such a comparison called?
   (A) Simile
   (B) Hyperbole
   (C) Pun
   (D) Oxymoron
   (E) Synesthesia

3. What is the author's attitude toward his subject matter?
   (A) We have much to fear from death's embrace, he says.
   (B) Death ought to hold little fear.
   (C) We ought to be terrified of the suddenness of death; the author recommends suicide.
   (D) Life usually terminates abruptly, but this is good, for it relieves us of the trials of parenthood.
   (E) Life is a boring affair at best and death is preferable for it is exciting.

4. How does the author's use of comparison illuminate his theme?
   (A) It shows that the mother–child relationship is central to Nature.
   (B) It really doesn't illuminate the theme to any great extent; that is done through poetic devices.
   (C) It portrays life's dilemma accurately, as our "toys" often break and we may not always be solaced by others.
   (D) It pictures the approach of death, and casts it in a light of calm reassurance.
   (E) It describes the enormous difficulty of raising children and reassures us that all share this situation.

5. What are the "playthings" in line 10?
   (A) All the people and things with which we fill our lives
   (B) All the minor annoyances of daily life

287

(C) Status items
(D) Leisure activities
(E) Wicked and evil habits

6. What does the use of the word "playthings" tell you about the speaker's view of life?
   (A) Life is best appreciated by the young.
   (B) Life is an extended childhood.
   (C) Man is immature and subject to folly all his life.
   (D) Man is unaware of the true value of life until it is terminated.
   (E) Life is a bitter affair at best.

7. What is the form of this poem?
   (A) An ode
   (B) Free verse
   (C) A sonnet
   (D) A ballad
   (E) Light verse

8. What is the prevailing foot of this poem?
   (A) Dactyl
   (B) Spondee
   (C) Trochee
   (D) Iamb
   (E) Anapest

9. What is the rhyme scheme of this poem?
   (A) *abbaabba cdecde*
   (B) *ababcdcdefefgg*
   (C) *aaaa bbbb cccc dd*
   (D) *aaba aaba cde cde*
   (E) None of the above; it is unrhymed.

10. What is the tone of this poem?
    (A) Euphuistic
    (B) Baroque

(C) Gentle and contemplative
(D) Bewildered
(E) Straightforward

11. The speaker shifts point of view in which of the following lines?
    (A) Line 9
    (B) Line 4
    (C) Line 5
    (D) Line 3
    (E) Line 2

12. Which line best states the poem's meaning?
    (A) Line 14
    (B) Line 9
    (C) Line 4
    (D) Line 11
    (E) Line 12

13. The author states that
    (A) life far exceeds death
    (B) we have little to fear from death because the afterlife exceeds all our expectations
    (C) we have an enormous amount to fear from death
    (D) we shall never know what awaits us after death
    (E) there is nothing after life

14. The poet's attitude toward life and death shows that he was most likely influenced by
    (A) the death of a loved one
    (B) the Transcendentalists of the 1830–1860's
    (C) the rhythm of nineteenth-century slave verse
    (D) the Puritan attitudes of the seventeenth century
    (E) the Revolutionary War

Part B: Time—20 minutes

Write a brief essay in which you demonstrate how the author of "Nature" views life, death, and eternity. Be sure to draw specific examples from the poem.

SECTION 2

Part A: Time—45 minutes

Directions: Read the following passage carefully; then write the assignment given after the passage.

CAPTAIN JOHN SMITH AMONG THE INDIANS

The winter [of 1607] approaching, the rivers became so covered with swans, geese, ducks, and cranes, that we daily feasted with good bread, Virginia peas, pumpkins, putchamins, fish, fowl, and diverse sorts of wild beasts as fat as we could eat them, so that none of our tuftaffety humorists desired to go for England.

But our comedies never endured long without a tragedy; some idle exceptions being muttered against Captain Smith for not discovering the head of Chicka-hamania River, and taxed by the Council to be too slow in so worthy an attempt. The next voyage he proceeded so far that with much labor by cutting of trees asunder he made his passage; but when his barge could pass no farther, he left her in a broad bay out of danger of shot, commanding none should go ashore till his return: himself with two English and two savages went up higher in a canoe, but he was not long absent but his men went ashore, whose want of government gave both occasion and opportunity to the savages to surprise one George Cassen, whom they slew, and much failed not to have cut off the boat and all the rest.

Smith, little dreaming of that accident, being got to the marshes at the river's head, twenty miles in the desert, had his two men slain (as is supposed) sleeping by the canoe, whilst himself by fowling sought them victual; who, finding he was beset with two hundred savages, two of them he slew, still defending himself with the aid of a savage his guide, whom he bound to his arm with his garters and used him as a buckler; yet he was shot in his thigh a little and had many arrows that stuck in his clothes but no great hurt, till at last they took him prisoner.

When this news came to Jamestown, much was their sorrow for his loss, few expecting what ensued.

Six or seven weeks those barbarians kept him prisoner, many strange triumphs and conjurations they made of him, yet he so demeaned himself amongst them, as he not only diverted them from surprising the fort, but procured his own liberty, and got himself and his company such estimation amongst them, that those savages admired him more than their own Quiyoucko-sucks. The manner how they used and delivered him is as follows.

The savages having drawn from George Cassen whither Captain Smith was gone, prosecuting that opportunity they followed him with three hundred bowmen, conducted by the King of Pamaunkee, who in divisions searching the turnings of the river, found Robinson and Emry by the fireside; those they shot full of arrows and slew. Then finding the Captain, as is said, that used the savage that was his guide as his shield (three of them being slain and divers others so galled) all the rest would not come near him. Thinking thus to have returned to his boat, regarding them as he marched more than his way, slipped up to the middle in an oozy creek and his savage with him; yet durst they not come to him till being near dead with cold, he threw away his arms. Then according to their composition they drew him forth and led him to the fire, where his men were slain. Diligently they chafed his benumbed limbs.

He demanding for their captain, they showed him Opechankanough, King of Pamaunkee, to whom he gave a round ivory double compass dial. Much they marveled at the playing of the fly and needle, which they could see so plainly, and yet not touch it because of the glass that covered them. But when he demonstrated by that globelike jewel the roundness of the earth, the skies, the sphere of the sun, moon, and stars, and how the sun did chase the night round about the world continually; the greatness of the land and sea, the diversity of nations, variety of complexions, and how we were to them antipodes, and many other suchlike matters, they all stood as amazed with admiration.

—*John Smith*

Directions: Write an essay in which you evaluate the author's purpose in writing and publishing this selection. Take into account the time period in which it was written as well as the way in which the action is described.

Part B: Time—30 minutes

Directions: Read the following passage carefully and consider the questions which follow it.

From SINNERS IN THE HANDS OF AN ANGRY GOD

THE wrath of God is like great waters that are dammed for the present; they increase more and more and rise higher and higher, till an outlet is given; and the longer the stream is stopped, the more rapid and mighty is its course when once it is let loose. 'Tis true that judgment against your evil work has not been executed hitherto; the floods of God's vengeance have been withheld; but your guilt in the meantime is constantly increasing, and you are every day treasuring up more wrath; the waters are continually rising and waxing more and more mighty; and there is nothing but the mere pleasure of God that holds the waters back, that are unwilling to be stopped, and press hard to go forward. If God should only withdraw his hand from the floodgate it would immediately fly open, and the fiery floods of the fierceness and wrath of God would rush forth with inconceivable fury, and would come upon you with omnipotent power; and if your strength were ten thousand times greater than it is, yea, ten thousand times greater than the strength of the stoutest, sturdiest devil in hell, it would be nothing to withstand or endure it.

The bow of God's wrath is bent, and the arrow made ready on the string, and justice bends the arrow at your heart and strains the bow, and it is nothing but the mere pleasure of God, and that of an angry God, without any promise or obligation at all, that keeps the arrow one moment from being made drunk with your blood.

Thus are all you that never passed under a great change of heart by the mighty power of the Spirit of God upon your souls; all that were never born again and made new creatures, and raised from being dead in sin to a state of new and before altogether unexperienced light and life (however you may have reformed your life in many things, and may have had religious affections, and may keep up a form of religion in your families and closets and in the house of God, and may be strict in it), you are thus in the hands of an angry God; 'tis nothing but his mere pleasure that keeps you from being this moment swallowed up in everlasting destruction.

However unconvinced you may now be of the truth of what you hear, by and by you will be fully convinced of it. Those that are gone from being in the like circumstances with you, see that it was so with them; for destruction came suddenly upon most of them; when they expected nothing of it, and while they were saying, Peace and Safety. Now they see that those things that they depended on for peace and safety were nothing but thin air and empty shadows.

The God that holds you over the pit of hell much as one holds a spider or some loathsome insect over the fire, abhors you, and is dreadfully provoked; his wrath toward you burns like fire; he looks upon you as worthy of nothing else but to be cast into the fire; he is of purer eyes than to bear to have you in his sight; you are ten thousand times so abominable in his eyes as the most hateful and venomous serpent is in ours. You have offended him infinitely more than ever a stubborn rebel did his prince; and yet it is nothing but his hand that holds you from falling into the fire every moment. 'Tis ascribed to nothing else, that you did not go to hell the last night; that you were suffered to awake again in this world after you closed your eyes to sleep and there is no other reason to be given why you have not dropped into hell since you arose in the morning, but that God's hand has held you up. There is no other reason to be given why you have not gone to hell since you have sat here in the house of God, provoking his pure eyes by your sinful wicked manner of attending his solemn worship. Yea, there is nothing else that is to be given as a reason why you don't this very moment drop down into hell.

O sinner! Consider the fearful danger you are in. 'Tis a great furnace of wrath, a wide and bottomless pit, full of the fire of wrath, that you are held over in the hand of that God whose wrath is provoked and incensed as much against you as against many of the damned in hell. You hang by a slender thread with the flames of divine wrath flashing about it.

—Jonathan Edwards

1. What is the *tone* of this passage?
2. What is the *style?*
3. What is the relationship between the *style* and *content?*
4. What is the speaker's attitude toward people? Toward God?
5. How do the *tone* and *style* underscore and support his attitude?

Write an essay in which you show how the author's tone and style are effective in giving his view of God's attitude toward man.

SECTION 3

Time—60 minutes

Choose two literary works in which a character views the past with such feelings as reverence, bitterness, or longing. With clear evidence drawn from the works, show how the characters' views of the past are used to develop a theme in the work. You may wish to select your examples from the list of authors provided, but any two works of comparable literary excellence may be used.

F. Scott Fitzgerald   Toni Morrison

John Updike   Charles Dickens

Bernard Malamud   Henry James

Arthur Miller   Ernest Hemingway

Henrik Ibsen   Theodore Dreiser

ANSWERS AND EXPLANATIONS FOR SAMPLE EXAMINATION A

Section 1, Part A: "Nature"

1. **(C)** Henry Wadsworth Longfellow (1807–1882) is using the Italian (also known as Petrarchan) sonnet form to compare death to sleep, a common theme in sonnets. Lines 1–8 describe a mother leading her child to bed and rest at day's end; lines 9–14 describe Nature leading man to his final sleep.

2. **(A)** Longfellow is using a simile here, a direct comparison of two unlike objects, using "like" or "as." The first line, "*As* a fond mother . . . " tells us this. Hyperbole, (B), is overstatement or great exaggeration for effect. A pun, (C), is the humorous use of words to stress their different meanings, or the use of words that are alike or almost alike in sound but different in meaning; a play on words (*e.g.*, "tail" and "tale"). An oxymoron, (D), consists of contradictory terms brought together to express a paradox in order to establish a strong poetic effect. See poetry section for examples. Synesthesia, (E), occurs when the stimulus applied to one sense triggers another, for example, when hearing a certain sound induces the visualization of color.

3. **(B)** Longfellow's use of the mother-child comparison is intended to reassure the reader and to remove death's sting. Furthermore, words such as "gently" in line 11 suggest the calmness with which we ought to approach death. The final line clarifies his attitude: What lies after our mortal existence far exceeds what meager "playthings" we might have relinquished and the afterlife promises far more splendid treasures (lines 8, 14).

4. **(D)** See explanatory answer for question 3.

5. **(A)** As a child has his treasures, so adults fill their lives with the people and things they value.

6. **(B)** Longfellow does not condemn man for his diversions, as answer (C) implies. Rather, man is unaware of what lies beyond, and man remains in a state of childlike innocence, not realizing what is of value until he has passed through life.

7. **(C)** A sonnet is a lyric poem of 14 lines written in iambic pentameter. Originated by the Italian poets during the thirteenth century, it reached perfection a century later in the work of Petrarch, and later came to be known as the Italian or Petrarchan sonnet. When the English poets of the sixteenth century discovered Petrarch, they were challenged by his format and adopted the

number of lines but changed the rhyme scheme, as will be discussed later. An ode, (A), is an elaborate lyric verse which usually deals with an important and dignified theme. Free verses, (B), has unrhymed lines without regular rhythm. A ballad, (D), is a simple verse which tells a story to be sung or recited. Light verse, (E), falls into a general group of poems written to entertain. Epigrams and limericks show the less serious side of light verse; parody or satire illustrate its more profound aspects.

8. **(D)** Meter is the rhythm of poetry, a pattern of stressed and unstressed syllables measured in units called "feet." This is more fully explained in the Poetry Section. Sonnets are constructed of iambs. An iambic foot consists of an unstressed syllable followed by a stressed one (˘ ´). Other poetic feet include: (A) dactyl: stressed, unstressed, unstressed (´ ˘ ˘); (B) spondee: stressed, stressed (´ ´); (C) trochee: stressed, unstressed (´ ˘); and (E) anapest: unstressed, unstressed, stressed (˘ ˘ ´).

9. **(A)** This is the rhyme scheme of the Italian sonnet. The first group, called the octave, presents the poet's subject; the second group, called the sestet, indicates the importance of the facts set forth in the octave. The sestet lines may resolve the problem presented in the octave. The rhyme scheme of a poem is determined by assigning a letter to each new sound found at the end of a line of verse. (See the Poetry Section for more detail).

10. **(C)** The tone of a poem is derived from the author's attitude toward his audience and subject matter. Here, the tone is gentle and contemplative, as the mother-child situation suggests. (A) Euphuistic describes a very ornate and affected style characterized by euphemism. (B) A baroque tone would be elaborate and extravagantly ornamented. (D) Far from bewildered, the speaker is certain that the unknown afterlife exceeds that which we know. (E) The compassion and tenderness evidenced argue against a straightforward tone.

11. **(A)** Line 9: "So Nature deals with us . . . ."

12. **(A)** The final line (line 14) sums up Longfellow's point, as discussed previously.

13 **(B)** See answer 3.

14. **(B)** The Transcendentalists believed that there was some knowledge of reality or truth that man grasps not through logic or the laws of nature but through his intuition. There is obviously no other way Longfellow could have knowledge of the afterlife. (A) We have no way of knowing from the poem if the poet had suffered a personal loss. (C) This answer would be absurd in reference to Longfellow. (D) The Puritans preached God's wrath and the fearsomeness of the afterlife for all but a very few who were "elect" or saved. There was no way of knowing prior to death if one was saved or not. (E) The Revolutionary War is too general a response to suffice as a correct answer.

Section 1, Part B

The author's view of life and death were explained earlier. The essay should stress this view with specific examples drawn from the poem.

Section 2, Part A

John Smith's famous account is our first advertisement, intended to convince people that, contrary to truth, the New World was a land of plenty (see first paragraph). It was intended to draw single young men hungry for adventure, hence the references to exciting captures and rescues. Also, Smith was not above promoting his own interests and depicting himself as a great leader of men. He hoped to attain greater position and power, but was replaced by other leaders. The essay must stress the references to an abundance of food and adventure. It should also mention that much of what is described is greatly exaggerated, as in the adventure of Smith facing 200 savages or impressing the Indian leader with his compass.

Section 2, Part B

Edwards' "terror" sermon illustrates the Puritan belief in the ultimate depravity of man and the unlimited power and beneficence of God. The tone is angry, strong, biting, and vituperative: It is intended to frighten man into abandoning his wicked ways and following God. The style relies upon figures of speech, such as similes, metaphors, etc. Examples are found in the second paragraph ("bow of God's wrath") and fifth paragraph ("a spider or some loathsome insect" and "offended him infinitely more than ever a stubborn rebel did his prince"). Edwards does not have an overly elaborate style. The figures of speech are used to best advantage because there are only three in the selection. The *style* works very well with the *content,* for the use of figures of speech underscores God's hatred of man. The speaker obviously feels people are all wicked sinners and deserve to be denied God's grace if they do not repent of their evil ways. God, in contrast, is all-powerful, capable of forgiving even the most wicked of men. It is only God's grace that allows man to survive as long as he has. The *tone* and *style* reinforce the content, adding up to what has been called a "fire and brimstone" sermon.

Section 3

F. Scott Fitzgerald's *The Great Gatsby* centers around Jay Gatsby's attempt to recapture the past in the form of his first love, Daisy Buchanan. Gatsby, a gangster and bootlegger, partially succeeds in winning Daisy from her husband, wealthy and amoral Tom Buchanan, but never realizes that she is not what he believes her to be and that one cannot recapture the past. This is shown in a conversation he has with the narrator, Nick Carraway, when Nick tells Gatsby that one cannot regain the past. "Of course you can," Gatsby replies, supremely confident that with enough money and possessions, he can succeed in turning the clock back five years. Gatsby's attitude toward the past is one of "reverence" and "longing," and the theme developed by the novel is that one can never recapture what is gone. Arthur Miller's *The Crucible* shows how John Proctor, the farmer who had had an affair with the serving girl, Abigail Williams, tries to erase the bitterness of the past to clear his family of the charge of witchcraft. Updike's *Rabbit, Run* would also suit here, as would Thornton Wilder's *Our Town.*

Sample Examination B

SECTION 1

Part A: Time—25 minutes

Directions: Read the poem that follows and answer all the questions about it.

UPON THE BURNING OF OUR HOUSE
JULY 10TH, 1666

In silent night when rest I took,
For sorrow near I did not look,
I waken'd was with thund'ring noise
And piteous shrieks of dreadful voice.
5 That fearful sound of fire and fire,
Let no man know is my desire.

I, starting up, the light did spy,
And to my God my heart did cry
To strengthen me in my distress
10 And not to leave me succorless.
Then coming out beheld a space,
The flame consume my dwelling place.

And, when I could no longer look,
I blest his Name that gave and took,
15 That laid my goods now in the dust:
Yea so it was, and so 'twas just.
It was his own: it was not mine;
Far be it that I should repine.

He might of all justly bereft,
20 But yet sufficient for us left.
When by the ruins oft I past,
My sorrowing eyes aside did cast,
And here and there the places spy
Where oft I sat, and long did lie.

25 Here stood that trunk, and there that chest;
There lay that store I counted best:
My pleasant things in ashes lie,

And them behold no more shall I.
Under thy roof no guest shall sit,
30 Nor at thy table eat a bit.

No pleasant tale shall e'er be told,
Nor things recounted done of old.
No candle e'er shall shine in thee,
Nor bridegroom's voice ere heard shall be.
35 In silence ever shalt thou lie;
Adieu, adieu; all's vanity.

Then straight I gin my heart to chide,
And did thy wealth on earth abide?
Didst fix thy hope on mould'ring dust,
40 The arm of flesh didst make thy trust?
Raise up thy thoughts above the sky
That dunghill mists away may fly.

Thou hast an house on high erect,
Fram'd by that mighty Architect,
45 With glory richly furnished,
Stands permanent tho' this be fled.
It's purchased, and paid for too
By him who hath enough to do.

A prize so vast as is unknown,
50 Yet, by his gift, is made thine own.
There's wealth enough, I need no more;
Farewell my pelf, farewell my store.
The world no longer let me love,
My hope and treasure lies above.

—*Anne Bradstreet*

1. Many people try to find logical explanations for unfortunate events. Does the poet, anywhere in the poem, attempt to place blame for the fire?
   (A) She attributes the cause to God, but not the blame.
   (B) Initially she blames the bridegroom, but realizes that it is really God's fault by line 40.
   (C) She blames the initial builder for his use of substandard materials and workmanship.
   (D) She really doesn't care that much about the loss of her possessions, for she already has another house in a better neighborhood.
   (E) She blames God, for He cruelly took back His possessions, as line 17 shows.

2. The "arm of flesh" in line 40 refers to
   (A) hope, promise
   (B) death, decay
   (C) secular, mundane concerns
   (D) the destruction of the fire
   (E) spiritual renewal

3. The poet's attitude toward her home
   (A) remains the same throughout the poem
   (B) changes in the seventh stanza, best summarized in lines 37–42
   (C) changes in the fifth stanza, best summarized in line 26
   (D) is never really made clear, and is especially ambiguous in the eighth stanza
   (E) is not important to the meaning of this poem

4. The poet speaks of two homes in this poem. Who is the nominal owner of each?
   (A) The bridegroom owned the first home; the wealthy architect the second.
   (B) The poet owns the first home; the bridegroom the second.
   (C) The poet owns both homes.
   (D) The plantation overseer owns both homes.
   (E) The poet is the nominal owner of the first home; God, the second.

5. In a philosophical sense—the way the poet really intends it—who is the true owner of both homes?
   (A) The poet feels she owns all homes, but she does have a mortgage on the first.
   (B) God owns both homes, for the poet believes that everything man has is a gift from God.
   (C) The homes are both really unowned, as line 47 and 44 reveal.
   (D) Mankind owns both homes, for all possessions are commonly shared.
   (E) The reader is never sure of ownership here, for it is not critical to the poet's message.

6. "Pelf" in line 52 most nearly means
   (A) a home
   (B) furniture
   (C) money or riches
   (D) a small shop
   (E) furs

7. The connotation of the word "pelf" is
   (A) the poet's earthly nature that must be overcome if she is to find salvation
   (B) the poet's greedy attitude toward her possessions
   (C) The poet's cavalier attitude toward her possessions
   (D) the poet's secret love of death and desire for release from travails
   (E) the poet's deep love of God and His kingdom

8. When the poet finds herself unable to look at the fire any longer, she
   (A) curses God and His unjust actions
   (B) blesses God, but finds His action incomprehensible
   (C) consoles herself with plans for the new house on which a famous architect is already working
   (D) consoles herself with the thought of the new house her husband is building high on the hill
   (E) blesses God, for she believes His actions were just

9. Which adjective best describes the language of the poem?
   (A) Ironic
   (B) Argumentative
   (C) Colloquial
   (D) Pedantic
   (E) Highly figurative

10. Which of the following is the most accurate description of the way material possessions are treated in the poem?
    (A) Their value diminishes when compared to God's treasures.
    (B) Although initially highly valued, the author realizes by the end of the poem that she can easily replace her goods. Thus, their value diminishes.
    (C) Select items—her trunk and chest especially—mean more than anything else to the author.
    (D) They were never highly regarded.
    (E) She is just thankful that her family has been spared.

11. The verse pattern here is
    (A) free verse

(B) rhymed couplets
(C) sprung rhythm
(D) highly alliterative
(E) irregular

(B) first
(C) third
(D) seventh
(E) ninth

12. Judging from the situation and its description, most probably
    (A) this is a true story
    (B) this never could have occurred
    (C) the author is not very religious
    (D) this happened to someone the author knew very well
    (E) this is a totally false story

13. The attitude of the speaker can best be described as
    (A) ironic
    (B) sarcastic
    (C) moody
    (D) religious
    (E) irreligious

14. "The world no longer let me love,/My hope and treasure lies above" makes a suitable ending for all of the following reasons EXCEPT:
    (A) The ending shows the speaker's growing realization of God's majesty, and proves the theme.
    (B) The first thing the speaker did when she saw the fire was pray to God.
    (C) The author is really not very devout.
    (D) The thought behind the words helps console the author on the loss of her possessions.
    (E) The destruction of her worldly goods was followed by prayer to God.

15. In which stanza does the speaker's attitude toward her home change?
    (A) sixth

16. Which line best summarizes her change in feeling?
    (A) "And to my God my heart did cry" (line 8)
    (B) "Then straight I gin my heart to chide" (line 37)
    (C) "Thou hast a house on high erect" (line 43)
    (D) "I blest his Name that gave and took" (line 14)
    (E) "In silent night when rest I took" (line 1)

17. The point of view in this poem is
    (A) objective
    (B) limited omniscient
    (C) omniscient
    (D) first-person participant
    (E) first-person observer

18. In the eighth stanza, the "house on high erect" stands for
    (A) heaven
    (B) her newly constructed house on the hill
    (C) her store
    (D) the richly furnished home provided by her architect friend
    (E) none of the above

19. The literary device in the eighth stanza is called
    (A) metaphor
    (B) understatement
    (C) paradox
    (D) oxymoron
    (E) hyperbole

Part B: Time—35 minutes

One can imagine how sacred home was in the colonial period when Anne Bradstreet wrote this verse: a place of refuge against hostile Indians and bitter weather; a place of order in an alien wilderness. Discuss Bradstreet's attitude toward her loss. Be sure to include specific references from the poem.

SECTION 2

Time—60 minutes

Directions: Read the following passage carefully. Then write an essay in which you describe the author's attitude toward America. What points does he make toward his conclusion?

WHAT IS AN AMERICAN?

What, then, is the American, this new man? He is neither an European nor the descendant of an European; hence that strange mixture of blood, which you will find in no other country. I could point out to you a family whose grandfather was an Englishman, whose wife was Dutch, whose son married a French woman, and whose present four sons have now four wives of different nations. *He* is an American, who, leaving behind him all his ancient prejudices and manners, receives new ones from the new mode of life he has embraced, the new government he obeys, and the new rank he holds. He becomes an American by being received in the broad lap of our great Alma Mater. Here individuals of all nations are melted into a new race of men, whose labours and posterity will one day cause great changes in the world. Americans are the western pilgrims who are carrying along with them that great mass of arts, sciences, vigour, and industry which began long since in the East; they will finish the great circle. The Americans were once scattered all over Europe; here they are incorporated into one of the finest systems of population which has ever appeared, and which will hereafter become distinct by the power of the different climates they inhabit. The American ought therefore to love this country much better than that wherein either he or his forefathers were born. Here the rewards of his industry follow with equal steps the progress of his labour; his labour is founded on the basis of nature, self-interest; can it want a stronger allurement? Wives and children, who before in vain demanded of him a morsel of bread, now, fat and frolicsome, gladly help their father to clear those fields whence exuberant crops are to arise to feed and to clothe them all, without any part being claimed, either by a despotic prince, a rich abbot, or a mighty lord. Here religion demands but little of him: a small voluntary salary to the minister and gratitude to God; can he refuse these? The American is a new man, who acts upon new principles; he must therefore entertain new ideas and form new opinions. From involuntary idleness, servile dependence, penury, and useless labour, he has passed to toils of a very different nature, rewarded by ample subsistence. This is an American.

British America is divided into many provinces, forming a large association scattered along a coast of 1,500 miles extent and about 200 wide. This society I would fain examine, at least such as it appears in the middle provinces; if it does not afford that variety of tinges and gradations which may be observed in Europe, we have colours peculiar to ourselves. For instance, it is natural to conceive that those who live near the sea must be very different from those who live in the woods; the intermediate space will afford a separate and distinct class.

Men are like plants; the goodness and flavour of the fruit proceeds from the peculiar soil and exposition in which they grow. We are nothing but what we derive from the air we breathe, the climate we inhabit, the government we obey, the system of religion we profess, and the nature of our employment. Here you will find but few crimes; these have acquired as yet no root among us. I wish I were able to trace all my ideas; if my ignorance prevents me from describing them properly, I hope I shall be able to delineate a few of the outlines; which is all I propose.

Those who live near the sea feed more on fish than on flesh and often encounter that boisterous element. This renders them more bold and enterprising; this leads them to neglect the confined occupations of the land. They see and converse with a variety of people; their intercourse with mankind becomes extensive. The sea inspires them with a love of traffic, a desire of transporting produce from one place to another, and leads them to a variety of resources which supply the place of labour. Those who inhabit the middle settlements, by far the most numerous, must be very different; the simple cultivation of the earth purifies them, but the indulgences of the government, the soft remonstrances of religion, the rank of independent freeholders, must necessarily inspire them with sentiments, very little known in Europe among a people of the same class. What do I say? Europe has no such class of men; the early knowledge they acquire, the early bargains they make, give them a great degree of sagacity. As freemen, they will be litigious; pride and obstinacy are often the cause of lawsuits; the nature of our laws and governments may be another. As citizens, it is easy to imagine that they will carefully read the newspapers, enter into every political disquisition, freely blame or censure governors and others. As farmers, they will be careful and anxious to get as much as they can, because what they get is their own. As northern men, they will love the cheerful cup. As Christians, religion curbs them not in their opinions; the general indulgence leaves every one to think for themselves in spiritual matters; the law inspects our actions; our thoughts are left to God. Industry, good living, selfishness, litigiousness, country politics, the pride of freemen, religious indifference, are their characteristics. If you recede still farther from the sea, you will come into more modern settlements; they exhibit the same strong lineaments, in a ruder appearance. Religion seems to have still less influence, and their manners are less improved.

Now we arrive near the great woods, near the last inhabited districts; there men seem to be placed still farther beyond the reach of government, which in some measure leaves them to themselves. How can it pervade every corner, as they were driven there by misfortunes, necessity of beginnings, desire of acquiring large tracks of land, idleness, frequent want of economy, ancient debts; the reunion of such people does not afford a very pleasing spectacle. When discord, want of unity and friendship, when either drunkenness or idleness prevail in such remote districts, contention, inactivity, and wretchedness must ensue. There are not the same remedies to these evils as in a long-established community. The few magistrates they have are in general little better than the rest; they are often in a perfect state of war, that of man against man, sometimes decided by blows, sometimes by means of the law; that of man against every wild inhabitant of these venerable woods, of which they are come to dispossess them. There men appear to be no better than carnivorous animals of a superior rank, living on the flesh of wild animals when they can catch them, and when they are not able, they subsist on grain. He who would wish to see America in its proper light and have a true idea of its feeble beginnings and barbarous rudiments must visit our extended line of frontiers, where the last settlers dwell and where he may see the first labours of settlement, the mode of clearing the earth, in all their different appearances, where men are wholly left dependent on their native tempers and on the spur of uncertain industry, which often fails when not sanctified by the efficacy of a few moral rules. There, remote from the power of example and check of shame, many families exhibit the most hideous parts of our society. They are a kind of forlorn hope, preceding by ten or twelve years the most respectable army of veterans which come after them. In that space, prosperity will polish some, vice and the law will drive off the rest, who, uniting again with others like themselves, will recede still farther, making room for more industrious people, who will finish their improvements, convert the log-house into a convenient habitation, and rejoicing that the first heavy labours are finished, will change in a few years that hitherto barbarous country into a fine, fertile, well-regulated district. Such is our progress; such is the march of the Europeans toward the interior parts of this continent. In all societies there are off-casts; this impure part serves as our precursors or pioneers; my father himself was one of that class, but he came upon honest principles and was therefore one of the few who held fast; by good conduct and temperance, he transmitted to me his fair inheritance, when not above one in fourteen of his contemporaries had the same good fortune.

Forty years ago, this smiling country was thus inhabited; it is now purged, a general decency of manners prevails throughout, and such has been the fate of our best countries.

Exclusive of those general characteristics, each province has its own, founded on the government, climate, mode of husbandry, customs, and peculiarity of circumstances. Europeans submit insensibly to these great powers and become, in the course of a few generations, not only Americans in general, but either Pennsylvanians, Virginians, or provincials under some other name. Whoever traverses the continent must easily observe those strong differences, which will grow more evident in time. The inhabitants of Canada, Massachusetts, the middle provinces, the southern ones, will be as different as their climates; their only points of unity will be those of religion and language.

—*J. Hector St. John de Crèvecoeur*

SECTION 3

Time—60 minutes

Private vs. public conscience—the desire to do what an individual perceives as right vs. the responsibility of carrying out the dictates of society—figures as a central conflict in many important works of literature. Select one literary work in which a character is faced with the choice of doing what he/she believes to be right or what society demands. You may select from the following works or from another of comparable quality.

Madame Bovary   The Adventures of Huckleberry Finn

The Crucible   The Scarlet Letter

Ethan Frome   Jude the Obscure

Sister Carrie   The Red Badge of Courage

ANSWERS AND EXPLANATIONS FOR SAMPLE EXAMINATION B

Section 1, Part A

At the age of 18, Anne Bradstreet, the author of "Upon the Burning of Our House," came to America with her husband, settling in the Massachusetts Bay Colony. She had received a better education than most women of her day, and in spite of the demands made upon her as the mother of eight children, she found time to write poetry. Her brother-in-law took some of her verse back with him to England and had it published, establishing her as the first published poet of the New World. This particular poem is based on a true incident, as the date below the title suggests.

1. **(A)** Lines 14–18 tell us that God "gave and took" and that His actions were "just." The other house she mentions is not a physical house at all, as in choice (D), and she assigns no blame to God.

2. **(C)** Rather than an "arm of flesh," anchored to the mundane world, she knows now she ought to have realized that her "hope and treasure [lie] above" (last line).

3. **(B)** As mentioned in question 2 she now realizes that she ought to "Raise up [her] thoughts above the sky" to assuage her the loss of her home. There is another home—heaven—awaiting her on high, much more splendid than her temporal one.

4. **(E)** The word "nominal" is important here, for God actually owns all, as she realizes. The second home is heaven.

5. **(B)** See the third stanza.

6. **(C)** "Pelf" most nearly means accumulated goods. Do not be confused by choice (D), a small shop. The author uses the word "store" in line 52 to indicate a group of objects that she owns, not sells.

7. **(A)** She values her possessions very highly, especially since she would be unable to replace most of them, for there was no insurance and she lacked the means to send back to England for all the items, even if they were all available. Nonetheless, she believes that she must reject her reliance on earthly things if she is to achieve God's grace in heaven. These items are meaningless, of course, when she compares them to what God has to offer in salvation. Obviously, Bradstreet was very religious.

8. **(E)** See stanza 3.

9. **(E)** The language uses many figures of speech (see Poetry Unit). (A) The term ironic means that the words express a meaning that is often the direct opposite of what is intended; Bradstreet makes her meaning quite clear. (B) There is no argumentative tone here; she assumes that her reader will agree with her conclusion. (C) Colloquial language is characteristic of ordinary conversation rather than formal speech or writing. Bradstreet uses a great many inversions ("For sorrow near I did not look" [line 2] rather than "I did not look near for sorrow") and thus her language is not characteristic of the way people usually speak. (D) The term pedantic refers to an excessive or inappropriate show of learning, which is not the case here, although it was typical of much of the writing of the seventeenth century.

10. **(A)** See previous discussions.

11. **(B)** In the first stanza, for example, "took" and "look"; "noise" and "voice"; "fire" and "desire" all rhyme. Thus, the rhymes are in pairs, also called couplets. (A) Free verse has unrhymed lines without regular rhythm. (C) Sprung rhythm is characterized by the use of strongly accented syllables pushed up against unaccented syllables. It was brought into favor by Gerard Manley Hopkins in the late nineteenth and early twentieth centuries. (D) Alliteration is not a verse pattern. It refers to repeated sounds throughout a poem. (E) Rhymed couplets cannot be considered irregular verse.

12. **(A)** From Bradstreet's use of detail and description, as well as the obvious emotion and date on the top of the poem, we can infer that this is a true story.

13. **(D)** As discussed earlier, the poem reveals the speaker's deeply religious attitude. Nowhere is she sarcastic or ironic about her subject.

14. **(C)** As mentioned before, she is highly religious.

15. **(D)** As mentioned previously.

16. **(B)** As mentioned previously.

17. **(D)** The author is a participant in the action, as mentioned above. Far from objective, (A), she is very much involved in what happened. Omniscient (B,C) means having complete or infinite knowledge, and this could be true only in God's case, in her way of thinking. She finds out what is happening as events unfold.

18. **(A)** As mentioned previously.

19. **(A)** A metaphor is a comparison of two unlike objects; here she compares heaven to a house. (B) Paradox is a statement which appears self-contradictory, but underlines a basis of truth, while an oxymoron, (D), consists of contradictory terms brought together to express strong effects. Hyperbole, (E), is exaggeration.

Section 1, Part B

The essay must stress that Bradstreet does not dismiss her worldly possessions lightly—they were of enormous value to her—and she is dismayed by the loss of a gathering place for her family and friends. No more will people visit and eat under her roof (stanza 5); no more will marriages take place (stanza 6); no more pleasant evenings will be spent telling stories (stanza 6). Nonetheless, she is highly devout and solaces herself with the thought of God's grandeur that awaits her in heaven.

Section 2

This selection, from J. Hector St. John de Crèvecoeur's *Letters from an American Farmer,* reveals his affection for and deep faith in the promise of the New World. "Here individuals of all nations are melted into a new race of men, whose labours and posterity will one day cause great changes in the world," he says. This and the next few lines can be cited as examples of his belief in America's promise. In America, man is rewarded for his labor, and all people gladly contribute to the common cause.

Section 3

The Adventures of Huckleberry Finn provides a fine example of the conflict of self vs. society in the character of Huck, who must go against all that he has been taught about slavery to effect the rescue of Jim. He finds Jim a far finer human being than the hypocritical Widow Douglas, who tells Huck not to smoke yet takes snuff, and who tells him to respect all men yet owns Jim and his family. His decision at the fork of the Mississippi River, Cairo,—"All right, then, I'll go to hell"—shows that he will relinquish conventional, public morality to embrace what he feels is right, even if it means that he will suffer everlasting damnation for it.

In *Ethan Frome,* the main character, Ethan, is also faced with a public vs. private conscience decision: Should he leave his wife, the sickly Zeena, for the young and vibrant Mattie Silver, whose very name rings with the promise of bright, shiny things? In Dreiser's *Sister Carrie,* should sister Carrie live with a man without benefit of matrimony? Should she use him to further her career? Should the soldier in *The Red Badge of Courage* stand in battle and risk being killed, as conventional morality demanded, or should he turn and run, as his private conscience advised? Should Reverend Dimmesdale in *The Scarlet Letter* reveal that he is Hester Prynne's lover? Should he acknowledge their child and shoulder his portion of sin and guilt, or should he suffer in silence and self-torment?

Sample Examination C

SECTION 1

Part A: Time—45 minutes

Questions 1–13 refer to the following poem.

TO S. M., A YOUNG AFRICAN PAINTER ON SEEING HIS WORKS

To show the lab'ring bosom's deep intent,
And thought in living characters to paint,
When first thy pencil did those beauties give,
And breathing figures learnt from thee to live,
5 How did those prospects give my soul delight,
A new creation rushing on my sight!
Still, wondrous youth! each noble path pursue;
On deathless glories fix thine ardent view:
Still may the painter's and the poet's fire,
10 To aid thy pencil and thy verse conspire!
And may the charms of each seraphic theme
Conduct thy footsteps to immortal fame!
High to the blissful wonders of the skies
Elate thy soul, and raise thy wishful eyes.
15 Thrice happy, when exalted to survey
That splendid city, crowned with endless day,
Whose twice six gates on radiant hinges ring:

Celestial Salem blooms in endless spring.
Calm and serene thy moments glide along,
20 And may the muse inspire each future song!
Still, with the sweets of contemplation blessed,
May peace with balmy wings your soul invest!
But when these shades of time are chased away,
And darkness ends in everlasting day,
25 On what seraphic pinions shall we move,
And view the landscapes in the realms above!
There shall thy tongue in heavenly murmurs flow,
And there my muse with heavenly transport glow;
No more to tell of Damon's tender sighs,
30 Or rising radiance of Aurora's eyes;
For nobler themes demand a nobler strain,
And purer language on the ethereal plain.
Cease, gentle Muse! the solemn gloom of night
Now seals the fair creation from my sight.

—*Phillis Wheatley*

1. What has S. M. done to win the poet's admiration?
   (A) He can make people come alive on canvas and reveal the human soul in art.
   (B) He is both a poet and a painter, as line 9 reveals.
   (C) He has built a radiant city with 12 gates (lines 16–17).
   (D) He has died after a glorious career as a painter, poet, builder—a man of the world.
   (E) He was a noble Greek warrior as well as a painter.

2. "Seraphic" in line 11 most nearly means
   (A) a long, flowing robe; hence, a long, involved theme
   (B) a singer of melodious songs
   (C) foreign, mysterious
   (D) angelic
   (E) colorful, vivid

3. What hopes does the poet have for S. M.'s future?
   (A) That he will always burn with creative energy
   (B) That his work will attain immortality
   (C) That his soul will ascend to heaven
   (D) None of the above
   (E) All of the above

4. What do "shades of time" symbolize in line 23?
   (A) Temporal, unsubstantial life in heaven
   (B) Temporal, unsubstantial life on earth
   (C) Temporal, unsubstantial life devoid of art
   (D) The specific cares and woes of all painters, permanent and universal
   (E) The dull, dark days common to even the most talented

5. What may "darkness" symbolize in line 24?
   (A) The suffering the Roman slaves experienced each day
   (B) The blindness of the poet Homer
   (C) Death
   (D) The suffering the black slaves experienced daily
   (E) The suffering of a person who never received adequate recognition for his work

6. What does the poet envision for both herself and the painter?
   (A) A life of promise and hope
   (B) A life of creativity and perpetual bloom
   (C) A realm of noble companions
   (D) A better command of the resources of the temporal world
   (E) Nothing better than what they now have

7. The poet's style is marked by
   (A) metaphysical conceits
   (B) ironic commentary
   (C) inverted phrases
   (D) an unusual rhyme scheme
   (E) onomatopoeia

8. How does what the poet envisions differ from the life both poet and painter lead?
   (A) They will be three times happier.
   (B) They will finally be able to move to Salem.
   (C) All people will be able to be artists.
   (D) All people will again be young and vigorous.
   (E) They will no longer be hostages to other men.

9. What does "everlasting day" symbolize in line 24?
   (A) Heaven

   (B) Salem
   (C) Greece during the Golden Age
   (D) Africa
   (E) It has no symbolic meaning.

10. The metaphors in lines 29 and 30 are derived from
    (A) romance
    (B) religion
    (C) art
    (D) mythology
    (E) music

11. Which term best describes the tone of this poem?
    (A) Resigned
    (B) Formal, lofty
    (C) Angry
    (D) Despairing
    (E) Informal, relaxed

12. The theme of this poem can most precisely be stated as follows:
    (A) Artists will finally be appreciated only when they are dead.
    (B) Slaves will be released from bondage and enjoy endless creativity when they enter heaven.
    (C) Heaven is for the talented; there they can flourish and grow.
    (D) Art is the highest human attainment.
    (E) None of the above.

13. The rhyme scheme of this poem is
    (A) *abcd abcd efgh efgh*
    (B) *aaab bbbc ddde*
    (C) *abba cddc effg*
    (D) *aa bb cc dd*
    (E) *abc abc def def*

Questions 14–26 are based on the following poem.

HIS EXCELLENCY GENERAL WASHINGTON

Celestial choir! enthron'd in realms of light,
Columbia's scenes of glorious toils I write.
While freedom's cause her anxious breast alarms,
She flashes dreadful in refulgent arms.
5 See mother earth her offspring's fate bemoan,
And nations gaze at scenes before unknown!
See the bright beams of heaven's revolving light

Involved in sorrows and the veil of night!
The goddess comes, she moves divinely fair,
10 Olive and laurel binds her golden hair:
Wherever shines this native of the skies,
Unnumber'd charms and recent graces rise.
Muse! bow propitious while my pen relates
How pour her armies through a thousand gates;

15 As when Eolus heaven's fair face deforms,
Enwrapped in tempest and a night of storms;
Astonish'd ocean feels the wild uproar,
The refluent surges beat the sounding shore,
Or thick as leaves in Autumn's golden reign,
20 Such, and so many, moves the warrior's train.
In bright array they seek the work of war,
Where high unfurl'd the ensign waves in air.
Shall I to Washington their praise recite?
Enough thou know'st them in the fields of fight.
25 Thee, first in place and honours,—we demand
The grace and glory of thy martial band.
Fam'd, for thy valour, for thy virtues more,
Here every tongue thy guardian aid implore!

One century scarce performed its destin'd round,
30 When Gallic powers Columbia's fury found;
And so may you, whoever dares disgrace
The land of freedom's heaven-defended race!
Fix'd are the eyes of nations on the scales,
For in their hopes Columbia's arm prevails.
35 Anon Britannia droops the pensive head,
While round increase the rising hills of dead.
Ah! cruel blindess to Columbia's state!
Lament thy thirst of boundless power too late.
Proceed, great chief, with virtue on thy side,
40 Thy every action let the goddess guide.
A crown, a mansion, and a throne that shine,
With gold unfading, *Washington,* be thine.

—*Phillis Wheatley*

14. What purpose do the two opening lines serve?
    (A) They introduce the poem and state its subject.
    (B) They establish the tone and theme.
    (C) They explain Washington's role as a leader.
    (D) They explain the suitability of Washington as a subject.
    (E) They establish the poet's unconventional style.

15. What is Columbia?
    (A) A metaphor for the future
    (B) A metaphor for the past
    (C) A metaphor for the Gallic powers
    (D) A metaphor for Washington
    (E) The personification of America

16. What figure of speech is used in line 2?
    (A) Metaphor
    (B) Simile
    (C) Irony
    (D) Symbolism
    (E) Personification

17. Lines 2–22 describe Columbia. What impression do they give?
    (A) She is a shining goddess gracing the land.
    (B) She is a symbol of freedom.
    (C) She is a symbol of military might.
    (D) None of the above.
    (E) All of the above.

18. How does the poet regard Washington?
    (A) He is the unquestioned leader of Columbia's army, strong and virtuous.

    (B) He is a strong leader, but by no means omnipotent.
    (C) He is brave and forceful, but subject to enormous human doubt.
    (D) He is a fine leader, but no match for the Gallic powers.
    (E) He is soon to be replaced by Columbia, a true leader.

19. The poet views England as
    (A) a fair, honest power
    (B) a greedy, imperialist power
    (C) a true friend to Washington
    (D) a fair-weather friend
    (E) The poet makes no comment on England.

20. How do the other countries regard the struggle between England and the colonies?
    (A) They place their hopes in France.
    (B) They place their hopes in America.
    (C) They have made no formal declaration of where their hopes lie.
    (D) They are filled with fear.
    (E) They believe this is a no-win situation.

21. The rhyme scheme of this poem is
    (A) aa bb cc dd
    (B) *abc abc def def*
    (C) *abba cddc effg*
    (D) *aaab bbbc ddde*
    (E) There is no rhyme scheme; this poem is written in free verse.

22. "Celestial choir" (line 1) is an example of
    (A) personification

(B) symbolism
(C) alliteration
(D) metaphor
(E) irony

23. What will be the outcome of the struggle discussed in this poem?
    (A) Britain will win.
    (B) France will win.
    (C) No one will win.
    (D) America will win.
    (E) The Gallic powers will win.

24. What two subjects are combined in the close of the poem?
    (A) France and England
    (B) Columbia and Washington
    (C) England and Washington
    (D) Gallic powers and Washington
    (E) Columbia and France

25. What opinions and hopes are voiced at the end of the poem?
    (A) Both France and England will enjoy victory and crowning glory.
    (B) Both England and the Gallic powers will enjoy victory and crowning glory.
    (C) Both America and Washington will enjoy victory and crowning glory.
    (D) No one will win.
    (E) Only in heaven will the outcome be made evident.

26. The tone of the poem is
    (A) enervated
    (B) elevated
    (C) sarcastic
    (D) ironic
    (E) peaceful

Part B: Time—60 minutes

Compare the style, tone, and poetic devices employed in the two poems you have just read by Phillis Wheatley. Show both similarities and differences. Do you believe they were written in the same time period?

SECTION 2

Time—45 Minutes

Using any novel from the list below or any other novel of comparable quality, show how the main character is unwilling or unable to accept members of his community or family and is thus isolated and alone. Also explain how the author prepares the reader for this rejection of human companionship. Consider at least two elements of fiction such as theme, symbol, setting, characterization, or any other aspect of the writer's craft in your discussion.

Ethan Frome

The Scarlet Letter

The American

Hamlet

The Adventures of Huckleberry Finn

Gulliver's Travels

The Sound and the Fury

Invisible Man

The Sun Also Rises

McTeague

SECTION 3

Time—30 Minutes

In his Preface to *The House of the Seven Gables* (1851), Hawthorne explained some differences between the romance and the novel:

> When a writer calls his work a Romance, it need hardly be observed that he wishes to claim a certain latitude, both to its fashion and material, which he would not have felt himself entitled to assume, had he professed to be writing a Novel. The latter form of composition is presumed to aim at a very minute fidelity, not merely to the possible, but to the probable and ordinary course of man's experience. The former—while, as a work of art, it must rigidly subject itself to laws, and while it sins unpardonably, so far as it may swerve aside from the truth of the human heart—has fairly a right to present that truth under the circumstances, to a great extent, of the writer's own choosing or creation. If he think fit, also, he may so manage his atmospherical medium as to bring out or mellow the lights and deepen and enrich the shadows of the picture. He will be wise, no doubt, to make a very moderate use of the privileges here stated, and, especially, to mingle the Marvellous rather as a slight, delicate, and evanescent flavor, than as any portion of the actual substance of the dish offered to the public.

Select any novel that you have read that shows elements of romance. Isolate at least three examples of how the work functions as a Romance and show how they are evident in the novel. You may consider works by Hawthorne, or any other author whose works are suitable: Cooper, Melville, Thackeray, Faulkner, (Harriet Beecher) Stowe, or H. Rider, for example.

ANSWERS AND EXPLANATIONS FOR SAMPLE EXAMINATION C

Section 1, Part A

1. **(A)** The first two lines of the poem explain the basis for the poet's admiration of S. M. He can "show the lab'ring bosom's deep intent" (line 1), which is closest in meaning to "reveal the human soul in art." He is also able to paint "living characters" (line 2) or "make people come alive on canvas." (B) is incorrect, for the author is not saying that S. M. is both a painter and a poet, rather, she refers to him as the painter and herself as the poet, as "wondrous youth" pursues different "noble" paths. (C) is also wrong, because S. M. has not built the city 12 gates (heaven). (D) is wrong because S. M. has not yet died. (E) is incorrect, because S. M. is a young African painter, as the title indicates, not a Greek warrior.

2. **(D)** "Seraphic" means angelic, and relates to the discussion of heaven in the rest of the poem. The word "immortal" in line 12 is a context clue.

3. **(E)** The poet wishes that (A), he will always burn with creative energy (see line 20); (B) his work will attain immortality (see line 12); and (C), his soul will ascend to heaven (lines 20–34).

4. **(B)** We know that "shades of time" in line 23 stands for temporal, unsubstantial life on earth, as the following line, "darkness ends in everlasting day," tells us. The rest of the poem refers to heaven and the afterlife, another clue.

5. **(D)** The word "darkness" in line 24 refers to the suffering of black slaves, as shown by the

title, ". . . a Young African Painter." We are given no indication that any other answers are suitable.

6. **(B)** Lines 27, 28, 31, and 32 indicate that the author envisions an eternity of creativity in heaven. (D) is incorrect, for the ending of the poem moves the action to heaven. (C) is incorrect, for the poet does not indicate that heaven will be populated with any but themselves

7. **(C)** is the best answer, as a great many of the poet's sentences are inverted. For example, "May peace with balmy wings your soul invest!" (line 22) may be stated as "May your soul be invested with peace on balmy wings!" (A) is incorrect, since this poem contains no extended comparison of two unlike objects. (B) is incorrect, for the author is not ironic in her discussion. Rather, she is very serious and straightforward in her admiration of S. M.'s talent and future. (D) The rhyme scheme is common, made up as it is of rhymed couplets (pairs). (E) is wrong, for onomatopeia is the use of words whose sound suggests their meaning.

8. **(E)** is the answer, as lines 23 and 24 show.

9. **(A)** "Everlasting day" is a metaphor for heaven.

10. **(D)** Damon and Aurora are figures from Roman mythology. (A) Romance is incorrect, for, as discussed later in this practice exam, it is a genre that allows the writer greater use of the marvelous and the mysterious than the novel. It bears no reference to the two mythical characters cited above. (B) is incorrect, for neither of these are religious figures. (C) and (E) are also wrong, for these figures do not pertain to art or music.

11. **(B)** The elevated, formal tone is evident in the poet's use of language (see first two lines, for example), lofty themes (ascension to heaven and everlasting creativity), and style (word choice, poetic contractions). (A) The poet is not resigned at all. Rather, she sees a brilliant future for them both. (C) The poet is not angry, for the painter's skill inspires her admiration and she foresees a glorious afterlife. (D) and (E) are incorrect for the reasons cited above.

12. **(B)** The title and the last half of the poem tells us that the theme here concerns the author's belief that she and S. M. will be released from their earthly bondage to enjoy everlasting creativity in heaven. (A) is wrong, for the poet appreciates S. M. now, and he is not dead. (C) While heaven may indeed be for the talented, (B) is a more complete answer. (D) The poet does not state this belief in the poem.

13. **(D)** The poem is written in rhymed couplets (pairs): intent/paint (aa); give/live (bb); delight/sight (cc); etc.

14. **(A)** The poet will write of Columbia's "glorious toils," as she states in line 2. (B) The theme and tone are *introduced*, but not established. (C) and (D) Washington has not yet been mentioned. (E) The poet's style is very conventional.

15. **(E)** Columbia stands for America, as the poem tells of America's quest for freedom under General Washington.

16. **(E)** The author assigns human qualities to a non-living object when she makes America, or Columbia, a person. Columbia "toils" and experiences "anxious breast alarms" (lines 2–3). Line 4 assigns gender: "She flashes dreadful in refulgent arms."

17. **(E)** All of the above are correct. The poet admires America enormously.

18. **(A)** The poet believes in Washington without reservation. The praise increases as the poem continues; the final four lines sum up the poet's admiration.

19. **(B)** See lines 35–40, as Britannia (England) is defeated by America's great chief, who has virtue on his side.

20. **(B)** All place their hopes in America.

21. **(A)** This poem, like the previous one, is written in rhymed couplets: light/write (aa); alarms/arms (bb); bemoan/unknown (cc).

22. **(C))** Alliteration is the repetition of two or more initial sounds within a line of poetry or prose. Thus, the two C's or "celestial choir" show alliteration. All the other answers have been previously explained; see the Poetry Unit for further explanation of terms.

23. **(D)** The final four lines make it clear that America, under the leadership of Washington, will attain victory.

24. **(B)** Line 37 discusses Columbia; line 42, Washington. It is also clear that Washington will be in charge of Columbia/America.

25. **(C)** See answer 23.

26. **(B)** The poem's tone is elevated, as it employs a great many lofty words and phrases to praise Washington. Metaphors like "celestial choir" in line 1 further serve to raise the tone and underscore the theme. (A) Enervated means weakened, and is not to be confused with elevated. (C) The poet is not at all sarcastic toward her subject; her admiration is genuine.

Section 1, Part B

Both poems were written by the same person, Phillis Wheatley (c. 1753–1784). She was born in Africa and brought to Boston at the age of eight on a slave ship. By the time she was 13, she was translating Latin and writing poetry, for her owner, John Wheatley, encouraged her studies. Considered a member of the family and never treated as a slave, she was granted her freedom at the age of 20. Her later life was marred by great unhappiness: Her marriage was unsuccessful and two of her three children died young. She died alone and in poverty at the age of 31, her death coinciding with that of her third child. They were buried together in an unmarked grave.

The style, tone, and poetic devices employed in the two poems are the same. Wheatley was fond of classical literature and modeled her poetry after such contemporary English poets as Pope and Gray. We find that the style is elevated, employing sophisticated language, poetic contractions, and frequent use of figurative language. She was especially fond of alliteration, metaphor, and personification. Both poems use images of heaven, the first discussing the afterlife of the poet and S. M., the second linking Washington's quest to a heavenly undertaking. This would of course be shown by isolating specific lines from both poems and comparing them. The tone in both poems is the same: elevated and formal with lofty diction. This too would be shown by specific reference to the poems. All the similarities should allow the conclusion that the poems were written in the same period.

Section 2

In *Gulliver's Travels,* the main character, Gulliver, lost during a ship voyage, encounters three different versions of eighteenth-century civilization. He finds each repellent in different ways, and ends up living with a civilization of horses, totally rejecting "Yahoos," or human beings. Theme and setting would be appropriate for discussion here, as you would draw specific examples from the book.

Hamlet would be another good choice for the question, as the main character, Hamlet, attempts to establish contact with members of his family and community but finds that his efforts are rebuffed or misunderstood. Hamlet, who returned from school to attend his father's funeral, has discovered that his mother has married his father's brother a scant two months after his father's death. He finds himself unable to talk to his mother after she has remarried with such unseemly haste, and he distrusts his uncle, which turns out to be very wise indeed. His lover, Ophelia, is of no help either, for her father, Polonius, has told her to rebuff Hamlet's overtures. Thus, she returns his letters and gifts and denies him access to her. His two old friends, Rosencrantz and Guildenstern are turncoats, accepting pay from Hamlet's uncle, King Claudius, to spy on their friend. The famous "to be or not to be" speech shows his isolation. Characterization and theme would be considered here.

Frank Norris' *McTeague* is also suitable, but in a very different way. Unlike Hamlet,

McTeague is not a man who thinks a great deal about his actions. An unlicensed dentist on Polk Street in San Francisco at the turn of the century, McTeague is never very articulate or sure of himself. When his cousin Marcus reveals that McTeague lacks a license (Marcus is jealous that McTeague has successfully wooed the delicate Trina and won the lottery), he quickly reverts to an animal-like state and loses any veneer of civilization. Thus, he stops keeping himself clean, well fed, or neat, and he and Trina move from one hellish apartment to another, until he finally murders her to find the gold she has hidden. Like a wild animal, he runs for the desert, rejecting all human companionship. Setting (wretched apartments and the desert) and theme (overriding greed) would be suitable for discussion.

Ralph Ellison's *Invisible Man* is also fitting, as the main character, a black man alienated from all society, describes how he gradually came to reject all human companionship. He is invisible because people refuse to see him, refuse to recognize a black man in America, as he shows by tracing childhood and college humiliations. Any of these tragic stories would serve to show why he has rejected all human companionship and has gone underground.

Section 3

A romance is characterized by removal from reality and a certain use of the mysterious. Very often there will be a handsome hero on a shining white horse, a dastardly villain, or fair maiden in need of rescue. There may also be daring rescues and hairbreadth escapes, as well as various mysterious happenings. *The Blithedale Romance*, for example, describes the mysterious death of Zenobia, the beautiful and unusual dark heroine, as well as the strange performances of Westervelt and his Veiled Lady. *The House of the Seven Gables*, also by Hawthorne, describes the mysterious curse of the Maules, who were all supposed to die gurgling on blood. Maule's Well, where the curse originated, was said to be haunted. In the *Scarlet Letter*, Reverend Dimmesdale rips apart his vestment before the entire community to reveal mystery. Some say they see the very semblance of an A, identical to that displayed on the chest of his lover, Hester Prynne, all these years. Others swear that his breast is as clean as that of a new born babe's. The entire matter of the A on Dimmesdale's chest weaves through the book, as the evil Chillingworth dances with glee when he believes he has discovered, very early on, that he has seen it on the minister's chest. Even Chillingworth is removed from reality, as his eyes glow an evil red.

Any of Cooper's leatherstocking tales would suffice to answer this question. The *Deerslayer*, for example, describes how Natty Bumppo, a young man reared by the Delaware Indians, attempts to rescue Hist, his best friend Chingachgook's girl, from an unfriendly tribe of Huron Indians and is in turn captured himself. After a great deal of talk and various acts of torture, the Deerslayer (Natty) is rescued by his friend and the entire cavalry. The Deerslayer manages to kill a great many of the Hurons and general carnage results. This is the good guy–bad guy/daring rescue version of romance.